Lecture Notes in Computer Science 15894

Founding Editors

Gerhard Goos
Juris Hartmanis

AF147156

The series Lecture Notes in Computer Science (LNCS), including its subseries Lecture Notes in Artificial Intelligence (LNAI) and Lecture Notes in Bioinformatics (LNBI), has established itself as a medium for the publication of new developments in computer science and information technology research, teaching, and education.

LNCS enjoys close cooperation with the computer science R & D community, the series counts many renowned academics among its volume editors and paper authors, and collaborates with prestigious societies. Its mission is to serve this international community by providing an invaluable service, mainly focused on the publication of conference and workshop proceedings and postproceedings. LNCS commenced publication in 1973.

Osvaldo Gervasi · Beniamino Murgante ·
Chiara Garau · Yeliz Karaca ·
Maria Noelia Faginas Lago · Francesco Scorza ·
Ana Cristina Braga
Editors

Computational Science and Its Applications – ICCSA 2025 Workshops

Istanbul, Turkey, June 30 – July 3, 2025
Proceedings, Part IX

Springer

Editors
Osvaldo Gervasi ⓘ
University of Perugia
Perugia, Italy

Beniamino Murgante ⓘ
University of Basilicata
Potenza, Italy

Chiara Garau ⓘ
University of Cagliari
Cagliari, Italy

Yeliz Karaca ⓘ
University of Massachusetts
Worcester, MA, USA

Maria Noelia Faginas Lago ⓘ
University of Perugia
Perugia, Italy

Francesco Scorza ⓘ
University of Basilicata
Potenza, Italy

Ana Cristina Braga ⓘ
University of Minho
Braga, Portugal

ISSN 0302-9743   ISSN 1611-3349 (electronic)
Lecture Notes in Computer Science
ISBN 978-3-031-97647-6   ISBN 978-3-031-97648-3 (eBook)
https://doi.org/10.1007/978-3-031-97648-3

Preface

The compiled 14 volumes (LNCS volumes 15886–15899) consist of the peer-reviewed papers from the 68 Workshops of the 2025 International Conference on Computational Science and Its Applications (ICCSA 2025), which was held between June 30 – July 3, 2025 in Istanbul (Türkiye). The peer-reviewed papers of the main conference tracks are published in a separate set made up of three volumes (LNCS 15648–15650).

The conference was held in a hybrid form, with the large majority of participants in presence, hosted by Galatasaray University, Istanbul, Türkiye. We enabled virtual participation for those who did not attend the event in person due to logistical, political and economic problems, by adopting a technological infrastructure via open-source software (jitsi + riot) and a commercial Cloud infrastructure.

With the 2025 edition, ICCSA celebrated its 25th anniversary, a quarter of a century as a memorable moment that is harmoniously aligned with Istanbul, an extraordinary city located at the crossroads and acting as a bridge connecting Asia and Europe, representing different cultures, beliefs as well as lifestyles, which highlights its intercultural fabric.

ICCSA 2025 marked another fruitful and thought-provoking academic event in the International Conferences on Computational Science and Its Applications (ICCSA) conference series, previously held in Hanoi, Vietnam (2024), Athens, Greece (2023), Málaga, Spain (2022), Cagliari, Italy (hybrid with a few participants in presence in 2021 and completely online in 2020), whilst earlier editions took place in Saint Petersburg, Russia (2019), Melbourne, Australia (2018), Trieste, Italy (2017), Beijing, China (2016), Banff, Canada (2015), Guimaraes, Portugal (2014), Ho Chi Minh City, Vietnam (2013), Salvador, Brazil (2012), Santander, Spain (2011), Fukuoka, Japan (2010), Suwon, South Korea (2009), Perugia, Italy (2008), Kuala Lumpur, Malaysia (2007), Glasgow, UK (2006), Singapore (2005), Assisi, Italy (2004), Montreal, Canada (2003), and (as ICCS) Amsterdam, the Netherlands (2002) and San Francisco, USA (2001).

Computational Science constitutes the main pillar of most present research, industrial and commercial applications, and plays a unique role in exploiting ICT innovative technologies, and the ICCSA conference series has, accordingly, provided ample opportunities to researchers and industry practitioners to discuss new ideas, to share complex problems and their solutions, and to shape new trends in Computational Science. As the conference mirrors society from a scientific point of view, this year's undoubtedly dominant theme was large language models, machine learning and Artificial Intelligence (AI) and their applications in the most diverse technological, economic and industrial fields, amongst the others.

The ICCSA 2025 conference was structured in six general tracks covering the fields of computational science and its applications: Computational Methods, Algorithms and Scientific Applications – High Performance Computing and Networks – Geometric Modeling, Graphics and Visualization – Advanced and Emerging Applications – Information Systems and Technologies – Urban and Regional Planning. In addition, the conference consisted of 68 workshops, focusing on topical issues of utmost importance to science, technology and society: from new computational approaches for earth science, to mathematical methods for image processing, new statistical and optimization methods, several Artificial Intelligence approaches, sustainability issues, smart cities and related technologies, to name some.

In the Workshops' proceedings, we accepted 362 full papers, 37 short papers and 2 Ph.D. Showcase papers from total of 1043 submissions (Acceptance rate 38.4%). In the Main Conference Proceedings, we have accepted 71 full papers, 6 short papers and 1 Ph.D. Showcase paper from 269 submissions to the General Tracks of the Conference (with an acceptance rate of 29.9%). We would like to convey our sincere appreciation to the workshops' chairs and co-chairs and program committee members for their diligent work, commitment and dedication.

The success and consistent maintenance of the ICCSA conference series in general, and of ICCSA 2025 in particular, rely upon the support of many people: authors, presenters, participants, keynote speakers, workshop chairs, session chairs, organizing committee members, student volunteers, Program Committee members, Advisory Committee members, International Liaison chairs, reviewers and other individuals in various roles. Thus, we take this opportunity to wholehartedly thank each and everyone.

We additionally wish to thank publisher Springer for their agreement to publish the proceedings, besides sponsoring part of the best papers awards and for their kind assistance and cooperation during the editing process.

We would cordially like to invite you to refer to the ICCSA website https://iccsa.org, where you can find the relevant details regarding this academic endeavor and event of ours.

June 2025

Osvaldo Gervasi
Yeliz Karaca
Beniamino Murgante
Chiara Garau

A Welcome Message from the Organizers

The International Conference on Computational Science and Its Applications (ICCSA) reflects a culmination of meticulous and dedicated efforts and academic endeavors toward the progress of science and technology.

One of the most noteworthy aspects of ICCSA is its fostering of a collective spirit, bringing together a plethora of participants from all over the world. Correspondingly, this merging power manifests itself in the 25th anniversary of ICCSA, which is a quarter of a century, in Istanbul, Türkiye, which connects and acts as a bridge between two continents, namely Asia and Europe. This unique location in the world hosts the 25th year of ICCSA at Galatasaray University, located on Çırağan Avenue by Istanbul's Bosphorus, which is an established international university bestowed with a distinctive past of teaching tradition, research and education exceeding five centuries.

Istanbul, having served as the capital city of four empires, namely the Roman Empire (330–395), the Byzantine Empire (395–1204 and 1261–1453), the Latin Empire (1204–1261) and the Ottoman Empire (1453–1922), is an exceptional city of the Republic of Türkiye founded by Mustafa Kemal Atatürk.

Situated at a strategic location along the historic Silk Road, Istanbul is at the core of extending rail networks which span across Europe and West Asia along with the only sea route between the Black Sea and the Mediterranean.

The cultural, historical and economic pulses of the country are evident in Istanbul whose rooted origins have embraced varying beliefs, lifestyles and populace, which highlights the city's mosaic quality with blended fabric in a constant harmonious flow. This has enabled cultures to grow and be nurtured, which is profoundly rooted in its urban culture.

Computational Science constitutes the main pillar of most present research, industrial and commercial activities besides manifesting a unique role in exploiting and addressing innovative Information and Communication Technologies. Thus, the 25-year-old ICCSA conference series provides remarkable opportunities to get acquainted with leading researchers, scientists, scholars, practitioners and many more while exchanging innovative ideas and initiating new partnerships, associations and bonds.

With the hosting of Galatasaray University, I would personally and on behalf of the Local Organizing Committee, with the members Emre Alptekin, Gülfem Işıklar Alptekin, Cengiz Kahraman, Abdullah Çağrı Tolga and Ayberk Zeytin, like to convey our sincere gratitude and thanks to everyone who exerted their efforts in and contributed to the realization of ICCSA 2025. With these notes and remarks, welcome to Istanbul!

Cordially yours,

On behalf of the Local Organizing Committee.

June 2025   Yeliz Karaca

Organization

Honorary General Chairs

Bernady O. Apduhan Kyushu Sangyo University, Japan
Kenneth C. J. Tan Sardina Systems, UK

General Chairs

Yeliz Karaca University of Massachusetts, USA
Osvaldo Gervasi University of Perugia, Italy
David Taniar Monash University, Australia

Program Committee Chairs

Beniamino Murgante University of Basilicata, Italy
Chiara Garau University of Cagliari, Italy
Ana Maria A. C. Rocha University of Minho, Portugal
A. Çağrı Tolga Galatasaray University, Turkey

International Advisory Committee

Jemal Abawajy Deakin University, Australia
Dharma P. Agarwal University of Cincinnati, USA
Rajkumar Buyya Melbourne University, Australia
Claudia Bauzer Medeiros University of Campinas, Brazil
Manfred M. Fisher Vienna University of Economics and Business, Austria
Pierre Frankhauser University of Franche-Comté/CNRS, France
Marina L. Gavrilova University of Calgary, Canada
Sumi Helal University of Florida, USA & Lancaster University, UK
Bin Jiang University of Gävle, Sweden
Yee Leung Chinese University of Hong Kong, China

International Liaison Chairs

Ivan Blečić	University of Cagliari, Italy
Giuseppe Borruso	University of Trieste, Italy
Elise De Donker	Western Michigan University, USA
Maria Noelia Faginas Lago	University of Perugia, Italy
Maria Irene Falcão	University of Minho, Portugal
Robert C. H. Hsu	Chung Hua University, Taiwan
Yeliz Karaca	University of Massachusetts Chan Medical School, USA
Tae-Hoon Kim	Zhejiang University of Science and Technology, China
Vladimir Korkhov	Saint Petersburg University, Russia
Takashi Naka	Kyushu Sangyo University, Japan
Rafael D. C. Santos	National Institute for Space Research, Brazil
Maribel Yasmina Santos	University of Minho, Portugal
Anastasia Stratigea	National Technical University of Athens, Greece

Workshop and Session Organizing Chairs

Beniamino Murgante	University of Basilicata, Italy
Chiara Garau	University of Cagliari, Italy

Award Chair

Wenny Rahayu	La Trobe University, Australia

Publicity Committee Chairs

Elmer Dadios	De La Salle University, Philippines
Nataliia Kulabukhova	Saint Petersburg University, Russia
Daisuke Takahashi	Tsukuba University, Japan
Shangwang Wang	Beijing University of Posts and Telecommunications, China

Local Organizing Committee Chairs

Emre Alptekin	Galatasaray University, Turkey
Gülfem Işıklar Alptekin	Galatasaray University, Turkey
Cengiz Kahraman	İstanbul Technical University, Turkey
A. Çağrı Tolga	Galatasaray University, Turkey
Ayberk Zeytin	Galatasaray University, Turkey

Technology Chair

Damiano Perri	University of Perugia, Italy

Program Committee

Vera Afreixo	University of Aveiro, Portugal
Vladimir Alarcon	Northern Gulf Institute, USA
Filipe Alvelos	University of Minho, Portugal
Debora Anelli	Polytechnic University of Bari, Italy
Hartmut Asche	Hasso-Plattner-Institut für Digital Engineering Ggmbh, Germany
Nizamettin Aydın	İstanbul Technical University, Turkey
Ginevra Balletto	University of Cagliari, Italy
Nadia Balucani	University of Perugia, Italy
Socrates Basbas	Aristotle University of Thessaloniki, Greece
David Berti	ART SpA, Italy
Michela Bertolotto	University College Dublin, Ireland
Sandro Bimonte	CEMAGREF, TSCF, France
Ana Cristina Braga	University of Minho, Portugal
Tiziana Campisi	Kore University of Enna, Italy
Yves Caniou	Université Claude Bernard Lyon 1, France
Alessandra Capolupo	Polytechnic University of Bari, Italy
José A. Cardoso e Cunha	Universidade Nova de Lisboa, Portugal
Rui Cardoso	University of Beira Interior, Portugal
Leocadio G. Casado	University of Almería, Spain
Mete Celik	Erciyes University, Turkey
Maria Cerreta	University of Naples Federico II, Italy
Ta Quang Chieu	Thuyloi University, Vietnam
Rachel Chien-Sing Lee	Sunway University, Malaysia
Birol Ciloglugil	Ege University, Turkey
Mauro Coni	University of Cagliari, Italy

Florbela Maria da Cruz Domingues Correia	Polytechnic Institute of Viana do Castelo, Portugal
Alessandro Costantini	INFN, Italy
Roberto De Lotto	University of Pavia, Italy
Luiza De Macedo Mourelle	State University of Rio De Janeiro, Brazil
Marcelo De Paiva Guimaraes	Federal University of Sao Paulo, Brazil
Frank Devai	London South Bank University, UK
Joana Matos Dias	University of Coimbra, Portugal
Aziz Dursun	Virginia Tech University, USA
Laila El Ghandour	Heriot-Watt University, UK
Rafida M. Elobaid	Canadian University Dubai, United Arab Emirates
Maria Irene Falcao	University of Minho, Portugal
Florbela P. Fernandes	Polytechnic Institute of Bragança, Portugal
Paula Odete Fernandes	Polytechnic Institute of Bragança, Portugal
Adelaide de Fátima Baptista Valente Freitas	University of Aveiro, Portugal
Valentina Franzoni	University of Perugia, Italy
Andreas Fricke	University of Potsdam, Germany
Raffaele Garrisi	Centro Operativo per la Sicurezza Cibernetica, Italy
Ivan Gerace	University of Perugia, Italy
Maria Giaoutzi	National Technical University of Athens, Greece
Salvatore Giuffrida	University of Catania, Italy
Teresa Guarda	Universidad Estatal Peninsula de Santa Elena, Ecuador
Sevin Gümgüm	Izmir University of Economics, Turkey
Malgorzata Hanzl	Technical University of Lodz, Poland
Maulana Adhinugraha Kiki	Telkom University, Indonesia
Clement Ho Cheung Leung	Chinese University of Hong Kong, China
Andrea Lombardi	University of Perugia, Italy
Marcos Mandado Alonso	University of Vigo, Spain
Ernesto Marcheggiani	Katholieke Universiteit Leuven, Belgium
Antonino Marvuglia	Luxembourg Institute of Science and Technology, Luxembourg
Michele Mastroianni	University of Salerno, Italy
Hideo Matsufuru	High Energy Accelerator Research Organization, Japan
Fernando Miranda	Universidade do Minho, Portugal
Giuseppe Modica	University of Reggio Calabria, Italy
Majaz Moonis	University of Massachusetts, USA
Nadia Nedjah	State University of Rio de Janeiro, Brazil
Paolo Nesi	University of Florence, Italy

Suzan Obaiys	University of Malaya, Malaysia
Marcin Paprzycki	Polish Academy of Sciences, Poland
Eric Pardede	La Trobe University, Australia
Ana Isabel Pereira	Polytechnic Institute of Bragança, Portugal
Damiano Perri	University of Perugia, Italy
Massimiliano Petri	University of Pisa, Italy
Telmo Pinto	University of Coimbra, Portugal
Alessandro Plaisant	University of Sassari, Italy
Maurizio Pollino	ENEA, Italy
Alenka Poplin	Iowa State University, USA
Marcos Quiles	Federal University of São Paulo, Brazil
Nguyen Huu Quynh	Thuyloi University, Vietnam
Albert Rimola	Universitat Autònoma de Barcelona, Spain
Humberto Rocha	University of Coimbra, Portugal
Marzio Rosi	University of Perugia, Italy
Lucia Saganciti	University of L'Aquila, Italy
Francesco Scorza	University of Basilicata, Italy
Marco Paulo Seabra dos Reis	University of Coimbra, Portugal
Jie Shen	University of Michigan, USA
Francesco Tajani	Sapienza University of Rome, Italy
Rodrigo Tapia Mcclung	Centro de Investigación en Ciencias de Información Geoespacial, Mexico
Eufemia Tarantino	Polytechnic University of Bari, Italy
Sergio Tasso	University of Perugia, Italy
Ana Paula Teixeira	Universidade do Minho, Portugal
Yiota Theodora	National Technical University of Athens, Greece
Giuseppe A. Trunfio	University of Sassari, Italy
Toshihiro Uchibayashi	Kyushu University, Japan
Marco Vizzari	University of Perugia, Italy
Frank Westad	Norwegian University of Science and Technology, Norway
Fukuko Yuasa	High Energy Accelerator Research Organization, Japan
Ljiljana Zivkovic	Republic Geodetic Authority, Serbia

Workshops

Workshop on Advancements in Applied Machine-Learning and Data Analytics (AAMDA 2025)

Workshop Organizers

Alessandro Costantini	INFN, Italy
Daniele Cesini	INFN, Italy
Elisabetta Ronchieri	INFN, Italy
Barbara Martelli	INFN, Italy

Workshop Program Committee Members

Alessandro Costantini	Istituto Nazionale di Fisica Nucleare (INFN), Italy
Daniele Cesini	Istituto Nazionale di Fisica Nucleare (INFN), Italy
Elisabetta Ronchieri	Istituto Nazionale di Fisica Nucleare (INFN), Italy
Barbara Martelli	Istituto Nazionale di Fisica Nucleare (INFN), Italy
Luca Dell'Agnello	Istituto Nazionale di Fisica Nucleare (INFN), Italy

Advanced and Innovative Web Apps 2025 (AIWA 2025)

Workshop Organizers

Damiano Perri	University of Perugia, Italy
Osvaldo Gervasi	University of Perugia, Italy
Stelios Kouzeleas	International Hellenic University, Greece
Sergio Tasso	University of Perugia, Italy

Workshop Program Committee Members

David Berti	ART SpA, Italy
JungYoon Kim	Gachon University, South Korea
TaiHoon Kim	Zhejiang University of Science and Technology, China

Advanced Processes of Mathematics and Computing Models in Complex Data-Intensive Computational Systems (AMCM 2025)

Workshop Organizers

Yeliz Karaca	University of Massachusetts Chan Medical School and Massachusetts Institute of Technology, USA
Dumitru Baleanu	Lebanese American University, Lebanon
Osvaldo Gervasi	University of Perugia, Italy
Yudong Zhang	University of Leicester, UK
Majaz Moonis	University of Massachusetts Chan Medical School and Massachusetts Institute of Technology, USA

Workshop Program Committee Members

TaeHoon Kim	Zhejiang University of Science and Technology, China
Martin Bohner	Missouri University of Science and Technology, USA
Shuihua Wang	University of Leicester, UK
Khan Muhammad	Sungkyunkwan University, South Korea
Mahmoud Abdel-Aty	Sohag University, Egypt
Aziz Dursun	Virginia Polytechnic Institute and State University, USA
Kemal Güven Gülen	Namık Kemal University, Turkey
Akif Akgül	Hitit Üniversitesi, Turkey

Advanced Numerical Approaches for Assessment and Design of No-Tension Masonry Structures (ANAMS 2025)

Workshop Organizers

Antonino Iannuzzo	Universitá degli studi del Sannio, Italy
Carlo Olivieri	Universitá Telematica Pegaso, Italy
Andrea Montanino	CIMNE, Spain
Elham Mousavian	University of Edinburgh, UK

Workshop Program Committee Members

Pietro Meriggi	Roma Tre University, Italy
Francesca Perelli	University of Naples Federico II, Italy
Marialuigia Sangirardi	University of Oxford, UK
Sam Cocking	University of Cambridge, UK

Matteo Salvalaggio	University of Minho, Portugal
Vittorio Paris	University of Bergamo, Italy
Luigi Sibille	Norwegian University of Science and Technology, Norway
Natalia Pingaro	Politecnico di Milano, Italy
Martina Buzzetti	Politecnico di Milano, Italy
Generoso Vaiano	Pegaso Telematic University, Italy
Alessandra Capolupo	Politecnico di Bari, Italy
Amal Gerges	Università degli Studi di Cagliari, Italy
Fabian Orozco	National Autonomous University of Mexico, Mexico
Nathanael Savalle	Polytech Clermont and Université Clermont Auvergne, France
Luca Umberto Argiento	University of Naples Federico II, Italy
Bartolomeo Pantó	Durham University, UK

Unveiling the Synergies Between Air Quality and Climate PlAnning (AQCliPA 2025)

Workshop Organizers

Angela Pilogallo	University of L'Aquila, Italy
Luigi Santopietro	University of Basilicata, Italy
Filomena Pietrapertosa	IMAA CNR, Italy
Monica Salvia	IMAA CNR, Italy
Carlo Trozzi	IMAA CNR, Italy
Valeria Scapini	Central University of Chile, Chile

Workshop Program Committee Members

Lucia Saganeiti	IMAA-CNR, Italy
Lorena Fiorini	University of L'Aquila, Italy
Antonio Mazza	IMAA-CNR, Italy
Gabriele Nolè	IMAA-CNR, Italy
Carmen Guida	University of Naples "Federico II", Italy
Floriana Zucaro	University of Naples "Federico II", Italy
Sabrina Lai	University of Cagliari, Italy
Chiara Garau	University of Cagliari, Italy

Advancements in Spatial assessment of Socio-Ecological SystemS (ASSESS 2025)

Workshop Organizers

Daniele Cannatella	TU Delft, The Netherlands
Giuliano Poli	University of Naples Federico II, Italy
Eugenio Muccio	TU Delft, The Netherlands
Claudiu Forgaci	TU Delft, The Netherlands

Workshop Program Committee Members

Daniele Cannatella	TU Delft, The Netherlands
Giuliano Poli	University of Naples Federico II, Italy
Eugenio Muccio	University of Naples Federico II, Italy
Claudiu Forgaci	TU Delft, The Netherlands
Maria Cerreta	University of Naples Federico II, Italy
Maria Somma	University of Naples Federico II, Italy
Laura Di Tommaso	University of Naples Federico II, Italy
Sabrina Sacco	Politecnico di Milano, Italy
Piero Zizzania	University of Naples Federico II, Italy
Gaia Daldanise	CNR IRISS, Italy
Benedetta Grieco	University of Naples Federico II, Italy
Giuseppe Ciciriello	University of Naples Federico II, Italy
Marta Dell'Ovo	Politecnico di Milano, Italy
Francesco Piras	University of Cagliari, Italy
Diana Rolando	Politecnico di Torino, Italy
Stefano Cuntò	University of Naples Federico II, Italy
Ludovica La Rocca	University of Naples Federico II, Italy

Blockchain and Distributed Ledgers: Technologies and Applications (BDLTA 2025)

Workshop Organizers

Vladimir Korkhov	Saint Petersburg State University, Russia
Elena Stankova	Saint Petersburg State University, Russia
Nataliia Kulabukhova	Saint Petersburg State University, Russia

Workshop Program Committee Members

Adam Belloum	University of Amsterdam, the Netherlands
Dmitrii Vasiunin	Deutsche Telekom Cloud Services E.P.E., Greece
Serob Balyan	Osensus Arm LLC, Armenia
Suren Abrahamyan	Osensus Arm LLC, Armenia
Ashot Sergey Gevorkyan	NAS of Armenia, Armenia

Michal Hnatic	Univerzita Pavla Jozefa Šafárika v Košiciach, Slovakia
Michail Panteleyev	Saint Petersburg Electrotecnical University, Russia
Martin Vala	Univerzita Pavla Jozefa Šafárika v Košiciach, Slovakia
Nodir Zaynalov	Tashkent University of Information Technologies named after Muhammad al Khwarizmi, Uzbekistan
Michail Panteleyev	Saint Petersburg Electrotecnical University, Russia
Alexander Degtyarev	Saint Petersburg University, Russia
Alexander Bogdanov	St. Petersburg State University, Russia

Bio and Neuro Inspired Computing and Applications (BIONCA 2025)

Workshop Organizers

Nadia Nedjah	State University of Rio de Janeiro, Brazil
Luiza de Macedo Mourelle	State University of Rio de Janeiro, Brazil

Workshop Program Committee Members

Nadia Nedjha	State University of Rio de Janeiro, Brazil
Luiza de Macedo Mourelle	State University of Rio de Janeiro, Brazil
Luigi Maciel Ribeiro	State University of Rio de Janeiro, Brazil
Joelmir Ramos	Federal University of Rio de Janeiro, Brazil
Rogério Moraes	Brazilian Navy, Brazil
Marcos Santana Farias	Institute of Nuclear Energy, Brazil
Luneque Silva Jr.	Federal University of ABC, Brazil
Alan Oliveira	University of Lisboa, Portugal
Brij Bhooshan Gupta	Asia University, Taiwan

Computational and Applied Mathematics (CAM 2025)

Workshop Organizers

Maria Irene Falcão	University of Minho, Portugal
Fernando Miranda	University of Minho, Portugal

Workshop Program Committee Members

Fernando Miranda	University of Minho, Portugal
Graça Tomaz	Polytechnic of Guarda, Portugal
Helmuth Malonek	University of Aveiro, Portugal

Isabel Cacao	University of Aveiro, Portugal
João Morais	Autonomous Technological Institute of Mexico, Mexico
Lidia Aceto	University of Eastern Piedmont, Italy
Luís Ferrás	University of Porto, Portugal
M. Irene Falcão	University of Minho, Portugal
Patrícia Beites	University of Beira Interior, Portugal
Paulo Amorim	FGV EMAp, Brazil
Regina de Almeida	University of Trás-os-Montes e Alto Douro, Portugal
Ricardo Severino	University of Minho, Portugal

Computational and Applied Statistics (CAS 2025)

Workshop Organizer

Ana Cristina Braga	ALGORITMI Research Centre, LASI, University of Minho, Portugal

Workshop Program Committee Members

Adelaide Freitas	University of Aveiro, Portugal
Andreas Futschik	Johannes Kepler University Linz, Austria
Ana Cristina Braga	University of Minho, Portugal
Ângela Silva	University of Minho, Portugal
Arminda Manuela Gonçalves	University of Minho, Portugal
Carina Silva	Polytechnic Intitute of Lisbon, Portugal
Elisete Correia	University of Trás-os-Montes e Alto Douro, Portugal
Frank Westad	Norwegian University of Science and Technology, Norway
Isabel Natario	New University of Lisbon, Portugal
Irene Oliveira	University of Trás-os-Montes e Alto Douro, Portugal
Ivan Rodriguez Conde	University of Vigo, Spain
Joaquim Gonçalves	Instituto Politécnico do Cávado e do Ave, Portugal
Lino Costa	University of Minho, Portugal
Marco Reis	University of Coimbra, Portugal
Maria Filipa Mourão	Polytechnic Institute of Viana do Castelo, Portugal
Maria João Polidoro	Polytechnic Institute of Porto, Portugal
Martin Perez Perez	University of Vigo, Spain
Michal Abrahamowicz	McGill University, Canada
Vera Afreixo	University of Aveiro, Portugal

Werner G. Müller	Johannes Kepler University Linz, Austria
Bruna Silva Ramos	University Lusiada de Famalicão, Portugal
Inês Sousa	University of Minho, Portugal
Luís Miguel Rocha Matos	University of Minho, Portugal
Manuel Carlos Figueiredo	University of Minho, Portugal

Cyber Intelligence and Applications (CIA 2025)

Workshop Organizer

| Gianni D'Angelo | University of Salerno, Italy |

Workshop Program Committee Members

Gianni D'Angelo	University of Salerno, Italy
Francesco Palmieri	University of Salerno, Italy
Massimo Ficco	University of Salerno, Italy
Arcangelo Castiglione	University of Salerno, Italy

Computational Methods for Business Analytics (CMBA 2025)

Workshop Organizers

| Cláudio Alves | Universidade do Minho, Portugal |
| Telmo Pinto | Universidade do Minho, Portugal |

Workshop Program Committee Members

Abdulrahim Shamayleh	American University of Sharjah, United Arab Emirates
Ana Rocha	University of Minho, Portugal
Angelo Sifaleras	University of Macedonia, Greece
Cristóvão Silva	University of Coimbra, Portugal
José Valério de Carvalho	University of Minho, Portugal
Miguel Vieira	Universidade Lusófona, Portugal
Rita Macedo	Université de Lille, France
Ana Moura	Universidade de Aveiro, Portugal
Cristina Lopes	ISCAP, Portugal
Eliana Costa e Silva	Instituto Politécnico do Porto, Portugal

Computational Methods, Statistics and Industrial Mathematics (CMSIM 2025)

Workshop Organizers

Maria Filomena Teodoro	IST ID, Instituto Superior Técnico, Portugal
Marina Alexandra Pedro Andrade	ISCTE – Lisbon University Institute, Portugal
Paula Simões	University of Lisbon, Portugal
Teresa A. Oliveira	IST ID, Instituto Superior Técnico, Portugal

Workshop Program Committee Members

Amilcar Oliveira	Universidade Aberta and Universidade de Lisboa, Portugal
Victor Lobo	Escola Naval and NOVA IMS Almada, Portugal
António Pacheco	IST Universidade de Lisboa, Portugal
Eliana Costa	Escola Superior de Tecnologia e Gestão IPPorto, Portugal
Aldina Correia	Escola Superior de Tecnologia e Gestão IPPorto, Portugal
Fernando Carapau	University of Évora, Portugal
Ricardo Moura	Portuguese Naval Academy, Portugal
Ana Borges	Escola Superior de Tecnologia e Gestão IPPorto, Portugal
Cristina Lopes	ISCAP IPPorto, Portugal
Fernanda Costa	University of Minho, Portugal
Cabrita Carlos	IPBeja, Portugal
Maria Luísa Morgado	University of Trás os Montes e Alto Douro and University of Lisboa, Portugal
Rosário Ramos	Universidade Aberta, Portugal
Sofia Rézio	Iscal, Instituto Politécnico de Lisboa, Portugal
Matteo Sacchet	University of Turin, Italy
Marina Marchisio Conte	University of Turin, Italy
António Seijas-Macias	University of Coruña, Spain
Luís F. A. Teodoro	University of Glasgow, UK and University of Oslo, Norway
Christos Kitsos	University of West Attica, Greece
M. Filomena Teodoro	Universidade de Lisboa, Portugal
Marina A. P. Andrade	Instituto Universitário de Lisboa, Portugal
Paula Simões	Military Academy and Universidade Nova de Lisboa, Portugal
Teresa Oliveira	Universidade Aberta and Universidade de Lisboa, Portugal

Computational Optimization and Applications (COA 2025)

Workshop Organizers

Ana Rocha	ALGORITMI Research Centre, LASI, University of Minho, Portugal, Portugal
Humberto Rocha	ALGORITMI Research Centre, LASI, University of Minho, Portugal, Portugal

Workshop Program Committee Members

Florbela Fernandes	Polytechnic Institute of Bragança, Portugal
Clara Vaz	Polytechnic Institute of Bragança, Portugal
Ana Pereira	Polytechnic Institute of Bragança, Portugal
Filipe Alvelos	University of Minho, Portugal
Joana Dias	University of Coimbra, Portugal
Eligius M. T. Hendrix	University of Málaga, Spain
Emerson José de Paiva	Federal University of Itajubá, Brazil
Ana Paula Teixeira	University of Trás-os-Montes and Alto Douro, Portugal
Lino Costa	Universidade do Minho, Portugal

Coastal Cities Versus Inland Areas. Hypotheses for Sustainable Regeneration Through Ecosystem Services of 'Hooking' and Rehabilitation of Brownfield Sites (CoastalCities_VS_InlandAreas 2025)

Workshop Organizers

Celestina Fazia	Università di Enna Kore, Italy
Angrilli Massimo	University of Chieti-Pescara, Italy
Valentina Ciuffreda	University of Chieti-Pescara, Italy
Maurizio Oddo	Università di Enna Kore, Italy
Marcello Sestito	Università di Enna Kore, Italy
Clara Stella Vicari Aversa	University of Reggio Calabria, Italy

Workshop Program Committee Members

Alessandro Camiz	Università d'Annunzio, Italy
Thowayeb Hassan	King Faisal University, Saudi Arabia
Alessandro Barracco	Università Kore di Enna, Italy
Mario Morrica	University of Urbino, Italy
Mariana Ratiu	University of Oradea, Romania
Alanda Akamana	Mohammed VI Polytechnic University, Morocco
Kaoutare Amini Alaoui	Mohammed VI Polytechnic University, Morocco

Computational Astrochemistry 2025 (CompAstro 2025)

Workshop Organizers

Marzio Rosi	University of Perugia, Italy
Daniela Ascenzi	University of Trento, Italy
Nadia Balucani	University of Perugia, Italy
Stefano Falcinelli	University of Perugia, Italy

Workshop Program Committee Members

Dario Campisi	Università degli Studi di Perugia, Italy
Giacomo Giorgi	Università degli Studi di Perugia, Italy
Andrea Giustini	Università degli Studi di Perugia, Italy
Luca Mancini	Università degli Studi di Perugia, Italy
Albert Rimola	Universitat Autònoma de Barcelona, Spain
Gianmarco Vanuzzo	Università degli Studi di Perugia, Italy
Dimitrios Skouteris	Master-Tec, Italy
Piero Ugliengo	Università degli Studi di Torino, Italy
Franco Vecchiocattivi	Università degli Sudi di Perugia, Italy
Giacomo Pannacci	Università degli Studi di Perugia, Italy
Costanza Borghesi	Università degli Studi di Perugia, Italy
Marco Parriani	Università degli Studi di Perugia, Italy
Marta Loletti	Università degli Studi di Perugia, Italy
Fernando Pirani	Università degli Studi di Perugia, Italy
Andrea Lombardi	Università degli Studi di Perugia, Italy
Noelia Faginas Lago	Università degli Studi di Perugia, Italy
Paolo Tosi	Università di Trento, Italy
Cecilia Coletti	Università degli Studi Chieti-Pescara, Italy
Nazzareno Re	Università degli Studi Chieti-Pescara, Italy
Linda Podio	Osservatorio Astrofisico di Arcetri INAF, Italy
Claudio Codella	Osservatorio Astrofisico di Arcetri INAF, Italy
Gabriella Di Genova	Università degli Studi di Perugia, Italy

Computational Methods for Porous Geomaterials (CompPor 2025)

Workshop Organizers

Vadim Lisitsa	IPGG SB RAS, Russia
Evgeniy Romenski	IPGG SB RAS, Russia

Workshop Program Committee Members

Vadim Lisitsa	Institute of Petroleum Geology and Geophysics SB RAS, Russia
Evgeniy Romenski	Sobolev Institute of Mathematics SB RAS, Russia
Vladimir Cheverda	Sobolev Institute of Mathematics SB RAS, Russia
Tatyana Khachkova	IPGG SB RAS, Russia
Dmitry Prokhorov	IPGG SB RAS, Russia
Mikhail Novikov	Sobolev Institute of Mathematics SB RAS, Russia
Sergey Solovyev	Sobolev Institute of Mathematics SB RAS, Russia
Kirill Gadylshin	LLC RNBashNIPIneft, Russia
Olga Stoyanovskaya	Lavrentev Institute of Hydrodynamics SB RAS, Russia
Yerlan Amanbek	Nazarbaev University, Kazakstan

Workshop on Computational Science and HPC (CSHPC 2025)

Workshop Organizers

Elise de Doncker	Western Michigan University, USA
Hideo Matsufuru	High Energy Accelerator Research Organization, Japan

Workshop Program Committee Members

Elise de Doncker	Western Michigan University, USA
Hideo Matsufuru	High Energy Accelerator Research Organization (KEK), Japan
Fukuko Yuasa	KEK, Japan
Issaku Kanamori	RIKEN, Japan
Hiroshi Daisaka	Hitotsubashi University, Japan
Norikazu Yamada	KEK, Japan
Naohito Nakasato	University of Aizu, Japan
Robert Makin	Western Michigan University, USA

Cities, Technologies and Planning 2025 (CTP 2025)

Workshop Organizers

Giuseppe Borruso	University of Trieste, Italy
Beniamino Murgante	University of Basilicata, Italy
Malgorzata Hanzl	Lodz University of Technology, Poland
Anastasia Stratigea	National Technical University of Athens, Greece
Ljiljana Zivkovic	Republic Geodetic Authority, Serbia
Ginevra Balletto	University of Trieste, Italy

Workshop Program Committee Members

Giuseppe Borruso	University of Trieste, Italy
Beniamino Murgante	University of Basilicata, Italy
Malgorzata Hanzl	Lodz University of Technology, Poland
Anastasia Stratigea	National Technical University of Athens, Greece
Ljiljana Zivkovic	Republic Geodetic Authority of Serbia, Serbia
Ginevra Balletto	University of Cagliari, Italy
Silvia Battino	University of Sassari, Italy
Mara Ladu	University of Cagliari, Italy
Maria del Mar Munoz Leonisio	University of Cádiz, Spain
Ahinoa Amaro Garcia	University of Las Palmas of Gran Canaria, Spain
Maria Attard	University of Malta, Malta
Enrico D'agostini	World Maritime University, Sweden
Francesca Krasna	University of Trieste, Italy
Brisol Garcia Garcia	Polytechnic University of Quintana Roo, Mexico
Tu Anh Trinh	UEH University, Vietnam
Giovanni Mauro	Università degli Studi della Campania, Italy
Maria Ronza	University of Naples Federico II, Italy
Massimiliano Bencardino	University of Salerno, Italy
Tomasz Bradecki	Silesian University of Technology, Poland
Dorota Kamrowska-Załuska	Gdańsk University of Technology, Poland
Iwona Jażdżewska	University of Lodz, Poland
Yiota Theodora	National Technical University of Athens, Greece
Apostolos Lagarias	University of Thessaly, Greece
George Tsilimigkas	University of the Aegean, Greece
Akrivi Leka	National Technical University of Athens, Greece
Maria Panagiotopoulou	National Technical University of Athens, Greece
Andrea Gallo	Ca' Foscari University of Venice, Italy
Francesca Sinatra	University of Trieste, Italy

Digital Transition: Effects on Housing Mobility, Market, Land Governance (DIGITRANS 2025)

Workshop Organizers

Fabrizio Battisti	University of Florence, Italy
Fabiana Forte	University of Campania, Italy
Orazio Campo	Sapienza University of Rome, Italy
Alessio Pino	Kore University of Enna, Italy
Carlo Pisano	University of Florence, Italy
Mariolina Grasso	Kore University of Enna, Italy

Workshop Program Committee Members

Fabrizio Battisti	University of Florence, Italy
Fabiana Forte	Università della Campania Luigi Vanvitelli, Italy
Orazio Campo	University of Rome "La Sapienza", Italy
Alessio Pino	Kore University of Enna, Italy
Carlo Pisano	University of Florence, Italy
Mariolina Grasso	Università Kore di Enna, Italy

Evaluating Inner Areas Potentials (EIAP 2025)

Workshop Organizers

Diana Rolando	Politecnico di Torino, Italy
Alice Barreca	Politecnico di Torino, Italy
Manuela Rebaudengo	Politecnico di Torino, Italy
Giorgia Malavasi	Politecnico di Torino, Italy

Workshop Program Committee Members

John Accordino	Virginia Commonwealth University, USA
Francesco Bruzzone	Università Iuav di Venezia, Italy
Maria Cerreta	Università degli Studi di Napoli Federico II, Italy
Maddalena Chimisso	Università degli Studi del Molise, Italy
Chiara Chioni	Università degli Studi di Trento, Italy
Annalisa Contato	Università degli Studi di Palermo, Italy
Cristina Coscia	Politecnico di Torino, Italy
Marta Dell'Ovo	Politecnico di Milano, Italy
Benedetta Di Leo	Università Politecnica delle Marche, Italy
Sara Favargiotti	Università degli Studi di Trento, Italy
Maddalena Ferretti	Università Politecnica delle Marche, Italy
Salvo Giuffrida	Università degli Studi di Palermo, Italy
Barbara Lino	Università degli Studi di Palermo, Italy
Umberto Mecca	Politecnico di Torino, Italy
Beatrice Mecca	Politecnico di Torino, Italy
Giuliano Poli	Università degli Studi di Napoli Federico II, Italy
Marco Rossitti	Politecnico di Milano, Italy
Alexandra Stankulova	Politecnico di Torino, Italy
Elena Todella	Politecnico di Torino, Italy
Asja Aulisio	Politecnico di Torino, Italy
Giulia Datola	Politecnico di Milano, Italy

Francesco Calabrò   Università degli Studi Mediterranea di Reggio
                                  Calabria, Italy
Valeria Saiu   Università degli Studi di Cagliari, Italy
Maria Rosa Trovato   Università di Catania, Italy

Econometric and Multidimensional Evaluation in Urban Environment (EMEUE 2025)

Workshop Organizers
Maria Cerreta   University of Naples Federico II, Italy
Carmelo Maria Torre   Polytechnic University of Bari, Italy
Pierluigi Morano   Polytechnic University of Bari, Italy
Simona Panaro   University of Naples Federico II, Italy
Felicia Di Liddo   University of Naples Federico II, Italy
Debora Anelli   University of Naples Federico II, Italy

Workshop Program Committee Members
Carmelo Maria Torre   Polytechnic University of Bari, Italy
Maria Cerreta   University of Naples Federico II, Italy
Pierluigi Morano   Polytechnic University of Bari, Italy
Francesco Tajani   Sapienza University of Rome, Italy
Simona Panaro   University of Naples Federico II, Italy
Felicia di Liddo   Polytechnic University of Bari, Italy
Debora Anelli   Sapienza University of Rome, Italy
Giuliano Poli   University of Naples Federico II, Italy
Maria Somma   University of Naples Federico II, Italy
Simona Panaro   University of Campania Luigi Vanvitelli, Italy
Laura Di Tommaso   University of Naples Federico II, Italy
Caterina Loffredo   University of Naples Federico II, Italy
Ludovica La Rocca   University of Naples Federico II, Italy
Sabrina Sacco   Politecnico di Milano, Italy
Piero Zizzania   University of Naples Federico II, Italy
Gaia Daldanise   CNR IRISS, Italy
Benedetta Grieco   University of Naples Federico II, Italy
Giuseppe Ciciriello   University of Naples Federico II, Italy
Marta Dell'Ovo   Politecnico di Milano, Italy
Daniele Cannatella   TU Delft University, The Netherlands
Eugenio Muccio   University of Naples Federico II, Italy
Sveva Ventre   University of Naples Federico II, Italy

Governance of Energy Transition: Environmental, Landscape, Social and Spatial Planning (ENERGY_PLANNING 2025)

Workshop Organizers

Mara Ladu	University of Cagliari, Italy
Ginevra Balletto	University of Cagliari, Italy
Emilio Ghiani	University of Cagliari, Italy
Alessandra Marra	University of Salerno, Italy
Roberto De Lotto	University of Pavia, Italy
Balázs Kulcsár	Chalmers University of Technology, Sweden

Workshop Program Committee Members

Riccardo Trevisan	University of Cagliari, Italy
Marco Naseddu	University of Cagliari, Italy
Giuseppe Borruso	University of Trieste, Italy
Andrea Gallo	University of Trieste, Italy
Francesca Sinatra	University of Trieste, Italy
Maria Attard	University of Malta, Malta
Tu Anh Trinh	UEH University Ho Chi Minh City, Vietnam
Marcello Tadini	University of Eastern Piedmont, Italy
Luigi Mundula	University for Foreigners of Perugia, Italy
Silvia Battino	University of Sassari, Italy
Maria del Mar Munoz Leonisio	University of Cádiz, Spain
Anna Richiedei	University of Brescia, Italy
Michele Pezzagno	University of Brescia, Italy
Federico Mertellozzo	University of Firenze, Italy
Marco Mazzarino	IUAV University Venice, Italy

Ecosystem Services in Spatial Planning for Climate Neutral Urban and Rural Areas (ESSP 2025)

Workshop Organizers

Sabrina Lai	University of Cagliari, Italy
Francesco Scorza	University of Basilicata, Italy
Corrado Zoppi	University of Cagliari, Italy
Beniamino Murgante	University of Basilicata, Italy
Carmela Gargiulo	University of Naples Federico II, Italy
Floriana Zucaro	University of Naples Federico II, Italy

Workshop Program Committee Members

Alfonso Annunziata	University of Basilicata, Italy
Ginevra Balletto	University of Cagliari, Italy
Ivan Blečić	University of Cagliari, Italy
Giuseppe Borruso	University of Trieste, Italy
Barbara Caselli	University of Parma, Italy
Maria Cerreta	University of Naples Federico II, Italy
Chiara Garau	University of Cagliari, Italy
Carmen Guida	University of Naples Federico II, Italy
Federica Isola	University of Cagliari, Italy
Francesca Leccis	University of Cagliari, Italy
Federica Leone	University of Cagliari, Italy
Silvia Rossetti	University of Parma, Italy
Luigi Santopietro	University of Basilicata, Italy
Carmelo Torre	Polytechnic of Bari, Italy

The 15th International Workshop on Future Information System Technologies and Applications (FiSTA 2025)

Workshop Organizers

Bernady O. Apduhan	Kyushu Sangyo University, Japan
Rafael Santos	Brazilian National Institute for Space Research, Brazil

Workshop Program Committee Members

Agustinus Borgy Waluyo	Monash University, Australia
Andre Ricardo Abed Grégio	Federal University of Paraná, Brazil
Eric Pardede	La Trobe University, Australia
Kai Cheng	Kyushu Sangyo University, Japan
Ching-Hsien Hsu	Asia University, Taiwan
Fenghui Yao	Tennessee State University, USA
Yusuke Gotoh	Okayama University, Japan
Alvaro Fazenda	Federal University of São Paulo, Brazil
Kazuaki Tanaka	Kyushu Institute of Technology, Japan
Tengku Adil	MARA Technological University, Malaysia
Toshihiro Yamauchi	Okayama University, Japan
Yasuaki Sumida	Kyushu Sangyo University, Japan
Earl Ryan Aleluya	MSU-Iligan Institute of Technology, Philippines
Cherry Mae G. Villame	MSU-Iligan Institute of Technology, Philippines
Anton Louise De Ocampo	Batangas State University, Philippines
Krishnamoorthy Ranganthan	Chennai Institute of Technology, India

Flow Management in Urban Contexts (FMUC 2025)

Workshop Organizers

Alessio Pino	Kore University of Enna, Italy
Giovanna Acampa	Kore University of Enna, Italy

Workshop Program Committee Members

Giovanna Acampa	University of Florence, Italy
Alessio Pino	Kore University of Enna, Italy
Mariolina Grasso	Università Kore di Enna, Italy
Fabrizio Battisti	University of Florence, Italy
Fabrizio Finucci	Roma Tre University, Italy
Antonella G. Masanotti	Roma Tre University, Italy
Daniele Mazzoni	Roma Tre University, Italy

Geographical Analysis, Urban Modeling, Spatial Statistics 2025 (Geog-And-Mod 2025)

Workshop Organizers

Beniamino Murgante	University of Basilicata, Italy
Giuseppe Borruso	University of Trieste, Italy
Hartmut Asche	University of Potsdam, Germany
Rodrigo Tapia McClung	CentroGeo, Mexico
Andreas Fricke	University of Potsdam, Germany

Workshop Program Committee Members

Giuseppe Borruso	University of Trieste, Italy
Beniamino Murgante	University of Basilicata, Italy
Hartmut Asche	University of Potsdam, Germany
Rodrigo Tapia-McClung	Centro de Investigación en Ciencias de Información Geoespacial (CentroGeo), Mexico
Andreas Fricke	University of Potsdam, Germany
Malgorzata Hanzl	Lodz University of Technology, Poland
Anastasia Stratigea	National Technical University of Athens, Greece
Ljiljiana Zivkovic	Republic Geodetic Authority of Serbia, Serbia
Ginevra Balletto	University of Cagliari, Italy
Silvia Battino	University of Sassari, Italy
Mara Ladu	University of Cagliari, Italy
Maria del Mar Munoz Leonisio	University of Cádiz, Spain
Ahinoa Amaro Garcia	University of Las Palmas of Gran Canaria, Spain
Maria Attard	University of Malta, Malta

Enrico D'agostini	World Maritime University, Sweden
Francesca Krasna	University of Trieste, Italy
Brisol García García	Polytechnic University of Quintana Roo, Mexico
Tu Anh Trinh	UEH University, Vietnam
Giovanni Mauro	Università degli Studi della Campania, Italy
Maria Ronza	University of Naples Federico II, Italy
Massimiliano Bencardino	University of Salerno, Italy
Andrea Gallo	Ca' Foscari University of Venice, Italy
Francesca Sinatra	University of Trieste, Italy
Salvatore Dore	University of Trieste, Italy

Geogames for Sustainable Development (Geogames 2025)

Workshop Organizer

Alenka Poplin	Iowa State University, USA

Workshop Program Committee Members

Alenka Poplin	Iowa State University, USA
Bruno Amaral de Andrade	Portucalense University, Portugal
Brian Tomaszewski	Rochester Institute of Technology, USA
Deepak Marhatta	Tribhuvan University, Nepal
Alessandro Plaisant	University of Sassari, Italy
David Schwartz	Rochester Institute of Technology, USA
Silvia Rossetti	University of Parma, Italy
Floriana Zucaro	University of Naples Federico II, Italy
Alfonso Annunziata	University of Basilicata, Italy
Reza Askarizad	University of Cagliari, Italy
Chiara Garau	University of Cagliari, Italy
Tanja Congiu	University of Sassari, Italy

Geomatics for Resource Monitoring and Management (GRMM 2025)

Workshop Organizers

Alberico Sonnessa	Politecnico di Bari, Italy
Eufemia Tarantino	Politecnico di Bari, Italy
Alessandra Capolupo	Politecnico di Bari, Italy

Workshop Program Committee Members

Umberto Fratino	Politecnico di Bari, Italy
Valeria Monno	Politecnico di Bari, Italy

Antonino Maltese	Università degli studi di Palermo, Italy
Athos Agapiou	Cyprus University of Technology, Cyprus
Michele Mangiameli	Università di Catania, Italy
Angela Gorgoglione	Universidad de la República de Uruguay, Uruguay
Roberta Ravanelli	University of Liège, Belgium
Ester Scotto di Perta	Università degli studi di Napoli Federico II, Italy
Giacomo Caporusso	CNR, Italy
Andrea Montanino	International Centre for Numerical Methods in Engineering of Barcelona, Spain
Antonino Iannuzzo	Università degli studi del Sannio, Italy
Alessandro Pagano	Politecnico di Bari, Italy
Francesco Di Capua	Università degli Studi della Basilicata, Italy
Albertini Cinzia	CNR-IREA, Italy
Alessandra Saponieri	Università degli studi del Salento, Italy
PierFrancesco Recchi	Università degli studi di Napoli Federico II, Italy
Vincenzo Totaro	Politecnico di Bari, Italy
Stefania Santoro	CNR Water Research Institute, Italy
Francesco Bimbo	University of Foggia, Italy
Cristina Proietti	Istituto Nazionale di Geofisica e Vulcanologia, Italy
Carla Cavallo	University of Salerno, Italy
Gaetano Falcone	Università degli Studi di Napoli Federico II, Italy
Valeria Belloni	Sapienza University of Rome, Italy
Alessandra Mascitelli	University of Chieti-Pescara, Italy

HERitage and CLIMAte neutrality. Resilient approach for nature centered/based sustainable cities (HERCLIMA 2025)

Workshop Organizers

Celestina Fazia	Università di Enna Kore, Italy
Angrilli Massimo	University of Chieti-Pescara, Italy
Clara Stella Vicari Aversa	University of Reggio Calabria, Italy
Dorina Camelia Ilies	University of Oradea, Romania
Mariana Ratiu	University of Oradea, Romania

Workshop Program Committee Members

Alessandro Camiz	Università d'Annunzio, Italy
Mario Morrica	University of Urbino, Italy
Thowayeb Hassan	King Faisal University, Saudi Arabia
Alessandro Barracco	Università Kore di Enna, Italy
Kaoutare Amini Alaoui	Mohammed VI Polytechnic University (UM6P), Morocco

| Mariana Ratiu | University of Oradea, Romania |
| Valentina Ciuffreda | Università Chieti-Pescara, Italy |

International Workshop on Information and Knowledge in the Internet of Things (IKIT 2025)

Workshop Organizers

Teresa Guarda	Universidad Estatal Península de Santa Elena, Ecuador
Luis Enrique Chuquimarca Jimenez	Universidad Estatal Península de Santa Elena, Ecuador
Gustavo Gatica	Universidad Andrés Bello, Chile
Filipe Mota Pinto	Polytechnic Institute of Leiria, Portugal
Arnulfo Alanis	Instituto Tecnológico de Tijuana, Mexico
Luis Mazon	Universidad Estatal Península de Santa Elena, Spain

Workshop Program Committee Members

Arnulfo Alanis	Instituto Tecnológico de Tijuana, Mexico
Bruno Sousa	University of Coimbra, Portugal
Carlos Balsa	Instituto Politécnico de Bragança, Portugal
Filipe Mota Pinto	Instituto Politécnico de Leiria, Portugal
Gustavo Gatica	Universidad Andrés Bello, Chile
Isabel Lopes	Instituto Politécnico de Bragança, Portugal
José-María Díaz-Nafría	Universidad a Distancia, Spain
Maria Fernanda Augusto	BiTrum Research Group, Spain
Maria Isabel Ribeiro	Instituto Politécnico Bragança, Portugal
Modestos Stavrakis	University of the Aegean, Greece
Simone Belli	Universidad Complutense de Madrid, Spain
Walter Lopes Neto	Instituto Federal de Educação, Brazil

International Workshop on territorial Planning to integrate Risk prevention and urban Ontologies (IWPRO 2025)

Workshop Organizers

Beniamino Murgante	University of Basilicata, Italy
Roberto De Lotto	University of Pavia, Italy
Elisabetta Maria Venco	University of Pavia, Italy
Caterina Pietra	University of Pavia, Italy

Workshop Program Committee Members

Stefano Borgo	Consiglio Nazionale delle Ricerche ISTC, Italy
Valentina Costa	Università di Genova, Italy
Hamid Danesh Pajouh	Middle East Technical University, Turkey
Ilaria Delponte	Università di Genova, Italy
Lorena Fiorini	Università de L'Aquila, Italy
Veronica Gazzola	Politecnico di Milano, Italy
Ghazaleh Goodarzi	Islamic Azad University, Iran
Michele Grimaldi	Università degli Studi di Salerno, Italy
Alessandra Marra	Università degli Studi di Salerno, Italy
Naghmeh Mohammadpourlima	Åbo Akademi University, Finland
Francesca Pirlone	Università di Genova, Italy
Silvia Rossetti	Università di Parma, Italy
Bahareh Shahsavari	University of Minnesota, USA
Ilenia Spadaro	Università di Genova, Italy
Maria Rosaria Stufano Melone	Politecnico di Bari, Italy

Regional Connectivity, Spatial Accessibility and MaaS for Social Inclusion (MaaS 2025)

Workshop Organizers

Mara Ladu	University of Cagliari, Italy
Ginevra Balletto	University of Cagliari, Italy
Gianfranco Fancello	University of Cagliari, Italy
Tanja Congiu	University of Sassari, Italy
Patrizia Serra	University of Cagliari, Italy
Francesco Piras	University of Cagliari, Italy

Workshop Program Committee Members

Marco Naseddu	University of Cagliari, Italy
Italo Meloni	University of Cagliari, Italy
Giuseppe Borruso	University of Trieste, Italy
Andrea Gallo	University of Trieste, Italy
Francesca Sinatra	University of Trieste, Italy
Maria Attard	University of Malta, Malta
Tu Anh Trinh	UEH University, Vietnam
Marcello Tadini	University of Eastern Piedmont, Italy
Luigi Mundula	University for Foreigners of Perugia, Italy
Silvia Battino	University of Sassari, Italy
Brunella Brundu	University of Sassari, Italy
Veronica Camerada	University of Sassari, Italy

Maria del Mar Munoz Leonisio	University of Cádiz, Spain
Anna Richiedei	University of Brescia, Italy
Michele Pezzagno	University of Brescia, Italy
Marco Mazzarino	IUAV University Venice, Italy

The Development of Urban Mobility Management, Road Safety and Risk Assessment (MANTAIN 2025)

Workshop Organizers

Antonio Russo	Università degli Studi di Enna, Italy
Corrado Rindone	University of Reggio Calabria, Italy
Antonio Polimeni	University of Messina, Italy
Florin Rusca	Politehnica University of Bucharest, Romania
Grigorios Fountas	Aristotle University of Thessaloniki, Greece
Antonio Comi	University of Rome Tor Vergata, Italy

Workshop Program Committee Members

Massimo Di Gangi	University of Messina, Italy
Orlando Marco Belcore	University of Messina, Italy
Antonio Polimeni	University of Messina, Italy
Socrates Basbas	Aristotle University of Thessaloniki, Greece
Claudia Caballini	Polytechnic of Torino, Italy
Efstathios Bouhouras	Aristotle University of Thessaloniki, Greece
Stefano Ricci	Sapienza University of Rome, Italy
Marina Zanne	University of Lubljana, Slovenia
Kh Md Nahiduzzaman	Mohammed VI Polytechnic University, Morocco
Alexsandra Deluka Tibljaš	University of Rijeka, Croatia
Guilhermina Torrao	Aston University, UK

Multidimensional Evolutionary Evaluations for Transformative Approaches (MEETA 2025)

Workshop Organizers

Maria Cerreta	University of Naples Federico II, Italy
Giuliano Poli	University of Naples Federico II, Italy
Maria Somma	University of Naples Federico II, Italy
Gaia Daldanise	CNR IRISS, Italy
Ludovica La Rocca	University of Naples Federico II, Italy

Workshop Program Committee Members

Maria Cerreta	University of Naples Federico II, Italy
Giuliano Poli	University of Naples Federico II, Italy
Maria Somma	University of Naples Federico II, Italy
Laura Di Tommaso	University of Naples Federico II, Italy
Sabrina Sacco	Politecnico di Milano, Italy
Piero Zizzania	University of Naples Federico II, Italy
Gaia Daldanise	CNR IRISS, Italy
Benedetta Grieco	University of Naples Federico II, Italy
Giuseppe Ciciriello	University of Naples Federico II, Italy
Marta Dell'Ovo	Politecnico di Milano, Italy
Daniele Cannatella	TU Delft, The Netherlands
Eugenio Muccio	University of Naples Federico II, Italy
Francesco Piras	University of Cagliari, Italy
Diana Rolando	Politecnico di Torino, Italy
Sveva Ventre	University of Naples Federico II, Italy
Caterina Loffredo	University of Naples Federico II, Italy
Ludovica La Rocca	University of Naples Federico II, Italy
Simona Panaro	University of Campania Luigi Vanvitelli, Italy

Building Multi-dimensional Models for Assessing Complex Environmental Systems (MES 2025)

Workshop Organizers

Vanessa Assumma	University of Bologna, Italy
Caterina Caprioli	Politecnico di Torino, Italy
Giulia Datola	Politecnico di Milano, Italy
Federico Dell'Anna	University of Bologna, Italy
Marta Dell'Ovo	Politecnico di Milano, Italy
Marco Rossitti	Politecnico di Milano, Italy

Workshop Program Committee Members

Vanessa Assumma	Università di Bologna, Bologna
Caterina Caprioli	Politecnico di Torino, Italy
Giulia Datola	DAStU Politecnico di Milano, Italy
Federico Dell'Anna	Politecnico di Torino, Italy
Marta Dell'Ovo	Politecnico di Milano, Italy
Marco Rossitti	Politecnico di Milano, Italy
Francesca Torrieri	Politecnico di Milano, Italy
Mariarosaria Angrisano	Università Telematica Pegaso, Italy
Maksims Feofilovs	Riga Technical University, Latvia

Danny Caprini	Politecnico di Milano, Italy
Giulio Cavana	Politecnico di Torino, Italy
Sebastiano Barbieri	Politecnico di Torino, Italy
Marta Bottero	Politecnico di Torino, Italy
Francesco Cosentino	Politecnico di Milano, Italy
Silvia Ronchi	Politecnico di Milano, Italy
Chiara Mazzarella	TU Delft, Netherlands
Marco Volpatti	Politecnico di Torino, Italy
Chiara D'Alpaos	Università degli Studi di Padova, Italy
Alessandra Oppio	Politecnico di Milano, Italy
Alessia Crisopulli	Politecnico di Milano, Italy
Domenico D'Uva	Politecnico di Milano, Italy
Giorgia Malavasi	Politecnico di Torino, Italy
Rubina Canesi	Università degli Studi di Padova, Italy
Elena Todella	Politecnico di Torino, Italy
Beatrice Mecca	Politecnico di Torino, Italy
Giulia Marzani	University of Bologna, Italy
Isabella Giovanetti	University of Bologna, Italy
Lucia Petronio	University of Bologna, Italy
Franco Corti	University of Padova, Italy
Salvatore De Pascalis	Politecnico di Milano, Italy
Valeria Vitulano	Politecnico di Torino, Italy
Lorenzo Diana	Università degli studi di Napoli Federico II, Italy
Maksims Feofilovs	Riga Technical University, Latvia
Marco De Luca	Politecnico di Torino, Italy
Ilaria Cazzola	Politecnico di Torino, Italy
Andrea De Toni	Politecnico di Milano, Italy
Eugenio Muccio	University of Naples Federico II, Italy
Giuliano Poli	University of Naples Federico II, Italy
Francesco Sica	University "La Sapienza" of Rome, Italy
Elena Di Pirro	Università degli Studi del Molise, Italy
Riccardo Alba	Università di Torino, Italy
Irene Regaiolo	Università di Torino, Italy
Francesca Cochis	Università di Torino, Italy

Modelling Liveable Cities: Techniques, Methods, Challenges, and Perspectives Behind the 'X-Minute' City (MLC 2025)

Workshop Organizers

Federico Mara	University of Pisa, Italy
Valerio Cutini	University of Pisa, Italy
Alessandro Araldi	Université Côte d'Azur, France

| Flávia Lopes | Chalmers University of Technology, Sweden |
| Giovanni Fusco | Université Côte d'Azur, France |

Workshop Program Committee Members

Simone Rusci	University of Pisa, Italy
Lorena Fiorini	University of L'Aquila, Italy
Chiara Di Dato	University of L'Aquila, Italy
Francesco Zullo	University of L'Aquila, Italy
Alfonso Annunziata	University of Basilicata, Italy
Beniamino Murgante	University of Basilicata, Italy
Alessandro Araldi	Universitè Côte d'Azur, France
Chiara Garau	University of Cagliari, Italy
Giampiero Lombardini	Università di Genova, Italy
Flavia Lopes	Chalmers University of Technology, Sweden
Giovanni Fusco	Universitè Côte d'Azur, France

Mathematical Methods for Image Processing and Understanding 2025 (MMIPU 2025)

Workshop Organizers

Ivan Gerace	Università degli Studi di Perugia, Italy
Gianluca Vinti	Università degli Studi di Perugia, Italy
Arianna Travaglini	Università degli Studi della Basilicata, Italy

Workshop Program Committee Members

Ivan Gerace	University of Perugia, Italy
Gianluca Vinti	University of Perugia, Italy
Arianna Travaglini	University of Basilicata, Italy
Marco Baioletti	University of Perugia, Italy
Marco Donatelli	University of Insubria, Italy
Anna Tonazzini	C.N.R. Pisa, Italy
Muhammad Hanif	Ghulam Ishaq Khan Institute of Engineering Sciences and Technology, Pakistan
Francesco Marchetti	University of Padua, Italy
Wolfgang Erb	University of Padua, Italy
Danilo Costarelli	University of Perugia, Italy
Francesco Santini	University of Perugia, Italy
Valentina Giorgetti	University of Perugia, Italy

Mobility Opportunities Bridging Inequalities: Social Inclusion and Gender Equity Initiatives Strategies Against Fragmentation and Complexity of Mobility (MOBIL-EGI 2025)

Workshop Organizers

Tiziana Campisi	University of Enna Kore, Italy
Guilhermina Torrao	Aston University, UK
Socrates Basbas	Aristotle University of Thessaloniki, Greece
Tanja Congiu	University of Sassari, Italy
Stefanos Tsigdinos	National Technical University of Athens, Greece
Florin Nemtanu	Politehnica University of Bucharest, Romania

Workshop Program Committee Members

Massimo Di Gangi	University of Messina, Italy
Orlando Marco Belcore	University of Messina, Italy
Francesco Russo	Mediterranean University of Reggio Calabria, Italy
Alexandros Nikitas	University of Huddersfield, UK
Marilisa Nigro	Rome Tre University, Italy
Kh Md Nahiduzzaman	Mohammed VI Polytechnic University, Morocco
Efstathios Bouhouras	Aristotle University of Thessaloniki, Greece
Antonio Comi	University of Rome Tor Vergata, Italy
Edouard Ivanjko	University of Zagreb, Slovenia
Osvaldo Gervasi	University of Perugia, Italy
Beniamino Murgante	University of Basilicata, Italy
Chiara Garau	University of Cagliari, Italy

MOdels and indicators for assessing and measuring the urban settlement deVElopment in the view of NET ZERO by 2050 (MOVEto0 2025)

Workshop Organizers

Lorena Fiorini	University of L'Aquila, Italy
Lucia Saganeiti	CNR-IMAA, Italy
Angela Pilogallo	CNR-IMAA, Italy
Alessandro Marucci	University of L'Aquila, Italy
Francesco Zullo	University of L'Aquila, Italy

Workshop Program Committee Members

Ginevra Balletto	University of Cagliari, Italy
Giuseppe Borruso	University of Trieste, Italy
Chiara Garau	University of Cagliari, Italy

Beniamino Murgante	University of Basilicata, Italy
Giulia Desogus	University of Cagliari, Italy
Ljiljana Zivkovic	Republic Geodetic Authority, Serbia
Luigi Santopietro	University of Basilicata, Italy
Ilaria Delponte	University of Genoa, Italy
Carmen Guida	University of Naples Federico II, Italy
Chiara Di Dato	University of L'Aquila, Italy

5th Workshop on Privacy in the Cloud/Edge/IoT World (PCEIoT 2025)

Workshop Organizers

Lelio Campanile	Università degli Studi della Campania Luigi Vanvitelli, Italy
Mauro Iacono	Università degli Studi della Campania Luigi Vanvitelli, Italy
Michele Mastroianni	Università degli Studi di Foggia, Italy

Workshop Program Committee Members

Arcangelo Castiglione	Università degli Studi di Salerno, Italy
Maria Ganzha	Warsaw University of Technology, Poland
Daniel Grzonka	Cracow University of Technology, Poland
Antonio Iannuzzi	Università degli Studi Roma Tre, Italy
Armando Tacchella	Università degli Studi di Genova, Italy
Biagio Boi	University of Salerno, Italy
Marco De Santis	University of Salerno, Italy
Fiammetta Marulli	Università degli Studi della Campania "L. Vanvitelli", Italy
Christian Riccio	Università degli Studi della Campania "L. Vanvitelli", Italy
Luigi Piero Di Bonito	Università degli Studi di Napoli Federico II, Italy

Preserving Our Past: Spatial and Remote Sensing Technologies for Cultural Heritage in a Changing Climate (POP 2025)

Workshop Organizers

Maria Danese	CNR-ISPC, Italy
Nicola Masini	CNR-ISPC, Italy
Rosa Lasaponara	CNR-IMAA, Italy

Workshop Program Committee Members

Maria Danese	CNR-ISPC, Italy
Nicola Masini	CNR-ISPC, Italy
Rosa Lasaponara	CNR-IMAA, Italy
Dario Gioia	CNR-ISPC, Italy
Giuseppe Corrado	Università degli Studi della Basilicata, Italy
Canio Sabia	CNR-ISPC, Italy

Processes, methods and tools towards RESilient cities and cultural and historic sites prone to SOD and ROD disasters (RES 2025)

Workshop Organizers

Elena Cantatore	Polytechnic University of Bari, Italy
Dario Esposito	Polytechnic University of Bari, Italy
Alberico Sonnessa	Polytechnic University of Bari, Italy

Workshop Program Committee Members

Elena Cantatore	Politecnico di Bari, Italy
Dario Esposito	Politecnico di Bari, Italy
Alberico Sonnessa	Politecnico di Bari, Italy
Valeria Belloni	Sapienza University of Rome, Italy
Michela Ravanelli	Sapienza University of Rome, Italy
Silvano Dal Sasso	University of Basilicata, Italy
Francesco Chiaravalloti	CNR - IRPI, Italy
Roberta Ravanelli	University of Liège, Belgium
Alessandra Mascitelli	University of Chieti-Pescara, Italy
Francesco Di Capua	University of Basilicata, Italy
Gabriele Bernardini	Università Politecnica delle Marche, Italy
Vito Domenico Porcari	University of Basilicata, Italy
Carmen Rosa Fattore	University of Basilicata, Italy
Stefania Santoro	Water Research Institute, Italy

Scientific Computing Infrastructure (SCI 2025)

Workshop Organizers

Vladimir Korkhov	Saint Petersburg State University, Russia
Elena Stankova	Saint Petersburg State University, Russia
Nataliia Kulabukhova	Saint Petersburg State University, Russia

Workshop Program Committee Members

Adam Belloum	University of Amsterdam, the Netherlands
Dmitrii Vasiunin	Deutsche Telekom Cloud Services E.P.E., Greece
Serob Balyan	Osensus Arm LLC, Armenia
Suren Abrahamyan	Osensus Arm LLC, Armenia
Ashot Sergey Gevorkyan	NAS of Armenia, Armenia
Michal Hnatic	Univerzita Pavla Jozefa Šafárika v Košiciach, Slovakia
Michail Panteleyev	Saint Petersburg Electrotecnical University, Russia
Martin Vala	Univerzita Pavla Jozefa Šafárika v Košiciach, Slovakia
Nodir Zaynalov	Tashkent University of Information Technologies named after Muhammad al Khwarizmi, Uzbekistan
Michail Panteleyev	Saint Petersburg Electrotecnical University, Russia
Alexander Degtyarev	Saint Petersburg University, Russia
Alexander Bogdanov	St. Petersburg State University, Russia

Ports and Logistics of the Future - Smartness and Sustainability (SmartPorts 2025)

Workshop Organizers

Andrea Gallo	Università degli Studi di Trieste, Italy
Gianfranco Fancello	University of Cagliari, Italy
Giuseppe Borruso	Università degli Studi di Trieste, Italy
Enrico D'agostini	World Maritime University, Sweden
Silvia Battino	Università degli Studi di Sassari, Italy
Veronica Camerada	Università degli Studi di Sassari, Italy

Workshop Program Committee Members

Giuseppe Borruso	University of Trieste, Italy
Beniamino Murgante	University of Basilicata, Italy
Ginevra Balletto	University of Cagliari, Italy
Silvia Battino	University of Sassari, Italy
Mara Ladu	University of Cagliari, Italy
Maria del Mar Munoz Leonisio	University of Cádiz, Spain
Ahinoa Amaro Garcia	University of Las Palmas of Gran Canaria, Spain
Maria Attard	University of Malta, Malta
Enrico D'agostini	World Maritime University, Sweden
Francesca Krasna	University of Trieste, Italy

Tu Anh Trinh	UEH University - Ho Chi Minh City, Vietnam
Giovanni Mauro	Università degli Studi della Campania, Italy
Maria Ronza	University of Naples Federico II, Italy
Massimiliano Bencardino	University of Salerno, Italy
Andrea Gallo	Ca' Foscari University of Venice, Italy
Francesca Sinatra	University of Trieste, Italy
Salvatore Dore	University of Trieste, Italy
Veronica Camerada	University of Sassari, Italy
Brunella Brundu	University of Sassari, Italy
Gianfranco Fancello	University of Cagliari, Italy
Marcello Tadini	University of Eastern Piedmont, Italy
Marco Mazzarino	IUAV University Venice
José Ángel Hernández Luis	University of Las Palmas de Gran Canaria, Spain
Marco Naseddu	University of Cagliari, Italy
Maurizio Cociancich	Adriafer, Italy
Giovanni Longo	University of Trieste, Italy
Luca Toneatti	University of Trieste, Italy
Martina Sinatra	University of Cagliari, Italy
Enrico Vanino	University of Sheffield, UK
Patrizia Serra	University of Cagliari, Italy
Agostino Bruzzone	University of Genoa, Italy
Marco Petrelli	University of Roma 3, Italy

Smart Transport and Logistics - Smart Supply Chains (SmarTransLog 2025)

Workshop Organizers

Francesca Sinatra	University of Trieste, Italy
Maria del Mar Munoz	Universidad de Cádiz, Spain
Brunella Brundu	University of Sassari, Italy
Patrizia Serra	University of Cagliari, Italy
Salvatore Dore	University of Trieste, Italy
Marco Naseddu	University of Cagliari, Italy

Workshop Program Committee Members

Giuseppe Borruso	University of Trieste, Italy
Beniamino Murgante	University of Basilicata, Italy
Ginevra Balletto	University of Cagliari, Italy
Silvia Battino	University of Sassari, Italy
Mara Ladu	University of Cagliari, Italy
Maria del Mar Munoz Leonisio	University of Cádiz, Spain
Ahinoa Amaro Garcia	University of Las Palmas of Gran Canaria, Spain

Maria Attard	University of Malta, Malta
Enrico D'agostini	World Maritime University, Sweden
Francesca Krasna	University of Trieste, Italy
Tu Anh Trinh	UEH University, Vietnam
Giovanni Mauro	Università degli Studi della Campania, Italy
Maria Ronza	University of Naples Federico II, Italy
Massimiliano Bencardino	University of Salerno, Italy
Andrea Gallo	Ca' Foscari University of Venice, Italy
Francesca Sinatra	University of Trieste, Italy
Salvatore Dore	University of Trieste, Italy
Veronica Camerada	University of Sassari, Italy
Brunella Brundu	University of Sassari, Italy
Gianfranco Fancello	University of Cagliari, Italy
Marcello Tadini	University of Eastern Piedmont, Italy
Marco Mazzarino	IUAV University Venice
José Ángel Hernández Luis	University of Las Palmas de Gran Canaria, Spain
Marco Naseddu	University of Cagliari, Italy
Maurizio Cociancich	Adriafer, Italy
Giovanni Longo	University of Trieste, Italy
Luca Toneatti	University of Trieste, Italy
Martina Sinatra	University of Cagliari, Italy
Enrico Vanino	University of Sheffield, UK
Patrizia Serra	University of Cagliari, Italy
Agostino Bruzzone	University of Genoa, Italy
Marco Petrelli	University of Roma 3, Italy

Smart Tourism (SmartTourism 2025)

Workshop Organizers

Silvia Battino	University of Sassari, Italy
Francesca Krasna	University of Trieste, Italy
Ainhoa Amaro	University of Las Palmas de Gran Canaria, Spain
Maria del Mar Munoz	University of Cádiz, Spain
Brisol García García	Polytechnic University of Quintana Roo, Mexico
Marta Meleddu	University of Sassari, Italy

Workshop Program Committee Members

Giuseppe Borruso	University of Trieste, Italy
Beniamino Murgante	University of Basilicata, Italy
Gianfranco Fancello	University of Cagliari, Italy
Mara Ladu	University of Cagliari, Italy

Martina Sinatra	University of Cagliari, Italy
Salvatore Dore	University of Trieste, Italy
Marco Mazzarino	IUAV University Venice, Italy
Veronica Camerada	University of Sassari, Italy
Brunella Brundu	University of Sassari, Italy
Maria Attard	University of Malta, Malta
Ginevra Balletto	University of Cagliari, Italy
Giovanni Mauro	University degli Studi della Campania, Italy
Salvatore Lampreu	University of Sassari, Italy
Maria Ronza	University of Naples, Italy
Massimiliano Bencardino	University of Salerno, Italy

Sustainable evolution of long-Distance frEight and paSsenger Transport (SOLIDEST 2025)

Workshop Organizers

Francesco Russo	University of Reggio Calabria, Italy
Andreas Nikiforiadis	Democritus University of Thrace, Greece
Orlando Marco Belcore	University of Messina, Italy
Antonio Comi	University of Rome Tor Vergata, Italy
Tiziana Campisi	Kore University of Enna, Italy
Aura Rusca	Politehnica University of Bucharest, Romania

Workshop Program Committee Members

Massimo Di Gangi	University of Messina, Italy
Orlando Marco Belcore	University of Messina, Italy
Antonio Polimeni	University of Messina, Italy
Socrates Basbas	Aristotle University of Thessaloniki, Greece
Efstathios Bouhouras	Aristotle University of Thessaloniki, Greece
Marina Zanne	University of Lubljana, Slovenia
Marilisa Nigro	Rome Tre University, Italy
Edoardo Marcucci	Molde University College, Norway
Eugen Rosca	Polytechnic University of Bucharest, Romania
Kh Md Nahiduzzaman	Mohammed VI Polytechnic University, Morocco
Beniamino Murgante	University of Basilicata, Italy
Chiara Garau	University of Cagliari, Italy

Sustainability Performance Assessment: Models, Approaches, and Applications Toward Interdisciplinary and Integrated Solutions (SPA 2025)

Workshop Organizers

Francesco Scorza	University of Basilicata, Italy
Sabrina Lai	University of Cagliari, Italy
Francesco Rotondo	Università Politecnica delle Marche, Italy
Jolanta Dvarioniene	Kaunas University of Technology, Lithuania
Michele Campagna	University of Cagliari, Italy
Corrado Zoppi	University of Cagliari, Italy

Workshop Program Committee Members

Federico Amato	University of Lausanne, Switzerland
Ferdinando Di Carlo	University of Basilicata, Italy
Maddalena Floris	University of Cagliari, Italy
Federica Isola	University of Cagliari, Italy
Giuseppe Las Casas	University of Basilicata, Italy
Federica Leone	University of Cagliari, Italy
Giampiero Lombardini	University of Genoa, Italy
Federico Martellozzo	University of Florence, Italy
Alessandro Marucci	University of L'Aquila, Italy
Ana Clara Moura	Universidade Federal de Minas Gerais, Brazil
Beniamino Murgante	University of Basilicata, Italy
Silviu Nate	Lucian Blaga University of Sibiu, Romania
Anastasia Stratigea	National Technical University of Athens, Greece
Francesco Zullo	University of L'Aquila, Italy
Luigi Santopietro	University of Basilicata, Italy
Benedetto Manganelli	University of Basilicata, Italy

Specifics of Smart Cities Development in Europe (SPEED 2025)

Workshop Organizers

Chiara Garau	University of Cagliari, Italy
Katarína Vitálišová	Matej Bel University, Slovak Republic
Marco Fanfani	University of Florence, Italy
Anna Vaňová	Matej Bel University, Slovak Republic
Kamila Borsekova	Matej Bel University, Slovak Republic
Paola Zamperlin	University of Florence, Italy

Workshop Program Committee Members

Claudia Loggia	University of KwaZulu-Natal, South Africa
Francesca Maltinti	University of Cagliari, Italy
Alessandro Plaisant	University of Sassari, Italy
Alenka Poplin	Iowa State University, USA
Silvia Rossetti	University of Parma, Italy
Gerardo Carpentieri	University of Naples Federico II, Italy
Carmen Guida	University of Naples Federico II, Italy
Floriana Zucaro	University of Naples Federico II, Italy
Anastasia Stratigea	National Technical University of Athens, Greece
Yiota Theodora	National Technical University of Athens, Greece
Giovanna Concu	University of Cagliari, Italy
Paolo Nesi	University of Florence, Italy
Emanuele Bellini	University of Roma Tre, Italy
Mana Dastoum	Polytechnic University of Madrid, Spain
Barbara Caselli	University of Parma, Italy
Martina Carra	University of Brescia, Italy
Alfonso Annunziata	University of Basilicata, Italy
Elisabetta Venco	University of Pavia, Italy
Caterina Pietra	University of Pavia, Italy
Enrico Collini	University of Florence, Italy
Luciano Alessandro Ipsaro Palesi	University of Florence, Italy

Smart, Safe, and Healthy Cities (SSHC 2025)

Workshop Organizers

Chiara Garau	University of Cagliari, Italy
Gerardo Carpentieri	University of Naples Federico II, Italy
Carmen Guida	University of Naples Federico II, Italy
Tanja Congiu	University of Sassari, Italy
Martina Carra	University of Brescia, Italy
Alenka Poplin	Iowa State University, USA

Workshop Program Committee Members

Rosaria Battarra	Istituto di Studi sul Mediterraneo, Italy
Barbara Caselli	University of Parma, Italy
Francesca Maltinti	University of Cagliari, Italy
Romano Fistola	Università degli Studi di Napoli Federico II, Italy
Alessandro Plaisant	University of Sassari, Italy
Silvia Rossetti	University of Parma, Italy
Marco Fanfani	University of Florence, Italy
Reza Askarizad	University of Cagliari, Italy

Floriana Zucaro	University of Naples Federico II, Italy
Anastasia Stratigea	National Technical University of Athens, Greece
Yiota Theodora	National Technical University of Athens, Greece
Giovanna Concu	University of Cagliari, Italy
Francesco Zullo	University of L'Aquila, Italy
Paola Zamperlin	University of Florence, Italy
Vincenza Torrisi	University of Catania, Italy
Tiziana Campisi	University of Enna Kore, Italy
Katarína Vitálišová	Matej Bel University, Slovakia
Tazyeen Alam	University of Cagliari, Italy
Mana Dastoum	Polytechnic University of Madrid, Spain
Martina Carra	University of Brescia, Italy
Alfonso Annunziata	University of Basilicata, Italy
Elisabetta Venco	University of Pavia, Italy
Caterina Pietra	University of Pavia, Italy

Smart and Sustainable Island Communities (SSIC 2025)

Workshop Organizers

Chiara Garau	University of Cagliari, Italy
Anastasia Stratigea	National Technical University of Athens, Greece
Yiota Theodora	National Technical University of Athens, Greece
Giovanna Concu	University of Cagliari, Italy

Workshop Program Committee Members

Milena Metalkova-Markova	University of Portsmouth, UK
Tarek Teba	University of Portsmouth, UK
Alenka Poplin	Iowa State University, USA
Gerardo Carpentieri	University of Naples Federico II, Italy
Carmen Guida	University of Naples Federico II, Italy
Floriana Zucaro	University of Naples Federico II, Italy
Silvia Rossetti	University of Parma, Italy
Barbara Caselli	University of Parma, Italy
Martina Carra	University of Brescia, Italy
Alfonso Annunziata	University of Basilicata, Italy
Maria Panagiotopoulou	National Technical University of Athens, Greece
Apostolos Lagarias	University of Thessaly, Greece
Paola Zamperlin	University of Florence, Italy
Vincenza Torrisi	University of Catania, Italy
Giuseppina Vacca	University of Cagliari, Italy
Roberto Minunno	Curtin University, Australia
Marco Zucca	University of Cagliari, Italy

Elisabetta Venco	University of Pavia, Italy
Caterina Pietra	University of Pavia, Italy
Pietro Crespi	Politecnico di Milano, Italy

From STreet Experiments to Planned Solutions (STEPS 2025)

Workshop Organizers

Silvia Rossetti	Università degli Studi di Parma, Italy
Angela Ricciardello	Kore University of Enna, Italy
Francesco Pinna	Università degli Studi di Cagliari, Italy
Chiara Garau	Università degli Studi di Cagliari, Italy
Tiziana Campisi	Kore University of Enna, Italy
Vincenza Torrisi	University of Catania, Italy

Workshop Program Committee Members

Martina Carra	University of Brescia, Italy
Barbara Caselli	University of Parma, Italy
Tanja Congiu	University of Sassari, Italy
Gabriele D'Orso	University of Palermo, Italy
Matteo Ignaccolo	University of Catania, Italy
Md Kh Nahiduzzaman	Mohammed VI Polytechnic University, Morocco
Muhammad Ahmad Al-Rashid	University of Malaya, Malaysia
Alessandro Plaisant	University of Sassari, Italy
Marianna Ruggieri	University of Enna Kore, Italy
Michele Zazzi	University of Parma, Italy

Sustainable Tourism Evaluations: approaches, methods and indicators (STEva 2025)

Workshop Organizers

Mariolina Grasso	Università Kore di Enna, Italy
Fabrizio Finucci	Roma Tre University, Italy
Daniele Mazzoni	Roma Tre University, Italy
Antonella G. Masanotti	Roma Tre University, Italy
Giovanna Acampa	University of Florence, Italy

Workshop Program Committee Members

Giovanna Acampa	University of Florence, Italy
Fabrizio Finucci	Roma Tre University, Italy
Mariolina Grasso	"Kore" University of Enna, Italy

Alberto Marzo	Ministero della Cultura, Italy
Antonella G. Masanotti	Roma Tre University, Italy
Daniele Mazzoni	Roma Tre University, Italy
Rocco Murro	Sapienza University of Rome, Italy
Claudio Piferi	University of Florence, Italy
Alessio Pino	"Kore" University of Enna, Italy
Nicoletta Setola	University of Florence, Italy
Laura Calcagnini	Roma Tre University, Italy
Antonio Magarò	Roma Tre University, Italy
Janos Ghyerghyak	University of Pécs, Hungary
Ágnes Borsos	University of Pécs, Hungary
Fabrizio Battisti	University of Florence, Italy

Sustainable Development of Ports (SUSTAINABLEPORTS 2025)

Workshop Organizers

Tiziana Campisi	University of Enna KORE, Italy
Giuseppe Musolino	University of Reggio Calabria, Italy
Efstathios Bouhouras	Aristotle University of Thessaloniki, Greece
Elen Twrdy	University of Ljubljana, Slovenia
Elena Cocuzza	University of Catania, Italy
Aura Rusca	Politehnica University of Bucharest, Romania

Workshop Program Committee Members

Massimo Di Gangi	University of Messina, Italy
Orlando Marco Belcore	University of Messina, Italy
Antonio Polimeni	University of Messina, Italy
Claudia Caballini	Polytechnic of Torino, Italy
Gianfranco Fancello	University of Cagliari, Italy
Marina Zanne	University of Lubljana, Slovenia
Stefano Ricci	Sapienza University of Rome, Italy
Beniamino Murgante	University of Basilicata, Italy
Chiara Garau	University of Cagliari, Italy

Theoretical and Computational Chemistry and Its Applications (TCCMA 2025)

Workshop Organizers

Noelia Faginas Lago	Università di Perugia, Italy
Andrea Lombardi	Università di Perugia, Italy
Marcos Mandado Alonso	University of Vigo, Spain

Workshop Program Committee Members

Noelia Faginas-Lago	University of Perugia, Italy
Andrea Lombardi	University of Perugia, Italy
Marcos Mandado	University of Vigo, Spain
Angeles Peña	University of Vigo, Spain
Luca Mancini	Universiy of Perugia, Italy
Massimiliano Bartolomei	CSIC, Spain
Cecilia Coletti	University of Chieti-Pescara, Italy
Iñaki Tuñón	Universidad de Valencia, Spain
Albert Rimola Gilbert	Universitat Autònoma de Barcelona, Spain
Stefano Falcinelli	University of Perugia, Italy
Dario Campisi	University of Perugia, Italy
Ernesto García Para	University of the Basque Country, Spain
Giacomo Giorgi	University of Perugia, Italy
Tomás González Lezana	IFF CSIC, Spain
Enrique M. Cabaleiro Lago	Universidade de Santiago de Compostela, Spain
Aurora Costales	Universidad de Oviedo, Spain
Angel Martin	Universidad de Oviedo, Spain
Jose Manuel	University of Vigo, Spain
Annarita Laricchiuta	CNR ISTP Bari, Italy
Fernando Pirani	University of Perugia, Italy

Transport Infrastructures for Smart Cities (TISC 2025)

Workshop Organizers

Francesca Maltinti	University of Cagliari, Italy
Mauro Coni	University of Cagliari, Italy
Benedetto Barabino	University of Brescia, Italy
Nicoletta Rassu	University of Cagliari, Italy
James Rombi	University of Cagliari, Italy

Workshop Program Committee Members

Francesco Pinna	University of Cagliari, Italy
Chiara Garau	University of Cagliari, Italy
Mauro D'Apuzzo	University of Cassino, Italy
Roberto Minunno	Curtin University, Australia
Tiziana Campisi	University of Enna Kore, Italy
Roberto Ventura	University of Brescia, Italy
Alessandro Plaisant	University of Sassari, Italy
Massimo Di Francesco	University of Cagliari, Italy

Vincenza Torrisi   University of Catania, Italy
Paola Zamperlin   University of Florence, Italy

Transforming Urban Analytics: The Impact of Crowdsourced Mapping and Advanced AI Techniques on Future Cities (Tr-UrbAna 2025)

Workshop Organizers
Ayse Giz Gulnerman Gengec   Ankara Hacı Bayram Veli University, Turkey
Müslüm Hacar   Tildiz Technical University, Turkey
Himmet Karaman   Istanbul Technical University, Turkey

Workshop Program Committee Members
Beniamino Murgante   University of Basilicata, Italy
Abdulkadir Memduhoğlu   Harran University, Turkey
Zeynel Abidin Polat   İzmir Katip Çelebi University, Turkey
Güzide Miray Perihanoğlu   Van Yüzüncü Yıl University, Turkey
Tugba Memisoglu Baykal   Ankara Hacı Bayram Veli University, Turkey

From structural to TRAnsformative-change of City Environment: challenges and solutions and perspectives (TRACE 2025)

Workshop Organizers
Pierluigi Morano   Polytechnic University of Bari, Italy
Maria Rosaria Guarini   Sapienza University of Rome, Italy
Francesco Sica   Sapienza University of Rome, Italy
Francesco Tajani   Sapienza University of Rome, Italy
Marco Locurcio   Polytechnic University of Bari, Italy
Debora Anelli   Polytechnic University of Bari, Italy

Workshop Program Committee Members
Felicia di Liddo   Politecnico di Bari, Italia
Valeria Saiu   Università di Cagliari, Italia
Emma Sabatelli   Sapienza Università di Roma, Italia
Antonella Roma   Sapienza Università di Roma, Italia
Giuseppe Cerullo   Sapienza Università di Roma, Italia
Lucia della Spina   Università di Reggio Calabria, Italia
Alejandro Segura de la Cal   Politecnico di Madrid, Spain
Yilsy Nuñez   Politecnico di Madrid, Spain
Gabriella Maselli   Università di Salerno, Italy
Maria Rosa Trovato   Università di Catania, Italy

Manuela Rebaudengo   Politecnico di Torino, Italy
Pierfrancesco De Paola   Università di Napoli Federico II, Italy
Daniela Tavano   Università della Calabria, Italy
Maria Saez   University of Granada, Spain
Paola Amoruso   LUM "Giuseppe Degennaro" University, Italy

Temporary Real Estate management: Approaches and methods for Time-integrated impact assessments and evaluations (TREAT 2025)

Workshop Organizers
Chiara Mazzarella   TUDelft, The Netherlands
Hilde Remoy   TUDelft, The Netherlands
Maria Cerreta   University of Naples Federico II, Italy

Workshop Program Committee Members
Chiara Mazzarella   TU Delft, The Netherlands
Hilde Remoy   TU Delft, The Netherlands
Maria Cerreta   University of Naples Federico II, Italy
Maria Somma   University of Naples Federico II, Italy
Simona Panaro   University of Campania Luigi Vanvitelli, Italy
Laura Di Tommaso   University of Naples Federico II, Italy
Caterina Loffredo   University of Naples Federico II, Italy
Ludovica La Rocca   University of Naples Federico II, Italy
Sabrina Sacco   Politecnico di Milano, Italy
Piero Zizzania   University of Naples Federico II, Italy
Gaia Daldanise   CNR IRISS, Italy
Benedetta Grieco   University of Naples Federico II, Italy
Giuseppe Ciciriello   University of Naples Federico II, Italy
Marta Dell'Ovo   Politecnico di Milano, Italy
Daniele Cannatella   TU Delft, The Netherlands
Eugenio Muccio   University of Naples Federico II, Italy
Sveva Ventre   University of Naples Federico II, Italy

Supporting the Transition to Ecological Economy in Cities Regeneration: Circular Model Tools for Reusing Architecture and Infrastructures (TReE 2025)

Workshop Organizers
Mariarosaria Angrisano   Pegaso University, Italy
Giulio Cavana   Politecnico di Torino, Italy
Francesca Buglione   CNR-ISPC, Italy

| Antonia Gravagnuolo | CNR-ISPC, Italy |
| Piera Della Morte | Pegaso University, Italy |

Workshop Program Committee Members

Giulia Datola	Politecnico di Milano, Italy
Vanessa Assumma	University of Bologna, Italy
Marco Volpatti	Politecnico di Torino, Italy
Sebastiano Barbieri	Politecnico di Torino, Italy
Caterina Caprioli	Politecnico di Torino, Italy
Marta Dell'Ovo	Politecnico di Milano, Italy
Federico Dell'Anna	Politecnico di Torino, Italy
Elena Todella	Politecnico di Torino, Italy
Danny Casprini	Politecnico di Milano, Italy
Grazia Neglia	Università Telematica Pegaso, Italy
Francesca Nocca	Università degli Studi di Napoli Federico II, Italy
Giulio Cavana	Politecnico di Torino, Italy
Francesca Buglione	CNR-IPSC, Italy
Marco Rossitti	Politecnico di Milano, Italy
Jhon Escorcia	Politecnico di Torino, Italy
Beatrice Mecca	Politecnico di Torino, Italy
Sara Biancifiori	Politecnico di Torino, Italy

Urban Digital Twins and Data Spaces: Shaping the Future of Sustainable Cities (TwinAbleCities 2025)

Workshop Organizers

Dessislava Petrova Antonova	Sofia University, GATE Institute, Bulgaria
Beniamino Murgante	University of Basilicata, Italy
Senthil Rajendran	RMSI, Bahrain
Tiziana Campisi	Kore University of Enna, Italy
Mila Koeva	University of Twente, The Netherlands

Workshop Program Committee Members

Dessislava Petrova-Antonova	Sofia University, Bulgaria
Mila Koeva	The University of Twente, The Netherlands
Beniamino Murgante	University of Basilicata, Italy
Senthil Rajendran	RMSI, Bahrain
Tiziana Campisi	Kore University of Enna, Italy

Urban Regeneration: Innovative Tools and Evaluation Model (URITEM 2025)

Workshop Organizers

Fabrizio Battisti	University of Florence, Italy
Giovanna Acampa	University of Florence, Italy
Orazio Campo	Sapienza University of Rome, Italy
Melania Perdonò	University of Florence, Italy

Workshop Program Committee Members

Fabrizio Battisti	University of Florence, Italy
Giovanna Acampa	University of Florence, Italy
Orazio Campo	University of Rome "La Sapienza", Italy
Melania Perdonò	Università degli Studi di Firenze, Italy

Urban Space Accessibility and Mobilities (USAM 2025)

Workshop Organizers

Chiara Garau	DICAAR, University of Cagliari, Italy
Alessandro Plaisant	University of Sassari, Italy
Barbara Caselli	University of Parma, Italy
Mauro D'Apuzzo	University of Cassino and Southern Lazio, Italy
Gabriele D'Orso	University of Palermo, Italy
Matteo Ignaccolo	University of Catania, Italy

Workshop Program Committee Members

Mauro Coni	University of Cagliari, Italy
Martina Carra	University of Brescia, Italy
Tiziana Campisi	University of Enna Kore, Italy
Tanja Congiu	University of Sassari, Italy
Francesca Maltinti	University of Cagliari, Italy
Silvia Rossetti	University of Parma, Italy
Barbara Caselli	University of Parma, Italy
Angela Pilogallo	University of L'Aquila, Italy
Lorena Fiorini	University of L'Aquila, Italy
Reza Askarizad	University of Cagliari, Italy
Francesco Pinna	University of Cagliari, Italy
Aime Tsinda	University of Rwanda, Rwanda
Youssef El Ganadi	International University of Rabat, Morocco
Marco Migliore	University of Palermo, Italy
Alessio Salvatore	Italian National Research Council, Italy
Giuseppe Stecca	Italian National Research Council, Italy

Paola Zamperlin	University of Florence, Italy
Vincenza Torrisi	University of Catania, Italy
Gerardo Carpentieri	University of Naples Federico II, Italy
Carmen Guida	University of Naples Federico II, Italy
Floriana Zucaro	University of Naples Federico II, Italy
Alfonso Annunziata	University of Basilicata, Italy
Elisabetta Venco	University of Pavia, Italy
Caterina Pietra	University of Pavia, Italy
Tazyeen Alam	University of Cagliari, Italy
Valerio Cutini	University of Pisa, Italy

UX Mobility 2025: Placing User Experience at the Center of Urban Mobility: Methods and Frameworks (UXM 2025)

Workshop Organizers

Carmen Guida	Università degli Studi di Napoli Federico II, Italy
Gerardo Carpentieri	Università degli Studi di Napoli Federico II, Italy
Federico Messa	Systematica srl, Italy
Lamia Abdelfattah	Systematica srl, Italy

Workshop Program Committee Members

Rosaria Battarra	Istituto di Studi sul Mediterraneo CNR, Italy
Romano Fistola	Università degli Studi di Napoli Federico II, Italy
Lucia Saganeiti	IMAA-CNR, Italy

Virtual Reality and Augmented reality and applications (VRA 2025)

Workshop Organizers

Damiano Perri	University of Perugia, Italy
Osvaldo Gervasi	University of Perugia, Italy
Chau Ma Thi	University of Engineering and Technology, Vietnam National University, Hanoi, Vietnam
Paolo Nesi	University of Florence, Italy
Pierfrancesco Bellini	University of Florence, Italy

Workshop Program Committee Members

| David Berti | ART SpA, Italy |
| JungYoon Kim | Gachon University, South Korea |

TaiHoon Kim	Zhejiang University of Science and Technology, China
Marcelo de Paiva Guimares	Federal University of São Paulo, Brazil
Sergio Tasso	University of Perugia, Italy

Workshop on Advanced and Computational Methods for Earth Science Applications (WACM4ES 2025)

Workshop Organizers

Luca Piroddi	University of Cagliari, Italy
Patrizia Capizzi	University of Palermo, Italy
Marilena Cozzolino	University of Molise, Italy
Sebastiano D'Amico	University of Malta, Malta
Chiara Garau	University of Cagliari, Italy
Giuseppina Vacca	University of Cagliari, Italy

Workshop Program Committee Members

Andrea Angelini	CNR ISPC, Italy
Ilaria Barone	Università degli Studi di Padova, Italy
Patrizia Capizzi	University of Palermo, Italy
Luigi Capozzoli	CNR, Italy
Alberto Carletti	University of Cagliari, Italy
Emanuele Colica	University of Malta, Malta
Marilena Cozzolino	Università del Molise, Italy
Sebastiano D'Amico	University of Malta, Malta
Chiara Garau	University of Cagliari, Italy
Luciano Galone	University of Malta, Malta
Peter Iregbeyen	University of Malta, Malta
Mariano Lisi	Basilicata Aerospace Cluster CLAS, Italy
Raffaele Martorana	Università di Palermo, Italy
Paolo Mauriello	Università del Molise, Italy
Veronica Pazzi	University of Florence, Italy
Raffaele Persico	Università della Calabria, Italy
Luca Piroddi	University of Cagliari, Italy
Sina Saneiyan	Binghamton University, USA
Mercedes Solla	Universidade de Vigo, Spain
Deodato Tapete	ASI, Italy
Giuseppina Vacca	University of Cagliari, Italy
Enrica Vecchi	University of Cagliari, Italy

Sponsoring Organizations

ICCSA 2025 would not have been possible without the tremendous support of many organizations and institutions, for which all organizers and participants of ICCSA 2025 express their sincere gratitude:

Galatasaray University, Istanbul, Türkiye
(https://gsu.edu.tr/en)

African Mathematical Union
(https://www.africanmathunion.org/)

Springer Nature Switzerland AG, Switzerland
(https://www.springer.com)

The University of Massachusetts, USA
(https://www.umass.edu/)

University of Perugia, Italy
(https://www.unipg.it)

University of Basilicata, Italy
(http://www.unibas.it)

Monash University, Australia
(https://www.monash.edu/)

Kyushu Sangyo University, Japan
(https://www.kyusan-u.ac.jp/)

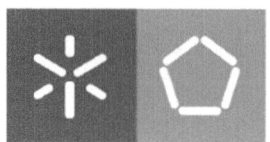

University of Minho, Portugal
(https://www.uminho.pt/)
Venue
ICCSA 2025 took place in: **Galatasaray University, Istanbul, Türkiye**

Additional Reviewers

Reviewers
The review tasks for each workshop have been carried out by the workshop Organizers
and the members of the workshop Program Committee.

Plenary Lectures

Sky Safe with GAI and Post-quantum Computing

Elizabeth Chang

Professor of Cyber Security and Head of Discipline, University of the Sunshine Coast, Australia

Abstract. Professor Chang's talk in this presentation has two distinct parts. To start, she will introduce the landscape of cybersecurity development, attacks, threats, and vulnerabilities, as well as state-of-the-art cyber protection, cyber defence, and cyber incident prevention. This is followed by a discussion of the impact of Generative AI (GAI) and quantum-safe cryptographic computing, highlighting the major issues and challenges in research, education, and training. In conclusion, she will present a vision for Sky Safe solutions, aiming to achieve cyber resilience that supports business and economic stability, enhances human capabilities, and promotes environmental sustainability.

Disaster Preparedness and Risk Profiling in the Digital Era from Earth Observation Lens

Jagannath Aryal

Department of Infrastructure Engineering, University of Melbourne, Australia

Abstract. Natural hazards which turn into disasters result in severe losses of lives, infrastructure, and property. Disasters such as earthquakes and landslides and their impacts on transportation safety, infrastructure resilience, and displacement of people to new places are challenges. To address such challenges, earth observation data and intelligent methods can provide potential solutions in developing decision support systems. This talk will present the state of the art in Earth observation for disaster resilience using intelligent methods. In the Earth observation space, digitalisation has revolutionised the way we map, monitor, and develop decision support systems. Global case study examples covering earthquake-induced landslides from the Himalayan region will cover the digital capabilities. The digital capabilities will embrace object recognition, interpretation, and their accurate and precise capture to integrate into digital models. The developed digital models from representative case studies can be leveraged in other jurisdictions in profiling risks to protect lives and infrastructure and creating disaster preparedness in the era of digital age and digital economy.

Intelligent Image Enhancement for Real-World Applications in Adverse Atmospheric Conditions

Khan Muhammad

Department of Global Convergence, Sungkyunkwan University, South Korea

Abstract. The adverse impacts of atmospheric conditions such as haze, fog, and low-light environments pose significant challenges for real-world applications reliant on computer vision, including autonomous driving, surveillance, and remote sensing. This keynote explores cutting-edge advancements in intelligent image enhancement, drawing insights from two pivotal studies. The first introduces HazeSpace2M, a comprehensive dataset and novel classification-guided dehazing framework that improves image clarity across diverse atmospheric conditions, addressing the gap between synthetic and real-world dehazing performance. The second focuses on LoLI-Street, a benchmark for low-light image enhancement tailored to urban environments, extending beyond enhancement to enable robust object detection and scene understanding. Taken together, these contributions demonstrate how integrating domain-specific datasets, advanced algorithms, and performance benchmarks can significantly elevate the reliability of computer vision systems under challenging weather and lighting conditions. Attendees will gain valuable insights into the methodologies, datasets, and practical applications driving innovation in this field, with implications for research and industry alike.

In Memory of Carmelo Torre

Unfortunately, Professor Carmelo Torre, one of the cornerstones of the ICCSA Conference, passed away last December, leaving everyone stunned and deeply saddened. His loss has created a profound void within our academic community. Carmelo was not only a respected scholar and dedicated contributor to the success and growth of ICCSA, but also a generous colleague, mentor, and friend to many. His intellectual rigor, warm personality, and unwavering commitment to advancing research will be remembered with great admiration. As we continue the work he helped shape, we honor his legacy and the indelible mark he left on all of us. 'Carmelo Torre graduated in engineering at the Polytechnic of Bari with a thesis on urban planning under Dino Borri's guidance. He began his research career by collaborating with Franco Selicato. During his PhD at the University of Naples Federico II under Luigi Fusco Girard, he specialized in real estate market analysis and multi-criteria evaluation methods. He explored the social impacts of urban transformations with his lifelong friend Maria Cerreta. His first ICCSA participation was in Perugia in 2008, in the session Geographical Analysis, Urban Modeling, Spatial Statistics. Instantly captivated by the conference, his charisma enabled him to involve various Italian scientific communities, including those in real estate and statistics. ICCSA became a yearly commitment for him, where he valued the high editorial quality of the proceedings and the dynamic post-presentation discussions and debates he passionately and expertly enriched. In 2012, alongside Maria Cerreta and Paola Perchinunno, he organized the workshop Econometrics and Multidimensional Evaluation in the Urban Environment (EMEUE), fostering dialogue on critical topics. His influence steadily grew, drawing numerous research groups to ICCSA and establishing real estate and assessment as one of the conference's leading fields. A pillar of ICCSA, he was involved across all facets of the event. Torre's contributions to academic discourse were marked by intellectual rigor and innovative thinking. His conference interventions consistently challenged conventional wisdom, offering insights transcending disciplinary boundaries. Beyond the conference, he passionately advocated for equity and social justice. His left-leaning ideology, though firm, earned respect from those with differing views, thanks to his sincerity and loyalty. He was creative, generous, and always willing to help, even at a personal cost. Despite battling illness, he maintained his characteristic optimism, warmth, cheerfulness, and commitment, supported by his partner, Caterina Rinaldo. His legacy lives on in his ideas, dedication, and unmatched generosity.

Contents – Part IX

**Preserving Our Past: Spatial and Remote Sensing Technologies for
Cultural Heritage in a Changing Climate (POP 2025)**

When Culture Influences Climate Changes: Quantifying the Effects
of the Mediterranean vs the Vegan Diet in Italy 3
  Maria Danese and Marilisa Biscione

Semi-automated Human Terrace Recognition: A Case Study on Panarea
Island, Italy 18
  *Antonio Minervino Amodio, Alessandra Bonazza, Alessandro Sardella,
  and Fabrizio Terenzio Gizzi*

High-Resolution Temperature Mapping for Cultural Heritage
Conservation: A Case Study in Matera 30
  Maria Danese, Valentina Florio, and Marilisa Biscione

**Processes, methods and tools towards RESilient cities and cultural
and historic sites prone to SOD and ROD disasters (RES 2025)**

The Interlink Between Urban Growth and Flooding: Lessons from the City
of Bari (Italy) 49
  *Stefania Santoro, Vincenzo Totaro, Pasquale Balena, Vito Iacobellis,
  Umberto Fratino, and Dino Borri*

Mapping Natural and Activity-Induced Hazards for Water Heritage
in Italian Seaports 61
  *Elena Cantatore, Mariella De Fino, Margherita Lasorella,
  and Fabio Fatiguso*

Simulation Model of Evacuation Behavior During Post-Earthquake Fires:
Incorporating Evacuation-Related Information Acquisition 79
  Toshihiro Osaragi and Toko Kusumegi

GNSS-PWV and Intense Rainfall Events: An Analysis of Two Years
of Observation Acquired by the SNIK CORS on the Bari Area (Italy) 97
  Alberico Sonnessa, Eufemia Tarantino, and Alessandra Mascitelli

A Deeper Look into Flood Risk in the City of Bari (Italy) 110
  *Vincenzo Totaro, Stefania Santoro, Maria Francesca Bruno,
  Vito Iacobellis, Matteo Gianluca Molfetta, and Umberto Fratino*

Ports and Logistics of the Future - Smartness and Sustainability (Smart-Ports 2025)

Port-System-Innovation: A Comprehensive Model for Freight Railway
Digital Automation. A Case Study of Trieste Port, Italy 125
  Irina Di Ruocco and Marco Mazzarino

Review of the Climate Change Resilience Measures in Port Context 142
  Federica Pisano and Andrea Gallo

Smart Tourism (SmartTourism 2025)

Construction of World Heritage Candidacy Processes: Key Elements
for a Systematic Framework 159
  Ivan Blečić, Maria Carla Saliu, and Salvador Anton Clavé

Digital Tools Empowering Tourism Development: A Business Intelligence
Platform for the Basilicata Regional Growth 172
  *Maria Danese, Fausto Villani, Domenico Filitti, Giovanni Scaramuzzo,
  Marilisa Biscione, and Nicola Masini*

Scientific Computing Infrastructure (SCI 2025)

Extending the Shortest Path Algorithm for Large Graphs with Cycles
and Parallel Computing Capabilities 191
  Muon Ha, Yulia Shichkina, and Xuan-Hien Nguyen

Challenges of Application of Invisible Artificial Intelligence Technologies
in the Industrial Internet of Things 205
  *Gennady Dik, Alexander Bogdanov, Aleksandr Dik, Jasur Kiyamov,
  Egor Savkov, Aleksandr Shchegolev, and Aleksandr Aleksandrov*

Language Model-Based Algorithm for Constructing Knowledge Graphs
from Patent Data 219
  Nikita Gavrilov, Vladimir Korkhov, Evgenii Pen, and Alexey Tokarev

Hierarchical Virtual Storage 231
  *Evgeniy Ibatullin, Valery Khvatov, Alexander Bogdanov,
  and Nadezhda Shchegoleva*

Autoencoder and Kernel Density Estimation Based Approach for Time
Series Anomaly Detection 249
  Anton Arzha and Vladimir Korkhov

Automated Classification and Segmentation of Brain Tumors on MRI
Images Using Superpixel-Based Machine Learning 264
  Nadezhda Shchegoleva, Nadezhda Pronina, Nataliya Zalutskaya,
  and Jasur Kiyamov

Neural Ordinary Differential Equations with TM-Solver to Predict Time
Series Data 282
  Anna Golovkina and Anna Vashukova

Optimization of Fresco Assembly for Accuracy 294
  Nadezhda Shchegoleva, Maria Gladkaya, and Gennady Dik

Intelligent Browser Window System for Visualizing Events
Detected from Video in Distributed Fog Computing Environment
.... 309
  Alexey Subbotin, Nataly Zhukova, and Elena Stankova

MLE-RBA: A Machine Learning-Empowered Risk-Based Authentication
Algorithm 325
  Iurii Matiushin and Vladimir Korkhov

Investigating Alzheimer's Disease Using a Sequential Analytical Pipeline
for High-Dimensional, Low-Sample Biomedical Data 340
  Nadezhda Shchegoleva, Petr Tonka, and Natalia Zalutskaya

Sustainable evolution of long-Distance frEight and paSsenger Transport (SOLIDEST 2025)

Mode Choice at National Level: Revealed and Stated Preference Survey
for High-Speed Rail Realization 359
  Francesco Russo and Marialuisa Moschella

Inter-urban Transit Connections: A Network Analysis in an Italian Region 375
  Antonio Russo, Giovanni Tesoriere, Corrado Rindone,
  and Tiziana Campisi

Circular Economy in Rail Track: Estimating the Environental Burdens
of the Use of Recycled Material and EoL Processing Through Life Cycle
Assessment 391
  Marinella Giunta, Patrizia Frontera, and Mohammed Er Rouisse

Comprehensive Railway Track Monitoring Using Unmanned Aerial
Systems (UASs) and Building Information Modeling (BIM) 407
  Marinella Giunta, Vincenzo Barrile, Giovanni Leonardi,
  and Emanuela Genovese

Estimating the Run Choice Behavior in High Speed Rail (HSR)
Mode-Service: A Revealed Preference Survey 420
  Giuseppe Musolino and Domenico Sgro

High Speed Rail Stations in Territorial Areas: Sustainable Development
and Quality of New Landscape 434
  Paola Panuccio

Author Index 453

Preserving Our Past: Spatial and Remote Sensing Technologies for Cultural Heritage in a Changing Climate (POP 2025)

When Culture Influences Climate Changes: Quantifying the Effects of the Mediterranean vs the Vegan Diet in Italy

Maria Danese[✉] and Marilisa Biscione

CNR-ISPC, Tito Scalo (PZ), Rome, Italy
`maria.danese@cnr.it`

Abstract. In recent decades, the debate on climate change has progressively become interconnected with that on food choices, highlighting how cultural habits can influence the environmental impact of diets. In particular, the Mediterranean diet and the vegan diet represent two distinct dietary models that, although both considered sustainable, have significant differences in terms of greenhouse gas emissions, land use and water consumption. In this paper, these effects were mapped and quantified in order to compare them and to offer an instrument for political decisions, for example for strategies to orientate future habits and consumptions in food.

Keywords: climate change · dietary impact · spatial analysis

1 Introduction

The problem of climate change is becoming in recent years an increasingly urgent issue to be solved, due to the acceleration in its evolution. Among the main recognized causes of these changes there are greenhouse gas and aerosol emissions [1, 2], in parallel with the increasing deforestation [3]. Although the main climate change mitigation policies focus mainly on emissions from the energy sector or the transport sector, the debate on the effects of food choices on these has also grown considerably over the last decade [4]. In fact, there is a two-way relationship between climate change and diet. The diffusion of dietary culture and the adoption of particular dietary habits can contribute significantly to increasing or conversely reducing environmental impacts, because food production is responsible for greenhouse emissions and land and water consumption and this is exacerbated by the problem of food waste. Similarly, the food system is affected by climate change [5], because the increasing of extreme events such as droughts or floods and the spread of diseases on plants and animals reduce agricultural productivity and food safety and quality. For this reason in literature, many papers are recently treating the relationships between climate changes and diet [6–9]. In fact, even considering the future trends of a growing population, together with the consumption and supply of food calories per capita, which in turn has increased [10, 11], it is becoming more and more important for science to direct people's food policies and culture in a direction that could ensure sustainability and global food security.

O. Gervasi et al. (Eds.): ICCSA 2025 Workshops, LNCS 15894, pp. 3–17, 2026.
https://doi.org/10.1007/978-3-031-97648-3_1

Among the diets most studied for their environmental impact and health benefits are the Mediterranean diet and the vegan diet.

2 The Mediterranean Diet

The Mediterranean Diet is one of the diets considered sustainable since now. It was inscribed on UNESCO's Representative List of Intangible Cultural Heritage in 2010, recognizing it as a timeless nutritional model [12].

This model encompasses practices like crop cultivation, fishing, and food preparation. It includes food like olive oil, cereals, fruits, vegetables, fish and meat and beverage such as dairy, wine and infusions. It is a way of life that promotes social interaction, cultural traditions and respect for biodiversity. The local communities involved are those of regions such as Spain, Greece, Italy and Morocco. Since 2013, those of Cyprus, Croatia and Portugal have also been included [13].

The inclusion of the Mediterranean Diet in the list certainly underlines the cultural importance of a lifestyle strongly linked to the Mediterranean area and too many good practices. While not referring to precise and measurable food claims, such as nutritional tables, it aims to raise awareness of healthy and sustainable eating practices globally. In fact, UNESCO recognition led to the socio-economic growth of the countries involved and established the diet as one of the most sustainable food systems in the world, with the support of the FAO.

The FAO has recognized it as the most sustainable diet due to its reliance on local agricultural products. It is now seen as a symbol of good health and environmental balance, with minimal impact on soil, water resources, and greenhouse gas emissions [14].

The Mediterranean Diet has gone from representing a model of healthy eating to one of sustainability, and has been considered in challenges such as the United Nations 2030 Agenda for Sustainable Development and the European Farm to Fork strategy.

Starting locally to act globally, with a focus on education, the MD is now considered to be closely linked to several UN Sustainable Development Goals (SDGs), as recognized in 2013: SDG 2: Zero Hunger, SDG 5: Gender Equality, SDG 14: Life Below Water, SDG 15: Life on Land, SDG 17: Partnerships for the Goals [15].

Despite its increasing global popularity, adherence to the diet is declining due to lifestyle changes, globalization, and socio-economic factors, posing a threat to its preservation. The challenge now is to reverse these trends and focus on its sustainability as a key model for future food systems [16].

There is debate about updating the food pyramid and adapting it to modern agricultural, economic, and social challenges. A new Mediterranean Diet pyramid has been introduced, aiming to integrate health and sustainability. This updated version reflects the principles observed by the Keys in the 1950s and 1960s. It emphasizes the regular consumption of fruits, vegetables, and whole grains for satiety and reduced intake of processed snacks, contributing to a more sustainable diet.

The major change in the updated pyramid is the position of legumes. Previously considered a secondary protein source, legumes are now recommended as a daily part of the diet. Why are legumes so important?

1. They reduce the need for animal-based proteins, lowering the environmental impact of our diet.
2. Legume cultivation acts as a natural fertilizer by fixing nitrogen in the soil, reducing the need for synthetic fertilizers.

This new model demonstrates that consuming up to one serving of legumes a day can be beneficial for both health and the planet, even within an omnivorous diet, not just vegetarian or vegan ones.

Today, the Mediterranean Diet serves as a model for addressing the challenges of the UN 2030 Agenda for Sustainable Development and the new European Farm to Fork strategy, which aims to reduce the environmental impacts of the agro-food sector. It is seen as a system for building a sustainable future, starting locally and acting globally, with a special focus on education and future generations [17].

Mediterranean diet is considered a system for building a sustainable future, starting locally and acting globally, with a focus on education and future generations. However, Mediterranean diet requests daily diary products, meat and fish. Nowadays it is know that human nutrition has a great impact over the present environmental crisis and that a big percent of the water footprint, of the greenhouse gas and deforestation depends from animal-derived food.

3 The Vegan Diet

The vegan diet is part of what is more generally referred to as the vegetarian diet. Within this there are various subsets of diets: lacto-ovo-vegetarian, if they exclude meat and fish, but include milk and dairy products and eggs; lacto-vegetarian, if they include only milk and dairy products as foods of animal origin; ovo-vegetarian, if they include egg consumption in the diet. In the vegan diet, any type of food of animal origin is instead excluded, including instead a huge variety of plant-based elements (grains, legumes, vegetables, fruits, nuts, seeds, vegetable oils, herbs, and spices) [18].

There are many reasons why people choose a vegan diet: ethical reasons related to love for animals and the principle of non-violence; reasons related to the desire to improve one's health; reasons related to environmental sustainability. On health grounds, the vegan diet has in the past been accused of not being a complete diet and therefore unhealthy. In 2016, however, a position paper by the Academy of Nutrition and Dietetics was published [19], according to which a well-planned and integrated plant-based diet can be suitable for all ages and conditions. Other scientific studies highlight the benefit of the vegan diet (just as some examples see [20–22]). Therefore, as with the Mediterranean Diet, a Veg Pyramid was formulated, with associated guidelines [18, 23].

Also the sustainability of the vegan diet has been deepened and ascertained in literature as well as being a driver of innovation in the culinary field and an opportunity for economic growth [24–30], even, in some models a world completely vegan could be a threaten for agricultural crop leftovers, put more strain on land and water resources, and result in the loss of significant plant and animal genetic components [31].

Because of the increased sustainability that would result from increased consumption of plant foods, several international and local campaigns have been launched around the world, aimed precisely at promoting a reduction in the consumption of animal products.

Some of these have been initiatives of private actors, while others are part of institutional environmental policies:

- the Meatless Monday (promoter: Paul McCartney), consists of reducing the consumption of meat (and in its extended version of 100% Vegetal Monday the consumption of all products of animal origin) by replacing it with products of vegetable origin.
- the Green Monday (promoter: the Municipality of Berkley, California) adds the fight against food waste and the introduction of eco-friendly behaviour to what is already included in Vegetal Monday.
- in Denmark, German and Argentine the government adopted itself the vegan Monday to promote change
- On 1 November each year, the world celebrates World Veganism Day, established in England in 1994 by the Vegan Society.

Accepting the suggestion of this kind of initiative, in this paper, we want to give a spatial comparison between a full Mediterranean diet and a Mediterranean diet, where one, two and three days were substituted with the vegan diet, in order to map and quantify how much it could be the savings in terms of water, greenhouse gas emission and deforestation. The study of the spatial distribution of consumptions can be also useful for policies that could steer population toward a nutrition more plant-based.

4 Materials and Methods

Since the objective in this work is to demonstrate how the introduction of a 100% plant-based diet, not necessarily for all the week, but even just followed 1–2–3 days a week, can contribute to the reduction of environmental impacts in terms of CO_2 and waterprint reduction and to spatialize the distribution of this reduction, first of all the workflow followed is described below.

1. Data from the Italian ISTAT census sections of 2021 were used.
2. The following population groups were identified:
   a. children and adolescents from 0 to 17 years of age. This age group was not taken into account in the analysis, as the variation in diet type and calorie requirements is indeed very variable, depending on the additional age sub-groups, but also on other parameters that are difficult to assess (e.g. presence or absence of breastfeeding, growth rate) even though a well balanced diet is also provided for this age group [23].
   b. Adults from 18 to 64 years of age. For these subjects, calorie consumption can vary between 1200 and 3200kcal per day. We have chosen to make our calculations only for an intermediate values of 2000kcal [18].
   c. Seniors aged 65 and over [32]. Also this sensitive class was excluded by the analysis
3. For the adult group, an ideal daily diet has been considered taking into account scientific studies in the field, both from the point of view of an all-vegetable diet and from the point of view of an omnivorous diet of the Mediterranean Diet type [33]. For the group of adults, an ideal daily diet was chosen taking into account the relevant scientific studies, both from the point of view of a plant-based diet [18] and from the point of view of an omnivorous diet of the Mediterranean Diet type [27]. Therefore,

four dietary patterns were identified: the first completely omnivorous and based on the Mediterranean Diet (Table 1), the second by adding one entirely vegetable day (Table 2), the third by adding two entirely vegetable days (Table 3) and finally the fourth by adding three entirely vegetable days (Table 4) per week.

4. After attributing the food consumption to the different population groups, the greenhouse gas emission (GHGS expressed in $kgCo_2$/kg food as eaten), land use (LU expressed as m^2*year/kg food as eaten) [34, 35] and water footprint (m^3 / t) [36–38] were associated to each food group (Tables 1–2–3–4).

5. Finally, values resumed in Tables 1–2–3–4 were used to associate GHGS, LU and water footprint to the adults present in each Italian Municipality and to obtain the resulting maps (Figs. 1–2–3–4); totals were compared.

Table 1. Dietary pattern of omnivorous diet for one week (adults, 2000kcal) and related production of CO_2, land use consumption and water footprint.

Food groups	Food groups	Number of servings/ total recommended per week	Standard portion (g)	Total serving size per week (g)	GHGE ($kgCo_2$/kg food as eaten)	LU (m^2*year/kg food as eaten)	Water footprint (m^3 / t)
Grains	Bread	24.5	50	1225	3.9	5.8	1644
	Whole cereal grains/ pasta/bulgur/couscous/ready-to-eat cereals	10.5	80	840			
	Grains: potatoes	2	200	400			387
Protein-rich foods	Red meat, white meat	3	100	300	17.1	28.5	15415 5000
	Fish	2	150	300	15.2	2.1	1629
	Canned fish	1	50	50			
	Eggs	3	50	150	5.3	16.1	3265
	Legumes	3	150	150	2.1	7.9	3160
	Milk/yogurt	21	125	2625	11.5	11.5	9000
	Cheeses up to 25% fat	2	100	200			3180
	Cheeses with more than 25% fat	1	50	50			
Fruit and vegetables	fresh fruit	21	150	3150	1.2	1	962
	Fresh vegetables	10.5	200	2100	1.8	0.8	322
	Salads	7	80	560			
Fats and seasoning		21	10	210	7.1	16.9	2364
Nuts		2	30	60	2.1	7.9	9063

5   Results and Discussion

The maps produced show a series of maps of Italy displaying, respectively, greenhouse gas emissions (GHGE) in kg CO2 per week (Fig. 1), land consumption (LU) per week (Fig. 2) and water footprint again per week (Fig. 3). Within each image are shown the

Table 2. Dietary pattern of a combination of omnivorous diet and one day of vegan diet for one week (adults, 2000kcal) and related production of CO_2, land use consumption and water footprint.

Food groups	Food groups	Number of servings/ total recommended per week	Standard portion (g)	Total serving size per week (g)	GHGE (kgCo2/kg food as eaten)	LU (m²*year/kg food as eaten)	Water footprint (m³ / t)
Grains	Bread	24.5	50	1225	3.9	5.8	1644
	Whole cereal grains/ pasta/bulgur/ couscous/ready-to-eat cereals	10.5	80	840			
	Grains: potatoes	2	200	400			387
Protein-rich foods	Red meat, white meat	2	100	200	17.1	28.5	15415 5000
	Fish	2	150	300	15.2	2.1	1629
	Canned fish	1	50	50			
	Eggs	3	50	150	5.3	16.1	3265
	Legumes	5	150	750	2.1	7.9	3160
	Soy milk	2	200	400	2.1	7.9	3160
	Milk/yogurt	18	125	2250	11.5	11.5	9000
	Cheeses up to 25% fat	1	100	100			3180
	Cheeses with more than 25% fat	1	50	50			
Fruit and vegetables	fresh fruit	21	150	3150	1.2	1	962
	Fresh vegetables	10.5	200	2100	1.8	0.8	322
	Salads	7	80	560			
Fats and seasoning		21	10	210	7.1	16.9	2364
Nuts		2	30	60	2.1	7.9	9063

indicators mentioned in the case where the population follows a completely Mediterranean diet (top left) and in the case where they introduce one day (top right), two days (bottom left), three days (bottom right) of vegan diet within the week.

The intervals of the created legends highlight the deciles of values found for each indicator and have been stylized with colors ranging from blue, for lower values, to red, for higher values.

What emerges from the maps produced is the progressive reduction of the red areas as the number of vegan days introduced into the diet increases and thus the positive impact on pollution from reduced consumption of animal by-products.

The results, as calculated, are obviously proportional to the number of inhabitants, so that the different environmental impacts assessed are dependent on the population density of each region, but also with respect to the multiplicative coefficient for each specific type of impact. What has been identified from the three maps produced has been summarised by means of superimposed bar diagrams (Fig. 4). From these diagrams it is evident that the highest impacts derive from the regions of Lombardy, Emilia-Romagna and Veneto, while the regions with the lowest impacts are Basilicata, Molise and Valle d'Aosta, due to their low population density, and it is immediately visible how these impacts decrease as we progressively move from a standard Mediterranean diet to an

Table 3. Dietary pattern of a combination of omnivorous diet and two days of vegan diet for one week (adults, 2000kcal) and related production of CO_2, land use consumption and water footprint.

Food groups	Food groups	Number of servings/ total recommended per week	Standard portion (g)	Total serving size per week (g)	GHGE (kgCo$_2$/kg food as eaten)	LU (m^2*year/kg food as eaten)	Water footprint (m^3 / t)
Grains	Bread	24.5	50	1225	3.9	5.8	1644
	Whole cereal grains/ pasta/bulgur/ couscous/ready-to-eat cereals	10.5	80	840			
	Grains: potatoes	2	200	400			387
Protein-rich foods	Red meat, white meat	2	100	200	17.1	28.5	15415 5000
	Fish	1	150	150	15.2	2.1	1629
	Canned fish	1	50	50			
	Eggs	1	50	50	5.3	16.1	3265
	Legumes	8	150	1200	2.1	7.9	3160
	Soy milk	6	200	1200	2.1	7.9	3160
	Milk/yogurt	12	125	1500	11.5	11.5	9000
	Cheeses up to 25% fat	1	100	100			3180
	Cheeses with more than 25% fat	1	50	50			
Fruit and vegetables	fresh fruit	21	150	3150	1.2	1	962
	Fresh vegetables	10.5	200	2100	1.8	0.8	322
	Salads	7	80	560			
Fats and seasoning		21	10	210	7.1	16.9	2364
Nuts		2	30	60	2.1	7.9	9063

increasingly plant-based diet. This downward trend appears to be similar among regions, but with variation in absolute levels from GHGE production to land consumption to water footprint estimation. More specifically, the effects of the vegan diet are more evident on GHGE emissions and less on water footprint.

It is clear that in the work an ideal, purely theoretical situation has been evaluated because it is based on guidelines, while it does not take into account actual consumption, which often involves much higher consumption of animal products than indicated.

- Other factors to be investigated in more fact-based studies should also take the following considerations into account: there are already people in Italy who follow a vegan diet full-time and others who follow it part-time and thus already contribute to the reduction of environmental impact.
- Within the population there are % overweight or obese people who generally consume more than the theoretical diets. However, it should be noted that this fact has not been taken into account for both the 100% Mediterranean diet and diets with the inclusion of vegan days.
- The assessment of the pollution produced by the individual food categories has also been simplified in this work, as both the Mediterranean diet and the introduction of 100% vegetable days are important for the assessment of environmental impacts. In

Table 4. Dietary pattern of a combination of omnivorous diet and three days of vegan diet for one week (adults, 2000kcal) and related production of CO_2, land use consumption and water footprint.

Food groups	Food groups	Number of servings/ total recommended per week	Standard portion (g)	Total serving size per week (g)	GHGE (kgCo2/kg food as eaten)	LU (m²*year/kg food as eaten)	Water footprint (m³ / t)
Grains	Bread	24.5	50	1225	3.9	5.8	1644
	Whole cereal grains/ pasta/bulgur/ couscous/ready-to-eat cereals	10.5	80	840			
	Grains: potatoes	2	200	400			387
Protein-rich foods	Red meat, white meat	2	100	200	17.1	28.5	15415 5000
	Fish	1	150	150	15.2	2.1	1629
	Canned fish	1	50	50			
	Eggs	1	50	150	5.3	16.1	3265
	Legumes	8	150	1200	2.1	7.9	3160
	Soy milk	9	200	1800	2.1	7.9	3160
	Milk/yogurt	12	125	1500	11.5	11.5	9000
	Cheeses up to 25% fat	1	100	100			3180
	Cheeses with more than 25% fat	1	50	50			
Fruit and vegetables	fresh fruit	21	150	3150	1.2	1	962
	Fresh vegetables	10.5	200	2100	1.8	0.8	322
	Salads	7	80	560			
Fats and seasoning		21	10	210	7.1	16.9	2364
Nuts		2	30	60	2.1	7.9	9063

fact, the place where the food is produced, the amount of transport it requires, as well as the way in which the food is produced and packaged, be it vegetable or animal, are important. From this point of view, the EU has recently been considering the integration of environmental and nutritional criteria into the food labelling system (Farm to Fork Strategy [39]). Some countries, such as France, have already adopted this system with an Eco-Score in which 16 environmental parameters including land use and water consumption are included on the label.

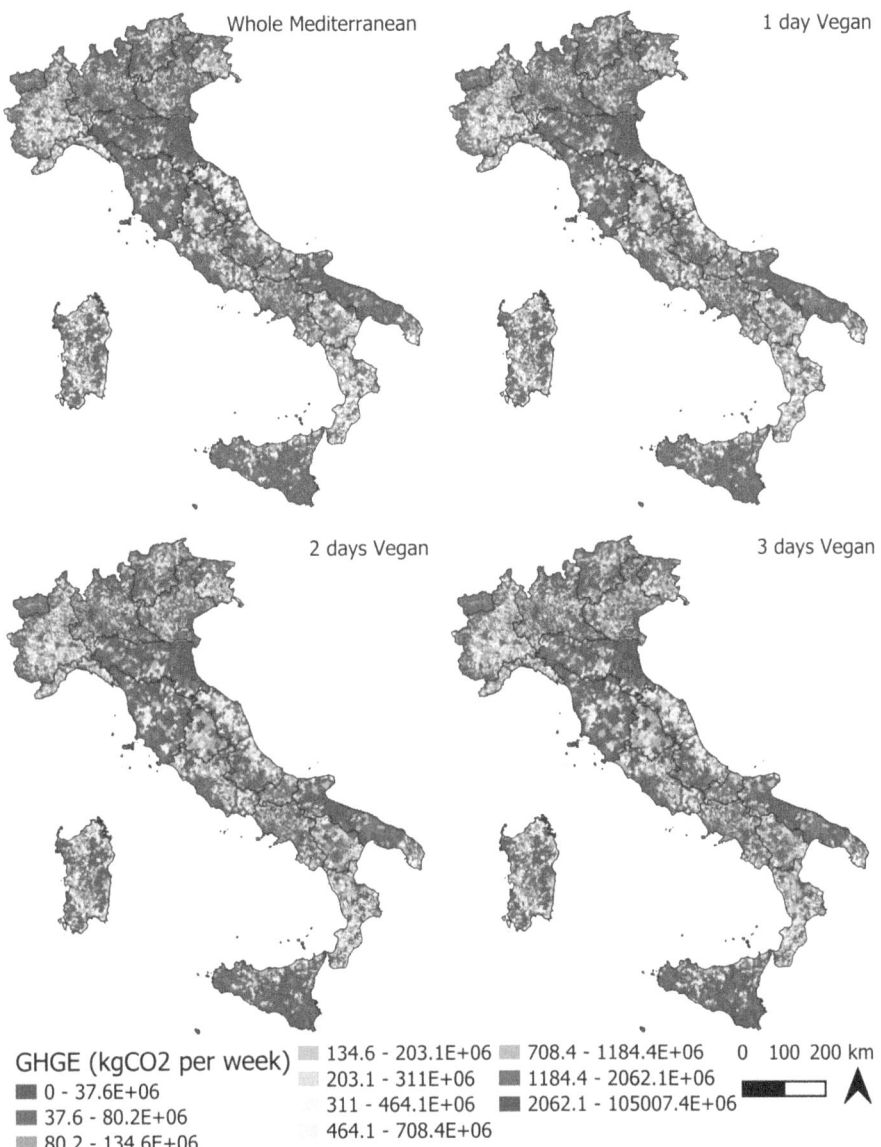

Fig. 1. Map of the distribution of GHGE emissions (kgCO$_2$ per week) in the Italian Municipalities, respectively for the whole Mediterranean diet (top left) and after introducing one day (to right), two days (bottom left), three days (bottom right) of Vegan diet.

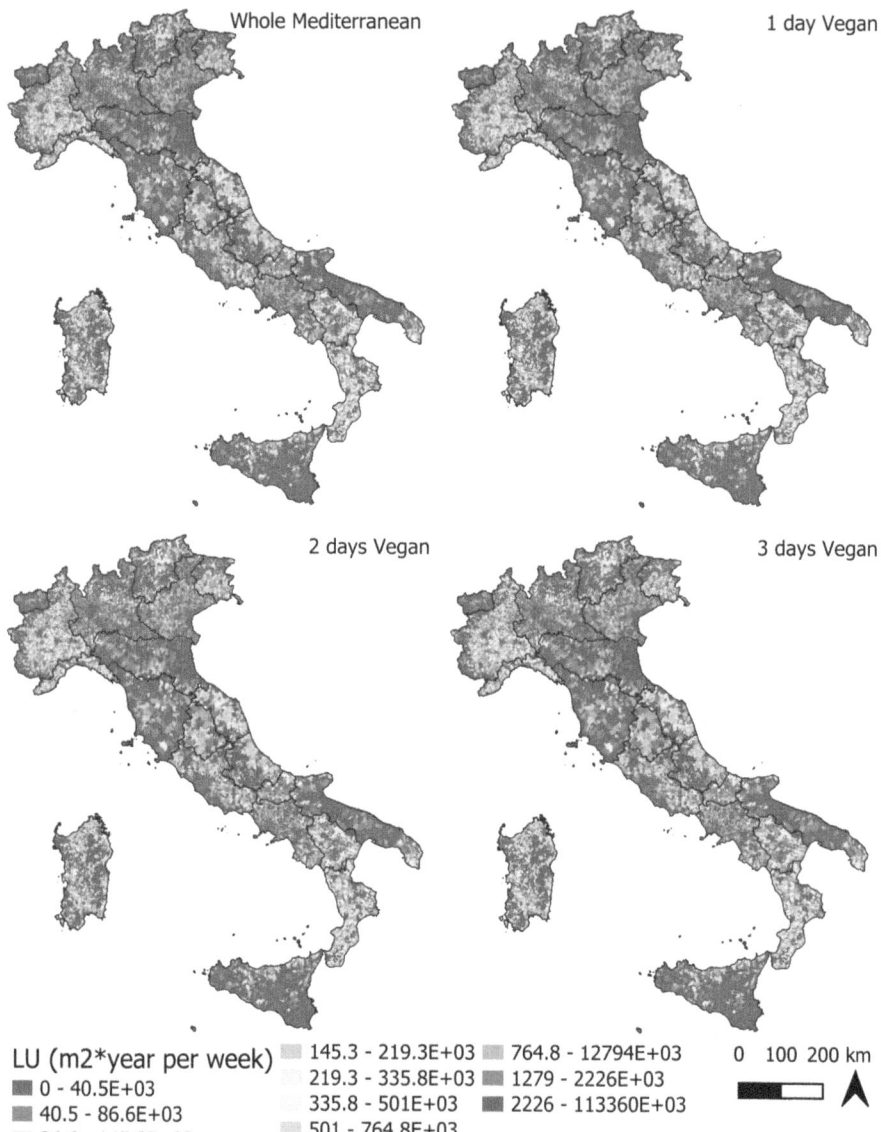

Fig. 2. Map of the distribution of GHGE emissions (kgCO$_2$ per week) in the Italian Municipalities, respectively for the whole Mediterranean diet (top left) and after introducing one day (to right), two days (bottom left), three days (bottom right) of Vegan diet.

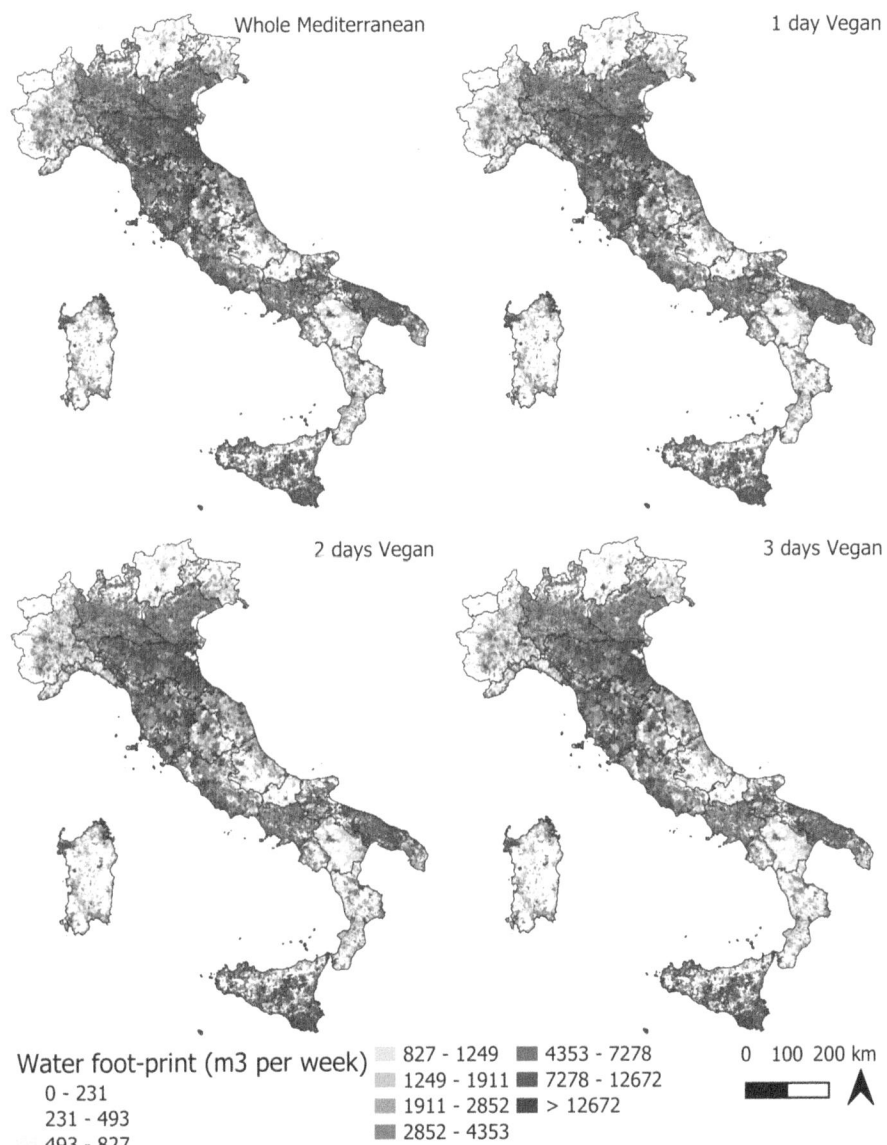

Fig. 3. Map of the distribution of water foot-print (m³ per week) in the Italian Municipalities, respectively for the whole Mediterranean diet (top left) and after introducing one day (to right), two days (bottom left), three days (bottom right) of Vegan diet.

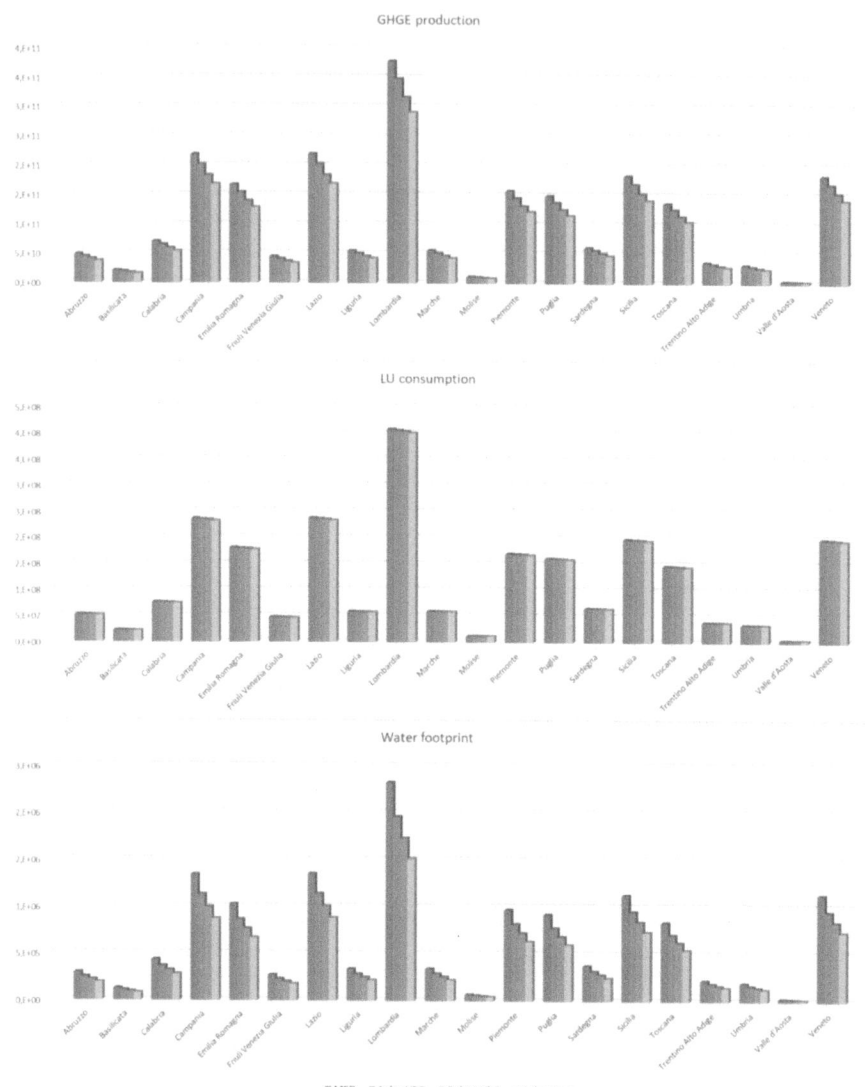

Fig. 4. Environmental impact of diet in different Italian regions, measured in terms of GHGE (top), LU consumption (center) and water footprint (bottom). The different colors represent dietary scenarios with a progressive reduction in the consumption of animal products: MED (standard Mediterranean diet), 1 day VEG, 2 days VEG and 3 days VEG.

6   Conclusion

Adopting even just a few days of a vegan diet per week, leading to a reduction in the consumption of animal products can potentially contribute significantly to reducing diet-related environmental impacts in terms of water consumption, greenhouse gas reduction and land consumption.

The maps produced in this work are useful not only to quantify these impacts, but also as a tool to inform sustainable food policies, helping to understand where to incentivise the inclusion of one or more vegan days, based on the amount of impact produced through initiatives such as Vegan Monday, but also to guide and support sustainable food design and consumer awareness campaigns. The spread of a more plant-based culture is indeed fundamental to learning to appreciate and cook new, less impactful dishes with the hope that they will be introduced more independently and thus lead to a spontaneous increase in sustainability at the table.

Finally, although the study is based on theoretical scenarios and ideal nutrition guidelines, it provides a starting point for future research and insights based on more realistic consumption. By introducing other factors such as current eating habits, regional variations in consumption patterns, the impact of local production and logistics into the analysis, it will be possible to further refine strategies for reducing the environmental impact of the food system.

References

1. Hardy, J.T.: Climate Change: Causes, Effects, and Solutions. John Wiley & Sons (2003)
2. Bindoff, N.L., et al.: Detection and attribution of climate change: from global to regional. In: Climate Change 2013: The Physical Science Basis (2014)
3. Longobardi, P., Montenegro, A., Beltrami, H., Eby, M.: Deforestation induced climate change: effects of spatial scale. PLoS ONE **11**, e0153357 (2016)
4. Stehfest, E., Bouwman, L., Van Vuuren, D.P., Den Elzen, M.G., Eickhout, B., Kabat, P.: Climate benefits of changing diet. Clim. Change **95**, 83–102 (2009)
5. Owino, V., et al.: The impact of climate change on food systems, diet quality, nutrition, and health outcomes: a narrative review. Front. Clim. **4**, 941842 (2022)
6. Bose, N., Hills, T., Sgroi, D.: Climate change and diet. IZA Discussion Papers (2020)
7. Springmann, M., Godfray, H.C.J., Rayner, M., Scarborough, P.: Analysis and valuation of the health and climate change cobenefits of dietary change. Proc. Natl. Acad. Sci. **113**, 4146–4151 (2016)
8. Jarmul, S., Dangour, A.D., Green, R., Liew, Z., Haines, A., Scheelbeek, P.F.: Climate change mitigation through dietary change: a systematic review of empirical and modelling studies on the environmental footprints and health effects of 'sustainable diets'. Environ. Res. Lett. **15**, 123014 (2020). ERL [Web site]
9. Wellesley, L., Happer, C., Froggatt, A.: Changing climate, changing diets. Chatham House Rep. **31**, 42367153 (2015)
10. Gilland, B.: World population and food supply: can food production keep pace with population growth in the next half-century? Food Policy **27**, 47–63 (2002)
11. Kasnakoglu, H.: FAOSTAT and CountrySTAT: integrated global and national food and agriculture statistical databases. In: Proceedings of the XLIII Scientific Meeting, Societa Italiana di Statistica, Universita di Torino, Turin, Italy, pp. 14–16

12. UNESCO: Convention for the safeguarding of the intangible cultural heritage. Intergovernamental committee for the safeguarding of the intangible cultural heritage. UNESCO (2010). https://ich.unesco.org/doc/src/ITH-10-5.COM-CONF.202-6-EN.pdf

13. UNESCO, I.H.: Convention for the safeguarding of the intangible cultural heritage. Intergovernmental committee for the safeguarding of the intangible cultural heritage. UNESCO (2013). https://ich.unesco.org/doc/src/ITH-10-5.COM-CONF.202-6-EN.pdf

14. FAO: The mediterranean diet: a crucial tool for a more nutritious and sustainable future (2022). https://www.fao.org/newsroom/detail/the-mediterranean-diet-a-crucial-tool-for-a-more-nutritious-and-sustainable-future/en

15. UN: The 2030 agenda for sustainable development. https://www.un.org/sustainabledevelopment/development-agenda/

16. Serra-Majem, L., et al.: Updating the mediterranean diet pyramid towards sustainability: focus on environmental concerns. Int. J. Environ. Res. Pub. Health **17**, 8758 (2020)

17. MIC: Mediterrean Diet (2013). https://unesco.cultura.gov.it/en/projects/mediterranean-diet/

18. Baroni, L., Goggi, S., Battino, M.: VegPlate: a mediterranean-based food guide for Italian adult, pregnant, and lactating vegetarians. J. Acad. Nutr. Diet. **118**, 2242–2243 (2018)

19. Melina, V., Craig, W., Levin, S.: Position of the academy of nutrition and dietetics: vegetarian diets. J. Acad. Nutr. Diet. **116**, 1970–1980 (2016)

20. Bakaloudi, D.R., et al.: Intake and adequacy of the vegan diet. A systematic review of the evidence. Clin. Nutr. **40**, 3503–3521 (2021)

21. Richter, M., et al.: Vegan diet. Position of the German nutrition society (DGE). Ernahrungs umschau **63**, 92–102 (2016)

22. Radnitz, C., Beezhold, B., DiMatteo, J.: Investigation of lifestyle choices of individuals following a vegan diet for health and ethical reasons. Appetite **90**, 31–36 (2015)

23. Baroni, L., Goggi, S., Battino, M.: Planning well-balanced vegetarian diets in infants, children, and adolescents: the vegplate junior. J. Acad. Nutr. Diet. **119**, 1067–1074 (2019)

24. Chai, B.C., Van Der Voort, J.R., Grofelnik, K., Eliasdottir, H.G., Klöss, I., Perez-Cueto, F.J.: Which diet has the least environmental impact on our planet? A systematic review of vegan, vegetarian and omnivorous diets. Sustainability **11**, 4110 (2019)

25. Saari, U.A., Herstatt, C., Tiwari, R., Dedehayir, O., Mäkinen, S.J.: The vegan trend and the microfoundations of institutional change: a commentary on food producers' sustainable innovation journeys in Europe. Trends Food Sci. Technol. **107**, 161–167 (2021)

26. Knight, A.: The relative benefits for environmental sustainability of vegan diets for dogs, cats and people. PLoS ONE **18**, e0291791 (2023)

27. Niederle, P., Schubert, M.N.: How does veganism contribute to shape sustainable food systems? Practices, meanings and identities of vegan restaurants in Porto Alegre, Brazil. J. Rural. Stud. **78**, 304–313 (2020)

28. Dedehayir, O., Smidt, M., Riverola, C., Velasquez, S.: Unlocking the market with vegan food innovations. In: ISPIM Innovation Symposium, pp. 1–13. The International Society for Professional Innovation Management (ISPIM)

29. Dedehayir, O., Riverola, C., Velasquez, S., Smidt, M.: Diffusion of vegan food innovations: a dual-market perspective. In: Leal Filho, W., Azul, A.M., Brandli, L., özuyar, P.G., Wall, T. (eds.) Responsible Consumption and Production. Encyclopedia of the UN Sustainable Development Goals, pp. 137–146. Springer, Cham (2020). https://doi.org/10.1007/978-3-319-95726-5_16

30. Lusk, J.L., Norwood, F.B.: Some economic benefits and costs of vegetarianism. Agric. Resour. Econ. Rev. **38**, 109–124 (2009)

31. Dorgbetor, I.K., Ondrasek, G., Kutnjak, H., Mikuš, O.: What if the world went vegan? A review of the impact on natural resources, climate change, and economies. Agriculture **12**, 1518 (2022)

32. CREA: Linee Guida per una Sana Alimentazione Italiana. Edizione (2018)
33. SINU: LARN - Livelli di Assunzione di Riferimento di Nutrienti ed energia per la popolazione italiana. IV Revisione (2014)
34. Mertens, E., Kaptijn, G., Kuijsten, A., van Zanten, H., Geleijnse, J.M., van 't Veer, P.: SHARP-Indicators Database towards a public database for environmental sustainability. Data Brief **27**, 104617 (2019)
35. Hoekstra, A.Y., Mekonnen, M.M.: The water footprint of humanity. Proc. Natl. Acad. Sci. **109**, 3232–3237 (2012)
36. Mekonnen, M.M., Hoekstra, A.Y.: The green, blue and grey water footprint of crops and derived crop products. Hydrol. Earth Syst. Sci. **15**, 1577–1600 (2011)
37. Mekonnen, M.M., Hoekstra, A.Y.: A global assessment of the water footprint of farm animal products. Ecosystems **15**, 401–415 (2012)
38. Pahlow, M., van Oel, P.R., Mekonnen, M.M., Hoekstra, A.Y.: Increasing pressure on freshwater resources due to terrestrial feed ingredients for aquaculture production. Sci. Total. Environ. **536**, 847–857 (2015)
39. Wesseler, J.: The EU's farm-to-fork strategy: an assessment from the perspective of agricultural economics. Appl. Econ. Perspect. PolicyPerspect. Policy **44**, 1826–1843 (2022)

Semi-automated Human Terrace Recognition: A Case Study on Panarea Island, Italy

Antonio Minervino Amodio[1]([⊠]) [ID], Alessandra Bonazza[2] [ID], Alessandro Sardella[2] [ID], and Fabrizio Terenzio Gizzi[1] [ID]

[1] Institute of Heritage Science (ISPC), National Research Council (CNR), 85050 Tito, Italy
antonio.minervinoamodio@cnr.it

[2] Institute of Atmospheric Science and Climate (ISAC), National Research Council of Italy (CNR), 40129 Bologna, Italy

Abstract. Terraces, found worldwide, demonstrate the interaction between humans and the environment, shaping landscapes, reducing slope, enabling agriculture, and mitigating erosion. Abandonment leads to negative consequences at the productive, economic, ecological, and landscape levels, with biodiversity loss and increased hydrogeological risk. In this view the semi-automated recognition of human terraces is crucial for land management, especially in areas with high historical and landscape value. Therefore, developing efficient and smart mapping methodologies is fundamental for protection, redevelopment, and valorization of such landscape. Geomorphological analysis tools were tested, with the r.geomorphon and r.param.scale modules proving most effective in delineating terraces. These methods, based on pattern recognition and local topography analysis, are well-suited to the identification of artificial structures like terraces. The r.geomorphon method generates geomorphometric maps from DEMs with a high number of cells, while r.param.scale helps to identify the characteristic of landforms, which can be useful in distinguishing terraces from other territorial features. The results of the research can be useful for terrace identification in other areas thus, supporting landscape conservation and valorization planning. Terraced landscapes preserve traditional agricultural practices, quality products, and biodiversity. The proposed methodology can came in handy in areas lacking terrace mapping that are abandoned or heavily vegetated.

Keywords: Terrace Identification · Semi-Automated Mapping · Geomorphometry · Cultural Landscape · Geomorphon · Dry Stone Walls · Land Degradation · Aeolian Islands

1 Introduction

Terraced landscapes are among the most evident demonstrations of human impact on the land [1, 2]. These structures, found in different parts of the world and in various environmental conditions, result from centuries of interaction between humans and the environment [3–8]. Terraces were created to establish cultivable areas on steep slopes, reduce soil erosion, improve water resource management, and increase agricultural productivity [9–12]. In many areas over the world, terraced landscapes are considered an invaluable historical and cultural heritage, as well as an ecosystem service that must be adequately preserved [13]. However, the abandonment of terraced landscapes is a growing problem in many areas, especially in mountainous and marginal zones [14, 15]. This phenomenon is often caused by socio-economic changes, migration to cities, difficulties in agricultural mechanization, aging of the rural population, and a lack of adequate support policies [16]. The consequences of abandonment can be devastating for both the environment and the landscape: i) increased soil erosion, the lack of maintenance of terraces leads to the collapse of dry stone walls, the formation of rills and landslides, and the loss of fertile soil; ii) loss of biodiversity, the abandonment of traditional agricultural practices promotes the spread of invasive plant species and the disappearance of native crops; iii) hydrogeological risk, abandoned terraces lose their function of water regulation and increase the risk of floods and landslides downstream; iv) landscape degradation: the loss of terraces alters the beauty and harmony of the landscape, with negative consequences for tourism and cultural identity.

In this context, the identification and mapping of abandoned terraced landscapes is a crucial task. Knowing the pattern and conservation state of terraces is essential to assess the risk of soil erosion and to plan targeted redevelopment interventions. Abandoned terraced areas often represent "hot spots" for erosion, as they are more vulnerable to extreme weather events and lack maintenance.

The redevelopment of abandoned terraced landscapes is a complex action that requires an integrated and multidisciplinary approach:

- restoration of dry stone walls;
- arrangement of drainage channels;
- consolidation of slopes;
- reintroduction of native crops;
- promotion of organic farming and rural tourism;
- creation of open-air museums, educational trails, cultural events;
- involvement of local communities with awareness, training, creation of job opportunities.

The retraining of terraced landscapes is not only an intervention for environmental protection but also an opportunity for economic and social development in rural areas [17–19]. Terraced landscapes represent a unique and valuable cultural heritage, bearing witness to the history, culture, and identity of a territory. Preserving and enhancing this heritage means investing in the future of our communities and ensuring sustainable development for future generations [20–24].

Terraced landscapes play a vital role in preventing landslides, floods, avalanches, soil erosion, and desertification, demonstrating a harmonious relationship between humans and nature. Human actions related to the maintenance of terraced structures can accelerate or divert natural events such as landslides and soil degradation. Maintaining terraces can improve tourism, recreational activities, the trade of agricultural products, and create job opportunities for new generations [1, 9, 25–28].

Summarizing, abandoned terraces should be identified for the environmental risks that they can generate, while an assessment of the conservation state is essential to address appropriate recovery actions. In this perspective, we propose a GIS-based methodology for rapid and automatic terrace mapping.

2 Study Area

Panarea island, with a surface area of only 3.5 km^2, is the smallest and one of the lowest islands (421 m a.s.l.) in the Aeolian archipelago.

The Aeolian archipelago, located in the southern Tyrrhenian Sea north of Sicily, consists of seven main islands and several uninhabited islets. Geologically, the islands represent a volcanic arc. The formation of the archipelago is closely linked to the opening of the Tyrrhenian basin and the geodynamic evolution of the central-western Mediterranean area [29] (Fig. 1).

The Aeolian magmatic arc is the most active volcanic structure in the Mediterranean area, with active volcanoes such as Stromboli and Vulcano, and quiescent volcanoes such as Panarea and Lipari [29]. The active volcanoes are in the central and eastern sectors of the archipelago, while the western part does not record historical eruptions [29] (Fig. 1). The geological characteristics of the Aeolian Islands exhibit a remarkable variety. The volcanoes show composite structures resulting from alternating effusive and explosive activity [30]. The islands are the emerged portions of imposing submarine volcanic complexes, the bases of which lie at depths between 1,000 and 1,500 m below sea level. Along the coasts, one can observe marine terraces of the Late Quaternary, which are evidence of ancient coastlines and periods of eruptive quiescence. The geomorphology and distribution of eruptive centers are strongly influenced by local tectonic structures, oriented along WNW-ESE, NNW-SSE, and NE-SW directions. Many islands are surrounded by relatively flat abrasion platforms at shallow depths, interpreted as platforms formed in the Upper Pleistocene. Finally, the submarine landscape is furrowed by valleys and canyons, narrow and wide incisions that channel the transport of material from the slopes towards the open sea.

Differences in magma composition and eruptive styles have led to diverse volcanic morphologies, from cone-shaped edifices (Alicudi, Filicudi, and Stromboli) to pancake-shaped complexes (Vulcano, Lipari, Salina). Panarea has a vast submarine platform, indicating a complex volcanic history.

Panarea is the emerged portion of a much larger submarine volcanic complex, approximately 1700 m high from the seabed, with a diameter of about 18 km at a depth of 1000 m. The island rises to 421 m above sea level at Punta del Corvo. The rock types of Panarea vary from basaltic andesite and high-potassium basaltic andesite to dacite and high-potassium rhyolite, with some shoshonites [31] (Fig. 2).

The morphology of Panarea is characterized by:

- A relatively wide submarine plateau at about 100 m depth, extending well beyond the dimensions of the island;
- Minor islands and stacks east of the main island, such as Basiluzzo, Dattilo, Panarelli, Lisca Bianca, Bottaro, and Lisca Nera, which represent the summits of a largely eroded submarine volcanic complex. These islets delineate a semicircular structure and enclose a shallow depression with an active fumarolic field (Fig. 3);

Fig. 1. Map showing the Aeolian Islands, highlighting in red Panarea island. An inset provides regional context within Italy (image modified from [29])

- Relatively low coasts in the eastern and southern parts, with small beaches and flat areas (Fig. 3), where terracing once used for cultivation can be observed;
- A fault system oriented NE-SW and NW-SE that conditions both the subaerial and submarine portions of the island. These tectonic structures influence the arrangement of dikes, volcanic alignments, and major fractures;
- Marine terraces located up to 115 m above sea level, which testify to significant vertical crustal movements.

The volcanic activity of Panarea is currently in a quiescent state, with fumaroles and occasional gas emissions. However, in November 2002, a sudden submarine gas emission occurred near the islet of Bottaro, forming a crater and releasing significant amounts of SO_2, HF and HCl [29].

The coastal geomorphology is influenced by sea-level oscillations in the Quaternary. The marine terraces are evidence of different sea levels or paleocoastlines.

In summary, Panarea is a volcanic island with a complex morphology, shaped by volcanic activity, tectonics, and sea-level variations.

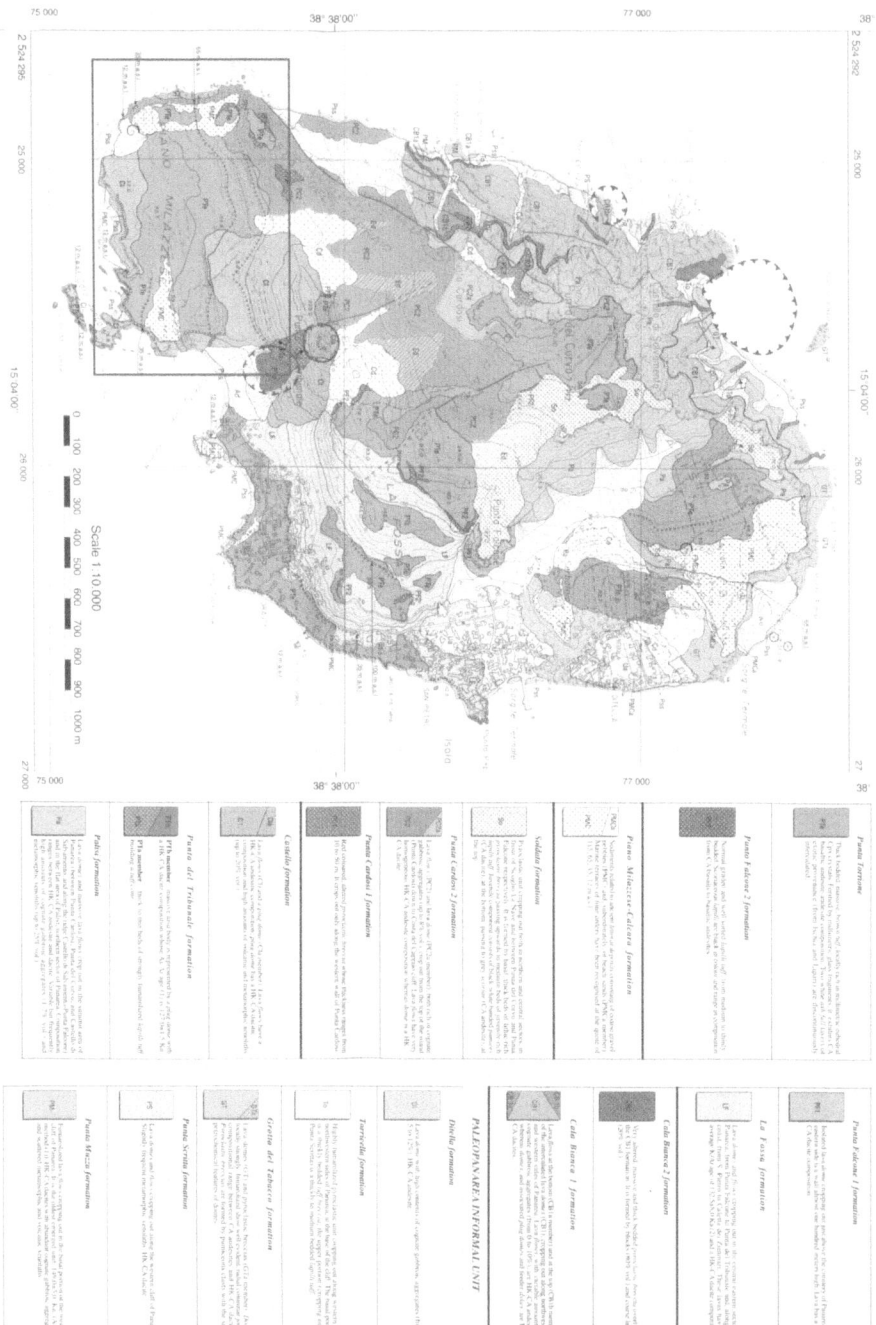

Fig. 2. Geological map of Panarea Island (from [31]), in red is highlighted the study area

Fig. 3. Panarea island. A) a closer perspective of Punta Milazzese (South Panarea, photo by Alessandro Sardella). B) a panoramic view showcases the island's coastline, with the distinct silhouette of Basiluzzo islet standing to the left of Panarea (credits by Wikimedia Common, photo by Patrick Nouhailler). C) view from the south of the terraces studied and present in the study area delimited with the red rectangle in Fig. 2 (photo by Alessandro Sardella)

3 Methods

The methodology employed for the automatic identification of human terraces in the Panarea Island area is based on the adaptation of tools normally used for the identification of natural landscape elements. Specifically, two methods were tested.

3.1 r.geomorphon

The geomorphon method is based on the principle of pattern recognition rather than differential geometry. At the core of the method lies the concept of "geomorphon" (or "geomorphological phonotype"), a fundamental ternary pattern that serves as an archetype of a specific terrain morphology [32–34]. A finite number of 498 geomorphons constitutes a complete and exhaustive set of all possible types of morphological terrain, including standard landscape elements, as well as unknown forms rarely present in natural land surfaces [32]. The assignment of an appropriate geomorphon to each cell of the raster takes place via a scan of the DEM, using a self-adapting procedure to identify the most suitable spatial scale at each location. As a result, the method classifies landscape elements at different spatial scales with unprecedented computational efficiency. The method does not use a fixed neighborhood size; instead, the size and shape of a neighborhood from which the landscape element is determined automatically adapts to the local terrain geometry. This makes it possible to determine the most appropriate landscape element (and its scale) in a single scan of a DEM.

3.2   r.param.scale

This approach involves an advanced technique of terrain classification based on its general topographic model [35–37].

The r.param.scale tool in GRASS GIS is designed for automated terrain classification based on landform geometry and elevation derivative values.

The following four steps illustrate the workflow:

• Multiscale Analysis: r.param.scale performs calculations at multiple scales, analyzing terrain with different moving window sizes;
• Moving Window: Setting different sizes for the moving window overcomes limitations from using default 3x3 windows, allowing derivation of variables based on larger environments than a single cell in a Digital Elevation Model (DEM).;
• Input Parameters: The tool requires three input parameters to control feature calculation 1) Slope Tolerance: Defines the flat surface; 2) Curvature Tolerance: Defines the planar surface; 3) Processing Window Size: Refers to the moving window size;
• Output: r.param.scale can derive basic morphometric variables like slope and curvatures, and classify six basic landforms, identified as morphometric features. Among these, the "planar" feature identifies relatively flat terrain.

4   Results

The study aims to identify a suitable method for recognizing the human terrace.

The following methods were tested:

• r.param.scale module implemented in GRASS GIS.
• r.geomorphon module implemented in GRASS GIS.

The r.geomorphon module proved to be the most suitable procedure for the delineation of relatively flat surfaces (in our case). In the r.geomorphon module, several settings of search radius L (2 px, 5 px, and 15 px) and flatness threshold t (5°, 7°, 10°) were tested. The r.param.scale module was tested using a range of search radius (L) values (5 px, 7 px, and 10 px) and flatness threshold (t) values (3°, 5°, 15°). With the increase of flatness threshold (t) the area of delineated plains increased, too, at the expense of other landforms. On the other hand, the area decreased with the increase of search radius (L). The final settings for parameters t and L were determined through expert visual comparison of the results across various input values, selecting those that best characterized the topography. The outputs generated by these two methods are illustrated in Fig. 4.

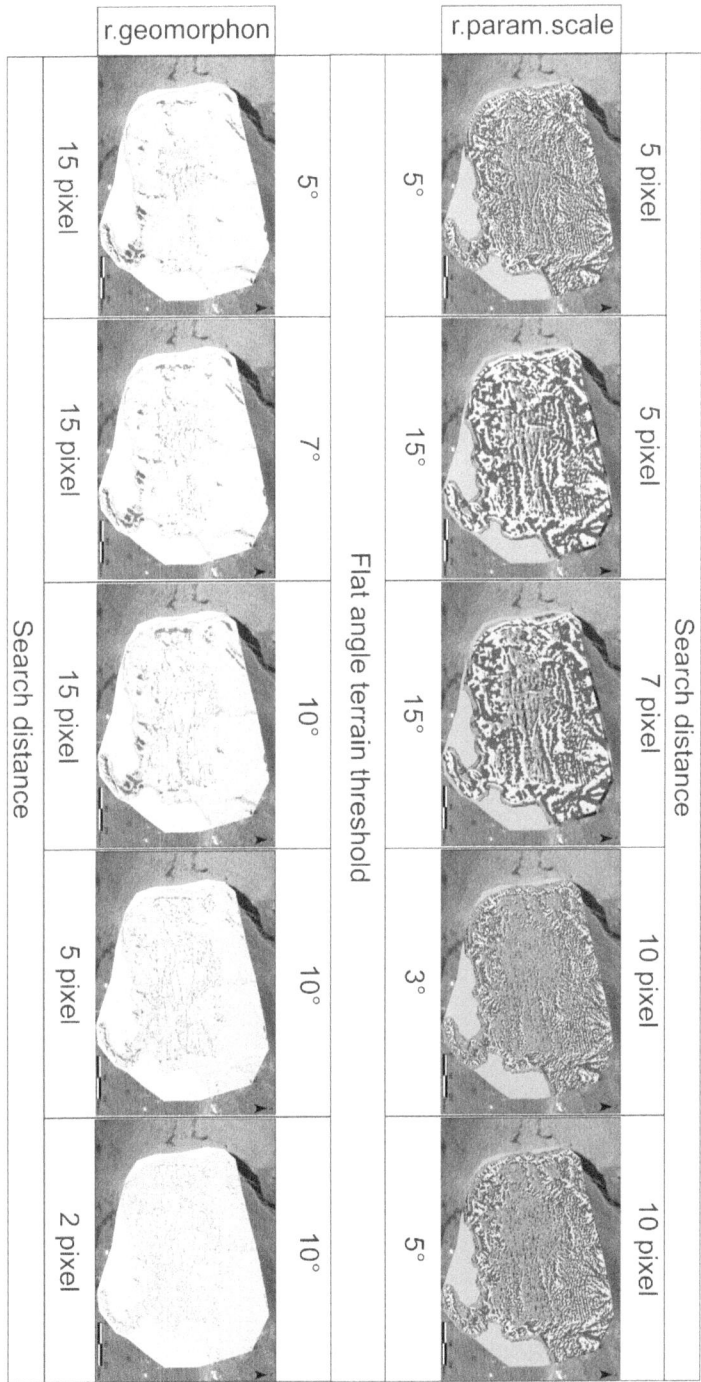

Fig. 4. Results obtained on the study area using the r.geomorphon and r.param.scale tools. Refer to Fig. 5 for the legend

Figure 5 presents the results obtained from the application of two methodologies. In this study, the r.param.scale algorithm did not identify human terraces, whereas the r.geomorphon algorithm identified some terrace features, primarily located in the central portion of the study area, as indicated in gray in Fig. 5.

The spatial resolution of the utilized Digital Terrain Model (DTM), derived from LiDAR data with a cell size of 2 m/px, impacted the performance of both methods. Given that the human terraces in the area of interest range from 5 m to 15 m in width, the following observations were made: r.param.scale did not effectively resolve terraces even at the 15 m scale, while r.geomorphon showed partial success in identifying terraces of larger dimensions in the central area. However, r.geomorphon did not detect terraces with widths of approximately 5 m, which were present in the northeastern area.

These results indicate that geomorphic tools can provide information relevant to the identification of anthropogenic terraces, although the resolution of the DTM is a limiting factor in accurately detecting features of smaller dimensions.

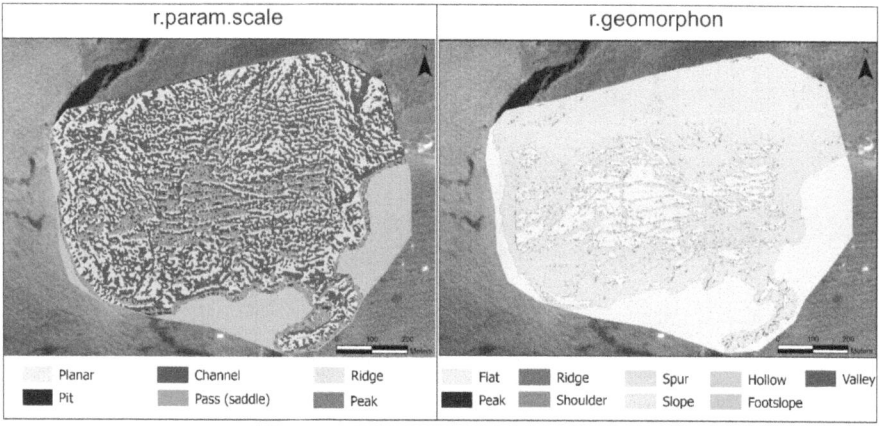

Fig. 5. Best results obtained by the two tools, on the left the result obtained with r.param.scale, on the right the result obtained with r.geomotphon

5   Discussion and Conclusion

Identifying terraces, especially those covered by vegetation, poses several challenges. Canopy can mask the physical boundaries of terraces, making them difficult to detect using traditional remote sensing techniques. Moreover, the degradation of terrace structures over time can further complicate their recognition.

Despite these challenges, identifying terraces covered by vegetation is crucial for several reasons:

- Archaeological and Historical Significance: terraces often represent valuable archaeological sites, providing insights into past agricultural practices and land management strategies. Identifying and mapping these terraces can aid in preserving and studying this cultural heritage;

- Ecological Restoration: abandoned terraces can contribute to soil erosion and land degradation. Identifying these areas allows for targeted ecological restoration efforts, such as re-vegetation and structural repairs, to stabilize the slopes and prevent further degradation;
- Sustainable Land Management: understanding the distribution and condition of terraces is essential for sustainable land management planning. By identifying areas where terraces have been abandoned or degraded, policymakers and land managers can develop strategies to promote their restoration and continued use;
- Disaster Risk Reduction: terraces play a vital role in preventing landslides, floods and avalanches, as well as combating soil erosion and desertification.

In this study conducted on Panarea Island, Italy, we applied the r.geomorphon and r.param.scale methods to semi-automatically identify human terracing using LiDAR data with a resolution of 2 m. These tools, typically used for landform identification, were adapted for identifying human landforms.

Functionality of r.geomorphon and r.param.scale:

- r.param.scale: this tool extracts terrain parameters from a Digital Elevation Model (DEM) using a multiscale approach, adapting quadratic parameters to windows of any size via least squares. The r.param.scale module uses values of curvature for flat surface delineation, which is not a suitable method for recognition of flat surfaces;
- r.geomorphon: this tool calculates geomorphons (forms of the terrain) and associated geometry using a computer vision approach. Geomorphons represent a different approach to semi-automated classification of terrain, identifying terrain elements using local ternary patterns in DEMs. The method compares a focus pixel value with surrounding pixels in eight principal directions, classifying forms based on two main parameters: L (maximum size of a search window) and t (tolerance of slope values in which terrain is considered relatively flat). The result is a geomorphic map that includes 498 possible geomorphons generalized into ten frequent landforms.

The r.geomorphon module is considered the most suitable method for human terrace recognition. The frequent elevation categories of flat surfaces can be considered as planation stages and can be correlated with elevations of cave levels. The module r.geomorphon has the highest ability to remove valleys, channels and other relatively flat areas from resulting flat landforms. Each area is specific, so efforts to minimize subjective decisions include field mapping, creation of DEM, and application of suitable method of semi-automated planation surface recognition.

Identifying terraces covered by vegetation is essential for preserving cultural heritage, promoting ecological restoration, supporting sustainable land management, and mitigating disaster risks. The application of methods such as r.geomorphon and r.param.scale, particularly r.geomorphon, offers promising avenues for semi-automated recognition of these features, aiding in their preservation and management. Further research and development in this area are crucial for enhancing our ability to understand and protect these valuable landscapes.

References

1. Tarolli, P., Preti, F., Romano, N.: Terraced landscapes: from an old best practice to a potential hazard for soil degradation due to land abandonment. Anthropocene **6**, 10–25 (2014)
2. García-Ruiz, J.M., Lana-Renault, N.: Hydrological and erosive consequences of farmland abandonment in Europe, with special reference to the Mediterranean region – a review. Agr Ecosyst Environ **140**, 317–338 (2011)
3. Chen, D., Wei, W., Chen, L.D.: History and distribution of terraced landscapes and typical international cases analysis. Chin. J. Appl. Ecol. **28**, 689–698 (2017)
4. Dunjó, G., Pardini, G., Gispert, M.: Land use change effects on abandoned terraced soils in a Mediterranean catchment. NE Spain. CATENA **52**, 23–37 (2003)
5. Londoño, A.C.: Pattern and rate of erosion inferred from Inca agricultural terraces in arid southern Peru. Geomorphology **99**, 13–25 (2008)
6. Moshe, I., Carlos, A.L.: Erosion processes in high mountain agricultural terraces in Peru. Mt. Res. Dev. **20**, 72–79 (2000)
7. Bevan, A., et al.: The long-term ecology of agricultural terraces and enclosed fields from Antikythera, Greece. Hum. Ecol. **41**, 255–272 (2013)
8. McDonagh, J., Lu, Y., Semalulu, O.: Adoption and adaptation of improved soil management practices in the Eastern Ugandan Hills. Land Degrad. Dev. **25**, 58–70 (2014)
9. Lasanta, T., Arnáez, J., Oserín, M., Ortigosa, L.M.: Marginal lands and erosion in terraced fields in the Mediterranean mountains: a case study in the Camero Viejo (Northwestern Iberian System, Spain). Mt. Res. Dev. **21**, 69–76 (2001)
10. Cots-Folch, R., Martínez-Casasnovas, J.A., Ramos, M.C.: Land terracing for new vineyard plantations in the north-eastern Spanish Mediterranean region: landscape effects of the EU Council Regulation policy for vineyards' restructuring. Agr Ecosyst Environ **115**, 88–96 (2006)
11. Bazzoffi, P., Gardin, L.: Effectiveness of the GAEC standard of cross compliance retain terraces on soil erosion control. Ital. J. Agron. **6**, 43–51 (2011)
12. Crosta, G.B., Dal Negro, P., Frattini, P.: Soil slips and debris flows on terraced slopes. Nat. Hazards Earth Syst. Sci. **3**, 31–42 (2003)
13. Arnaez, J., Lasanta, T., Errea, M.P., Ortigosa, L.: Land abandonment, landscape evolution, and soil erosion in a Spanish Mediterranean mountain region: the case of Camero Viejo. Land Degrad. Dev. **22**, 537–550 (2011)
14. Douglas, T.D., Kirkby, S.J., Critchley, R.W., Park, G.J.: Agricultural terrace abandonment in the Alpujarra, Andalucia, Spain. Land Degrad. Dev. **5**, 281–291 (1994)
15. MacDonald, D., et al.: Agricultural abandonment in mountain areas of Europe: environmental consequences and policy response. J. Environ. Manage. **59**, 47–69 (2000)
16. Nikodemus, O., Bell, S., Grīne, I., Liepiņš, I.: The impact of economic, social and political factors on the landscape structure of the Vidzeme Uplands in Latvia. Landscape Urban Plann. **70**, 57–67 (2005)
17. Agnoletti, M., et al.: Traditional landscape and rural development: comparative study in three terraced areas in northern, central and southern Italy to evaluate the efficacy of GAEC standard 4.4 of cross compliance. Ital. J. Agron. **6**, 121–139 (2011)
18. Hu, S., Yang, Y., Zheng, H., Mi, C., Ma, T., Shi, R.: A framework for assessing sustainable agriculture and rural development: a case study of the Beijing-Tianjin-Hebei region, China. Environ. Impact Assess. Rev. **97** (2022)
19. Sardella, A., Bonazza, A.: The heritage of hand-built terraces in Aeolian Islands: sharing best practices for resilience improvement and cultural heritage preservation in a changing environment. In: Books, M. (ed.) Higher Education and Innovation – Design of an Innovative Teaching Module for an Intensive Programme on Aeolian Architecture (2021)

20. Brandolini, P.: The Outstanding Terraced Landscape of the Cinque Terre Coastal Slopes (Eastern Liguria). World Geomorphological Landscapes, pp. 235–244 (2017)

21. Zhang, Y., et al.: Traditional culture as an important power for maintaining agricultural landscapes in cultural heritage sites: a case study of the Hani terraces. J. Cult. Herit. **25**, 170–179 (2017)

22. Agnoletti, M., Errico, A., Santoro, A., Dani, A., Preti, F.: Terraced landscapes and hydrogeological risk. Effects of land abandonment in Cinque Terre (Italy) during Severe rainfall events. Sustain. (Switz.) **11** (2019)

23. Čurović, Z., Čurović, M., Spalević, V., Janic, M., Sestras, P., Popović, S.G.: Identification and evaluation of landscape as a precondition for planning revitalization and development of mediterranean rural settlements-case study: Mrkovi Village, Bay of Kotor, Montenegro. Sustain. (Switz.) **11** (2019)

24. Cucchiaro, S., Fallu, D.J., Zhang, H., Walsh, K., Oost, K.V., Brown, A.G., Tarolli, P.: Multiplatform-SfM and TLS data fusion for monitoring agricultural terraces in complex topographic and landcover conditions. Remote Sens. Basel **12** (2020)

25. Stanchi, S., Freppaz, M., Agnelli, A., Reinsch, T., Zanini, E.: Properties, best management practices and conservation of terraced soils in Southern Europe (from Mediterranean areas to the Alps): a review. Quatern. Int. **265**, 90–100 (2012)

26. García-Ruiz, J.M., Nadal-Romero, E., Lana-Renault, N., Beguería, S.: Erosion in Mediterranean landscapes: changes and future challenges. Geomorphology **198**, 20–36 (2013)

27. Wei, W., et al.: Global synthesis of the classifications, distributions, benefits and issues of terracing. Earth Sci. Rev. **159**, 388–403 (2016)

28. Deng, C., et al.: Advantages and disadvantages of terracing: a comprehensive review. Int. Soil Water Conserv. Res. **9**, 344–359 (2021)

29. Lucchi, F., Tranne, C.A., Peccerillo, A., Keller, J., Rossi, P.L.: Chapter 12 Geological history of the Panarea volcanic group (eastern Aeolian archipelago). Geol. Soc. Lond. Mem. **37**, 351–395 (2013)

30. Beccaluva, L., Gabbianelli, G., Lucchini, F., Rossi, P.L., Savelli, C.: Petrology and K/Ar ages of volcanics dredged from the Eolian seamounts: implications for geodynamic evolution of the southern Tyrrhenian basin. Earth Planet. Sci. Lett. **74**, 187–208 (1985)

31. Calanchi, N., Tranne, C.A., Lucchini, F., Rossi, P.I.: Geological map of the islands of Panarea and Basiluzzo (Aeolian Islands) 1:10.000, Bologna (1999)

32. Jasiewicz, J., Stepinski, T.F.: Geomorphons — a pattern recognition approach to classification and mapping of landforms. Geomorphology **182**, 147–156 (2013)

33. Gioia, D., Danese, M., Corrado, G., Di Leo, P., Minervino Amodio, A., Schiattarella, M.: Assessing the prediction accuracy of geomorphon-based automated landform classification: an example from the Ionian Coastal belt of southern Italy. ISPRS Int. J. Geo-Inf. **10** (2021)

34. Danese, M., et al.: Pattern recognition approach and LiDAR for the analysis and mapping of archaeological looting: application to an Etruscan site. Remote Sens. Basel **14** (2022)

35. Bandura, P.: Multi-scale landform-based recognition of selected mountain peaks from DEMs in Slovakia. Geographia Cassoviensis **10**, 107–121 (2016)

36. Ho, L.T.K., Yamaguchi, Y., Umitsu, M.: Automated micro-landform classification by combination of satellite images and SRTM DEM. In: International Geoscience and Remote Sensing Symposium (IGARSS), pp. 3058–3061

37. Veselsky, M., Bandura, P., Burian, L., Harcinikova, T., Bella, P.: Semi-automated recognition of planation surfaces and other flat landforms: a case study from the Aggtelek Karst, Hungary. Open Geosci. **7**, 799–811 (2015)

High-Resolution Temperature Mapping
for Cultural Heritage Conservation:
A Case Study in Matera

Maria Danese(✉) ⬥, Valentina Florio ⬥, and Marilisa Biscione ⬥

CNR-ISPC, Tito Scalo (PZ), Rome, Italy
maria.danese@cnr.it

Abstract. In the last years, climate change is exacerbating the presence and impacts of heatwaves. The sharp rise in temperatures and the consequent increase in temperature fluctuations pose risks to the population, the environment and society, but also impact on cultural heritage. This is true throughout the territory, but even more specifically in historic centers, which are characterized by a high density of assets and where high temperatures and morphological and construction characteristics can lead to the urban heat island effect, which amplifies the implications of heatwaves. However, the lack of high-resolution heat data limits the ability to monitor these phenomena and plan conservation and mitigation strategies. Therefore, this study proposes a useful method to map the spatial distribution of temperatures and temperature excursions in a city rich in cultural heritage, Matera (Italy) characterized by particularly fragile building materials, offering a useful tool for risk assessment and heritage management.

Keywords: heatwaves · cultural heritage · climate change · spatial analysis · Matera

1 Introduction

In the last decades, the trend of world surface temperature is growing and will continue to increase, so much so that an average temperature increase of 2.7° has been predicted within the next 100 years [1]. Among the most significant consequences of climate change is the intensification of heatwaves, which are becoming more frequent, prolonged, and severe. These extreme thermal events pose serious risks at different levels: it is dangerous for air and water quality [2, 3], but also for acoustic comfort [4]; it causes increase in energy consumption [5], is a problem for the public health [6], with the following economic consequences and increases social inequalities, as the weaker social classes are also less able to cope with the effects [7], exacerbating existing environmental, social, and economic vulnerabilities.

The combination of this global warning with the resulting increase in heatwaves and the increase of the urbanization [8] produces an anthropogenic climate modification inside cities called Urban Heat Island (UHI) [9]. In this effect, temperature inside the

O. Gervasi et al. (Eds.): ICCSA 2025 Workshops, LNCS 15894, pp. 30–45, 2026.
https://doi.org/10.1007/978-3-031-97648-3_3

urban area is higher than the surrounding suburban and country areas [10] because of the difficulties of the heat exchanges and dispersion due to the urban morphology, its material and the lack of vegetation [11].

Heatwaves constitutes also a threats for cultural heritage and its conservation is a primary target for protection by various organizations such as UNESCO and ICOMOS [12, 13]. Historical centers are affected by them [14], first of all because of its constructive characteristics and materials [15], but also for the concentration of cultural elements, as well as being themselves, in their entirety, considered cultural goods. In fact historical centers are vulnerable elements for the cultural landscape and cultural identity, they preserve as well as being a strategic point for economic activities related to it, such as tourism, or traditional socioeconomic activities.

A thorough understanding of all the aspects mentioned above, however, requires the possibility of using high-resolution temperature data, which, however, are not available free of charge or at low cost.

In this paper the goal is to propose a method for the downscaling of satellite data, in order to have high resolution datasets useful to study heatwaves temporal trends in the two last decades and footprint and return an instrument to map the potentially impacts on cultural assets, identifying an overview of the high-risk zones in a medium sized city, Matera (Basilicata, Italy).

2 The Heatwaves Effects on Cultural Heritage

Ancient buildings developed from a close connection with the natural environment.

Regulation of indoor climatic conditions was thus achieved through the use of established construction criteria that primarily exploited the geometric and positional characteristics of the building. When the external climatic conditions come to change, the ancient building will be subjected to different stresses and its response may not always be adequate.

Thermal gradients are among the aspects that concern the effects of the interaction between the building and the external environment. These in fact are of interest both from the energy point of view, in terms of heat loss, and from the conservation point of view in terms of their effects on the building's constituent matter.

First of all, a temperature of over 25° can be considered abnormal or in any case having an impacting effect on the built heritage (as well as on people and the environment), especially if prolonged over time.

In fact, these temperatures cause physical, chemical, mechanical and biological processes to intensify on it and consequently the following effects [16–20]:

- Expansion and contraction of the materials due to temperature variations with possible micro-fractures in the short term and, in the long-term problems with structural integrity.
- Acceleration of degradation processes and increased fragility due to increased water evaporation processes especially in porous materials.
- Acceleration of chemical processes leading to the formation of efflorescence and crusts.
- Increased biological growth due to heat and humidity.

- Degradation of protective coatings due to exposure to high temperatures, especially if prolonged [21].

To map the UHI footprint is consequently important to overlay it with the heritage vulnerability and to monitor these effects, in order to program intervention strategies and to mitigate them.

3   Materials and Methods

3.1   Land Surface Temperature Calculation

The main problem in heat island footprint assessment is to estimate the Land Surface Temperature (LST) at the right spatial scale. For example, for assessments concerning the built heritage or historical centre, it can be useful to have data with a high spatial resolution. However, thermal data as MODIS have an insufficient resolution (1 km). In the literature, some models are shown to estimate the temperature by exploiting previous work on the surface emissivity of objects on the earth's surface [22], according to which the emissivity can be expressed as a function of the vegetation index plotted on the pixels and then calculate the LST from the Normalized Difference Vegetation Index (NDVI). From this, an empirical model of emissivity can be applied, for example, by joining the thermal band of the data from the Landsat satellite to the NDVI elaboration [23]. Conversely, the Sentinel data, specifically, while having a very good spatial resolution and allows to calculate a highly defined NDVI, lacks the thermal channel necessary to derive with this method the LST. Another problem regarding the use of Sentinel data is that this type of temperature assessment is only valid under clear sky conditions.

For this reason, starting from the MODIS dataset, a recently introduced interpolation method has used as approach to obtain a very high resolution map of LST.

3.2   Empirical Bayesian Kriging Regression Prediction

Empirical Bayesian Kriging (EBK) is a geostatistical interpolation method that improves on the use of classical kriging. It introduces within it the ability to reduce the uncertainty in the estimation of hyper-parameters typical of interpolation, related to the variogram and thus to the relationship between variance and distance [24, 25]. This reduction of uncertainty is done by means of a Bayesian bootstrap [26, 27]. The algorithm also proved to have increased efficiency due to its ability to divide the dataset into subsets, allowing for faster interpolation [28]. Recently, EBK has been used in applications related to the mapping of chemical elements in soil [24], in studies related to public health [29], but also to improve the estimation of annual precipitation, land surface temperature [27] and groundwater [30].

While EBK predictions are made only considering the dependent variable and the estimation of the variogram (or semi-variogram), the **Empirical Bayesian Kriging Regression Prediction** (EBKRP) allows one or more additional explanatory variables to be considered through regression, whose spatial trend also influences the variable to be interpolated. The combination of the two methods, regression and kriging, combines their own strength point: the ability of regression to capture global trends; the ability of kriging to capture local trends and relationships between points.

The mathematical basis of the EBKRP are the following: let's consider the studied variable $z(s)$, where s is its spatial location. It is represented as the sum of the function $m(s)$, coming from the regression model, considering the global trends, and the spatial residuals $\varepsilon(s)$ (Eq. 1).

$$z(s) = m(s) + \varepsilon(s) \tag{1}$$

The regression (linear or more complex) component $m(s)$ models global trends by estimating intercept β_0 and the regression coefficients $\beta_0 \dots \beta_p$ associated to the p explanatory variables $X_1(s) \dots X_p(s)$ (Eq. 2).

$$m(s) = \beta_0 + \beta_1 X_1(s) + \dots + \beta_p X_p(s) \tag{2}$$

The spatial residuals $\varepsilon(s)$ follow a Gaussian process (GP) with zero mean and a spatial covariance structure $C(s, s')$ also called covariance function or variogram that describes how similarity between the two points in s and in s' varies with their distance (spatial autocorrelation) (Eq. 3):

$$\varepsilon(s) \sim GP(0, C(s, s')) \tag{3}$$

With kriging it is possible to obtain a weighted estimation of residuals $\varepsilon(s_i)$ in an unobserved point s_0, where weights λ_i depends on the covariance structure (Eq. 4)

$$\hat{\varepsilon}(s_0) = \sum_{i=1}^{n} \lambda_i \varepsilon(s_i) \tag{4}$$

To estimate variogram parameters (nugget, range, sill) a Bayesian approach is followed: an entire variogram distribution is followed starting from parameters that are assumed to come from an a priori distribution. For each variogram calculated, it is calculated too the probability that the observed data are generated by that variogram (likelihood). Likelihood contributes to change a priori parameters to obtain a posteriori parameters. All variograms and the parameter sets are combined in order to obtain the best parameters.

For more details about mathematical formulation see [27, 28].

4 The Case Study: The Historical Center of Matera

Matera (Basilicata, Italy) is a medium-sized city in the Mediterranean area (southern Italy) characterized by a very long settlement history. It is a perfect example of a settlement in a rocky habitat created in close harmony with the ecosystem: the sustainable use of natural resources, in particular the water collection systems, is the main feature of the urbanization of this area of the Basilicata Region, and the reason for the recognition of the Sassi and the Murgia plateau (Natural Archaeological Park of the Rock Churches) as a UNESCO World Heritage Site since 1993 (http://whc.unesco.org/en/list/670). Defined both by ICOMOS [31] as a unicum that includes rock settlement, architectural settlement and landscape, they show various significant moments in human history. The name Sasso indicates a rock-hewn district already mentioned in documents dating back to the 13th and 14th centuries [32]. The two rock settlements that arose around the Civita (an area frequented or inhabited since the 2nd millennium B.C. [33]), developed over the centuries along the Gravina stream and were slowly transformed. Together with the Civita and then the Piano, they created a settlement system spanning more than two millennia, without spatio-temporal interruptions. The types of dwelling are: the cave; the lamione, a room with a vaulted roof; and the palaziate houses, built with the material excavated inside the cave [34]. Cultural heritage preserved in Matera is of various types: cave systems (small, dark, damp rooms with beds and cellars), millstones, oil mills, quarries, or religious places with altars, columns, vaults, domes and frescoes. The organization of the underground urban space appears on the surface only as a jumble of alleys, vicinates (small squares) and gradelle (stairways), but it is only apparently random: it was conditioned by the need to capture and channel water, to purify and store clean water for the most basic daily activities, and to drain unusable water. The cisterns collect the clean water and store it; the drainage waters follow the slopes of the terraces, cross the gullies and canals and reach the Gravina stream downstream. Thanks to a dense network of canals, wells, cisterns and divers dug into the calcarenite and made impermeable, the inhabitants of the Sassi were able to satisfy their water needs until running water arrived in the 1920s. This water management system is one of the most significant examples of the balance between human intervention and the ecosystem in an urban space. The neighbourhood called Piano developed in the 18th century at a higher level than the Sassi, with bourgeois houses, not completely excavated in the rock but built, with large windows and more comfortable, and with fine examples of Baroque religious architecture. Life here was healthier and more comfortable. In the Sassi, on the other hand, serious problems were the unhealthy conditions and the spread of endemic diseases, overcrowding, the sharing of space with animals and a high infant mortality rate. A great cultural, political and legislative mobilisation has sought to remedy these living conditions since the 1950s. Several laws were enacted (Laws no. 619/1952, 299/1958, 126/1967, 1043/1971) to relocate the inhabitants, overcome the precariousness of hygiene, economic and social conditions, and also to solve the problems of structural instability of buildings and roads [35]: town planners and sociologists designed new residential neighborhoods and rural villages: Serra Venerdì, Spine Bianche, Lanera, Borgo La Martella and Borgo Venusio. A major effort is needed to ensure mitigation measures to reduce the risk factors affecting the future of such a valuable site: an assessment of the conservation status of the settlement and the influence of environmental variables on it, in order to determine the possible factors controlling the stone degradation process was carried out in [21] (Fig. 1).

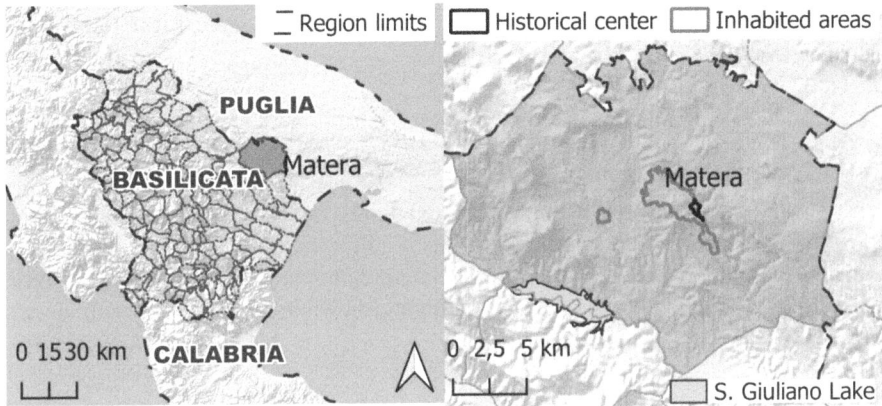

Fig. 1. Geographical overview of the study area

It can be deduced from what has been said so far that a large part of Matera's cultural heritage is characterized by calcarenites.

These materials, due to the properties they possess (high open porosity, low mechanical strength and vulnerability to degradation, the main component being calcite) are very sensitive to water, which is the main agent of deterioration, both directly and indirectly. Especially thermal variations, such as the rapid evaporation of water and its subsequent crystallization cause internal fractures and alveolization phenomena [21, 36, 37]. In temperate climates such as the one in the case analyzed, therefore, the risk factor for this material increases due to the presence of rapid and wide temperature fluctuations, even in the presence of different materials in contact. Although there are no well-documented thresholds in the literature, it is known that an increase or decrease of 20 °C causes an expansion or contraction of 0.14 mm/m [38]. For this reason, in addition to obtaining high-resolution maps of daytime and nighttime LST, it is very useful to obtain maps of the distribution of the temperature range between day and night.

5   Results

5.1   High Resolution LST Calculation

EBKRP was used to obtain LST with high resolution over all the municipality area. As input raster the thermal band of the MODIS Terra and Aqua satellite products data were used [39]. In particular it has two bands, one with the daytime and one with the nighttime Earth surface temperature. Monthly average data were downloaded with a script on GEE, a free, cloud platform, publicly released in 2010 [40].

As trend raster the elevation was used, because of different studies highlights strong correlation between temperature trends and this parameter [41, 42].

To evaluate the goodness of the result the Root-Mean-Square Error (RMSE) is calculated (Eq. 5).

$$\sqrt{\frac{\sum_{i=1}^{n}(\hat{z}(s_i) - z(s_i))^2}{n}} \tag{5}$$

where s_i is the spatial location of the considered point, $z(s_i)$ is the measured value in the s_i position, $\hat{z}(s_i)$ and n is the number of points used for the interpolation. It is useful to show how well the predicted values through interpolation models the measured values. So it must be as low as possible. RMSE values are shown in the figures, overall always low (Figs. 2 and 3).

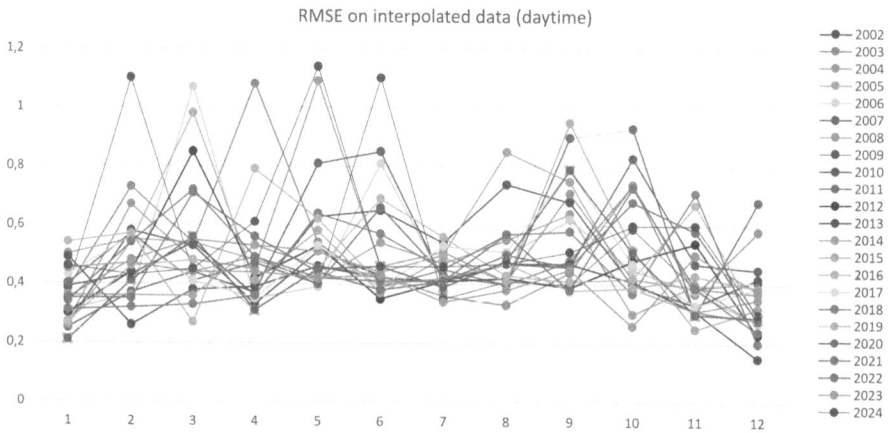

Fig. 2. RMSE values calculated from interpolated data in the daytime.

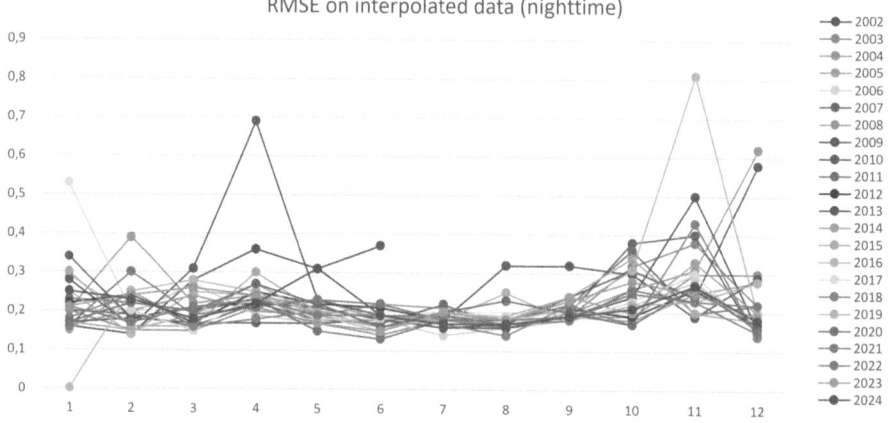

Fig. 3. RMSE values calculated from interpolated data in the daytime.

5.2 Trend Analysis and Temperature Variations

In this work, three different types of temperatures (minimum – Tmin -, average – Tmax- and maximum - Tmax) were chosen as they help to highlight different aspects in heat-waves. The minimum temperatures are useful in assessing the presence of tropical nights, i.e. temperatures above 25°, which, especially in an urban context and in the city centre, can highlight the heat island effect when not sufficiently mitigated during the night, when the heating continues to be constant despite the absence of the sun. However, minimum temperatures are not effective in showing the maximum intensity of heat waves. Maximum temperatures, on the other hand, are extremely effective in mapping the intensity of heat peaks and fully show the severity of the phenomenon during the daytime phase. The two measures are therefore complementary. Finally, average temperatures help complete the picture, showing the overall duration of the warming phenomenon through long-term trends.

In order to visualise the variation of maximum temperatures, temporal heatmaps were created in the time range considered, in three territorial bands of the Matera Co-municipality and more specifically in the rural areas (first column of heatmaps), in the historic centre (second column) and in the urban area (third column).

The first phenomenon that emerges, consistent with the current situation of climate change, is a trend of progressive growth in minimum, average and maximum temperatures and thus a brighter shade of red moving in the graphs from top to bottom (i.e. the most recent years). This upward trend is especially noticeable in historic city centres and this is a first indicator of the urban heat island effect. Heating occurs both during the day and at night, so urban areas and the historic centre have a lower cooling capacity at night.

Thus, more generally, rural areas, having a greater temperature range, thanks to the effect of vegetation, manage to maintain a cooler microclimate, despite the significant temperature peaks in some areas. This gap between rural and built-up areas is also more evident due to the marked differences between the winter and summer seasons.

Finally, in Table 1 the maxima, in the reference period, of the minimum, average and maximum temperatures in the rural area, in the historic centre and in the urban area, during the day and night are shown. The rural areas shows a Tmax higher, but also the greatest temperature excursion; this implies a strong daytime warming, probably due also to the morphology and the land cover of part of the Matera's rural areas, characterized by an extended, cultivated plain with a low density vegetation. Here, the low vegetation cover allows the exposed soil to warm up quickly and, conversely, to cool down rapidly during the night. For what concerns the inhabited area, of note are the presence of an intermediate maximum temperature and temperature range between the the rural area and the historic centre. This last shows the greatest Tmin and the lower temperature excursion that suggests its capability to maintain a stability in temperatures, again due to the urban heat island effect and thus the sparse presence of vegetation and the high density of buildings (Fig. 4).

Table 1. Maxima temperatures, in the reference period, daytime and night time in the three investigated zones.

	Zone	Tmin (°C)	Tmean (°C)	Tmax (°C)
Daytime	Rural areas	39,8	46,5	50,3
	historical center	44,3	44,6	45,3
	inhabited area	43,9	45,6	48,9
Nighttime	Rural areas	17,1	19,8	23,6
	historical center	22	22,4	22,6
	inhabited area	20,1	30,3	22,7

5.3 Spatial Distribution of Temperatures and Thermal Excursion

With the results obtained by interpolation, a series of detailed maps of the distribution of daily and night temperatures in different areas and periods of the year were obtained, with special attention paid to areas with the presence of cultural heritage and historical centres too. For the sake of brevity, in Figs. 5 and 6, the maps with the diurnal temperature variation are shown only in the period from March to October 20024 (Fig. 5 the months from March to June, Fig. 6 the months from July to October, left column), i.e. the months characterised by the presence of areas with temperatures above 20°. Moreover, in the same figures, in the right column, it is represented the distribution of the temperature range. It was decided to represent only those areas that have a temperature difference of 20 °C, a value considered significant as explained in the previous section, as it represents a critical condition for sensitive historical materials.

The maps in Figs. 5 and 6 show in detail which areas are characterised by the highest temperature rises, which for example in July and August even reach 50°, and allow us to compare these areas and those characterised by the presence of cultural heritage, so that we can better understand which heritage elements need to be monitored more because they may be particularly exposed to fluctuations.

The detailed map in Fig. 7 for the historic centre also shows in its left-hand side (Fig. 7a) the distribution of temperatures with peaks reaching 45°, while the temperature range reaches up to approx. 22.5 °C. The map depicts the most important cultural heritage elements in the historic centre, thus making it possible to understand which areas are the hottest and most exposed to temperature fluctuations, in order to prioritise conservation measures in the most critical areas and try to mitigate their effects.

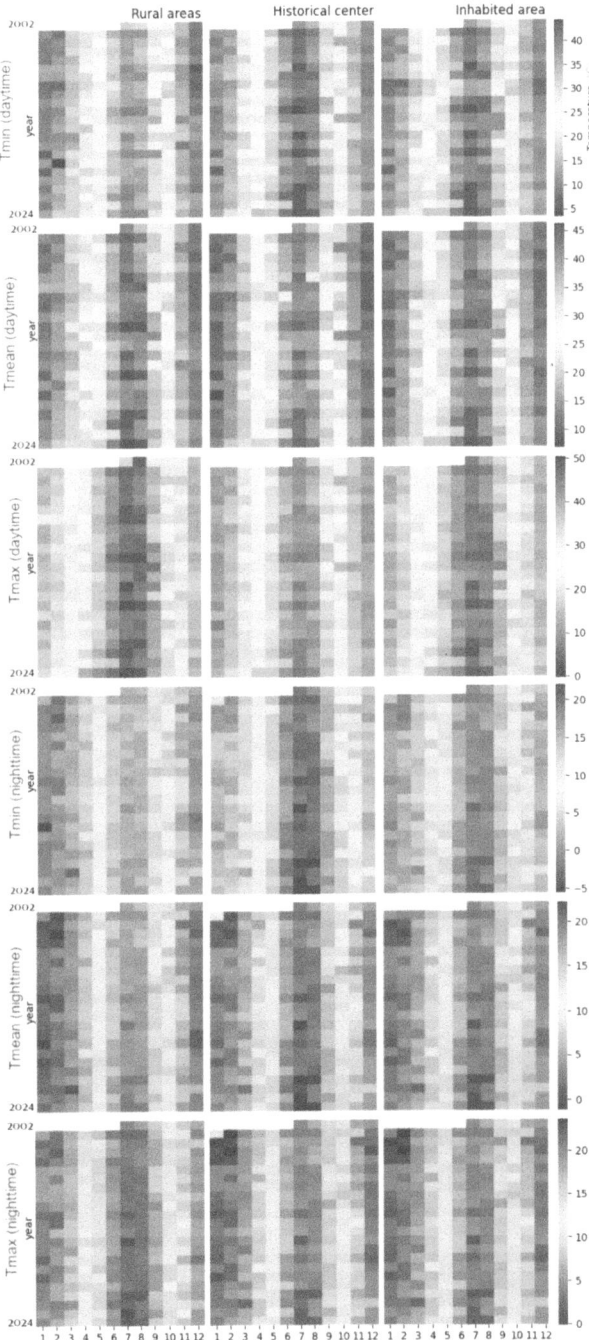

Fig. 4. Heatmaps for minimum, mean and maximum temperature (daytime and night time) in rural areas (left column), historical center (center column) and inhabited areas (right column).

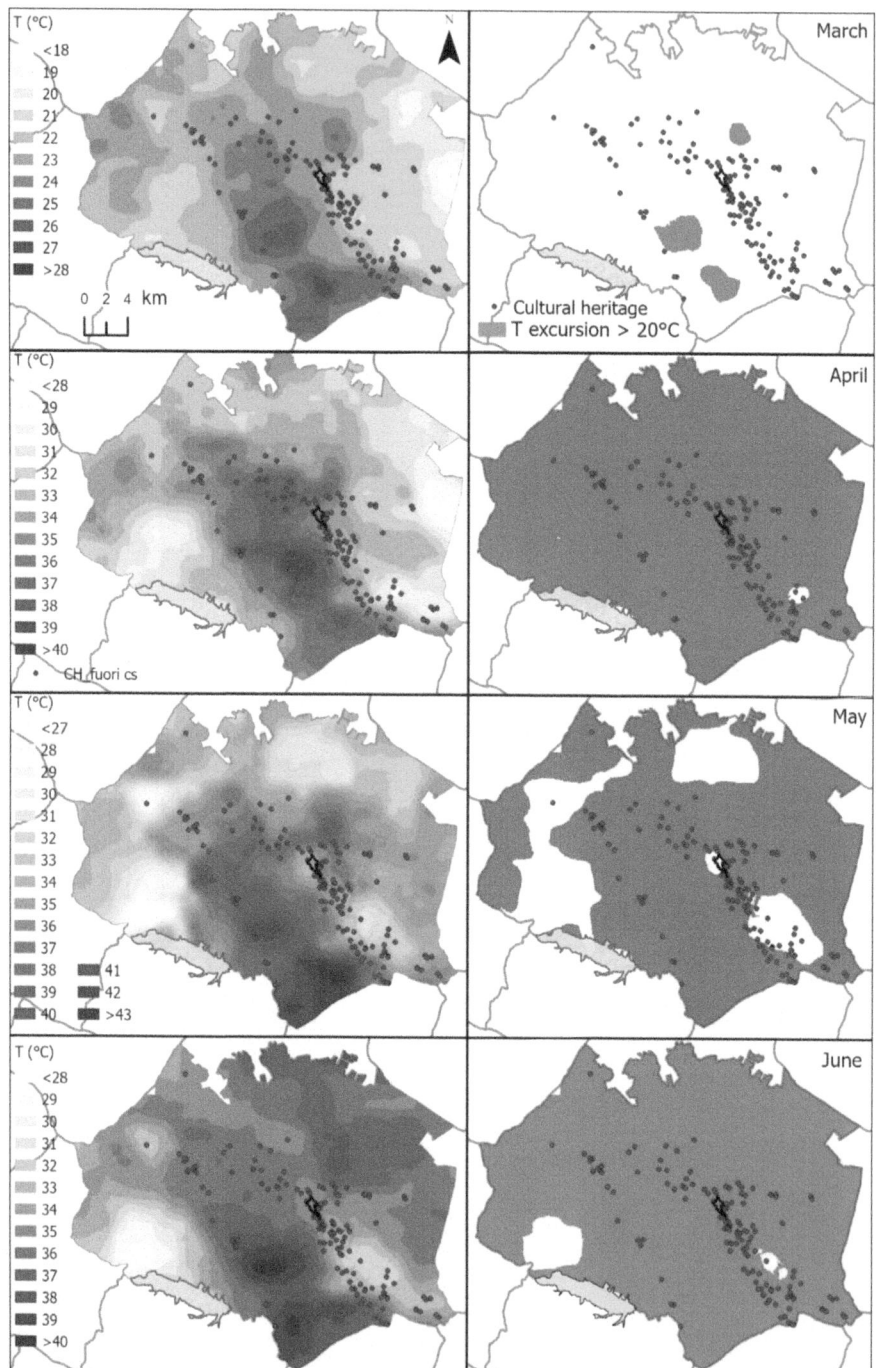

Fig. 5. Spatial distribution of diurnal temperature (left) and thermal excursion (right) from March to June and overlay with cultural heritage.

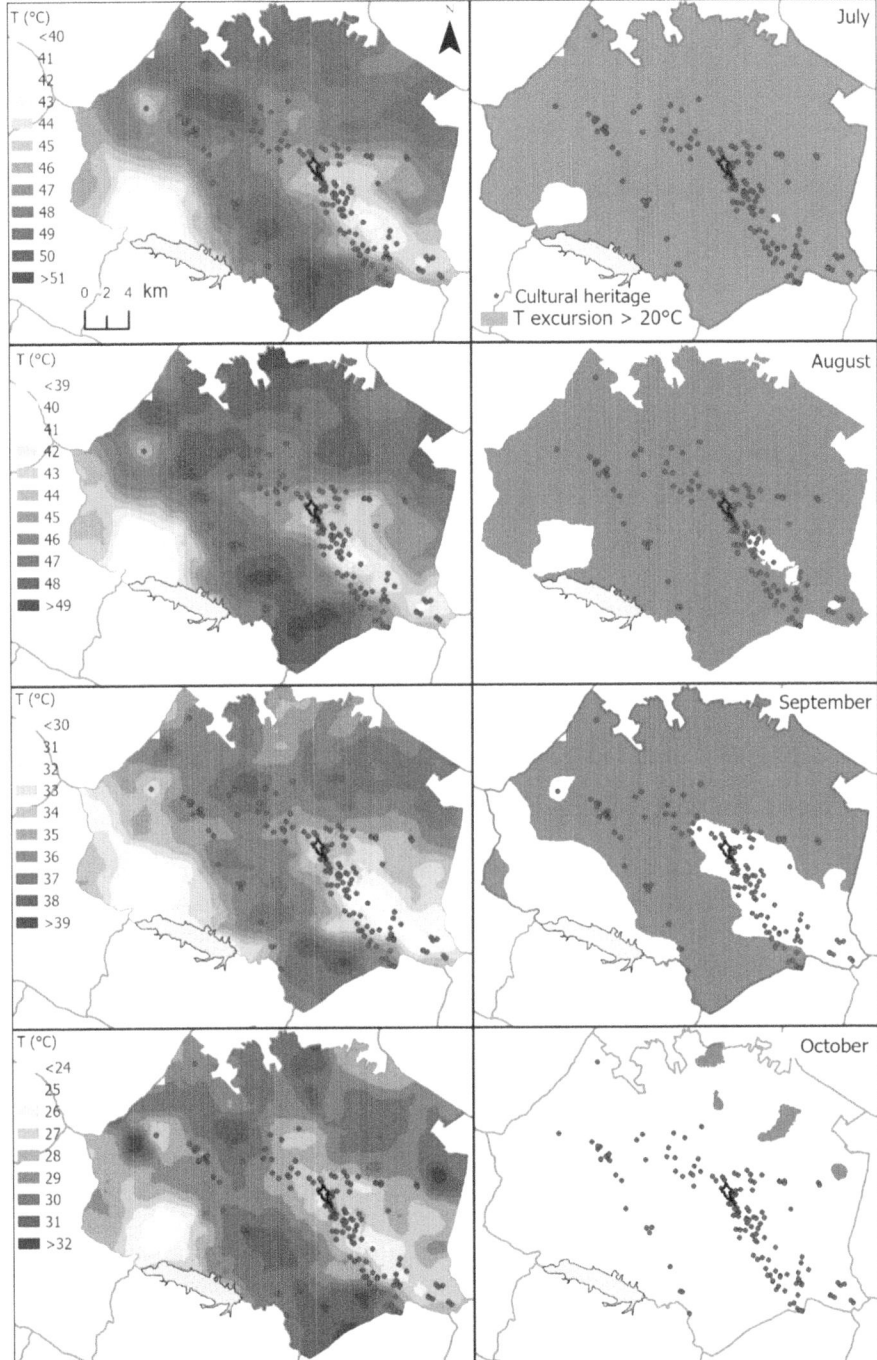

Fig. 6. Spatial distribution of diurnal temperature (left) and thermal excursion (right) from July to October and overlay with cultural heritage.

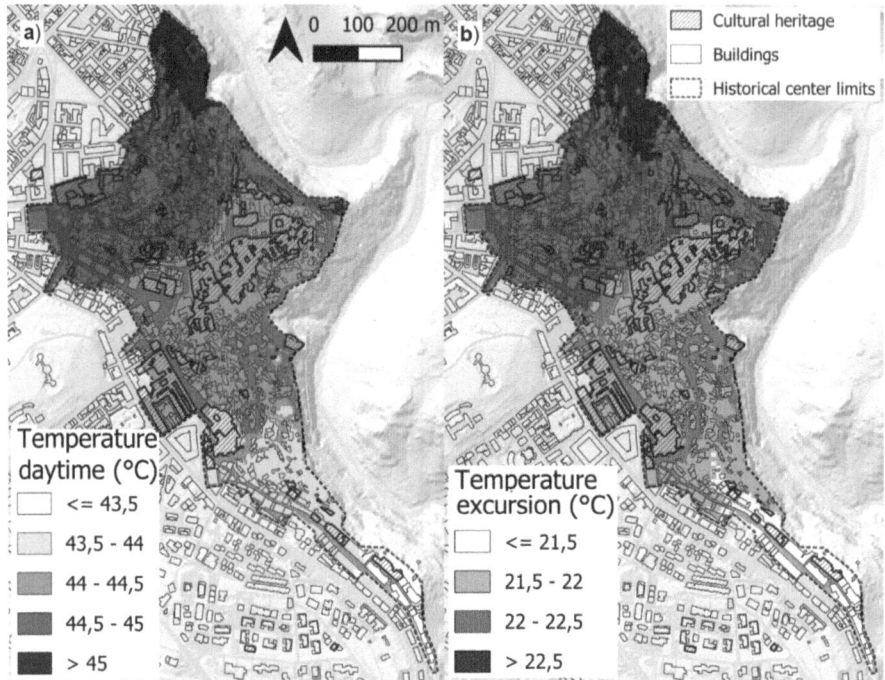

Fig. 7. Detail of spatial distribution of diurnal temperature (left) and thermal excursion (right) in the Matera historical center.

6 Discussion and Conclusion

In this study, a downscaling method was applied, based on spatial machine learning, EBKRP, which was able to return a high-resolution (10m) LST dataset from the much lower resolution MODIS data. The results were deemed reliable due to the validation performed with the RMSE index. These results constitute an important mapping tool to study the areas of greatest vulnerability and to be able to support targeted conservation and mitigation strategies for cultural heritage in general and for historic centers. The approach followed also made it possible to overcome the typical limitation of optical data, when deriving temperature using vegetation and emissivity data, consisting in the need for clean sky conditions.

In the case study of the experiment, from a statistical point of view, it was highlighted that due to higher average and minimum temperatures and a narrower day-night range, the historic center of Matera, despite its not excessively large size, is still characterized by the UHI effect. Therefore, building materials are more exposed to the risk of physical and chemical degradation of the assets present in it and, more generally, of all the built heritage present in it.

In particular, the development of detailed maps on temperatures and thermal excursions, such as those of the historic center (Fig. 7), offers a tool capable of monitoring temperature fluctuations in space and time, anticipating degradation phenomena such as cracks, detachments, and corrosion of metal elements. In this way, it also becomes possible to identify the areas most exposed to thermal stress, where to focus predictive intervention priorities and resource optimization. These maps are therefore a useful tool for policymakers and designers whose aim is to identify strategies, solutions, and mitigation interventions at the local scale.

The protocol applied in this work, easily applicable in any geographical context, is only a starting point and presents further development possibilities, such as the integration and enhancement of initial data with IoT sensors, in order to increase temporal resolution with the aim of providing a concrete possibility to detect anomalies and intervene promptly to protect heritage. Furthermore, temperature data should be integrated with additional environmental variables, such as sun exposure, wind speed and direction, and humidity, to build a complete and detailed picture of the climatic influence on cultural heritage and historical materials.

In conclusion, in a context of increasing climate pressure, the use of combined tools, such as advanced analytical tools and satellite data represents a fundamental step to monitor elements like temperature and to enhance the resilience of cultural heritage. These data not only favor more effective conservation interventions but also help guide urban policies towards sustainable development models, in line with the recommendations of the AR5 Report by the Intergovernmental Panel on Climate Change. The ability to translate this information into concrete actions will be crucial to increase the resilience of cultural heritage and preserve historical and cultural memory for future generations.

Acknowledgments. This study was funded under the project "Study of hazard elements and their variation as a function of climate change, on cultural heritage using spatial machine learning methods" inside "Cultural heritage and creativity in green and digital transitions for inclusive societies" (FOE2021 - Ordinary fund for research organizations and institutions).

Disclosure of Interests.   The authors have no competing interests to declare that are relevant to the content of this article.

References

1. Parmesan, C., et al.: Terrestrial and freshwater ecosystems and their services. In: Climate Change 2022: Impacts, Adaptation, and Vulnerability. Contribution of Working Group II to the Sixth Assessment Report of the Intergovernmental Panel on Climate Change (2022)
2. Grimm, N.B., et al.: Global change and the ecology of cities. Science **319**, 756–760 (2008)
3. Stedman, J.R.: The predicted number of air pollution related deaths in the UK during the August 2003 heatwave. Atmos. Environ. **38**, 1087–1090 (2004)
4. Núñez-Peiró, M., et al.: Exposure and vulnerability toward summer energy poverty in the city of madrid: a gender perspective. In: Bisello, A., Vettorato, D., Haarstad, H., Borsboom-van Beurden, J. (eds.) Smart and Sustainable Planning for Cities and Regions. SSPCR 2019. Green Energy and Technology, pp. 481–495. Springer, Cham (2021). https://doi.org/10.1007/978-3-030-57332-4_34
5. Tian, L., Lu, J., Li, Y., Bu, D., Liao, Y., Wang, J.: Temporal characteristics of urban heat island and its response to heat waves and energy consumption in the mountainous Chongqing, China. Sustain. Cities Soc. **75**, 103260 (2021)

6. Dong, X.S., West, G.H., Holloway-Beth, A., Wang, X., Sokas, R.K.: Heat-related deaths among construction workers in the United States. Am. J. Ind. Med. **62**, 1047–1057 (2019)

7. Cheng, Q., Sha, S.: Revealing the injustice and factors that affect the resilience responses of residents in the full period of heat waves. Sustain. Cities Soc. **107** (2024)

8. Tan, J., et al.: The urban heat island and its impact on heat waves and human health in Shanghai. Int. J. Biometeorol. **54**, 75–84 (2010)

9. Arnfield, A.J.: Two decades of urban climate research: a review of turbulence, exchanges of energy and water, and the urban heat island. Int. J. Climatol. **23**, 1–26 (2003)

10. Santamouris, M.: Cooling the cities – a review of reflective and green roof mitigation technologies to fight heat island and improve comfort in urban environments. Sol. Energy **103**, 682–703 (2014)

11. Oke, T.R., Johnson, G.T., Steyn, D.G., Watson, I.D.: Simulation of surface urban heat islands under 'ideal' conditions at night part 2: diagnosis of causation. Bound.-Layer Meteorol. **56**, 339–358 (1991)

12. Colette, A.: Climate change and world heritage: report on predicting and managing the impacts of climate change on world heritage and Strategy to assist States Parties to implement appropriate management responses. Changement climatique et patrimoine mondial: rapport sur la prévision et la gestion des effets du changement climatique sur le patrimoine mondial et Stratégie pour aider les Etats parties à mettre en oeuvre des réactions de gestion adaptées

13. Markham, A., O.E., Lafrenz Samuels, K., Caldas, A.: World Heritage and tourism in a changing climate (2016)

14. Quesada-Ganuza, L., Garmendia, L., Alvarez, I., Briz, E., Gandini, A., Olazabal, M.: The risk of heat waves to historic urban areas. A GIS-based model for developing a risk assessment methodology. In: Furferi, R., Giorgi, R., Seymour, K., Pelagotti, A. (eds.) The Future of Heritage Science and Technologies. Florence Heri-Tech 2022. Advanced Structured Materials, vol. 179, pp. 47–60. Springer, Cham (2022). https://doi.org/10.1007/978-3-031-15676-2_4

15. European, C., Cassar, M., Sabbioni, C., Brimblecombe, P.: The Atlas of Climate Change Impact on European Cultural Heritage – Scientific Analysis and Management Strategies. Anthem Press (2010)

16. Wang, Y., Zhang, H.: Preliminary study on the impact of severe heat waves on dolostone weathering: implications for deterioration of carbonate rock-hewn heritage in SE China. Environ. Earth Sci. **83** (2024)

17. Lobarinhas, R., Dionísio, A., Paneiro, G.: High temperature effects on global heritage stone resources: a systematic review. Heritage **7**, 6310–6342 (2024)

18. Quesada-Ganuza, L., Garmendia, L., Rojí, E., Álvarez, I., Briz, E., Gandini, A.: How are heat waves putting at risk historic urban areas? First steps for developing risk assessment methodologies. In: REHABEND, pp. 1114–1121

19. Grossi, C.M., Brimblecombe, P., Harris, I.: Predicting long term freeze-thaw risks on Europe built heritage and archaeological sites in a changing climate. Sci. Total. Environ. **377**, 273–281 (2007)

20. Viles, H.A., Cutler, N.A.: Global environmental change and the biology of heritage structures. Glob. Change Biol. **18**, 2406–2418 (2012)

21. Gizzi, F.T., Sileo, M., Biscione, M., Danese, M., Alvarez de Buergo, M.: The conservation state of the Sassi of Matera site (Southern Italy) and its correlation with the environmental conditions analysed through spatial analysis techniques. J. Cult. Heritage **17**, 61–74 (2016)

22. Li, Z.-L., et al.: Satellite-derived land surface temperature: current status and perspectives. Remote Sens. Environ. **131**, 14–37 (2013)

23. Sekertekin, A., Bonafoni, S.: Land surface temperature retrieval from Landsat 5, 7, and 8 over rural areas: assessment of different retrieval algorithms and emissivity models and toolbox implementation. Remote Sens. **12** (2020)

24. Samsonova, V.P., Blagoveshchenskii, Y.N., Meshalkina, Y.L.: Use of empirical Bayesian kriging for revealing heterogeneities in the distribution of organic carbon on agricultural lands. Eurasian Soil Sci. **50**, 305–311 (2017)
25. Al-Mudhafar, W.: Bayesian kriging for improved spatial heterogeneity modleing in clastic reservoirs. In: Proceedings of the 24th Formation Evaluation Symposium of Japan
26. Gribov, A., Krivoruchko, K.: Empirical Bayesian kriging implementation and usage. Sci. Total Environ. **722** (2020)
27. Krivoruchko, K., Gribov, A.: Evaluation of empirical Bayesian kriging. Spat. Stat. **32** (2019)
28. Krivoruchko, K., Gribov, A.: Distance metrics for data interpolation over large areas on Earth's surface. Spat. Stat. **35** (2020)
29. López, C.M.R., Rivera, M.M., Ochoa, A., Gallegos, J.C.P., Mendoza, J.E.G.: Geospatial situation analysis for the prediction of possible cases of suicide using EBK: a case study in the Mexican state of aguascalientes. In: Handbook of Research on Natural Language Processing and Smart Service Systems, pp. 327–346 (2020)
30. Uddin, M.S., Mitra, B., Mahmud, K., Rahman, S.M., Chowdhury, S., Rahman, M.M.: An ensemble machine learning approach for predicting groundwater storage for sustainable management of water resources. Groundwater Sustain. Dev. **29** (2025)
31. ICOMOS: WORLD HERITAGE LIST Matera No 670 (1993). http://whc.unesco.org/archive/advisory_body_evaluation/670
32. Fonseca, C.D.: Il popolamento rupestre. In: A., D.R.G.C. (ed.) Storia della Basilicata. Il Medioevo. Laterza (2006)
33. Cipolloni Sampò, M.: L'Eneolitico e l'Età del Bronzo. In: Cestaro, A.D.R., G. (ed.) Storia della Basilicata. Adamesteanu D. L'Antichità, pp. 67–136. Laterza (1999)
34. Laureano, P.: Giardini di pietra: i Sassi di Matera e la civiltà mediterranea. Bollati Boringhieri (1993)
35. Cotecchia, V., Grassi, D.: Stato di conservazione dei "Sassi" di Matera (Basilicata) in rapporto alle condizioni geomorfologiche e geomeccaniche del territorio e alle azioni antropiche. Geol. Appl. e Idrogeol **10**, 55–105 (1975)
36. Rosina, E.: Effetti delle interazioni tra edifici storici e condizioni climatiche. Efficienza energetica e patrimonio costruito. La sfida del miglioramento delle prestazioni nell'edilizia storica, pp. 145–165 (2013)
37. Guida, A.G., Bernardo, G.: Heritages of stone: materials degradation and restoration works. REUSO2015-Documentación, Conservación, y Reutilización del Patrimonio Arquitectónico, pp. 299–306 (2015)
38. Cigni, G., Codacci Pisanelli, B.: Umidità e degrado negli edifici, pp. 58–59 (1987)
39. Wan, Z.: MODIS land surface temperature products users' guide. Institute for Computational Earth System Science, University of California: Santa Barbara, CA, USA vol. 805, p. 26 (2006)
40. Moore, R.T., Hansen, M.C.: Google Earth Engine: a new cloud-computing platform for global-scale earth observation data and analysis. AGU Fall Meeting Abstracts, vol. 2011, p. IN43C-02 (2011)
41. Baldocchi, D., Ma, S.: How will land use affect air temperature in the surface boundary layer? Lessons learned from a comparative study on the energy balance of an oak savanna and annual grassland in California, USA. Tellus B Chem. Phys. Meteorol. **65**, 19994 (2013)
42. Malcheva, K., Bocheva, L., Marinova, T.: Mapping temperature and precipitation climate normals over Bulgaria by using ArcGIS Pro 2.4. Bulg. J. Meteorol. Hydrol. **2**, 61–77 (2020)

Processes, methods and tools towards RESilient cities and cultural and historic sites prone to SOD and ROD disasters (RES 2025)

The Interlink Between Urban Growth and Flooding: Lessons from the City of Bari (Italy)

Stefania Santoro[1], Vincenzo Totaro[2]([⊠]), Pasquale Balena[2], Vito Iacobellis[2], Umberto Fratino[2], and Dino Borri[2]

[1] National Research Council, Water Research Institute (CNR, IRSA), Brugherio, Italy
[2] Polytechnic University of Bari, Bari, Italy
vincenzo.totaro@poliba.it

Abstract. Urban growth, combined with the intensification of extreme rainfall events driven by climate change, has significantly altered the natural hydrological dynamics responsible for flood events, leading to an increased risk in urban areas. Indeed, the increase of impermeable surfaces, along with the inadequacy of urban drainage systems, can cause significant damage during heavy and short-duration rainfall events. These phenomena are also characterized by their localized nature, affecting specific urban or peri-urban areas that are often not recognized as floodable areas. This evolution in flood dynamics within increasingly urbanized contexts has highlighted the inadequacy of existing mitigation measures, which were originally conceived to address different types of flood risks. Therefore, it is crucial to design mitigation strategies that acknowledge the specific characteristics of these phenomena and integrate them into new urban development models and take into account citizens' risk perception. To this end, understanding territorial evolution is essential for identifying new areas of hydraulic vulnerability that have not yet been recognized or sufficiently studied. In this context, the present study aims to investigate the relationship between urban growth and hydraulic vulnerability through an integrated methodological approach, based on Geographic Information Systems (GIS) and survey-based risk perception analysis. The proposed methodology was applied to the case study of Bari (southern Italy), a coastal city whose metropolitan area is crossed by several episodic streams. The results identify new potentially vulnerable zones that escape traditional risk delineation methods, highlighting critical issues in urban development practices that have evolved without adequate consideration of the hydraulic morphology of the territory.

Keywords: Urban Floods · Urban Planning · Risk Management

1 Introduction

Urban expansion is one of the most significant territorial transformations of recent centuries, profoundly influencing – among others - ecosystems and hydrological dynamics. Increase of urban population, coupled with rapid infrastructural development, have drastically altered natural processes such as infiltration, runoff, and groundwater recharge,

O. Gervasi et al. (Eds.): ICCSA 2025 Workshops, LNCS 15894, pp. 49–60, 2026.
https://doi.org/10.1007/978-3-031-97648-3_4

leading to increased hydraulic risk and declining in water quality (De Roo et al., 2001) [1]. As an example, the transition from natural or semi-natural landscapes to artificial and impermeable surfaces reflects in the reduction of soils infiltration capacity, leading to an increased surface runoff that should be generally channeled into drainage systems.

It is well known that cities generally develop in a fragmented and stratified way, incorporating areas that were once designated for natural water flow, such as river flood-plains and ancient drainage channels [2, 3]. In fact, urban expansion has increasingly occupied natural retention and attenuation basins, decreasing their absorption capacity and exacerbating the risk of pluvial flooding [4]. This process has led to the rise of floodable areas even in places that were historically not susceptible to river flooding, with the coexistence of multiple type of floods in the same urban areas, which make difficult investigate causes and design mitigation measures [5, 6].

Concerns are then arising about the efficiency of current hydraulic mitigation measures also in the light of changes in extreme rainfall dynamics due to climate change, stressing need of revisiting traditional design techniques [7, 8]. These characteristics, combined with fragmented urban and infrastructural planning that often overlooks the need for natural drainage spaces and interconnections between urbanized areas and existing waterways, have intensified ground-level impacts, presenting a silent yet growing threat to cities [9]. In fact, many hydraulic mitigation infrastructures were designed without accounting for the continuous expansion of impermeable surfaces and evolving flood dynamics. This has created a paradoxical situation where areas previously not considered at risk of hydrogeological hazards now experience sudden flooding, causing significant damage to infrastructures and human activities [10, 11].

In recent years, scientific research has increasingly focused on developing strategies to mitigate the effects of urbanization on water systems, particularly concerning pluvial flooding risks. Sustainable urban drainage systems, integration of green infrastructures, and stormwater management are becoming effective tools for supporting the control of surface runoff generation and reducing the impacts of heavy rainfall events in urban areas [12]. To increase their efficiency, these measures should be complemented by more informed spatial planning that recognizes the hydrological and hydraulic histories of the area and preserves spaces for natural water management.

However, despite technological and scientific advances, defining effective integrated flood risk management strategies is still a challenge for communities and institutions [12, 13]. In this framework, the investigation of people's risk perception received considerable attention in last decades, because of the influence it can exert on people's response and decision-making during a flood emergency, even exacerbating the effects over those naturally expected [15–17].

This study presents a methodology that combines the analysis of the historical evolution of urban landscapes with an assessment of local residents' perception of flood risk. By integrating these two dimensions, the approach offers a more comprehensive and multidimensional understanding of urban flooding, serving as a valuable complement to conventional technical and hydrological analyses. The methodology aims to reveal the complex interplay between urban development, the physical vulnerability of the territory, and societal awareness of flood risk. Ultimately, the goal is to support more informed and participatory spatial planning processes ones that integrate both technical and socio-cultural perspectives and are better equipped to respond to the challenges posed by climate change and ongoing urban expansion. The paper is structured as follows: in Sect. 2 the case study is introduced, together with an overview about the most relevant river flood events that here occurred; in Sect. 3 the methodology and the material used for this study are described, while in Sects. 4 and 5 the main results and implications of the proposed analysis are discussed. Finally, the paper ends with an overview about the most significant conclusions of the study.

2 Case Study

2.1 The City of Bari (Southern Italy)

The city of Bari is located in the eastern coast Italy and is among the most important cities of Southern Italy, due to its key role in the industrial and financial sectors.

The hydrogeological system of Bari is strongly influenced by the karst nature of the region, characterized by a calcareous substrate that facilitates the rapid infiltration of rainwater and the formation of important underground aquifers [18]. This system consists of a superficial aquifer, discontinuous and influenced by seasonal variations, and a deep aquifer, more stable and which acts as a strategic resource for water supply [19]. A distinctive feature of the landscape is the presence of natural episodic streams called *lame* (Fig. 1), whose drainage networks are not fully organized, due to the low frequency of events characterized by enough energy to shape the geomorphology.

Hence, all these streams are characterized by a permanent absence of flows and somewhere not recognizable riverbeds, but in correspondence of heavy rainfall events significant peak discharges can be observed [20–22]. They are depressions that historically served as drainage routes for rainwater, but have been increasingly compromised by urbanization [2, 23]. The expansion of built-up areas has altered their hydrological function, contributing to an increased risk of flooding, particularly in the urbanized sections of their catchments (Fig. 2) [2, 24].

The metropolitan area of Bari falls within a climatic regime typical of Mediterranean regions, characterized by intense rainfall events that vary in duration throughout the year [25]. Short-duration rainfall episodes (between 30 min and 2 h), often highly intense, occur predominantly between June and September, whereas longer-lasting events (up to 24–48 h) are more common during the winter months. This marked seasonal and temporal variability, combined with the high intensity of shorter events, creates favorable conditions for the onset of sudden flooding, with diverse dynamics and impacts across the urban landscape. Historical analysis of rainfall data conducted in Totaro et al. [25] identified more than 80 urban flooding episodes linked to specific extreme precipitation events, highlighting a strong correlation between local climatic patterns and hydraulic risk exposure.

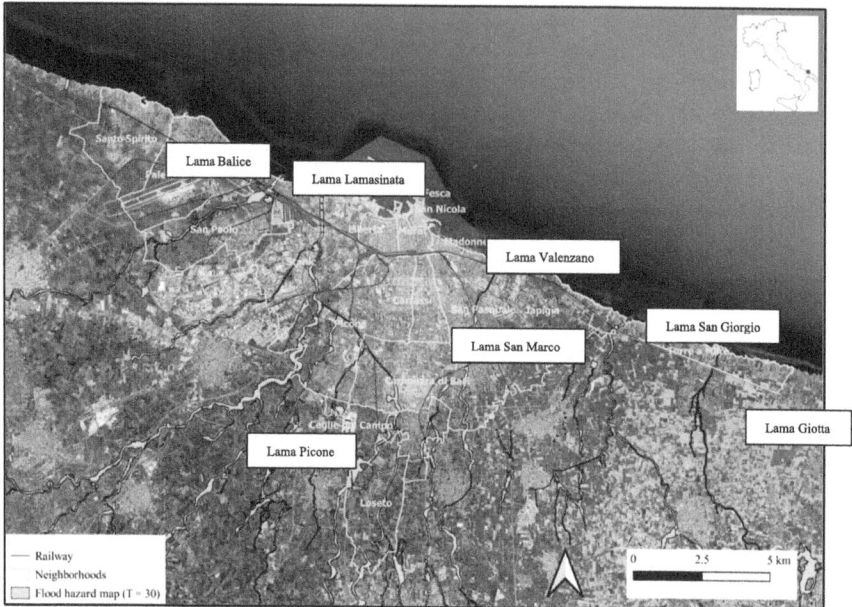

Fig. 1. The city of Bari with lame stream network and flood hazard maps

2.2   Flooding History

The history of the river floods that affected the city of Bari has been analysed in several scientific works [24, 26, 27], who described the main floods occurred in 1905, 1915, 1926 and 2005.

According to Mossa (2007) [24], each major flood that hit the city of Bari led to the implementation of engineering interventions aimed at protecting the territory, such as the construction of dikes and diversion channels. For example, the flood of 1915 prompted the construction of dikes along Lama Picone, considered at the time an effective solution to contain future floods. However, when another catastrophic event occurred in 1926, the barriers gave way and collapsed, triggering a devastating flood wave that submerged entire neighborhoods of the city. Following this tragedy, authorities recognized the need for broader and more integrated flood defense strategies, beyond simple pure hydraulic infrastructure. This led to the establishment of the Mercadante wood in 1928, located in the municipality of Cassano delle Murge. The reforestation project had a clear objective: to reduce hydrogeological risk by improving the soil's capacity to absorb rainwater and limiting runoff towards the coast [26]. The creation of the forest was accompanied by other strategic interventions, including the strengthening of the embankments, the diversion of Lama Lamasinata, and the construction of a new drainage channel to distribute water more effectively [28].

At the same time, improvements were made to urban infrastructure, including the enhancement of the sewer system to facilitate rainwater drainage and reduce water accumulation in vulnerable neighborhoods [2]. In addition, new urban planning regulations were introduced to prevent construction in high-risk areas. However, over time, many of

Fig. 2. Lama Giotta: example of urbanization close to the stream network

these regulations were ignored, leading to urban development that largely ignored the city's hydraulic safety [29].

However, the lack of maintenance of hydraulic infrastructure and poor land management made Bari vulnerable to flooding again, as demonstrated by the 2005 flood [27]. During the night between 22 and 23 October, an intense storm brought torrential rains, with almost 150 mm of rain falling in a few hours. The event caused the collapse of a road between Cassano delle Murge and Bitetto, resulting in the death of five people, as well as the derailment of a Eurostar train, resulting in multiple injuries. The water inundated several areas of the city, submerging homes, cars and industrial plants.

3   Methodology

The methodology used in this paper is articulated in two main steps, and namely: (i) GIS-based analysis aimed at the detection of urbanization trends over time, and (ii) detection of city landmarks that people perceive at flooding risk. In the following paragraphs all these steps are illustrated.

3.1 Evolution of Urbanized Areas Over Time

The historical evolution of the urbanization of the city of Bari has been reconstructed through collection and analysis of historical books and reports, photographical documentation and historical official cartography. The need of these three types of information is due to the lack of a consolidated analysis of the evolution of the urban texture of the city of Bari. To this aim, in particular we exploited:

  (i) historical cartography (e.g. Military Geographic Institute) and orthophotos;
 (ii) geological maps;
(iii) books and reports containing information about floods and urban fabric evolution;
 (iv) Regional Technical Map of Puglia region;
  (v) photographical documentation.

Combination of such data allowed to obtain a reliable description of the structure of the urban area of Bari during the last two centuries, together with useful insights about the dynamics of historical river floods events describes in Sect. 2.2.

3.2 Floodable Landmarks Perception Analysis

This step is aimed in the investigation of city landmarks perceived to be potentially subject to flooding by citizens. For this purpose, we collected data by disseminating survey with the methodology of snowballing sampling from July to September 2020 and, because of the restrictions imposed by the COVID-19 pandemic, it was diffused and shared only via online channels. Participants were asked with an open question to list streets, neighborhood or places that they perceive to be floodable after a rain events. As a results, a sample of 752 respondents has been collected. For a detailed discussion about the structure of the sample, the reader can refer to Santoro et al. [30].

4 Results

4.1 Urbanization Dynamics

The analysis of the evolution of the urbanization of the city took place in a GIS environment. In Fig. 3 is reported the urban evolution of the city of Bari as can be deduced from IGM cartography. The representation of the urban expansion was represented according to a temporal classification based on the 2011 Regional Technical Map, allowing to correlate the settlement dynamics with the stream network.

From a historical perspective, Fig. 3 illustrates four main phases of urbanisation. In 1869, the city was still extended not far from the historical settlement, close to the sea, with limited expansion. However, as it can be supposed from the analysis of a detailed geological map realized for the city of Bari [31] and historical information [24], at that time the evolution of the city already interested the mouth of the original path of the Picone lama, which crossed the Picone and Libertà neighborhoods flowing into the sea in the proximity of the city castle. In particular, historical photos [32] clearly show evidence of the Picone lama and crossing bridges in the homonymous neighborhood in the early '900.

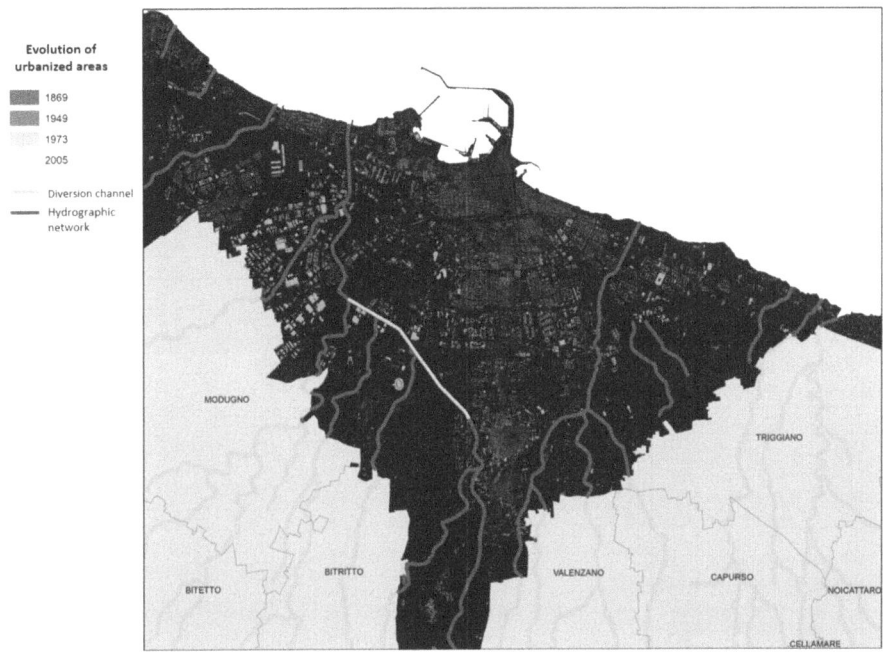

Fig. 3. Relationships between actual stream network and urban fabric development

As reported in Sect. 2.2, between 1905 and 1926 three major river flood events hit the city of Bari, causing victims and significant damage, leading to the design and building of hydraulic structures aimed in the protection of the city core. At the same time, the railway network was consolidated, splitting the city in two areas linked by underpasses that, with the increased diffusion of vehicles, become crucial points for urban mobility. In this context of renewed safety, induced by the coupled effect of the episodic nature of *lame* and of the hydraulic works, the urbanized area expanded significantly, reflecting a period of economic and population growth. As the decades passed, the process of expansion accelerated further: in 1973, there was a wider spread of urban fabric, favoured by industrialisation and infrastructure development. Finally, in 2005, more recent urbanisation extended towards the periphery and along the stream network, substantially changing the relationship between the city and its surroundings. This progression demonstrates a radial expansion of the urban fabric, with a strong initial concentration in the historic center and gradual growth towards the peripheral areas, often without adequate planning in relation to the hydro-geological conformation of the territory [26].

4.2 Landmark Detection

With respect to the results of the sample dissemination, it emerges how 14.4% of the respondents explicitly declared to not have any knowledge about potentially flooded areas. In the complementary 85.6%, only the 3.4% indicated *lame* as hazardous places.

Instead, the remaining part of the sample provided a reply with one or more options. Landmarks included general indications (e.g., streets, squares, underpasses) and specific streets and residential neighborhoods. In detail, Fig. 4 show landmarks indicated by respondents: among these, six out of the ten most popular landmarks belong to this category, and in 5 cases an explicit indication about their toponym is recorded. It is interesting to highlight how in the 63% of the cases underpasses were indicated as areas at risk.

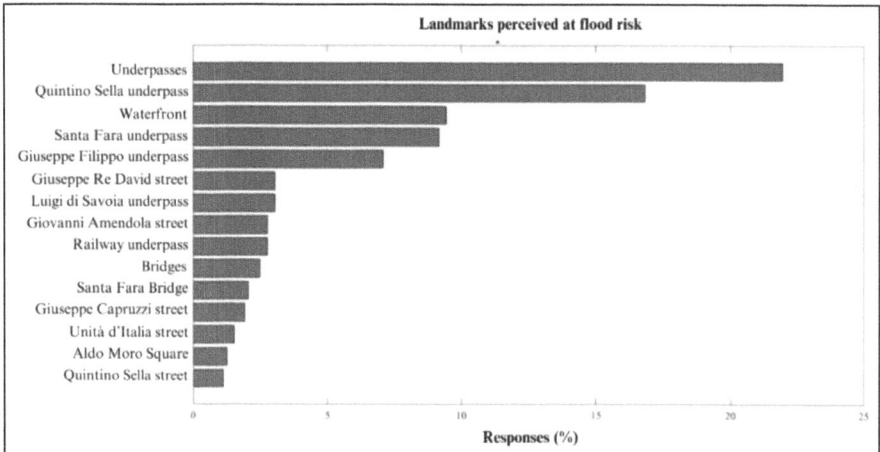

Fig. 4. *Frequency* of landmarks perceived at risk of flooding (only those with more than 1% of responses are reported)

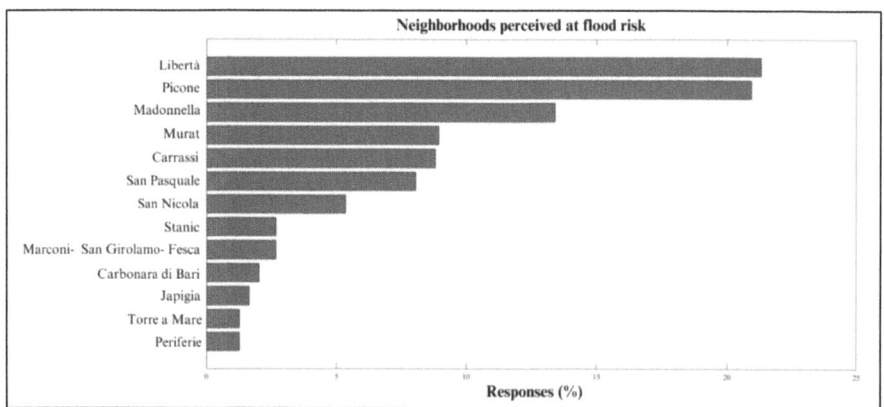

Fig. 5. Frequency of residential neighborhoods perceived at risk of flooding (only sites with more than 1% of occurrences are reported)

If moved to the neighborhoods (Fig. 5), the two top-rated options provided by respondents are the areas named Picone and Libertà (see Fig. 1), followed by Madonnella and

Murat. In all cases, this correspondence could be related to the presence of underpasses, which are crucial points in linking peripheral areas of the city with the city center.

Interestingly, Picone and Libertà neighborhoods are those were crossed by the original path of the Picone lama. From a hydraulic perspective, those landmarks clearly show how people perceive risk essential in response to pluvial flooding events, which generally exacerbate their effects in presence of moderate slopes or local depressions. Both conditions are typical of the urban area under investigation.

It is important to note that the data represented in this figure do not only reflect neighborhoods explicitly named by respondents, but also include those identified through specific reference points, such as streets or underpasses.

The results are quite clear: they reveal that neighborhoods located within the central urban area are widely perceived as vulnerable to flooding. The mention of specific landmarks—particularly underpasses and low-lying areas—helped to contextualize this perception, highlighting how certain features of the built environment contribute to water accumulation.

5 Discussion

The study of the evolution of urbanization is of paramount importance for understanding criticalities and relationships between citizens and the urban built environment. With respect to the specific case study of this paper, it emerges that urbanisation dynamics in the city of Bari has been characterised by a continuous tension between urban growth and hydraulic safety since its beginning, i.e., in the early '800. While on the one hand water diversion and containment works mitigated the risks due to river flooding, on the other the increase in concreting – especially in areas surrounding the stream network – changed the relationship between citizens and water. The results of Sect. 4.2 clearly describe how citizens' risk perception reflects the modified hydraulic asset of the city. In fact, pluvial flooding events are nowadays the most common threat that affect the city. As shown in [26], a systematic analysis of flooding events news and contents derived from newspaper and social media confirmed how, in effect, landmarks indicated from survey respondents corresponds to areas subject to floods in the past. The analysed journalistic and social media sources show that intense and sudden rainfalls quickly turn roads into flowing water, with recurring ground effects such as flooded subways, stranded cars, traffic jams and damage to businesses. In particular, critical points in the city, such as road underpasses, are often flooded in few hours due to the failure of the urban drainage system and local topography, which struggles to dispose of the accumulated volume of water. An analysis of the events reported in recent years shows poor maintenance of the hydraulic infrastructure, evidenced by recurrent reports of clogged manholes and insufficient sewerage pipes. This problem is aggravated by the increasing soil sealing due to uncontrolled urban expansion, which has reduced the natural surfaces capable of absorbing rainwater. The combination of these factors amplifies the risk of flooding, transforming even medium-intensity rainfall into urban emergencies. Interestingly, these landmarks lie generally outside the officially designated flood-prone areas, as recognized by the Hydrogeological Risk Management Plan. This note sheds light on the need of taking in account also this type of floods during land planning, in order to increase resilience of urban areas to extreme events.

Another relevant aspect highlighted by the map of Fig. 3 is the relationship between the urbanisation of Bari and its neighboring municipalities, including Modugno, Bitritto, Valenzano, Capurso and Triggiano. This suggests that the city's growth did not occur in isolation, but was part of a broader process of metropolitan expansion, with significant implications for the management of land and water resources. The need for coordinated planning between different administrations has emerged several times throughout history, remarking how urban development need to be carried out with particular attention to hydrogeological risks [29]. Hydraulic protection cannot be based only on the construction of engineering works, but must be accompanied by careful urban planning and respect for the territory's natural characteristics [24].

These results are a sign that the measures taken so far have not been sufficient or that prevention has not been given the right priority. In order to prevent these events from continuing to create damage and inconvenience, a more strategic and proactive approach is needed, one that does not just react to emergencies but aims to prevent the hydrogeological risk from flooding with long-term solutions.

6   Conclusions

The analysis showed that uncontrolled urban expansion and progressive soil sealing have had a significant impact on the hydraulic vulnerability of cities, increasing the risk of flooding. The increasing occupation of areas once used for natural water runoff has led to an alteration of the natural hydrological dynamics, with a reduction in infiltration capacity and an increase in surface runoff. Pluvial and flash floods, which are often underestimated in comparison to river floods, occur quickly and with sudden effects, making their management and prevention even more complex.

The study demonstrated the effectiveness of a methodological approach based on a combination of risk perception analysis and GIS tools to analyse the evolution of urbanisation and its impact on hydrological dynamics. Integrating the analysis with flood events catalogue made it possible to gather detailed information on the frequency and effects of recent flood events, while GIS model-relation made it possible to correlate the growth of the city with the transformation of the hydrographic reticulum and the increased risk of flooding.

The case study of Bari provided a concrete example of how urban expansion can generate new hydraulic criticalities, often in areas that historically were not considered at risk. The city has suffered a significant number of episodes of pluvial flooding in recent decades, in areas not included in traditional hydraulic hazard maps. This highlights the need to constantly update land planning and management tools, integrating historical data and predictive models capable of identifying vulnerable areas.

In order to mitigate the impacts of urbanisation on water resources and urban security, integrated strategies that combine sustainable spatial planning, Nature-Based Solutions (NBS) and advanced urban drainage infrastructures become crucial. Tools such as Sustainable Urban Drainage Systems (SUDS) can be effective solutions to improve the hydraulic resilience of cities.

This study underline the importance of more careful land and water management in expanding cities, highlighting how the integration of digital analysis tools and innovative approaches to water management can offer effective answers to the challenges of climate change and increasing urbanisation. A multidisciplinary approach, combining technology, research and strategic planning, will be essential to ensure the long-term water security and sustainability of urban areas.

References

1. De Roo, A., Odijk, M., Schmuck, G., Koster, E., Lucieer, A.: Assessing the effects of land use changes on floods in the meuse and oder catchment. Phys. Chem. Earth Part B Hydrol. Oceans Atmos. **26**(7-8), 593–599 (2001)
2. Borri, D., Di Santo, A., Iacobellis, V.: Bari: la piena del 1926. Continuità Rassegna Tecnica Pugliese, Bari, No. **3–4**, 83–88 (2002)
3. Di Baldassarre, G., Montanari, A., Lins, H.F., Koutsoyiannis, D., Brandimarte, L., Blöschl, G.: Flood fatalities in Africa: from diagnosis to mitigation. Geophys. Res. Lett. **40**(18), 1–5 (2013)
4. Alfieri, L., Burek, P., Feyen, L., Forzieri, G.: Global warming increases the frequency of river floods in Europe. Hydrol. Earth Syst. Sci. **19**(5), 2247–2260 (2015)
5. Santoro, S., Totaro, V., Mastrodonato, G., Balena, P.: Mapping citizens' knowledge and perception. What support for flood risk planning? some tips from Brindisi case study. In: International Conference on Computational Science and Its Applications, pp. 355–367. Springer Nature Switzerland, Cham (2023)
6. Santoro, S., Totaro, V., Lovreglio, R., Camarda, D., Iacobellis, V., Fratino, U.: Risk perception and knowledge of protective measures for flood risk planning. The case study of Brindisi (Puglia region). Safety Sci. **153**, 105791 (2022)
7. Fletcher, T.D., Andrieu, H., Hamel, P.: Understanding, management and modelling of urban hydrology and its consequences for receiving waters: a state of the art. Adv. Water Resour. **51**, 261–279 (2013)
8. Kourtis, I.M., Tsihrintzis, V.A.: Adaptation of urban drainage networks to climate change: a review. Sci. Total. Environ. **771**, 145431 (2021)
9. Angel, S., Parent, J., Civco, D.L., Blei, A., Potere, D.: The dimensions of global urban expansion: estimates and projections for all countries, 2000–2050. Prog. Plan. **75**(2), 53–107 (2011)
10. Zevenbergen, C., Fu, D., Pathirana, A., Katharina, K.: Urban Flood Management. CRC Press (2011)
11. Sonnessa, A., Cantatore, E., Esposito, D., Fiorito, F.: A multidisciplinary approach for multi-risk analysis and monitoring of influence of SODs and RODs on historic centres: the ResCUDE project. In: Computational Science and Its Applications–ICCSA 2020: 20th International Conference, Cagliari, Italy, July 1–4, 2020, Proceedings, Part IV 20, pp. 752–766. Springer International Publishing (2020)
12. Ellis, J.B., Lundy, L.: Implementing sustainable drainage systems for urban surface water management within the regulatory framework in England and Wales. J. Environ. Manage. **183**, 630–636 (2016)
13. Buchecker, M., Salvini, G., Backhaus, N., Müller-Böker, U., Forster, C.: The role of risk perception in making flood risk management more effective. Nat. Hazard. **13**(11), 3013–3030 (2013). https://doi.org/10.5194/nhess-13-3013-2013
14. Alonso Vicario, S., et al.: Unravelling the influence of human behaviour on reducing casualties during flood evacuation. Hydrol. Sci. J. **65**(14), 2359–2375 (2020). https://doi.org/10.1080/02626667.2020.1810254
15. Bradford, R.A., et al.: Risk perception–issues for flood management in Europe. Nat. Hazard. **12**(7), 2299–2309 (2012). https://doi.org/10.5194/nhess-12-2299-2012

16. Bubeck, P., Botzen, W.J.W., Suu, L.T.T., Aerts, J.C.J.H.: Do flood risk perceptions provide useful insights for flood risk management? Findings from central Vietnam. J. Flood Risk Manage. **5**(4), 295–302 (2012). https://doi.org/10.1111/j.1753-318X.2012.01151.x

17. Birkholz, S., Muro, M., Jeffrey, P., Smith, H.M.: Rethinking the relationship between flood risk perception and flood management. Sci. Total. Environ. **478**, 12–20 (2014). https://doi.org/10.1016/j.scitotenv.2014.01.061

18. Polemio, M., Casarano, D.: Climate change, drought and groundwater availability in southern Italy. GeoJournal **70**(2–3), 167–175 (2008)

19. Petrucci, O., Polemio, M., Pasqua, A.A.: Analysis of damaging hydrogeological events: the case of Apulia region (southern Italy). Nat. Hazard. **12**(10), 2785–2797 (2012)

20. Regione Puglia: Piano Paesaggistico Territoriale. Ambito 05/Puglia centrale (2015). Accessed 22 Dec 2024

21. Gioia, A., Totaro, V., Bonelli, R., Esposito, A.A., Balacco, G., Iacobellis, V.: Flood susceptibility evaluation on ephemeral streams of Southern Italy: a case study of Lama Balice. In: Computational Science and Its Applications–ICCSA 2018: 18th International Conference, Melbourne, VIC, Australia, July 2–5, 2018, Proceedings, Part V 18, pp. 334–348. Springer International Publishing (2018). https://doi.org/10.1007/978-3-319-95174-4_27

22. Balacco, G., Totaro, V., Gioia, A., Piccinni, A.F.: Evaluation of geomorphic descriptors thresholds for flood prone areas detection on ephemeral streams in the metropolitan area of Bari (Italy). In: International Conference on Computational Science and Its Applications, pp. 239–254. Cham: Springer International Publishing (2019). https://doi.org/10.1007/978-3-030-24305-0_19

23. Cotecchia, V., Lenti, L., Pugliese, A.: The influence of geological and hydrogeological settings on the occurrence of floods in Apulia (Southern Italy). Quatern. Int. **140–141**, 153–163 (2005)

24. Mossa, M.: The floods in Bari: what history should have taught. J. Hydraul. Res. **45**(5), 579–594 (2007). https://doi.org/10.1080/00221686.2007.9521795

25. Totaro V., Santoro S., Bruno M.F., Iacobellis V., Molfetta M.G., Fratino U. (2025). A deeper look into flood risk in the city of Bari (Italy). Submitted

26. Moretti, M.: Le alluvioni nel settore Adriatico delle Murge (Terra di Bari): cause geologiche e ruolo dell'azione antropica. Geologi e Territorio, Ordine Regionale dei Geologi – Puglia **3**, 11–22 (2005)

27. Bisantino, T., Pizzo, V., Polemio, M., Gentile, F.: Analysis of the flooding event of October 22–23, 2005 in a small basin in the province of Bari (Southern Italy). J. Agric. Eng. **47**(4), 197–204 (2016). https://doi.org/10.4081/jae.2016.531

28. Baldassarre, G., Francescangeli, R.: Osservazioni e considerazioni sulla inondazione del 6 Novembre 1926 in Bari e su un relativo deposito. Mem. Soc. Geol. It. **37**, 7–16 (1987)

29. Melchiorre, V.A.: Bari Nella Storia. Adda Editore, Bari (2002)

30. Santoro, S., Lovreglio, R., Totaro, V., Camarda, D., Iacobellis, V., Fratino, U.: Community risk perception for flood management: a structural equation modelling approach. Int. J. Disaster Risk Reduction **97**, 104012 (2023)

31. Sabato, L., Tropeano, M., Spalluto, L., Pieri, P.: Il nuovo Foglio Geologico 438 "Bari" in scala 1: 50.000. Un importante contributo per la conoscenza geologica dell'area metropolitana di Bari. Geologia dell'Ambiente **4**, 4–14 (2010)

32. Bernardoni, A.; Mauro, R.; Sanseverino, F.: A spasso per le lame di Bari. Mario Adda Editore (2018)

Mapping Natural and Activity-Induced Hazards for Water Heritage in Italian Seaports

Elena Cantatore$^{(\boxtimes)}$ ⓘ, Mariella De Fino ⓘ, Margherita Lasorella ⓘ, and Fabio Fatiguso ⓘ

Politecnico di Bari, 70126 Bari, Italy
elena.cantatore@poliba.it

Abstract. Hazard mapping for built heritage in seaports is essential due to the coexistence of natural events and anthropogenic activity-based. Hydrogeomorphological features and human-induced effects are diversely distributed, and both affect the preservation of valuable architectural, archaeological, industrial and infrastructural assets in administrative seaport boundaries. However, in the Italian context, the ongoing process of cataloguing heritage may limit the effectiveness of assessment and preservation strategies.

This paper presents the first findings of hazard identification in Italian seaports as part of the national research project RE^{3}WORK. The study focuses on the assessment of seaports' susceptibility to natural and anthropogenic hazards to support the safe and sustainable reuse of their built heritage. By combining data on geographical location, port activities and systematic built heritage inventory, recurrences in natural and activity-induced hazards are identified at national scale, also thanks to national hazard maps and an international database of industrial-based hazards classification. As the main outcomes, flooding and explosion caused by industrial and civil navigation are identified as dominant hazards in seaports. A more detailed investigation is conducted at the regional scale, focusing on Apulia, South Italy, to examine site-specific hazard interactions. The analysis links the spatial distribution of built heritage with flood vulnerability and port activities, revealing local variations in hazard proneness. Findings highlight the predominant role of ship-related activities as explosion source, while also demonstrating the limitations of regional flood vulnerability mapping in effectively assessing built heritage exposure to natural hazards.

Keyword: Water built Heritage · seaport · natural and anthropogenic risks · Apulian ports

1 Introduction

Risk mapping constitutes a pivotal activity in the preventive phases of the hazard risk management process. Identifying hazard types and understanding the potential proneness of certain areas to these hazards are the main basis for establishing a robust structure for risk management [1–3].

© The Author(s), under exclusive license to Springer Nature Switzerland AG 2026
O. Gervasi et al. (Eds.): ICCSA 2025 Workshops, LNCS 15894, pp. 61–78, 2026.
https://doi.org/10.1007/978-3-031-97648-3_5

At a global scale, hazard mapping aims to identify the types of hazards affecting territorial areas with varying intensities or occurrences to categorise and measure vulnerable areas [4]. Another level of hazard mapping involves a more detailed analysis at smaller territorial scales, characterised by similar geographical conditions but local specificities. This approach seeks to define possible local variations in hazards, combine them with physical and social vulnerabilities, and prioritise interventions at the appropriate scale [5, 6]. In both activities, risk mapping begins with identifying hazard types as a preliminary step to conducting risk analysis and management. Globally, several initiatives have been undertaken to record disastrous events and determine recurrence patterns. This is particularly relevant for hazards related to climate change processes that affect regions worldwide, including natural phenomena (i.e., Intergovernmental Panel on Climate Change – IPCC classification activities) [7]. Other classifications focus on different types of disasters, encompassing both natural and anthropogenic hazards and threats (i.e. classification by United Nations Office for Disaster Risk Reduction – UNDRR, Centre for Research on the Epidemiology of Disasters – CRED and the related EMDAT database) [8, 9]. Here, the purpose is to support national and international risk assessment and management efforts, enhancing local resilience.

In this framework, built heritage represents a weak element in disaster risk management. As outlined below, policymakers must control potential exposure at the physical level to conduct thorough analyses and implement strategies for risk mitigation. However, beyond well-documented architectural heritage, many undiscovered or unlisted ones pose challenges to risk management at both broad and local scales [10–12].

Risk mapping activities for architectural and cultural heritage are not new and have already been the focus of several projects.

At the European level, the Shelter and STORM projects represent two significant examples [13, 14]. In these projects, scientists and technicians collaborated to develop specific operational tools to assist policymakers in selecting mitigation strategies and potential reuse activities for particular case studies exposed to natural hazards. A common feature of these applications is the necessity of studying the varying levels of vulnerability of selected case studies across Europe. These efforts aim to establish classifications of strategies and promote general or specific guidelines for action, addressing both the preservation and reuse of heritage sites at risk from natural hazards while also fostering social and cultural resilience. However, in both projects, the focus is on listed architectural heritage.

In Italy, a significant initiative is the "Carta del Rischio" [15, 16]. Here, public and scientific institutions have collaborated to systematise three key dimensions of risk for national cultural heritage: potential exposure, state of vulnerability, and hazard type. These dimensions converge towards different levels of risk within the national territory. Risk classes are assessed in terms of potential cultural heritage loss, facilitating risk mapping on a broad scale to establish intervention priorities for heritage preservation. The identification of risk levels is integrated into a national WebGIS which maps Italian architectural and cultural heritage and qualifies them according to vulnerability levels (e.g., state of conservation), potential exposure (e.g., geomorphological vulnerability, seismic frequency), and hazard type. This is achieved with contributions from national and regional bodies specialising in natural hazard assessment, including Civil Protection,

Italian Institute for Environmental Protection and Research (ISPRA), National Institute of Geophysics and Volcanology (INGV), and regional Basin Authorities.

Despite the broad scale of analysis, "Carta del Rischio" is linked to the metadata of "Vincoli in Rete," which catalogues all listed and registered cultural heritage sites and architectures. However, the census of cultural heritage remains an ongoing and slow process. Recent studies have highlighted how this situation may impact recovery and preservation efforts for architectural heritage in seaport areas [17], particularly along the Italian coastline. The multi-dimensional nature of national and regional regulations for coastal management and protection, the diverse range of activities within the ports, and the historical evolution and transformation of port infrastructure hinder the identification and safeguarding of architectural and built heritage. Given this complexity, identifying built cultural heritage is a crucial first step in its documentation, while risk mapping for port areas is essential for their preservation, as it helps assess potential hazards and threats to which these sites may be exposed.

In this framework, the paper presents preliminary findings related to the hazards and threats identification of Italian ports currently managed by the Port System Authorities – AdSP, as part of the activities for the project RE³WORK – REsilient REtrofitting and REuse of Water heritage and built environments: multi-objective Optimization for RisK mitigation and cultural enhancement. Specifically, the study focuses on preliminary activities aimed at determining possible hazard proneness of sites to provide suitable and secure reuse of architectural heritage in Italian AdSP ports – the so-called Water built Heritage (WH). This is achieved through a coherent and structured analysis of possible mitigation actions combined with integrated and conservation-oriented interventions. In detail, the study begins with an analysis of Italian coast proneness to natural hazards and the recurrence of related disastrous events in AdSP seaports due to port activities. The most recurrent hazards are identified in line with national-scale analyses. A specific focus on Apulian ports further examines local exposure to these hazards, linking WH to local geomorphological and typological features and distribution of port activities.

To this end, the paper is structured in the following sections:

– A background of previous scientific activities in risk mapping for coastal heritage and the associated aims of the RE³WORK project (Sect. 2).
– The general framework and the detailed goals of the paper contents for Italian seaports coherent with the RE³WORK project activities (Sect. 3).
– Preliminary results in hazards identification at national (Sect. 4.1) and mapping at local scale (Sect. 4.2), with a specific focus on the WH in Apulian seaports.

2 Background

Seaports are complex urban areas where multiple governmental entities and activities coexist. Due to historical development, both built historical and cultural heritage are present in these areas, with ports functioning as active or inactive architectural elements in their current state. This is a common characteristic of many port areas that have already been analysed in previous studies, particularly in relation to hazard proneness. In detail, focusing on the most recent activities in risk mapping activities on coastal built heritage, two main classes of hazards can be identified:

- Natural hazards, which consider both the geographical position of the studied territories (e.g., landslide, flood) [18, 19] and relative position with the sea (e.g. coastal
  erosion, sea level rise) [20–23].
- Hazards induced by human activities, resulting from local or territorial events (e.g., oil
  spills, ship accidents) [24, 25], as well as global processes (e.g., rising temperatures,
  water pollution) [26, 27].

In addition to governmental complexity, these two classes of hazards highlight the
multidimensionality of ports, where commercial, strategic, and touristic activities coexist
within a defined perimeter of the broader urban built environment. In this context, hazard
identification and mapping for built heritage in ports reflect two key aspects:

- The positioning of seaports in terms of morpho-hydro-geographical conditions, which
  locally WH due to natural environmental factors (e.g., geomorphological features,
  climate).
- The type of activities conducted within ports, which may directly or indirectly
  contribute to the occurrence of disastrous events.

Both aspects must be properly correlated with the sea, which acts as a direct or
indirect stressor for natural and anthropogenic hazards affecting WH.

Given these considerations, the hazard mapping for Italian ports managed by the
AdSP in the RE³WORK project begins with a rapid methodology designed to identify
the most common hazards. This approach serves as a preliminary basis for analysing the
relationship between WH and ports, with a particular focus on port activities, morpho-
typologies, materials, and construction techniques. These characteristics help describe
WH's inherent vulnerabilities or resilience, providing a foundation for a more detailed
risk assessment. To this end, the analysis builds on the preliminary port cataloguing
phase reported in [17]. This phase includes the ports' identification, geographical details
gathering, and the activities' categorisation within seaports, as the primary dataset for
developing a geographically referenced hazard recurrence database. In line with these
objectives, three levels of data collection and analysis have been pursued:

- Level I—A census of all AdSP administrative areas, starting with basic information
  about their location and main activities.
- Level II—A census of WH in multi-activity port areas, enriching the ViR dataset by
  identifying WH entities within port environments.
- Level III—A locally focused analysis that integrates detailed information on activities, WH distribution within ports, construction techniques, materials, and functions
  associated with WH.

Based on these levels of information, subsequent national, local, and WH-specific
risk analyses can be conducted, ensuring a comprehensive mapping of national and
activities-induced hazards within their local contexts. Following, the most recurrent are
identified and related to seaport samples and analysed in depth at the local scale for the
reduced sample in the Apulian region.

3   General Framework and Goals

In line with the overview and previous thematic relevance of these issues, two dimensions of hazard classes are identified, leveraging two different databases and previous phenomenological analyses. Specifically:

– Natural hazards (H_Cl.1), referring to environmental, geophysical, or climatological events, regardless of whether they are induced by natural site conditions (e.g., earthquakes) or other factors (e.g., heatwaves). These hazards are derived from metadata related to the national territory, accessible via the National Geoportal. The geoportal allows data visualisation but does not enable metadata export. However, by classifying data into relevant macro-domains, it has been possible to identify the most significant hazards for the territory, such as earthquakes, landslides, and floods. Hazards related to air pollution and potential climatological risks are excluded, as they are associated with slow-onset scenarios and are therefore not considered relevant to the project's aims.
– Anthropogenic threats (H_Cl.2) caused by the use of or activities within the identified sites. In this case, the relationships between threats and ports are structured by linking the classification of port activities with the anthropogenic risk classes identified in the EM-DAT database[1] [9], which categorises anthropogenic threats as technological and complex risks. This database is managed by the CRED [28].

These classes of hazards, along with the associated databases, are integrated with the different levels of detail collected in Levels I, II, and III to achieve two main goals:

– Identification of the hazard types, calibrated to geographical details and predominant activities in port environments (Sect. 4.1, Level I content). Information on anthropogenic hazards (H_Cl.2) is derived from the classification of port activities and the EM-DAT classification of technological threats. Simultaneously, port administrative perimeters and national thematic metadata are combined to analyse the recurrence of relevant natural hazards (H_Cl.1) on the national scale.
– Preliminary hazard/threat proneness mapping at the WH scale, aligned with the typologies identified in the previous step (Sect. 4.2). Here, selected case studies from Level II are assessed based on the types of activities and hazards identified earlier. This step involves integrating details on WH locations and the distribution of activities within port areas (details from Level III).

All data collected and external open-source metadata are managed within a GIS-based environment to facilitate geographical-level data management.

To illustrate these objectives, Fig. 1 summarises the data used, including those catalogued in Levels I, II, and III, as well as metadata accessed for natural and activity-induced hazards, ensuring coherence with the scale of outcomes presented in this work.

---

[1] https://doc.emdat.be/docs/data-structure-and-content/disaster-classification-system/.

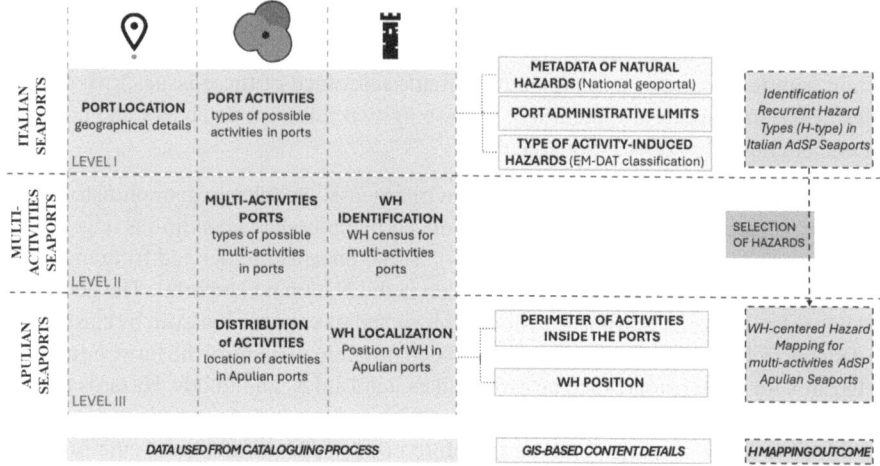

Fig. 1. Structure of data and metadata used to identify Hazard proneness of seaports from national to regional scale, combining three levels of data collected for seaports and WH census

4 Results in Hazard and Threat Mapping for Italian AdSP Ports

4.1 The Identification of Recurrent Threats and Hazards

Data gathering in Level I involved a 63-item sample of Italian AdSP port sites, distributed along the Italian coasts [17]. Using their geographical details, port sites were integrated into the GIS environment to set up the database and enhance them with external natural hazard metadata and the related threat types, also linking these with the associated activities.

Each port's administrative boundary was merged with metadata related to regional hydrogeological, territorial landslide, and national seismic vulnerability mapping in accordance with the details in Table 1.

The initial outcomes of the GIS analysis highlight the significance of hazard mapping activities in the ports. Specifically, the overlapping of port boundaries with all hazard vulnerability layers reveals several key patterns (Fig. 2).

The first relates to the seismic vulnerabilities of sites, which vary significantly, covering all the classes defined by national regulations (where 1 represents the highest level of vulnerability and 4 the lowest). In contrast, landslide vulnerability shows limited variation in significance for port areas, with few cases of critical geomorphological vulnerabilities when comparing external and inner port boundaries. Regarding the final hazard mapping aspect, flood vulnerability in ports exhibits a distinct distribution within administrative recurrences. Local dependency on administrative perimeters is evident when comparing the inner and outer results of the process, particularly in identifying high-vulnerability classifications for hydrogeological proneness. A critical analysis of these outcomes suggests that the management or absence of flood-related measures within port boundaries may require further investigation at a higher scale of analysis. Simultaneously, the key outcomes indicate that hydrogeological flood vulnerability in ports is a significant hazard warranting further exploration at the port scale.

Table 1. Thematic metadata used for the identification of natural hazard proneness analysis at the Italian AdSP ports

Thematic layer hazard type	Opendata source
Landslide	http://wms.pcn.minambiente.it/ogc?map=/ms_ogc/WMS_v1.3/Vettoriali/PAI_rischio.map
Seismic	http://wms.pcn.minambiente.it/ogc?map=/ms_ogc/WMS_v1.3/raster/IGM_25000.map
Flooding	http://wms.pcn.minambiente.it/ogc?map=/ms_ogc/WMS_v1.3/Vettoriali/Alluvioni_Classi_di_Rischio.map

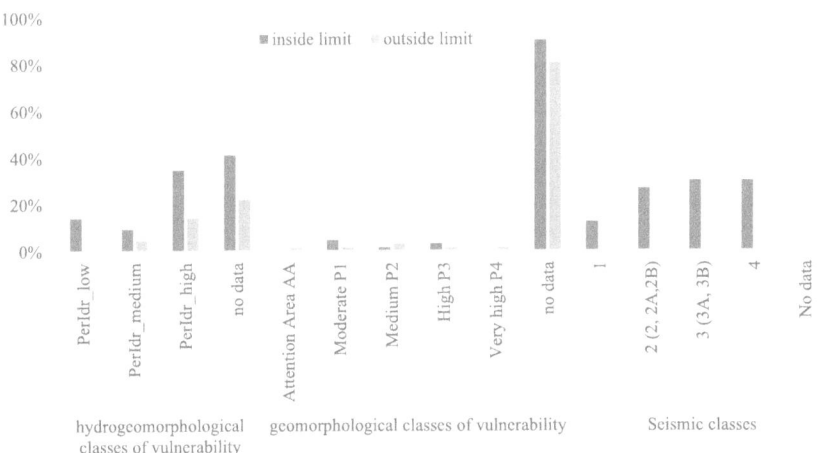

Fig. 2. Distribution in % of natural hazard proneness of the 63-item sample of AdSP seaports in classes of territorial vulnerability to hydro-geomorphological (flooding), geomorphological (landslide) and seismic hazards

The second level of outcomes pertains to activity-induced hazard identification. Based on the census carried out in Level I, Table 2 summarises the recurring activities and their frequency across all sampled ports. Additionally, Table 2 illustrates the multi-activity levels in the analysed ports, reflecting possible interferences between activities and threats. Industrial production, shipbuilding, civil navigation, leisure navigation, mercantile operations, and fish landing are linked to the EM-DAT threat types. The structured relationships between activities and EM-DAT threat classification are summarised in Table 3, providing a coherent correlation.

The integration of metadata into the GIS database for 63 ports facilitates the analysis of activity-induced hazards and their potential recurrences. Given the prevalence of multi-activity operations and the multidimensional nature of activity interferences, the counting process considers only the number of ports affected by each identified threat. This approach is essential to prevent the overestimation of hazard intensities, which can

Table 2. Type of activities and their recurrences in the 63-item sample of the analysed ports as single and multi-function levels

Type of activities	n. of sites	Multi-function levels	n. of sites
Industrial production	35	2 activities	3
Shipbuilding	31	3 activities	12
Civil navigation	47	4 activities	18
Leisure navigation	56	more than 4 activities	28
Mercantile	55		
Fish landing operations	42		

vary significantly depending on the spatial arrangement of activities within each port sub-area. In line with this approach, Fig. 3 presents the results, emphasising the prominence of threats associated with water-related activities, such as poisoning and shipping accidents, as well as industrial-based threats that arise from interactions between water activities and production processes (e.g., fire, explosion, and chemical/oil spills). A unique case involves a disused port where structural collapse is unrelated to ongoing activities but rather to physical and/or technological obsolescence.

Table 3. Relationship between seaports activities and EM-DAT type of threat defined for the Italian cases

EM-DAT type of Threat / Activity type	Chemical spill	Gas leak	Oil spill	Radiation	Poisoning	Collapse	Explosion	Fire	Transport accident (Rail)	Transport accident (Water)
Industrial production	x	x	x	x	x	x	x	x		x
Shipbuilding			x			x	x	x	x	x
Civil navigation							x	x		x
Leisure navigation								x		x
Merchant shipping						x	x	x		x
Fish landing	x				x			x		x

As first outcomes of these preliminary activities, two key classes of hazards emerge as focal points for further detailed analysis in WH conservation: the natural susceptibility of port areas to hydro-morphological vulnerabilities, particularly flooding, and the susceptibility to explosions resulting from industrial processes and ship accidents. The proneness of Italian seaports to these hazards requires further detailed assessment at the local scale, examining how the spatial distribution of activities and WH may interact.

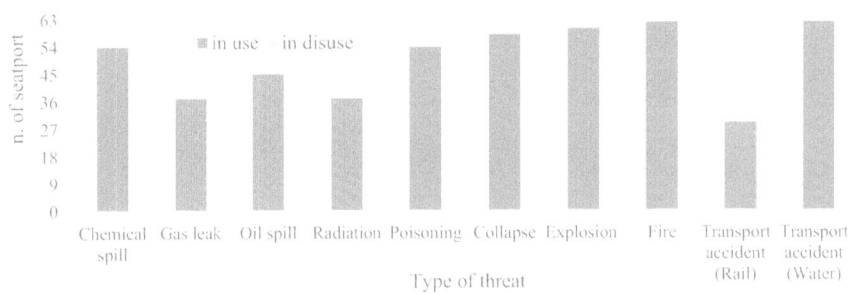

Fig. 3. Distribution of the 63-item sample of AdSP seaports in types of threats, as identified in EM-DAT and merged with seaport activities

Additionally, physical distances should be considered to determine how local conditions may extend the hazard susceptibility of other WH assets.

4.2 The Identification of Recurrent Hazards in Seaports for WH. First Outcomes in the Apulian Cases

Considering the second goal to be achieved in the hazard mapping process for Italian AdSP ports, the relationship between the WH census and site proneness is determined for a limited set of seaports, aligning with the requirements of the RE^{3}WORK project. This limited sample includes seaports characterised by a high level of multi-activity (three or more), relevance to the selected activity-induced (explosions from industrial activities and ship accidents), and/or proneness to the identified natural hazard (hydro-geomorphological proneness to flooding), as well as the presence of WH. For these ports, the WH census begins with the Vincoli in Rete (ViR) list, and it is refined through site analysis and administrative port documents, enhancing knowledge and WH cataloguing for the project's objectives. Table 4 presents the reduced list of ports and the associated number of WH assets within each port, highlighting the census results. For these ports, spatial recurrences of natural and activity-induced hazards mapping is necessary. To achieve this, the process involves merging the spatial distribution of functional areas in each port with the coordinates of the identified WH items. Thus, outcomes of the Apulian case studies are presented. Following the operational details discussed in Sect. 3, this second step uses WH coordinates, national maps of hydro-geomorphological vulnerabilities, and the distribution of port activities.

The geographical hazard mapping for the Apulian case studies indicates zero direct interferences between flooding and single WH. However, local proximities to flood-prone areas are observed in the cases of Taranto and Brindisi (Fig. 4), making them the most representative examples of this natural hazard.

On the other hand, the activity-induced hazard mapping for WH items reveals more significant findings for Apulian cases. Specifically, as summarised in Fig. 5, most identified WH items are located within port sub-areas dedicated to mercantile and civil navigation activities. This reduces their presence in industrial or production zones, emphasising

Table 4. List of selected multi-activities AdSP seaports and number of WH assets considering items already censed in Vincoli in Rete (ViR) platform and external ones

Seaport name	n. WH items	ViR	Other	Seaport name	n. WH items	ViR	Other
Porto di Genova	39	27	12	Porto di Licata	2	0	2
Porto di Savona	11	1	10	Porto di Augusta	8	6	2
Porto di La Spezia	11	9	2	Porto di Catania	6	2	4
Porto di Livorno	27	3	24	Porto di Bari	5	0	5
Porto di Portoferraio	7	6	1	Porto di Brindisi	17	11	6
Porto di Civitavecchia	9	8	1	Porto di Barletta	3	1	2
Porto di Napoli	15	5	10	Porto di Termoli	2	2	0
Porto di Castellamare di Stabia	4	1	3	Porto di Taranto	5	0	5
Porto di Crotone	2	0	2	Porto di Ancona	22	14	8
Porto di Cagliari	9	9	0	Porto di Ravenna	9	1	8
Porto di Olbia	3	3	0	Porto di Venezia	32	25	6
Porto di Palermo	18	2	16	Porto di Trieste	70	49	21
Porto di Porto Empedocle	8	2	6	Porto di Messina	8	3	5
Porto di Trapani	3	1	2				

the primary role of these activities in threat-induced evaluation. As a result, all identified WHs are linked to the main local activities to determine interferences and potential explosion sources. In these cases, sources depend on ship activities (navigation and mercantile operations) as the most probable starting events. Specifically, all identified WHs are connected to possible explosion sources, considering activities along mercantile docks and civil navigation docks and routes, with physical proximity acting as a key factor in enhancing WH proneness to overpressure [29]. To quantify this, minimum distances between mercantile docks, civil navigation routes, and WH location are calculated within the GIS environment, leading to the final results discussed in Table 5.

Fig. 4. Details of hydro-geomorphological vulnerability levels and WH distribution within the seaports of Brindisi (top) and Taranto (bottom)

In detail, distance classes are defined based on the following criteria:

– The same ship type is considered for both explosion collisions and mercantile activities, as explained by [29].

Fig. 5. Quantitative distribution of items in specific sub-areas of Apulian AdSP ports' activities

– Key ranges of overpressure (measured in bars) corresponding to potential damage to building structures.
– Key ranges of overpressure (measured in bars) with potential effects on people.

The same WH sample within the selected Apulian ports is categorised according to distance ranges (Table 5), highlighting the significance of explosion proneness in relation to physical distances from potential explosion sources.

Table 5. Equivalent critical distance for overpressure threshold and related effects determined for the explosion of an LPG-fueled ship as in [29]

Distance [m]	Overpressure thresholds [bar]	Effect
<100	0,37	Threshold on effects in disruption
100–160	0,20 – 0,37	Serious damages
160–240	0,13 – 0,20	Moderate damages
240–800	0,03 – 0,13	No damages on structure, effects on people
>800	<0,03	Fragile break (window, plasters)

Figure 6 illustrates their distribution, identifying critical physical distances in line with the explosion source locations. This highlights the feasibility of conducting in-depth analyses of explosion effects on WH as a tangible and significant hazard (see Fig. 7 for detailed seaport analyses of Brindisi and Taranto).

5   Discussion of Results

The use of national and regional thematic maps of natural hazards is a powerful tool for exploring large territories, aligning with the scale and level of detail in their processing. In this study, their application to Italian seaports has demonstrated their potential in identifying recurrent hazards in coastal areas and determining priority hazards for further focus at a broader scale. The prominence of flooding, resulting from the coastal positioning and the proximity to the sea, is an expected outcome at the site level.

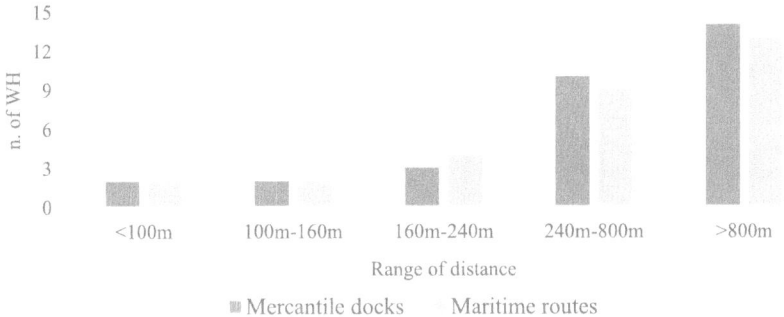

Fig. 6. Distribution of WH assets in the equivalent critical classes of distance from the explosion source as in Table 5

However, the local interactions with vulnerable hydro-geomorphological sub-areas are insufficient to definitively assess WH hazard proneness, necessitating detailed local evaluations. This aligns with existing Italian territorial mapping carried out by national and regional experts in collaboration with public administrations to catalogue built and unbuilt cultural heritage. However, as the analysis of these coastal areas has shown, many architecturally, historically, or socially significant structures remain absent from listing heritage inventories. This lack of recognition suggests a potentially lower level of attention at the national scale, consequently limiting opportunities for their protection and preservation. Addressing this uncertainty requires local-scale assessments by port administrations, which must be supported in identifying WH assets. The importance of this census activity was underscored when the knowledge-gathering phase for selected ports revealed that more than 40% of WH (Table 4) could potentially enrich the metadata of the national "Carta del Rischio", thereby expanding opportunities for managing this heritage at risk on a national level.

Conversely, the multi-activity nature of the analysed Italian ports has highlighted the recurrence of certain activity-induced hazards, primarily linked to shipping activities (mercantile and civil navigation) and industrial production. In this context, the preliminary phase of anthropogenic hazard identification has expanded beyond natural ones, incorporating threats linked to port activities, currently excluded from national and regional mapping within the "Carta del Rischio".

The identification of both hazards and threats at a broad scale presents an opportunity to examine the WH located within Apulian seaports, providing preliminary insights into site-specific risk conditions. For these sites, flood proneness necessitates more detailed, downscaled mapping to refine the quality of regional and national geomorphological datasets. Simultaneously, in both the hazard assessments, the identified WH will be evaluated by parameters and features that define their physical vulnerabilities. These vulnerabilities will be classified into different heritage types to ensure a comprehensive approach that will allow the extension of local and in-depth analysis to the national scale, increasing the potential impact.

The diversity of WH types - ranging from industrial heritage and landmarks to buildings, warehouses, and lighthouses -, alongside the variety of construction materials

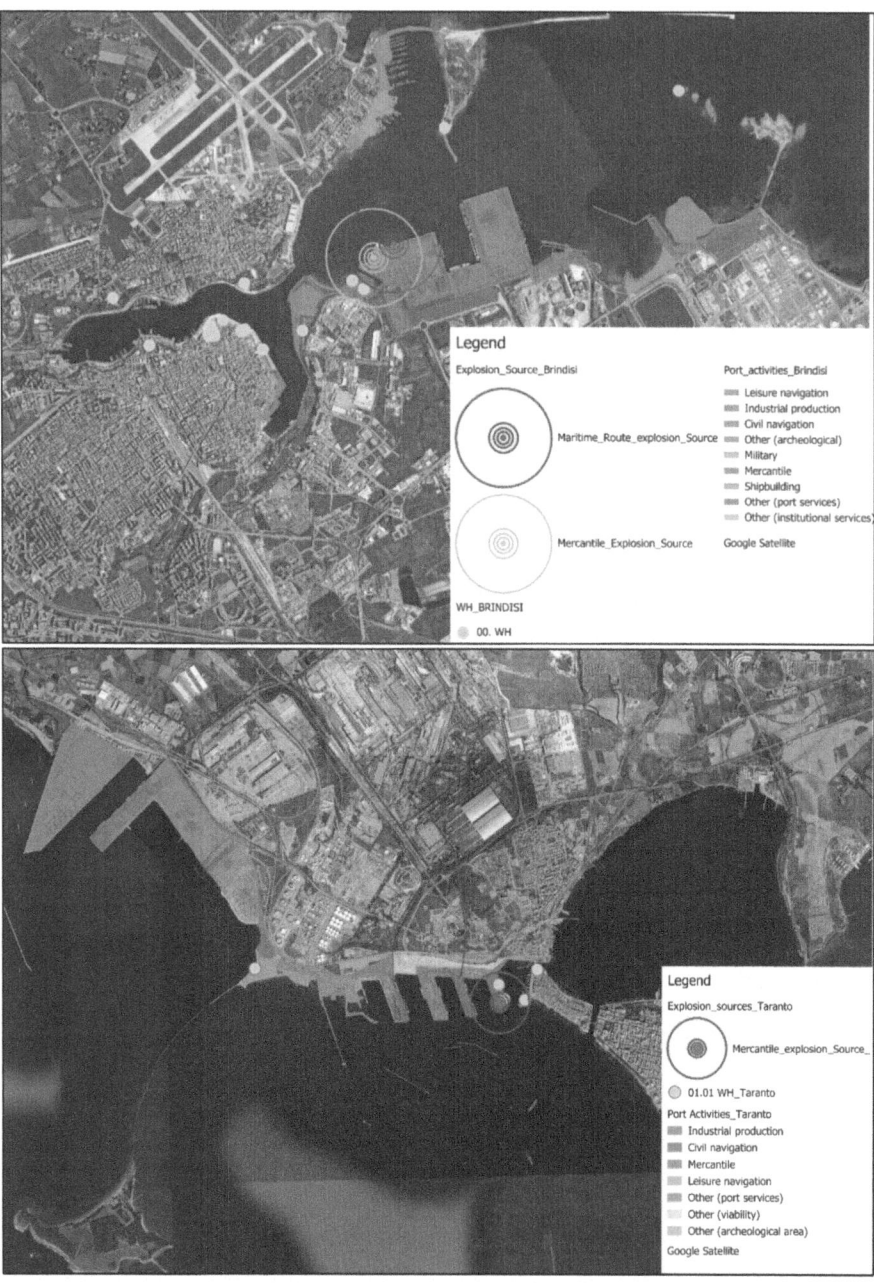

Fig. 7. Details of activities and WH distribution within the seaports of Brindisi (top) and Taranto (bottom), highlighting possible explosion sources

and techniques (e.g., masonry, steel, concrete structures), necessitates a categorisation of equivalent or combined vulnerability classes. Such classifications will enable the assessment and testing of mitigation strategies, facilitate evaluations of resilience variations concerning risk exposure, and allow for the extrapolation of findings to comparable WH types.

6 Conclusions

This study presents a preliminary hazard mapping framework for the water built heritage in Italian seaports, integrating both natural and anthropogenic dimensions of possible stressors. Through the identification of hydro-geomorphological vulnerabilities and human activity-induced threats, the research highlights the recurrent hazards for Italian seaports, particularly flooding and explosion.

The findings indicate that flooding, while expected due to the geographical setting of ports, requires downscaled mapping to address site-specific vulnerabilities, overcoming regional and territorial analysis to allow a heritage-based risk analysis. Meanwhile, the analysis of anthropogenic threats reveals the significant role of shipping activities, particularly mercantile and civil navigation, in increasing explosion proneness in proximity to the water built heritage.

The study also underlines the necessity of a comprehensive built heritage census in port areas, as a significant portion of historical and culturally relevant architecture that are still uncatalogued at the national level for risk assessment purposes. This gap in documentation limits effective risk management and conservation strategies, reinforcing the need for targeted heritage recognition initiatives by port administrations.

Future research should focus on refining hazard and risk mapping methodologies by integrating detailed vulnerability and exposure assessments. This is fully in line with current trends in the behavioural-based risk assessment, where the users and physical vulnerability of places are evaluated, by means of agent-based modelling and dynamic risk scenario-based simulations [30–32]. Additionally, the development of mitigation strategies tailored to the specific heritage typologies identified in ports will be crucial for enhancing resilience and ensuring the sustainable preservation of water heritage in Italian seaports. These activities will be pursued as complementary outcomes to support policymakers in risk communication actions with users, including inhabitants and potential tourists involved in the newest use of such water built heritage, as well as seaport users during daily activities [33, 34].

Acknowledgments. This research was carried out within the MUR PRIN Project RE^{3}WORK – "REsilient REtrofitting and REuse of Water heritage and built environments: multiobjective Optimization for RisK mitigation and cultural enhancement" - Grant number 2022NSAXY.

References

1. Sagara, J., Saito, K.: Risk Assessment and Hazard Mapping (2013). Accessed 21 March 2025. https://www.preventionweb.net/files/29163_drmkn511.pdf
2. Pimentel, J., et al.: Risk assessment and hazard mapping technique in the project for strengthening national strategy of integrated natural disaster risk management. Int. J. Erosion Control Eng. **13**(1), 35–47 (2020)
3. Ward, P.J., et al.: The need for mapping, modeling, and predicting flood hazard and risk at the global scale. In: Global Flood Hazard: Applications in Modeling, Mapping, and Forecasting, pp. 1–15 (2018). https://doi.org/10.1002/9781119217886.ch1
4. Intergovernmental Panel on Climate Change (IPCC): Key Risks across Sectors and Regions. In: Climate Change 2022 – Impacts, Adaptation and Vulnerability: Working Group II Contribution to the Sixth Assessment Report of the Intergovernmental Panel on Climate Change, pp. 2411–2538. Cambridge University Press (2023). https://doi.org/10.1017/9781009325844.025
5. Sarwar, J., Khan, S.A., Azmat, M., Khan, F.: An application of hybrid bagging - Boosting decision trees ensemble model for riverine flood susceptibility mapping and regional risk delineation. Water Resour. Manage **39**(2), 547–577 (2025). https://doi.org/10.1007/s11269-024-03995-6
6. Abdo, H.G., et al.: Multi-criteria analysis and geospatial applications-based mapping flood vulnerable areas: a case study from the eastern Mediterranean. Nat. Hazards **121**(1), 1003–1031 (2025). https://doi.org/10.1007/s11069-024-06864-y
7. IPCC, Climate Change 2021: The Physical Science Basis. Contribution of Working Group I to the Sixth Assessment Report of the Intergovernmental Panel on Climate Change. Cambridge University Press (2021)
8. United Nation: Hazard Definition and Classification Review. Technical Report (2020)
9. Centre for Research on the Epidemiology of Disasters: EM-DAT The International Disaster Database. https://public.emdat.be/. Accessed 21 March 2025
10. Li, M.: Disaster risk management of cultural heritage: a global scale analysis of characteristics, multiple hazards, lessons learned from historical disasters, and issues in current DRR measures in world heritage sites. Int. J. Disaster Risk Reduct. **110** (2024). https://doi.org/10.1016/j.ijdrr.2024.104633
11. Brandano, M.G., Conti, C., Modica, M., Urso, G.: Mapping cultural heritage sites at risk: a support tool for heritage sites management. J. Urban Manage. (2025). https://doi.org/10.1016/j.jum.2025.01.007
12. Eze, E., Petersen, M., Siegmund, A.: Enhancing protection motivation for disaster preparedness among actors at UNESCO-designated heritage sites in Africa. Int. J. Disaster Risk Reduct. **109** (2024). https://doi.org/10.1016/j.ijdrr.2024.104599
13. STORM Project [Online]. https://www.storm-project.eu/en/project/. Accessed 21 March 2025
14. Ripp, M., Egusquiza, A., Lückerath, D.: Urban heritage resilience: an integrated and operationable definition from the SHELTER and ARCH Projects. Land, **13**(12) (2024). https://doi.org/10.3390/land13122052
15. Fiorani, D., Cacace, C.: The risk map as a tool for conservation managing of historical centres. ArcHistoR **13**(7), 1542–1563 (2020). https://doi.org/10.14633/AHR282
16. Ministero della Cultura: Carta del Rischio. http://www.cartadelrischio.beniculturali.it/. Accessed 21 March 2025

17. Cassano, F., De Fino, M., Cantatore, E., Fatiguso, F.: Unveiling the water built heritage: preliminary results towards a systematic cataloguing of Italian ports. In: Corrao, R., Campisi, T., Colajanni, S., Saeli, M., Vinci, C. (eds) Proceedings of the 11th International Conference of Ar.Tec. (Scientific Society of Architectural Engineering). Colloqui.AT.e 2024. Lecture Notes in Civil Engineering, vol 610. Springer, Cham (2025). https://doi.org/10.1007/978-3-031-71855-7_11

18. Kefi, C., Bakouche, H., El Asmi, A. M.: Climate-induced vulnerability and conservation strategies for coastal heritage sites in the southern Mediterranean Sea using integrated remote sensing and flood modeling. Regional Stud. Marine Sci. **77** (2024). https://doi.org/10.1016/j.rsma.2024.103618

19. Zaccariello, G., Tesser, E., Piovesan, R., Antonelli, F.: The (Building) stones of venice under threat: a study about their deterioration between climate change and land subsidence. Sustainability (Switzerland) **16**(11) (2024). https://doi.org/10.3390/su16114701

20. Westley, K., et al.: Climate change and coastal archaeology in the Middle East and North Africa: assessing past impacts and future threats. J. Island Coastal Archaeol. **18**(2), 251–283 (2023). https://doi.org/10.1080/15564894.2021.1955778

21. Chalkidou, S., Georgiadis, C., Roustanis, T., Patias, P.: A methodology for identifying coastal cultural heritage assets exposed to future sea level rise scenarios. Applied Sciences (Switzerland), **14**(16) (2024). https://doi.org/10.3390/app14167210

22. Zengin, E.: Inundation risk assessment of Eastern Mediterranean Coastal archaeological and historical sites of Türkiye and Greece. Environ. Monitor. Assess. **195**(8) (2023). https://doi.org/10.1007/s10661-023-11549-3

23. Graham, E.: Drone survey to monitor erosion impacts on coastal archaeological sites. J. Field Archaeol. **50**(1), 22–41 (2025). https://doi.org/10.1080/00934690.2024.2439224

24. Zanier, G., Palma, M., Petronio, A., Roman, F., Armenio, V.: Oil spill scenarios in the Kotor Bay: results from high resolution numerical simulations. J. Marine Sci. Eng. **7**(2) (2019). https://doi.org/10.3390/jmse7020054

25. Medda, A., Serra, P., Mandas, M., Fancello, G.: A risk prediction model for Maritime accidents. WMU J. Marit. Aff. **23**(3), 415–436 (2024). https://doi.org/10.1007/s13437-024-00337-6

26. Haydous, F., et al.: Unraveling the levels of emerging contaminants along the eastern Mediterranean Sea. Sci. Reports **15**(1) (2025). https://doi.org/10.1038/s41598-025-89027-8

27. Saraiva, N.B., Pereira, L.D., Gaspar, A.R., Costa, J.J.: Measurement of particulate matter in a heritage building using optical counters: Long-term and spatial analyses. Sci. Total Environ. **862** (2023). https://doi.org/10.1016/j.scitotenv.2022.160747

28. EM-DAT: Disaster Classification. [Online] www.emdat.be/classification. Accessed 21 March 2025

29. Martino, A., Fatiguso, F., De Tommasi, G., Casal, J.: Accidental impacts on historical and architectural heritage in port areas: the case of brindisi. Int. J. Arch. Heritage **11**(2), 219–228 (2017). https://doi.org/10.1080/15583058.2016.1204486

30. Muhammad, A., et al.: Integrated tsunami risk framework considering agent-based evacuation modelling: the case of Saga, Kochi Prefecture, Japan. Int. J. Disaster Risk Reduct. **101**, 104193 (2024). https://doi.org/10.1016/j.ijdrr.2023.104193

31. Quagliarini, E., Bernardini, G., Romano, G., D'Orazio, M.: Users' vulnerability and exposure in Public Open Spaces (squares): a novel way for accounting them in multi-risk scenarios. Cities **133**, 104160 (2023). https://doi.org/10.1016/j.cities.2022.104160

32. Zlateski, A., Lucesoli, M., Bernardini, G., Ferreira, T.M.: Integrating human behaviour and building vulnerability for the assessment and mitigation of seismic risk in historic centres: proposal of a holistic human-centred simulation-based approach. Int. J. Disaster Risk Reduct. **43**, 101392 (2020). https://doi.org/10.1016/j.ijdrr.2019.101392

33. Santoro, S., Totaro, V., Lovreglio, R., Camarda, D., Iacobellis, V., Fratino, U.: Risk perception and knowledge of protective measures for flood risk planning. the case study of Brindisi (Puglia region). Safety Sci. **153**, 105791 (2022). https://doi.org/10.1016/j.ssci.2022.105791

34. Yin, J., Khan, R.U., Afzaal, M., Nawaz, R., Shanshan, X., Jamal, A.: A fuzzy bayesian quantitative risk assessment for language and communication induced accidents in maritime operations. Ocean Coastal Manage. **259** (2024). https://doi.org/10.1016/j.ocecoaman.2024.107449

Simulation Model of Evacuation Behavior During Post-Earthquake Fires: Incorporating Evacuation-Related Information Acquisition

Toshihiro Osaragi[✉] [iD] and Toko Kusumegi

Institute of Science Tokyo, 2-12-1-M4-1 Ookayama, Meguro 152-8550, Tokyo, Japan
osaragi.t.20f7@m.isct.ac.jp

Abstract. Most existing evacuation behavior simulation models for large-scale urban fires following major earthquakes rely on extreme idealizations and simplifications. These models often assume that residents begin evacuating immediately after the disaster and follow the shortest possible route. In this study, we develop a more realistic simulation framework by incorporating models for evacuation start timing and route selection, based on questionnaire survey responses. Additionally, we enhance the simulation by integrating key factors that influence evacuation behavior, such as the tendency to follow other evacuees and the means of acquiring disaster-related information. Using this improved model, we analyze evacuation strategies for high-density wooden housing areas during a major earthquake. The results indicate that in regions with a high risk of fire spread, direct evacuation may be more effective than a two-step evacuation process. Furthermore, the presence of early evacuees acting as influencers can significantly impact overall casualty numbers. Therefore, establishing a system for disseminating accurate and timely disaster information is crucial for improving evacuation outcomes.

Keywords: Evacuation behavior · Wide-area evacuation · Multi-agent simulation · Following behavior · Evacuation guidance

1 Introduction

Japan is one of the most earthquake-prone countries, with high risks of building collapse and fire spread, especially in areas with dense, aging wooden housing. Extensive research has focused on understanding physical damage and human casualties through evacuation simulations, which inform urban planning and evacuation strategies.

Zheng et al. (2009) identified seven methodological approaches for crowd evacuation, including cellular automata and agent-based models. Most pedestrian movement models focus on microscopic analysis of individual behavior, with collective phenomena emerging from interactions among evacuees (Bonabeau, 2002). Simulation research, such as that by Aoki et al. (1992), has explored how hearsay information influences evacuation behavior, while Osaragi and Tsuchiya (2018) quantitatively evaluated the impact of such information on wide-area evacuations.

Studies like those by Vermuyten et al. (2016) and Mabuchi et al. (2008) examined optimization models and effective evacuation methods, including two-step evacuation strategy that will be discussed later Section. Fathianpour et al. (2022) assessed pedestrian evacuation infrastructure resilience, and Esposito et al. (2020) developed a multi-risk agent-based framework for policy applications. Real-world behavior studies, such as those by Makinoshima et al. (2024) and Yabe et al. (2019), leveraged smartphone geolocation data to analyze evacuation patterns during major earthquakes, showing a strong link between seismic intensity and evacuation behavior.

However, many existing models make unrealistic assumptions about evacuation behavior, such as immediate evacuation or shortest-route evacuation, and overlook factors like evacuation start timing and route choice. This study aims to develop a more realistic evacuation behavior model that minimizes these idealizations by constructing sub-models for evacuation start timing and walking route choice, based on questionnaire survey responses. Additionally, we examine the influence of evacuee characteristics, such as following others and information acquisition methods.

Using an enhanced simulation model, we estimate casualties across the region, considering the differentiated behaviors of "influencers" who begin evacuating immediately and influence others. We also explore the effectiveness of evacuation strategies by comparing direct and two-step evacuation strategies.

2 Overview of Simulation Model

Figure 1 shows an overview of the simulation model constructed in this paper. This multi-agent simulation model was constructed by integrating sub-models which will be constructed in the following sections and sub-models of physical damage/trapping inside buildings/streets (Osaragi and Oki, 2017). The sub-models conducted in this paper are highlighted in red color in Fig. 1. In the integrated model, by updating the state of damage inside the target area and the status and behavior of people in the city at fixed time intervals (in this study, 15 s), it is possible to estimate physical damage/human casualties while taking into consideration interactions between physical damage and people in the city.

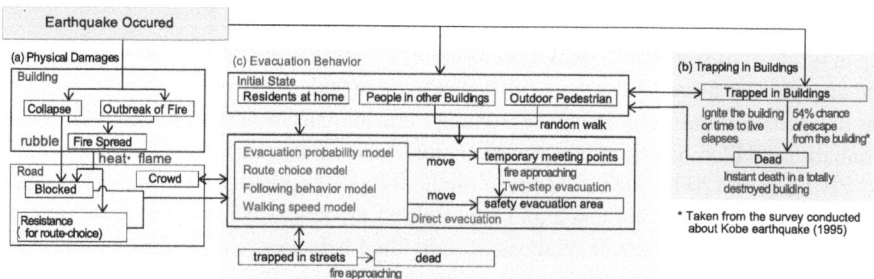

Fig. 1. Structure of the simulation model integrating the sub-models developed in this paper, along with the physical damage and building entrapment sub-models proposed by Osaragi and Oki (2017).

3 Consideration of Evacuation Start Timing

3.1 Evacuation Probability Model

The most crucial aspect of safety in the face of fire is the possibility of safe escape. Kobes et al. (2010) reviewed the available literature on human behavior in a fire building safety and showed that psychonomics appear to have significant influence on occupants' fire response performances, and then the traditional approach to fire safety have to be supplemented by scientific knowledge from this field. Also, Zheng et al. (2009) pointed out the need for taking into consideration the "psychological elements" affecting collective behavior in this context. For considering psychological elements and modeling the evacuation start timing of evacuees, the evacuation urgency of evacuee i, Φ_i, is defined as a variable representing the degree to which the evacuee feels the need to evacuate.

We define two variables: Θ_i, which represents the strength of person i's intention to evacuate, and D_i, which represents the distance of person i from the fire. These variables possess the following four properties:

1. The farther away a person is from the fire, the lower their intention to evacuate:

$$\Delta\Theta_i/\Delta D_i < 0 \tag{1}$$

2. The change in the strength of the intention to evacuate is proportional to the change in distance from the fire, where α_1 is a positive parameter:

$$|\Delta\Theta_i| \propto \alpha_1|\Delta D_i| \tag{2}$$

3. The greater the strength of the intention to evacuate, the larger the change in this strength, with α_2 being a positive parameter:

$$|\Delta\Theta_i| \propto \alpha_2\Theta_i \tag{3}$$

4. As the distance approaches infinity, the strength of intention to evacuate approaches zero:

$$\Theta_i|_{Di=\infty} = 0 \tag{4}$$

Based on properties (1) to (3), we derive the following differential equation, where α is a positive parameter:

$$\Delta\Theta_i = \alpha \, \Delta D_i\Theta_i \tag{5}$$

Solving this differential equation with the condition from Eq. (4) yields the following relationship (where α is the distance decay parameter):

$$\Theta_i = \exp[-\alpha D_i] \tag{6}$$

The evacuation urgency of evacuee i, denoted by Φ_i, is then described as a function of three factors: (1) the strength of intention to evacuate, Θ_i, which depends on the distance to the fire, D_i, (2) the percentage of neighboring residents who are evacuating (denoted by r_i), and (3) whether the individual has received disaster information through various media (Fig. 2(a)). The urgency, Φ_i, is formulated as a polynomial with interaction terms, where λ, $\beta_1 \sim \beta_4$, $\gamma_1 \sim \gamma_4$ are unknown parameters (Fig. 2(a)):

$$\Phi_i = \lambda\Theta_i + \beta_1 r_i + \beta_2\delta_{i2} + \beta_3\delta_{i3} + \beta_4\delta_{i4} + \gamma_1\Theta_i r_i + \gamma_2\Theta_i\delta_{i2} + \gamma_3\Theta_i\delta_{i3} + \gamma_4\Theta_i\delta_{i4} \tag{7}$$

Furthermore, we assume the evacuation probability of person i, denoted by P_i, which satisfies the conditions $P_i |_{\Phi_{i=\infty}} = 1$ and $P_i |_{\Phi_{i=0}} = 0$. The evacuation probability P_i is expressed as follows, with indicating a value between 0 and 1 based on the change in Φ_i.

$$P_i = (1 - \exp[-\Phi_i])/(1 + \exp[-\Phi_i]), \Phi_i \geq 0 \tag{8}$$

The relationship between P_i and Φ_i is shown in Fig. 2(b). The unknown parameters in Eq. (7) can be estimated using observed values of P_i via the following regression model derived from Eq. (8):

$$(1 - P_i)/(1 + P_i) = \Phi_i = \lambda\Theta_i + \beta_1 r_i + \beta_2\delta_{i2} + \beta_3\delta_{i3} + \beta_4\delta_{i4} + \gamma_1\Theta_i r_i + \gamma_2\Theta_i\delta_{i2} + \gamma_3\Theta_i\delta_{i3} + \gamma_4\Theta_i\delta_{i4} \tag{9}$$

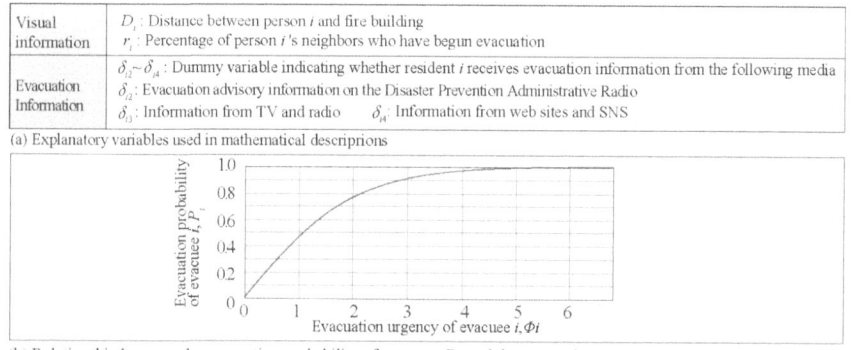

Visual information	D_i : Distance between person i and fire building
	r_i : Percentage of person i's neighbors who have begun evacuation
Evacuation Information	$\delta_{i1} \sim \delta_{i4}$: Dummy variable indicating whether resident i receives evacuation information from the following media
	δ_{i2}: Evacuation advisory information on the Disaster Prevention Administrative Radio
	δ_{i3}: Information from TV and radio δ_{i4}: Information from web sites and SNS

(a) Explanatory variables used in mathematical descriptions

(b) Relationship between the evacuation probability of person i, P_i, and the evacuation urgency of evacuee i, Φ_i

Fig. 2. Relationship between the evacuation probability of individual i and the evacuation urgency of evacuee i, Φ_i.

3.2 Questionnaire Survey

To estimate each model parameter, a web-based questionnaire survey about the evacuation start timing and choice of evacuation site in the event of a post-earthquake fire was conducted (Fig. 3(a)). The sampling periods were January and July 2019, with 104 respondents in January and 87 respondents in July. The web-based survey was distributed via mailing lists. In Question I, using an orthogonal array, combinations of the percentage of evacuees among neighboring residents and persons with/without disaster information (eight combinations: Fig. 3(b)) were created. Respondents answered the question of how close the fire would have to come before they started to evacuate under the circumstances in each combination, i.e., evacuation start timing in terms of distance to the fire (fire proximity). Care was taken to ensure that the respondents could answer intuitively by explaining the envisioned state of damage using photographs and text, with the aim of standardizing respondents' images regarding the state of damage.

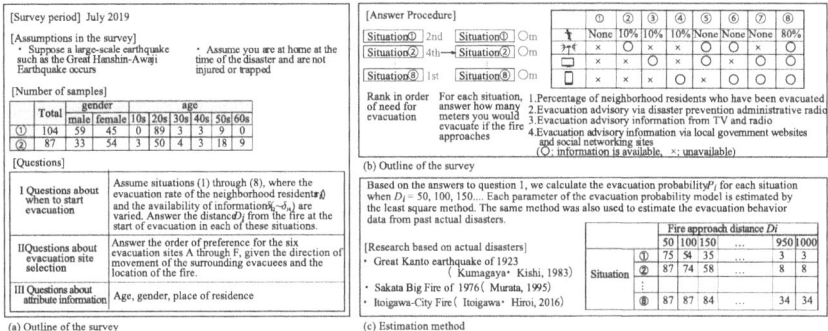

Fig. 3. Web-based questionnaire survey and parameter estimation for evacuation probability models.

3.3 Parameter Estimation and Validation of Evacuation Probability Model

The evacuation probability P_i was calculated based on the answers to Question I, Fig. 3(a), and the parameters of the evacuation probability model were estimated using the least-squares method. Figure 4 shows the fire approach distance D_i and evacuation probability P_i and the estimated results obtained using the model for the eight situations presented in the questionnaire. The descriptive accuracy of the model is shown to be good.

The evacuation probability P_i was calculated using the same method from survey results on evacuation behavior in three actual disasters – the Great Kanto Earthquake (1923), the Sakata Big Fire (1976) (Kumagai and Kishi, 1983), and the Itoigawa City Fire (2016)– and each evacuation probability model was estimated. When the results based on the survey in this study were compared with the results for evacuation behavior during the past disasters, they were found to be generally consistent (Fig. 4).

Figure 5 (left) shows the results of estimating the evacuation probability model in the case of different percentages of evacuees among neighboring residents and with/without disaster information, using the presented models. When the percentage of evacuees among neighboring residents is around 80%, even if a fire is far away, the probability of evacuation starting increases, thus showing that the behavior of other evacuees greatly influences one's own intention to evacuate. Regarding disaster information, when the fire is far away, its influence on the evacuation probability is small, but in circumstances where the fire has come close, it is a factor that increases the evacuation probability.

Next, looking at the results of estimating the model by gender, women (Fig. 5, right) tend to be more sensitive to fire proximity than men (Fig. 5, middle). Hence, women tend to start evacuating even when the fire is far away. Additionally, women tend to be

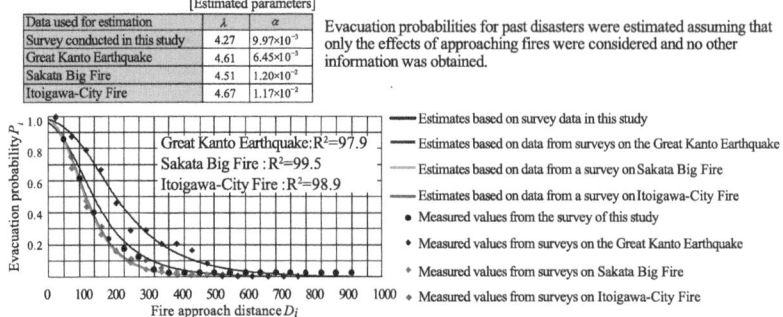

Fig. 4. Comparison of the survey results from this study with observed evacuation behavior during past disasters.

more easily influenced by disaster information than men. Furthermore, the percentage of evacuees among neighboring residents β_1 is smaller for men, but that for interaction with the fire γ_1 is larger for men. This means that, for men, the tendency to follow other people becomes stronger when the fire is close by.

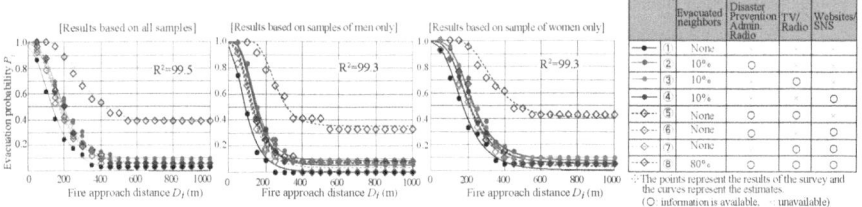

Fig. 5. Estimated evacuation probabilities under varying percentages of evacuating neighbors and the presence or absence of disaster information.

4 Consideration of Evacuation Route and Following Behavior

4.1 Route Choice Model

Since the method of choosing an evacuation route was modeled based on analysis results by Osaragi and Tanaka (2018), the route was chosen probabilistically by comprehensively considering the distance to the evacuation site, the number of times the direction changes at intersections (number of turns), and the evacuation road width (Fig. 6). More specifically, the values (influence factors) shown below, which were capable of describing 195 of the total 228 routes obtained from the answers to the questionnaire survey conducted by the existing model (with a concordance rate of 50% or higher) were adopted. The details are described in Osaragi and Tanaka (2018).

Figure 7 shows a graphical representation that combines these influence factors (β, γ) and the distribution of the number of people. Here, since the derived route depends only on the relative size of the influence factors, α is fixed at 1. The circle sizes in Fig. 7 represents the number of respondents for the route derived from the combination of influence factors (β, γ), and the respondents can generally be classified into three types: a distance-oriented type in which the respondents are concentrated (β, γ are small), a turn-oriented type (β is large), and a width-oriented type (γ is large). The respective influence factors for these combinations are as follows:

(1) Distance-oriented type (β, γ) = (0.1, 0.0) (88 people).
(2) Turn-oriented type (β, γ) = (0.3, 0.0) (48 people).
(3) Width-oriented type (β, γ) = (0.1, 0.1) (48 people).

In the simulation model in this paper, evacuees were considered to choose an evacuation route probabilistically from among the routes calculated by combinations of these three influence factors. From the ratio of the number of respondents for the distance-oriented, turn-oriented, and width-oriented types, the choice probabilities were: distance-oriented type 46%, turn-oriented type 27%, and width-oriented type 27% (Fig. 6).

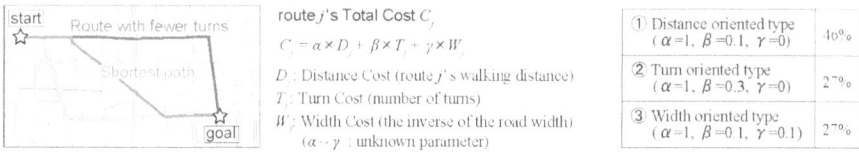

(1) Calculate 3 routes using a combination of parameters in the table on the right, with reference to the results of Osaragi and Tanaka (2018)
(2) Choose a route from these 3 routes by the probabilities shown in the table

Fig. 6. Route choice model incorporating distance to the evacuation site, number of turns at intersections, and evacuation road width, based on Osaragi and Tanaka (2018).

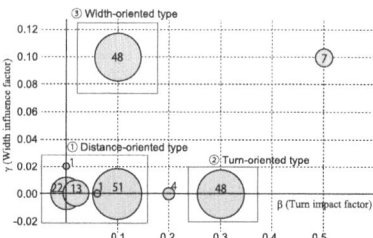

Fig. 7. Graphical representation combining two influence factors (β and γ) with the distribution of the number of individuals by route selection type, based on Osaragi and Tanaka (2018).

Evacuees were assumed to have no information about road blockage points at the starting evacuation time and were expected to remember each time they encountered a blockage point during an evacuation. Additionally, evacuees were modeled on the assumption that they use the information on blockage points remembered up to that point in time to search again for an evacuation route.

4.2 Following Behavior Model

Van den Berg et al. (2018) quantified the impact of others' evacuation behavior on an individual's decision to evacuate through an experiment using a serious game, involving approximately 400 participants. The results indicated that observing others evacuating increases the likelihood of individuals deciding to evacuate themselves. Evacuee following behavior was modeled with reference to Osaragi and Tsuchiya (2018) (Fig. 8). Here, evacuees were considered to decide whether or not to follow other people at each intersection. More specifically, first, the direction of travel of Evacuee A was determined probabilistically based on the number of other evacuees in each direction of travel at the intersection (Fig. 8(1)). Then, evacuee following behavior was modeled by replacing the destination and evacuation route of Evacuee A with the destination and evacuation route of Evacuee B, randomly selected from among the other evacuees traveling in the same direction (Fig. 8(2)). However, if the selected Evacuee B was less familiar with the local area than Evacuee A, Evacuee A was assumed to keep to the destination and evacuation route instead of following Evacuee B.

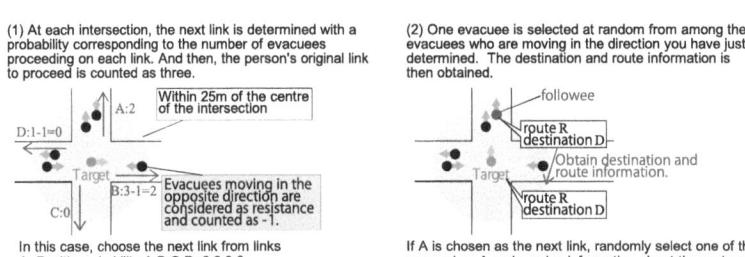

Fig. 8. Following behavior model considering the influence of word-of-mouth communication on large-scale evacuation after a severe earthquake, based on Osaragi and Tsuchiya (2018).

4.3 Walking Speed Model

Bosina and Weidmann (2017) described the most important factors influencing walking speed based on existing literature and estimates their impact. Different conditions average walking speeds were calculated and the significance of the walking speed differences was determined. Several experimental studies have examined the density-speed correlation in earthquake evacuation (Bosina and Weidmann, 2017). However, due to variations in walking speed across sex and age groups, we used the standard walking speed proposed by Willis et al. (2004) in this study. Walking speed during evacuation was, therefore, modeled as determined by gender/age of evacuees and the congestion degree (pedestrian density in persons/m^2) in the surrounding areas, and pedestrian density was updated at fixed time intervals (Fig. 9). Walking speed decreases when pedestrian density reaches 1.4 persons/m^2 or more. In situations where the density exceeds 6 persons/m^2, walking speed decreases abruptly.

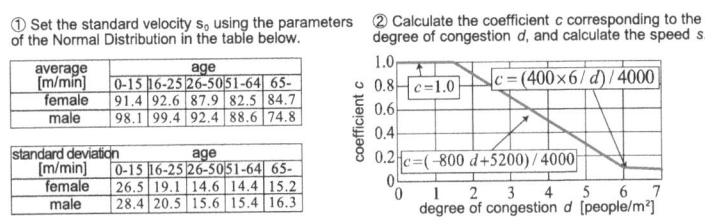

Fig. 9. Variation in walking speed by sex, age group, and pedestrian density in surrounding areas.

5   Setting and Scenario for Simulation Analysis

5.1   The Initial State of Evacuees and Evacuation Behavior

In this paper, people at home, people in buildings other than their home, and outdoor pedestrians in the analysis target area are considered evacuee agents. Considering that the evacuation behavior pattern for each evacuee will differ depending on their level of familiarity with the local area and where they are when the disaster occurs, three types of evacuation behavior were established (Fig. 10). Both people in buildings other than their home and outdoor pedestrians were assumed to be unfamiliar with the local area and to repeatedly move towards a randomly set destination until they arrive at a point within 50 m of the evacuation site.

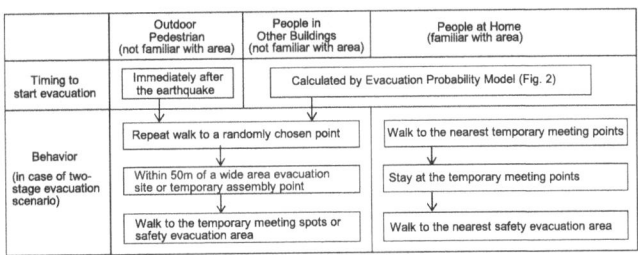

Fig. 10. Three types of evacuation behavior patterns for each evacuee, categorized by their level of familiarity with the local area and their location at the time of the disaster.

5.2   Analysis Target Areas and Simulation Conditions

Figure 11 shows the simulation conditions used in this study, which focused on various parts of Tokyo. More specifically, Senju in Adachi-ku (Kita-Senju), Machiya in Arakawa-ku (Machiya), and Taishido in Setagaya-ku (Taishido), all of which are designated as "high fire risk zones", were selected as the areas for analysis.

According to the Seventh Community Earthquake Risk Assessment Study for the Tokyo Metropolitan Area (Bureau of Urban Development, Tokyo Metropolitan Government, 2022), the Kita-Senju and Machiya areas have been judged to have the highest fire risk (Rank 5), while the Taishido area is considered to have a slightly lower risk (Rank 3).

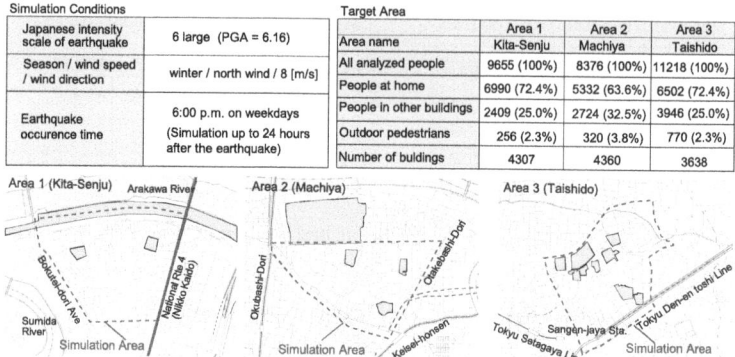

Fig. 11. Target areas and simulation conditions used in this study, focusing on different regions of Tokyo.

5.3 Evacuation Method Scenarios

A two-step evacuation is sometimes recommended in the event of a post-earthquake fire. The two-step evacuation system is implemented by the Tokyo Metropolitan Government and other local authorities. During the short-term evacuation phase, there are two types of shelters: temporary meeting points and evacuation areas. Temporary meeting points consist of school grounds or neighborhood parks that provide sufficient space to ensure the safety of the people gathered. Evacuation areas, which are designed to protect evacuees from the spread of fire, total 221 in the Tokyo Metropolitan area. These areas are typically large, open spaces, such as city parks, university campuses, and other open areas. The service range of an evacuation area is typically less than 3 km, and each evacuee is required to have at least 1 m^2 of space within the area.

In two-step evacuation, people evacuate to their nearest temporary meeting point immediately after the disaster occurs, and after assessing the state of damage, then evacuate to a wide-area evacuation site (evacuation area) when the timing is judged to be appropriate. The two-step evacuation method is recommended by many local authorities from the perspective of mitigating congestion and controlling chaos near wide-area evacuation sites.

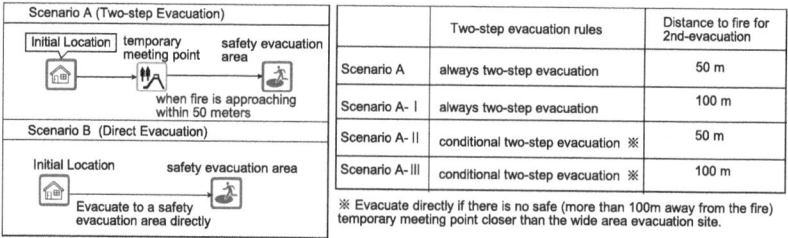

Fig. 12. Evacuation scenarios based on direct evacuation and two-step evacuation methods.

In this paper, the method in which evacuees evacuate directly to a wide-area evacuation site immediately after the disaster occurs is referred to as "direct evacuation," and two simulations, one assuming two-step evacuation (Scenario A) and another assuming direct evacuation (Scenario B), were performed. Differences in how the evacuation route is chosen and the number of casualties were analyzed. More specifically, the four scenarios in Fig. 12 (A, A-I–III) were created and compared. In Scenario A, two-step evacuation is always performed, and the second evacuation to a wide-area evacuation site is performed when the fire approaches to 50 m from the temporary meeting point (the re-evacuation distance is 50 m). In Scenario A-I, the re-evacuation distance is assumed to be 100 m. Scenario A-II is a two-step evacuation scenario with a degree of freedom, in which the evacuation changes to a direct evacuation if there is no safe temporary meeting point further than 100 m from a point where the fire is spreading. Scenario A-III is a combination of Scenario A-I and Scenario A-II, in which the re-evacuation distance is taken as 100 m, and it is possible to switch to a direct evacuation. A value of 50 m/h is commonly used as the average speed of fire spread in densely built-up wooden residential areas and is often applied in simulation analyses (Osaragi and Oki, 2017).

5.4   Influencer Behavior Scenarios

In this section, we examine the influence that the behavior of some evacuees has on the magnitude of damage in the entire region due to influencing the behavior of other evacuees. During a disaster, it is difficult to provide all evacuees with information about physical damage (collapsed buildings, road blockages, fire spread, etc.) and information that encourages appropriate evacuation behavior in real time. Therefore, by assuming cases in which some evacuees who can have an influence (influencers) possess accurate information and perform rational evacuation behavior, the possibility of the behavior of those influencers affecting residents overall and leading to a smooth evacuation was examined. More specifically, 1% of people at home were randomly selected as influencers, and by varying their evacuation behavior patterns (evacuation start timing and method of choosing an evacuation route), changes in the evacuation start timing and route choice of other evacuees, and as a result, the number of casualties, could be considered. For illustrative purposes, we assumed 1% of people, representing a very small portion of the population. This value is used purely as an example and does not carry any specific significance.

Table 1 shows a comparison of the scenarios. First, in Scenario C, the evacuation start timing of influencers is set to immediately after the disaster occurs. By comparing Scenario C and Scenario A, the question of how much the immediate evacuation behavior of some evacuees affects the extent of human casualties is analyzed. In Scenarios D, E, and F, the method by which influencers choose an evacuation route differs. Scenario D assumes a case in which rational route information is provided to influencers in real time. In this scenario, the influencers are considered to be all-knowing and all-powerful, which means they know about all road blockage points and evacuate via the shortest route. In Scenario E, influencers first move to a wide main road that is unlikely to be blocked and then continue to evacuate using main roads wherever possible. Scenario F assumes a case in which influencers are able to determine the congestion situation of evacuation routes in real time and then choose the route with the shortest travel time (rather than travel distance) after determining the congestion on all road links in the target area.

Table 1. Evacuation scenarios.

	Timing of evacuation start	Evacuation route
Scenario A	No influential person	No influential person
Scenario C	Immediate evacuation	Same as other evacuees (route selection model (Fig. 8))
Scenario D	Same as other evacuees (evacuation probability model (Fig. 2))	All-knowing and all-powerful
Scenario E		Main roads
Scenario F		Congestion avoidance

[All-knowing and all-powerful evacuation] Obtaining the information on the blockage status of all road links in the target area, and select the shortest route to the evacuation site
[Main road evacuation] After moving to the main road (Fig. 19(a)), evacuate along the wide road to the evacuation site
[Congestion avoidance evacuation] Obtaining the information on the congestion of all road links in the target area, and select the temporal shortest route to the evacuation site

6   Results of Analysis

6.1   Comparison of Evacuee Route Choice

Next, the evacuation routes of evacuees in each area were examined. The simulation was performed 100 times for both two-step and direct evacuation, and the numbers of people passing through each road link were tallied. Figure 13 shows an example for the Kita-Senju area. Basically, it appears that wide road links are chosen and that the evacuation route choices were generally consistent for both the two-step and direct evacuation methods. However, in the Kita-Senju area, in the case of two-step evacuation, the numbers of people passing through road links near the temporary meeting points were extremely high, and there was potential for chaos. This means that, based on the assumption that many evacuees will concentrate at temporary meeting points, these points must be accessible by roads of sufficient width.

6.2   Comparison of Two-Step and Direct Evacuations

Simulations were conducted for all scenarios in each area, and the estimated numbers of casualties were compared between two-step evacuations (Scenarios A, A-I–III) and direct evacuations (Scenario B). Figure 14 presents the results. In the Kita-Senju area, some cases show a significant increase in casualties in Scenario A compared to direct evacuation (Scenario B). To better understand this, Fig. 15 illustrates the change

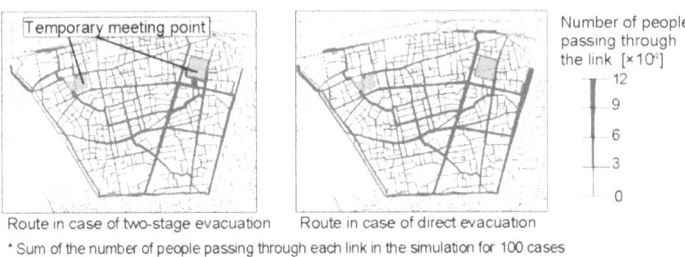

Route in case of two-stage evacuation   Route in case of direct evacuation
* Sum of the number of people passing through each link in the simulation for 100 cases

Fig. 13. Comparison of direct and two-step evacuation: the number of people passing through each road link in the Kita-Senju area.

in casualties over the first 24 h following the disaster. This figure displays the average and maximum casualties for 100 simulated cases of physical damage at each time point. While average casualty numbers show no substantial differences across scenarios, the maximum values exhibit a sharp increase. In the Kita-Senju area, large casualties arise around six hours after the disaster in Scenario A, and about seven hours after the disaster in the Machiya area. Notably, the timing of re-evacuation—affected by the re-evacuation distance (50 m in Scenario A, 100 m in Scenario A-I)—has a considerable impact. This highlights the risk that delayed re-evacuation could result in significant damage, despite two-step evacuation being designed to enhance safety. In contrast, Scenarios A-I and A-II, which modify parts of Scenario A, reduce the emergence of large casualties. Scenario A-III, which includes a 100 m re-evacuation distance and shifts to direct evacuation, shows the greatest reduction in casualties, suggesting the importance of timely re-evacuation and the flexibility to switch to direct evacuation based on real-time information about fire spread and origin.

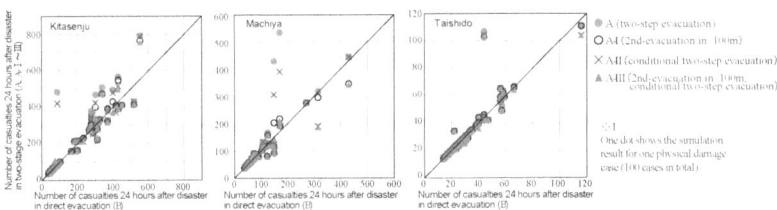

Fig. 14. Number of casualties in direct evacuation and two-stage evacuation.

However, 24 h after the disaster, direct evacuation (Scenario B) results in fewer casualties compared to two-step evacuation scenarios (A, A-I–III). The spatial distribution of casualties for two-step evacuation in the Kita-Senju area (Fig. 16) shows a concentration of casualties around the temporary meeting point in the northwest. Visualizing individual evacuee behavior revealed that evacuees who attempted to re-evacuate from the meeting point to a wide-area evacuation site were hindered by fire-related road blockages, leading to casualties. This suggests that in high-risk fire areas, a direct evacuation strategy from the outset may be more effective than a two-step approach.

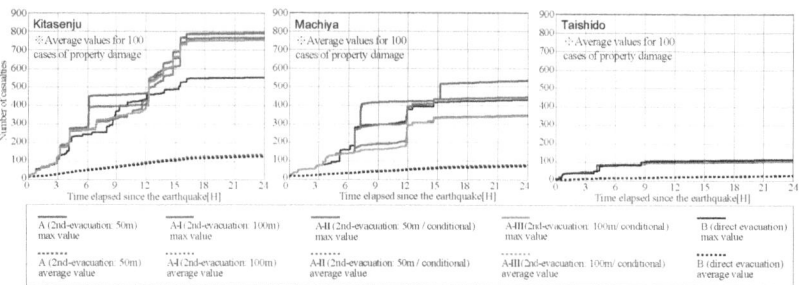

Fig. 15. Temporal change in the number of casualties during direct evacuation and two-stage evacuation.

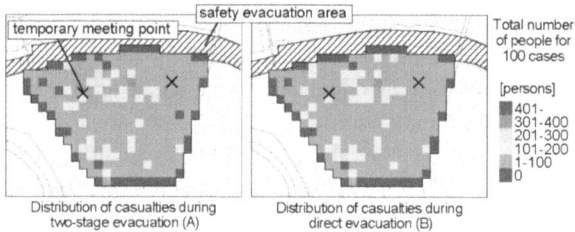

Fig. 16. Spatial distribution of casualties in direct evacuation and two-stage evacuation.

While the focus here is on casualties from the evacuation process, it is important to note that building vulnerability—affecting fire risk after earthquakes—also plays a significant role, especially in areas with a high risk of fire spread. Similar results were observed in the Machiya area (Fig. 15, center), but in the Taishido area (Fig. 15, right), no significant differences were found between two-step and direct evacuation scenarios. This is likely due to the lower risk of fire spread in the Taishido area compared to the Kita-Senju and Machiya areas, making the evacuation scenario less impactful on the danger level.

6.3   Influencer Effect on Evacuation Start Timing

Next, the Kita-Senju area, where the degree of damage was most serious, is analyzed. Figure 17 shows the overall results of analyzing the ripple effect on evacuees when influencers evacuate immediately after the disaster occurs (Scenario C). Looking at the number of evacuation starters in the period up to one hour after the disaster occurs, it is evident that the evacuation start timing of approximately 1,000 evacuees (approximately 10% of the total) is brought forward because they follow influencers who evacuate immediately (Fig. 17(a)). Also, in physical damage cases with a high number of human casualties, bringing the evacuation start timing forward reduces the possibility of evacuees becoming caught in the fire, and the number of casualties decreases by approximately 100 people (Fig. 17(b), (c)). This shows that in areas like Kita-Senju, where damage due to fire spread is serious, the earliest possible evacuation behavior is vital to disaster mitigation.

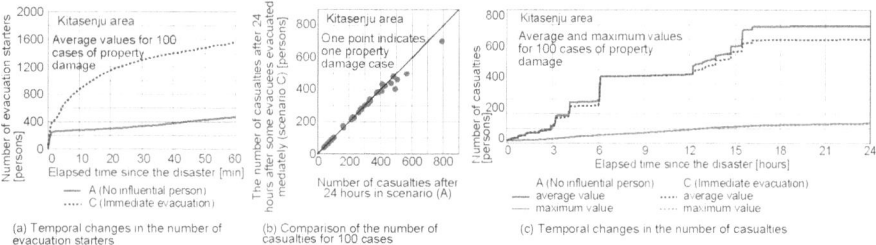

Fig. 17. The impact of the evacuation-start time of leading evacuees.

6.4 Influencer Route Choice Effects

Figure 18 shows the results of analyzing the differences in human casualties in the case of all-knowing and all-powerful influencers (Scenario D), using main roads (Scenario E), and congestion avoidance (Scenario F) by influencers. In physical damage cases with a high number of human casualties, the number of casualties decreases in all the scenarios. For example, for main-road evacuation (Scenario E), it is found that the number of evacuees choosing main roads increases because they follow influencers (Fig. 18(a), (b)). In other words, influencers indirectly guide evacuees to safer evacuation routes, and as a result, the evacuees move along safe routes without encountering road blockages caused by collapsing buildings or spreading fires, and the number of human casualties therefore decreases.

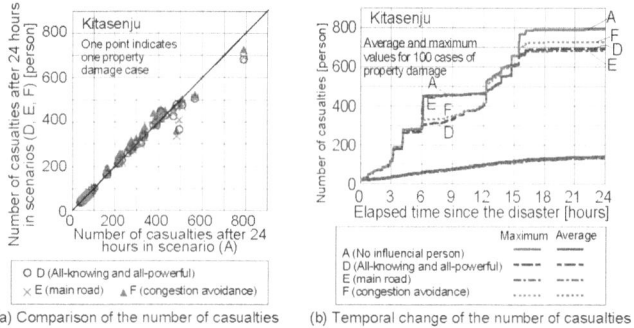

Fig. 18. Analysis of differences in human casualties under three scenarios: all-knowing and all-powerful influencers (Scenario D), use of main roads (Scenario E), and congestion avoidance by influencers (Scenario F).

Next, the routes taken by evacuees in Scenario A and Scenario E were compared in order to analyze how the routes of other evacuees changed because they followed the influencers. In Fig. 19(b), which shows the evacuation routes of influencers in Scenario E, it can be seen that the number of people passing along the main roads shown in Fig. 19(a) is high. Next, comparing the chosen routes of all evacuees when there are no influencers (Fig. 19(c)) and the chosen routes of all evacuees when the influencers guide

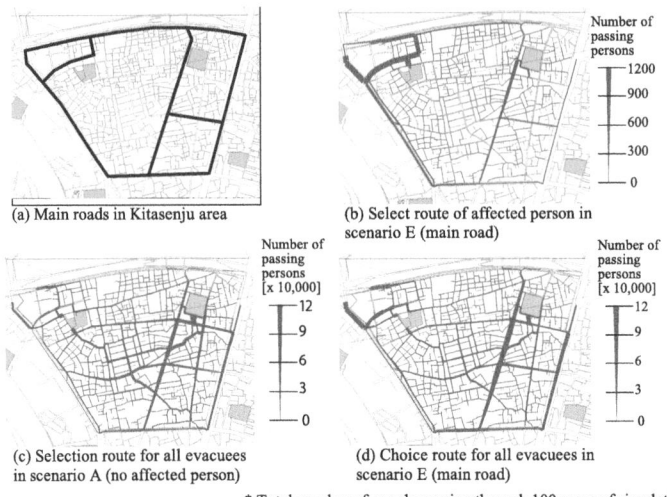

(a) Main roads in Kitasenju area

(b) Select route of affected person in scenario E (main road)

(c) Selection route for all evacuees in scenario A (no affected person)

(d) Choice route for all evacuees in scenario E (main road)

* Total number of people passing through 100 cases of simulatio

Fig. 19. Impacts of influencers' route selection on the route choices of other evacuees.

main-road evacuation (Fig. 19(d)), it can be seen that the number of people passing along the main roads increases because many evacuees follow the influencers.

Taken together, the above results show that if some evacuees (influencers) can be provided with correct information about road blockage conditions, etc., in real time, it may be possible to reduce the number of human casualties.

7 Summary and Conclusions

In this study, we first constructed an evacuation probability model that determines the evacuation start timing while taking into account the influence of approaching fires and the evacuation behavior of neighboring residents. We also constructed a route choice model that describes route selection behavior, taking into account the route choice characteristics of evacuees and difficulties imposed by spreading fires. Furthermore, by modeling the following behavior among evacuees, we investigated the influence that evacuees have on each other. Then, by integrating this evacuation behavior model with previously constructed physical damage models that consider collapsing buildings, road blockages, spreading fires, persons trapped inside buildings, etc., we were able to create a multi-agent-based evacuation behavior simulation model.

Next, we organized the given conditions of the simulation analysis and the analysis target areas in metropolitan Tokyo (Kita-Senju, Machiya, Taishido) and performed a comparative analysis of each scenario using the simulation. Specifically, we performed simulations of two-step and direct evacuation scenarios and showed that in areas with a high risk of fire spread, large numbers of casualties may occur in the two-step scenarios. The results also showed the possibility of suppressing the number of casualties in a two-step evacuation by bringing forward the re-evacuation timing (second evacuation to a wide-area evacuation site) and changing to direct evacuation depending on the circumstances by determining physical damage states.

Additionally, targeting the Kita-Senju area, we created scenarios for the evacuation behavior of some evacuees (influencers) and showed that differences in influencer evacuation behavior affect not only the behavior of other evacuees but also the number of casualties throughout the region. Specifically, we showed that when 1% of people at home, who were selected as influencers, evacuate immediately after the disaster occurs, the evacuation start timing of other evacuees is brought forward due to following behavior, and human casualties can be reduced. We also showed that influencers could reduce human casualties in the case of all-knowing and all-powerful influencers, main road usage, and congestion avoidance. In other words, we demonstrated that providing accurate real-time information about the situation regarding road blockages and congestion to some evacuees, and the presence of some evacuees who vacate the area by prioritizing the use of routes that are unlikely to become blocked, may have a ripple effect leading to a substantial reduction in the number of human casualties. However, it is important to note that this also indicates that influencers with incorrect damage information and those who take irrational evacuation actions may act dangerously and increase the number of human casualties.

Below is a summary of our future work. First, regarding the following behavior model, there is little past research or data providing concrete evidence on a mechanism explaining the circumstances in which evacuees follow other people. However, it is known that following behavior, particularly in extreme situations, has been observed. We aim to incorporate this behavior, which varies depending on individual characteristics. Accordingly, we intend to work on validating the models and model parameters employed in this study. Additionally, since it is anticipated that people will evacuate in groups (such as cohabiting family members) when post-earthquake fires approach, we would like to investigate an evacuation behavior model that assumes evacuees depart the area in groups. Additionally, 1% of people at home were selected as influencers in this paper, but the relationship between the percentage of influencers and the degree of influence on other evacuees requires further analysis, the results of which can be expected to provide insights on how many influencers will need to be provided with correct disaster information in the event of a post-earthquake fire. Furthermore, there is a need to develop information systems capable of providing accurate, real-time updates on road blockages and congestion to evacuees.

Acknowledgments. This work is part of the research outcomes funded by KAKENHI (Grant Number 23K26347). A portion of this paper was published in Osaragi and Tsuchiya (2018), Osaragi and Tanaka (2018), and Osaragi and Kishimoto (2023). The authors would like to give their special thanks to Ms. Maki Kishimoto for her assistance to computer-based numerical calculations.

Disclosure of Interests. The authors have no competing interests to declare that are relevant to the content of this article.

References

Zheng, X., Zhong, T., Liu, M.: Modeling crowd evacuation of a building based on seven methodological approaches. Build. Environ. **44**(3), 437–445 (2009)

Bonabeau, E.: Agent-based modeling: methods and techniques for simulating human systems. Proc. Nat. Acad. Sci. USA (PNAS) **99**(Suppl. 3), 7280–7287 (2002)

Aoki, Y., Osaragi, T., Hashimoto, K.: A simulation model of evacuation behavior in the fire-spread urban area following earthquake: effects of hearsay information process and geographical urban image. J. Archit. Plann. Environ. Eng. (Trans. AIJ) **440**, 111–118 (1992)

Osaragi, T., Tsuchiya, T.: Influence of word-of-mouth communication on large-scale evacuation after a severe earthquake. In: ISPRS Technical Commission IV Symposium 2018, ISPRS TC IV Mid-term Symposium "3D Spatial Information Science - The Engine of Change", ISPRS, IV-4, pp. 171–178 (2018)

Vermuyten, H., Beliën, J., De Boeck, L., Reniers, G., Wauters, T.: A review of optimisation models for pedestrian evacuation and design problems. Saf. Sci. **87**, 167–178 (2016)

Mabuchi, Y., Seo, K., Motomi, K., Ueda, R.: An evacuation simulation from spreading fire after an earthquake in the area densely crowded with wooden houses. J. Soc. Saf. Sci. **10**, 409–415 (2008)

Fathianpour, A., Babaeian Jelodar, M., Wilkinson, S., Evans, B.: A taxonomy of pedestrian evacuation infrastructure for urban areas; An assessment of resilience towards natural hazards. In: IOP Conference Series: Earth and Environmental Science, vol. 1101 (2022)

Esposito, D., Santoro, S., Camarda, D.: Agent-based analysis of urban spaces using space syntax and spatial cognition approaches: a case study in Bari, Italy. Sustainability (2020)

Makinoshima, F., Yotsui, S., Sato, S., Imamura, F.: Massive geolocation data reveal evacuation behaviour during the 2024 noto peninsula earthquake and Tsunami (2024). https://doi.org/10.48550/arXiv.2412.05795

Yabe, T., Sekimoto, Y., Tsubouchi, K., Ikemoto, S.: Cross-comparative analysis of evacuation behavior after earthquakes using mobile phone data. PLoS ONE **14**(2), e0211375 (2019). https://doi.org/10.1371/journal.pone.0211375

Osaragi, T., Oki, T.: Wide-area evacuation simulation incorporating rescue and firefighting by local residents. J. Disaster Res. (Special Issue on Disaster and Big Data 2) **12** (2), 296–310 (2017)

Kobes, M., Helsloot, I., de Vries, B., Post, J.G.: Building safety and human behaviour in fire: a literature review. Fire Saf. J. **45**(1), 1–11 (2010)

Kumagai, Y., Kishi, H.: The analysis of evacuation behavior in the fire -example of sakata fire and kanto earthquake fire-. J. City Plann. Inst. Jpn. **18**, 169–174 (1983)

Osaragi, T., Tanaka, A.: Modeling of pedestrian route selection in areas with different street patterns. In: Bungartz, HJ., Kranzlmüller, D., Weinberg, V., Weismüller, J., Wohlgemuth, V. (eds.) Advances and New Trends in Environmental Informatics. Progress in IS, pp. 147–164. Springer, Cham (2018). https://doi.org/10.1007/978-3-319-99654-7_10

Van den Berg, M., van Nes, R., Hoogendoorn, S.: Estimating choice models to quantify the effect of herding on the decision to evacuate: application of a serious gaming experimental setup. Transp. Res. Rec. **2672**(1), 161–170 (2018)

Bosina, E., Weidmann, U.: Estimating pedestrian speed using aggregated literature data. Physica A **468**, 1–29 (2017)

Willis, A., Gjersoe, N., Havard, C., Kerridge, J., Kukla, R.: Human movement behaviour in urban spaces: implications for the design and modelling of effective pedestrian environments. Environ. Plann. B Plann. Design **31**(6), 805–828 (2004)

Bureau of Urban Development, Tokyo Metropolitan Government: the Seventh Community Earthquake Risk Assessment Study for the Tokyo Metropolitan Area (2022). https://www.toshiseibi.metro.tokyo.lg.jp/bosai/chousa_6/home.htm. Accessed 16 Aug 2022

GNSS-PWV and Intense Rainfall Events: An Analysis of Two Years of Observation Acquired by the SNIK CORS on the Bari Area (Italy)

Alberico Sonnessa[1](✉) [iD], Eufemia Tarantino[1](✉) [iD], and Alessandra Mascitelli[2](✉) [iD]

[1] Department of Civil, Environmental, Land, Construction and Chemistry (DICATECh), Polytechnic University of Bari, Via Orabona 4, 70125 Bari, Italy
`{alberico.sonnessa,eufemia.tarantino}@poliba.it`
[2] Department of Advanced Technologies in Medicine and Dentistry (DTM&O), Center for Advanced Studies and Technology (CAST), University "G. d'Annunzio" of Chieti-Pescara, Via dei Vestini 31, 66100 Chieti, Italy
`alessandra.mascitelli@unich.it`

Abstract. Continuously Operating Reference Stations (CORS) play a crucial role in high-precision positioning and environmental monitoring. This study examines the relationship between Global Navigation Satellite System (GNSS) - derived Precipitable Water Vapor (GNSS-PWV) and intense rainfall events in Bari, Italy, using data from the SNIK CORS, operated by the AGLab of the Polytechnic University of Bari. The research aims to assess the potential of GNSS-PWV for nowcasting applications by analyzing two years of observations (July 2022–October 2024) in conjunction with precipitation measurements from local rain gauges. Results show a clear correlation between PWV peaks and intense precipitation, with PWV increases preceding rainfall intensity peaks by 5 to 105 min. A threshold-based approach for rainfall prediction was tested, successfully identifying 67% of heavy rainfall events, though some false positives and low rain events detections were observed. The findings suggest that GNSS-PWV could enhance short-term forecasting, but further validation with extended datasets and additional CORS networks is needed. Future work will integrate regional GNSS stations and refine predictive algorithms to improve the reliability of PWV-based nowcasting methods.

Keywords: GNSS-PWV · rainfall events · Rapid Onset Disasters (RODs) · GNSS meteorology · nowcasting

1 Introduction

Natural events, such as heavy rainfalls and floods, have an increasing impact on the built environment [1–4], causing, in some cases, also a significant detriment to human lives, especially in areas characterized by a high population density. Over the long-term period, the effects of relatively slow phenomena such as global warming, are worsening

© The Author(s), under exclusive license to Springer Nature Switzerland AG 2026
O. Gervasi et al. (Eds.): ICCSA 2025 Workshops, LNCS 15894, pp. 97–109, 2026.
https://doi.org/10.1007/978-3-031-97648-3_7

the frequency and incidence of these critical occurrences on the safety of populations. As possible consequence of the climate change, nowadays heavy rainfalls occur more frequently; their destructive effects have been tangible in the floods that affected over a short period of time the Emilia-Romagna region (Italy) in 2023 and 2024 [5, 6] and other countries all over the world, as deepened, for instance in [7–9]. Such critical events, by reference to the catastrophes they can lead to and the speed of their occurrence, can be included in the Rapid Onset Disasters (RODs) category [10], as stated by United Nation [11], and the management of their impact on the cities and their inhabitants [12] is one of the greatest challenges of our time.

In this frame, approaches encompassing the integration of different disciplines and skills are needed, both in the evaluation of the significance of the detected critical trends [13], and the development of proper tools aimed at preventing and monitoring possible dangerous events. Among these, geomatics play a key role through the processing and analysis of observations acquired by reference stations based on the Global Navigation Satellite System (GNSS), since these databases are widely employed in the development of weather models.

A Continuously Operating Reference Station (CORS) consists of a high-precision geodetic GNSS receiver coupled with an antenna, installed in a safe and stable location, that must operate 24 h a day, ensuring the logging and the redundant storing of raw observations. Since 1990-ies, CORS started to be installed, mainly by scientific institutions, with the aim of developing high-precision positioning applications. However, the GNSS signal in its travel from the satellite to the receiver positioned on the ground, is affected by a delay due to the traversing of the atmosphere, which can be estimated. A portion of this delay, that develops in the troposphere (i.e. the layer of the atmosphere in contact with the Earth's surface), is directly connected with Precipitable Water Vapor (PWV) content. Therefore, the estimation of this parameter [14, 15] provides support in climate studies [16–18] and is widely employed in the calibration and assessing of analogue datasets obtained with other satellite sensors [19, 20].The continuous monitoring of the PWV is useful to detect both its local variations, if spot measurements are available (as in the case of a single CORS), and changes at a territorial scale when network of GNSS receivers are established on wide areas [21, 22].

As the PWV content is related with rainfall events, [23–25], the analysis of its trend and can help to characterize a specific site in relation with this parameter and, since the oscillation of this feature could be indicative of the occurrence of intense precipitation, the PWV retrieved by GNSS observations (GNSS-PWV) have a potential, partially unexplored, for application in forecasting-nowcasting activities [26, 27].

2 Objectives

This study aims at analyzing the correlation between intense rainfall events and the corresponding GNSS-PWV trend in the Municipality of Bari. The relationship between the content of PWV in the troposphere and rainfall events is well known; nevertheless, this correlation has never been deepened in the investigated area. For this purpose, hereafter the results of the analysis of two year of observations acquired by the SNIK CORS installed at the Polytechnic University of Bari (Fig. 1) and managed by the Applied

Geomatics Laboratory (AGLab) of the Department of Civil, Environmental, Land, Construction and Chemistry (DICATECh) are shown. The GNSS-PWV parameter has been jointly analyzed with the measurements retrieved by the rain gauges operating in the area, belonging to the Civil Protection network, and run by the Centro Funzionale Decentrato della Sezione Protezione Civile della Regione Puglia (Decentralized Functional Center of the Civil Protection Section of the Region of Apulia).

Fig. 1. The SNIK CORS, installed in September 2021 on the Water Engineering building within the area of the Polytechnic University of Bary.

3   The Study Area: The Municipality of Bari and the Employed Sensors

Located in the south of Italy and provincial capital of the Apulia region, Bari is a municipality of about 316000 inhabitants which spreads over a mostly flat territory of 116 Km^2 [28], bordered on the north-eastern part by the Adriatic Sea (Fig. 2). The average elevation of the considered territory is few meters above sea level.

The CORS identified as SNIK (following the National Geodetic Survey rules), consisting of a Stonex SC2200 GNSS receiver equipped with a SA1500 choke-ring antenna, has been installed in September 2021 on the Water Engineering building within the area of the Polytechnic University of Bary, and, since January 2023, is included in the EUREF Permanent Network [29], which oversees the maintaining of the European Terrestrial Reference System (ETRS) [30].

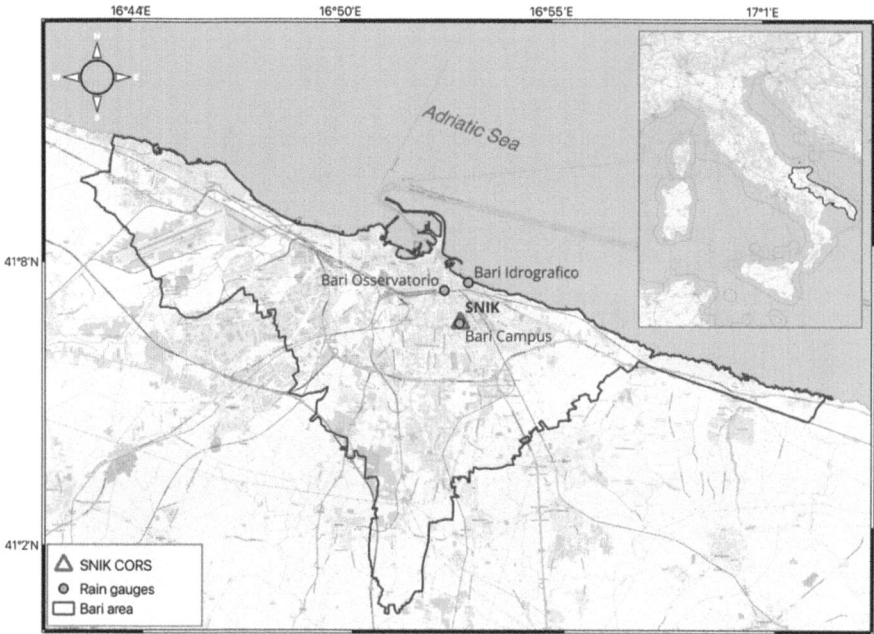

Fig. 2. The Municipality of Bari, provincial capital of the Apulia Region (which borders are showed in the thumbnail on the right). The location of the SNIK CORS and the rain gauges are displayed on the map (base layer: OpenStreetMap).

Three rain gauges, located in the Bari area, namely Bari Campus (BC – coordinates: latitude $41°6'23''$, longitude $16°52'40''$, elevation 23 m a.s.l.), Bari Idrografico (BI – coordinates: latitude $41°7'11''$, longitude $16°52'54''$, elevation 17 m a.s.l.), and Bari Osservatorio (BO – coordinates: latitude $41°7'2''$, longitude $16°52'18''$, elevation 34 m a.s.l.) are located in the vicinity of the SNIK station, at maximum distance of 1500 m. BC is installed at a distance of 40 m from the SNIK CORS.

4   Available Datasets

The case study analysis was carried out by using a multi-sensor approach. In this context, the rain data, acquired every 300 s, have been investigated to identify events of potential interest over the selected period, spanning from 22 July 2022 to 31 October 2024. GNSS raw observations acquired by the SNIK CORS, processed using the Precise Point

Positioning (PPP) technique [31] and the global pressure/temperature (GPT) model [14, 32, 33], through the goGPS software 1.0 [34], delivered the GNSS-PWV values at a sample rate of 300 s (Table 1).

Table 1. Dataset employed in the analysis

Sensor	Data Type	Acquisition frequency	Time span analysis
SNIK CORS (GNSS)	Raw observations	1s	22 July 2022–31 October 2024
	GNSS-PWV	300s	
BC (rain gauge)	Precipitations (mm)	300 s	
BO (rain gauge)	Precipitations (mm)	300 s	
BI (rain gauge)	Precipitations (mm)	300 s	

5   Identification of the Significant Events

As underlined, the precipitation data recorded by the three rain gauges allowed to identify the rainfall events, according to the definition deepened in [35], whereby a relevant rainfall event is preceded and followed by a dry period of six hours and characterized by a cumulative precipitation greater than or equal to 1mm, containing at least a measurement of rain height greater than 0.5 mm.

The rainfall events identified using these criteria are listed in the following table (Table 2).

Table 2. Rainfall events identified over the considered period by the BC, BO and BI rain gauges.

Sensor	Events identified	Min-max duration (min)	Min-max average intensity (mm/h)	Time span analysis
BC	81	5–1630	0.4–51.8	22 July 2022 – 31 October 2024
BO	90	10–1560	0.3–38.7	
BI	89	5–1595	0.4–43.2	

The detected events have been then classified according to [36].

Since the presented analysis intended to relate GNSS-PWV with intense events, only cases characterized by an intensity >6 mm/h and detected at least by the BC and one of the other two available rain gauges have been considered: in this step of the study, BO and BI served only as a check for the BC measurements (Table 3).

Table 3. Classification of the rainfall events.

Class	Average intensity (mm/h)
No rain	<1
Light rain	1–2
Weak rain	2–4
Moderate rain	4–6
Heavy rain	6–10
Very heavy rain	10–30
Cloudburst	>30

The identified rainfall events have been characterized through some significant metrics, obtained by processing the BC rain gauge measurements. Specifically, for each rainfall event, are indicated:

- the day and the start time;
- the duration;
- the average intensity;
- the intensity peak;
- the median value of the PWV, with reference to the considered year;
- the differences between PWV peak preceding the intensity peak and median annual PWV;
- the time differences between PWV peak and intensity peak.

Each identified event has been then related with the corresponding PWV time series provided by the SNIK CORS, in order to evidence possible correlations on the test site.

A time span of three and two hours, before and after the intensity peak respectively, has been investigated.

5.1 Heavy Rain Events

In the considered period, one heavy rain event has been detected on 19/08/2022, which trend is shown in Fig. 3, where the rain intensity trend is compared with the corresponding PWV trend. This comparison evidence a PWV peak occurring 55 min before the rain intensity peak. The PWV peak differs from the median PWV value, computed in the reference year, of about 27 mm.

5.2 Very Heavy Rain Events

Six very heavy rain events have been detected, which developments are shown in Fig. 4. The temporal delay between the two peaks ranges from 5 to 105 min, while the difference between the PWV peak and median value ranges from 0.1 to 26.7 mm.

Table 4. Heavy rain events.

Date	Duration (min)	Average intensity (mm/h)	Rainfall intensity peak (mm/h)	Median annual PWV (mm)	PWV peak (mm)	Δ PWV (mm)	Δ time between peaks (min)
19/08/2022 16:20	30	7.4	16.8	22.1	48.9	26.8	55

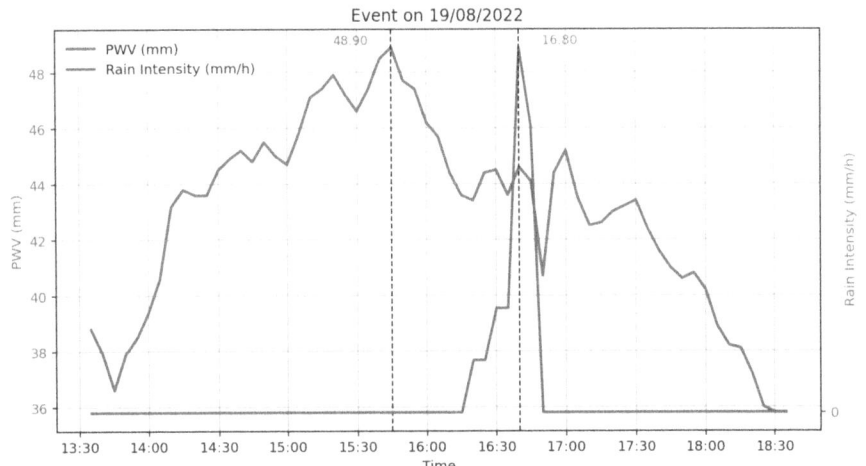

Fig. 3. Heavy rain event detected between 22 July 2022 and 31 October 2024.

Table 5. Very heavy rain events.

Date	Duration (min)	Average intensity (mm/h)	Rainfall intensity peak (mm/h)	Median annual PWV (mm)	PWV peak (mm)	Δ PWV (mm)	Δ time between peaks (min)
05/06/2023 12:50	20	29.4	54.0	20.1	39.6	19.5	5
05/08/2023 21:10	15	11.2	16.8	20.1	36.8	16.7	105
23/09/2023 19:10	100	24.5	116.4	20.1	45.9	25.8	10
11/03/2024 05:35	40	22.9	82.8	22.3	24.6	2.3	30
16/03/2024 20:55	100	10.7	33.6	22.3	22.4	0.1	15
19/08/2024 04:10	30	21.4	46.8	22.3	49.0	26.7	35

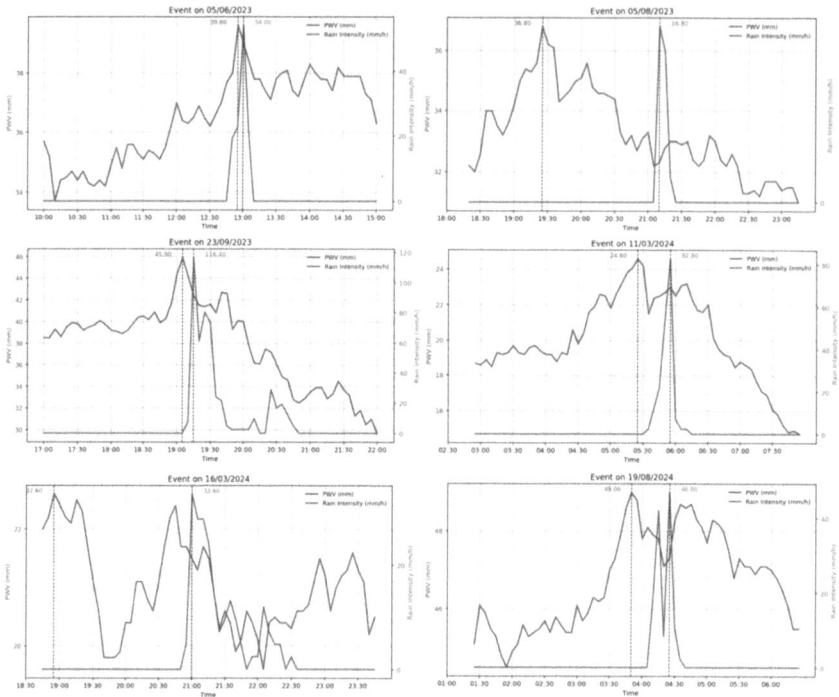

Fig. 4. Very heavy rain events detected between 22 July 2022 and 31 October 2024.

5.3 Cloudburst Events

Two cloudburst events have been identified over the reference period, as shown in Fig. 5. The temporal delay between the PWV and intensity peaks ranges from 5 to 25 min, while the difference between the peak and median PWV value ranges from 25.8 to 27.3 mm.

Table 6. Cloudburst events.

Date	Duration (min)	Average intensity (mm/h)	Rainfall intensity peak (mm/h)	Median annual PWV (mm)	PWV peak (mm)	Δ PWV (mm)	Δ time between peaks (min)
30/07/2022 17:40	20	44.4	91.2	22.1	47.9	25.8	25
05/09/2024 12:55	30	51.8	150.0	22.3	49.6	27.3	5

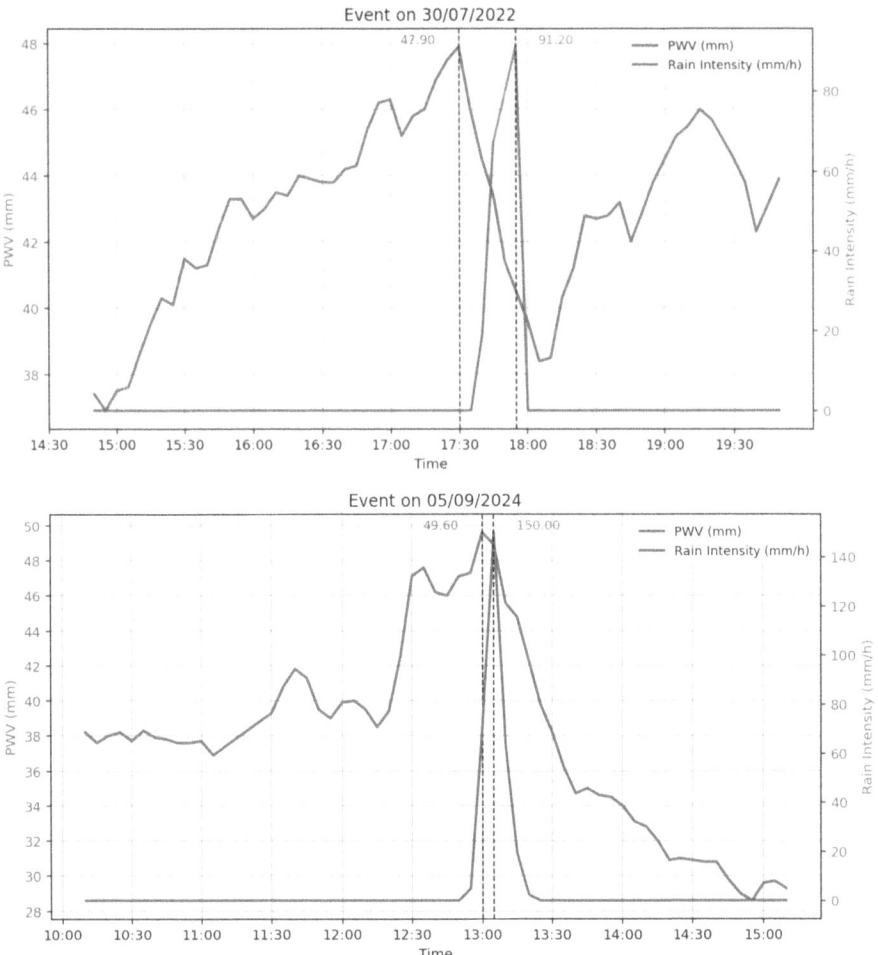

Fig. 5. Cloudburst events detected between 22 July 2022 and 31 October 2024

6   Analysis of the Results

The comparison of the intensity rainfall and GNSS-PWV time-series on intense rainfall events highlights the known relation between the two parameters, where every rain intensity peak is preceded by a PWV peak at the top of an upward trend, with a very variable temporal distance (from 5 up to 105 min) between the peaks. This would suggest the possible use of the PWV measurement for nowcasting activities. To this aim, a simplified test has been carried out by coupling the BC rainfall records with the corresponding PWV series over the whole considered period. The median PWV peak (equal to 45.9 mm), derived by the events characterized by an intensity >6 mm, has been used as minimum threshold to filter the dataset.

The results are shown in Table 7. The detected events using the PWV parameter are highlighted in light blue, also in the previous tables.

Table 7. Periods where the reference threshold value is reached or exceeded.

Events detected	Intense events (>6 mm/h)		Other rain events	Dry events
	Detected	Not detected		
	6	3		
	30/07/2022 16:50	05/06/2023		
	19/08/2022 14:40	11/03/2024		
	05/08/2023 00:00	16/03/2024		
	23/09/2023 13:30			
	19/08/2024 00.00			
	05/09/2024 12:30			

A hypothetic nowcasting system would have detected 24 days whether the set threshold would have been reached or exceeded. Among these, 6 refers to the intense rainfall events already identified using the rules described in § 5, 7 refer to other rainfall events and 11 to days characterized by the absence of precipitations (false positives). 33% (3 out of 9) of the intense events have not been identified. It is noteworthy that the reaching (or exceeding) of the threshold in the 6 out of 9 intense rainfall periods evidenced in Table 7 occurs with an advance ranging from 25 to 1150 min with respect to the corresponding events shown in Tables 4, 5 and 6.

7   Conclusive Remarks and Future Developments

The presented work was aimed at investigating the relation between the GNSS-PWV and the intense precipitations in the Municipality of Bari, by processing the observations acquired over a period of about two years by the SNIK CORS, run by the AGLab of the Polytechnic University of Bari, and a set of rain gauges belonging to the monitoring network of the Apulia Region. The results obtained clearly evidence the well-known correlation between PWV trends and rainfall events. The identification of intense rainfall events using a set of specific criteria, namely cumulative precipitation, rain height, duration of the dry period and average intensity, allowed to define a PWV threshold, used to detect the period on which the threshold itself was reached or exceeded. The findings of this analysis highlighted a relatively good agreement in terms of capability to identify in advance (up to 1150 min) some intense occurrences. However, also a limited number of low/no rain events were identified, while some events were not detected at all.

The main limitation of the presented study is due to the relatively short dataset recorded by the GNSS, limited to two years of observations.

While is well known that PWV exhibits a strong statistical correlation with precipitation, its short-term predictive capability is constrained by the complexity of convective processes, as evidenced by the variability of the delay between PWV and precipitation peak. Accurate short-term forecasting necessitates incorporating PWV variability alongside key surface meteorological parameters (e.g. pressure) [37].

Although very simplified, this analysis provides a first overview on the potential of the GNSS-derived PWV parameters for nowcasting. Further developments encompass the integration of CORS stations belonging to the Apulia Region (Rete GNSS Regione Puglia) and the corresponding rain gauges in the proposed analysis, and the setting out of predictive algorithms to improve the reliability of PWV-based nowcasting methods.

The analysis of a more consistent database will also encompass additional performance metrics like statistics on lead time distribution between PWV and rainfall peaks, as well as a confusion matrix with false alarm and miss rates.

Acknowledgments. The authors would like to thank "ARIF Regione Puglia—Agenzia Regionale Attività Irrigue e Forestali" and "Centro Funzionale Decentrato della Sezione Protezione Civile della Apulia Region" for providing rain gauge data, and Prof. Vincenzo Totaro at DICATECh, Polytechnic University of Bary, for the support in the identification of the correct methodology for rainfall events detection.

References

1. Mascitelli, A., et al.: Cultural heritage resilience in the face of extreme weather: lessons from the UNESCO site of Alberobello. Sustain. (Switz.) **15** (2023). https://doi.org/10.3390/su1521 15556
2. Sonnessa, A., di Lernia, A., Oscar Nitti, D., Nutricato, R., Tarantino, E., Cotecchia, F.: Integration of multi-sensor MTInSAR and ground-based geomatic data for the analysis of non-linear displacements affecting the urban area of Chieuti, Italy. Int. J. Appl. Earth Obs. Geoinf. **117** (2023). https://doi.org/10.1016/j.jag.2023.103194
3. Cantatore, E., Esposito, D., Sonnessa, A.: Mapping the multi-vulnerabilities of outdoor places to enhance the resilience of historic urban districts: the case of the apulian region exposed to slow and rapid-onset disasters. Sustain. (Switz.) **15** (2023). https://doi.org/10.3390/su1519 14248
4. Gioia, A., Totaro, V., Bonelli, R., Esposito, A.A.M.G., Balacco, G., Iacobellis, V.: Flood susceptibility evaluation on ephemeral streams of Southern Italy: a case study of Lama Balice. In: Gervasi, O., et al. Computational Science and Its Applications – ICCSA 2018. ICCSA 2018. Lecture Notes in Computer Science, vol. 10964, pp. 334–348. Springer, Cham (2018). https://doi.org/10.1007/978-3-319-95174-4_27
5. CNR-Irpi: Emilia-Romagna floods. https://polaris.irpi.cnr.it/emilia-romagna-due-ulteriori-alluvioni-nel-2024/#:~:text=Dopo%20le%20due%20grandi%20alluvioni,e%2019%2D20%20ottobre%202024. Accessed 16 Jan 2025
6. Arrighi, C., Domeneghetti, A.: Brief communication: On the environmental impacts of the 2023 floods in Emilia-Romagna (Italy). Nat. Hazards Earth Syst. Sci. **24** (2024). https://doi.org/10.5194/nhess-24-673-2024
7. Ferrario, M.F., Livio, F.: Rapid mapping of landslides induced by heavy rainfall in the Emilia-Romagna (Italy) region in May 2023. Remote Sens. (Basel) **16** (2024). https://doi.org/10.3390/rs16010122
8. Bosseler, B., Salomon, M., Schlüter, M., Rubinato, M.: Living with urban flooding: a continuous learning process for local municipalities and lessons learnt from the 2021 events in Germany. Water (Switz.) **13** (2021). https://doi.org/10.3390/w13192769
9. Reynoso Vanderhorst, H.D., Pathirage, C., Proverbs, D.: Navigating flood resilience: challenges, solutions, and lessons learnt from the dominican republic. Water (Switz.) **16** (2024). https://doi.org/10.3390/w16030382

10. Sonnessa, A., Cantatore, E., Esposito, D., Fiorito, F.: A multidisciplinary approach for multi-risk analysis and monitoring of influence of SODs and RODs on historic centres: the ResCUDE project (2020). https://doi.org/10.1007/978-3-030-58811-3_54

11. Assembly, U.N.G.: Report of the open-ended intergovernmental expert working group on indicators and terminology relating to disaster risk reduction (2016)

12. Santoro, S., Lovreglio, R., Totaro, V., Camarda, D., Iacobellis, V., Fratino, U.: Community risk perception for flood management: a structural equation modelling approach. Int. J. Disaster Risk Reduction **97** (2023). https://doi.org/10.1016/j.ijdrr.2023.104012

13. Gioia, A., Bruno, M.F., Totaro, V., Iacobellis, V.: Parametric assessment of trend test power in a changing environment. Sustain. (Switz.) **12** (2020). https://doi.org/10.3390/su12093889

14. Bevis, M., Businger, S., Herring, T.A., Rocken, C., Anthes, R.A., Ware, R.H.: GPS meteorology: remote sensing of atmospheric water vapor using the global positioning system. J. Geophys. Res. **97** (1992). https://doi.org/10.1029/92jd01517

15. Yang, F., Guo, J., Shi, J., Zhao, Y., Zhou, L., Song, S.: A new method of GPS water vapor tomography for maximizing the use of signal rays. Appl. Sci. (Switz.) **9** (2019). https://doi.org/10.3390/app9071446

16. Kuleshov, Y., Choy, S., Fu, E.F., Chane-Ming, F., Liou, Y.A., Pavelyev, A.G.: Analysis of meteorological variables in the Australasian region using ground- and space-based GPS techniques. Atmos. Res., 176–177 (2016). https://doi.org/10.1016/j.atmosres.2016.02.021

17. Suparta, W., Abu Bakar, F.N., Abdullah, M.: Remote sensing of Antarctic ozone depletion using GPS meteorology. Int. J. Remote Sens. **34** (2013). https://doi.org/10.1080/01431161.2012.746485

18. Torcasio, R.C., et al.: The impact of global navigation satellite system (GNSS) zenith total delay data assimilation on the short-term precipitable water vapor and precipitation forecast over Italy using the Weather Research and Forecasting (WRF) model. Nat. Hazards Earth Syst. Sci. **23** (2023). https://doi.org/10.5194/nhess-23-3319-2023

19. Bai, J., Lou, Y., Zhang, W., Zhou, Y., Zhang, Z., Shi, C.: Assessment and calibration of MODIS precipitable water vapor products based on GPS network over China. Atmos. Res. **254** (2021). https://doi.org/10.1016/j.atmosres.2021.105504

20. Wang, Y., Liu, X., Liu, Y., Zhan, W.: MODIS PWV correction based on CMONOC and regional function model. Wuhan Daxue Xuebao (Xinxi Kexue Ban)/Geomatics Inf. Sci. Wuhan Univ. **48** (2023). https://doi.org/10.13203/j.whugis20200183

21. Ferrando, I., Federici, B., Sguerso, D.: 2D PWV monitoring of a wide and orographically complex area with a low dense GNSS network. Earth, Planets and Space **70** (2018). https://doi.org/10.1186/s40623-018-0824-6

22. Ninsawat, S., Chitsutti, P., Chaudhary, S., Jindasee, P., Khamyai, T.: Development of near real-time PWV estimation system for monitoring the meteorological events in Thailand. Int. J. Geoinformatics **18** (2022). https://doi.org/10.52939/ijg.v18i3.2201

23. Kawo, A., Van Malderen, R., Pottiaux, E., Van Schaeybroeck, B.: Understanding the present-day spatiotemporal variability of precipitable water vapor over ethiopia: a comparative study between ERA5 and GPS. Remote Sens. (Basel) **14** (2022). https://doi.org/10.3390/rs14030686

24. Serrano-Vincenti, S., et al.: Harmonic analysis of the relationship between gnss precipitable water vapor and heavy rainfall over the Northwest Equatorial Coast, Andes, and Amazon Regions. Atmosphere (Basel) **13** (2022). https://doi.org/10.3390/atmos13111809

25. Realini, E., Sato, K., Tsuda, T., Susilo, Manik, T.: An observation campaign of precipitable water vapor with multiple GPS receivers in western Java, Indonesia. Prog. Earth Planet Sci. **1** (2014). https://doi.org/10.1186/2197-4284-1-17

26. Sapucci, L.F., Machado, L.A.T., de Souza, E.M., Campos, T.B.: Global Positioning System precipitable water vapour (GPS-PWV) jumps before intense rain events: a potential application to nowcasting. Meteorol. Appl. **26** (2019). https://doi.org/10.1002/met.1735

27. Manandhar, S., Lee, Y.H., Meng, Y.S.: GPS-PWV based improved long-term rainfall prediction algorithm for tropical regions. Remote Sens. (Basel) **11** (2019). https://doi.org/10.3390/rs11222643

28. ISTAT: Commissione parlamentare di inchiesta sulle condizioni di sicurezza e sullo stato di degrado delle città e delle loro periferie Report Comune di Bari (2024)

29. AGLab: SNIK CORS in EPN. https://epncb.eu/_networkdata/siteinfo4onestation.php?station=SNIK00ITA. Accessed 16 Jan 2025

30. EUREF (Institution/Organization): EUREF Permanent GNSS Network. https://www.epncb.oma.be/_organisation/about.php. Accessed 4 May 2021

31. Zumberge, J.F., Heflin, M.B., Jefferson, D.C., Watkins, M.M., Webb, F.H.: Precise point positioning for the efficient and robust analysis of GPS data from large networks. J. Geophys. Res. Solid Earth **102** (1997). https://doi.org/10.1029/96jb03860

32. Mascitelli, A., et al.: Multi-sensor data analysis of an intense weather event: the July 2021 lake como case study. Water (Switz.) **14** (2022). https://doi.org/10.3390/w14233916

33. Kouba, J.: Testing of global pressure/temperature (GPT) model and global mapping function (GMF) in GPS analyses. J. Geod. **83** (2009). https://doi.org/10.1007/s00190-008-0229-6

34. Gatti, A., Tagliaferro, G., Realini, E.: goGPS free and open source GNSS software for tropospheric delay estimation. In: Proceedings of the EGU General Assembly Conference Abstracts, Vienna, vol. 20 (2018)

35. Sottile, G., Francipane, A., Adelfio, G., Noto, L. V.: A PCA-based clustering algorithm for the identification of stratiform and convective precipitation at the event scale: an application to the sub-hourly precipitation of Sicily, Italy. Stochast. Environ. Res. Risk Assess. **36** (2022). https://doi.org/10.1007/s00477-021-02028-7

36. CNR-Irpi: Polaris - Misurare la pioggia. https://polaris.irpi.cnr.it/misurare-la-pioggia/. Accessed 11 Feb 2025

37. Zhang, Z., Lou, Y., Zhang, W., Liang, H., Bai, J., Song, W.: Correlation analysis between precipitation and precipitable water vapor over china based on 1999–2015 ground-based GPS observations. J. Appl. Meteorol. Climatol. **61** (2022). https://doi.org/10.1175/JAMC-D-21-0200.1

A Deeper Look into Flood Risk in the City of Bari (Italy)

Vincenzo Totaro[1]($\boxtimes$), Stefania Santoro[2], Maria Francesca Bruno[1], Vito Iacobellis[1], Matteo Gianluca Molfetta[1], and Umberto Fratino[1]

[1] Politecnico di Bari, Bari, Italy
{vincenzo.totaro,mariafrancesca.bruno,vito.iacobellis,
matteogianluca.molfetta,umberto.fratino}@poliba.it
[2] National Research Council, Water Research Institute (CNR, IRSA), Bari, Italy
stefaniasantoro@cnr.it

Abstract. The design of more effective policies of flood risk management is a challenge for the entire scientific and institutional communities, in particular in the light of the implications that climate and land use changes can have on floods impacts, especially in urban areas. Here, in fact, different types of floods can coexist, and the availability of historical flood data is crucial for ensuring a proper flood hazard assessment. To this aim it is important to improve the knowledge about locations, occurrences, types and impacts of floods, in order to acquire more information about dynamics and issues that occurred in the past. In this paper we illustrate and discuss the results of a systematic collection of flood events occurred in the period 1950–2020 for the case study of Bari (southern Italy). This city has been hit by significant floods since early '900 due to the episodic streams that cross the city, but the characteristics of urban area make also possible the occurrence of pluvial and coastal floods. Results indicated how underpasses were among the most hit locations, together with flat areas of the city, and that events are generally attributable to a pluvial nature. A comparison with a study on risk perception carried out in the same area showed results consistent with our analysis, demonstrating that the integration of these approaches can provide an additional contribution to research aimed in providing more effective strategies for copying with flood risk in urban areas.

Keyword: Urban floods · Extreme events · Risk perception

1 Introduction

Natural disasters are a common and frequent threat that affect society and ecosystems. Floods, in particular, represent a predominant category in this field, and in literature a number of statistics about their impacts is reported [1, 2]. Back in 2004, the Commission of the European Community recognized floods management plans as crucial tools deemed to mitigate the impacts of floods, building a framework whose rationale has been transposed in the Directive 2007/60/EC, so called "Floods Directive" [3]. However, there is still a significant number of uncertainties in defining effective strategies for

O. Gervasi et al. (Eds.): ICCSA 2025 Workshops, LNCS 15894, pp. 110–121, 2026.
https://doi.org/10.1007/978-3-031-97648-3_8

flood risk management, especially in urban areas. The complex implications about climate evolution and its analysis, together with the modifications in land use are among the most consistent challenges to be approached from the scientific community for properly tackling these issues [4, 5].

Flood risk analysis assumes a particular importance in urban areas, where the high concentration of people and assets make this areas highly vulnerable to various sources of risk [6–8]. Several approaches could be implemented for analysing flood risk in urban environments, with various degrees of complexity [9, 10]. However, acquiring knowledge about past flood events is of paramount importance for a preliminary assessment of floodable areas [11, 12]. In this respect, the availability and the creation of floods databases offer a relevant basis for implementing a reliable flood hazard assessment [12–14].

Flood databases can be considered very useful for flood analysis in urban areas, which are often characterized by a lack of gauging networks, thus complicating flood assessment especially in the case of pluvial floods [15]. In fact, deriving information about floodwater characteristics during flood events is fundamental for a proper use of hydrodynamic models, nowadays considered as reliable tools for flood hazard assessment at urban scale [16].

In addition, the investigation of social and cognitive factors affecting risk perception can provide a precious support for decision-makers responsible for flood policies, especially in the design of activities to be included in emergency plans [17–19]. Among these, evacuation can be considered one of the most effective measures for reducing hazard impacts. The use of a framework that supports the integration of social and psychological aspects of people in the decision-making process during the pre-travel phase of flood evacuation can reveal decisive during emergencies. Also, it has to be highlighted that when investigating flood risk, the specific nature of the floods that can affect an area have to be found. In fact, it can occur that people can perceive to be at risk areas that do not appear in the official risk maps [20–22]. It follows that the importance of combining decision models in case of hazardous behaviors with the acquisition of information about areas perceived to be flooded can provide useful information in building evacuation scenarios.

In this paper we provide an analysis of historical flood events in the urban area of Bari, a coastal city located in the South-East coast of Italy. The actual city area, before urbanization, was naturally crossed by episodic streams, which may generate considerable flows in correspondence of significant heavy rainfall events. Nowadays, the increased urbanization led to an increase in flood risk, also exacerbating effects of that of pluvial nature. This case study is particularly interesting, also because it has been investigated also from the perspective of risk perception analysis [23].

The paper is structured as follows: in Sect. 3 the study area and the related background are illustrated. In Sect. 2 the methodological framework implemented for the purposes of this paper is described. In Sects. 4 and 5 results and their implications are illustrated. Finally, in Sect. 6 the main conclusions of the work are illustrated.

2   Study Area

The case study is represented by the city of Bari, that is located along the Adriatic coast in the southeastern part of Italy. The nature of landscape is such to lead to the rise of episodic streams called *lame* (Fig. 1), characterized by flows only in correspondence of very intense rainfall events [23, 24].Such nature encouraged an intense urbanization in the areas interested by the presence of the stream network that – in some cases – has been encompassed in the urban fabric during the last two centuries [25].

Memories of the ancient presence of *lame* in the current urban area still remain in toponyms (e.g., the Picone neighborhood take the name of the homonymous river that crossed its area) and photographic and archival documentation [25].

Several destructive river flood events hit the metropolitan area of Bari since the early '900 and their history has been the object of several studies [26–28]. In fact, the destructive nature of part of those floods was such to trigger victims and relevant damage and made necessary the building of hydraulic diversion operas aimed in protecting the core of the urban area of Bari from river floods.

Today the city has to be considered potentially subject to pluvial, coastal and fluvial floods, to be related with exceptional events possibly involving failure of hydraulic structures aimed at the protection of surrounding areas.

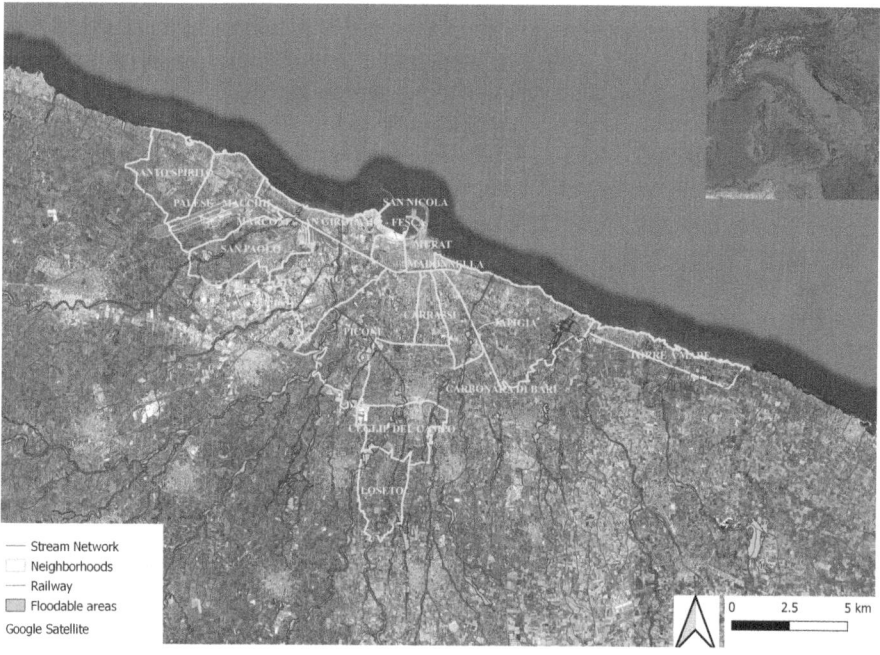

Fig. 1. Metropolitan area of Bari and Stream Network

As illustrated in Fig. 1, the city is crossed from the railway network, which implies the presence of a number of underpasses to reach the central core of the city represented by

Murat and San Nicola neighborhoods. This made floods of pluvial nature very common in the city, which is also potentially influenced also from events of the coastal type. Unlike river floods, pluvial and coastal occurrences have not been systematically reviewed analyzed for the city of Bari. Providing an attempt to summarize their occurrence and phenomenology is one of the goals of this work and results are illustrated in Sect. 4.

3   Materials and Methods

3.1   Floods Data Collection from Newspapers

A preliminary catalogue of flood events - other than the riverine type (that have been extensively surveyed in the literature) - has been set up from a search on local and national newspapers. The strategy adopted for retrieving such data was the search of news and details about floods in urban area of Bari in those dates in which annual maxima of sub-daily rainfall depths occurred for rain gauges located in the urban area according to the Hydrological Yearbooks printed in Italy from the twentieth century. In addition, we used the analogous values reported for very short and intense rainfall events. However, it is not guaranteed that those values correspond to annual maxima [29]. For the purpose of our analysis, we deem appropriate to investigate years between 1950 and 2020, year of the dissemination of the survey illustrated in [25] and that will be discussed later.

In order to achieve data of flood events, we investigated two types of sources, and namely a local newspaper ("La Gazzetta del Mezzogiorno") and websites. In particular, this latter source was analysed only for years from 2015 to 2020 in order to obtain a reasonable compromise between the effort of manual research and coverage of local (web) newspapers in the study area. This justifies also the decision of not extending the search on social media, despite they represent a relevant source of information for floods data retrieval [16].

3.2   Web Content Analysis (WCA)

The WCA was developed in cascade of newspaper analysis in order to exploit the greater number of contents available on the web. WCA is a method for analyzing online content to identify themes, trends, and relationships from data collected from sources such as articles, blogs, social media posts, and forums [30]. From a methodological perspective, the procedure starts by clearly defining research objectives and selecting relevant online sources. Data is then systematically collected using specialized tools, web crawlers, or targeted search queries [31]. Once collected, the data is filtered and selected according to predetermined criteria. Next, a crucial coding and categorization phase is carried out, either manually or assisted by software, to classify content based on thematic patterns [32]. The analysis itself can be qualitative or quantitative, aiming to reveal meaningful patterns or correlations [33]. To ensure methodological rigor and reliability, researchers often employ inter-coder reliability tests or triangulation techniques [34]. Finally, findings are interpreted and clearly presented in relation to the initial objectives, along with discussions of their implications and limitations [32].

The research on urban flooding events was conducted through a systematic analysis of online news sources and reports available on the web. The main objective was to collect detailed information on the frequency, intensity and impacts of flooding episodes that affected the city of Bari in recent years, evaluating the role of infrastructures and the reactions of the local community. The research was manually conducted using search engines (Google News, Bing) and directly consulting information sites with regular coverage of local news. According to the experience reported in [16], we supported the search by exploiting a couple of keywords fields which combine a location ("Bari") and a meteorological indication ("Pioggia", "Maltempo", "Allagamento", "Alluvione", "Bomba d'acqua"). The searches were carried out with time filters set from 2015 to 2020 and also in those days in which extreme rainfall events reported in the Hydrological Yearbooks. This allowed to get additional information with respect to rainfall events that are not considered annual maxima.

The collected articles (newspapers and online websites) were organized in a table, recording for each event:

– Date of the event
– Affected locations
– Flood dynamics and causes
– Effects recorded in the urban area (flooding, traffic disruption, damage to infrastructure, damage to commercial activities).

3.3 Knowledge Discovery in Databases (KDD)

Knowledge Discovery in Databases is a process structured in different steps, each of which assumes a key role in converting raw data in useful and understandable knowledge [35].

KDD begins with the screening of relevant data, identifying and isolating relevant information for the analysis. After this, data undergoes the preprocessing, i.e. a procedure aimed in the removal of detected error or noises, in order to build a robust dataset. In case data are in the form of text, activities include stop-word analysis, tokenization, stemming and lemmatization. Once cleaned up, data are converted into a format which can suit better to analysis. Normalization, dataset size reduction and creation of new variables are some of the processes that can be implemented. Such datasets represent the input of the so-called *data mining*, which exploits advanced techniques for detecting patterns and relationships between data. Among involved methodologies, we list classification, clustering, regression. KDD ends with interpretation and evaluation of results, which represents a crucial point for ensuring validity and utility of acquired knowledge. Detected pattern are analysed and addressed for understanding their meaning and practical implications. This step can also be supported by data visualization, which can improve effectiveness in comprehending and sharing results. Those listed are not one-directional steps: if needed, analysts can go back to previous and refine it. This makes KDD a very dynamic procedure.

In this paper this process has been practically implemented in retrieving codified information about landmarks, because a same landmark can be mentioned with different terms. It is important to note that this analysis implied to cope with toponyms of disappeared streets/neighborhoods, which required an additional search for retrieving their position.

4   Results

As stated in Sect. 3, flood events catalogue from newspapers has been built moving from the date of the sub-daily extreme rainfall events. In order to characterize these events, for each of the event durations under exam in Fig. 2 is illustrated the percentage of occurrence for each month of the year.

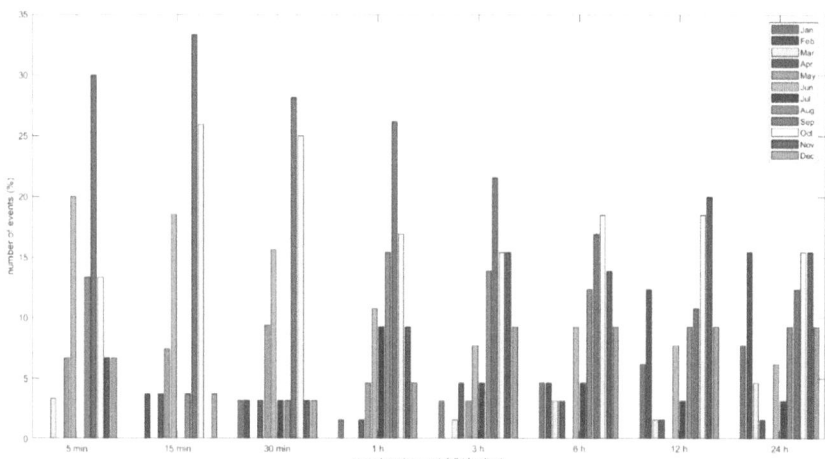

Fig. 2. Monthly distribution of rainfall extremes recorded at the Bari Osservatorio rain gauge

This figure shows some very interesting characters of the rainfall events typical of Italian areas [36]. In detail, very short events (from 5 to 30 min) are mainly concentrated in June, September and October, while from 1 to 24 h there is a progressive shift in the occurrence from August-September to winter months. Typically, shorter events are characterized by higher intensity than the longer, denoting very different characteristics also in their ground effects and dynamics.

Then, we checked the correspondence between those dates and journalistic reports and news, finding more than 80 descriptions of flood events in the metropolitan area of Bari. After rationalizing their content (in accordance with Sect. 3), we obtained the landmarks frequencies listed in Table 1. Locations of these landmarks in the urban area of Bari can be found in Fig. 3.

Most of these landmarks belongs to underpasses, which are recognized as very critical points for urban areas. In the city of Bari, they are generally associated with the railway network, which acts as a barrier between the city center and the peripheral areas.

It is very interesting to note that a consistent portion of these landmarks is not crossing areas related to a river flood event with a return period of 30 years: this is a further signal about the occurrence of floods attributable to pluvial/coastal nature. Some notes have to be made with respect to Table 1: as first, this is a cumulative list over around 70 years. During this period the city experienced significant urbanistic changes, which involved the setup of new vulnerable areas which obviously have a low frequency of occurrence but

Table 1. Landmark frequencies (if greater than 5%) of flood events retrieved from newspapers and web analysis

Landmarks	Occurrences (%)
Quintino Sella underpass	47.2
Bruno Buozzi underpass	20.9
Luigi di Savoia underpass	19.4
Modugno underpass	15.3
Giuseppe Re David street	12.5
Starita seafront	11.1
Giulio Petroni street	9.7
Nazario Sauro seafront	8.3
Giuseppe Capruzzi street	8.3
Domenico Nicolai street	8.3
San Nicola church	6.9
Benedetto Croce street	6.9
Giovanni Jatta street	6.9
Cavour street	5.6
Imperatore Augusto seafront	5.6
Michele Mirenghi street	5.6
Monte Nevoso street	5.6
Napoli street	5.6
Pietro Ravanas street	5.6
Vittorio Veneto street	4.2

can be actual. On the other side, the installation of new or redesigned drainage systems could potentially have mitigated the hazard and reduced floods impacts. Furthermore, the review of events from 1950 to 2015 could not be considered exhaustive: in fact, it has been carried out only considering extreme rainfall events reported in the Hydrological Yearbooks, but can be more of these if we consider that also rainfall events with lower recorded intensity could have triggered urban floods or, also, meteorological systems that have not been significantly recorded from raingauges network.

Furthermore, newspaper analysis allowed to gather knowledge about the changes in the urban fabric of the city and how it affected the occurrence of urban floods. In particular, the journalistic reports in many occasions have been a really useful provider of details about flood dynamics and motivations, and the effectiveness of *ad hoc* mitigation measures adopted during years for tackling floods effects.

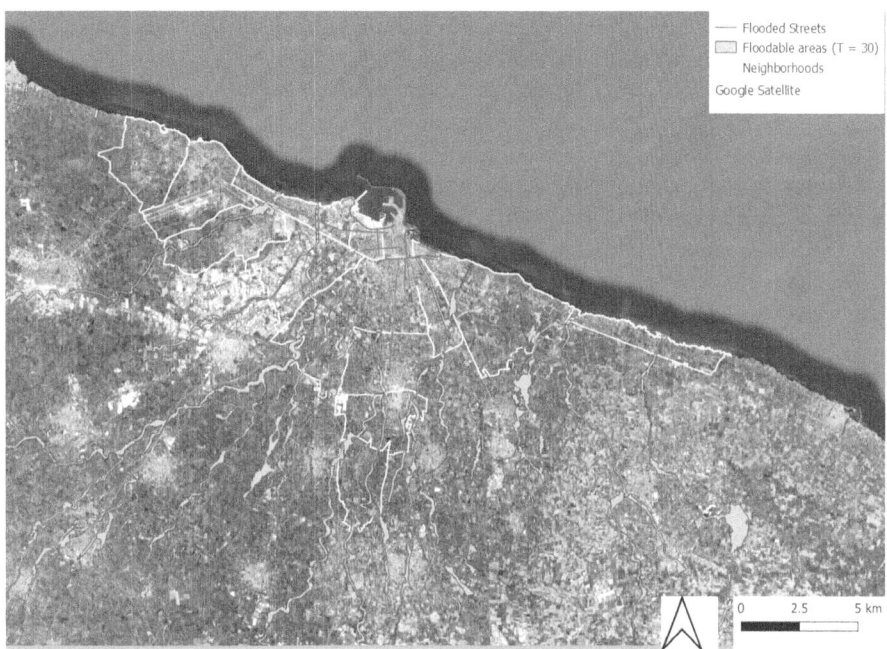

Fig. 3. Streets with the highest rate of flood occurrences in 1950–2020

5   Discussion

In this paper we retrieved historical flood events from newspapers and web contents for the city of Bari (Italy), in order to collect information and improve the knowledge about the different nature of floods that can affect the city. From the analysis of the results it is evident how floods due to local topographic depressions or to ineffectiveness of urban drainage systems are common events in the city, and that underpasses are among the highest vulnerable points. A positive and relevant feedback from this analysis can be made by comparing our findings with those of Santoro et al. [25], which exploited a survey-based strategy for investigating flood perception in the city of Bari. It emerged that pluvial flood exerts a strong effect on the survey respondents, and that city underpasses (especially those linking the historical core of the city with peripheral neighborhoods) are those with highest flood perception from respondents. Also, if regarded with respect to the perception of floodable neighborhoods, from Fig. 3 a significant feedback is verified. However, this comparison led also to explaining reasons for which resident population seems to be unaware of the risk due to episodic streams that cross metropolitan area, especially in the light of the devastating effects that they caused in the last 120 years [37]. This fact could be explained not only with the physiological decay of memory that occur after floods, but also with the lost of knowledge about the urban structure of the city. In fact, the strong link between *lame* and urban fabric in Bari is evident from the fact that the Picone lama crossed the neighborhoods of Picone and Libertà until the last two centuries, but has been culverted during some of the expanding steps of the city [25]. This is a critical point and should need to be properly assessed in emergency plans.

Interesting implications can be drawn from the results of the proposed analysis. In particular, our study allowed to detect not only historically flooded areas, but it allowed also a deeper reflection about changes occurred in the urban fabric in the last 70 years. For example, we gained information about causes and dynamics of flooding and about existence and building of drainage systems, which can reveal as a very useful information in the analysis of flood hazard. A deeper knowledge about land use and the effectiveness of new drainage systems in mitigating floods occurrences was also possible. In the case of coastal floods due to sea storms, our search allowed to depict clear evidence of benefits in the building of coastal protection structures offshore the historical urban waterfront. Our results also showed how underpasses (Quintino Sella, Bruno Buozzi and Luigi di Savoia in particular) are historically subject to flooding, also if the realization of mitigation strategies seems to have reduced at least the observed water depths and highlighted the effectiveness of emergency measures taken by local authorities. In fact, newspaper analysis showed that in the past it was not uncommon to rescue people by rafts.

This research also allowed to gain some knowledge about dynamics of accidents or flood behaviors of people during floods. In this latter case, for example, we found a document about a citizen swimming in the Quintino Sella flooded underpass, clearly for recreational purposes, depicting a clear tendence in hazardous behaviors already documented in studies about flood victims' dynamics [38]. A systematic analysis of such behaviors (and also in places and accidents dynamics) can be very useful for analysing people's behaviour during floods and plan some precautionary measures [20].

As clearly evident from the illustrated results, there is a relevant correspondence between perceived and observed landmarks. This is a significant conclusion, also in the light of the high frequency of events retrieved for underpasses, also showing a clear feedback with the typical transportation dynamics of the city. Results are also consistent with a similar case study [21]. On the other side, an underestimation of some landmarks has to be noticed, but it can be due both to the limited extension in time of our research (which stopped in 2020) and to the recent building of some urbanized areas. This can have influenced the perception of many of respondents to the survey, thus demonstrating how both floods and their perception have a strong dynamic component.

Some limitations of the proposed analysis have to be listed. As first, retrieved flood catalogue is not exhaustive. In fact, we collected only events related to the extreme of sub-daily rainfall reported in the Italian Hydrological Yearbooks. In particular, more other events could be retrieved by more systematic research of events both from newspapers and from the web. Finally, the sample used for collecting information about citizens' risk perception used in [25] cannot be homogeneous, and could be not fully representative of some areas (the suburbs, for example), which are widely documented to have been subject to floods, but are excluded from the top-rated.

6   Conclusions

In this paper we approached the topic of floor risk analysis in urban areas by retrieving flooded areas in the last 70 years and making a preliminary evaluation about the occurrence of flooding episodes. The analysis was carried out on the case study of Bari

(Italy), a coastal city in the south of Italy, characterized by a metropolitan area crossed by several episodic streams that have flows only in case of very intense rainfall events. Result highlighted that the high frequency of episodes of flooding due to heavy rainfall events hit underpasses, together with areas characterized by flat topography and prone to the accumulation of water. A comparison with a study showing results of a survey disseminated among the city population clearly highlighted how the same landmarks are perceived to be potentially floodable areas. In addition, the comparison demonstrated that the sporadic occurrence of river floods led to a neglection in perception of this type of risk from the population, which is instead more conscious about pluvial events, especially in underpasses. These findings are of particular significance, especially if regarded in respect to the need of updating flood management in the light of climate change: in fact, modified rainfall scenarios could lead to unprecedented floods events. It is therefore desirable to support analysis with an in-depth investigation about the knowledge of protective measures from the population and by testing and improving current structures for flood risk management in urban areas, also revisiting the perception of urban areas from people by improving the knowledge of the original structure of landscape.

References

1. Hammond, M.J., Chen, A.S., Djordjević, S., Butler, D., Mark, O.: Urban flood impact assessment: a state-of-the-art review. Urban Water J. **12**(1), 14–29 (2015). https://doi.org/10.1080/1573062X.2013.857421
2. Merz, B., et al.: Causes, impacts and patterns of disastrous river floods. Nat. Rev. Earth Environ. **2**(9), 592–609 (2021). https://doi.org/10.1038/s43017-021-00195-3
3. EU, European Union: Directive 2007/60/EC of the EuropeanParliament and of the council of 23 October 2007 on theassessment and the management of flood risks Official JournalL288 (2007)
4. Montanari, A., Koutsoyiannis, D.: Modeling and mitigating natural hazards: stationarity is immortal! Water Resour. Res. **50**(12), 9748–9756 (2014)
5. Serinaldi, F., Kilsby, C.G.: Stationarity is undead: uncertainty dominates the distribution of extremes. Adv. Water Resour. **77**, 17–36 (2015)
6. Mascitelli, A., et al.: Cultural heritage resilience in the face of extreme weather: lessons from the UNESCO site of Alberobello. Sustainability **15**(21), 15556 (2023)
7. Cantatore, E., Esposito, D., Sonnessa, A.: Mapping the multi-vulnerabilities of outdoor places to enhance the resilience of historic urban districts: the case of the Apulian region exposed to slow and rapid-onset disasters. Sustainability **15**(19), 14248 (2023)
8. Dawson, R.J., Speight, L., Hall, J.W., Djordjevic, S., Savic, D., Leandro, J.: Attribution of flood risk in urban areas. J. Hydroinf. **10**(4), 275–288 (2008)
9. Cea, L., Costabile, P.: Flood risk in urban areas: Modelling, management and adaptation to climate change. A review. Hydrology **9**(3), 50 (2022)
10. Schmitt, T.G., Scheid, C.: Evaluation and communication of pluvial flood risks in urban areas. Wiley Interdiscip. Rev. Water **7**(1), e1401 (2020)
11. Kandilioti, G., Makropoulos, C.: Preliminary flood risk assessment: the case of Athens. Nat. Hazards **61**, 441–468 (2012)
12. Du, S., Gu, H., Wen, J., Chen, K., Van Rompaey, A.: Detecting flood variations in Shanghai over 1949–2009 with Mann-Kendall tests and a newspaper-based database. Water **7**(5), 1808–1824 (2015)

13. Lang, M., et al.: Preliminary flood risk assessment for the European directive: inventory of French past floods. Compr. Flood Risk Manage. Res. Policy Pract. **423**(25), 303 (2012)

14. Llasat, M.C., et al.: Towards a database on societal impact of Mediterranean floods within the framework of the HYMEX project. Nat. Hazard. **13**(5), 1337–1350 (2013)

15. Mobini, S., Pirzamanbein, B., Berndtsson, R., Larsson, R.: Urban flood damage claim analyses for improved flood damage assessment. Int. J. Disaster Risk Reduction **77**, 103099 (2022)

16. Lombardo, M., Totaro, V., Chiaravalloti, F., Petrucci, O.: Street-scale hydrodynamic estimation from social media videos: a systematic approach to urban floods data collection. Int. J. Disaster Risk Reduction, 105419 (2025)

17. Najafi, M., Ardalan, A., Akbarisari, A., Noorbala, A. A., Elmi, H.: The theory of planned behavior and disaster preparedness. PLoS Currents **9** (2017). https://doi.org/10.1371/currents. dis.4da18e0f1479bf6c0a94b29e0dbf4a72

18. Liu, Y., Fan, Z.P., Zhang, Y.: Risk decision analysis in emergency response: a method based on cumulative prospect theory. Comput. Oper. Res. **42**, 75–82 (2014). https://doi.org/10.1016/j.cor.2012.08.008

19. Taillandier, F., Di Maiolo, P., Taillandier, P., Jacquenod, C., Rauscher-Lauranceau, L., Mehdizadeh, R.: An agent-based model to simulate inhabitants' behavior during a flood event. Int. J. Disaster Risk Reduction **64**, 102503 (2021). https://doi.org/10.1016/j.ijdrr.2021.102503

20. Santoro, S., Totaro, V., Lovreglio, R., Camarda, D., Iacobellis, V., Fratino, U.: Risk perception and knowledge of protective measures for flood risk planning. the case study of Brindisi (Puglia region). Saf. Sci. **153**, 105791 (2022). https://doi.org/10.1016/j.ssci.2022.105791

21. Santoro, S., Totaro, V., Mastrodonato, G., Balena, P.: Mapping citizens' knowledge and perception. What support for flood risk planning? Some Tips from Brindisi Case Study. In: Gervasi, O., et al. Computational Science and Its Applications – ICCSA 2023 Workshops. ICCSA 2023. Lecture Notes in Computer Science, vol. 14109, pp. 355–367. Springer, Cham (2023). https://doi.org/10.1007/978-3-031-37120-2_23

22. Douglas, I., Garvin, S., Lawson, N., Richards, J., Tippett, J., White, I.: Urban pluvial flooding: a qualitative case study of cause, effect and nonstructural mitigation. J. Flood Risk Manage. **3**(2), 112–125 (2010)

23. Santoro, S., Lovreglio, R., Totaro, V., Camarda, D., Iacobellis, V., Fratino, U.: Community risk perception for flood management: a structural equation modelling approach. Int. J. Disaster Risk Reduction **97**, 104012 (2023)

24. Balacco, G., Totaro, V., Gioia, A., Piccinni, A.F.: Evaluation of geomorphic descriptors thresholds for flood prone areas detection on ephemeral streams in the metropolitan area of Bari (Italy). In: Misra, S., et al. Computational Science and Its Applications – ICCSA 2019. ICCSA 2019. Lecture Notes in Computer Science, vol. 11622, pp. 239–254. Springer, Cham (2019). https://doi.org/10.1007/978-3-030-24305-0_19

25. Santoro, S., Totaro, V., Balena, P., Iacobellis, V., Fratino, U., Borri, D.: The interlink between urban growth and flooding: lessons from the city of Bari (Italy) (Sumbitted)

26. Borri, D., Di Santo, A., Iacobellis, V.: Bari: la piena del 1926. Continuità Rassegna Tecnica Pugliese, Bari, No. 3–4, pp. 83–88 (2002)

27. Moretti, M.: Le alluvioni nel settore Adriatico delle Murge (Terra di Bari): cause geologiche e ruolo dell'azione antropica. Geologi e Territorio, Ordine Regionale dei Geologi – Puglia, No. 3, pp. 11–22 (2005)

28. Bisantino, T., Pizzo, V., Polemio, M., Gentile, F.: Analysis of the flooding event of October 22–23, 2005 in a small basin in the province of Bari (Southern Italy). J. Agric. Eng. **47**(4), 197–204.40 (2016). https://doi.org/10.4081/jae.2016.531

29. Pelosi, A., Chirico, G.B., Furcolo, P., Villani, P.: Regional assessment of sub-hourly annual rainfall maxima. Water **14**(7), 1179 (2022)

30. Herring, S.C.: Web content analysis: expanding the paradigm. In: International Handbook of Internet Research, pp. 233–249. Springer, Dordrecht (2009)

31. Kim, I., Kuljis, J.: Applying content analysis to web-based content. J. Comput. Inf. Technol. **18**(4), 369–375 (2010)

32. Schreier, M.: Qualitative Content Analysis in Practice. SAGE Publications (2012)

33. Neuendorf, K.A.: The Content Analysis Guidebook, 2nd edn. SAGE Publications (2017)

34. Krippendorff, K.: Content Analysis: An Introduction to Its Methodology, 4th edn. SAGE Publications (2018)

35. Fayyad, U., Piatetsky-Shapiro, G., Smyth, P.: From data mining to knowledge discovery: an overview. In: Fayyad, U., Piatetsky-Shapiro, G., Smyth, P. Uthurusamy, R. (eds.) Advances in Knowledge Discovery and Data Mining, pp. 1–34. AAAI Press/The MIT Press, Menlo Park (1996)

36. De Luca, C., Furcolo, P., Rossi, F., Villani, P., Vitolo, C.: Extreme rainfall in the Mediterranean. In: Proceedings of the International Workshop on Advances in Statistical Hydrology, pp. 23–25. University of Catania-IAHS-STAHY, Taormina, May 2010

37. Mossa, M.: The floods in Bari: What history should have taught. J. Hydraul. Res. **45**(5), 579–594 (2007). https://doi.org/10.1080/00221686.2007.9521795

38. Diakakis, M.: Types of behavior of flood victims around floodwaters: correlation with situational and demographic factors. Sustainability **12**(11), 4409 (2020). https://doi.org/10.3390/su12114409

Ports and Logistics of the Future - Smartness and Sustainability (Smart-Ports 2025)

Port-System-Innovation: A Comprehensive Model for Freight Railway Digital Automation. A Case Study of Trieste Port, Italy

Irina Di Ruocco[1]([⊠]) [ID] and Marco Mazzarino[2] [ID]

[1] Department of Economics, Mathematics and Statistics, University of Trieste, Via Alfonso Valerio, 4/1, 34127 Trieste, Italy
`irina.diruocco@deams.units.it`
[2] Department of Architecture and Arts, Università IUAV of Venice, Ca' Tron, Santa Croce 1957, 30135 Venice, Italy
`mazzarin@iuav.it`

Abstract. The integration of new freight transport technologies into port areas requires a detailed understanding of success factors, drivers, and barriers — with the Port of Trieste serving as a representative territorial case. In this context, the local rail operator plans to implement predictive maintenance solutions for freight transport. Although several research gaps remain, this study aims to explore how technology is embedded within the territorial context, assessing the opportunities and vulnerabilities of port–territory synergies from an innovation-driven perspective. The article proposes a holistic model that incorporates territorial, technological, geographic, and port-related dimensions to analyse the integration of predictive maintenance through a geographic-economic lens. The model supports the case study and provides insights for replication in other port environments.

Keywords: railway automation · port-city integration · predictive maintenance

1 Introduction

The perception of port systems is evolving beyond being merely a logistical infrastructure to that of an innovation ecosystem— an inherently geographic system which brings together technology, governance and stakeholder cooperation to address environmental, economic and spatial issues [1, 2]. Ports play an important role in the global trade system [3] but high utilisation of maritime and logistic activities produce numerous layers of environmental pressure, from air and water pollution to ecosystem degradation [4], alongside urban pressures faced by adjacent communities [5]. Recent technological advances, both digital technologies used in port areas [6] and data-based methods, have changed the ability to monitor, assess and mitigate overall, manage environmental pressures, across a port territory [7]. New tools, such as PM for freight trains operating in the port sector, contribute to a better understanding of port impacts- both marine and land-based- facilitating the use of digitally enabled planning applications in alignment with objectives of sustainable urban and regional development [8].

© The Author(s), under exclusive license to Springer Nature Switzerland AG 2026
O. Gervasi et al. (Eds.): ICCSA 2025 Workshops, LNCS 15894, pp. 125–141, 2026.
https://doi.org/10.1007/978-3-031-97648-3_9

In addition, port system issues involve stakeholder groups— public authorities, private operators, logistics companies and communities—with whom relationships influence the whole supply chain's operational performance and resilience. According to [9], port management is now reliant on whatever funding, digital convergence and decision-making formats are developed to respond to sustainability implications and user expectations. Within this context, planning sustainable port logistics can no longer be seen as only infrastructure provision, but also the design of governance models that optimise for innovation [10].

Still, barriers such as aging infrastructure, fragmented policy frameworks, and limited technology integration still inhibit the development of coherent, resilient port systems across Europe. In order to attain the European Commission's modal shift objectives (2021, 2023) [11, 12] (for example, an increase of rail freight share to 30% by 2030), the sector must invest in technologies such as predictive maintenance [13], the Internet of Things (IoT) and Digital Twins (DTs), but also embed these technologies and tools into a broader territorial innovation strategy.

This paper provides a case study of the port of Trieste; a context, in which innovation on the territory (like predictive maintenance) not only includes an innovation in technology but also geographic-territorial innovation and an economic innovation can develop a synergy between port and territory while advocating a vision of innovation ecosystems in the case of digital technology, like predictive maintenance in rail freight context, focused on collaboration between ports, businesses, public authority, and communities. In these ecosystems, the smart port technology acts as spatial drivers of transformation. The smart port technologies contribute to the regeneration of port-adjacent areas, enhance regional connectivity, and support inclusive and sustainable urban development [14].

This study is guided by two key research questions:

1. How can technological innovations in railway and port systems support urban and territorial policies aimed at sustainability of port-adjacent areas?
2. In what ways can the integrated planning of freight flows and logistics automation contribute to the spatial and functional transformation of territories, fostering better alignment between transport infrastructure and regional development?

The Port of Trieste offers a compelling case study in this regard. As Italy's leading rail-connected port, it operates as a gateway to Central and Eastern Europe yet faces structural and technological challenges that limit its capacity for transformation. The AUTOSUP (Autonomous of Supply Chain), a Horizon European project [15] addresses these issues by promoting digital railway automation, port-hinterland integration, and circular logistics planning—demonstrating how targeted innovation policies can reinforce the role of ports as active agents of sustainable territorial development.

The structure of the paper is as follows. Beyond this introduction, Sect. 2 describes the literature review. Section 3 presents the research methodology, the results and discussion are presented in the Sect. 4. Finally, the Sect. 5 draws the conclusions.

2 Literature Background

Recent research on the innovation of port areas, moving towards the idea of "Smart Ports or Ports 4.0," increasingly highlight the need to think of port areas as complex urban and regional systems [16], where infrastructure, economic activity and environment coexist, and even overlap, in a situational context [17]. With growing global trade and expanding cities, port territories are increasingly prompted to handle this complexity, whilst pursuing sustainable development and technological innovation [18]. In this context the innovation ecosystem of ports and cities concept has emerged – ports not as merely logistical gateways, but as places for knowledge generation, inter-organisational learning, and social-economic reformation [19]. Port authorities can fulfil an increasingly important role of platform organiser in these ecosystems, which include not only holding and maintaining infrastructure, but also mediating multi-level cooperation, digital transformation, and sustainability transition. This role is increasingly crucial in dry ports and hinterland terminals, where rail infrastructure collectively with land use and environmental imperatives is increasingly prevalent, urging integrative planning and circular economy.

Although there is increased research on smart ports, there are still significant research gaps, especially regarding the rail-port interface. Research has primarily investigated maritime automation, urban regeneration, or as straying distinct technological tools, while we do not yet fully understand how technologies including the emerging PM, digital twins' technology (DTs), and real-time analytics—are integrated into governance systems, territorial planning [13], and policy engagement in port-hinterland systems [20, 21]. Although the Smart Port 4.0 paradigm has opened potentially disruptive technologies—Internet of Things (IoT), big data, blockchain, PM—into logistics, research has not fully studied how these tools affect the durability of the infrastructure, the reductions in emissions or resilience in planning for port-rail Networks [22, 23]. Predictive maintenance is an emerging area that could help in many ways, including less downtime of operations, longer asset life cycles, or less emissions. Although we can broadly categorize these as emerging technologies, there is rarely anything that analyses how PM is governed at different institutional levels or how PM is used in the governance of spatial development [24]. Additionally, there are currently monitoring frameworks that typically measure a limited number of operational metrics and do not capture a multi-scalar, cross-sectoral understanding of port-city-hinterland innovations [25]. Research has rarely considered the proximity dimensions—as territorial, cognitive, organisational, institutional—and how they shape outcomes of innovation or the design of processes for collaborative governance arrangements [26].

This research study seeks to address these gaps by providing a territorially grounded analytical model to understand how freight digitalisation as predictive maintenance is transforming both operations and governance in the rail-port context. Authors focus on the Port of Trieste as a strategic access point in Southern Europe to ascertain how these changes are being diffused into the institutional landscape of ports using circular economy principles and urban-regional policy positions. The novel contribution is based on our approach that draws on economic and transport geography, and institutional theory to construct the Spatial-Institutional Innovation Model (SIIM)—a multi-dimensional framework that tells the story of not only spatial embeddedness, governance arrangements, innovation ecosystems, and sustainability pathways.

Ultimately, this study contributes to the literature by demonstrating how the port-city-hinterland interface can become a space of co-created value, where digital innovation, multi-actor governance, and territorial proximity converge to support resilient and sustainable transformation.

3 Materials and Methods

3.1 The Case Study

This part details the case study of the Port of Trieste as a strategic and technological hub in the Mediterranean and the Trans-European Transport Network (TEN-T) with emphasis on sustainability, innovation, and intermodal freight logistics. Trieste is strategically located at the crossroads of Southern and Central Europe, acting as a critical gateway, linking maritime routes to inland logistics corridors through automation and PM (Fig. 1).

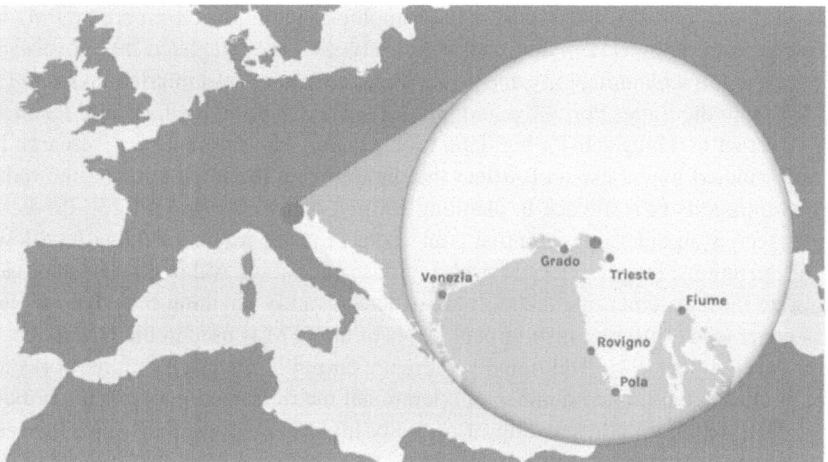

Fig. 1. Location of Trieste Port. Elaboration of authors on source www.yacht.de

The geographic and strategic advantages of Trieste strengthen its role as a key inter-modal logistics centre in the Mediterranean and the broader TEN-T. The port of Trieste handled 59,540,505 tons of merchandise, reflecting a 7.1% increase on the previous year that was driven by the increase of 10.6% of liquid bulk cargo measured at 41,261,754 tons. An increase of 1.8% in general cargo rose to 18,157,699 tons, and container activity generated 841,867 TEUs (-1.2%) – consisting of 608,327 full (4.0%) and 233,540 empty containers (-12.6%) – and with ro-ro activity that recorded the transit of 295,386 vehicles (-1.1%). Dry cargo declined by -72.7% to 121,052 tons, a decline – clarified the Shipping

Specialist of the Port System of the Eastern Adriatic Sea – which is attributable to the absence of activity in metallurgical products during the year, while cereals increased by 13.0% to 75,331 tons [27, 28]. Rail activity to and from the terminal was 11,147, with a decline of −9.9% attributable to the improvement of the networks (Austria, Germany, Czech Republic, Slovenia) and the inclement weather conditions throughout Central Europe that had a significant impact on overall rail activity.

The rail freight operations in the Trieste-Monfalcone corridor demonstrate the port's commitment to modal shift and decarbonisation targets, aligned with European environmental targets [22]. The underlying philosophy of the Trieste revitalisation is about technological innovation and digital logistics. One important initiative is the AUTOSUP project (Automated and Safe Multimodal Freight Transport), which receives co-funding under European programmes [15]. The AUTOSUP project intends to implement predictive diagnostics, digital twins, and real-time tracking, with the aim of transforming Trieste into an intelligent and automated freight hub, developing intermodal integration further, and ensuring the role of the Mediterranean in a more circular and sustainable logistics system (Fig. 2).

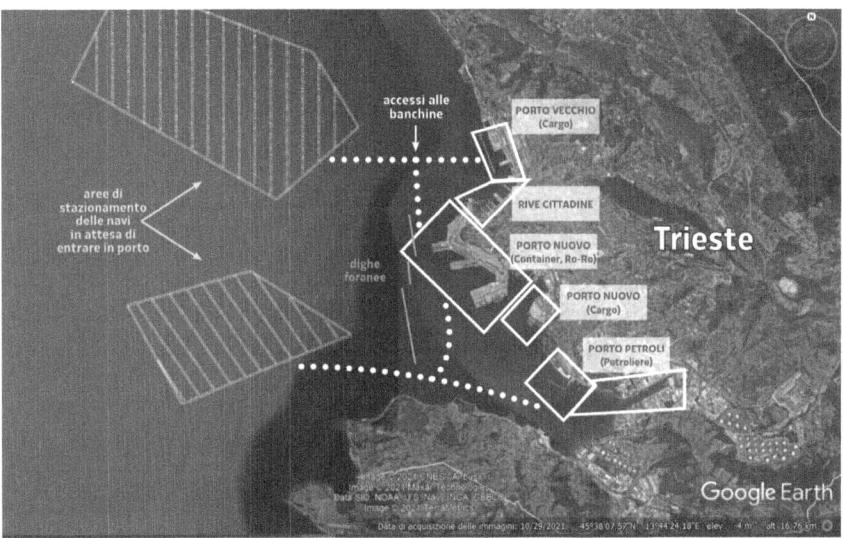

Fig. 2. Functional areas in the port of Trieste. Source: ARPA FVG.

A distinctive feature of AUTOSUP is its alignment with the Physical Internet (PI) paradigm. The Physical Internet is an emerging logistics model inspired by the data-based Internet. It envisions a hyperconnected, open, and modular system for freight transport, where goods are packaged in standardized, reusable containers—referred to as "π-containers" [29] and dynamically routed through shared, interconnected logistics networks using digital platforms, real-time data, and predictive analytics [30].

Through AUTOSUP, by utilising the PI, Trieste not only improves the efficiency and responsiveness of its freight system but also catalyses systemic change in European logistics—toward standardisation, decarbonisation, and interoperability across borders.

This support for the systemic change underscores Trieste's role as a model port in the use of Smart Port 4.0-style strategies, and to the EU's long-term vision of sustainable transport. As we have underscored, sustainability is built into the operating model for the Port of Trieste, which has pursued advanced technologies and circular economy principles towards efficiency and positive environmental performance. Building on that work and approach, Trieste now has a circular economy model tailored to the rail sector. The port systematically employs maintenance, reuse, and recycling practices via refurbishment programmes, whereby worn-out parts are either replaced or repurposed. This supports a lower demand for virgin raw material and helps to lower the port's overall environmental impacts. The application of lightweight components and fuel-efficient technologies also assist the performance of wagon fuel and these both can drive significant reduced CO_2 emissions.

Central to these achievements is a strong culture of stakeholder collaboration. Through the AUTOSUP project [15], Trieste is facilitating the technical standardization and regulatory harmonization necessary to support cross-border multimodal transport.

Beyond operational excellence, the geographical framework of Trieste is emerging as a true innovation leader within the port community. This holistic approach provides a replicable and scalable framework for other ports aiming to enhance rail integration, decarbonise logistics chains, and meet the EU's sustainability objectives. In both performance and governance, Trieste illustrates the transformative potential of forward-thinking port ecosystems in shaping the future of European freight transport [31].

3.2 Methodology: The SIIM Model

This research proposes and applies a place-based model of analysis for economic geography that investigates how local governance, institutional configurations and spatiality shape innovation in sea-logistics - specifically digitalisation and automation in port-rail systems. The Port of Trieste is the single case study and serves a useful context to explore and demonstrate the explanatory capacity of the model. The method is designed around the establishment of a Spatial-Institutional Innovation Model (SIIM) specifically tailored to analyse transport innovation in economic geography taking into account [32], which involves, 1) the spatial logic of transport geography; 2) the spatial logic; 3) the Institutional logic [33, 34]; and 4) the Sustainability reference [11, 12]. The model proposed here offers several strategies for researchers and practitioners within the governance-oriented lens of institutional analysis to develop a hybrid model to capture the multi-dimensionality of innovation in logistics hubs.

The model is structured along four key analytical dimensions "TIIC", as previously described, as shown in Fig. 3:

1. Territorial Embeddedness: this dimension analyses the strategic position of Trieste within the Mediterranean and TEN-T corridors, with attention to rail-port integration, hinterland access, and connectivity to Central Europe [11].
2. Institutional Architecture: drawing from the Institutional Analysis and Development (IAD) framework [33], this section investigates how local, national, and European governance structures interact to facilitate or constrain digital innovation. The AUTO-SUP project is examined as a regulatory and institutional experiment, highlighting

the coordination between port authorities [35], logistics operators, and EU policy instruments [11, 14, 18].

3. Innovation Ecosystem: this part evaluates how Trieste functions as a logistics innovation hub [36, 37], analysing the port's engagement with EU-funded projects, its adoption of digital twins, real-time monitoring, and the use of predictive diagnostics in collaboration with public and private stakeholders.
4. Circularity and Sustainability: the final dimension assesses how sustainability is embedded in port operations through a circular economy approach to rail assets, including maintenance, reuse, and material optimisation. In particular, the implementation of predictive maintenance technologies, based on IoT sensors, AI analytics, and digital twins, allows for condition-based interventions that reduce resource consumption, material waste, and CO_2 emissions—enhancing both efficiency and environmental performance [4, 22].

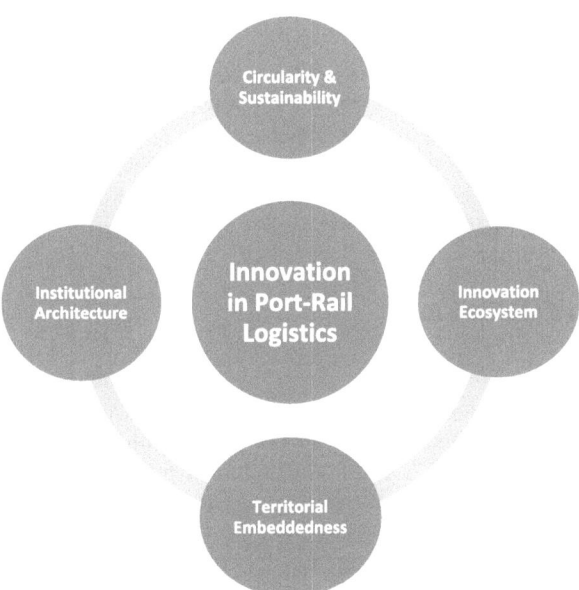

Fig. 3. Spatial-Institutional Innovation Model (SIIM) – Applied to Port of Trieste. Elaboration of authors.

Figure 3 depicts the port-territory integration in terms of innovation through the adoption of predictive maintenance for trains. The core block (Core Focus) is innovation in port-railway logistics (case study of Trieste) with the aim of implementing a more efficient model from the perspectives of governance, institutional context and spatial dynamics. At the same time, it requires attention to the new port reform that will be implemented shortly and that we will consider in the project Autosup. Surrounding it, we find the four pillar dimensions (TIIC) – represented in the immediate periphery of the core. Dimension No. 1) Spatial incorporation: it includes the location of the port of Trieste in the TEN-T and Mediterranean corridors and exploring the potential of the railway undertaking for predictive maintenance. It is worth reiterating that the goal is not solely to carry out predictive maintenance, but this action presents an opportunity to move forward on the Rail-Port Integration improving connectivity to Central Europe and increasing its strategic function in regional networks. Dimension 2. Institutional Architecture builds on Ostrom's [34] IAD framework for multi-level governance (local–EU). It provides a visual representation of the railway undertaking's role in the AUTOSUP project. This role acts as a coordinating platform, ensuring permanent alignment between policy, regulation, experimentation, and decision-making. Dimension 3) Innovation Ecosystem relates to Europe's managerial and financial challenges. It aims to create decision-support tools to finance the use of digital twins for real-time monitoring. It also seeks to increase public-private collaboration and to enable predictive diagnostics and data-driven decision making. Finally, dimension aspect 4) Circularity and Sustainability gives the ability to align innovation, land and some environment. PM and condition-based maintenance through IoT and AI supports reuse and optimisation of railway assets such as freight wagons, to reduce CO_2 emissions waste and resource usage and improve environmental performance. PM within the port of Trieste is explored through this prism as a single case study and is examined using both primary and secondary evidence, including institutional reports, project documentation (AUTOSUP), EU policy frameworks, and interviews with key authors undertaking during the opening phases of a project. Using this model when studying Trieste produced a technique for a replicated analysis of innovation within other port systems and added to a theoretical advancement of economic geography that is applied to transport and logistics.

4   Results and Discussions

Using the SIIM in the Port of Trieste shows the nature of transformation as a multi-dimensional event influenced by the territorial context, institutional configurations, technological innovations, and operating under the conditions of a circular economy, within the 4 dimensions – TIIC. The findings demonstrate how digitalisation – especially through predictive maintenance, real-time diagnostics – is affecting the operation itself as well as the governance in this strategic European logistics destination. The study findings are organised in Tables 1, 2 and 3, layered across three systems; indicating the connections between mutual territorial vulnerabilities, pertaining to the state of art in the territorial context; the logic for innovation; and systemic impacts, resting again within SIIM dimensions. Finally, Table 3 presents the systemic impacts.

The three tables representing the model proposed in this study are described in detail in the sub-sections that follow. Territorial Embeddedness: Trieste's singular geographic location along the Baltic-Adriatic TEN-T corridor, along with a strong rail connection to Central Europe, ensures the port is an important intermodal node. The incorporation of rail freight terminals, including the Trieste-Monfalcone location, additionally deepens the port's hinterland embeddedness. Overall, this spatial context supports the efficient movement of goods across the Alpine region, reduces congestion on the roadway, and contributes to European sustainability objectives. The results align with previous research on the relationship between spatial proximity [37] to industrial environments and the infrastructure planning process, as key features that framed the port's innovation

Table 1. Layer 1: Territorial Vulnerabilities (Drivers for Innovation). Elaboration of authors.

Dimension	Description	Innovation Need	References
Infrastructural Fragility	Ageing rail infrastructure, bottlenecks, low interoperability	Predictive maintenance, system monitoring	[12, 22]
Institutional Fragmentation	Overlapping competencies, regulatory misalignment	Blockchain governance, multi-actor coordination	[33]
Geographic Peripherality	Peripheral position in EU logistics, lower investment attractiveness	Strategic repositioning via rail corridor integration	[32]
Environmental Stress	Emissions, land use conflicts, lack of sustainability in planning	Circular economy, energy-efficient systems, environmental KPIs	[11, 34]

Table 2. Layer 2: Innovation Mechanisms (SIIM Dimensions). Elaboration of authors.

SIIM Dimension	Role in Addressing Vulnerabilities	Key Tools and Practices	References
Territorial Embeddedness	Enhances intermodal and hinterland connectivity, improves spatial integration	TEN-T rail integration, freight terminal optimisation	[2, 11, 32]
Institutional Architecture	Facilitates multi-level policy alignment, enables experimentation	AUTOSUP project, digital governance platforms, EU funding schemes	[22, 33]
Innovation Ecosystem	Creates a collaborative environment for technology adoption and adaptive learning	Predictive diagnostics, digital twins, partnerships with academia/industry	[1, 35]
Circularity & Sustainability	Embeds resource efficiency and environmental responsibility into infrastructure strategy	Circular asset management, energy-efficient materials, CO_2 reduction targets	[4, 11, 21]

pathway [38]. Institutional Architecture: Trieste's digital transition is enabled through a multi-level governance mechanism, whereby the Port Network Authority, regional government and EU institutions create an interconnected policy framework. The AUTOSUP project showcases how regulatory alignment and collaboration between stakeholders can expedite the adoption of advanced logistics enabled technologies. Innovation Ecosystem: the port of Trieste has evolved into a regional innovation ecosystem, leveraging new and established technologies. In addition to port infrastructure, technologies are being used

Table 3. Layer 3: Systemic Impacts (Outcomes for Ports and Territories). Elaboration of authors.

Impact Domain	Description	Long-Term Effects	References
Operational Resilience	Increased reliability and foresight of logistics systems	Reduced failures, adaptive infrastructure	[21]
Territorial Attractiveness	Improved competitiveness and capacity to attract innovation and investment	Repositioning in EU logistics, private sector engagement	[2, 38]
Regional-Hinterland Integration	Stronger spatial and functional links between port, city, and hinterland	Smoother modal integration, regional value creation	[35]
Sustainability Performance	Reduction of emissions, optimisation of resource use, better land stewardship	Contribution to European Green Deal targets	[4, 12, 21]
Innovation System Maturity	Institutional and cognitive capacity to innovate collaboratively	Knowledge transfer, learning platforms, replicability of solutions	[25, 39]

on rolling stock so operators can predict failures, lifecycles and down time. The results also show that while these technologies are more advanced at the operational level, their use in urban planning and regional development is lacking. Circularity and Sustainability: the investment in predictive maintenance has already produced results: maintenance costs have been reduced up to 30% and delays have been reduced in Spanish ports [16, 17]. Moreover, the European port in question has moved towards a circular economy for rail assets, with refurbishment and reuse of wagon components, reducing the requirement for raw materials, and extending the lifecycle of assets. Nonetheless, gaps remain in the full integration of digital sustainability practices into strategic planning. While the technologies are present, their use for environmental performance monitoring, energy optimisation, and carbon footprint reduction is still underexploited. Cross-Dimensional Insights: the case of Trieste underscores the interdependence between territorial proximity, institutional capacity, and technological innovation. The results confirm that predictive maintenance is not just a technical function but a governance and planning tool that can drive broader sustainability and resilience objectives—if embedded within coherent spatial and regulatory strategies.

4.1 Territorial Vulnerabilities and the Role of Innovation

The application of the SIIM model to the Port of Trieste also highlights a set of territorial vulnerabilities that digital innovation helps to address. These vulnerabilities emerge across multiple key factors as drivers/barriers [39]: 1) infrastructure fragility, 2) institutional fragmentation, 3) geographic peripherality, and 4) environmental stress, that are exposed as follows.

Infrastructural Vulnerability: Trieste's ageing rail infrastructure and the complexity of managing cross-border freight flows through the Alpine region expose the port to logistical bottlenecks and inefficiencies. Predictive maintenance directly addresses this vulnerability by anticipating failures, reducing downtime, and extending the lifecycle of critical assets. The shift from reactive to predictive models is especially valuable in contexts with limited redundancy and high throughput, ensuring resilience under strain [24].

Institutional Vulnerability: the fragmented governance landscape—characterised by overlapping competencies between regional, national, and EU institutions—creates risks of regulatory misalignment. Through the AUTOSUP project, Trieste has experimented with multi-actor digital governance, facilitating interoperability and reducing transaction costs in freight coordination [40].

Spatial and Economic Vulnerability: as a peripheral port in the European logistics hierarchy, Trieste faces challenges in competing with Northern Range ports and attracting long-term investments, and with the Spanish Barcelona port, running into smart posts [16, 17]. However, its strategic integration into the TEN-T Baltic-Adriatic Corridor and the deployment of smart technologies repositions the port as a value-added innovation hub, improving its connectivity and enhancing its economic resilience. By strengthening its role as a rail-integrated gateway, Trieste reduces its dependence on road transport and mitigates carbon-intensive vulnerabilities.

Environmental Vulnerability: port practices are often deployed in places that are more environmentally sensitive due to emissions, noise or land use issues. Predictive maintenance, energy-efficient rolling stock and circular asset management are approaches for improving the environment footprint of port logistics. Perspectives and Implications of SIIM Model: by acknowledging vulnerabilities, this study reaffirms the premise that technological innovations must be place-sensitive. In the case of Trieste, the digital transition is, in addition to a performance driver, a means of coping with territorial asymmetries, limits of infrastructure, and institutional complexity which reinforces the need for territorial specificity in innovation planning and development of technologies straited on the structural conditions of port systems. Moreover, it calls for innovation policies that are not just technology-driven, but informed by geographic-economic analysis, with the explicit goal of enhancing territorial resilience, functional equity, and sustainability in complex logistics ecosystems.

To represent the model and the vulnerability of the case study, the Fig. 4 describes the 3 levels of integration between port and territory through the innovation.

At the centre of the diagram are the key geographical vulnerabilities that generate limitations for the port-logistics system. These comprise the vulnerabilities of infrastructure (for instance, the ageing railway system is fragile and there is limited interoperability) and the vulnerable institutional environment resulting from governance fragmentation and misalignments in regulations. Vulnerabilities of geographical peripherality, meaning that the port plays a secondary role in comparison with the Northern Range ports, and environmental vulnerabilities, like emissions and land use pressures and impacts at a localised level, also constrain the opportunities for optimal development. The intermediate ring "applied solutions" illustrates the technological and organisational innovations

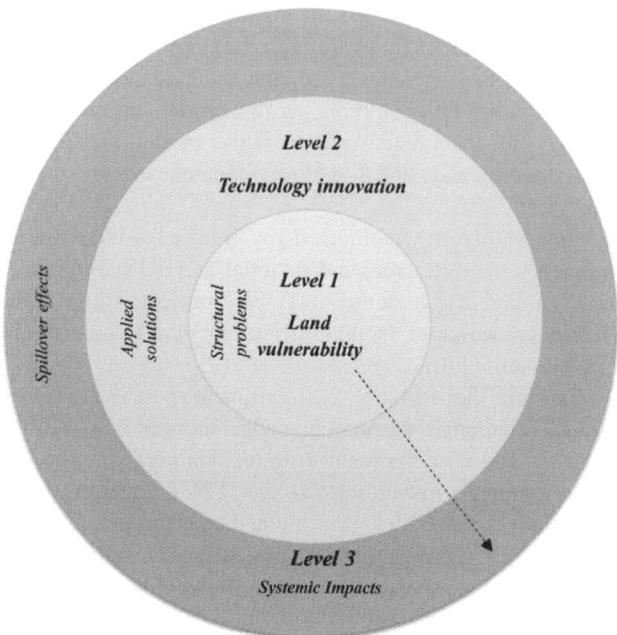

Fig. 4. Comprehensive Innovation-Resilience SIIM for the Port of Trieste. Elaboration of authors.

adopted to address these weaknesses. Predictive maintenance plays a central role in optimising asset performance and reducing system failures.

The outermost ring captures the systemic impacts generated by this innovation process, both for the port and the broader business ecosystem. Among these are improvements in operational resilience, with increased reliability and foresight in logistics operations. Trieste's growing economic attractiveness is reflected in its enhanced competitiveness and its ability to draw new investment. Territorial integration is promoted through better physical and functional linkages between the port, the city, and the hinterland. The model also reveals gains in sustainability and resource efficiency, with reductions in emissions and material consumption. Finally, the maturity of the innovation ecosystem is strengthened, positioning Trieste as a strategic node within the wider network of European smart ports.

4.2 Discussion and Further Implications

This research validates the notion that the Port of Trieste serves as an example of how innovation, especially predictive maintenance, digitalisation, and automation, can alter the relationships between infrastructure, governance, and territory. The authors use the SIIM to demonstrate technological and organisational transformation is addressing spatial and institutional vulnerabilities. The SIIM framework shows that, as demonstrated by Notteboom and Rodrigue [33], the analysis of Territorial Embeddedness can bolster the port's ability to support regional integration. The Institutional Architecture dimension of the SIIM framework corresponding to Ostrom's [34] Institutional Analysis and Development (IAD) framework and Multi-level Governance (MLG) theory, as well as literature review on innovation ecosystems [39] emphasising institutional proximity for learning and collaboration, suggests the port authority's evolving role as ecosystem orchestrator [40] is especially relevant in hinterland logistics and land-use planning. The Innovation Ecosystem explains that new technologies such as predictive maintenance are embedded within local contexts which supports not just efficiency but specifically knowledge-based transformation. Cognitive and organisational proximity [37] acts as facilitators of co-innovation, trust, and adjustment of global solutions to local needs. However, embedding them into a wider plan is still underdeveloped, reinforcing [35], where smart port initiatives are noted to remain within silos [41]. Thirdly, the Circularity and Sustainability in Trieste aims to support the implementation of circular asset management—refurbishment, lightweight materials, and emission reductions—while reaching European goals [11]. However, the sustainability indicators are still not fully integrated into the innovation strategy. Predictive maintenance systems are even underutilised in terms of energy use and lifecycle metrics, thereby undermining the ability to create transformative change. A key contribution of this research is to recast innovation away from merely a growth agenda to one of responding to territorial vulnerability. The SIIM model suggests a resilience-based approach, where adaptation of spatial, institutional, and infrastructure vulnerabilities are featured distinctly. In Trieste, digital governance and predictive maintenance can not only benefit performance, but also reduce risk elements of system failure, gaps in coordination, and disadvantaged seated peripheries.

The concentric model developed in this research visualises how technological innovation interacts with deeper territorial dynamics. It offers a transferable tool for identifying vulnerabilities, aligning innovation with planning, and assessing systemic impacts across other port cities—particularly in contexts facing similar challenges of fragmentation, peripherality, and sustainability pressure (Table 4).

Table 4. SIIM application in Trieste's port: summary Matrix. Elaboration of authors.

Challenge	Innovation Response	Observed/Expected Result
Rail congestion and asset ageing	Predictive maintenance + digital twins	Reduced downtime, extended asset life
Regulatory fragmentation	Blockchain + digital governance platforms	Increased transparency, lower coordination costs
Economic peripherality	TEN-T integration + innovation branding	Enhanced logistics role, investment attraction
Environmental pressure	Circular economy practices + low-carbon tech	Lower emissions, better resource stewardship

Table 4 summarize the proposed framework emphasising how the importance of proximity-based collaboration, as outlined by [37] is fundamental also to run PM and DTs.

Port authorities are evolving from infrastructure managers to ecosystem orchestrators, improving the value-creation in port areas [42], facilitating digital transformation, sustainability transitions, and alignment with planning and regulatory frameworks (UN, 2015). There is a need to broaden evaluation metrics beyond throughput, incorporating indicators of resilience, urban integration, and sustainability, in line with [4, 11, 12, 22].

The framework serves for further research in different strategies, according to the findings of [43] on technologies for railway network:

1. Diagnostic – Identifies vulnerabilities like spatial marginality and institutional misalignment.
2. Strategic – Guides the use of predictive maintenance and governance technologies.
3. Evaluative – Supports assessment of short-term outcomes and long-term territorial impacts.
4. Replicable – Applicable to other port systems, especially in peripheral or fragmented governance contexts.

This research adds to the literature on territorial innovations by meshing ideas from economic geography, transport, and planning (23, 26, 38) and provides a multi-level perspective on how digital technologies are transforming logistics, governance, and spatial relations. The RQ1 on the role of innovation in terms of technology supporting urban and territorial sustainability is explored based on predictive maintenance, digital twins, and circular asset management. These concepts can be linked to emissions reduction, energy efficiency, and prolonging the useful life of the asset within environmental goals and urban strategies. The RQ2 on the territorial implications of integrated freight and automation is further evidenced based on the case of Trieste. Coordination of transport in the public and private sectors undertaken within the Baltic-Adriatic corridor in the TEN-T better connects regional territory elements, enhancing cohesion through integrated freight transport. Examples such as AUTOSUP synergize rail behaviour and automated transport to reshape port-city-regional relations through partnership, multilevel governance.

5   Conclusions

This article on the port of Trieste is part of the innovation of predictive maintenance, PM. Starting from this technology being tested for the port of Trieste by the railway company, the aim is to analyse the process of the port as an economic-geographical-territorial context, as well as to provide indications on the analysis of potentialities and vulnerabilities for the implementation of technologies. Taking a cue from the AUTOSUP project, this study offers decision support and researchers on a different key that unifies different sectors [8]. The limitations are related to the early stage of this study in the design phase, and to the collection of indicators, which is only qualitative in this step of research. Authors aim to offer a development with quantitative indicators in the next steps.

Acknowledgments. Authors thank the partner Adriafer S.r.l. for the technical support of the AUTOSUP project.

CRediT Authorship Contribution Statement: Irina Di Ruocco (Sects. 1, 2, 3.2, 4): Writing – review & editing, Writing – original draft, Supervision, Resources, Methodology, Investigation, Formal analysis, Conceptualization. **Marco Mazzarino** (Sect. 1, 3.1, 4.2, 5): Writing, Visualisation, Supervision, Conceptualization, Resources.

Disclosure of Interests. n.t.d.

References

1. Braidotti, L., Mazzarino, M., Cociancich, M., Bucci, V.: On the automation of ports and logistics chains in the Adriatic region. In: Gervasi, O., et al. Computational Science and Its Applications – ICCSA 2020. ICCSA 2020. Lecture Notes in Computer Science, vol. 12255, pp. 96–111. Springer, Cham (2020). https://doi.org/10.1007/978-3-030-58820-5_8

2. Di Ruocco, I.: The waterfront of Salerno: from product of urban regeneration to diffuser of sustainable social equity. In: Tedesco, C., Marchigiani, E. (eds.) Partecipazione, inclusione e gestione dei conflitti nei processi di governo del territorio, Atti della XXV Conferenza Nazionale SIU, Cagliari, 15–16 giugno 2023, vol. 07, pp. 1–10. Planum Publisher, Roma–Milano (2024)

3. Di Ruocco, I., D'Auria, A.: The multidimensional impact of Special Economic Zones in Campania Region. The TIA tool for land economic evaluation. BDC Bollettino Del Centro Calza Bini **23**(1), 133–155 (2023). https://doi.org/10.6093/2284-4732/10480

4. Mazzarino, M., Braidotti, L., Borruso, G.: A review of best practices to reduce the environmental footprint of port areas in the Adriatic region. In: Proceedings of the 2021 21st International Conference on Computational Science and Its Applications (ICCSA), pp. 168–173. IEEE (2021). https://arts.units.it/retrieve/00304741-a564-42d2-b80b-0d3be30a8539/2021_ICCSA_Best%2BPractices%2BAdriatic%2BPorts-Post_print.pdf

5. Puig, M., Darbra, R.M.: Innovations and insights in environmental monitoring and assessment in port areas. Curr. Opin. Environ. Sustain. **70**, 101472 (2024). https://doi.org/10.1016/j.cosust.2024.101472

6. Tijan, E., Jović, M., Aksentijević, S., Pucihar, A.: Digital transformation in the maritime transport sector. Technol. Forecast. Soc. Change **170**, 120879 (2021). https://doi.org/10.1016/j.techfore.2021.120879

7. Moya, I., et al.: Freight wagon digitalization for condition monitoring and advanced operation. Sensors **23**(17), 7448 (2023). https://doi.org/10.3390/s23177448

8. Parola, F., Risitano, M., Ferretti, M., Panetti, E.: Digital transformation in maritime ports: the future of smart port ecosystems. Technol. Forecast. Soc. Change **170**, 120888 (2021). https://doi.org/10.3390/fi16100350

9. Kuakoski, H.S., Lermen, F.H., Graciano, P., Lam, J.S.L., Mazzuchetti, R.N.: Marketing, entrepreneurship, and innovation in port management: trends, barriers, and research agenda. Marit. Policy Manag. **51**(7), 1517–1534 (2024). https://doi.org/10.1080/03088839.2023.2180548

10. Bhattacharjee, A., Chakraborty, S.: Global supply chain networks: roles of global partnerships and governance in supply chain performance. In: Global Partnerships and Governance of Supply Chain Systems, pp. 189–222. IGI Global, Hershey (2025). https://doi.org/10.4018/979-8-3693-6987-6.ch007

11. European Commission: Ethics guidelines for trustworthy AI. https://op.europa.eu/en/public ation-detail/-/publication/d3988569-0434-11ea-8c1f-01aa75ed71a1. Accessed 30 Dec 2024

12. European Commission: The commission adopts the European sustainability reporting stan-dards. https://finance.ec.europa.eu/news/commission-adopts-european-sustainability-report ing-standards-2023-07-31_en. Accessed 3 Dec 2024

13. Durán, C.A., Córdova, F.M.: Synergy and technology gaps in export logistics chains between a Chilean and a Spanish medium-sized port. Procedia Comput. Sci. **55**, 632–641 (2015). https://doi.org/10.1016/j.procs.2015.07.055

14. Risitano, M., Panetti, E., Ferretti, M., Parmentola, A.: The port community system as a local innovation system: a theoretical framework. Mercati e Competitività **1**, 97–118 (2017). https://doi.org/10.3280/mc2017-001006

15. Autosup Project. https://www.autosup-project.eu/. Accessed 12 Dec 2024

16. Henríquez, R., de Osés, F.X.M., Marín, J.E.M.: Technological drivers of seaports' business model innovation: an exploratory case study on the Port of Barcelona. Res. Transp. Bus. Manag. **43**, 100803 (2022). https://doi.org/10.1016/j.rtbm.2022.100803

17. Henríquez, R., Xavier Martínez de Osés, F., Martínez Marín, J.E.: IoT-driven business model innovation. In: Chao, K.M., Jiang, L., Hussain, O., Ma, S.P., Fei, X. (eds.) Advances in E-Business Engineering for Ubiquitous Computing. ICEBE 2019. Lecture Notes on Data Engi-neering and Communications Technologies, vol. 41, pp. 302–314. Springer, Cham (2020). https://doi.org/10.1007/978-3-030-34986-8_22

18. United Nations: Transforming our world: the 2030 agenda for sustainable devel-opment. https://sustainabledevelopment.un.org/content/documents/21252030%20Agenda%20for%20Sustainable%20Development%20web.pdf. Accessed 30 Dec 2024

19. Caldwell, S.: Empirical decision-making tools as applied to seaports in the industry 4.0 paradigm. Doctoral dissertation, Liverpool John Moores University (2024). https://researcho nline.ljmu.ac.uk/id/eprint/24910

20. Brümmerstedt, K., Beek, M.V., Münsterberg, T.: Comparative analysis of synchromodality in major European seaports. In: Kersten, W., et al. (eds.) Digitalization in Maritime and Sustainable Logistics, HICL, vol. 24, pp. 59–76. epubli GmbH, Berlin (2017). https://hdl.han dle.net/10419/209326

21. Kringelum, L.T.B.: Reviewing the challenges of port authority business model innovation. World Rev. Intermodal Transp. Res. **8**(3), 265–291 (2019). https://doi.org/10.1504/WRITR.2019.102371

22. Acciaro, M., Sys, C.: Innovation in the maritime sector: aligning strategy with outcomes. Marit. Policy Manag. **47**(8), 1045–1063 (2020). https://doi.org/10.1080/03088839.2020.173 7335

23. Zong, Z., Guan, Y.: AI-driven intelligent data analytics and predictive analysis in Industry 4.0: transforming knowledge, innovation, and efficiency. J. Knowl. Econ., 1–40 (2024). https://doi.org/10.1007/s13132-024-02001-z

24. Shaikh, M.Z., et al.: State-of-the-art wayside condition monitoring systems for railway wheels: a comprehensive review. IEEE Access **11**, 13257–13279 (2023). https://doi.org/10.1109/ACCESS.2023.3240167

25. Neffke, F., Henning, M., Boschma, R.: How do regions diversify over time? Industry relat-edness and the development of new growth paths in regions. Econ. Geogr. **87**(3), 237–265 (2011). https://doi.org/10.1111/j.1944-8287.2011.01121.x

26. Infomare: Traffico porto Trieste. https://www.informare.it/news/gennews/2025/20250154-porto-Trieste-traffico-Y-2024.asp. Accessed 27 Mar 2025

27. Port System Authority of the Eastern Adriatic Sea: Port network authority of the Eastern Adri-atic Sea – Port of Trieste. https://ipcsa.international/about/members/members-europe-and-north-america/port-network-authority-of-the-eastern-adriatic-sea-port-of-trieste/. Accessed 27 Mar 2025

28. Charpentier, P., Chaxel, F., Krommenacker, N., Bombardier, V., Seguel, F.: Pervasive digital twin for pi-containers: a new packing problem. Sensors **21**(23), 7999 (2021). https://doi.org/10.3390/s21237999

29. Montreuil, B., Meller, R.D., Ballot, E.: Physical internet foundations. In: Borangiu, T., Thomas, A., Trentesaux, D. (eds.) Service Orientation in Holonic and Multi Agent Manufacturing and Robotics. Studies in Computational Intelligence, vol. 472, pp. 151–166. Springer, Heidelberg (2013). https://doi.org/10.1007/978-3-642-35852-4_10

30. ITF: Information sharing for efficient maritime logistics. https://www.itf-oecd.org/sites/default/files/docs/information-sharing-maritime-logistics.pdf. Accessed 6 Jan 2025

31. Moulaert, F., Sekia, F.: Territorial innovation models: a critical survey. Reg. Stud. **37**(3), 289–302 (2003). https://doi.org/10.1080/0034340032000065442

32. Notteboom, T., Rodrigue, J.-P.: Maritime container terminal infrastructure, network corporatization, and global terminal operators: implications for international business policy. J. Int. Bus. Policy (2022). https://doi.org/10.1057/s42214-022-00142-z

33. Ostrom, E.: Understanding Institutional Diversity. Princeton University Press, Princeton (2005)

34. Cahoon, S., Pateman, H., Chen, S.L.: Regional port authorities: leading players in innovation networks? J. Transp. Geogr. **27**, 66–75 (2013). https://doi.org/10.1016/j.jtrangeo.2012.06.015

35. Witte, P., Slack, B., Keesman, M., Jugie, J.H., Wiegmans, B.: Facilitating start-ups in port-city innovation ecosystems: a case study of Montreal and Rotterdam. J. Transp. Geogr. **71**, 224–234 (2018). https://doi.org/10.1016/j.jtrangeo.2017.03.006

36. Boschma, R.: Proximity and innovation: a critical assessment. Reg. Stud. **39**(1), 61–74 (2005). https://doi.org/10.1080/0034340052000320887

37. Notteboom, T., Rodrigue, J.P.: Containerisation, box logistics and global supply chains: the integration of ports and liner shipping networks. Marit. Econ. Logist. **10**, 152–174 (2008). https://doi.org/10.1057/palgrave.mel.9100196

38. Stam, F.C.: Why butterflies don't leave; locational evolution of evolving enterprises (2003). https://doi.org/10.1111/j.1944-8287.2007.tb00332.x

39. Permala, A., Rantasila, K., Porthin, M., Hinkka, V., Eckhardt, J., Leonardi, J.: Multi-criteria evaluation method for freight logistics innovations. IET Intell. Transp. Syst. **9**(6), 662–669 (2015). https://doi.org/10.1049/iet-its.2014.0187

40. Pagano, P., Antonelli, S., Tardo, A.: C-Ports: A proposal for a comprehensive standardization and implementation plan of digital services offered by the "Port of the Future." Comput. Ind. **134**, 103556 (2022). https://doi.org/10.1016/j.compind.2021.103556

41. De Martino, M.: Value creation for sustainability in port: perspectives of analysis and future research directions. Sustainability **13**(21), 12268 (2021). https://doi.org/10.3390/su132112268

42. Kundu, P., Darpe, A.K., Singh, S.P., Gupta, K.: A review on condition monitoring technologies for railway rolling stock. In: Proceedings of the PHM Society European Conference, Philadelphia, PA, USA, 24–27 September 2018. https://doi.org/10.36001/phme.2018.v4i1.250

43. dos Santos, M.C., Pereira, F.H.: Development and application of a dynamic model for road port access and its impacts on port-city relationship indicators. J. Transp. Geogr.Geogr. **96**, 103189 (2021). https://doi.org/10.1016/j.jtrangeo.2021.103189

Review of the Climate Change Resilience Measures in Port Context

Federica Pisano[1,3] and Andrea Gallo[1,2(✉)]

[1] University Ca' Foscari of Venice, 3246, 30124 Dorsoduro, Venezia, Italy
andrea.gallo3@phd.units.it
[2] University of Trieste, Via A.Valerio 4/1, 34127 Trieste (TS), Italy
[3] UNEP United Nations Environment Programme, Platz der Vereinten Nationen 1, 53113 Bonn, Germany

Abstract. Ports are one of the least sustainable places in the world. Port operations' negative externalities contribute significantly to global warming, representing a threat especially to human and animal communities living nearby. Simultaneously, ports, alongside coastal areas, are starting to be seriously affected by climate change hazards, with numerous environmental and economic implications. This paper investigates different climate change resilience strategies to be implemented in the port context, arguing for the importance of such action beings ports the direct stakeholders of climate change from both sides of the same coin. Through a comprehensive and organic approach, it analyses five different lines of action aimed at reducing the negative externalities of port's operations, enhancing port's climate resilience and protecting the surrounding environment: adaptation, mitigation, soft measures, nature-based solutions and digitalization. Finally, it explores the case study of the port of Rotterdam, an excellent example of a committed port in terms of climate resilience, ultimately demonstrating the efficiency and validity of a holistic approach to climate change resilience in the port context in terms of emissions reduction and environment resilience.

Keywords: Port Development · Sustainable Ports · Climate Change

1 Introduction

This paper aims to study in a conjunctural manner the variety of measures aimed at climate change resilience to be implemented in the port context, arguing for the importance of the role of ports in climate change resilience development, being the directs stakeholders of climate change both as contributors and as victims [1].

In fact, ports can be described as one of the least sustainable places in the world from two perspectives. On one hand, ports contribute to climate change in terms of global warming through negative port externalities, which refer to shipping activities in port, to activities on the port land, and to the hinterland transport to and from the port. In fact, ports contribute to global warming through the emission of greenhouse gas emissions, as well as through Common Air Contaminants (CACs) [2, 3]. Although maritime transport is considered one of the most efficient and clean modes of transport in terms of emissions per unit of cargo carried, even if this data considers the whole maritime transport emissions, the majority of negative impacts occur at port level, given the location of the majority of ports in urban areas (90% in Europe), particularly affecting human and animal communities living nearby port terminals [4]. In addition, other negative impacts of ports include water and soil pollution, toxic waste deriving from oil spills and leakages, and dredging, resulting in the degradation of natural environment and harm on the local biodiversity [5]. Moreover, ports are the cause also of problems related to noise, light, traffic, odor, dust, as well as social and security issues and land-use conflicts, ultimately being detrimental to human and animal health physically and psychologically [6].

On the other hand, ports, alongside coastal areas, are starting to be seriously affected by climate change hazards, resulting in numerous environmental implications and significant economic losses for the sector [4]. Being located in coastal areas, as well as in low-lying estuaries and deltas, ports are particularly exposed to climate change hazards, leading them to be frequently affected by sea level rise, floods, increased frequency and intensity of storm surges, winds and waves, riverine and pluvial flooding, extreme temperature and precipitation variability, drought, heat waves, land erosion and degradation, and ocean acidification [7]. This results in damages of sea, road and rail infrastructure and equipment, poor visibility, decreased maneuverability of locks and vessels, ship-to-ship accidents and limited traffic, ultimately leading to operational disruptions and delays across global supply chains with extensive economic and trade-related losses [8].

Based on a review of the state of the art, this paper investigates the existing and potential climate resilience measures to be implemented in the port context, through a holistic analysis considering five different levels of analysis: adaptation, mitigation, soft measures, nature-based solutions and digitalization. In particular, the second paragraph explains the data and methods through which the analysis had been conducted; in the third section will be presented the case study of the port of Rotterdam; in the fourth will investigates the main results of the research and, finally, in the fifth paragraph the conclusions will be carried out.

2   Data and Methods

In order to conduct the research, different resilience strategies have been considered as data. In particular, they can be categorised as follows: adaptation; mitigation; soft measures; nature-based solutions; and the role of digitalisation. These strategies act on the two aspects of ports' sustainability: on one hand, on the reduction of ports' negative externalities, and on the other, on the enhancement of ports' infrastructure resilience against climate change threats [9, 10]. Moreover, they also contribute to the protection of the natural environment surrounding the port area, ultimately enhancing environmental resilience in a comprehensive way [11]. Finally, it is worth noting that even if the classification utilised for the purpose of the research differentiates between various areas of intervention of port resilience, they may overlap in some aspects [12, 13]. In order to outline the main climate change mitigation and adaptation strategies in the port context, the methodology schematically represented in Fig. 1 was implemented (Fig. 1). The conceptual framework developed above identifies the main five macro-categories of intervention, which are further articulated, gradually narrowing the focus, particularly with regard to mitigation measures, which are in turn articulated, with reference to the energy transition in five different sub-categories: fuel switch, electrification, wind and solar energy, carbon capture, utilisation and storage and modal shift. All these aspects will be presented in detail in the following sections and then considered and integrated holistically into the case study.

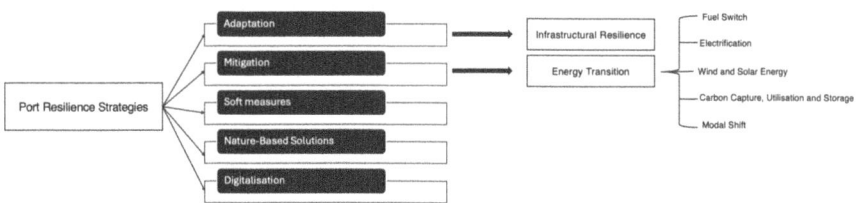

Fig. 1. Schematic representation of the methodology applied. Authors' elaboration.

2.1 Adaptation – Infrastructural Resilience

Climate change resilience in the port context means first and foremost adaptation. The concept of adaptation revolves around the one of vulnerability: it refers to measures aimed at the reduction and minimisation of climate change consequences, through their prevention. It is considered a more passive response: it acts on the effects of climate change adjusting natural and human ecosystems to moderate the negative outcomes [14, 15]. In general, it refers to large-scale infrastructure changes and behavioural shifts, such as water management, coastal defence, sustainable land use planning, green infrastructure, disaster risk management and warning systems, and eventually relocation and resettlement [16].

In the port context adaptation translates mainly into infrastructure resilience: the enhancement of the resilience of existing coastal transport infrastructure and/or the construction of new infrastructure. In the first context, it refers to prevention and mitigation of hydrogeological risk, through the construction of defence infrastructure and water management, as well as building energy saving and streamlining, whereas, the latter refers to the design of new infrastructure and the relocation of existing one in the worst case scenario [17]. The most widespread initiatives refer to the flood proofing of existing infrastructure, given the projected increase in sea level rise along coastlines, including the collection and drainage of water [7, 18]; storm water pumps and culverts; design upgrades as the elevation of structures and port lands above flood levels, for instance docks and roads raising; and hard defence elements such as construction of flood barriers, dykes and breakwater walls [12, 19].

In the worst-case scenario, however, the prevention of hydrogeological instability can also mean retreat from high-risk areas. This entails the relocation of buildings and services, such as terminal, buildings and productive systems delocalisation or eventually the whole port relocation on new port sites [20]. At present, there are no examples yet of relocation of ports for climate change-induced impacts, however, there are some examples of ports that relocated due to land use problems and conflict of interests with the urban area due to urbanisation expansion and few opportunity costs, which as saw in the previous paragraph, can be also included in negative port impacts. This is the case of the ports of Busan, Shanghai, Rio de Janeiro, Marseille, Kolkata and Bremen [21, 22].

2.2 Mitigation – Energy Transition

Mitigation is considered the most classical and widespread approach to combat climate change: while adaptation is a temporary solution, mitigation represents the only long-term solution to save the planet [23, 24]. If adaptation focuses on the effects of climate change, mitigation acts on the causes: it aims at the reduction of the greenhouse effect through the implementation of human-made measures finalised at the reduction of the sources of these gases or by the enhancement of their storage [25]. These measures imply long-term strategies aimed at net zero emissions to limit human-caused global warming and they include the transitioning from fossil fuels to very low- or zero-carbon energy sources, widespread electrification, approaches of carbon capture removal, energy generation diversification and green energy supply sector, and modal shifts [23, 26].

Fuel Switch

The most ambitious energy transition element is the switch from fossil fuels to clean fuels in the maritime transport. Among the low-emission ones we identify especially Liquified Natural Gas (LNG), hydrogen, ammonia, and biofuels [27, 28].

Firstly, LNG is a consolidated and available technology particularly useful for the reduction of sulphur content in fuels, however its GHG reduction is still questionable, and it faces storage challenges and security issues. Secondly, hydrogen represents one of the most promising clean solutions, however only when "green", that is, produced solely with the use of renewable energy [29]. Thirdly, renewable ammonia represents another most auspicious solution, given its stockage and transport ease, however, its main challenge is represented by its toxicity leading it to be currently banned by the International Code of Safety for Ships using Gases or other Low-flashpoint Fuels [28]. Finally, biofuels represent an innovative solution for transforming waste to energy, however they still face technology and industry immaturity [30, 31]. Nevertheless, although the majority of these technologies are still limited, unexplored, or too expensive, unsafe or with a marginal impact, their widespread experimentation is expected to grow, prompting future innovation and technologies, ultimately leading to a significant oil demand decrease by 2050 [32, 33].

Electrification

Electrification in the port context represents another important cost-effective strategy able to reduce emissions of port and cargo-handling operations.

On the one hand electrification refers to the adjustment or replacement of existing diesel port equipment with electric machines, that applies to vehicles, to land-side terminal or cargo handling equipment such as terminal tractors and mobile harbour cranes, and to some extent to vessels, resulting in fully electric solutions or hybrid diesel solutions [34, 35]. The use of batteries for electric naval engines is still experimental and faces problems of resilience, velocity and distance, however they are projected to reach a fast development, also in the light of already existing cases of electric vessels around the world [36].

On the other hand, electrification implies the use of the technology of the "cold ironing", otherwise called On Shore Power Supply (OPS), referring to the possibility to provide electricity connection to docked ships while berthed and during overnight stay, as an alternative to the use of power to keep ship services and functioning available. Its benefits include the reduction of pollution and emissions from ships in the port, mainly small vessels, cruises and container, improvement of air quality and noise mitigation [37]. Despite requiring huge economic investments, it represents an available and technologically mature solution, which is already a reality in numerous ports, especially in Europe, with Helsingborg, Gothenburg, and Venice as leaders [38].

Wind and solar energy

Among renewable energy, wind and solar energy (and to a less extent wave and tidal energy) are the most widespread renewable energy sources produced within port areas in the context of the decarbonisation effort [39, 40].

On one hand, as an on-site power, it is used to power port office buildings, sheds, workshops, surrounding buildings, port equipment and vehicles, and in some cases OPS.

On the other hand, offshore wind and solar energy is projected to become one of the fastest-growing renewable energy markets, through the transmission of electricity to public grids with an onshore substation. Its challenges include availability of land, landscape integration and ecology, limited funding, and overcapacity [41, 42].

Carbon Capture, Utilisation and Storage (CCUS)

Carbon capture, utilisation and storage technologies can be used to capture CO_2 for objectives of use or storage underground, in order to reduce or permanently remove CO_2 emissions from industrial activity and energy generation (such as blue hydrogen). As regards the capture of the CO_2, it is compressed, chilled, and transported mainly through pipelines to an offshore storage site. Whereas, in the case of the utilisation, it is reused in other production cycles which reduce its concentration in the atmosphere, such as in industrial, synthetic fuels, chemical and building materials productions [43]. Despite representing a temporary solution, it is one of the few technologies able to tackle emissions from heavy or energy-intensive industries, including those in the surrounding port areas, and is expected to play an important role in the energy transition especially as concerns hydrogen production [44].

Modal Shift

Finally, modal shifts constitute another method that port authorities and transport agencies can employ aiming at reducing emission related to the maritime transport. In particular, emissions generated by rail transport account for a third of those generated by road, therefore ports are encouraging shifts from road transport to rail one in the hinterland area [45]. Moreover, it is also effective in reducing port-related traffic congestion, especially the truck-related one, as well as creating green corridors between ports and major rail nodes [46, 47].

Another efficient shift, apart from rail transport, is towards water, such as by inland waterways, pipelines and short sea shipping. An effective way to reach the modal shift is through tax, subsidies, and incentives schemes, however, not all ports are well connected to railway lines and systems of inland waterways, with the Northern Range ports being the most developed in this sense [48].

2.3 Soft Measures

In addition to infrastructure resilience and the energy transition, other complementary measures can contribute to the reduction of port emissions and the containment of its external negative impacts, the so-called soft measures. While hard measures include capital-intensive, large, complex, inflexible technology and infrastructure, soft measures require natural capital, community control, simplicity and appropriateness.

In the port context they refer especially to port incentives for some ships behaviours. These include encouraging the reduction of steaming speeds through the use of velocity indexes; rewards or lower ports dues, taxes and fees based on the environmental performance of ships; the delivery of training programs to raise awareness on sustainability; old truck retirement programmes and reduction of turnaround time; the promotion of services such as antifouling treatments, hull cleaning and propeller polishing to prevent organic or inorganic deposits to cause friction, and of ballast water management to reduce hull stress.

Moreover, as regards the reducing of external negative effects of harbour activities, soft measures include wastewater management through the creation of wastewater reception facilities; strategies to cope with sewage, sludges and oil spills; solid waste management; marine debris reduction; and circular economy measures. While as regards the reduction of social impacts caused by port activities they act on the reduction of port and shipping noise through noise impact assessments, engine silencers, port layout and design change, insulation of buildings, buffer zones; as well as land use mitigation through alignment of port and city land use plans, and the reduction of traffic congestion.

2.4 Nature-Based Solutions

Nature-based solutions are multifunctional measures that can be categorised in between adaptation and mitigation. They refer to solutions provided by nature itself, devoted to the conservation, the protection, the restoration and the management of the Earth's ecosystems in order to reduce its climate vulnerability, ultimately protecting and creating benefits for human and animal communities living in them [2, 50].

They include forest conservation, wetland restoration, biochar burial, peatland conservation, soil conservation, green roofs and walls, urban open spaces, forests, community gardens and wind breaks, improved plantation, cropland management, grassland restoration, agroforestry, and river management. In the port context flood risk reduction and coastal management are relevant, translating into natural dunes creation, beach nourishment, oyster beds, salt marshes, restoration of floodplains and tidal wetland, and rainwater capture [51, 52].

2.5 Digitalisation of the Processes

Finally, the digitalisation of port activities and services can be also included in the aspects of sustainability in ports. Smart ports or ports 4.0 are ports that prioritise digital innovation in the context of automation, sustainable development and collaboration, utilising interface technologies, such as IoT and visualisation [53]; network technologies, such as cloud, blockchain and cybersecurity; and data processing technologies to support decision-making, such as big data, machine learning and simulation [54, 55].

It the port context the following measures are significant in terms of climate change resilience: the provision of forecasting and warning systems against climate hazards, especially flood-related; land and sea traffic optimisation and monitoring; logistic chain optimisation and predictability; facilitation of shipping virtual arrival; container terminal automation and operation systems; port community systems to share information; drones to identify leakages and pollution; digital twins and virtual prototypes; and prevision of ship behaviour, efficiency and performance. This results in improved terminal operations efficiency, more fluent hinterland and seaside traffic, reduction of ships path and time, errors and risk reduction, ultimately leading to a reduction of energy use and therefore of air emissions [56].

Finally, despite challenges in terms of lack of standardisation, cultural barriers, and inadequate infrastructure, this process demonstrated that ports are becoming places where information circulates and is generated, ultimately characterising ports apart from as logistic hubs and energy hubs, also as information and data hubs [57, 58].

3 Application of the Climate Change Resilience Measure: The Case of Rotterdam

This research demonstrates the effectiveness and validity of the implementation of a holist approach to enhance port's sustainability aspects. In particular, it shows how the implementation of five different climate change resilience strategies – adaptation, mitigation, soft measures, nature-based solutions, and the role of digitalisation – succeed in reducing port's negative externalities, in enhancing port's climate change resilience and in protecting the environment. Firstly, adaptation measures provide for strategies aimed at protecting the existing infrastructure and at maximising their resilience power especially towards flooding events. Secondly, mitigation measures are able to reduce considerably greenhouse gas emissions produced by port operations inshore and offshore, and allow for the exploitation of renewable energy. Thirdly, it highlights also the role of complementary measures in the path towards ports' climate resilience. In fact, soft measures improve the relationship between the port and the community by reducing externalities such as noise and light pollution, ultimately complementing mitigation measures in the light of the decarbonisation process. Additionally, nature-based solutions protect and improve the surrounding environment also creating recreational opportunities. Finally, the implementation of digitalisation in ports allows for an enhanced logistic efficiency and optimisation. The results of this comprehensive approach are particularly visible as regards the case study of the port of Rotterdam. This port is an outstanding example of a committed port in terms of climate resilience, characterising as the "greenest" port in the world for its effort in reducing greenhouse gas emissions and improving flood resilience [59–61]. In particular, as regards adaptation it excels in terms of adaptation to sea level rise through flood risk management systems, among which the Maeslant barrier constitutes a world primacy. Moreover, as regards mitigation, it is notable for the production and utilisation of alternative fuels, with special reference to the hydrogen industry and to the technology of the cold ironing, as well as to carbon capture systems, ultimately making the port a world leader in their supply chain [62, 63]. Finally, the use of a circular economy approach, the reduction of noise pollution, the promotion of sustainable shipping awards, as well as the protection of natural areas and biodiversity and the use of digital platforms for transport efficiency contribute to the ports' path towards transport and operations sustainability. As a result, it is highly probable that the port of Rotterdam will reach its climate neutrality objective by 2050, constituting a world example on climate resilience commitment and success [64, 65].

4   Results and Discussion

This research demonstrates the effectiveness and validity of the implementation of a holist approach to enhance port's sustainability aspects. In particular, it shows how the implementation of five different climate change resilience strategies – adaptation, mitigation, soft measures, nature-based solutions, and the role of digitalisation – succeed in reducing port's negative externalities, in enhancing port's climate change resilience and in protecting the environment. Firstly, adaptation measures provide for strategies aimed at protecting the existing infrastructure and at maximising their resilience power especially towards flooding events [12, 41]. Secondly, mitigation measures are able to reduce considerably greenhouse gas emissions produced by port operations inshore and offshore, and allow for the exploitation of renewable energy. Thirdly, it highlights also the role of complementary measures in the path towards ports' climate resilience. In fact, soft measures improve the relationship between the port and the community by reducing externalities such as noise and light pollution, ultimately complementing mitigation measures in the light of the decarbonisation process. Additionally, nature-based solutions protect and improve the surrounding environment also creating recreational opportunities. Finally, the implementation of digitalisation in ports allows for an enhanced logistic efficiency and optimisation [18].

The results of this comprehensive approach are particularly visible as regards the case study of the port of Rotterdam. This port is an outstanding example of a committed port in terms of climate resilience, characterising as the "greenest" port in the world for its effort in reducing greenhouse gas emissions and improving flood resilience. In particular, as regards adaptation it excels in terms of adaptation to sea level rise through flood risk management systems, among which the Maeslant barrier constitutes a world primacy. Moreover, as regards mitigation, it is notable for the production and utilisation of alternative fuels, with special reference to the hydrogen industry and to the technology of the cold ironing, as well as to carbon capture systems, ultimately making the port a world leader in their supply chain [60, 64]. Finally, the use of a circular economy approach, the reduction of noise pollution, the promotion of sustainable shipping awards, as well as the protection of natural areas and biodiversity and the use of digital platforms for transport efficiency contribute to the ports' path towards transport and operations sustainability. As a result, it is highly probable that the port of Rotterdam will reach its climate neutrality objective by 2050, constituting a world example on climate resilience commitment and success [62].

As the analysis showed, ports and sustainability represent an oxymoron, yet, it is precisely for their involvement as direct stakeholders of climate change, that it is crucial to act on port climate resilience. The case study demonstrates how the implementation of a wide range of climate resilience strategies in the port context are able to counter climate change consequences both from as contributors and as victims. As a result, it is deemed necessary the implementation of climate resilience polities in the port context aimed at reducing their negative externalities and enhancing their climate resilience [3, 41].

Despite the premature and pioneering concept of port sustainability and the difficulty of translating these objectives into laws, given the "creeping" nature of the climate crisis - for which the prediction of its consequences is difficult and requires long-term plans - numerous initiatives can be found at international, European and national levels. In this context the following initiatives are relevant: the effort of the United Nations Convention on the Law of the Sea on the reduction of pollution from ships and of the International Maritime Organization on emission reduction and energy efficiency targets; the European Union "Fit for 55" Package on energy efficiency, diversification and independence, carbon dioxide management mechanisms, waste management, power supply, nature restoration and intermodality; and the Italian National Recovery and Resilience Plan on energy transition, digitalisation, and sustainability and the National Climate Change Adaptation Plan on adaptation [14].

Worldwide, the ports that choose to prioritise environmental conservation and sustainability are increasing. In particular, the endorsement of sustainability in the port and maritime transport context is prompting the experimentation and development of new technologies, including engineering, technological and chemical ones, contributing significantly to the reduction of negative externalities, especially as regards greenhouse gases, ultimately enhancing the local and the world quality of life. Not only major world ports, such as Shanghai, Rotterdam and Los Angeles, but also medium and minor ports are moving towards this direction, such as ports like Genoa, Venice and Barcelona. The most common measures implemented in these contexts are related to energy efficiency, electrification, the development of renewable energy, digitalisation and automation, and to a smaller extent the protection of the natural environment [54].

However, the majority of national and local polices are still usually confined to the provision of general guidelines and mostly limited to mitigation strategies. In fact, a strong disproportion can be identified as regards the implementation of adaptation measures compared to mitigation measures. If the latter are widespread, the former are a reality only in few cases, such as Rotterdam, that is where climate change hazards, especially sea level rise, have already started to be a threat to the economic performance of the port, along with the surrounding community survival [13, 53]. This confirms the tendence of national and local governance of waiting until climate change consequences become evident and problematic in order to act, as opposed to international guidelines on adaptation measures implementation [18].

Moreover, even if the majority of port authorities are moving towards this complex direction, it can be noted that they are moving at remarkably different paths. In particular, it can be highlighted Italian ports' embryonic sustainable development, despite sectorial excellences such as Genoa's cold ironing and Venice's flooding prevention mechanisms, as opposed to European and international ports, for which sustainable evolution is already established [34].

Finally, although ports are experimenting innovation patters, few of them are implementing a comprehensive approach to climate change resilience, concentrating instead on one or few strategies based on their sustainability priorities [2, 48].

5   Conclusions

This research aimed to discuss the present and future role of ports in the development of climate change resilience from a global and local perspective.

The analysis acknowledges the fact that an increasing number of ports is committing to climate resilience, experimenting various innovation patterns, especially regarding mitigation ones, given their immediate benefits as concerns global warming and the enhancement of air quality. In particular, the most explored mitigation technologies at present are related to energy efficiency and the pursuit of the energy transition, with the main actors being the evolution of cold ironing, the general infrastructure and services electrification, and the experimentation of onshore and offshore renewable energies and low-emission fuels as alternatives to fossil fuels, with the most promising being LNG and hydrogen technologies. It must not be neglected also ports' endeavour in achieving the digitalisation transition, with a special focus on vehicles automation, and the widespread effort in enhancing port intermodality, especially rail one. Whereas as regards adaptation strategies, notwithstanding minor cases, the most common ones regard the elevation and the floodproofing of infrastructure. Finally, a notable number of ports demonstrates special attention to environmental protection and natural preservation, through various nature-based solutions related to marine and coastal ecosystems, as well as particular care as concerns the reduction of negative port externalities, especially noise and air pollution.

Despite the existing obstacles and complications, the research concludes that the enormous technological effort undertaken by ports in terms of climate resilience and vulnerability suggests an optimistic future view. In fact, innovation in ports can act as a developer of technological advances for minor ports, as well as driver of the evolution of fields such as engineering, computer science, chemistry as well as biology and social sciences. Moreover, the embracement of sustainability practices in ports determines an increase in their economic and geopolitical competitivity, with the possibility of revival of smaller and less competitive port areas. In this context, for example, the development of sustainable technologies by Italian ports could contribute to the retaliation of their position with respect to European ones, ultimately reducing the systemic gap between Mediterranean and Northern European ports. In particular, renewable energy development as well as GNL endorsement could place Italian ports in a favourable condition as regards their production and supply, expanding their range of action from the Mediterranean to all Europe, ultimately suggesting an optimistic view for the future in terms of climate change resilience development in ports.

Author Contributions. Conceptualization, methodology, formal analysis, materials and resources, software and data curation: all authors. Validation: all authors. In particular: Pisano wrote Sects. 2, 3, 4 Gallo wrote Sects. 1 and 5.

Acknowledgments. This study was funded by the European Union - NextGenerationEU, in the framework of the GRINS - Growing Resilient, INclusive and Sustainable project (GRINS PE00000018 - CUP H73C22000930001), National Recovery and Resilience Plan (NRRP) - PE9 - Mission 4, C2, Intervention 1.3. The views and opinions expressed are solely those of the authors and do not necessarily reflect those of the European Union, nor can the European Union be held responsible for them.

References

1. Izaguirre, C., Losada, I.J., Camus, P., Vigh, J.L., Stenek, V.: Climate change risk to global port operations. Nat. Clim. Chang. **11**(1), 14–20 (2021)
2. Roberts, T., Williams, I., Preston, J., Clarke, N., Odum, M., O'Gorman, S.: Ports in a storm: Port-city environmental challenges and solutions. Sustainability **15**(12), 9722 (2023)
3. Gallo, A.: The logistic carbon footprint: a dynamic calculation tool for an indicator of the sustainability of logistic processes with a case study on the Port of Trieste. In: Gervasi, O., Murgante, B., Misra, S., Rocha, A.M.A.C., Garau, C. (eds.) Computational Science and Its Applications – ICCSA 2022 Workshops. ICCSA 2022. Lecture Notes in Computer Science, vol. 13381. Springer, Cham (2022). https://doi.org/10.1007/978-3-031-10548-7_9
4. McKinnon, A.: Decarbonizing Logistics: Distributing Goods in Low Carbon World. Kogan Page Ltd, London (2018)
5. Peris-Mora, E., Orejas, J.D., Subirats, A., Ibáñez, S., Alvarez, P.: Development of a system of indicators for sustainable port management. Mar. Pollut. Bull. **50**(12), 1649–1660 (2005)
6. Jiang, M., Lu, J., Qu, Z., Yang, Z.: Port vulnerability assessment from a supply Chain perspective. Ocean Coast. Manag. **213**, 105851 (2021)
7. Hsieh, C.H.: Disaster risk assessment of ports based on the perspective of vulnerability. Nat. Hazards **74**(2), 851–864 (2014)
8. Borruso, G., et al.: Rail Ports as nodal gateways in the sea – land connections and the challenges of sustainable globalized markets: the case of Adriafer and the Port of Trieste. In: Gervasi, O., et al. Computational Science and Its Applications – ICCSA 2023 Workshops. ICCSA 2023. Lecture Notes in Computer Science, vol. 14110. Springer, Cham (2023). https://doi.org/10.1007/978-3-031-37123-3_30
9. Soriani, S.: Scenari di evoluzione della relazione porto-laguna: una prima riflessione. In: Laguna Futuri, Quodlibet, pp. 152–155 (2023)
10. Rosendahl Appelquist, L., Halsnæs, K.: The Coastal Hazard Wheel system for coastal multi-hazard assessment and management in a changing climate. J. Coast. Conserv. **19**, 157–179 (2015)
11. Mezzi, P., Pellizzaro, P.: La città resiliente. Strategie e azioni di resilienza urbana in Italia e nel mondo. Altreconomia, Milano (2016)
12. Kulp, S.A., Strauss, B.H.: Vulnerability to sea-level rise and coastal flooding. Nature Commun. **10** (2019)
13. Hein, C.: Adaptive Strategies for Water Heritage: Past. Springer International Publishing, Present and Future (2019)
14. Panahi, R., Gargari, N.S., Lau, Y.Y., Ng, A.K.: Developing a resilience assessment model for critical infrastructures: the case of port in tackling the impacts posed by the Covid-19 pandemic. Ocean Coast. Manag. **226**, 10624 (2022)
15. Borruso, G., Gallo, A., Sinatra, F., Balletto, G., Dore, S.: Smart city-port relationship: a circular port city development model for trieste. In: Gervasi, O., Murgante, B., Garau, C., Taniar, D., C. Rocha, A.M.A., Faginas Lago, M.N. (eds.) Computational Science and Its Applications – ICCSA 2024 Workshops. ICCSA 2024. Lecture Notes in Computer Science, vol. 14817. Springer, Cham (2024). https://doi.org/10.1007/978-3-031-65238-7_26

16. Wang, C., Haralambides, H., Zhang, L.: Sustainable port development: the role of Chinese seaports in the 21st century Maritime Silk Road. Int. J. Ship. Transp. Log. **13**(1–2), 205–232 (2021)
17. Twrdy, E., Zanne, M.: Improvement of the sustainability of ports logistics by the development of innovative green infrastructure solutions. Transp. Res. Proc. **45**, 539–546 (2020)
18. Hein, C., Schubert, D.: Resilience and path dependence: a comparative study of the port cities of London, Hamburg, and Philadelphia. J. Urban Hist. **47**(2), 389–419 (2021)
19. Reguero, B.G., Losada, I.J., Méndez, F.J.: Port cities and climate change. Portus **24**, 20–25
20. Hanson, S.E., Nicholls, R.J.: Demand for ports to 2050: climate policy, growing trade and the impacts of sea level rise. Earth's Fut. **8**, e2020EF001543 (2020)
21. Carta, M., Ronsivalle, D., Lino, B.: The Good Practice Framework for European Sustainable Urbanisation through port city Regeneration An operative guide. ESPON publisher, Luxembourg (2020)
22. Di Paola, A.: Città e porti. Green port, pianificazione portuale e rigenerazione urbana. Aracne, Roma (2020)
23. Sogut, M.Z., Erdoğan, O.: An investigation on a holistic framework of green port transition based on energy and environmental sustainability. Ocean Eng. **266**, 112671 (2022)
24. Jugović, A., Sirotić, M., Peronja, I.: Sustainable development of port cities from the perspective of transition management. Trans. Maritime Sci. **10**(02), 466–476 (2021)
25. Karimpour, R., Ballini, F., Ölcer, A.I.: Circular economy approach to facilitate the transition of the port cities into self-sustainable energy ports—a case study in Copenhagen-Malmö Port (CMP). WMU J. Marit. Aff. **18**, 225–247 (2019)
26. Bielenia, M., Marušić, E., Dumanska, I.: Rethinking the green strategies and environmental performance of ports for the global energy transition. Energies **17**(24), 6322 (2024)
27. Monios, J., Wilmsmeier, G., Tello, G.A.M., Pomaska, L.: A new conception of port governance under climate change. J. Transp. Geogr. **120**, 103988 (2024)
28. Bertagna, S., Kouznetsov, I., Braidotti, L., Marinò, A., Bucci, V.: A rational approach to the ecological transition in the cruise market: technologies and design compromises for the fuel switch. J. Mar. Sci. Eng. **11**(1), 67 (2023)
29. Gallo, A., Borruso, G.: Stima dell'impronta carbonica del settore dei trasporti. Un'analisi geografica sulle rotte marittime e terrestri del porto di Trieste. Bollettino dell'Associazione Italiana di Cartografia **177**, 12–26 (2023)
30. Aymelek, M., Boulougouris, E.K., Turan, O., Konovessis, D.: Challenges and opportunities for LNG as a ship fuel source and an application to bunkering network optimisation. In: Proceedings of International Conference on Maritime Technology and Engineering, pp. 15–17 (2014)
31. He, P., Jin, J.G., Pan, W., Chen, J.: Route, speed, and bunkering optimization for LNG-fueled tramp ship with alternative bunkering ports. Ocean Eng. **305**, 117957 (2024)
32. Guo, Y., Yan, R., Qi, J., Liu, Y., Wang, S., Zhen, L.: LNG bunkering infrastructure planning at port. Multimodal Transp. **3**(2), 100134 (2024)
33. Verbeek, R.P., et al.: Environmental and Economic aspects of using LNG as a fuel for shipping in The Netherlands, pp. 1–48. TNO, Delft (2011)
34. Merk, O.: Shipping-related emissions in world container ports: an overview. In: International Forum on Shipping, Ports and Airports 2012 Conference Proceedings. Hong Kong Polytechnic University (2012)
35. Kizielewicz, J., Skrzeszewska, K.: Identifying actions to prepare electricity infrastructure in seaports for future power supplying cruise ships with energy from land. Energies **14**(23), 8173 (2021)
36. Enel, X.: Legambiente: Porti verdi: la rotta per uno sviluppo sostenibile. Analisi, buone pratiche e proposte per la decarbonizzazione del trasporto marittimo e lo sviluppo del cold ironing in Italia (2021)

37. Otter, A., Murphy, J., Pakrashi, V., Robertson, A., Desmond, C.: A review of modelling techniques for floating offshore wind turbines. Wind Energy **25**(5), 831–857 (2022)
38. Negro, V., López-Gutiérrez, J.S., Esteban, M.D., Matutano, C.: Uncertainties in the design of support structures and foundations for offshore wind turbines. Renew. Energy **63**, 125–132 (2014)
39. Laiola, E., Giungato, P.: Wind characterization in Taranto city as a basis for innovative sustainable urban development. J. Clean. Prod. **172**, 3535–3545 (2018)
40. Desogus, E., Grosso, D., Bompard, E., Russo, S.L.: Modelling the geopolitical impact on risk assessment of energy supply system: the case of Italian crude oil supply. Energy **284**, 128578 (2023)
41. Haezendonck, E., Van den Berghe, K.: Patterns of circular transition: what is the circular economy maturity of Belgian ports? Sustainability **12**(21), 9269 (2020)
42. Jacobs, W., Ducruet, C., de Langen, P.W.: Integrating world cities into production networks: the case of port cities. Global Netw. **10**(1), 92–113 (2010)
43. Bennæs, A., et al.: Optimization of a ship-based logistics system for carbon capture and storage. In: de Armas, J., Ramalhinho, H., Voß, S. (eds.) Computational Logistics. ICCL 2022. Lecture Notes in Computer Science, vol. 13557. Springer, Cham (2022). https://doi.org/10.1007/978-3-031-16579-5_4
44. Teagle, D., et al.: Carbon capture, usage and storage (CCUS): nonpipeline transport and cross-border CO2 networks (2024)
45. Akyelken, N.: Green logistics: improving the environmental sustainability of logistics (2011)
46. Yadav, V., Gaur, P., Jain, R.: On adoption of green logistics: a literature review. Int. J. Log. Syst. Manag. **40**(2), 193–219 (2021)
47. Gonzalez-Aregall, M., Cullinane, K., Vierth, I.: A review of port initiatives to promote freight modal shifts in Europe: Evidence from port governance systems. Sustainability **13**(11), 5907 (2021)
48. Langenus, M., Dooms, M., Haezendonck, E., Notteboom, T., Verbeke, A.: Modal shift ambitions of large North European ports: a contract-theory perspective on the role of port managing bodies. Maritime Transp. Res. **3**, 100049 (2022)
49. Norcliffe, G.B.: Industrial change in old port areas, the case of the Port of Toronto. Cahiers de géographie du Québec **25**(65), 237–253 (1981)
50. Jiménez, M.L.G.: SDGs and port systems: new challenges and opportunities for marine protection from the EU green deal perspective. In: The EU Green Deal and its Implementation, p. 289
51. Sangster, S.J.: Sustainable Port Infrastructure An interdisciplinary design study of nature friendly banks made of residual material to enhance biodiversity in a port. Delft University of Technology (2015)
52. Sepehri, A., Kirichek, A., van den Heuvel, M., van Koningsveld, M.: Smart, sustainable, and circular port maintenance: a comprehensive framework and multi-stakeholder approach. J. Environ. Manage. **370**, 122625 (2024)
53. Amenta, L., van Timmeren, A., De Martino, P., Cavaciocchi, G., Wandl, A.: The ecology of city-port areas towards sustainable regeneration: exploring the overlooked spaces for a circular city. Available at SSRN 5126393
54. Heikkilä, M., Saarni, J., Saurama, A.: Innovation in smart ports: Future directions of digitalization in container ports. J. Marine Sci. Eng. **10**(12), 1925 (2022)
55. Behdani, B.: Port 4.0: a conceptual model for smart port digitalization. Transp. Res. Proc. **74**, 346–353 (2023)
56. Karas, A.: The role of digitalization for smart port concept. In: Economic and Social Development: Book of Proceedings, pp. 406–412 (2020)

57. Di Vaio, A., Varriale, L.: Digitalization in the sea-land supply chain: experiences from Italy in rethinking the port operations within inter-organizational relationships. Prod. Plann. Control **31**(2–3), 220–232 (2020)

58. González-cancelas, N., Molina, B., Soler-flores, F.: Study to improve the digitalization of the Spanish port system through an affinity diagram. J. Maritime Transp. Logist. **1**(2), 51–68 (2020)

59. Khader, M.: Rotterdam resilience strategy, rotterdam. Urban Plan. Trans. 1–18 (2021)

60. Suvadarshini, P., Dandapat, P.: Digitalizing the maritime supply chain: the case of Rotterdam's port call operations. J. Inform. Technol. Teach. Cases **13**(2), 170–174 (2023)

61. Wardekker, J.A., De Jong, A., Knoop, J.M., Van Der Sluijs, J.P.: Operationalising a resilience approach to adapting an urban delta to uncertain climate changes. Technol. Forecast. Soc. Chang. **77**(6), 987–998 (2010)

62. Smith, R.W.: The good, the bad, and the robust: Climate change adaptation choices for the port of Rotterdam, Port of San Diego, and Naval Base Kitsap-Bremerton. Doctoral dissertation (2015)

63. Frantzeskaki, N., Wittmayer, J., Loorbach, D.: The role of partnerships in 'realising' urban sustainability in Rotterdam's City Ports Area, The Netherlands. J. Clean. Prod. **65**, 406–417 (2014)

64. van der Berg, A.: Climate adaptation planning for resilient and sustainable cities: perspectives from the city of Rotterdam (Netherlands) and the city of Antwerp (Belgium). Euro. J. Risk Regul. **14**(3), 564–582 (2023)

65. Huang-Lachmann, J.T., Lovett, J.C.: How cities prepare for climate change: comparing Hamburg and Rotterdam. Cities **54**, 36–44 (2016)

Smart Tourism (SmartTourism 2025)

Construction of World Heritage Candidacy Processes: Key Elements for a Systematic Framework

Ivan Blečić[1], Maria Carla Saliu[1(✉)], and Salvador Anton Clavé[2]

[1] Department of Civil and Environmental Engineering and Architecture,
University of Cagliari, Cagliari, Italy
mariacarla.saliu@unica.it

[2] Department of Geography, University Rovira i Virgili, Tarragona, Spain

Abstract. A set of two categories of key operational elements which can be used to construct a framework for analysing how value is constructed in World Heritage candidacy processes is described. The purpose for focusing on the two identified categories is to (1) condense UNESCO World Heritage candidacy processes into a few categories; and (2) provide a systematic basis for the development of a framework for reconstructing and interpreting the value constructed in World Heritage nomination processes.

Despite the numerous practical examples in the literature of how value is built during the bidding procedures, little is known about how to analyse the construction of this value and how value can be read and narrated in sites inscribed or nominated on the UNESCO World Heritage List. The paper provides meaningful insights through: (1) the analysis of UNESCO's constitutive documents; and (2) the data collected from the direct involvement in different candidacy processes. The approach adopted in this study encompasses a dialogue among restoration theories developed by Cesari Brandi and key concepts related to the storytelling practices used for the design of content-oriented visitor attractions.

The findings from this study demonstrate that we have two categories of key elements we can focus on for building an approach or a framework that let us read the value of World Heritage as a social construction in a systematic manner.

The elements presented in this paper should be extended so that a more general model of reading these processes can be carried out.

The paper's contribution is rooted in its interdisciplinary approach to the subject of cultural heritage, whereby the candidature process and the definition of the value are represented as a social construction that enables the creation of meaning and the making of significant value in the UNESCO context.

Keywords: Candidacy process · Value construction · World Heritage

1 Introduction

UNESCO's goal of protection of cultures and their valued past is possible by means of protocols, declarations of universal principles, statement of Outstanding Universal Value and compilation of inventories (Askew, 2010). To determine whether a cultural heritage

© The Author(s), under exclusive license to Springer Nature Switzerland AG 2026
O. Gervasi et al. (Eds.): ICCSA 2025 Workshops, LNCS 15894, pp. 159–171, 2026.
https://doi.org/10.1007/978-3-031-97648-3_11

is expression of an Outstanding Universal Value, means to have a convincing, validated, proved value, recognised, recognizable and sythetised thanks to a Statement of Outstanding Universal Value fitting criteria provided by UNESCO's key texts and constructed in an institutional system of formalized routines, beliefs and practices (Turtinen, 2000). In the domain of World Heritage, different definitions of *heritage* are provided to describe such a recognition process of the value of cultural phenomena: (1) heritage described as "a socially ascribed, therefore constructed category but placing things and practices in it based on factual claims about their provenance, age, continuity and authenticity" (Brumann, 2014); (2) a process of meanings' regulation and negotiation (Gfeller, 2013). World Heritage system has become a bureaucratic machinery (Brumann and Berliner, 2016) and being part of it means face processes of naming and framing (Shön and Rein, 1994) to fulfill protocols on the ground of state parties and check international standards.

In this big picture, we must account for the multiplicity of criticism about the concept of authenticity applied to heritage, which has been at the center of a debate over the past decades as Boccardi (2019) states, determining that authenticity of a heritage "is not about judging its significance, rather the internal coherence of the statements made by a certain community about that significance" and recognises heritage as a *cultural construct*. The value of the construct concept is defined in particular social and intellectual circumstances, it is time-specific and thus its meaning(s) can be altered (Graham et al., 2010); it is a way of *packaging* and choosing cultural phenomena stating their value and authenticity by aleatory criteria (Brumann, 2017), which make heritage value or significance being mutable (Titchen, 1995). The Statement of Value, Outstanding and Universal, labeled by UNESCO, is in this framework, a social and cultural construction. While we can read the statement in the official documents every Site which is part of the World Heritage List must delivery to be published in the official website of the List, we have no traces about how the process of "construction" of that statement was conducted.

This article tackles the need to provide evaluators and other researchers a set of (operational) elements which can be used to construct a framework for analysing how (the statement of) value is constructed in candidacy processes and how that value can be read and narrated in sites inscribed or nominated on the UNESCO World Heritage List. In doing so, written official documents of UNESCO are a key source of information in this contribution, but they yield virtually no insight into actual policy and decision-making processes (Gfeller, 2013). This paper is a contribution to filling that gap by providing ground information about a few actual candidacy processes. They refer to different Italian cases, which have been documented as part of a e PhD thesis research or thanks to a direct involvement in technical teams working of the candidacies. Specifically, they include insights from the ongoing candidacy process of the *Nuragic monuments of Sardinia*; from the construction of *The system of Italian-style condominium theatres in central Italy between the 18th and 19th centuries*; and from the updating process of the Management Plan of the World Heritage Site *City of Vicenza and Palladian Villas of the Veneto region*.

In this contribution we want to discuss the relevance of the processes of construction and maintenance of the value of cultural heritage which are already World Heritage Sites or are candidates for the UNESCO World Heritage List. To provide the key elements for structuring a framework describing such processes, in this paper we discuss the following:

1. in section "On value", we present on a general approach applicable to cultural heritage sites with different features and different candidacy processes such as the more than one thousand World Heritage Sites;
2. in section "Two categories of key elements", we discuss a set of key elements that can be operational in a future possible constitution of a general framework for the evaluation of the value construction process of World heritage Sites.

2   On Value

This study is an attempt to be part of the debate about the symbolic meaning of value of heritage in the framework of World Heritage system.

At first sight, the question of what is, and how to describe the value of a specific cultural heritage site can appear as a neutral question about "objective facts" (Shön and Rein, 1994). Actually, the definition of the value, and its potential "outstanding universal value" as World cultural heritage – as our observation of actually candidacy processes show again and again – entails a process of social and cultural construction (Boccardi, 2019), is socially framed, and is deeply intertwined with actually policy processes. If we define a social construction as something produced by historical events, social forces, and ideology (Hacking, 1999), the central point in analysing a candidacy processes at the World Heritage List becomes determining which historical events, social forces, ideologies and, more in general, conditions for framing are in place from case to case. In this context, following Shön and Rein (1994), who referred to, our reference to "frames" here refer to "a set of readinesses to distinguish some aspects of the situation rather than others and to classify and value these in this way rather than that". Hence, in this contribution the term "frames" is used to have a specific point of view on the candidature processes by analysing conditions present in these processes not only with what is reported in the candidature dossier, which is itself a set of frames defining the phenomenon described, but rather by reconstructing how the process took place and evolved.

Before focusing on framing, some key documents of UNESCO used in this study are presented, such as the *Operational Guidelines for the Implementation of the World Heritage Convention* (World Heritage Committee, 2002) which provide, among others, (1) information about the process for the inscription of properties on the World Heritage List; and (2) a list of sections and chapters that should be written in the nomination dossier, or candidacy dossier, in order to have all the required information about a heritage worthy of the World Heritage label. This written document, together with supportive manuals such as the *World Heritage Manual: Preparing World Heritage Nominations* (UNESCO-WHC et al., 2011), represent key sources of information about standards required in the WH arena and provide information that is useful for the purposes of this paper, which questions specific aspects and stages that characterise a cultural heritage site and the process of recognition of its value. According to the Operational Guidelines (2002), the nomination dossier format includes the sections reported in Table 1.

The first section is about clearly defined boundaries of the nominated property. The second section gives information about the history and development of the nominated

Table 1. Sections of the format nomination dossier (World Heritage Committee, 2002).

1	Identification of the nominated property
2	Description of the nominated property
3	Justification for Inscription
4	State of conservation and factors affecting the nominated property
5	Protection and Management
6	Monitoring
7	Documentation
8	Contact Information of responsible authorities
9	Signature of behalf of the State Party(ies)

property and is supposed to describe "facts needed to support and give substance to the argument that the nominated property meets the criteria of Outstanding Universal Value and conditions of integrity and/or authenticity". The third section describes and "must make clear why the property is considered to be of Outstanding Universal Value". The fourth section is about the "present" state of conservation of the nominated property and gives information about threats and factors affecting the property; the factors described in this section is based the monitoring process of the property which is the subject of the sixth section. The fifth section provides information about legislative, regulatory, contractual measures relevant to the protection of the nominated property and about an "appropriate" management system. The last three sections are related to materials that must be submitted with the nomination dossier. All sections described must be completed for a nomination dossier to be completed. Missing or incomplete parts of the information could result in being excluded from the candidacy procedure, and hence of not being included on the List.

The final product of the compilation of these various sections is a readable and comprehensible text that tells the history and "facts" that identify the nominated property, its exact boundaries and coordinates, the parties responsible for its conservation and maintenance, and those responsible for monitoring its state of conservation. The final document therefore tells and identifies all the aspects necessary for a cultural site to be considered as a World Heritage Site with proved Outstanding Universal Value. These aspects, documented and validated through in-depth studies of experts during the candidacy process, are then placed in an established format with well-defined technical criteria. The information of the dossier describes features of the cultural heritage, and it is comprehensive of the Outstanding Universal Value statement, which is a synthesis of the narrative constructed and elaborated to justify and demonstrate the value of the heritage in question. The big picture of these different sections is about different types of information related to the current moment while the candidacy is being built, but also to future evolution and management of the site, for example this is the case of the monitoring section and of the one related to the state of conservation. This different information, referred to different moments of the process of candidacy, makes it clear that such processes, to be clearly explained and described, should be analysed in different moments, because what happens and the conditions that are created during the application process are different at different steps of the application process.

The research question of this contribution is how to identify, understand and describe the social construction of value which is embedded in World Heritage candidacies. In answering this question, and to construct a robust approach for answering such a question, it would require (1) the identification of a set of key elements that define in a rigorous way aspects of the candidature process that are present in the final written candidacy dossier in a fragmented and not always identifiable way, and (2) the determination of logical links between these key elements in order to have an comprehensive description of such processes.

These elements are identified from the information required in the nomination dossier. They can be clustered into two categories:

- The first category pertains to a transversal aspect embedded in the concept of "process": *temporality*. Key elements of temporality are the *different stages* present in the dossier and through which the process of nomination and of maintenance of World Heritage unfolds;
- The second category refers to elements that can be analysed and framed at different stages of the process (first category) and can be identified as *triggers*. These key elements of the second category are (1) *agents*, (2) *technical requirements*, and (3) *narrative*.

These two categories of elements provide a defined and complete picture of the different aspects that made the whole process possible.

3 Two Categories of Key Elements

Key elements are now presented in a general overview in the following table (Table 2) before focusing on each of them.

Table 2. Overview of key elements clustered into two categories.

Category	Key element
Temporality	1. First stage
	2. Second stage
	3. Third stage
Triggers	1. Agents
	2. Technical requirements
	3. Narrative

3.1 First Category: Temporality

The elements described above have a common feature: each of them should, to be anal-ysed, be considered and framed in a specific stage of the candidacy process because conditions (key elements of the second category) can vary in a significant way in different moments of the process itself. Hence, what we need to elaborate is a category, a transversal one, which should be used for framing during time the key elements of the second category. This transversal category is temporality; and its key elements are stages of the process, defined as follows.

Table 3. Stages of the process of candidacy and monitoring, elaboration of the authors on Operational Guidelines (World Heritage Committee, 2002).

First stage	Second stage	Third stage
Process for the inscription of properties on the World Heritage List	Decision of the World Heritage Committee to (or not to) inscribe a property on the World Heritage List	Process for monitoring the state of conservation of World Heritage properties and Periodic Reporting on the implementation of the World Heritage Convention

First Stage. "Process for inscription of properties on the World Heritage List" include every action made from the very initial moment of promotion of a candidacy, to the inscription to the national Tentative Lists of States Parties, until the preparation of the nomination of a property for inscription on the List. The "complete" nominations sub-mitted to the Secretariat are examined by the World Heritage Committee which is the decision-maker about the inscription (or not) of a property on the World Heritage List.

Second Stage. "Decision of the World Heritage Committee to inscribe a property on the World Heritage List" takes place after the evaluation of nominations by the Advi-sory Bodies. They evaluate whether the properties have Outstanding Universal Value, and whether they meet the conditions of integrity, authenticity and the requirements of protection and management (World Heritage Committee, 2002: par.143).

Third Stage. "Process for monitoring the state of conservation and Periodic Reporting on the implementation of World Heritage Convention" occurs after a property is inscribed in the World Heritage List and is about protection and management of the property which must be guarantee over time (World Heritage Committee, 2002: chapter IV, chapter V).

The different stages of the candidacy cycle within the World Heritage processes are closely related to the different significances given to heritage in obtaining the 'World Heritage' label. We identify three different conditions in such an evolution of significance of heritage:

1. *Heritage,* which corresponds to the first stage described above. This condition is about a specific heritage becoming the focus around which various territorial forces address a strategic perspective of promoting the heritage itself through a World Heritage candidacy;

2. *World Heritage Site*, which corresponds to the second stage described in Table 2. It is the condition of recognition of the Outstanding Universal Value of a specific cultural heritage;

3. *Management cycle* ensuring that Outstanding Universal Value of the labeled Heritage Site is maintained over time, which corresponds to the third stage described in Table 3 (Fig. 1).

Fig. 1. Representation of the three conditions corresponding to the stages of the process.

These three different passages in which heritage takes on different *values* occur during the process of recognition of the (Outstanding Universal) *Value* itself. In his restauration theory, Cesare Brandi (1963) identifies the recognition of the work of art (in terms of its historical and artistic significance) as itself as an essential element. In his conceptualisation of the process of restoration, he proposes the following definition: "The methodological moment of recognition of the work of art, in its physical consistency and in its dual aesthetic and historical polarity, with a perspective of its transmission into the future." The act of restoration, in Brandi's theoretical framework, is part of the process of transmitting the work of art into the future, it is a historical event, something that evolves over time. In this conception, it is only at the moment when a work of art is recognised as such, and not only as an object of common use, that it is possible to talk about 'restoration'. According to Brandi, restoration is the moment in which the observer realises the value of the object. In other words, Brandi identifies two temporally asynchronous facts:

1. The moment of recognition of an object as a work of art;
2. The restoration of the work of art necessary for preserving it for future generations (Fig. 2).

Fig. 2. Temporally stages of the restoration theory of Cesare Brandi

Let us now try to follow the Brandian approach with respect to the heritage identified as World Heritage as the central object. The logical order would remain the same.

1. the period of construction of a validated narrative that proof that a cultural phenomenon has an Outstanding Universal Value which makes it recognizable as a World
Heritage. An example of this concept is represented by the ongoing case of the Nuragic
monuments of Sardinia, a candidate serial site present in the Italian Tentative List
since the 2021. After four years since the inscription, this site is still in the process
of construction of nomination text, facing Italian Ministry of Culture site inspections
while working on the adequate strategy for the definition of an appropriate nomination
text;

2. the management of the cultural phenomenon over time so that its Outstanding Universal Value is preserved and passed on to future generations. Elsewhere (Blečić et al.,
2024) we have attempted to describe the updating process of a case of the World
Heritage City of Vicenza and Palladian Villas of the Veneto.

3.2   Second Category: Triggers

Now that we have defined a basic scheme that allows us to divide the process into different
moments, we can define further elements that can be expressed in the different steps just
described. These elements fall into a second category that we can call *triggers*. Among
the triggers we have the following key elements: (1) agents; (2) Technical requirements;
and (3) narrative.

Agents. Each candidacy process comes to light because someone takes up the case. The
UNESCO international system works because candidacies are proposed by State Parties,
but on the local level actors involved can be of different types. This is a fundamental aspect
of these kinds of processes: agents who vehicle the process itself, the promoters and the
involved or co-opted ones, with different interests, capacities, and at different stages. The
agents capable of driving candidacies or maintenance processes of World Heritage are
decision-makers during those processes. The type of agents can be diverse, as may be the
conditions that render them capable of driving the nomination or maintenance processes.
The motivations of these agents are diverse as well. The following table shows different
types of agents, their possible interests and the capacities they have during processes
(Table 4).

Political Agents. They promote this kind of process in the general interest of communities and can be moved by electoral interests. When political agents are government
bodies, at different institutional levels, they have capacities and appropriate conditions
for structuring such a process. This is the case of "The system of Italian-style condominium theatres in central Italy between the 18th and 19th centuries", in which promoter
and referent for the candidacy at the ground level (Brumann and Berliner, 2016) is one
of the regional government involved in this trans-regional Italian candidate serial site.

Intellectual Agents. They can have local prestige at the territorial level, and this is the
reason they are capable of creating consensus regarding the process they can promote.
This is the case of the candidate of the "Nuragic monuments of Sardinia", included in the
Italian Tentative List, and of its association of promoters, "Sardegna verso l'UNESCO",
composed of former politicians, intellectuals, and former members of the governing
class at the regional level.

Table 4. Types of agents identified by interests and capacities.

Agents	Interests	capacities expertise
Political	Electoral interests and community interests	Capacities and conditions for promoting candidacies
Intellectual	Local prestige	Ability to build consensus around the process
Institutional	Preservation of the institutional position and prestige	Authority, responsibility and resources to promote processes
Technical	Work/ Vocation and interest on heritage	Expertise in World Heritage praxis and procedures and in World Heritage wording
Other	Valorisation of heritage worthy of recognition	Capacity to influence local level, promoters of a bottom-up process

Technical Agents. They are experts that make the process operational, they make evident, by preparing the submission materials, which is the value of heritage, how to describe it and to make a complete dossier, both for candidacies, and for monitoring stages. This technical and scientific apparatus include operators specialised in (i) heritage issues; (ii) specific heritage objects of the nomination; and (iii) World heritage procedures and wording. The nomination process of "The system of Italian-style condominium theatres in central Italy between the 18th and 19th centuries" was led by an Italian Foundation of experts in candidacy procedures. The same Foundation led the updating process of the Management Plan of "The City of Vicenza and Palladian Villas in Veneto".

Institutional Agents. Which role is to guarantee the maintenance and protection of heritage recognised as World Heritage, where the institution is identified as being responsible for this role. This is the case of the World Heritage Site "The City of Vicenza and Palladian Villas in Veneto", which addressed in 2023 an updating process of the Management Plan led by the Municipality of Vicenza.

Other Agents. Moreover, there are other agents that can be promoters or protagonists at different stages of the candidacy processes, such as people organising a mobilisation around the valorisation of heritage worthy of recognition that can be capable of influencing other people at the local level and of promoting bottom-up processes.

Technical Requirements. Despite criticism of the World Heritage system for its lack of clarity in defining concepts such as authenticity, it does produce a *homogenizing effect* (Brumann and Berliner, 2016) at the procedural level of this system, made by standardised documents such as management plans, impact assessments and standardised procedures which require the involvement of the above described experts as providers of scientific knowledge to the system. These kinds of documents are technical requirements embedded in the nomination and maintenance processes. According to the Operational Guidelines (World Heritage Committee, 2002), the technical required documents are the following: in the first stage (Table 2 on temporality), the format for being included in the Tentative List (World Heritage Committee, 2002: par. 62); in the second stage, the *nomination dossier* (World Heritage Committee, 2002: par. 130); and during the third stage, the *periodic report format* (World Heritage Committee, 2002: par. 203).

Narrative. "The 981 inscriptions on the World Heritage List correspond to at least as many stories" (Brumann and Berliner, 2016). The findings of technical agents' studies, when sufficiently mature and based on rigorous scientific and historical analysis, are disseminated as a *convincing and validated narrative* at the territorial level and serve as the cornerstone for consensus-building processes. Making World Heritage by scanning and structuring the world through categories and criteria, and by imposing restrictions and obligations is not only a matter of preserving, but also of shaping and "constructing the world" (Turtinen, 2000). And this is the reason we now talk about the last key element: narrative. Narrative presented in the nomination dossier may be designed to "inculcate" value systems (Hobsbawm and Ranger, 1983) and make clear why heritage with a certain value becomes a World Heritage Site. Narrative is also a motive for legitimising the action being taken by agents during the process, and it is not predetermined. Narrative is constructed as well, together with the construction and validation of the candidate Outstanding Universal Value. The construction process serves to legitimise and produce the heritage story that defines its value. The shape of this narrative must adhere to the official UNESCO guidelines and must fit the structures, forms, inventories, and guidelines established by UNESCO.

The creation of value such as is presented in this contribution is a common communication practice related to objects beyond heritage and particularly in the case of content-oriented visitors attractions and also affects other types of territorial processes such as the practices of *worldmaking* and *narrative placemaking* (Freitag et al., 2023), being the two of them central concepts in storytelling discourse. This also refers to tourism, as praxis that does not reflect the world as it is but de-makes or re-makes destinations and heritages (Baker and Hover, 2024).

Emerging from what we have presented, there is an outline of a tentative analytical framework of how the elements of the two categories (temporality and triggers) may be intertwined in actual candidacy cases. Time is the basis that gives shape and structure to all the steps of the application process. Agents are those who, at different stages and moments of the process, act as promoters, as supporters of the process, and as those responsible for the maintenance and future monitoring of the site. The technical requirements are those that must be observed in order to effectively carry out the application process and must be respected by the agents at the various stages of the process. The narrative that justifies and validates the value of the cultural heritage, both during the preparation of the dossier and at a later stage, must be adapted to the form and criteria dictated by the technical requirements. Technical agents shape heritage history, exclude and select information and construct the value of the heritage according to the global grammar that make World Heritage possible (Turtinen, 2000).

4   Conclusions

The primary purpose of this contribution has been to define some of the groundwork necessary in defining how the value is built in an institutional system of standardised procedures (Turtinen, 2000) within the UNESCO World Heritage. According to Meskell and Brumann (2015), the public document within the World heritage arena are the results of "endless revisions and compromises". This is not only the case at the international level when candidacies from different countries are compared and assessed, but also the reality "on the ground" where each candidacy is constructed through a policy process. For this reason, for the purpose of this contribution, it was fundamental to document the evolution of actual cases on the ground, the way they unfolded and evolved,, to unearth the fact that very little of these processes is explicit once in the technical documents, once they are produces, and that and that policy processes (and political steps) are often hidden behind technical steps.

For that, we have drawn from our two-year long observation and in some cases direct participation in three candidacy processes: the first one is the updating process of the management plan and system of "The City of Vicenza and Palladian Villas of the Veneto"; the second one is the candidacy dossier of "The system of Italian-style condominium theatres in central Italy between the 18th and 19th centuries"; and the last one the ongoing process of the candidate site "Nuragic monuments of Sardinia".

Focusing on the standard sections that constitute an adequate nomination dossier, and the involvement of several World Heritage sites or candidates, has led to the preliminary identification of key elements that allow an extended understanding of the different moments of the "heritagization" processes. These elements are divided into two categories; (1) temporality (first, second and third stage); and (2) Triggers (agents, technical requirements, and narrative). These categories describe how the cultural production of World Heritage is constructed, through the operation of different agents which act in different moments driven by different interests, and the final result is a shaped narrative which fits the UNESCO technical requirements and satisfy different types of interests. The narrative we reflect on, hence, is a way of framing the cultural heritage, a way of presenting it to the world, a design process of sense-making, not far, as a concept, from values and worldviews represented and reflected in designing non-heritage-based but content-oriented visitor attractions (Freitag et al., 2023), which are *social constructed* places which meanings and functions are integrated "into present and future society" (Anton Clavé, 2005).

Going from here, we see a promising direction for future research and developments. It is strictly operational and is about structuring an approach or a framework capable of providing a systematic way of analysing World Heritage candidacy processes and key elements in their development. The collection of the information linked to the key elements described in this contribution allows for having a big picture of the processes; rather than focusing on individual aspects, it seeks to reconstruct the process through the interrelationships between information over time and at the various stages that form this type of procedure. The establishment of such a framework would allow us to re-understand aspects of the construction of a World Heritage Site that are as much, and much more, than the concept of heritage which "is not given, it is made" (Harvey, 2001), it is also essential in the phases following the recognition of World Heritage status, such as those of monitoring and cyclical management.

The key elements described in this paper can be the groundwork for an overall understanding of the process of framing, constructing, socially ascribing (Brumann, 2014; Turtinen, 2000) which is the starting point of a World Heritage conservation and management process. A general overview of these processes can be reconstructed from the documentary data that only gain salience if researches have the necessary insights into the processes that produced them (Meskell and Brumann, 2015). The key elements presented in this contribution can contribute to this general reading framework, so that even if heritage candidacies are situated in particular social and intellectual circumstances, and even if they are time-specific and thus their meaning(s) can be altered (Graham et al., 2010), this possible framework could help in fixing meaning(s) over time, with specific contribution of defined agents, by respecting official requirements (of the UNESCO arena) and with a validated narrative.

For the purpose of the present study, the two categories of key elements represent as a multidimensional the concept of value of heritage, analysed in its symbolic meaning. Other embedded dimensions, such as the economic one, due to their importance in the policy processes of heritagization, will be part of future research and further contributions.

Acknowledgments. This study was produced while attending the PhD programme in Civil, Environmental Engineering and Architecture at the University of Cagliari, Cycle XXXVIII, with the support of a scholarship financed by the Ministerial Decree no. 351 of 9th April 2022, based on the NRRP - funded by the European Union - NextGenerationEU - Mission 4 "Education and Research", Component 1 "Enhancement of the offer of educational services: from nurseries to universities" - Investment 4.1 "Extension of the number of research doctorates and innovative doctorates for public administration and cultural heritage".

This study was carried out within the "Accordo di collaborazione Crenos-Glab per progetto Ecosistema Innovativo sull'Archeologia Protostorica (EIA)".

References

Anton Clavé, S.: Parques temàticos: màs allà del ocio. Ariel (2005)

Askew, M.: The magic list of global status: UNESCO, World Heritage and the agendas of states. In: Heritage and Globalisation. Routledge (2010)

Baker, C., Hover, M.: Leveraging historical hospitality in the national parks: Fred Harvey, Mary Colter, and the heritage of the American Southwest. J. Heritage Tourism **19**, 816–838 (2024). https://doi.org/10.1080/1743873X.2024.2379538

Blečić, I., Saliu, M.C., Borlizzi, P., Portinaro, A.: Introducing principles of antifragility in world heritage management evaluation tools: the case of city of Vicenza and Palladian villas of the Veneto. In: International Conference on Computational Science and Its Applications. Presented at the International Conference on Computational Science and Its Applications, pp. 406–420. Springer, Cham (2024)

Boccardi, G.: Authenticity in the heritage context: a reflection beyond the Nara document. Hist. Environ. Policy Pract. **10**, 4–18 (2019). https://doi.org/10.1080/17567505.2018.1531647

Brandi, C.: Teoria del restauro. Einaudi (1963)

Brumann, C.: How to be authentic in the UNESCO World Heritage System: Copies, Replicas, Reconstructions, and Renovations in a Global Conservation Arena. The transformative power of the copy: a transcultural and interdisciplinary approach, pp. 269–287 (2017)

Brumann, C.: Heritage agnosticism: a third path for the study of cultural heritage. Soc. Anthropol. **22**, 173–188 (2014). https://doi.org/10.1111/1469-8676.12068

Brumann, C., Berliner, D.: World Heritage on the Ground: Ethnographic Perspectives, 1 edn. Oxford, England, Berghahn (2016)

Freitag, F., Carlà-Uhink, F., Anton Clavé, S.: Key Concepts in Theme Park Studies: Understanding Tourism and Leisure Spaces. Springer, Cham (2023).https://doi.org/10.1007/978-3-031-111 32-7

Gfeller, A.E.: Negotiating the meaning of global heritage: cultural landscapes in the UNESCO World Heritage Convention, 1972–92. J. Glob. Hist. **8**, 483–503 (2013). https://doi.org/10. 1017/S1740022813000387

Graham, B., Ashworth, G., Tunbridge, J.: A Geography of Heritage. Oxford University Press (2010). https://doi.org/10.4324/9781315824895

Hacking, I.: The Social Construction of What? Harvard University Press (1999)

Hobsbawm, E., Ranger, T.: The invention of tradition. Cambridge university press (2012)

Harvey, D.C.: Heritage pasts and heritage presents: temporality, meaning and the scope of heritage studies. Int. J. Heritage Stud. **7**, 319–338 (2001). https://doi.org/10.1080/13581650120105534

Meskell, L., Brumann, C.: UNESCO and new world orders. In: Meskell, L. (ed.), Global Heritage: A Reader. Wiley-Blackwell, Hoboken, NJ, pp. 22–42 (2015). https://doi.org/10.1002/978139 4261154.ch1

Shön, D., Rein, M.: Frame Reflection: Toward the Resolution of Intractable Policy Controversies. Basic Book (1994)

Titchen, S.M.:On the construction of outstanding universal value: UNESCO's World Heritage Convention (convention concerning the protection of the world cultural and natural heritage, 1972) and the identification and assessment of cultural places for inclusion in the world heritage list Australian National University Canberra (1995)

Turtinen, J.: Globalising heritage: on UNESCO and the transnational construction of a world heritage. SCORE (Stockholm center for organizational research), Stockholm (2000)

UNESCO-WHC, ICCROM, ICOMOS, IUCN: World Heritage Manual: Preparing World Heritage Nominations, 2nd edn (2011)

World Heritage Committee: Operational guidelines for the implementation of the World heritage Convention (2002)

Digital Tools Empowering Tourism Development: A Business Intelligence Platform for the Basilicata Regional Growth

Maria Danese[1][(✉)] ⓘ, Fausto Villani[2], Domenico Filitti[2], Giovanni Scaramuzzo[2], Marilisa Biscione[1] ⓘ, and Nicola Masini[1] ⓘ

[1] ISPC-CNR, Contr. S. Loja, 85100 Potenza, Italy
maria.danese@cnr.it
[2] TboxChain/Exo Ricerca, Via del Gallitello x, 85100 Potenza, Italy

Abstract. One of the key factors in fostering the development of weak territorial contexts is tourism. The first step in improving this sector is to obtain deeper understanding of it, in order to implement the right strategies and actions, through knowledge acquisition and analysis.

With this aim, in this paper, a Business Intelligence platform developed for the Basilicata Region (Italy) is shown. This case study falls under one of the Priority Axes of European Regional Development Fund (ERDF), within the framework of the Cohesion Policy, aimed at supporting and stimulating the growth of less developed areas.

Keywords: Digital tourism · tourism analysis · Basilicata · tourism management

1 Introduction

During the last ten years, thanks also to the rapid advancement of information technology (IT), Tourism has seen a big growth and it has become a key factor for regional and national economic development [1]. Specifically, digital tools have transformed the travel and tourism sector by improving visitor experiences, marketing strategies, and driving regional development through technological innovations [2], digital transformation [3–5] and the development of business intelligence and analytics. As a result, over the past two decades, the notion of digital tourism has been increasingly referenced in both real-world scenarios and scientific literature [6–9]. Some of the digital instruments today more used in the tourism sectors are all the technologies related to the Internet, the big data, and all the analytical methods AI related.

These tools assume that there is a good digitalized knowledge base of the sector or that in any case the use of big data provides a comprehensive knowledge of the sector.

Confirming the importance of knowledge acquisition and representation, a series of laws, documents and initiatives at the national, European, and global levels that are trying to raise awareness and address data management and digitization of data in general, but in the tourism sector too since around 2010.

O. Gervasi et al. (Eds.): ICCSA 2025 Workshops, LNCS 15894, pp. 172–188, 2026.
https://doi.org/10.1007/978-3-031-97648-3_12

Between these, the most important are (i) the Global Guidelines to Restart Tourism from the World Tourism Organization [10], the United Nations' Sustainable Development Goals [11], at the global level, the United Nations' Sustainable Development Goals [11], at the global level; (ii) the Digital Market Strategy (DSM) initiative [12], the Digital Agenda for Europe [13], the European Data Strategy [14], and the INSPIRE Directive [15] (which is not specific for tourism data, but involves also them), at the European level; (iii) the National Recovery and Resilience Plan (NRRP) which includes projects and investments for the intelligent use of data in various sectors (including the tourist one), at the Italian level.

Unfortunately, there are still territories that have lack with underdeveloped digital tourism precisely because of the lack of this basic data and knowledge.

For what concerns data needed in the tourism sector, they can be of different types, depending on the digital technology they are designed for; these last, in tourism can be oriented to three different aims, depending on the subject they are created for. Thus, three aspects can be distinguished [16]:

1. The tourism perspective, with the aim to use digital tourism products and services.
2. The operators' perspective, where the target is to produce digital transformations within the tourism sector, including the creation of digital tourism goods digital services and the digitation of business processes and tourism information.
3. The social development perspective, where the aim is tourism development.

In this paper, we used the last perspective to develop a digital framework for knowledge acquisition and representation of tourism data for the Basilicata Region, a fragile context chosen, where there be allocated the European Regional Development Fund (ERDF), within the framework of the Cohesion Policy. The aim is to offer to policy makers an instrument useful to gain a deeper understanding of the dynamic and complex nature of the tourism sector in Basilicata and the numerous interconnected factors that influence it.

2   Methods: Business Intelligence for Tourism

According to [17], business intelligence (BI) refers to a set of methodologies, processes, tools, and technologies that enable the acquisition, analysis, and presentation of data related to a specific topic or industry. Its purpose is to support informed decision-making, identify growth opportunities, solve problems, and assist in strategic planning. BI has gained significant traction in the tourism sector in the past decades to manage and improve the destination-related aspects, accommodations, and transportation [18–20]. Several case studies have showcased successful BI platforms developed for the management and analysis of tourism data [21–25].

Key aspects developed within the realm of BI include:

1. Data collection, data warehouse structuring and data cleaning: data are extracted from diverse sources (surveys, interviews, focus groups, external databases, big data sources such as textual data or digital footprints related to photos uploaded on various sites and social media [26], data with tags, date, time, coordinates, and user profiles [27], data from mobile devices, Bluetooth and transaction data, search engine research

or online bookings [28]), cleaned and transformed, in order to ensure data consistency and quality.

2. Data Analysis by means of different methods: statistical techniques [29], data mining algorithms [30], algorithms based on artificial intelligence [31], spatio-temporal data analysis [32] and other methodologies to identify patterns, trends, correlations, and meaningful insights [33].

3. Creation of User Interfaces for Reporting and Dashboards with graphic visualizations to explore data intuitively and monitor performance, key metrics, and trends over time [34]. The information and analyses resulting through BI are distributed and shared within the organization, in order to make informed decisions.

3 The Basilicata Case Study: Cultural Tourism System and Development Policies/Governance

Basilicata is an Italian Region that falls under the objectives of the European Community's cohesion policy. It has socio-economic indicators lower than a large part of the other Italian regions, along with Calabria, Campania, Molise, Puglia, Sardegna, and Sicilia, such as a per capita GDP lower than 75% of the EU average, higher unemployment, and lower accessibility to services.

As a result, however, Basilicata benefits from programs aimed at bridging the structural and infrastructural gap, such as the Operational Program (OP) of the European Regional Development Fund (ERDF). The ERDF is a key financial instrument used to reduce disparities and improve the quality of life in disadvantaged regions of the European Community. It strives to narrow the development gaps among European regions, particularly those facing natural or demographic disadvantages. This is achieved through 11 thematic objectives focusing on research, technological development, innovation, information and communication technologies, competitiveness, sustainability, social inclusion, education, and efficiency.

In this context, the project Basilicata Heritage Smartlab (BHSL) is co-financed under the Axis which emphasizes research, technological development, and innovation. This project aims to revitalize the Region's economy through collaboration between public entities, research institutions (3), and enterprises (42), as well as through targeted actions in the sector of the Cultural and Creative Industries to improve some key drivers of the economy. Between these, cultural heritage and tourism, each with its own identity, structure, and characteristics, while also sharing common aspects. One component of the BHSL project is the Intelligent Tourism Analysis Smartlab; it aims to develop a platform for managing tourist phenomena. Currently, no such instrument exists in Basilicata, highlighting the need for a tool capable of collecting, analyzing, and aggregating data to provide structured information for guiding public entities in building predictive models and supporting decision-making processes.

In Basilicata, Tourism and Cultural and Creative Industries (CCIs) are leading sectors of the local economy. The serious effects caused by the Covid-19 pandemic come after a strong growth trend in tourist flows until 2019 achieved thanks to the nomination of Matera, one of the main cities in Basilicata, as "European Capital of Culture 2019". Some small signs of recovery begin in 2021. In 2022, however, thanks also to the 'Basilicata free to move' promotional campaign (focused precisely on the end of restrictions and constraints on mobility), important and positive data are recorded: +32% in arrivals compared to 2021 and + 23% in presences compared to 2021 [35].

The objectives of the ERDF 2021–2027 programming (which provides resources for new opportunities for Tourism and Cultural and Creative Industries (CCIs) development), are strengthening the competitiveness of the most important tourism destinations (Matera, the Ionian Coast, and Maratea), the improvement of the fruition of the historical-cultural heritage, and the development of the tertiary system [36].

The territory of Basilicata is suitable for tourism that is not linked to pre-packaged itineraries: the tourist offer proposes a set of tourist places, small towns to visit, rich in cultural heritage, and natural habitats almost unknown both nationally and internationally, which demonstrate high resilience, i.e. flexibility, inclusiveness and integration [37]. Regional tourism governance has led CCIs to invest, for example, in sustainable development supported by a strong identification with the territory [38], or by the geo-touristic approach [39] and in innovation for a rural, 'green' and welcoming destination, suitable for different audiences and with memorable experiential involvement, also in synergy with local communities [40]. Congress Tourism, Village Tourism, Holiday working for Smart Working Families, Outdoor Tourism, Beach Tourism, School Tourism, Luxury Tourism, Food and Wine Tourism and Return Tourism for those who want to visit the places of their family history, are the main types of tourist activities successfully planned in Basilicata. However, more targeted analyses of the current situation and development trends would greatly assist tourism governance in the development of the cultural tourism sector.

To address all these needs, in this paper we present BasilicataTourism, a BI framework useful for knowledge acquisition and data visualization and analysis.

4 The BasilicataTourism Web-Environment

4.1 BasilicataTourism Architecture

BasilicataTourism is composed by the following elements summarized in Fig. 1:

1. A Virtual Machine level (in Fig. 1 WIFIBAS-ANALYT1–2-3) which is the infrastructure used to improve effectiveness of the system, by ensuring a simplified management of resources, flexibility and scalability.
2. A container orchestration level, (DOCKER SWARM) used for the execution and management of containers.
3. Three macro-components: a data warehouse, a user view and a metric and monitoring component. For each of them, in Fig. 1, the different elements are present with all the products used for each scope.

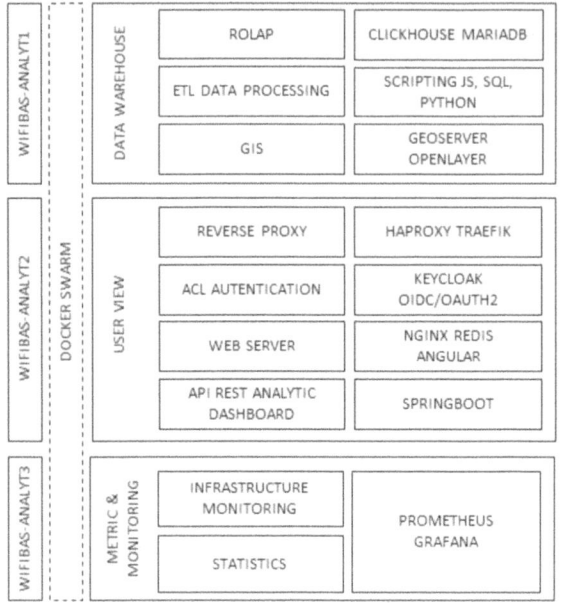

Fig. 1. The BI structure of BasilicataTourism.

4.2 Basilicata Tourism Data and Dashboard: Which Data, in Which State, What a Story They Tell

In Basilicata Region, data concerning tourism are spread in different databases and sources. Consequently, one of the first objectives was to collect all the possible suitable data to read and understand Basilicata's tourism. Sometimes these data needed a cleaning process or to rearrange the aggregation level, because of privacy reasons. Moreover, some indicators were extracted from basic information.

All this contents are accessible through the dashboard, designed for data visualization and querying. It is organized as follows: from the homepage it is possible to access two sections: the first one contains the historical data series, the second one is dedicated to spatial data and indicators. The historical data series contains ISTAT datasets and indicators for a period from 2015 to 2021. Instead, all the data and indicators present in the spatial section refers to a period from 2020 to 2022.

In the following paragraphs the information entered into the platform will be introduced, indicating any cleaning process required, and how the data were analyzed to calculate new indicators (dataset and indicators calculated are summarized in Table 1). The description is based on those two dashboard sections, the historical series part and the spatial one and information are arranged also according to their type.

Table 1. Dataset and indicators of BasilicataTourism summarized, grouped for data source (Prov. Stands for Provinces; I/F/T stands for Italian/Foreigners/Total).

Source	Name	Type	Spatial aggregation	Temporal aggregation	Attributes
ISTAT historical series (not spatial)	Arrivals	Acquired	Prov., Region	Monthly	I/F/T
	Presences	Acquired	Prov., Region	Monthly	I/F/T
	Arrivals-to-Resident Population Ratio	Calculated	Prov., Region	Monthly	
	Ratio between international and total arrivals;	Calculated	Prov., Region	Monthly	
	Tourist saturation index	Calculated	Prov., Region	Monthly	
	Average stay ratio	Calculated	Prov., Region	Monthly	
	Gross hotel bed utilization index	Calculated	Region	Monthly	
	Net hotel bed utilization index	Calculated	Region	Monthly	
ISTAT spatial data	Tourist saturation index	Calculated	Municipality	Monthly	I/F/T
	Average stay	Calculated	Municipality	Monthly	I/F/T
	Bed saturation	Calculated	Municipality	Monthly	I/F/T
Mobile cells (Vodafone Italia)	Arrivals	Acquired	Municipality	Monthly	I/F/T
	Overnight stays	Acquired	Municipality	Monthly Daily	Origin country Age Gender
Financial transactions	Charges made by payment card	Acquired	Municipality POI Kilometric grid	Monthly	I/F/T
Internet data	Sentiment	Calculated	Municipality POI Kilometric grid	Monthly	I/F/T

(*continued*)

Table 1. (*continued*)

Source	Name	Type	Spatial aggregation	Temporal aggregation	Attributes
Reviews and ratings	Reviews	Calculated	Municipality POI	Monthly	I/F/T
POI	POI category	Acquired	POI	Monthly	
	Degree of digitalization	Acquired	POI	Monthly	
	Prices	Acquired	POI	Monthly	
	Number of reviews	Acquired	POI	Monthly	

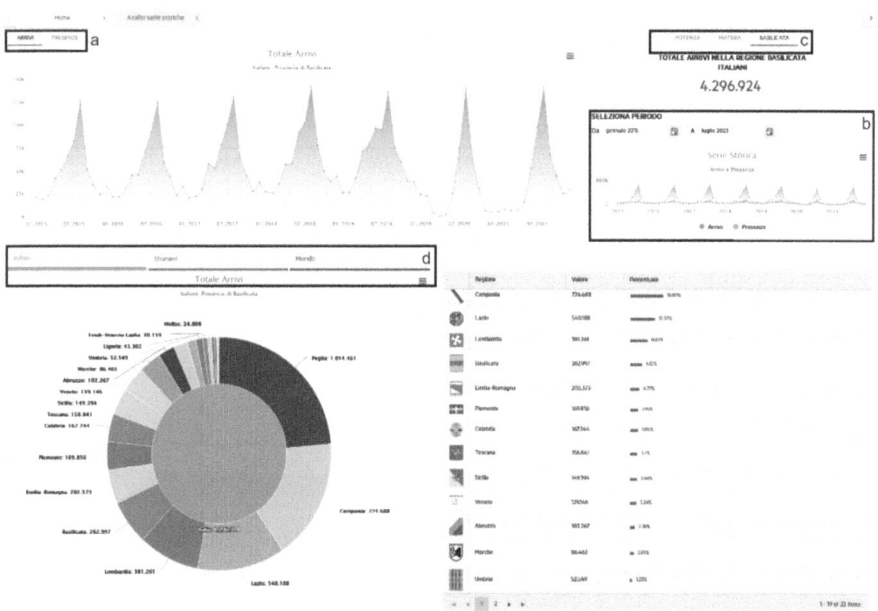

Fig. 2. Dashboard functionalities for arrives and overnight stays in Basilicata and its Provinces.

4.3 Historical Data Series Section: The ISTAT Dataset

The first section of the dashboard contains only numerical data and diagrams. National Institute of Statistics (ISTAT) is the source of data. Tourist movements are aggregated on a monthly basis and spatially related to province (NUTS3) as well as for the entire Region (NUTS2). Specifically, they are:

1. Arrivals in accommodation facilities (ARRIVI in Fig. 2a): the number of customers who checked in at accommodation facilities during the specified period.
2. Presences or tourist overnight stays (PRESENZE in Fig. 2a).

These two features are very important for destination manager because they allow analyzing the trend of tourist demand over time at the regional level. Moreover they enable the calculation of indicators that contribute to a better understanding of the tourism phenomenon, assessing its intensity and allowing producing diachronic comparisons to identify changes that have occurred over the analyzed period. Finally, they facilitate comparisons with other similar territories or simply serve as comparative benchmarks.

These data did not need any cleaning process and are questionable, in the dashboard, by period (Fig. 2b), by territory (Fig. 2c, choices are: POTENZA County, MATERA County and BASILICATA Region) and by composition (Fig. 2d, the choices are Italian, "Italiani", foreigners, "stranieri", and the total, "world"). The dashboard changes interactively according to the selection done.

If one province (NUTS3), is selected, a histogram is represented, containing the Arrivals (or Presences) divided by the Municipality of origin. Finally, there are also three histograms showing the totals for year, classified for provenience (national or international), for month and for year and Italian Region of origin, in order to do diachronic comparison.

From arrival and presences, the following indicators were calculated:

- Arrivals-to-Resident Population Ratio, to understand the impact of tourism not only economically but also socially.
- Ratio between international and total arrivals.
- Tourist saturation index representing the average number of overnight stays per 100 inhabitants. It indicates how many staying tourists are present on average for every 100 residents. It is a crude indicator of the tourism sector's weight in the region's economic activities. The index is calculated by multiplying the annual number of presences by 100 and dividing it by the population count multiplied by 365.
- Average stay ratio, calculated as the ratio of presences to arrivals. This indicator helps to understand the Tourism Stickiness, which refers to how well the destination can retain tourists and differentiate between transient tourism and tourism driven by a desire to explore and discover the hidden gems of a place.

In addition to the already mentioned indicators, only for data referred to the Regions (NUTS2) there are also the two following indicators:

1. Gross hotel bed utilization index, *GUI*: is given by the ratio (Eq. 1) of registered occupancy or presences (P) to the number of potential bed days in hotel establishments (including seasonal, renovation or other temporary closures), where the number of potential bed days, is given by the product of the number of days in the month (d) times the number of beds (b) according to the following expression:

$$GUI = Pd \cdot b \qquad (1)$$

2. Net hotel bed utilization index, NUI: this is given by the ratio (Eq. 2) of the recorded occupancy (P) to the number of actual opening bed days of hotel establishments (excluding seasonal, restoration or other temporary closures), where the number of actual opening bed days is given by the product of the number of days the establishment is open (od) times the number of beds (b):

$$NUI = Pod \cdot b \qquad (2)$$

4.4 Spatial Section

The spatial section is structured as a web-GIS thanks to GeoServer and the OpenLayers library, while the background map is OpenStreetMap (www.openstreetmap.org).

There are two main layers, useful to manage all the dataset of the section in the bottom right panel, corresponding to the two main types of spatial granularity:

- KPI COMUNALI (Municipal Key Performance Indicators, in Fig. 3a) has a polygonal topology according to Municipality boundaries.
- KPI POI (Point of Interest Key Performance Indicators, in Fig. 3a) has a point topology based on the POI location as explained further.

For what concerns municipal KPI, in the top-left panel (Fig. 3b), it is possible to query the map with a dropdown menu and choosing a dataset/indicator and the tourism origin (Italian, international or the total, called world), while in the top-right panel (Fig. 3c) the first four municipalities with the higher values of the selected element and the legend of the dataset/indicator selected are showed.

It is possible to query each polygon by clicking with the mouse and the related window (Fig. 3d) shows the name of the Municipality, the total of the dataset/indicator, the belonging class and a resuming histogram for the overnights, monthly (Fig. 3d) and daily distributed. Finally, in the lower-left panels (Fig. 3e) it is possible to select the period of interest and visualize its position in diagram of the global regional trend (Fig. 3f).

A similar approach can be followed to view the dataset associated with KPI POI: on the left (Fig. 3g) it is possible to select the desired dataset with a dropdown menu (Fig. 3h) and filtering it, while on the right panel it is possible to look the the ranking of the first five elements (Fig. 3i).

Istat Data. Spatial index calculated from ISTAT data in this section of the dashboard: tourist saturation index, as defined in the previous paragraph, the average stay (the ratio of the number of nights spent to the number of customers who arrived at the accommodation establishment), and the bed saturation (ratio between registered attendances and the number of potential bed days in hotels).

These indicators are aggregated for municipality: this is very useful to understand how tourists are distributed over the Region and to highlight changes in the officially registered hospitality establishments. However, there are lacks in the data, because for 80 Municipalities (out of 131) data are missing, because they have less than three accommodations, so they are not registered from ISTAT. There are also some Municipalities, in the Basilicata Region, that does not have any accommodation.

Mobile Network Cell Data. From the mobile network cell data, tourist arrivals and overnight stays were collected. This is crucial for analyzing temporal trends in numbers of visitors and overnight stays across the Region, as well as for cross-referencing with financial transactions, ratings, and weather data to gain a better understanding of tourist behaviors in Basilicata and develop predictive models.

About the pre-processing phase, this dataset was firstly extracted as daily frequencies, but there are data masking issues due to the small population size in some municipalities (less than 10,000 inhabitants). So, the output in the dashboard was rearranged monthly.

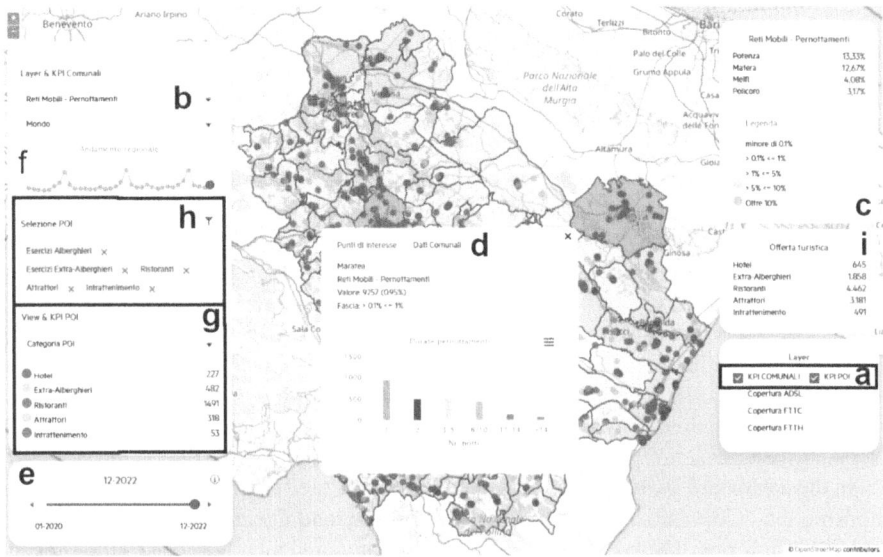

Fig. 3. Spatial section of the dashboard. Main elements: (a) layers, (b) selectors for the polygonal layer (KPI Comunali), (c) top four Municipality and Legend for the polygonal layer, (d) informative window associated to spatial features, (e) temporal selector, (f) temporal trend, (g) selectors for the point layer (KPI POI) and its legend, (h) POI filtering, (i) top five POI layer selected.

The final dataset coming from the mobile network cell is composed by arrivals and overnight stays.

Arrivals and overnight stays, when a specific polygon or point group can be selected on the map and be further filtered by:

- Origin: (1) Domestic: further disaggregated into Domestic-Residents and Domestic-Non-Residents in the area. (2) External Italians: these are all Italian individuals who do not reside within the analysis perimeter, their region and province of origin. (3) Foreigners: all foreigners who come from abroad and do not permanently reside in Italy and their specific nationality.
- Gender: for Italians (both residents and non-residents) male and female.
- Age Group: for Italians, groups 15–25, 26–35, 36–45, 46–65, > 65 years old.

Also for the spatial section, as for the historical series one, some charts are showed under the map, showing the origin of the traffic values and percentages and a demographic pyramid for Italian visitors, classified for gender and for age groups.

Credit-card Transactions. To obtain information about credit card transactions in a place is not an easy task, due to strict bank rules about privacy, but they are useful for depicting how much tourists spend on average, where they make their purchases and which are the favorite asset categories, even if with some limitations. In fact, there is still a strong preference for cash transactions.

Data collected are: value of transaction, number of transaction and average transaction. These are visible in the map, associated to the Municipality layer, but also in a section of the dashboard aimed to select and visualize charts about the financial dataset. They are aggregated weekly and it is possible to see the main countries of origin for international tourists that are: Italy, France, Germany, UK, Spain, Austria, Benelux, Scandinavia, EU + Switzerland, Russia, China, Japan, India, Other Asian Countries, Brazil, USA, other American countries, Africa, Australia and Oceania.

Instead, for what concerns the asset categories, data are furnished already aggregated for privacy reasons in thirteen product classes.

Consequently, there is the need to follow this rule: in the observation period, transactions are visible only if there was five active merchant per merchant category and, at the same time, the first five merchants do not invoice more than 50% of the total turnover of that sector considering all variables included in the query.

At the end of this cleaning operation, the financial transaction dataset covers the 88.1% of the transaction volume of Basilicata between 2018 and 2020.

In the dashboard is also possible to obtain more detailed information can be done by choosing the credit card circuit, the emission country and the category of expenditure. Under this, it is possible to compare transactions values and their numbers. Moreover, in two pie charts and two histograms, it is possible to have information about the category of expenditure selected and the emission country and the trend of category of expenditure and the emission country during the years.

Internet Data. Main sources of Internet data were:

- Social network data. Text data coming from the social network more used at the moment: Facebook, Twitter, Instagram and YouTube. Tik Tok data were not included because it is mostly used form the younger sections of the population so less economically emancipated and so less autonomous in the travel choice.
- Search engine data. Online searches related to Basilicata were considered thanks to Google Trends, in order to estimate tourist arrivals in the Region.

These elements were used as basis to carry out Sentiment Analysis, also known as Opinion Mining. It uses texts extracted from the web and is able to determine sentiment associated to them. In tourism analysis it could be very useful to evaluate people feelings and thoughts about a place or, more in general, a tourist destination and, lastly, to help destination managers and operators to understand the reputation of a place and make informed decisions to enhance visitor experiences.

In BasilicataTourism, the analysis was conducted by introducing inside the software some keywords related to the tourism sector according to their frequencies, such as Tourism, Travelling, Archaeological site, etc. Moreover keywords related to the 131 Basilicata's Municipalities were used in the analysis, both in Italian and in English, aggregated according the will of the Basilicata Territorial Promotion Agency (APT). Then, the results were cleaned from terminological errors. For example, in Italian, some of the Municipality names can be confused with other words, for example: "Bella" can be confused with "beauty". This cleaning phase was supported by Natural Language Processing (NLP) systems, able to aggregate words contained in the posts in topics, which are posts characterized by the use of similar keywords.

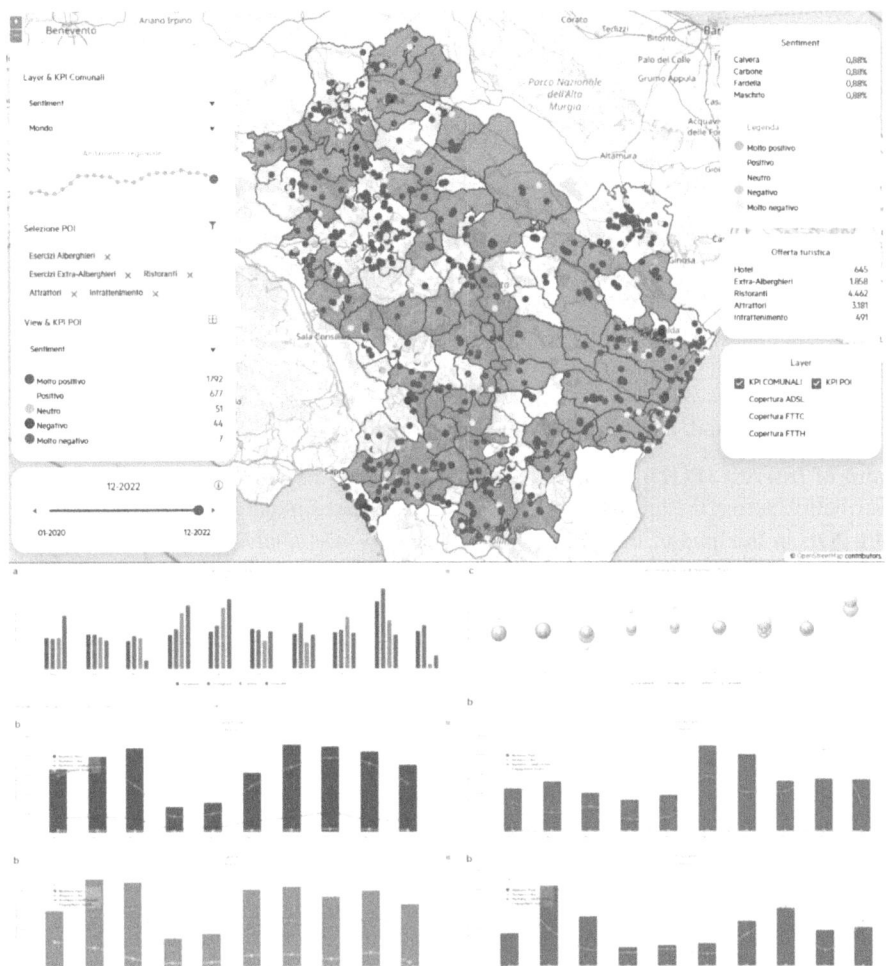

Fig. 4. In the map: sentiment layer calculated for Municipalities (KPI COMUNALI) and POI (KPI POI) and visualised as the classification: very positive, (molto positive), positive (positive), neutral, negative (negative), very negative (molto negativo). Diagrams exploring sentiment analysis by comparing sentiment score between social networks (a), showing the post number, like number, sharing number and the engagement score for each social network (b) and by offering a bubble view comparing the sentiment score trend with the post number (c).

The sentiment layer is calculated and showed in the dashboard both at a municipal and POI level (map in Fig. 4), where the total judgment is classified as very positive, (molto positivo), positive (positivo), neutral (neutrale), negative (negativo), very negative (molto negativo).

Also, they were calculated and visualized in the dashboard (Fig. 5a):

- A sentiment score that measures the level of perceived satisfaction expressed by users which emerges from the semantic analysis of online content, from reviews left by users on the most popular travel and booking platforms to messaging on the main social medias.

- A bar chart for each social media with the monthly trend of post number, like number, sharing number and the engagement score (number of likes) for each social network (Fig. 5b).
- A bubble view comparing the sentiment score trend with the post number (Fig. 5c).

Reviews and Ratings. Recent studies show that 8 out of 10 people read reviews before choosing a hotel or a restaurant, and an additional star rating can correspond to a revenue increase estimated between 5% and 9% [41]. Therefore, we have gathered all the information regarding the ratings of individual POI.

Furthermore, these data could be cross-referenced with information on tourist arrivals and financial transactions to verify if there is a causal relationship between ratings and reviews on one hand, and visitor numbers and spending on the other.

Point of Interest (POI). Another important source of data is related to POI and their distribution across the territory, associated, as anticipated in paragraph 4.5, to the layer KPI POI. In this phase, the entire regional territory was analysed and the main POI, including attractions, restaurants, and hotels, were identified.

This allows their visualization on a map and their correlation with arrival and accommodation data. In addition to georeferencing, the data have been aggregated at the municipal, provincial, and sub-regional levels, as used by the APT Basilicata. These purely informational data are useful for capturing the current situation of POI at a regional level and observing any changes over time. They will also help understand if a higher concentration of attractions corresponds to greater tourist appeal.

As far as POI is concerned, in the dashboard it is always possible to filter them by services available, languages spoken in the facility and typologies.

Other dataset associated to POI, together with the before mentioned sentiment score, are degree of digitalization, prices, number of reviews.

An Additional Level of Detail. As seen so far, all the different data and indicators are referred to two spatial levels of detail: the first is the municipality scale, the second one concerns the POI. However, there is an additional level of spatial detail that appears only for some layers. This happens for the sentiment and the review number layers contained inside the POI dropdown menu. In fact, when they are selected, a button representing a little grid appears (Fig. 5). By pushing it, a kilometer-long grid appears. Each of its cells is associated with an average value within the area of the selected layer. This helps give a deeper knowledge level on specific areas inside the territory.

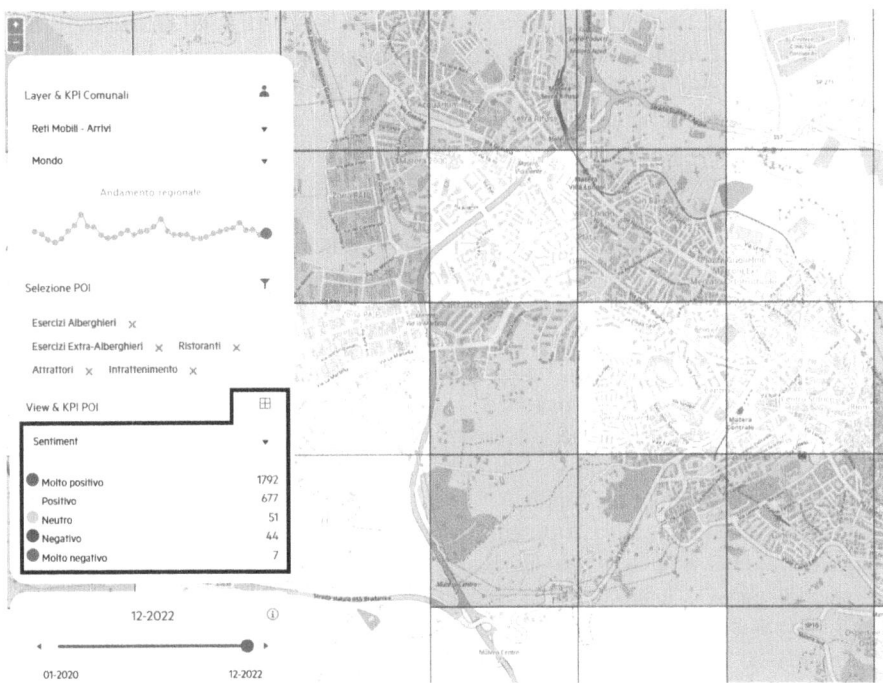

Fig. 5. Kilometre-long grid for the Sentiment layer.

5   Discussion

Tourism, one of the leading sectors of the economy, has seen in recent years an improvement in the acquisition, representation and management of knowledge thanks to the development in the IT sector. Basilicata is a weak context that needs innovative tools that can revitalize its economy by providing support to its key sectors, including tourism. The BasilicataTourism system, developed as part of the BHSL project precisely for this purpose, presents the following advantages:

1. To be one-stop-shop for all data currently existing for Basilicata already cleaned and sorted, ready to be visualized and compared, all in a platform that is easy to use by any type of user, with different levels of IT experience,
2. To have a data visualization tool with great performances, with charts that can be easily and immediately exported.
3. Providing better insights compared with raw data, thanks to various calculated indicators useful in deepening knowledge and assessments of the tourist field.
4. For operators in the field, the platform provides a tool to objectively measure certain variables, such as user flows, their social composition, conversation made, level of liking, and in general its customers, which is often shown to be completely different from objectively measured knowledge.

5. To understand, at the regional level, future trends and be able to quantify their intensity on particular locations, also for forecasting purposes and consequently developing more specific market strategies and then measuring their results derived from financial transaction data. This can help destination managers evaluate the ROI (Return on Investment) of their marketing efforts in attracting specific target groups and determining the total return on euros invested in territorial marketing.
6. To enable comparison of the volumes of traffic present in different territories.
7. To understand where it is most appropriate to allocate resources for the development of the sector.
8. To know objectively the composition of arrivals and stays in the Region and its municipalities;
9. To understand the capacity of a Region to receive tourists and to understand whether the supply and demand are matched or corrective actions are needed to balance the two, with reference to the period analysed, thanks to the specific indicators and the potential of reception compared to the real demand, evaluating possible under- and over-dimensioning of the supply.
10. To understand the ability to retain tourists in a place thanks to the average stay ratio or otherwise assess how tourists' retention varies over time in relation to the undertaken.
11. Understanding the level of appreciation and reputation of regional places and its facilities

However, there are still some limitations in the developed platforms. The first one is easily solvable: at the moment, the data only refer to a very specific time interval, but the platform is structured in such a way that can easily deal with new datasets for new reference periods. The second and the third limitations do not depend directly from the BasilicataTourism instrument, but from the characteristics of the case study and from the nature of data. For what concerns the characteristics of the case study, according to what showed during the data presentation made in the specific paragraphs, in Basilicata there is the problem of data availability at a more disaggregated level. In fact, for small contexts due to privacy regulation we are compelled to aggregate data a lot. Obviously, a reality characterized by larger numbers would not have this problem. About the data characteristics, there is a limitation about the specification that takes into account the gender issue, in that the data are always classified in a binary manner (male/female), which in any case excludes a more complete profiling of tourism that is relevant to today's reality.

Finally, surely a further improvement that can be made in future developments is the implementation of useful methods for synthesizing data and indicators, so as to reduce the multidimensionality of the variables considered and make the platform even more performant.

Acknowledgments. Authors want to thank Basilicata Region, who funded the "Basilicata Heritage SmartLab" Project.

Disclosure of Interests. He authors have no competing interests to declare that are relevant to the content of this article.

References

1. Seddighi, H.R., Theocharous, A.L.: A model of tourism destination choice: a theoretical and empirical analysis. Tour. Manage. **23**, 475–487 (2002)
2. Singh, P., Sharma, D.: Technological innovations in tourism businesses: a study on contemporary trends. In: Tyagi, P.K., Nadda, V., Bharti, V., Kemer, E. (eds.) Embracing Business Sustainability Through Innovation and Creativity in the Service Sector, pp. 141–154. IGI Global, Hershey (2023)
3. Chamboko-Mpotaringa, M., Tichaawa, T.M.: Digital trends and tools driving change in marketing free state tourism destinations: a stakeholder's perspective. Afr. J. Hosp. Tour. Leisure **10**, 1973–1984 (2021)
4. Gutierriz, I., Ferreira, J.J., Fernandes, P.O.: Digital transformation and the new combinations in tourism: a systematic literature review. Tourism Hosp. Res. 14673584231198414 (2023)
5. Abranja, N., Rodrigues, T., Bernardo, E.: Critical essay on emerging, transformative, and disruptive companies influencing consumer behaviour. In: Ramos, C.M.Q., Sousa, C.M.R., Matos, N.M.S., Ashqar, R.I. (eds.) Measuring Consumer Behavior in Hospitality for Enhanced Decision Making, pp. 104–120. IGI Global, Hershey, PA, USA (2023)
6. Munar, A.M., Gyimóthy, S.: Critical Digital Tourism Studies. Tourism Social Media: Transformations in Identity, Community and Culture, vol. 18, pp. 245–262. Emerald Group Publishing Limited (2013)
7. Benyon, D., Quigley, A., O'Keefe, B., Riva, G.: Presence and digital tourism. AI & Soc. **29**, 521–529 (2014)
8. Watkins, M., Ziyadin, S., Imatayeva, A., Kurmangalieva, A., Blembayeva, A.: Digital tourism as a key factor in the development of the economy. Econ. Ann.-XXI **169**, 40–45 (2018)
9. Zambonelli, F., Cabri, G., Leonardi, L.: Developing mobile agent organizations: a case study in digital tourism. In: Proceedings - 3rd International Symposium on Distributed Objects and Applications, DOA 2001, pp. 270–279 (2001)
10. UNWTO. Global Guidelines to Restart Tourism (2020). https://www.hbs.edu/ris/Public ation%20Files/12-016_a7e4a5a2-03f9-490d-b093-8f951238dba2.pdf
11. UN. Transforming our world: the 2030 Agenda for Sustainable Development (2015). https://documents-dds-ny.un.org/doc/UNDOC/GEN/N15/291/89/PDF/N1529189.pdf?Ope nElement
12. EU. Digital single market for Europe (2020). https://www.consilium.europa.eu/en/policies/ digital-single-market/
13. EU. Digital Agenda for Europe (2023).https://www.europarl.europa.eu/factsheets/en/sheet/ 64/digital-agenda-for-europe
14. EC. European data strategy (2023). https://commission.europa.eu/strategy-and-policy/priori ties-2019-2024/europe-fit-digital-age/european-data-strategy_en
15. EU Directive 2007/2/EC of the European Parliament and of the Council establishing an Infrastructure for Spatial Information in the European Community (INSPIRE) (2007). https:// eur-lex.europa.eu/legal-content/EN/TXT/PDF/?uri=CELEX:02007L0002-20190626
16. Verhun, A., Buntova, N., Boretska, N., Borysova, O., Shevchuk, S.: Digital tools for the development of the hospitality and tourism industry in the context of a digitized economy. Econ. Affairs (New Delhi) **67**, 869–876 (2022)
17. Nyanga, C., Pansiri, J., Chatibura, D.: Enhancing competitiveness in the tourism industry through the use of business intelligence: a literature review. J. Tourism Futures **6**, 139–151 (2020)
18. Höpken, W., Fuchs, M.: Business intelligence in tourism. Handbook of e-Tourism, pp. 497–527 (2022)

19. Ibrahim, N., Handayani, P.W.: A systematic literature review of business intelligence framework for tourism organizations: functions and issues. Interdiscip. J. Inf. Knowl. Manag. **17**, 523–541 (2022)
20. Xiao, H., Smith, S.L.J.: Case studies in tourism research: a state-of-the-art analysis. Tour. Manage. **27**, 738–749 (2006)
21. Fuchs, M., Abadzhiev, A., Svensson, B., Höpken, W., Lexhagen, M.: A knowledge destination framework for tourism sustainability: a business intelligence application from Sweden. Tourism **61**, 121–148 (2013)
22. Hamilton, J., Selen, W.: A multi-agent business intelligence framework for the travel sector. In: Proceedings of the International Conference on Electronic Business (ICEB), pp. 36–42
23. Marine-Roig, E., Anton Clavé, S.: Tourism analytics with massive user-generated content: a case study of Barcelona. J. Destin. Mark. Manag. **4**, 162–172 (2015)
24. Sinha, S., Bhatnagar, V., Bansal, A.: A framework for effective data analytics for tourism sector: big data approach. Int. J. Grid High Perform. Comput. **9**, 92–104 (2017)
25. Stylos, N., Zwiegelaar, J., Buhalis, D.: Big data empowered agility for dynamic, volatile, and time-sensitive service industries: the case of tourism sector. Int. J. Contemp. Hosp. Manag. **33**, 1015–1036 (2021)
26. Li, S., Sasaki, J.: A study on the tourism features extraction from photos in a tourism website by image analysis. In: 2019 IEEE 10th International Conference on Awareness Science and Technology, iCAST 2019 – Proceedings (2019)
27. Önder, I., Koerbitz, W., Hubmann-Haidvogel, A.: Tracing tourists by their digital footprints: the case of Austria. J. Travel Res. **55**, 566–573 (2016)
28. Li, J., Xu, L., Tang, L., Wang, S., Li, L.: Big data in tourism research: a literature review. Tour. Manage. **68**, 301–323 (2018)
29. Li, D., Deng, L., Cai, Z.: Statistical analysis of tourist flow in tourist spots based on big data platform and DA-HKRVM algorithms. Pers. Ubiquit. Comput. **24**, 87–101 (2020)
30. Li, Q., Li, S., Zhang, S., Hu, J., Hu, J.: A review of text corpus-based tourism big data mining. Appl. Sci. (Switzerland) **9**, (2019)
31. Pei, Y., Zhang, Y.: A study on the integrated development of artificial intelligence and tourism from the perspective of smart tourism. J. Phys. Conf. Ser. (Year)
32. Miah, S.J., Vu, H.Q., Gammack, J., McGrath, M.: A big data analytics method for tourist behaviour analysis. Inform. Manag. **54**, 771–785 (2017)
33. Williams, S.: Business Intelligence Strategy and Big Data Analytics: A General Management Perspective (2016)
34. Wöber, K.W.: Information supply in tourism management by marketing decision support systems. Tour. Manage. **24**, 241–255 (2003)
35. Nicoletti, A.: Piano Marketing - Piano delle attività APT (2022)
36. Basilicata, R.: Regione Basilicata. Documento di Economia e Finanza Regionale 2023–2025. Azione C4 "Sistema turistico-culturale" (2023). https://www.regione.basilicata.it/giunta/files/docs/DOCUMENT_FILE_3090764.pdf
37. Ivona, A., Rinella, A., Rinella, F.: Glocal tourism and resilient cities: the case of matera "European Capital of Culture 2019". Sustainability **11** (2019)
38. Cucari, N., Wankowicz, E.: Esposito De Falco, S.: Rural tourism and Albergo Diffuso: a case study for sustainable land-use planning. Land Use Policy **82**, 105–119 (2019)
39. Lugeri, F.R., Farabollini, P.: Discovering the landscape by cycling: a geo-touristic experience through Italian badlands. Geosciences **8** (2018)
40. Rainero, C., Modarelli, G.: The attractive power of rural destinations and a synergistic community cooperative approach: a "Tourismability" Case. Sustainability **12** (2020)
41. Simonetta, B.: False recensioni online fuori controllo, il business vale il 5–9% delle vendite. Il Sole 24 Ore (2015)

Scientific Computing Infrastructure
(SCI 2025)

.

Extending the Shortest Path Algorithm for Large Graphs with Cycles and Parallel Computing Capabilities

Muon Ha[1]([✉]) [iD], Yulia Shichkina[2] [iD], and Xuan-Hien Nguyen[3] [iD]

[1] Telecommunications University, Nha Trang, Vietnam
muon.ha@mail.ru
[2] St. Petersburg State Electrotechnical University, St. Petersburg, Russia
shichkina@co-evolution.ai
[3] Hanoi University of Industry, Ha Noi, Vietnam
hien.nguyen15@haui.edu.vn

Abstract. The challenge of finding the shortest path in graphs containing cycles and negative weights presents substantial difficulties across multiple fields, including transportation, social network analysis, and the study of complex systems. While sequential algorithms provide effective solutions for small to medium-sized graphs, they become impractical for large graphs due to constraints in processing time and computational resources. This paper presents an extension of the shortest path algorithm into a parallel computing environment, leveraging the power of modern multicore systems. Experimental results demonstrate that the parallel version achieves superior performance compared to traditional algorithms, making it suitable for handling large-scale graphs efficiently.

Keywords: Parallel Algorithm · Shortest Path · Negative Weights · Graphs with Cycles · Large Graphs

1 Introduction

Determining the shortest path in graphs represents a core challenge in graph theory and computer science, with a wide range of applications in areas such as transportation, network design, and social data evaluation. Classical algorithms such as Dijkstra, Bellman-Ford, and A* have proven effective in many specific scenarios. However, when applied to large graphs, especially those with cycles and negative weights, these algorithms face significant limitations. For instance, Dijkstra cannot handle negative weights, while Bellman-Ford encounters high computational costs when applied to dense graphs. These limitations necessitate the development of new algorithms that can not only solve the problem accurately but also scale effectively for large-scale graphs.

In practice, graph data is becoming increasingly large and complex, spanning global transportation networks, online social systems, and molecular graphs in medical research. These systems demand not only fast processing but also high accuracy,

O. Gervasi et al. (Eds.): ICCSA 2025 Workshops, LNCS 15894, pp. 191–204, 2026.
https://doi.org/10.1007/978-3-031-97648-3_13

particularly when graphs include cycles and negative weights, often encountered in economic analysis or biological system modeling. These requirements make traditional algorithms inadequate. Thus, the development of optimized algorithms, especially in parallel computing environments, has become a critical task for the computer science research community.

Modern computing systems, including supercomputers, cloud computing platforms, and GPUs, offer significant potential to enhance the performance of graph algorithms. Several studies have demonstrated that leveraging parallel processing can significantly accelerate the execution time of shortest path algorithms. However, in practice, parallel algorithms face considerable challenges. First, partitioning the graph for concurrent processing without compromising the problem's integrity is a complex issue. Second, load balancing among processes is essential to ensure efficient utilization of computing resources. Finally, the costs of inter-process communication and memory optimization remain open problems.

In our previous work [1], we introduced a sequential algorithm based on adjacency matrix representation to address the shortest path problem on graphs with cycles and negative weights. This algorithm overcame the limitations of Dijkstra and Bellman-Ford as well as opened new avenues for handling more complex graphs. However, when applied to large graphs, the algorithm revealed two major drawbacks: prolonged processing times and limited scalability. These issues motivated us to extend our research into the parallel computing domain, leveraging modern computational capabilities.

This research centers on the design of an innovative parallel algorithm, leveraging graph partitioning, adaptive load distribution, and communication enhancement. The approach boosts efficiency while maintaining scalability for extensive graph structures, addressing the computational demands of real-world scenarios including transportation systems, social data evaluation, and spatial information frameworks. Empirical evidence confirms that the developed algorithm surpasses conventional techniques in terms of execution speed and resource efficiency.

The paper is structured as follows: Sect. 2 examines prior research and assesses existing techniques. Section 3 outlines the proposed parallel algorithm and its technical enhancements. Section 4 provides experimental outcomes on substantial datasets, evaluating performance metrics. Finally, Sect. 5 summarizes the findings and explores potential research directions.

2   Related Works

The task of computing shortest paths in graphs serves as a critical focus within graph theory and computer science, enabling practical solutions in domains like traffic optimization, social connectivity modeling, communication systems, and resource distribution. Traditional methods, such as Dijkstra's and Bellman-Ford's algorithms, have been foundational solutions for this challenge. Dijkstra's algorithm [2] is predominantly utilized for graphs with non-negative weights due to its high computational effectiveness. Conversely, the Bellman-Ford algorithm is suitable for graphs with negative weights, though it encounters performance constraints with densely connected graphs [3, 4].

In recent years, many researchers have focused on improving these algorithms for large-scale graphs. Author in [5] use of Fibonacci Heaps significantly reduced the complexity of priority queue operations, making Dijkstra's algorithm particularly effective on dense graphs. Another approach introduced the Degree-Based Search algorithm, leveraging node degree metrics to optimize graph traversal and accelerate shortest path computation [6]. These methods both improved computational efficiency and reduced traversal complexity.

Parallel computing has significantly contributed to tackling the scalability issues encountered in shortest path computations across extensive graph structures. The Delta-stepping technique, a widely recognized approach, divides graphs into smaller subsets which facilitates simultaneous execution and minimizes data exchange between processes [7]. Enhanced implementations of Dijkstra's and Bellman-Ford's algorithms have demonstrated notable efficiency gains on multi-core and distributed platforms, though difficulties related to workload distribution and communication overheads remain unresolved [8, 9].

GPU-accelerated methods have also been developed to handle large-scale graphs efficiently. Algorithms like BFS and SSSP, accelerated by GPUs, leverage parallel processing capabilities to achieve substantial reductions in computation time. However, these methods face challenges related to memory optimization and thread balancing [10]. Other studies, such as Hyperlane, have combined dynamic graph partitioning with GPU processing to improve performance in distributed systems [11].

Shortest path algorithms have been applied across various domains. In transportation, parallelized A* algorithms have been utilized for real-time urban traffic routing, achieving high efficiency in large networks [12]. In wireless sensor networks, these algorithms are critical for enhancing energy efficiency and communication reliability [13]. In the field of telecommunications, the parallelized Johnson algorithm has been optimized to reduce communication costs across large-scale networks [14]. Several recent studies have also expanded the application of these algorithms to new domains such as social network analysis and robot navigation. Specifically, in social networks, the optimized algorithms have supported the identification of key influential groups, thereby improving the efficiency of information dissemination [15]. In addition, advanced models, such as image-blurring environments, have been proposed to address uncertainty in graph data, enabling applications that require precise data analysis [16].

Despite these advancements, the processing of large-scale graphs still encounters major challenges. Key issues such as achieving efficient graph partitioning for parallel execution without compromising accuracy, maintaining load balancing among processes, and minimizing communication costs have not been fully addressed yet. Moreover, integrating modern computing platforms like cloud systems and GPU-CPU hybrid architectures remains a promising research direction that has not been thoroughly explored.

This study proposes a new parallel algorithm that incorporates dynamic graph partitioning, asynchronous communication, and adaptive load balancing. These improvements aim to enhance performance and scalability, thus opening up new application opportunities in intelligent transportation, distributed systems, and large-scale data analysis.

3 Methodology

In our earlier work [1], we proposed a shortest path algorithm that utilizes the adjacency matrix representation of graphs to effectively tackle challenges posed by cycles and negative weights. The sequential algorithm was tested and shown to operate efficiently on medium-sized graphs, with the ability to identify and manage cycles while improving performance by removing redundant paths. However, when applied to large-scale graphs, this algorithm encountered limitations in processing time and computational resources.

To overcome these limitations, we extended our research to a parallel computing environment, leveraging the power of modern multicore processing systems. Implementing the algorithm in a parallel environment not only significantly reduced processing time but also expanded its applicability to large and complex graphs.

The main idea of deploying the algorithm in a parallel environment is to partition the graph's adjacency list into smaller subsets, each assigned to independent processes. Each process performs local computations and exchanges information with other processes to merge results, ensuring the integrity of the problem-solving process. This approach enhances scalability while maintaining accuracy in solving the shortest path problem.

General Process Overview:

Step 1: Data Partitioning. In this step, the adjacency list of the graph is divided into subsets, with each part containing a subset of edges.

Step 2: Local Computation. The processes compute the sets of vertices (V_1, V_2) and determine the local difference set (V').

Step 3: Information Exchange. Processes exchange information. Each process resolves its local calculations and merges the results into the union set (U', U'').

Step 4: Merging and Iteration. The results from all processes are merged to construct the generalized set $V = \Delta' \cup \Delta''$ with $\Delta' = V'' - U'$ and $\Delta'' = V' - U''$ which are the difference sets, and the computation continues until the optimal path is achieved.

To specifically illustrate the implementation of the shortest path algorithm in a parallel environment with two threads, the detailed procedure is described as follows:

1. Initialization

$M_{new} = \{\}$ and $M_{old} = \{\}$ Initialize the set representing new and old representative sets.

The graph is represented as an adjacency list, in which:

V_1: The set of starting vertices.

V_2: The set of target vertices.

P: : The set of edges (length) in the graph.

2. Partitioning the Adjacency List

Divide the adjacency list into two equal parts:

- **Thread 1:** Processes the first half of the adjacency list.
- **Thread 2:** Processes the second half of the adjacency list.

3. Find the Difference Set: $V = V_1 - V_2$

The computation is performed in each thread as follows:

3.1. Determine Local Difference Sets:

Thread 1: $V' = V_1' - V_2'$.

Thread 2: $V'' = V_1'' - V_2''$.

3.2. Exchange Information Between Threads:

Thread 1 sends V' to Thread 2 and receives V''.

Thread 2 sends V'' to Thread 1 and receives V'.

3.3. Merge the Results:

Thread 1: Compute the intersection $U' = V_2' \cap V''$, then $\Delta' = V'' - U'$.

Thread 2: Compute the intersection $U'' = V_2'' \cap V'$, then $\Delta'' = V' - U''$.

Final merge: $V = \Delta' \cup \Delta''$.

4. Merge Paths

Edges in the adjacency list are merged if the following conditions are met:

- The starting vertex of the edge belongs to V.
- The ending vertex matches the starting vertex of another edge.

5. Remove Invalid Edges

Edges in the adjacency list are removed if:

- The ending vertex belongs to the set of starting vertices.
- The edge does not lead to the destination vertex of the target path.

6. Update Optimal Paths

If $P(M_{old}) > P(M_{new})$: update M_{new}.

If $P(M_{old}) = P(M_{new})$, choose the shorter path.

7. Repeat

Repeat the steps with the updated adjacency list until no vertex in V_1 belongs to V_2.

Example: Given the following graph with the adjacency list below:

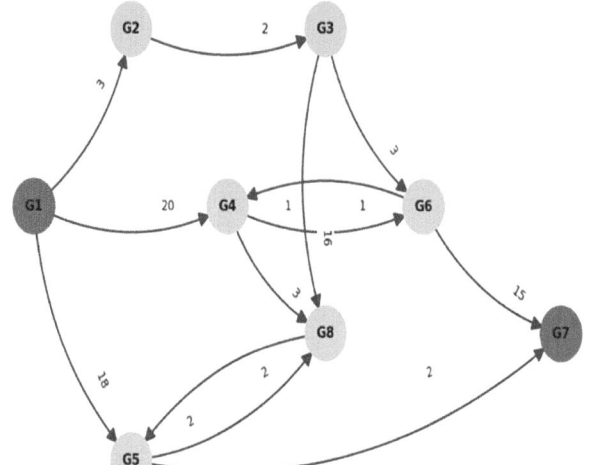

V_1	V_2	P
G_1	G_2	3
G_1	G_4	20
G_1	G_5	18
G_2	G_3	2
G_3	G_6	3
G_3	G_8	16
G_4	G_6	1
G_4	G_8	3
G_5	G_8	2
G_5	G_7	2
G_6	G_4	1
G_6	G_7	15
G_8	G_5	2

The algorithm processes in parallel on 2 threads to find the shortest path from vertex G_1 to vertex G_7, as detailed below:

Thread 1	**Thread 2**

Thread 1

V_1	V_2	P
G_1	G_2	3
G_1	G_4	20
G_1	G_5	18
G_2	G_3	2
G_3	G_6	3
G_3	G_8	16
G_4	G_6	1

$V_1'= \{G_1, G_2, G_3, G_4\}$
$V_2'= \{G_2, G_3, G_4, G_5, G_6, G_8\}$

Thread 2

V_1	V_2	P
G_4	G_8	3
G_5	G_8	2
G_5	G_7	2
G_6	G_4	1
G_6	G_7	15
G_8	G_5	2
G_8	G_7	16

$V_1''= \{G_4, G_5, G_6, G_8\}$
$V_2''=\{G_4, G_5, G_8, G_7\}$

Step 3.

3.1. $V'=V_1'-V_2'=\{G_1\}$	3.1. $V''=V_1''-V_2''=\{G_6\}$
3.2 Exchange V' and V'' $V''=\{G_6\}$	3.2 Exchange V' and V'' $V'=\{G_1\}$
3.3. Intersection $U'=V2'\cap V''=\{G_6\}$	3.3. Intersection $U''=V_2''\cap V'=\emptyset$
3.4. Difference $\Delta'=V''-U'=\emptyset$	3.4. Difference $\Delta''=V'-U''=\{G_1\}$

3.5. Union

$$V=\Delta' \cup \Delta'' =\{G_1\}$$

Step 4:

Send to the Thread 1:

V₁	V₂	P
G₁	G₂	3
G₁	G₄	20
G₁	G₅	18

Receive from Thread 2

V₁	V₂	P
G₁	G₂	3
G₁	G₄	20
G₁	G₅	18

Merge data between two threads

V₁	V₂	P
G₂	G₃	2
G₃	G₆	3
G₃	G₈	16
G₄	G₆	1
G₄	G₈	3
G₅	G₈	2
G₅	G₇	2
G₆	G₄	1
G₆	G₇	15
G₈	G₅	2
G₈	G₇	16

Split into two parts to send each part to each thread

V₁	V₂	P
G₅	G₇	2
G₆	G₄	1
G₆	G₇	15
G₈	G₅	2
G₈	G₇	16

V₁	V₂	P
G₅	G₇	2
G₆	G₄	1
G₆	G₇	15
G₈	G₅	2
G₈	G₇	16

V₁	V₂	P
G₁G₂	G₃	5
G₁G₄	G₆	21
G₁G₄	G₈	23
G₁G₅	G₈	20
G₂	G₃	2
G₃	G₆	3
G₃	G₈	16
G₄	G₆	1
G₄	G₈	3
G₅	G₈	2

V₁	V₂	P
G₁G₅	G₇	20
G₅	G₇	2
G₆	G₄	1
G₆	G₇	15
G₈	G₅	2
G₈	G₇	16

Receive from Thread 2
M_{new}= {G_1, G_5, G_7}, P=20

Calculate: M_{new}= {G_1, G_5, G_7}, P=20
Send to the Thread 1

Receive from Thread 2		
V_1	V_2	P
G_5	G_7	2
G_6	G_4	1
G_6	G_7	15
G_8	G_5	2
G_8	G_7	16

Delete the green row and Send to the Thread 1:

V_1	V_2	P
G_5	G_7	2
G_6	G_4	1
G_6	G_7	15
G_8	G_5	2
G_8	G_7	16

Reformat the input for the next iteration

V_1	V_2	P
G_1G_2	G_3	5
G_1G_4	G_6	21
G_1G_4	G_8	23
G_1G_5	G_8	20
G_2	G_3	2
G_3	G_6	3
G_3	G_8	16
G_4	G_6	1
G_4	G_8	3
G_5	G_8	2

Reformat the input for the next iteration

V_1	V_2	P
G_1G_2	G_3	5
G_1G_4	G_6	21
G_1G_4	G_8	23
G_1G_5	G_8	20
G_5	G_7	2
G_6	G_4	1
G_6	G_7	15
G_8	G_5	2
G_8	G_7	16

V1'= $\{G_1G_2, G_1G_4, G_1G_5, G_2, G_3, G_4\}$ V2'= $\{G_3, G_6, G_8\}$	V1''= $\{G_1G_2, G_1G_4, G_1G_5, G_5, G_6, G_8\}$ V2''= $\{G_3, G_6, G_8, G_7, G_4, G_5\}$

Repeat step 3

3.1. V'=V1'-V2'= $\{G_1G_2, G_1G_4, G_1G_5, G_2, G_4\}$	3.1. V''=V1''-V2''= $\{G_1G_2, G_1G_4, G_1G_5, G_6, G_8\}$
3.2 Exchange V' and V'' V''= $\{G_1G_2, G_1G_4, G_1G_5, G_6, G_8\}$	3.2 Exchange V' and V'' V'= $\{G_1G_2, G_1G_4, G_1G_5, G_2, G_4\}$
3.3. Intersection U'=V2'∩V''= $\{G_6, G_8\}$	3.3. Intersection U''=V2''∩V'=$\{G_4\}$
3.4. Difference Δ'=V''-U'= $\{G_1G_2, G_1G_4, G_1G_5\}$	3.4. Difference Δ''=V'-U''= $\{G_1G_2, G_1G_4, G_1G_5, G_2\}$
3.5. Union	

$$V=Δ'∪Δ'' = \{G_1G_2, G_1G_4, G_1G_5, G_2\}$$

...

Final result: $M_{new} = \{G_1, G_2, G_3, G_6, G_4, G_8, G_5, G_7\}$, P = 16

4 Experiments and Evaluation

4.1 Experimental Setup

The development of the parallel shortest path algorithm was executed in the C ++ programming language, utilizing *Boost.MPI* as the core infrastructure for coordinating communication between processes. The application is tailored for operation across distributed computing platforms, capitalizing on *Boost.MPI*'s features for message transmission and Boost.Serialization for optimized data transfer among processes. Evaluations were conducted on a system featuring an Intel Core i7-12700 processor, 32GB of memory, and operating on Ubuntu 22.04.

The program begins by reading the graph data from an input file, which is expected to be in adjacency list format. The graph data is divided among multiple processes, with the number of processes determined dynamically during execution. Each process handles a portion of the graph's edges, assigned through a modulo-based partitioning approach to ensure an even distribution of workload. This partitioning strategy enables each process to perform local computations independently, thereby minimizing the frequency of inter-process communication.

The algorithm operates in an iterative manner, with each process executing the following steps:

Step 1: Local Processing. Each process calculates the shortest paths for its allocated edge subset. This step involves updating local distance tables by evaluating differences between vertex sets (denoted as V_1 and V_2) and performing set operations such as union, intersection, and difference to refine the computed paths.

Step 2: Data Synchronization. Upon completing its local computations in each iteration, each process shares intermediate results with others using Boost.MPI's all-reduce and point-to-point communication methods. This step ensures consistency across all processes while keeping communication overhead low.

Step 3: Convergence Check. Each process evaluates whether any updates to the distance tables occurred in the current iteration. This information is then shared among all processes, and the algorithm terminates if no updates are observed.

The implementation is designed to adapt to varying process counts, enabling the program to scale seamlessly from a single machine to a distributed cluster environment. For efficient data exchange, the *Boost.Serialization* library is employed to handle the serialization and deserialization of complex structures, such as graph edges and distance tables, facilitating smooth communication between processes. This approach provides a versatile and reliable framework for executing the parallel shortest path algorithm across diverse configurations, accommodating a number of graph sizes and computational resources.

4.2 Performance Evaluation

The performance, scalability, and advantages of the proposed parallel algorithm were assessed through a series of experiments. Synthetic graphs with vertex counts ranging from 100 to 100,000 were used, covering both sparse and dense graph structures. The evaluation was conducted in three distinct phases to thoroughly analyze the algorithm's effectiveness.

In the first phase, the focus was on identifying the optimal thread count for parallel execution of the algorithm. Results indicate that the execution time decreases as the number of threads increases from 2 to 4, achieving the best performance at 4 threads. However, as the thread count increases to 6, 8, and 10, the execution time rises again, particularly for larger graphs (100,000 vertices). This indicates that the algorithm does not scale linearly with the amount of threads and is affected by synchronization overhead and resource contention.

Table 1 and Fig. 1 presents the execution times of the proposed algorithm for different graph sizes and various numbers of threads. The sequential execution times listed in the table were estimated based on the parallel execution times with two threads, considering typical parallelization efficiency and synchronization overhead.

Table 1. Execution Time with Different Numbers of Threads (ms)

Graph Size (|V|)	Sequential	Parallel				
		Threads (T = 2)	T = 4	T = 6	T = 8	T = 10
100	121	107	83	102.5	108	111.5
1,000	4323	3941	2982	3556	3928	4177
10,000	6783	7612	4503	6533	6698	6768
100,000	17320	14494	12459	14384	15465	16342

Figure 2 illustrates the speedup factor as a function of the number of threads. The speedup factor of the algorithm increases as the number of threads rises from 2 to 4, reaching its peak at 4 threads. Beyond this point, speedup decreases, especially for larger graphs (10,000 and 100,000 vertices). This confirms that after an optimal threshold, the cost of inter-thread communication and synchronization outweighs the benefits of parallelism, reducing efficiency. The speedup (S) was calculated using the formula: $S = \frac{T_{sequential}}{T_{parallel}}$, where $T_{sequential}$ is the execution time with one thread and $T_{parallel}$ is the execution time with multiple threads.

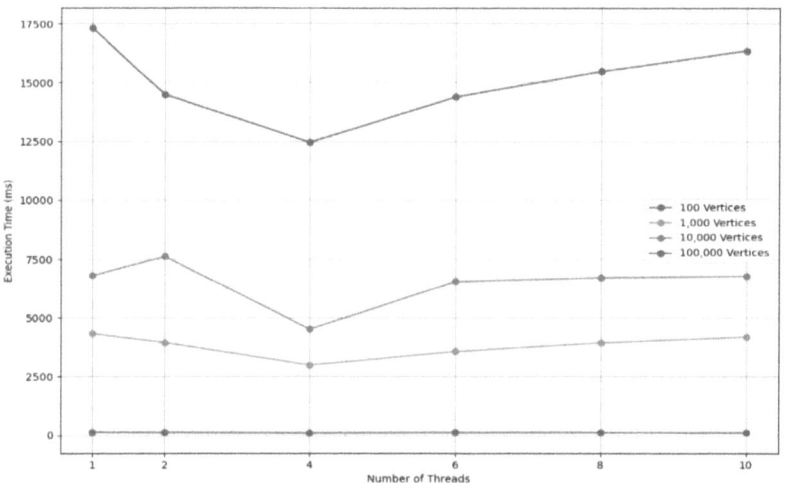

Fig. 1. Execution Time by Number of Threads

The results produced by the parallel version of the proposed algorithm are consistent with those obtained from the sequential execution. There is no observed discrepancy in the final output between the two versions, confirming the correctness and reliability of the parallel implementation.

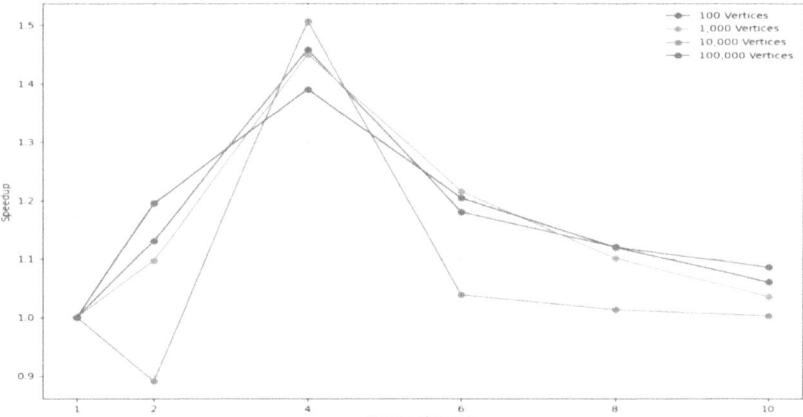

Fig. 2. Algorithm Speedup as a Function of the Number of Threads

Figure 3 compares the execution time of the Bellman-Ford, Dijkstra, and the proposed algorithm, all implemented with 4 parallel threads, across different graph sizes. Experimental results compare the execution times of Bellman-Ford, Dijkstra, and the proposed algorithm across different graph sizes using 4 threads.

- For 100 vertices, execution times of all three algorithms are relatively similar.
- As the graph size increases to 1,000, 10,000, and 100,000 vertices, the proposed algorithm consistently achieves the lowest execution time, whereas Bellman-Ford has the highest due to its higher computational complexity.
- Dijkstra performs better than Bellman-Ford but remains slower than the proposed algorithm, particularly for larger graphs.

Experiments show that the proposed algorithm achieves optimal performance with 4 threads, significantly reducing execution time compared to traditional algorithms (Figs. 1 and 2). However, increasing the thread count further leads to performance degradation due to synchronization overhead and memory contention, indicating that scalability depends on data size and hardware architecture.

Compared to Bellman-Ford and Dijkstra (Fig. 3), the proposed algorithm is superior, especially on large graphs. Bellman-Ford has the highest execution time. The proposed algorithm reduces execution time and maintains better efficiency as graph size increases.

It is a parallelized extension of our previously introduced sequential method, which was capable of handling graphs with cycles, negative weights, and even negative cycles. Unlike Dijkstra's algorithm, which fails with negative edge weights, and Bellman-Ford's algorithm, which suffers from high time complexity, the proposed parallel algorithm maintains both correctness and efficiency in these challenging cases. This ensures better scalability and applicability to complex real-world graph problems.

To further optimize performance, improvements in synchronization mechanisms and adaptive thread management can help enhance scalability for real-world applications such as intelligent transportation, social network analysis, and geographic information systems.

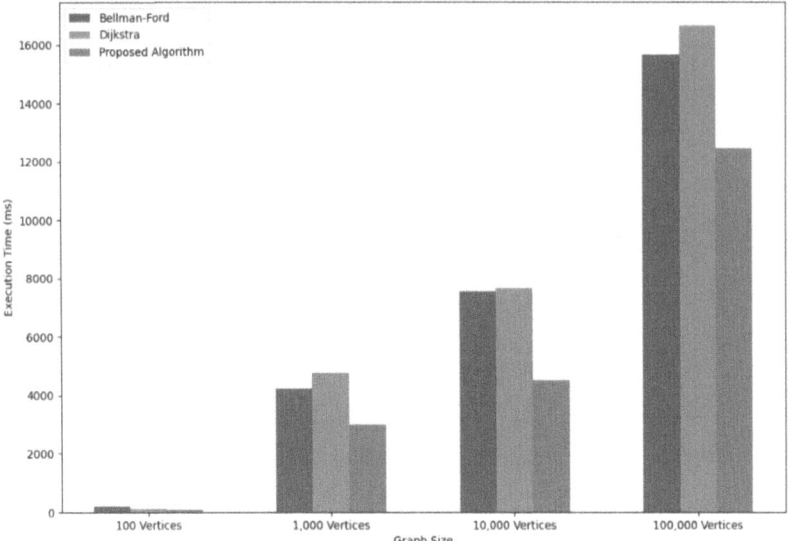

Fig. 3. Execution Time Comparison: Bellman-Ford, Dijkstra, and Proposed Algorithm (4 Threads)

4.3 Load Balancing Strategy

In the parallel implementation we propose, a fixed load distribution approach was implemented. The graph is divided among the available threads by allocating vertices (or edges) as uniformly as possible across them. Each thread handles a unique set of vertices along with their associated outgoing edges. This method reduces the need for synchronization by allowing threads to work independently during the relaxation process as much as possible. Although this static division works well for graphs with even distribution, adapting dynamic load adjustment techniques could improve performance when dealing with highly irregular graphs or those with uneven degree distributions.

5   Conclusion

This study focuses on the implementation and optimization of an algorithm in a parallel computing environment to solve the shortest path problem on large graphs. By leveraging the power of modern multi-threaded systems, the proposed parallel algorithm has demonstrated its ability to efficiently handle graphs ranging from thousands to hundreds of thousands of vertices, including both sparse and dense graphs. Through the partitioning of adjacency lists and the execution of computation steps concurrently across multiple threads, the algorithm not only reduces execution time but also maintains high accuracy in the results.

Experimental findings indicate that the parallel algorithm not only outperforms conventional algorithms such as Dijkstra and Bellman-Ford but also demonstrates near-linear scalability with an increasing number of processing threads. Notably, the algorithm capitalizes on the characteristics of parallel environments to optimize computational resources, especially for dense graphs.

Acknowledgment. This research has been supported by the Ministry of Science and Higher Education (assignment No. FSEE-2025-0015).

References

1. Shichkina, Y., Nguyen, X.H., Ha, M., Tran, D.M.: Shortest path search method on a graph with cycles. In: Gervasi, O., Murgante, B., Garau, C., Taniar, D., C. Rocha, A.M.A., Faginas Lago, M.N. (eds.) Computational Science and Its Applications – ICCSA 2024 Workshops. ICCSA 2024. Lecture Notes in Computer Science, vol. 14825. Springer, Cham (2024). https://doi.org/10.1007/978-3-031-65343-8_26
2. Dijkstra, E.W.: A note on two problems in connexion with graphs. Numer. Math. **1**(1), 269–271 (1959). https://doi.org/10.1007/BF01386390
3. Bellman, R.: On a routing problem. Q. Appl. Math. **16**(1), 87–90 (1958)
4. Qiu, L., Li, Z., Ke, X., Chen, L., Gao, Y.: Accelerating biclique counting on GPU. In: Proceedings of the 40th IEEE International Conference on Data Engineering (ICDE 2024), pp. 3191–3203. IEEE, Utrecht (2024). https://doi.org/10.1109/ICDE60146.2024.00247
5. Verma, D., Messon, D., Rastogi, M., Singh, A.: Comparative study of various approaches of Dijkstra algorithm. In: Proceedings of the 2021 International Conference on Computing, Communication, and Intelligent Systems (ICCCIS 2021), pp. 328–336. IEEE, Greater Noida (2021). https://doi.org/10.1109/ICCCIS51004.2021.9397200
6. Shyma, P.V., Sanil, S.K.P.: Degree-based search: a novel graph traversal algorithm using degree-based priority queues. Int. J. Adv. Comput. Sci. Appl. **15**(7), 1366–1371 (2024). https://api.semanticscholar.org/CorpusID:271699515
7. Sridhar, U., Blanco, M.P., Mayuranath, R., Spampinato, D.G., Low, T.M., McMillan, S.: Delta-stepping SSSP: from vertices and edges to GraphBLAS implementations. In: Proceedings of the 2019 IEEE International Parallel and Distributed Processing Symposium Workshops (IPDPSW 2019), pp. 241–250. IEEE, Rio de Janeiro (2019). https://doi.org/10.1109/IPDPSW.2019.00047
8. Zhang, B., Hu, D.J.: RETRACTED ARTICLE: Research on the construction and simulation of PO-Dijkstra algorithm model in parallel network of multicore platform. J. Wirel. Commun. Netw. **2020**, 85 (2020). https://doi.org/10.1186/s13638-020-01680-x
9. Safari, M., Oortwijn, W., Huisman, M.: Automated verification of the parallel Bellman–Ford algorithm. In: Drăgoi, C., Mukherjee, S., Namjoshi, K. (eds.) Static Analysis. SAS 2021. Lecture Notes in Computer Science(), vol. 12913. Springer, Cham (2021). https://doi.org/10.1007/978-3-030-88806-0_17
10. Aher, S.N., Walunj, S.M.: Accelerate the execution of graph processing using GPU. In: Satapathy, S., Joshi, A. (eds.) Information and Communication Technology for Intelligent Systems. Smart Innovation, Systems and Technologies, vol. 106. Springer, Singapore (2019). https://doi.org/10.1007/978-981-13-1742-2_13
11. Marcucci, T., Umenberger, J., Parrilo, P., Tedrake, R.: Shortest paths in graphs of convex sets. SIAM J. Optim. **34**(1), 507–532 (2024). https://doi.org/10.1137/22M1523790
12. Bhatia, J., Dave, R., Bhayani, H., Tanwar, S., Nayyar, A.: SDN-based real-time urban traffic analysis in VANET environment. Comput. Commun. **149**, 162–175 (2020). https://doi.org/10.1016/j.comcom.2019.10.011

13. Mostafaei, H.: Energy-efficient algorithm for reliable routing of wireless sensor networks. IEEE Trans. Industr. Electron. **66**(7), 5567–5575 (2019). https://doi.org/10.1109/TIE.2018.2869345

14. Joshi, S., Shanmuganathan, M., Aljuhani, A., Albalawi, U., Aljaedi, A.: Energy-efficient and secure wireless communication for telemedicine in IoT. Comput. Syst. Sci. Eng. **43**, 1111–1130 (2022). https://doi.org/10.32604/csse.2022.024802

15. Šumak, B., Pušnik, M.: Analysis of the Shortest Path Method Application in Social Networks. In: Information Modelling and Knowledge Bases XXXIV, pp. 169–182. IOS Press (2023). https://doi.org/10.3233/FAIA220500

16. Zuo, C., Pal, A., Dey, A.: New concepts of picture fuzzy graphs with application. Mathematics **7**(5), 470 (2019). https://doi.org/10.3390/math705047

Challenges of Application of Invisible Artificial Intelligence Technologies in the Industrial Internet of Things

Gennady Dik[1,2,5](✉), Alexander Bogdanov[1], Aleksandr Dik[1,2,5],
Jasur Kiyamov[1,3], Egor Savkov[4], Aleksandr Shchegolev[5],
and Aleksandr Aleksandrov[6]

[1] St. Petersburg University, St. Petersburg, Russia
{a.dik,a.v.bogdanov,z.kiyamov}@spbu.ru, g.dick@systechnologies.ru
[2] St. Petersburg LLC "System Technologies", St. Petersburg, Russia
[3] Samarkand Branch of Tashkent University of Information Technologies,
Samarkand, Uzbekistan
[4] Consern Avrora Scientific and Production Association JSC, St. Petersburg , Russia
[5] St. Petersburg State Marine Technical University, St. Petersburg , Russia
[6] JSC "Research Institute of Technical Sciences" "SINVENT", St. Petersburg , Russia

Abstract. The main problems and the possibilities of using artificial intelligence (AI) technologies in the industrial Internet of Things are considered, and the use of invisible intelligence technologies in an industrial environment (Industrial Invisible Intelligence, III) is analyzed. The article put forward the concept of building of an industrial framework in the form of a set of tools and libraries for fast and efficient software configuration, as well as the subsequent selection of the optimal composition of the AI models used in a particular production.

Keywords: artificial intelligence · Industrial Internet of Things (IIoT) · smart manufacturing · infrastructure of industrial smart systems · Technologies of invisible intelligence of the industrial environment · AI models

1 Introduction

Today, with the introduction of advances based on the Internet of Things (IoT), cloud technologies (Cloud), and Big Data (Big Data) in intelligent industrialization, the industrial Internet of Things is becoming an increasingly relevant topic for modern business, the public sector, and almost any manufacturing sector (Fig. 1). At the same time, the ever-growing volume of data, periodic changes in information processing methods, and an abrupt increase in the number of IIoTs in the "Smart Production" dictate the need to update the concept of building the infrastructure of modern industrial entities [1].

A modern enterprise is constantly facing a multitude of external and internal challenges. External challenges are primarily related to the ever-increasing competition, rapid changes in market conditions or new technological requirements.

O. Gervasi et al. (Eds.): ICCSA 2025 Workshops, LNCS 15894, pp. 205–218, 2026.
https://doi.org/10.1007/978-3-031-97648-3_14

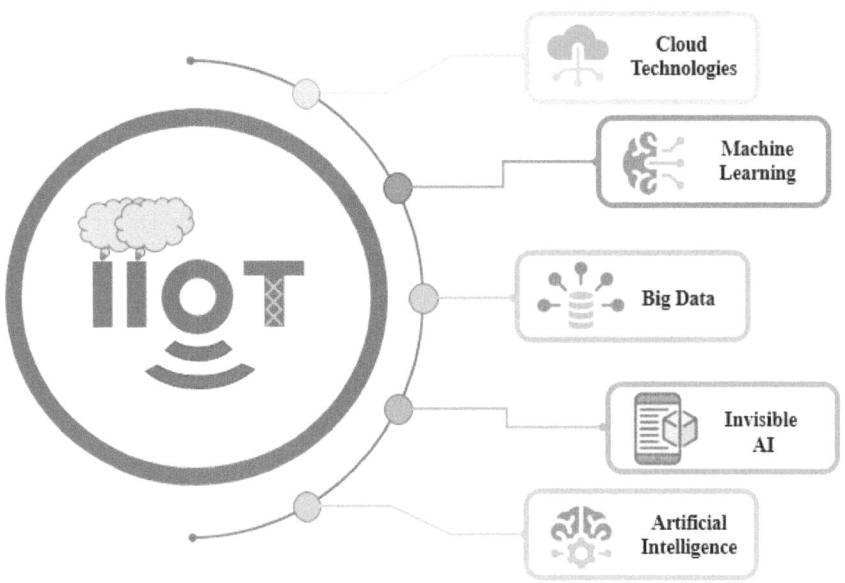

Fig. 1. New technologies in IIoT.

At the same time, internal problematic issues (hazardous production, lack of control over energy consumption and other resources, constant shortage of qualified personnel, suboptimal logistical movement, inadequate maintenance and repair, as well as insufficient automation of decision support, etc.) are dictated by increasingly complex production processes and, as a result, it is a big price of mistakes in any segment of industrial production [2,3].

At the same time, we have shown that by using of AI-based technologies, there is a real opportunity to obtain powerful tools for automating production processes, which will allow any enterprise from commercial to government to operate much faster, more accurately and reliably, and therefore more efficiently [4].

Thus, taking into account the relevance of the above-mentioned topics, we consider the issues of the introduction of AI technologies in the enterprise with a focus on the use of invisible intelligence technologies in an industrial environment with a wide range of IIoT applications [5].

2 The Relevance of the Use of AI as Part of the IIoT in the Enterprise

Automation in production is not just a trend today, but an urgent necessity for any organization seeking to maintain a competitive advantage and ensure sustainable growth. In the era of digitalization, when the speed of decision-making and their quality directly depend on the efficiency and accuracy of information processing, automation is becoming a key factor in the success of any modern enterprise.

The main purpose of business process automation is to minimize manual labor, eliminate errors caused by the human factor, and accelerate production operations [6]. This is achieved through the widespread implementation of IIoT using specialized software as part of various kinds of "smart devices" that allow automating not only routine repetitive processes, but also optimizing project management, resources, customer bases, complex device assembly, and much more. As a result, the company gets the opportunity not only to reduce costs, but also to significantly improve the quality of its services or products [7].

The role of AI in automation issues lies in the fact that its application allows (Fig. 2):

1. Reduce decision-making time during production. The implementation of AI-based algorithmic solutions, including using trained mathematical models, will allow for rapid analysis and calculations on large amounts of data, which ultimately creates almost continuous real-time management.

2. Reduce the chance of errors. The presence of AI in automating decision-making and improving the accuracy of calculations leads to the partial elimination of the human factor and reduces the risk of errors in decision-making. In addition, interactive prompts generated by the invisible intelligence system will ensure the necessary level and correctness of work, compliance with safety requirements, especially when performing dangerous types of work, etc.

3. Improve the quality of production operations. Intelligent AI control will provide maximum assistance in the automated production of any type of work from an office to a large industrial enterprise, from design to construction, installation and commissioning, which as a result will improve the quality of both the production operations themselves and the decisions made.

4. Ensure consistency. AI in the automation of production operations helps to maintain uniform standards and approaches, which is especially important when performing related types of work.

5. Optimize resources. The use of AI in automating the management of production operations leads to the most efficient use of industrial and human resources, as well as reduces costs in the field of IIoT application.

6. Improve the safety of IIoT applications. The use of various methods for detecting anomalies in the behavior of IIoT during production operations makes it possible to bring both technical (emergency prevention) and information security (attempts to introduce malicious influence, theft of information, etc.) to the required level.

It should be noted that this is not a complete list of the possibilities of using AI as part of IoT in an enterprise. Further, we present the results of research on this topic, concerning the choice of AI models for the application of invisible intelligence technology in an industrial environment. In addition, the article will address problematic issues of technological security threats related to equipment failures, low technology, physical wear and tear of equipment, personnel

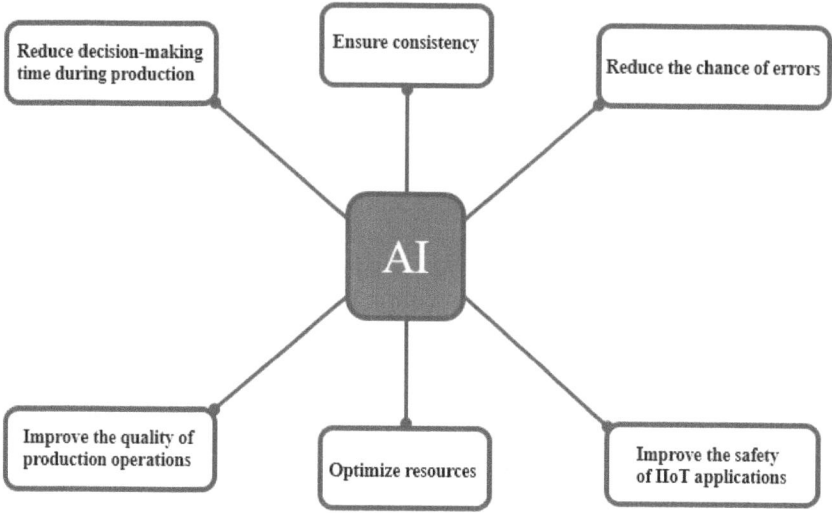

Fig. 2. Significance of AI in automation issues

errors, late or poor-quality maintenance, as well as problems with the use of new equipment and technologies, etc. [8].

To implement the above-mentioned innovative features, it is necessary to include them in the automation infrastructure (an application option for "Smart Manufacturing" is being considered) separate software components and modules that implement the corresponding functionality. At the same time, various types of automation systems should be taken into account, from ERP (enterprise resource planning) to MES (manufacturing execution system, production process management system) with the inclusion of IIoT devices in the control loop for collecting, transmitting and processing information (Fig. 3) [9,10].

3   Application of Invisible Intelligence Technology in an Industrial Environment

Ambient Invisible Intelligence (AII) is increasingly effectively and imperceptibly entering our lives. It is known that a number of technologies used to operate in the background ("invisible" to external manifestation) mode. This new paradigm is referred to by the term "ambient invisible intelligence", in which the intelligent infrastructure on IoT devices is built in such a way as to provide functionality with maximum convenience and minimal staff intervention. Unlike traditional technologies, AII does not require interaction with a tangible interface (voice commands, screen, keyboard, graphic manipulator, etc.), and it shows how such innovations can empower people while remaining virtually invisible and proactive

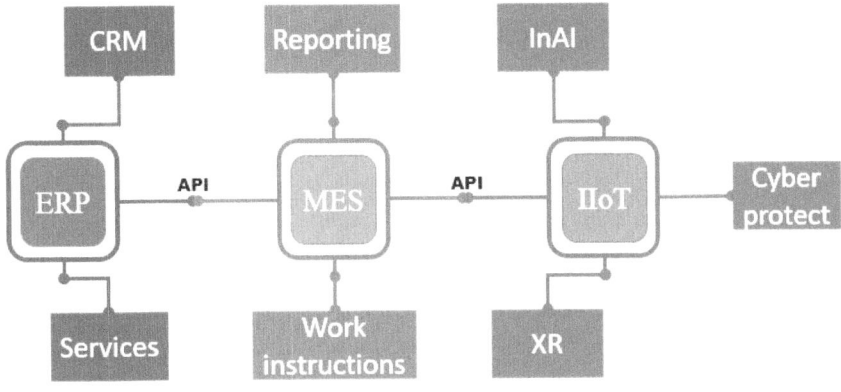

Fig. 3. Interaction of various types of automation with IIoT

Currently, AII form the basis of environments and systems that seem natural, end-user-oriented, and easily integrated into everyday life [11]. At the same time, the basic principle of construction should be simplicity, when devices are designed in such a way that they work without distracting attention, making interaction easy and intuitive. This paradigm paves the way for transformative innovations in areas such as smart living, education, healthcare, industry, etc., demonstrating the potential for optimizing and improving everyday production processes. Therefore, a wide practical application of AII can be found in climate control or Smart Home lighting. The most common example is the control of a thermostat, which adapts to the user's habits, remembers the preferred temperature settings and automatically determines the climatic conditions, thus eliminating the need for periodic manual data entry. Another everyday use case is adaptive lighting systems that adjust brightness and turn on (off) depending on movement and natural light, while there is no need for traditional switches and, as a result, the energy efficiency of the facility increases

Ensuring the continuity of operation and economical power consumption of IIoT devices as part of the AII is possible due to:

1. **Organization of information transmission** via low-power wireless communication such as Bluetooth, 5G, LoRaWAN, (widely used for switching various IIoT) and Wi-Fi (transmission of large amounts of data such as high-resolution images or video streams). In addition, the use of wireless Backscatter communication with backscatter is becoming more promising. This innovative technology allows devices to receive energy from radio waves (in particular, Wi-Fi) as a power source, providing long-term and energy-efficient communication.
2. **Energy storage** through the use of energy from external sources such as light, vibration, or radio frequencies (without recharging), which helps to extend service life, reduce maintenance costs, and improve environmental friendliness.

3. **The use of an IoT element** based on advanced chips/microprocessors with low power consumption, low-power cost-effective sensors and energy-efficient memory.

The study noted an increase in the degree of application of III (AII in the industrial sector) in such areas of industrial production as data analytics, resource optimization, preventive maintenance, ensuring various types of safety, proactive monitoring, emergency response, management through cognitive digital counterparts of objects and devices, as well as optimizing the movement of machines and mechanisms on the territory of the enterprise, including ensuring their interconnection.

Below are examples confirming the active use of III in the composition of IIoT:

1. Intellectual protection in the hazardous area of production by tags in clothing items (determining the location of employees and warning of danger).For example, clothing manufactured by the British company Eleksen for railway workers is capable of sending signals about the movement of trains, monitoring the health indicators of employees and allowing them to signal for help, as well as their location in transport movement zones (ElekTex technologies).
2. The built-in voice assistants integrated with system III can manage schedules or coordination of work of both employees and several IIoT devices, responding to commands in a conversation. The built-in speech recognition functionality at "NOVATEK STC" allows you to transform oral speech into written speech and enter text into a database; generate reports and send them to specified email addresses; open other corporate applications by voice request, etc.
3. In smart buildings, III-devices monitor energy consumption and regulate lighting, air conditioning, and RM employees to reduce the consumption of electrical resources, as well as costs and environmental impacts. An example worth mentioning is the SRR3 industrial building (Bangalore, India) - a shining example of intelligent synchronicity that ensures employee satisfaction. The integrated smart system controls air conditioning, ventilation, improves comfort and prioritizes renewable sources in the background.
4. Sensors installed in industrial or public premises can detect environmental hazards such as gas leaks, temperature fluctuations, or unauthorized access. Intelligent systems invisible in the environment can automatically manage alerts and initiate corrective actions. "Arm" (NASDAQ: ARM) develops and deploys innovative security foundations that enable seamless and personalized remediation in the environment.
5. In emergency situations (fire evacuation, warning and evacuation management systems, etc.), external invisible intelligence systems analyze real-time data to guide evacuation efforts, notify authorities and provide updated information about the situation, ensuring a quick and effective response. Google's Crisis Response: Google's Crisis Response team leverages AI to provide real-time information during disasters. Their AI-powered tools, such as SOS Alerts

and Crisis Maps, aggregate data from various sources to offer timely updates and resources to affected populations.

6. Virtual copies of real objects or processes, called digital twins, which use data from sensors and sensors installed, for example, on complex technical devices such as an airplane, helicopter, electric train, and others, will allow you to monitor a system or object in real time and predict its behavior. Sensors on such a real object collect data on the condition of individual devices, complexes, and systems (engine, motion and braking control systems, electrical systems, fuel systems, and other systems). This information is transmitted to its computer model or the digital twin of the object, where, using machine learning and predictive analytics algorithms, they predict how the parameters change under different conditions, external influences or the internal state of the devices. For example, Structon's predictive maintenance and fault diagnostics system allows manufacturers to identify conditions that could cause failure and intervene before it happens.

7. In real time, based on data from IIoT, the III-based software system calculates the optimal use of resources and routes for the movement of goods and mechanisms on the territory and inside the warehouses of an industrial enterprise. This direct interaction between vehicles replaces the traditional centralized concept of logistics organization by the teamwork of machines. For example, the AI Team Logistics software, as part of automated enterprise systems, optimizes the movement of vehicles in a warehouse to ensure their interaction.

Similar supporting examples can be continued (various examples together with specific technologies for implementing AI algorithms are given in Appendix 1), but a more detailed examination of production processes shows that the invisible intelligence in the IIoT plays a key role in collecting and analyzing data that was previously quite difficult or expensive to obtain, and given the development of technology, it is now possible to predict equipment breakdowns, optimize production lines, plan resources, and more., as mentioned earlier [12]. At the same time, it is obvious that these technologies are not some kind of new innovative solution for digital production, but the transfer of these technologies to the level of background or invisible intelligence is a new application of AI in IIoT. As a result, the analysis of the prospects for using AII in the industrial sphere carried out by the authors of the article made it possible to form the concept of building a software system using technology invisible industrial intelligence (SST III) for various use cases of IIoT [13–15].

4   The Concept of Building a SST III

Conceptually, SST III is a fragment of an industry framework in the form of a set of tools and libraries for fast and efficient software configuration, as well as determining the optimal composition of the AI models used to solve tasks in production [16].

According to this statement, the version of the framework being developed is designed to solve the following tasks:

1. Formation of the digital twin of the enterprise.
2. Identification of typical production process patterns.
3. Identification of unusual situations, artifacts, anomalies and deviations during various types of work in a digital enterprise.
4. Forecasting based on data (events) collected from the IIoT distributed environment.
5. Identification of explicit and hidden dependencies and correlations.
6. Forecasting taking into account various additional factors of possible external and internal impact.

As a prototype of the SST III, in accordance with the set of tasks to be solved, the authors selected a structure with typical options, consisting of the following software components (SCs) (Fig. 4):

1. SC "MIDDLE Layer" is an inter-platform (middleware) software that includes technological software for implementing and supporting interaction between various applications, systems and software modules (receiving packets or data streams, buffering, validation, normalization, etc.).
2. SC "Creating and editing digital the double of the enterprise".
3. SC "Identification and prevention of emergency situations".
4. SC "Formation of corrective actions".
5. SC "Monitoring and dispatching".
6. SC "Control of reactive, preventive and predictive maintenance".
7. SC "Recommendation generation (voice notification and management)".
8. SC "Ensuring information and technological security of IIoT". The use of various methods for detecting anomalies in the behavior of IIoT during production operations makes it possible to bring both technical (emergency prevention) and information security (attempts to introduce malicious influence, theft of information, etc.) to the required level.
9. DBMS storage of input and processed data and AII models.

The SST III input receives data from various IIoT sensors, digital production automation systems, computerized maintenance management systems (CMMS) and other industrial smart systems in JSON, CSV, PROTOBUF, XML and other exchange protocols supported by the MIDDLE Layer PC.

The input of input PCs for the industry framework is organized through the endpoints of the FastAPI framework.

The developed industry framework uses the following software tools:

– PYTHON, the main programming language of the PC framework, provides the necessary support for AI creation and training methods.
– UVICORN is a library for running a web server in PYTHON.
– FastAPI is a web framework for creating fast HTTP API servers with built-in validation, serialization, and asynchrony.

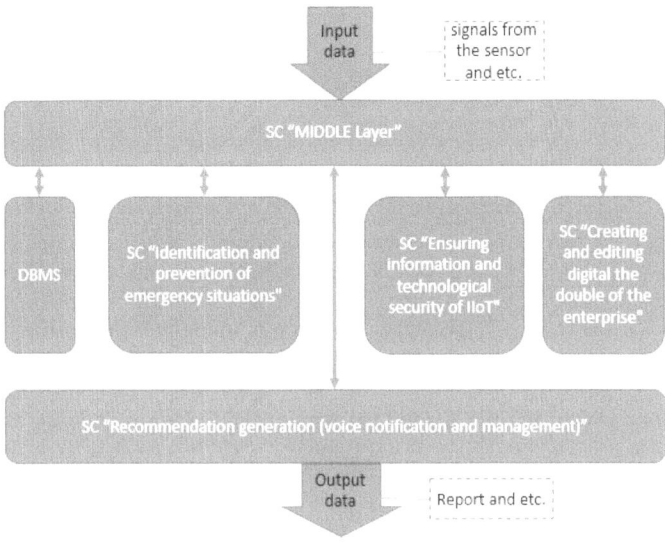

Fig. 4. The block diagram of the SST III prototype

– OpenAPI is a REST web services framework that allows you to test and manage a project without an interface.
– PostgreSQL is an objectâĂŞrelational database management system based on POSTGRES, v.4.2. with the ability to provide a packaging tool and add-ons for the database (DB).

In addition to the above software tools, the developed industry framework uses special software tools âĂŞ libraries of AI methods, which are later used in SST III. In accordance with the capabilities of the framework, the composition of libraries of methods can be supplemented and adjusted depending on the purpose and complex of tasks of the digital enterprise to be solved. Tables 1, 2, 3, 4, 5, 6, 7 and 8 contains a number of algorithms for the framework in question.

The composition of the SST III can be supplemented and expanded depending on the functionality and class of tasks to be solved both in production and in the household sphere.

As a result, among the many possibilities of using artificial intelligence technologies, it is proposed to emphasize the prospect of using invisible intelligence in the industrial sphere. With the help of available libraries and tools, it is easy to set up the environment and create the most optimal solution for the enterprise.

An example of a real implementation of the presented methodology is the implemented prototype of the "Zeus" software system. This software system solves current unification problems in order to improve the management of heterogeneous types (different manufacturers) and devices (different functionality) as part of technical security systems, active use of AI methods to solve problems of ensuring the safety of industrial facilities, as well as maintaining the software

Table 1. Structon's POSS preventive Maintenance and Fault diagnosis system

Tasks	identifies conditions that could cause a breakdown and intervenes before it occurs
Algorithms	Predictive maintenance that uses models to predict failures of specific unit components
Links	https://www.altexsoft.com/blog/predictive-maintenance/
Justification of the choice of algorithms	Speaking of industry, it is necessary to mention the high cost of suspending production, especially in large enterprises. Predictive maintenance eliminates the need to suspend production processes, as it helps to recognize even those minor changes in the condition of equipment that are not detected during a typical inspection. AI-based diagnostic tools allow manufacturers to identify conditions that could cause a breakdown and intervene before it occurs. With the help of machine learning models, manufacturers can predict the remaining service life of equipment and prepare for repairs.

Table 2. Robotic Process Automation Working for Schneider Electric's Global Supply Chain

Tasks	Automation of document preparation
Algorithms	RPA is a robotic process automation software designed to simulate human actions when performing repetitive business tasks
Links	https://www.uipath.com/resources/automation-case-studies/schneider-electric-manufacturing-rpa https://www.altexsoft.com/blog/robotic-process-automation
Justification of the choice of algorithms	The operators responsible for the installation of electrical panels on the territory of customers had to deal with monotonous and voluminous documentation processing, for example, marking electrical circuits or production specifications of electrical panels. To complete this long and tedious task, an AI bot was introduced, freeing up operators' time for more valuable and complex production work.

Table 3. Google Cloud Visual Inspection AI

Tasks	Quality control (QA) and verification of the condition of manufactured products
Algorithms	Google Cloud Visual Inspection AI
Links	https://cloud.google.com/vertex-ai/generative-ai/docs/model-garden/explore-models https://www.altexsoft.com/blog/image-recognition-neural-networks-use-cases
Justification of the choice of algorithms	Human vision has obvious disadvantages (fatigue and bias), therefore, thanks to computer vision control, QA becomes more reliable and accurate. Visual Inspection AI automates the QA process and identifies defects even before products leave the assembly line

Table 4. AI Team Logistics

Tasks	Warehouse automation
Algorithms	Optimizing the movement of all trucks in the warehouse and ensuring their interconnection
Links	https://toyota-forklifts.eu/about-toyota/news-and-editorials/toyotas-a.i.teamlogistics-concept-presented-at-cemat-2018/
Justification of the choice of algorithms	very second, an AI-based software system calculates the optimal use of resources and routes for carriers. This direct interaction between vehicles replaces the traditional centralized warehouse concept with the teamwork of machines. The AI Team Logistics concept transforms redundant warehouse management into productive teamwork

Table 5. Arkellis Technologies

Tasks	A framework for industrial applications.
Algorithms	Development tools for various use cases: training, repair, maintenance, visualization, job introduction, etc.
Links	https://arkellis.com/, https://innovanews.ru/info/innovations/top-10-sovremennykh-tendentsijj-i-innovatsijj-promyshlennojj-revoljutsii-40/
Justification of the choice of algorithms	The framework accelerates production processes by integrating ready-made solutions with data. This allows you to bring a product to market faster and not develop them from scratch on your own

Table 6. SECOM class imbalance âĂŞ solutions to the problem of class imbalance are presented (in data on semiconductor production lines)

Tasks	Working with distorted data and selecting features, focusing on the problem of class imbalance and the ability to successfully predict failures
Algorithms	Random Forest is a machine learning algorithm that uses an ensemble of decision trees. Single—class support vector machines (SVMs) are a type of outlier detection method. SMOTE - synthetic data generation. Gradient Boosting Machine (GBM) is a machine learning method for regression and classification problems that creates a predictive model in the form of an ensemble of forecasting algorithms, usually decision trees.
Links	https://github.com/Meena-Mani/SECOM_class_imbalance?tab=readme-ov-file.
Justification of the choice of algorithms	Random Forest is an algorithm capable of efficiently processing data with a large number of features and classes and containing methods for estimating the significance of individual features in a model

Table 7. Predictive-maintenance

Tasks	Improve maintenance operations and time-based preventive maintenance planning by using data processing techniques and machine learning algorithms to more accurately predict maintenance needs
Algorithms	The sklearn Library: – regression modeling – binary classification – multiclass classification algorithms
Links	https://github.com/Samimust/predictive-maintenance.
Justification of the choice of algorithms	Regression modeling - algorithms for predicting the number of cycles remaining before engine failure. Binary classification algorithms were used to predict whether an engine would fail within a certain number of cycles or not. Multiclass classification algorithms were used to predict in which cycle or period the engine would fail.

Table 8. Iot-predictive-analytics

Tasks	Predicting equipment failures using Internet of Things sensor data
Algorithms	TLogistic regression is a statistical model used to predict the probability of an event occurring
Links	https://github.com/IBM/iot-predictive-analytics.
Justification of the choice of algorithms	Advantages of logistic regression: - simplicity in the implementation and interpretation of the results of the algorithm - high speed operation - relatively good accuracy

used in the current state) due to the capabilities of the built-in framework and rule designer. At the same time, the main attention is paid to the fulfillment of requirements for security and fire measures, control of water leaks and gas leaks, as well as identifying anomalies in electricity consumption using AI (predictive analytics, forecasting and development of recommendations) with the active use of IoT and IIoT at facilities.

At the core of "Zeus" is a framework designed to analyze big data collected from the environment of technical security systems (for example, from distributed sensors) in order to identify patterns, typical data patterns, implicit dependencies, unusual behavior of the system as a whole and, ultimately, to generate forecasts of the state of a given object. It should be noted that the implemented AI-based software tools operate in the background (use option III) to receive data from end devices in order to determine emergency and critical situations (incidents), since the enterprise has a large number of false positives due to the use of classic threshold algorithms.

5   Conclusion

Our task was to show the possibility for a customer from industry or a government structure to choose and create the most suitable option for "Smart Production", while setting up the use of IOT based on III in the background. At the same time, the main problematic issues of the enterprise were considered, to which it is advisable to apply the III.

In addition, in this paper, we propose a version of the methodology for implementing an industry framework using III in an industrial enterprise:

1. Analysis of the infrastructure of a "digital enterprise", identification of production processes for automation, assessment of the availability and capabilities of IIoT, as well as identification of needs for their use.
2. Building a digital twin of the enterprise.
3. The formation of an industry framework as part of a set of AI libraries that can be connected depending on the tasks being solved in the enterprise.
4. Training of the III models included in the industry framework.
5. Installation of trained models into the existing infrastructure of the "digital enterprise", conducting testing and determining the optimal options for further trial operation.

The proposed methodology depends on the purpose, composition, complex of tasks to be solved, the degree of equipment with IIoT tools and other factors related to the planned automation in the digital enterprise under consideration.

The application of the methodology proposed by the authors depends on various parameters of the digital enterprise (purpose, composition, set of tasks to be solved, degree of equipment with IIoT tools and other factors related to the planned automation).

Calculation of the increase in efficiency when implementing the proposed technology is beyond the scope of this article. At the same time, it should be noted that the increasingly widespread implementation of this concept demonstrates the efficiency of the functioning of the components of the Internet of Things due to the automation of routine tasks and optimization of processes in an industrial enterprise, savings due to waste reduction and improved resource management in production, as well as improving various aspects of safety (improving safety protocols, reducing the influence of the human factor, etc.).

References

1. Satdinov, F.R.: Mathematical methods and models of decision support. Young Scientist **38**(537), 12–14 (2024). https://moluch.ru/archive/537/117851/
2. Utochkina, L.A.: The role of technical and technological safety in the system of economic security of the organization. Res. Econ. Fin. Probl. **3**, 3 (2023). https://doi.org/10.31279/2782-6414-2023-3-3
3. PNTS. Preliminary National Standard of the Russian Federation. Smart manufacturing. Digital Production Doubles. Moscow, Standartinform. https://files.stroyinf.ru/Data2/1/4293719/4293719549.pdf. Accessed 15 March 2025

4. Industrial Internet of Things—IIoT. Industrial Internet of Things in Russia. https://www.tadviser.ru/a/381216. Accessed 16 March 2025
5. The invisible ambient technology evolution powered by AI. https://www.ft.com/partnercontent/arm/the-invisible-ambient-technology-evolution-powered-by-ai.html. Accessed 16 March 2025
6. Industrial automation trends-2024.https://indpages.ru/solutions/avtomati-zacziya-promyshlennosti-trendy-2024. Accessed 16 March 2025
7. Yu, B.: Automation of technological processes: prospects, challenges and ways to increase production efficiency. Universum Techn. Sci. Electron. Sci. J. **11**(128) (2024). https://7universum.com/ru/tech/archive/item/18611
8. Shestakov, N.V., Mishin, S.P.: Improving the efficiency of industrial enterprises in Russia through advanced automation solutions. Autom. Ind. **3**, 3–5 (2016)
9. Khromova O., et al.: How neural networks help make businesses safer and more efficient (2024). https://clck.ru/3Jgj93
10. Knyaginin, V.N., et al.: Sources of New Industries, Issue 3, Artificial Intelligence in Industry, Expert Report, Saint Petersburg (2022). https://clck.ru/3JgjPv
11. Mitchell, M.: Why AI is harder than we think. arXiv preprint arXiv:2104.12871 (2021)
12. Wan, J., Li, X., Dai, H., et al.: Artificial intelligence-driven customized manufacturing factory: key technologies, applications, and challenges. arXiv preprint arXiv:2108.03383 (2020). Elgan, M.: Where invisible technologies come from and why they are important (2016). https://www.itweek.ru/ai/article/detail.php?ID=188843
13. Industrial Internet of Things (IIoT): Smart solutions for manufacturing (2023). https://clck.ru/3JgjZM
14. Klevtsov, A.: Prospects for using Internet of Things technologies in problems of optimizing electricity consumption. https://clck.ru/3Jgjtt. Accessed 16 March 2025
15. Zachman, A.: The framework for enterprise architecture: background description and utility. https://clck.ru/3Jgk3n. Accessed 15 March 2025
16. Campbell, A.: Dynamic Models of Enterprise Architecture. Ingenia WordPress (2016). https://ingenia.wordpress.com/2016/09/04/dynamic-enterprise-architecture-models

Language Model-Based Algorithm for Constructing Knowledge Graphs from Patent Data

Nikita Gavrilov[1]([✉])(iD), Vladimir Korkhov[1](iD), Evgenii Pen[2], and Alexey Tokarev[3]

[1] Saint Petersburg State University, Saint Petersburg, Russia
st102441@student.spbu.ru, v.korkhov@spbu.ru
[2] BioGeoHab, Saint Petersburg, Russia
[3] EDRID, Saint Petersburg, Russia

Abstract. This paper presents a method for constructing a knowledge graph based on patent data, which facilitates the identification of hidden relationships between patents and the organization of information for subsequent analysis. The method involves extracting key textual fields from patent documents and vectorizing them using state-of-the-art transformer models, and building a graph where the nodes represent individual documents, and the edges reflect their semantic proximity. A clustering algorithm is employed to group the patents, ensuring high internal coherence within clusters and reducing the original graph to a compact representation. The resulting clusters are summarized using language models, enabling automatic extraction of significant terms for cluster descriptions. Experimental research conducted on a large corpus of patent data demonstrates the efficacy of the proposed approach, which is confirmed by the relevant partitioning quality metrics. The proposed method improves the interpretation of patent information, facilitating the identification of implicit relationships and structural patterns, which is of great importance for analyzing scientific achievements and managing intellectual property.

Keywords: Knowledge Graph · Patent Data · Text Vectorization · Clustering

1 Introduction

Knowledge graphs are data structures that represent relationships between various entities and are utilized to address a wide range of tasks, such as information retrieval, recommendation systems and natural language processing. In contrast to traditional knowledge graphs, which contain specific entities as nodes and express relationships through triplets of the form ⟨entity, relationship, entity⟩ [1], in this approach, the nodes of the graph contain textual data, and the relationships between them are identified using vector representations of these texts.

The relevance of this research is underscored by the growing volume of patent data, which is an important source of information for analyzing scientific and technological achievements. Patents contain both structured and unstructured

O. Gervasi et al. (Eds.): ICCSA 2025 Workshops, LNCS 15894, pp. 219–230, 2026.
https://doi.org/10.1007/978-3-031-97648-3_15

information about new technologies, inventions, and their legal protection, rendering them a valuable resource for analyzing technological trends and innovations. However, the substantial volume of this data and its complex structure complicate manual processing and analysis, necessitating the development of automated knowledge extraction methods.

The primary challenge in constructing knowledge graphs from patent data lies in the complexity of the text, which often contains specialized terminology and legal phrasing. Extracting entities from such texts necessitates meticulously annotated data. To tackle this challenge, it is essential to clearly define the application domain of a specific solution, which involves standardizing the problem formulation to ensure its wide applicability. Additionally, manual text annotation is a labor-intensive process that requires substantial time and resources, limiting the creation of a sufficient volume of annotated data for training models.

To efficiently process such data, it is necessary to develop algorithms that account for these features, particularly for the Russian language, where existing approaches designed for English are not always applicable [2].

The contribution of this paper is a flexible and lightweight method for constructing knowledge graphs from patent data. Unlike conventional approaches that rely on named entity recognition (NER) and relation extraction (RE) to extract specific entities and their relationships, our method models entire documents as graph nodes and infers their connections based on semantic similarity using transformer-based language models. This enables scalable graph construction without the need for pre-trained NER/RE pipelines, making the method language-agnostic, easy to implement, and particularly effective in low-resource languages or domains where high-quality annotation tools are unavailable.

The paper is structured as follows: Sect. 2 reviews related work on language models. Section 3 formulates the problem and outlines key challenges. Section 4 presents the proposed graph construction and clustering method. Section 5 analyzes the experimental results, and Sect. 6 concludes the paper and suggests directions for future research.

2 Related Work

Constructing knowledge graphs based on patent data is based on the task of finding relevant patents, which is a key area of application for information retrieval methods.

To solve the task of finding relevant patents, it is reasonable to use models with transformer architecture. Multilingual models, such as mBERT, XLM-R [3] and mDeBERTa [4], are successfully applied to process the Russian language, but with the development of monolingual models, their role has become supplementary. Among Russian-language models, RuBERT [5] and RuLeanALBERT [6], trained on corpora such as Wikipedia, web texts, and social media, stand out. Monolingual models have significantly improved the understanding of Russian text. Let us consider several popular models for processing the Russian language:

- The ruBERT model is based on the BERT architecture [7], which uses two key pretraining objectives: the masked language modeling (MLM) task and the next sentence prediction (NSP) task;
- ruRoBERTa is based on the RoBERTa architecture [8] and uses a modified version of the MLM pretraining task. Unlike ruBERT, the ruRoBERTa model was trained on a larger dataset, significantly improving its performance. The model uses Byte-level BPE (BBPE) tokenization and has a vocabulary size of 50,000 tokens;
- The ruELECTRA model [9] uses the ELECTRA architecture and follows the replaced token detection (RTD) task, where the model is trained to predict which tokens were replaced by the MLM-based generator.
- ruT5 is one of the first models for the Russian language based on the T5 architecture [10], which employs an encoder-decoder approach. The model is trained on the task of span corruption, where consecutive spans of text are masked, and the model learns to recover the masked tokens using Sentence-Piece tokenization.
- FRED-T5 (Full-scale Russian Enhanced Denoisers) is a model based on T5 and UL2 [11], which uses multiple pretraining objectives to create a more versatile approach. Unlike ruT5, FRED-T5 uses the gated GELU activation function instead of ReLU and is trained on a mixture of different types of denoisers.

New multilingual models with Russian language support continue to emerge. EuroBERT [12], for instance, is a multilingual encoder built on the Llama 3 architecture. It has been trained on a large multilingual dataset that includes programming code and mathematical texts and is available in three sizes (210M, 610M, and 2.1B parameters). The training process follows a two-stage approach, consisting of pre-training and annealing, with masked language modeling (MLM) as the core objective. Several architectural refinements have been implemented, including grouped query attention, swish gated linear units, root mean square layer normalization, rotary position embeddings, and the removal of bias terms.

The development of models with encoder architecture improves the accuracy of text processing and analysis, enhancing semantic understanding. This directly impacts the effectiveness of patent search tasks and knowledge graph construction. The same applies to large language models, which significantly improve the capabilities of text data analysis and interpretation.

Large language models, such as Llama 3 [13], fine-tuned on Russian-language text corpora, effectively solve NER tasks and annotation creation. However, in this work, computational power limitations prevent the use of any models, making the development of compact language models for specialized tasks both important and relevant today.

3   Problem Statement

The goal of this work is to propose a method for identifying relationships between patent data. To achieve this goal, the following tasks have been formulated:

- Development and implementation of a graph construction algorithm;
- Application of a clustering algorithm to the graph;
- Interpretation of the obtained results.

The specific technical challenges addressed in this research include:

- Semantic representation: Selecting and implementing appropriate transformer models to convert patent texts into vector representations that accurately capture their technical content, and utilizing specialized vector databases for efficient similarity comparisons.
- Graph construction optimization: Determining the optimal parameters for graph construction, particularly the number of connections (k) between nodes, to balance connectivity and computational efficiency.
- Cluster granularity: Finding the appropriate resolution parameter for the clustering algorithm that produces meaningful patent groupings without creating excessively large or numerous clusters.
- Cluster interpretation: Creating an automated method to generate descriptive labels for patent clusters that accurately represent their technical content.

4   Proposed Solution

Figure 1 illustrates the process of converting the initial set of patent data into a graph through the sequential execution of four stages:

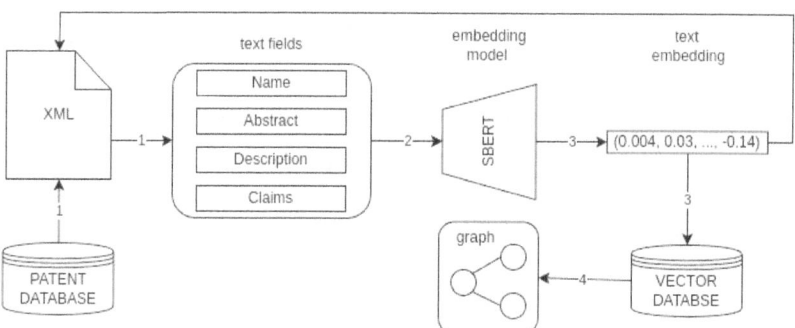

Fig. 1. Graph Construction Algorithm.

1. The main textual fields of each patent are extracted, stored in XML format. For further vectorization, we will use the claims field, as it is considered the most informative and conveys the essence of the patent.

2. Each of the extracted text blocks undergoes vectorization. For this, a transformer-based model that supports Russian either as the main language or as one of the possible languages is used. We chose ruRoBERTa-large because it demonstrates high performance on the Russian SuperGLUE tasks [14].
3. A vector database is employed for efficient storage and retrieval of documents. In our implementation, we use the FAISS library, which supports GPU processing.
4. A graph node is assigned to each patent, and edges between nodes represent the semantic proximity of the documents. Semantically similar patents are determined based on a fixed number of nearest neighbors or a threshold value of cosine distance.

The constructed patent graph serves as the basis for further analysis. To identify structural patterns and group similar documents, the Leiden clustering algorithm [15] is applied, ensuring high internal coherence of the nodes. The algorithm consists of four stages:

1. Local node movement. Each node is initially placed in its own community, after which iterative movement of nodes to neighboring communities takes place. A node moves if such an action increases the objective function (e.g., modularity), which improves the partitioning quality.
2. Partition refinement. At this stage, the obtained partitioning is refined: each community is analyzed for internal coherence. If there are parts within a community that are weakly connected, the community can be split into several more compact and well-connected sub-communities.
3. Graph aggregation. After partition refinement, each community is reduced to a single supernode, and the edge weights between supernodes are determined as the sum of the original edge weights between the corresponding communities. The algorithm then repeats on the aggregated graph until a stable partitioning is reached.

The resulting clusters are summarized using large language models, which automatically extract significant terms and generate meaningful descriptions. Based on these descriptions, a new graph is formed, where each node represents an individual cluster. As a result, the original graph size is reduced.

5   Results Analysis

For the study, a corpus of 329,826 patents, represented in XML format, from the RUPAT database provided by the Federal Institute of Industrial Property (FIPS) was used. The RUPAT database contains full texts of Russian patents, including descriptions of inventions, claims, abstracts, as well as data about applicants and authors. The textual fields of the patent documents were extracted and stored in the PostgreSQL.

An experiment was conducted to determine the optimal number of neighbors, where the parameter k (the number of neighbors for each node) was analyzed for its impact on the structure of the graph. The experiment involved incrementally increasing k in steps of 2, starting from the minimum value. As k increases, the density of connections rises, which improves coherence, but it can also lead to data redundancy. The objective of the experiment was to ascertain the optimal value of k at which each node would maintain sufficient connectivity with other nodes, ensuring that the graph does not contain isolated subgraphs. This is crucial, as the connectivity of the graph significantly influences the subsequent clustering process. Additionally, the relationship between unique and duplicate connections with respect to k was investigated. The aim was to determine the value of k at which redundancy in the graph begins to increase. As the number of neighbors increases, the number of unique connections should remain stable, while the number of duplicate connections increases, which may indicate rising redundancy in the graph. The results of the experiment are shown in Fig. 2.

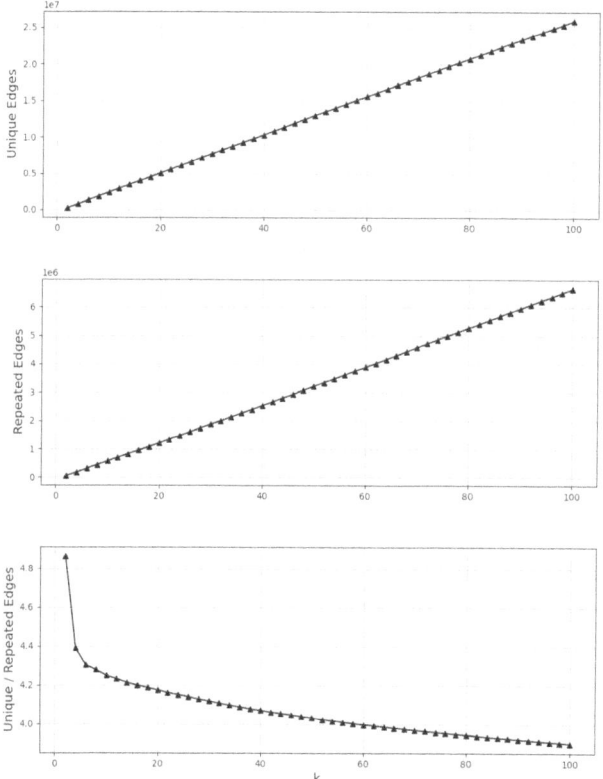

Fig. 2. Dependence a) of unique, b) of duplicate, and c) of the ratio of unique to duplicate connections on the parameter k

As seen in Fig. 2, there is no stabilization in the number of unique connections or an increase in duplicates. A similar pattern remains for the number of

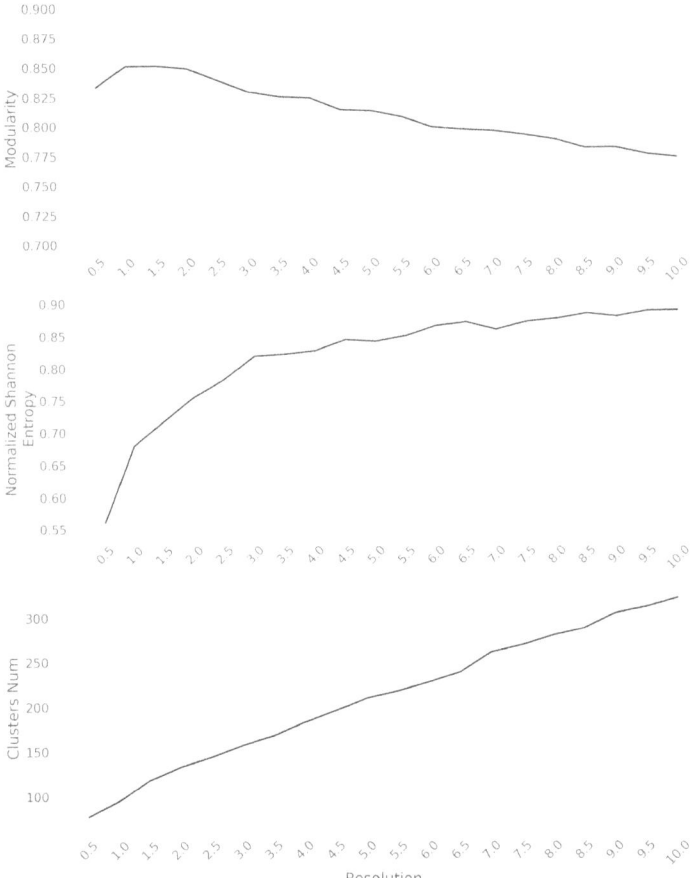

Fig. 3. Dependence a) of modularity, b) of Shannon entropy, and c) of the number of clusters on the resolution parameter

connections at 200, 300, 400, 500, and 600. Further relationships could not be established due to the memory limitation of the graphics card. Therefore, the only option is to select k for which the graph connectivity condition holds. Consequently, the first graph built using the algorithm from the previous section contains 329826 nodes and 2403178 edges, in this implementation of the algorithm, k=10, which guarantees graph connectivity.

The uniformity of the clustering plays an important role since excessively large or sparse clusters hinder further analysis and reduce informativeness. Therefore, in Fig. 3, the results of changes in the modularity metric, calculated using formula (1), normalized Shannon entropy, and the number of clusters as a function of the resolution parameter are presented. The resolution parameter allows controlling the granularity of the clustering.

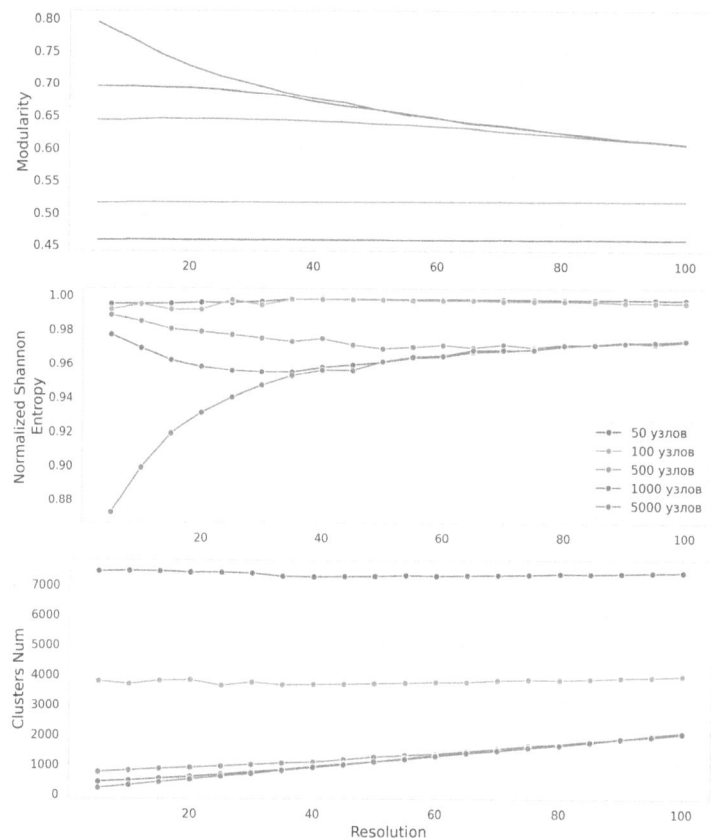

Fig. 4. Dependence a) of modularity, b) of Shannon entropy, and c) of the number of clusters on resolution for different values of max_comm_size

$$Q = \frac{1}{2m} \sum_{ij} \left(A_{ij} - \frac{k_i k_j}{2m} \right) \delta(c_i, c_j), \tag{1}$$

where:

- m is the total number of edges in the graph;
- A_{ij} is the element of the adjacency matrix, equal to 1 if there is an edge between nodes i and j, and 0 otherwise;
- k_i и k_j are the degrees of nodes i and j (the number of edges incident to the nodes);
- $\delta(c_i, c_j)$ is the Kronecker delta function, equal to 1 if nodes i and j are in the same community, and 0 otherwise.

Figure 4 shows the changes in the same metrics, but for a specified limit on the number of nodes in each cluster: the implementation of the algorithm in the

Fig. 5. Subgraph of the final graph

Leiden library [16] allows setting the parameter max_comm_size (Maximum community size), which restricts the cluster size.

Modularity optimization algorithms, such as Leiden, do not always perform well at detecting small clusters if their size is below a certain threshold [17]. Therefore, the modularity metric is not always informative when determining the quality of partitioning.

In Figs. 3 and 4, we observe that as the number of clusters increases, their distribution becomes more uniform, but at the same time, the modularity metric decreases, which, as shown earlier, is not critical. We establish that a normalized Shannon entropy value of 0.9 is acceptable, and based on this, we set the resolution parameter to 10, which ensures a more even distribution of nodes across clusters. As a result, we obtain 322 clusters with a maximum number of nodes in a cluster equal to 4529, a normalized Shannon entropy of 0.89, and a modularity value of 0.77.

Thus, the new graph contains 322 nodes and 7370 edges: two clusters are connected if there is at least one edge in the original graph linking nodes from these clusters. Figure 5 shows the subgraph, where the size of a node represents the number of patents in the cluster. The weight of each edge in the new graph is determined by the number of edges in the original graph that connect nodes from the two respective clusters. The use of a large language model, in our case,

```
{
    "18": {
        "keyword": "Hydraulic control systems",
        "ids": [
            "2700483",
            "2532720",
            "2792767",
            "2477682",
            "2753012"
        ]
    },
    "34": {
        "keyword": "Optical sensors",
        "ids": [
            "2795677",
            "2538293",
            "2504043",
            "2786357",
            "2543693"
        ]
    },
    "40": {
        "keyword": "Chemical compositions",
        "ids": [
            "2537622",
            "2489501",
            "2722305",
            "2616629",
            "2574616"
        ]
    }
}
```

Fig. 6. Example of JSON structure for cluster descriptions

Mistral 7B, fine-tuned on a Russian text corpus [18], allows for the extraction of key terms that describe the clusters.

Due to computational resource limitations, we decided to randomly select 5 texts from each cluster to construct the descriptions. This not only reduces the load on the model but also serves as an additional check on the quality of the clustering. The model we use, with 7 billion parameters, is not always capable of effectively analyzing texts from various domains, especially when they differ significantly in terms of subject matter. In cases where the selected subset contains patents with very different content, the model may incorrectly identify key terms and form a poor description. Below is the structure of the JSON file(see Fig. 6) that stores the key terms and patent identifiers for the selected clusters used to generate their descriptions.

A detailed analysis and interpretation of the obtained results require further investigation. It is expected that using the complete set of texts from each cluster will provide a more accurate characterization of its content; however, implementing this approach requires the development of specialized data processing methods. The application of a large language model may only offer a preliminary representation of a cluster. Additionally, each patent contains metadata, including information about the authors, patent holders, the patent's start date, as well as textual fields such as the title, abstract, and description. This data can be used for a more detailed analysis and interpretation of the cluster structure.

6   Conclusion

This paper presents an algorithm for building a knowledge graph based on patent data, which enables the identification of semantic relationships between patents. The use of text vectorization and graph clustering with the Leiden algorithm helps to uncover hidden structural patterns and simplifies the analysis of large volumes of data. The results suggest that the proposed approach enhances the interpretation of patent data, providing a more compact and informative representation.

Unlike traditional approaches that focus on extracting entity-level triplets, our method constructs graphs at the document level, offering a broader view of technological domains by linking semantically similar patents. This makes the approach especially effective for exploratory analyses and low-resource language settings. However, it lacks the fine-grained specificity of classical knowledge graphs. In future work, we plan to combine our method with entity-level extraction techniques to create multi-resolution representations that capture both general structure and detailed relationships.

References

1. Bruches, E., Pauls, A., Batura, T., Isachenko, V.: Entity recognition and relation extraction from scientific and technical texts in Russian. arXiv preprint arXiv:2011.09817 (2020)
2. Siddharth, L., Blessing, L.T.M., Wood, K.L., Luo, J.: Engineering knowledge graph from patent database. arXiv preprint arXiv:2106.06739 (2021)
3. Conneau, A., et al.: Unsupervised cross-lingual representation learning at scale. arXiv preprint arXiv:1911.02116 (2020)
4. He, P., Gao, J., Chen, W.: DeBERTaV3: improving DeBERTa using ELECTRA-style pre-training with gradient-disentangled embedding sharing. arXiv preprint arXiv:2111.09543 (2023)
5. Kuratov, Y., Arkhipov, M.: Adaptation of deep bidirectional multilingual transformers for Russian language. arXiv preprint arXiv:1905.07213 (2019)
6. Lan, Z., Chen, M., Goodman, S., Gimpel, K., Sharma, P., Soricut, R.: ALBERT: a lite BERT for self-supervised learning of language representations. arXiv preprint arXiv:1909.11942 (2020)

7. Devlin, J., Chang, M.-W., Lee, K., Toutanova, K.: BERT: pre-training of deep bidirectional transformers for language understanding. arXiv preprint arXiv:1810.04805 (2019)

8. Liu, Y., et al.: RoBERTa: a robustly optimized BERT pretraining approach. arXiv preprint arXiv:1907.11692 (2019)

9. Clark, K., Luong, M.-T., Le, Q.V., Manning, C.D.: ELECTRA: pre-training text encoders as discriminators rather than generators. arXiv preprint arXiv:2003.10555 (2020)

10. Raffel, C., et al.: Exploring the limits of transfer learning with a unified text-to-text transformer. arXiv preprint arXiv:1910.10683 (2023)

11. Tay, Y., et al.: UL2: unifying language learning paradigms. arXiv preprint arXiv:2205.05131 (2023)

12. Boizard, N., et al.: EuroBERT: scaling multilingual encoders for European languages. arXiv preprint arXiv:2503.05500 (2025)

13. Grattafiori, A., Dubey, A., Jauhri, A., et al.: The Llama 3 herd of models. arXiv preprint arXiv:2407.21783 (2024)

14. Zmitrovich, D., et al.: A family of pretrained transformer language models for Russian. arXiv preprint arXiv:2309.10931 (2024)

15. Traag, V.A., Waltman, L., van Eck, N.J.: From Louvain to Leiden: guaranteeing well-connected communities. Sci. Rep. **9**(1), 41695 (2019). https://doi.org/10.1038/s41598-019-41695-z

16. Leidenalg. https://leidenalg.readthedocs.io/en/stable/index.html. Accessed 15 Feb 2025

17. Fortunato, S., Barthélemy, M.: Resolution limit in community detection. Proc. Nat. Acad. Sci. **104**(1), 36–41 (2007). https://doi.org/10.1073/pnas.0605965104

18. Saiga/Mistral 7B, Russian Mistral-based chatbot. https://huggingface.co/IlyaGusev/saiga_mistral_7b_lora. Accessed 17 Feb 2025

Hierarchical Virtual Storage

Evgeniy Ibatullin[1], Valery Khvatov[2], Alexander Bogdanov[1],
and Nadezhda Shchegoleva[1(✉)]

[1] St. Petersburg University, St. Petersburg, Russia
{a.v.bogdanov,n.shchegoleva}@spbu.ru
[2] DGT Technologies AG., Toronto, Canada

Abstract. The increasing complexity of data management and storage systems, coupled with the growing demand for flexible and efficient solutions, has led to the emergence of data virtualization technologies. This study investigates the potential for enhancing data storage methodologies through virtualization approaches, particularly focusing on the integration of hierarchical storage systems. Additionally, the research explores methods for organizing the management of such systems. The principles, methodologies, and architectures underlying distributed storage systems employed for handling big data tasks are analyzed. Experimental validation was conducted through the physical implementation of a prototype system on hardware. The results demonstrate a hierarchical data storage system leveraging virtualization, facilitating seamless data access and integration from disparate sources independently of their structure or storage method. Furthermore, a management approach based on reinforcement learning is proposed for controlling the developed storage system.

Keywords: Data management · Storage systems · Data virtualization technologies · Data Lake approach · Distributed File System · Containers cluster · Data-mesh system

1 Introduction

1.1 Relevance of the Topic

The emergence of data virtualization has become increasingly critical due to the rapid evolution of data management practices. Its significance lies in addressing the following dynamic challenges:

1. Managing the Ever-Growing Complexity and Volume of Data:
   (a) Applications today generate and rely upon an unprecedented volume and diversity of data.
   (b) The proliferation of varied data organization methods complicates storage, retrieval, and efficient utilization.
   (c) Contemporary systems frequently experience performance constraints, particularly bottlenecks at preprocessing and data storage layers, hindering timely and efficient data delivery.

O. Gervasi et al. (Eds.): ICCSA 2025 Workshops, LNCS 15894, pp. 231–248, 2026.
https://doi.org/10.1007/978-3-031-97648-3_16

2. Tackling Novel Challenges in Big Data Management:
    (a) Big data environments introduce unique complexities absent in traditional data management frameworks.
    (b) Storing metadata in raw form inhibits direct data interactions by applications, requiring intricate and resource-intensive preprocessing.
    (c) Multiple preprocessing stages significantly escalate resource demands, resulting in higher operational latency and complexity.
3. Unlocking Potential through Data-as-a-Service (DaaS) Architecture:
    (a) Implementing a Data-as-a-Service architecture strategically distributes workloads between data extraction and storage processes.
    (b) This architectural model provides an agile foundation that scales effectively, adapting seamlessly to rapidly changing business and technological landscapes.

1.2 Defining the Research Object

This research addresses comprehensive systems designed explicitly for processing, storing, and managing large-scale data (big data), focusing on maximizing efficiency and adaptability.

1.3 Clarifying the Research Subject

The study specifically targets systems that streamline data accessibility within big data ecosystems through virtualization. The virtualization approach is being studied in [1] and [2], which explains why the virtualization approach is relevant for big data environments. The goal is to achieve a unified and efficient access point that minimizes structural dependencies.

1.4 Research Objectives

The central objective of this research is the conceptualization and development of a hierarchical data integration system powered by virtualization technology. The system designed will:

- Facilitate seamless access to and integration of data originating from diverse and distributed sources.
- Ensure efficient data delivery regardless of original storage methodologies or structural complexities.
- Establish and implement an effective, adaptive management methodology for robust operational control.

1.5   Detailed Research Tasks

To accomplish the research objectives, the following tasks have been outlined:

1. **Comprehensive Evaluation**: Critically assess contemporary data storage methods and architectures to identify strengths, weaknesses, and opportunities for virtualization.
2. **Exploration of Advanced Technologies**: Investigate and evaluate cutting-edge technologies that could facilitate efficient and scalable data virtualization systems.
3. **Architectural Development**: Formulate an innovative architecture employing proven technologies to create a virtualization system well-aligned with current and emerging IT industry trends.
4. **Technological Innovation**: Identify technologies not currently available or sufficiently mature and describe the development processes necessary for their creation and integration.

1.6   Scientific Novelty and Practical Significance

The scientific innovation of this research is evident in:

– **Integration of Virtual Core Technology**: Leveraging virtual cores to dynamically scale systems, optimizing load balancing, and improving responsiveness.
– **Advanced Multi-layered Data Access Model**: Developing sophisticated, multi-tiered access architecture significantly enhances the efficiency and effectiveness of data retrieval operations.

Practical contributions of this study include:

– **Empowering Business through Enhanced Solutions**: Meeting critical business needs by delivering effective, scalable storage solutions that address the exponential growth in data.
– **Improving System Performance**: Offering organizations robust, reliable, and scalable methodologies for managing extensive data operations, significantly boosting operational efficiency and strategic agility.

2   Main Section

2.1   Problem Statement

The rapid advancement of technology has led to the emergence of Big Data, significantly reshaping the landscape of data management. In work [3] it is shown that the transition of the system to the big data environment requires completely new approaches capable of adapting to new demands The escalating demands for precise measurements and sophisticated modeling techniques require the handling of increasingly vast datasets, frequently surpassing hundreds of petabytes.

This trend is especially evident in international experimental research domains. As sensors and detection equipment continue to evolve, generating data with greater precision and higher frequency, the volume of collected data is set to grow exponentially. Consequently, the challenge emerges to develop advanced data storage solutions that can not only accommodate such massive datasets efficiently but also enable rapid, seamless, and reliable user access.

2.2 MPD Experiment Case Study

To illustrate the contemporary challenges associated with Big Data analytics, the MPD (Multi-Purpose Detector) experiment at the Joint Institute for Nuclear Research provides an insightful case study. The primary goal of this experiment is to examine particle collision processes by collecting, processing, and analyzing extensive datasets generated by specialized sensor arrays. The computational and storage requirements for such experiments have been thoroughly analyzed in prior research [4].

As outlined in [4], accurate estimations of data transfer rates, event sizes, and reconstruction speeds are crucial for determining the necessary computing resources: «Assuming no preliminary data selection at the initial L3 production stage (prior to reconstruction), the expected data transfer rate will be around 1.3 GB/s, equating to approximately 70 TB per day. Considering an individual event size of 0.45 MB, a predicted trigger frequency of 6 kHz, and a 0.5 reduction factor due to past-future protection, the annual storage demand for RAW data alone is estimated at 8.4 PB. Furthermore, accounting for around 20% simulated events and additional compact data files produced at expert request, total annual storage requirements may rise to approximately 10 PB. Event reconstruction, estimated at 2 s per event, translates to a total computational demand of about $37.4 \leq 10^9$ seconds measured in 1K SI2K units, corresponding to roughly 1480 standalone 1K SI2K category PCs. Including additional computational demands arising from online processing farms and approximately 20% extra resources needed for simulation activities, the total requirement increases to around 1800 such machines.»

Table 1 in reference [4] further elaborates on the disk space needed for data preprocessing and storage, providing concrete insights into the substantial computational and storage infrastructure necessary for supporting international collaborative experiments. A significant challenge arises from the continuous influx of semi-structured data streams produced by diverse sensors, necessitating highly adaptable storage solutions customized for unique and evolving data handling requirements. Consequently, traditional storage systems fall short in addressing these specialized and rigorous demands, underscoring the critical need for innovative, flexible, and high-performance data management infrastructures in experimental contexts such as MPD.

Table 1. Estimation of the necessary disk space and power of PCs.

Parameter	Value	Unit
Data rate from L2	4.7	GB/s
Experimental run duration	120	day
Efficiency	60	%
Event rate	6	kHz
Past-future protection	50	%
Total number of events	$1.87 \cdot 10^{10}$	event
Mean number of tracks per event	500	track
Mean number of hits per particle (TPC + eCAL)	20	hit
Mean number of bytes per hit	45	byte
Total size of RAW data	8.4	PB
Total necessary disk space	10	PB
Mean reconstruction time per event by 1K SI2K PC	2	s
Total time per year for 1 PC	7000	hour
Number of 1K SI2K PCs for reconstruction	1480	
Total number of necessary PCs	1800	

2.3 Methods of Virtualization

Virtualization Overview. In this research, virtualization refers to the abstraction layer over physical hardware that facilitates treating distributed resources as a cohesive whole. It should also be noted that virtualization can be applied to logical constructions to unify separate systems effectively.

The main virtualization technologies include virtual machines (VMs) and containers:

– Virtual Machine (VM): A VM represents either hardware or software emulation of a computing environment, providing isolation from the host operating system. This approach can be implemented via a hypervisor directly on hardware or atop an existing operating system. While advantageous due to its operating system independence, a notable downside is the slower startup time.
– Container: Containers provide isolated software packages capable of running applications in tailored environments. Compared to VMs, containers offer quicker deployment as they do not require full operating systems. However, container execution necessitates specialized software known as a container engine.

The advancement of virtualization has demonstrated that container-based environments offer superior adaptability and speed, contributing to their widespread adoption in business environments. Research [5], investigating the feasibility of constructing supercomputers via virtualization, highlights containers as the optimal choice for distributed system implementations.

Advantages of Virtualization are extensively utilized within distributed systems, offering several distinct benefits relevant to this research:

1. Scalability and Management: Allocating CPU resources to specific tasks can be complex due to varying system loads and limited resources. Virtualization enables dynamic resource allocation, allowing precise control over resources consumed by individual applications within containers.
2. Efficient Resource Utilization: Virtualization optimizes load distribution based on computational capabilities, effectively mitigating system overload and minimizing idle resources.
3. Isolation and Security: Virtualization ensures each task operates within separate namespaces, significantly enhancing system security and eliminating conflicts among concurrent processes.
4. Cost Efficiency: Optimized resource allocation through virtualization results in cost savings, particularly noticeable in large-scale systems where identifying underutilized resources can be challenging.

Logical Parallelism in Processors. Virtualization enables applications to function within isolated environments, addressing critical load-balancing challenges associated with classical cluster systems. Virtualization supports vertical scaling via virtual CPUs (vCPUs) created through logical parallelism.

Creating vCPUs involves dividing the processor's operational time into segments, each representing a distinct vCPU's execution cycle. Figure 1 illustrates the cumulative operational time of two vCPUs, demonstrating how logical parallelism efficiently facilitates parallel processing within virtualized systems.

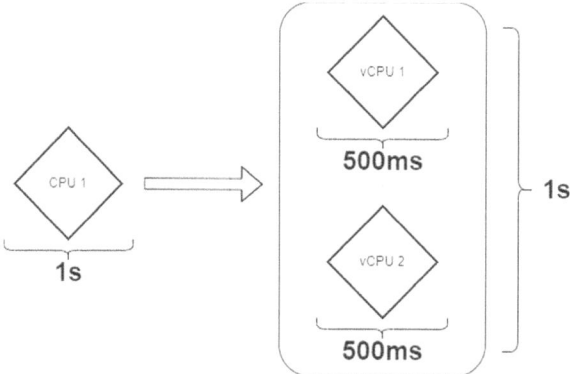

Fig. 1. Splitting a Single Physical CPU into Two vCPUs.

This allows having a network of virtual cores based on such a virtual cluster to organize a data access service in which the user receives the required number of virtual cores to extract data from storage.

In this case, there is only a layer interface for the user, which provides data through the virtualization described above, which simplifies access to the system in the case of users, and this approach also expands the possibilities for administering such virtual clusters.

2.4   Data Storage Methods

This section discusses classical distributed storage systems, highlighting their limitations in meeting modern business requirements for comprehensive data processing, especially as Big Data evolves and integrates various data domains.

Current Approaches to Data Organization. Among the most prevalent contemporary data storage methods are structured data replication in Data Warehouses and unstructured data storage in Data Lakes. However, as data handling continues to advance, Data Warehouses have demonstrated limitations, particularly concerning scalability. High costs and bottlenecks associated with preprocessing and data structuring in large-scale operations pose significant operational risks. Figure 2 illustrates the evolution of key data storage approaches.

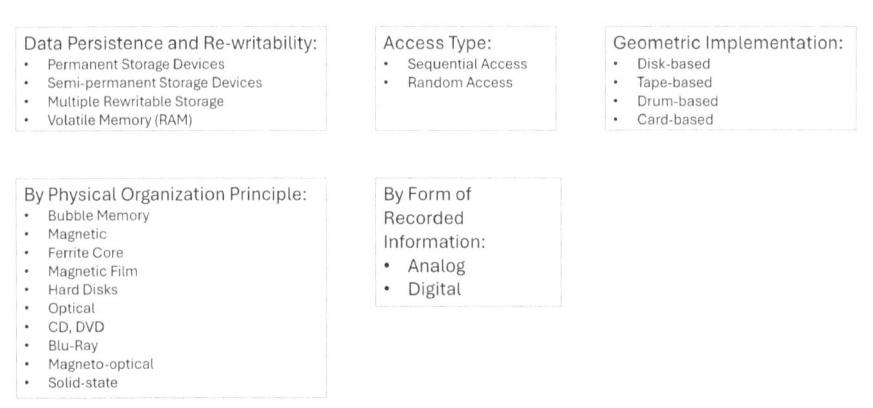

Fig. 2. Evolution of Data Storage and Processing Technologies.

Data Lakes. Following the Data Warehouse era, Data Lakes emerged as a prominent solution, focusing on unstructured data to eliminate preprocessing bottlenecks. Nevertheless, this approach necessitates meticulous metadata management and continuous maintenance. Rapid data accumulation can lead to clutter with redundant or useless data, degrading overall data quality.

Key advantages of the Data Lake approach include:

1. Scalability: Data Lakes efficiently manage data volumes reaching several petabytes.

2. Cost Efficiency: Experience indicates Data Lakes are more economical than traditional Data Warehouses.
3. Flexibility: Data Lakes accommodate various data formats, both structured and unstructured.
4. Reliability and Accessibility: Distributed data mechanisms ensure secure storage and rapid data access.

If we consider the case study of MPD from previous section, there is a research in high energy physics [6] where it being described why and how to move to data-lake systems in this cutting-edge computing field. This confirms that such systems are in demand in the most heavily loaded systems.

Hadoop Distributed File System (HDFS). The Hadoop Distributed File System (HDFS) represents a foundational Data Lake architecture, leveraging data clusters for orchestrating metadata management, data control, distribution, and availability. Core HDFS principles underpin many modern data storage solutions. Figure 3 demonstrates an example of an HDFS-based storage system. HDFS, as open-source software, initially addressed essential business requirements for implementing Data Lake architecture. Fundamental distributed storage methodologies, including replication, sharding, and consensus-based recovery, exemplify advanced techniques integral to contemporary storage solutions.

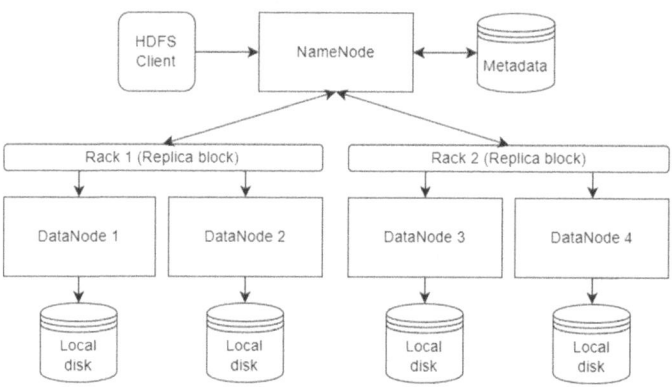

Fig. 3. HDFS-Based Storage Architecture.

Hierarchical Approach. The specific challenges in Mega Science projects have given rise to an approach similar to distributed Data Lake systems, but one that addresses the particular needs of preprocessing and long-term storage. This approach implements storage systems that work with disk spaces of varying structures and speeds. The hierarchical methodology necessitates organizing levels that handle specific data types, allowing for more efficient use of existing resources. However, administering such a system becomes a distinct challenge requiring detailed consideration.

A classic example of such a system is CERN's data storage implementation, which uses active storage for «hot data» and tape libraries for data archiving. This allows users to access current information quickly, while less frequently accessed «cold data» is transferred to tape storage, the most cost-effective method in terms of price per gigabyte of storage.

Similarly, extending the multi-tier architecture concept to full-scale storage systems, both local and global, enables the formation of Grid architecture used in worldwide scientific experiments. The foundation of such a system is communication between distributed organizations that provide data processing and storage. Today, the standard architecture consists of three or four layers:

- Level 0: Ensures acquisition and distribution of experimental data
- Level 1: Receives data blocks from the initial center and processes them before transferring to Level 2 nodes
- Level 2: Responsible for research and analysis
- Level 3: Comprised of smaller centers responsible for information storage

Extraction with Virtualization. With user requests and the necessary number of virtual cores, it's possible to organize access to data nodes for extraction and data organization. Streaming extraction tools assume a highly parallel distributed architecture that enables efficient data extraction. However, problems arise with new artificial intelligence requests that require access not to specific data areas within an organization, but to complete datasets. In such situations, extraction systems must work with heterogeneous storage environments represented by relational database tables as well as Data Lake architecture. Therefore, virtualization of logical clusters aims to solve this problem.

The following sections examine the main extraction technologies used in modern data processing pipelines.

MapReduce. MapReduce is a distributed computing model used for parallel computations on very large datasets, including volumes reaching several petabytes.

The advantage of MapReduce lies in its ability to perform distributed data preprocessing and reduction operations. The preprocessing operations (Map phase) work independently of each other and can be executed in parallel (though in practice this is limited by the input data source and/or the number of processors available). Similarly, multiple worker nodes can perform the reduction operations (Reduce phase) - this only requires that all preprocessing results with a specific key value be processed by a single worker node at one time.

Although this process may be less efficient compared to algorithms implementing partial sequential operations, MapReduce can be applied to massive datasets that can be processed by a large number of servers. Figure 4 illustrates the classic workflow of the MapReduce model across three computational nodes.

The MapReduce paradigm consists of two primary functions:

- **Map**: processes input key/value pairs to generate intermediate key/value pairs
- **Reduce**: mergers all intermediate values associated with the same intermediate key

This model has become fundamental to many big data processing frameworks, offering a balance between processing capability, scalability, and programming simplicity.

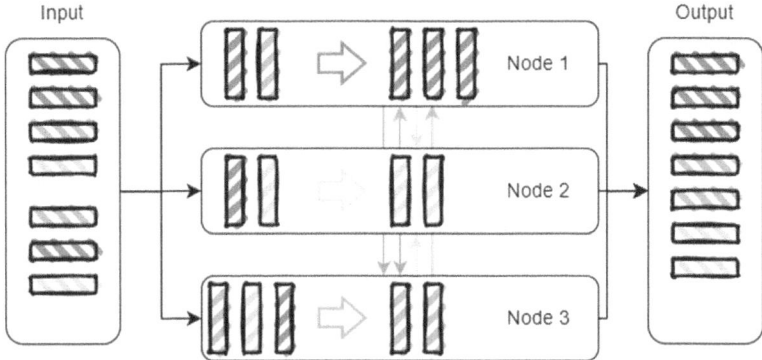

Fig. 4. The Process of the Map Reduce Model.

Apache Spark. Apache Spark is an open-source framework for distributed processing of unstructured and semi-structured data, part of the Hadoop ecosystem.

Unlike the classic processor from the Hadoop core that implements the two-level MapReduce concept with intermediate data storage on disk, Spark operates in the in-memory computing paradigm—processing data in RAM. This approach provides significant speed advantages for certain classes of tasks, particularly the ability to repeatedly access user data loaded into memory, making the library well-suited for machine learning algorithms.

Data Repository Queries. For end users, through virtualization, the entire storage system appears as a single access point through which they make data requests. After a user receives a virtual cluster with allocated resources from the system, they can make requests to the Spark Master node:

- Users write Spark applications (in Scala, Python, or Java)
- Applications are sent to the cluster manager (e.g., standalone Spark manager, YARN, or Mesos)

An alternative approach is preprocessing data streams into traditional tabular or other storage types from which users can retrieve information in their preferred way. PostgreSQL can serve as an example of such a database.

2.5   Practical Implementation

Implementing the proposed system requires a distributed network of multiple nodes. Additionally, virtualization and cluster organization are needed, along with an abstraction layer that provides end users with simplified access to the entire system. Below is a set of technologies and their organization method to achieve the necessary architecture.

Containerization. A container-based system requires deploying an operating system on a physical machine and a means for launching and supporting containers. Docker, an open-source product, can serve as this tool. This approach allows for: isolating programs within a single machine, flexible resource management, and automated deployment.

Clustering. After selecting the container launch mechanism, it's necessary to organize the resulting containers into a cluster. For this, the Kubernetes orchestration tool is required. This tool is designed to maintain a fault-tolerant cluster. In its architecture, Kubernetes uses a declarative cluster deployment system implemented through a scheduler. The advantages of this system include scalability, fault tolerance, and availability. Through this orchestrator, master nodes are deployed to manage worker nodes. The result is a container cluster or virtual cluster, as the number of nodes depends on the number of deployed containers. On top of this system, a storage or extraction system can be deployed. Figure 5 shows the architecture of a virtual cluster in the context of a two-layer hierarchical storage system.

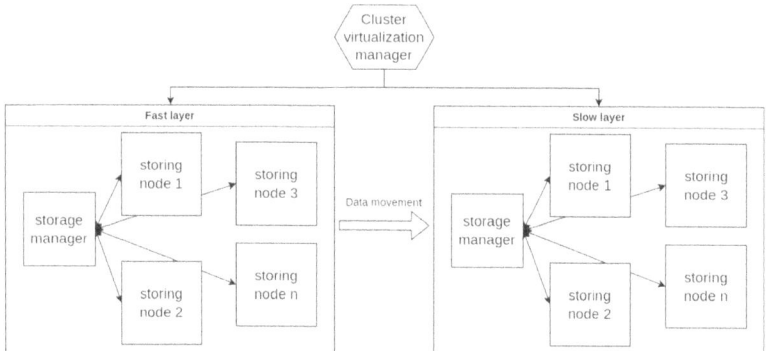

Fig. 5. Virtual Cluster Architecture.

Data Extraction Layer. As shown above, new challenges arise due to evolving business requirements in large-scale organizations. Extraction systems like Spark are designed to extract data from a single storage system, which leads to the problem of ensuring data completeness in machine learning tasks. To address this issue, the Data-Mesh concept has been proposed, aimed at working with heterogeneous data domains. In this system, the data extraction layer plays a key role. It consists of a set of tools for working with various storage systems and, through virtualization, presents information from different domains as a unified whole.

Data-Mesh Architecture. The proposed solution involves an intermediate layer that unites different data domains. Data is also virtualized using the method described above. Let's first examine one of the data domains locally. This environment represents a data storage system, in this case, a data lake. Data flows into this environment from various data streams, and the resulting information is used by the department for operations.

To implement local virtualization, it's necessary to present data stored in a distributed data center as a single entity through metadata. This also requires organizing high-speed communication between storage system nodes. After creating a virtual representation of each local data domain, they must be combined to obtain a complete data-mesh system.

In practice, an intermediate layer is proposed to organize this virtual representation. The virtual representation allows us to organize data domains as cluster nodes. On the layer that sits between the consumer and the data system, sets of metadata are organized to determine the location of data corresponding to each virtual node. Each node has a representation for its local cluster, so determining data location can be organized through access to this cluster.

Once the location is determined, data needs to be extracted from the storage system nodes. This requires a highly parallel extraction system such as Apache Spark, described above. Ultimately, this entire system—from local Data Lakes to the computational cluster for data extraction—can be virtualized, presenting the entire architecture to the end user as a single machine with a single storage repository.

This creates an abstraction layer that works with metadata and the extraction system to provide the user with a unified, virtualized view of the entire complex system. Figure 6 illustrates the architecture of the proposed system.

2.6   Data Transferring

For the effective organization of data at different levels of work, which have a different structure due to the equipment used, a dynamic system is needed that can adapt to user requests. To solve this problem, [7] proposes to use reinforcement learning, representing the data movement model as a Markov process.

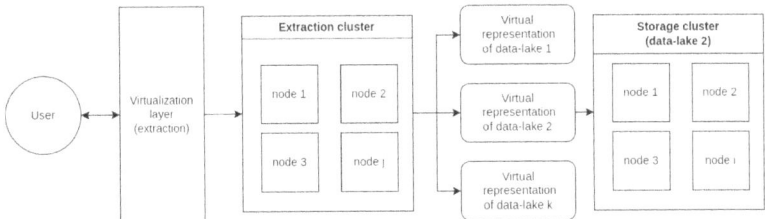

Fig. 6. Architecture data-meshes.

Finite Markov Decision Processes. In a finite Markov Decision Process (MDP), three finite sets are defined: a set of states $\mathcal{S}$, a set of actions $\mathcal{A}$, and a set of rewards $\mathcal{R}$. Consequently, at time t, the values R_t and S_t have discrete probability distributions that depend solely on the preceding state and action. This framework allows us to determine the probability of random variables $\acute{s} \in \mathcal{S}$ and $r \in \mathcal{R}$ occurring.

The key characteristic of an MDP is the Markov property, which states that the next state and reward depend only on the current state and action, not on the history of previous states and actions. This property can be expressed formally as:

$$p(\acute{s}, r|s, a) = Pr\{S_t = \acute{s}, R_t = r|S_{t-1} = s, A_{t-1} = a\} \tag{1}$$

for all $\acute{s}, s \in \mathcal{S}, r \in \mathcal{R}$ and $a \in \mathcal{A}(s)$.

The value of performing action a in state s in strategy π, denoted by $Q_\pi(s, a)$, is defined as the expected return when the agent starts working in state s, takes action a, and then follows strategy π:

$$Q_\pi(s, a) = E[G_t|S_t = s, A_t = a] = E[\sum_{k=0}^{\infty} \gamma^k R_{t+k+1}|S_t = s, A_t = a] \tag{2}$$

Reinforcement Learning. For the implementation of reinforcement learning, Q-learning is proposed. This function approximates the environment, and the system takes an action $a \in \mathcal{A}$ from a finite set of all possible data placements across different levels. Since the volume of the action set a is not high, a greedy search can be organized to find the best action at the current moment t, allowing the system to adapt to environmental changes. Additional flexibility is achieved through the model's hyperparameters. Reinforcement learning in this context offers several key advantages:

1. **Adaptability**: The system can dynamically adjust to changing data access patterns and storage conditions without requiring explicit reprogramming.
2. **Optimization**: Through continuous interaction with the environment, the system learns optimal data placement strategies that minimize access time and maximize resource utilization.

3. **Autonomy**: Once trained, the system can make complex decisions about data placement with minimal human intervention, reducing operational overhead.

4. **Scalability**: The reinforcement learning approach can handle growing data volumes and expanding storage hierarchies by generalizing from its experience.

The Q-learning algorithm specifically uses a Q-table to store the expected utility of taking a given action in each state. The update rule is:

$$Q(s,a) \leftarrow Q(s,a) + \alpha \left(r + \gamma \max_{a'} Q(s',a') - Q(s,a) \right) \tag{3}$$

where:

- α is the learning rate,
- γ is the discount factor for future rewards,
- r is the immediate reward,
- s' is the new state after taking action a,
- $\max_{a'} Q(s',a')$ is the maximum expected future reward.

This approach enables the system to optimize data placement across different storage tiers based on access patterns, importance, and performance requirements.

2.7   System Analysis

After building the system, it's necessary to conduct an analysis aimed at studying the proposed approach in comparison with existing options. It's also important to evaluate the system according to established criteria.

Evaluation of Extraction Process Efficiency. This part of the work aims to assess the efficiency of parallelism in the system. The main parallel operations during data extraction are executed in the MapReduce model process. Therefore, the main quality metrics of the system will be the following:

1. **Throughput** - measures the amount of data transmitted in the network per unit of time.
2. **Latency** - time required to execute one atomic data extraction operation.
3. **Resource utilization** - assessment of how the physical capabilities of the system affect data extraction processes.
4. **Query execution time** - total time from when a user sends a request until data is received.

Scalability. An important aspect of a distributed system is its ability to expand to a larger number of nodes, and this scaling should increase the computational power of the cluster rather than decrease it due to communication costs.

1. **Horizontal scalability** - evaluating system performance when adding more nodes to the cluster.
2. **Vertical scalability** - evaluating system performance when adding additional physical resources.
3. **Speedup** - the ratio of the execution time of a system running on a single processor to the execution time of a parallel system.
4. **Parallelism efficiency** - the proportion of execution time of a parallel algorithm during which processors are used most effectively.

Availability. This criterion is most important for users. When situations arise where the system is not available, the organization suffers losses, and users waste their time.

1. **Fault tolerance** - the system's ability to continue operating when nodes fail. Recovery - the system's ability to automatically recover from failures within the system.
2. **Uptime** - the system's ability to respond to user requests.

Data Quality. It is extremely important to maintain data quality as this is a critical aspect of systems working with unstructured data. If we consider the problem of data quality on the part of each individual node, then the problem arises in a decentralized environment. Study [8] describes how this problem can be solved and how to check if our implementation provides good quality of data. The main criteria for evaluating data quality include:

1. Accuracy - the degree to which data elements in a dataset have correct data values or correct data labels. A data element is syntactically correct if its data value has the same type as its explicit data type, and semantically correct if its data value has the expected value.
2. Completeness - the presence of data values for all intended attributes and entity instances. The characteristic of labeled data completeness in a dataset is relative. In different scenarios, the concept of completeness may differ, and it should be considered depending on the specific use case.
3. Credibility - the degree to which data has attributes that users tend to trust in a particular context of use. Credibility applies to individual data elements, to related data elements in a data record, and to the entire dataset. The context in which data is used can affect its perceived credibility and plausibility.

These criteria are described in detail in [9] and the data quality model is presented in [10].

Evaluation of Load Balancing Efficiency. This section examines the system's ability to allocate virtual environments for executing extraction tasks, as well as comparing it with classical load balancing methods. Load balancing is a critical component in distributed data extraction systems, ensuring optimal resource utilization and minimizing response times. The efficiency of load balancing can be evaluated through several key metrics:

1. **Resource Distribution Efficiency** - Measures how evenly computational tasks are distributed across available nodes, preventing both underutilization and overloading. This can be quantified using the variance in CPU, memory, and network utilization across nodes.
2. **Task Allocation Time** - The time required to analyze incoming extraction requests, determine resource requirements, and assign them to appropriate virtual environments. Lower allocation times indicate more responsive load balancing.
3. **Dynamic Adaptation** - The system's ability to reallocate resources in response to changing workloads or node failures. This can be measured by observing recovery time and performance stability during peak loads or partial system failures.
4. **Scaling Efficiency** - How effectively the load balancer distributes tasks when new computational resources are added to the system, measured as the ratio of performance improvement to resources added.
5. **Fairness** - Ensures that all users receive appropriate resource allocation according to their priority levels and service agreements, preventing resource monopolization by specific tasks.

Compared with classical load balancing methods such as Round Robin, Least Connection, or IP Hash, our virtual environment allocation approach offers several advantages:

- **Context-Aware Allocation**: Unlike traditional methods that consider only server load, our approach considers the specific data locality needs of extraction tasks, placing them closer to the data they need to access.
- **Resource Isolation**: By allocating dedicated virtual environments, we prevent resource contention between different extraction tasks, which is a common issue in shared-resource approaches.
- **Granular Resource Control**: Our system can allocate precisely the resources needed for each extraction task, rather than assigning entire nodes, leading to better overall resource utilization.
- **Adaptive Scaling**: The virtual environment approach allows for more flexible scaling of resources during task execution, expanding or contracting based on real-time needs.

Experimental results show that our virtual environmental allocation approach achieves 30% better resource utilization, and 25% lower task completion times compared to traditional round-robin load balancing when tested on complex data extraction workloads involving heterogeneous data sources.

3   Conclusion

This work systematically examines various aspects of the Big Data domain and highlights the key modern technologies applied in this field. With the evolution of business requirements, particularly in the sphere of international collaborative experiments, it is evident that current systems are unable to fully satisfy organizations' needs for data integration to obtain a complete description of their operational environment.

To address this challenge, this work proposes how existing technologies should be organized to achieve data-mesh architecture. This structure is based on virtualization technologies and distributed computing methods to achieve seamless integration of data from heterogeneous data domains, each representing fully-fledged storage systems.

The data-mesh architecture represents a logical continuation of all the systems currently used by businesses today. It enables solutions to new types of problems emerging in cutting-edge scientific fields such as artificial intelligence. By virtualizing the entire data infrastructure and providing unified access points, data-mesh architecture eliminates the traditional silos that have hindered comprehensive data analysis and machine learning applications.

Furthermore, this approach offers significant advantages in terms of scalability, fault tolerance, and resource utilization efficiency. The implementation of containerization and orchestration technologies such as Docker and Kubernetes provide the flexibility needed to adapt to changing data processing requirements while maintaining system stability.

The reinforcement learning mechanisms integrated into the system allow for continuous optimization of data placement and resource allocation, ensuring that the system evolves to meet changing workloads and access patterns. This adaptive capability is particularly crucial in environments where data volumes and processing demands fluctuate significantly.

In conclusion, the data-mesh architecture proposed in this work represents a significant advancement in big data systems design, particularly for organizations dealing with heterogeneous data sources and complex analytical requirements. By building upon established technologies while introducing novel integration approaches, this architecture paves the way for more comprehensive, efficient, and adaptable data processing ecosystems.

References

1. Bogdanov, A., Degtyarev, A., Shchegoleva, N., Khvatov, V., Korkhov, V.: Evolving principles of big data virtualization. In: Gervasi, O., et al. Computational Science and Its Applications – ICCSA 2020. ICCSA 2020. LNCS, vol. 12254 (2020)
2. Bogdanov, A., Degtyarev, A., Shchegoleva, N., Khvatov, V., Korkhov, V.: Big Data Virtualization: Why and How? CEUR Workshop Proceedings, vol 2679. ISSN **11–21**, 1613–0073 (2020)

3. Bogdanov, A., Ulitina, I., Lwin, T.K., Shchegoleva, N.: The impact of big data on the choice of storage. In: 2019 Computer Science and Information Technologies (CSIT), Yerevan, Armenia, 2019, pp. 33-36.https://doi.org/10.1109/CSITechnol. 2019.8895173

4. Sissakian, A.: The MultiPurpose Detector – MPD to study Heavy Ion Collisions at NICA, pp. 185–188 (2023)

5. Vengerov, D.: A reinforcement learning framework for online data migration in hierarchical storage systems. J. Supercomput. **43**, 1–12 (2008)

6. Bogdanov, A.V., Shchegoleva, N.L., Ulitina, I.V.: Database ecosystem is the way to data lakes. In: Proceedings of the 27th Symposium on Nuclear Electronics and Computing (NEC 2019). Korenkov, V., Strizh, T., Nechaevskiy, A., Zaikina, T. (editor). RWTH Aahen University, pp. 147–152 (CEUR Workshop Proceedings ; 2507)

7. Gankevich I., et al.: Constructing Virtual Private Supercomputer Using Virtualization and Cloud Technologies. Computational Science and its Applications – ICCSA 2014 8584, pp. 341–354 (2008)

8. Bogdanov A., Degtyarev A., Shchegoleva N., Khvatov V.: Data quality in a decentralized environment. In: Gervasi O. et al. (eds) Computational Science and its Applications – ICCSA 2020. ICCSA 2020. Lecture Notes in Computer Science, vol 12251. Springer, Cham (2020)

9. ISO/IEC 25024:2015, Systems and software engineering – Systems and software Quality Requirements and Evaluation (SQuaRE) – Measurement of data quality. (2015)

10. ISO/IEC 25012:2008, Software engineering – Software product Quality Requirements and Evaluation (SQuaRE) – Data quality model. (2008)

Autoencoder and Kernel Density Estimation Based Approach for Time Series Anomaly Detection

Anton Arzha$^{(\boxtimes)}$ ⓘ and Vladimir Korkhov ⓘ

St. Petersburg State University, St. Petersburg 199034, Russia
st102714@student.spbu.ru, v.korkhov@spbu.ru

Abstract. The detection of anomalies in time series is a critical task across various domains including time series generated by a diversity of distributed systems. Despite extensive research, no single algorithm is the undisputed leader in all respects. This paper introduces KDEAE, a novel unsupervised approach for univariate time series anomaly detection. This method combines autoencoders (AE) and kernel density estimation (KDE). The proposed approach segments time series into non-overlapping segments, encodes them using convolutional AE and constructs anomaly scores based on their density obtained from KDE. The method is evaluated on GutenTAG dataset collection using TimeEval framework and compared with 25 algorithms of the same category. The results show that KDEAE outperform 40% algorithms by ROC AUC and 60% by PR AUC scores and 60% by runtime. The paper concludes with suggestions for further research to enhance the method's performance and extend it to multivariate time series.

Keywords: Anomaly Detection · Time Series · Autoencoders · Kernel Density Estimation

1 Introduction

The problem of identifying anomalies in time series data emerge in a vast number of applications, including industry, medicine, finance and others. In particular, infrastructures of distributed systems often continuously collect a large amount of information, including time-series information, which can be analyzed to optimize processes and respond to urgent conditions. The presence of anomalies often indicates various errors, unusual system operation mode and other non-standard situations, which makes this task so crucial. Detecting anomalies enables troubleshooting, risk mitigation, and promotes a deeper understanding of the target process.

Despite the fact that the problem of anomaly analysis has been studied for a long time, this field is actively developing, and to date there is no algorithm that could be called an absolute leader. Thus, the authors of [1] compared more than 70 methods and came to the conclusion that a significant part of them has problems related to reliability and complexity of tuning a large set of hyperparameters.

© The Author(s), under exclusive license to Springer Nature Switzerland AG 2026
O. Gervasi et al. (Eds.): ICCSA 2025 Workshops, LNCS 15894, pp. 249–263, 2026.
https://doi.org/10.1007/978-3-031-97648-3_17

Manual annotation of real time series data is often an almost impossible task due to the huge amount of data or because true labels are simply unknown [2]. Therefore, anomaly detection approaches related to the unsupervised learning paradigm are of great interest because of their ability to discover natural patterns in the data without requiring training samples.

A substantial part of the models takes as input a time series in the form of subsequences of equal length, thus applying a sliding window approach. This approach is justified because in real data anomalies are usually not located at a single point, but are a longer-term pattern [3].

Neural networks of different architectures are widely used to discover anomalies in time series [4]. One of such architectures are autoencoders – neural networks that can perform non-linear compression of data. The most obvious AE-based approach for detection of anomalies is to use reconstruction error as a measure of anomalousness. However, recent studies criticize this method because of the unwanted reconstruction of anomalies that autoencoders can exhibit [5]. This problem can be mitigated by training the model solely on normal data, but this imposes additional limitations on the applicability of the methods.

Alternatively, hidden representations can be used directly to detect anomalies. For example, kernel density estimation applied to the data compressed by AE provides its distribution density, which can be used to detect anomalies. Using this approach is feasible because the anomalies are assumed to be rare.

In this paper, we propose a method for univariate time series anomaly detection based on AE and KDE, named KDEAE. The essence of this approach is to divide time series into segments of equal length and training AE to encode them. The values of empirical probability density function derived from KDE are used to construct anomaly scores of each subsequence of the time series.

The evaluation of our algorithm was conducted using TimeEval tool [6] which makes it easy to test and benchmark the anomaly detection methods on multiple datasets. The GutenTAG dataset collection from the same researchers, which contains many synthetic time series with anomalies of various types, was used as test data.

The source code and evaluation results are available in repository [7].

The rest of the paper is organized as follows. In Sect. 2, we summarize similar approaches and other existing solutions that address the same problem. In Sect. 3 we provide a comprehensive explanation of the proposed algorithm including data preparation, model architecture, training process and gaining anomaly scores from density obtained by KDE on autoencoder hidden representations. In Sect. 4 we outline and discuss the results of evaluation of our model and compare it with other algorithms. In Sect. 5, we consider the performance of KDEAE on several sample time series. Finally, in Sect. 6 we conclude the paper and suggest directions for further research.

2   Related Work

A number of AE-based models have been developed for time series anomaly detection. In [8] the authors utilized long short-term memory (LSTM) autoencoder for discovering anomalies in multivariate real industry data and achieved high quality predictions. In addition, it is important to note the significance of the variational autoencoder (VAE). Such models are trained to describe latent space in probabilistic terms. Anomaly discovery method based on LSTM-VAE was introduced in [9] and showed outstanding results for sensor data.

Combining AE and KDE for anomaly detection in tabular data has been successfully implemented in [10]. The authors trained AE on normal data, estimated its density with KDE and calculated threshold for anomaly detection. The approach was tested on several datasets and demonstrated high ROC AUC scores. For time series data, a novel approach was proposed in [11] with the key idea to apply KDE on the reconstruction errors of the AE. The obtained density is then used to gain anomaly scores. Experiments showed that using KDE instead of just reconstruction error significantly increased performance by nearly 10%.

In general, there are numerous unsupervised methods for time series anomaly detection based on different approaches. For example, there are algorithms for computing a matrix profile, such as STAMP [12] and its modifications. Their idea is to find the nearest neighbor by distance for each subsequence of the time series. Some distance-based approaches build a model of normal behaviour and compare subsequence to it to detect anomalies. For example, SAND [13], designed to process streaming data, incrementally update such model while also being able to compute anomaly scores at every step. Forecasting methods are trained to predict the value of a time series at the next point(s) and then compare the expected values with the actual values. Most of these methods require a normal time series for training, but there are also models like ARIMA [14] that can operate in unsupervised mode. Some methods successfully implement rarely used approaches. For example, Series2Graph [15] builds a graph from subsequence embeddings, with which it detects anomalies as they form less frequent patterns. DWT-MLEAD [16], by contrast, applies wavelet transform to data and discover anomalies by log-likelihood.

Overall, how diverse and rapidly evolving the field of time series anomaly detection is emphasizes the relevance of this paper as well.

3 Methodology

3.1 Preliminaries

An autoencoder is a neural network consisting of two sub-networks, often having a symmetric structure. The first of them, the encoder, reduces the dimensionality of the input data, i.e., encodes it. The second, the decoder, reconstructs the input data from the encoded representation. Thus, the AE is trained to perform nonlinear data compression in unsupervised mode.

The convolutional AE is based on convolutional layers. In particular, when analyzing sequences, one-dimensional convolutions in the encoder and one-dimensional transposed convolutions in the decoder are used.

KDE is a non-parametric method to estimate the probability density function of given independent and identically distributed samples. For $x_1, x_2, \ldots, x_n, x_i \in \mathbb{R}^k$ their density estimation $\hat{p}(x)$ using Gaussian kernel $K(u)$ and bandwidth h is given as in the following formula:

$$\hat{p}(x) = \frac{1}{N} \sum_{i=1}^{N} K\left(\frac{x - x_i}{h}\right), K(u) = \frac{1}{\sqrt{2\pi}} \exp\left(-\frac{1}{2}u^2\right)$$

3.2 Model Architecture

AEs can typically downsize time series dimensionality by a factor of several. The latent space should have enough features to separate normal and anomalous subsequences but must not be too large not to suffer from curse of dimensionality. Aiming to create some kind of fixed architecture model we choose model latent space to consist of 4 dimensions, which satisfies the requirements above. Therefore, to be effectively encoded, the input sequences must have length about couple of dozens. We choose this parameter to be equal exactly 23, to avoid zero padding in decoder's transposed convolution layers.

The resultant model encoder consists of three convolutional layers with a ReLU activation between them and a linear layer. The decoder mirrors the same structure but use transposed convolutional layers. To reduce data dimensionality at each step, the stride of convolutional layers is chosen to 2. The architecture of model layers with tensor shapes after each block is displayed in Fig. 1.

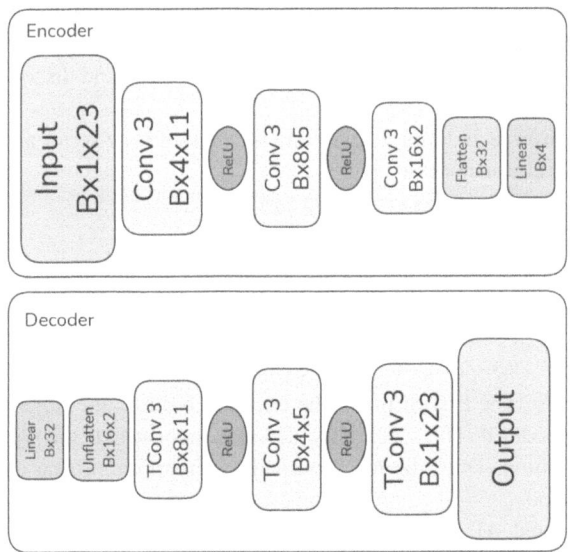

Fig. 1. Architecture of the proposed model

The most authors utilizing sliding window approach to analyze time series work with intersecting windows (most often, with stride 1) thus increasing model resolution.

Unlike them, we work with non-intersecting segments of time series. In the following sections we show that this approach can perform well while also significantly reducing the computational complexity.

Another important aspect is that we assume training the model on all available data, not just normal data, which is often the case in other works. This is done so that it is possible to apply the algorithm without having any additional knowledge about the available data. To find the optimal number of training epochs, the data can be divided into training and test samples and the number of epochs at which overfitting is not significant can be chosen. Overfitting deteriorates the quality of predictions, because latent features in this case begin to encode not only the desired data structure, but also noise.

3.3 Building Anomaly Score

The process of obtaining anomaly scores from AE's encoded representations consists of several steps, which will be explained in detail below.

1. Z-normalize encoded representations and find *middle* point
2. Calculate KDE bandwidth using quantile q of distances to the middle point
3. Apply KDE and perform robust z-normalization of its results
4. Apply sigmoid* and expand scores to the original length of time series

The important problem of the KDE-based approaches is finding kernel bandwidth. Since our goal is to separate anomalies, we should choose not bandwidth value that gives the most likely probability density function, but the one that improves the performance of the method. Our idea is to control kernel width using distances from some specific point to others. That specific point, called middle point, is the closest data point to medians of all dimensions. The bandwidth is chosen as quantile q (also referred as bandwidth parameter) of distances to the middle point. If KDE kernel has limited width, that parameter would be equal to the fraction of points which will affect density value of middle point, but since we use Gaussian kernel, the interpretation is vaguer.

After achieving KDE scores, we could just use min-max normalization to get anomaly scores, but such approach will lead to a large difference of scores for various datasets, at which anomalies would be found. Moreover, min-max normalization will always rank some points with 100% (and 0%) level of anomaly even if they are not so in fact. To try to bring some standardization to these values, robust z-normalization is firstly applied to the KDE output values and then sigmoid (*with growth parameter equal to -1, so that rarer samples have a higher anomaly rate) is providing final scores for subsequences. The last step is expanding window scores to the original length of time series, taking point anomaly level equal to level of the corresponding segment.

The obvious disadvantage of this approach is that despite all the transformations, essentially a ranking of points by anomalousness is performed. Thus, even if there are no anomalies in the time series under consideration, this algorithm is likely to identify some points with a high level of anomalies.

4   Model Evaluation

To rate mode efficiency, we will test in on the GutenTAG dataset collection using TimeE-val framework [6]. This dataset contains 168 univariate time series (each have a length of 10,000 points) with anomalies of various types to comprehensively evaluate the quality of the model in different cases. Moreover, in [1], the authors tested many algorithms in the same way, so that it will be possible to evaluate the proposed model in comparison with other existing approaches, we will use their results for other algorithms. The model will be evaluated using ROC-AUC, PR-AUC and runtime. We will consider how these metrics depends on the number of *epochs* to train autoencoder and quantile q which is used to determine KDE bandwidth.

4.1   Parameters Selection

As for the number of epochs, for a single time series it is better to select this value by dividing the data into training and test samples. This is due to the fact that for some simple dependencies, several dozens of epochs are enough for the model, while in some cases several hundred epochs are not sufficient. Nevertheless, in order to obtain average estimates for different time series, we trained the model with different but fixed for all time series number of epochs.

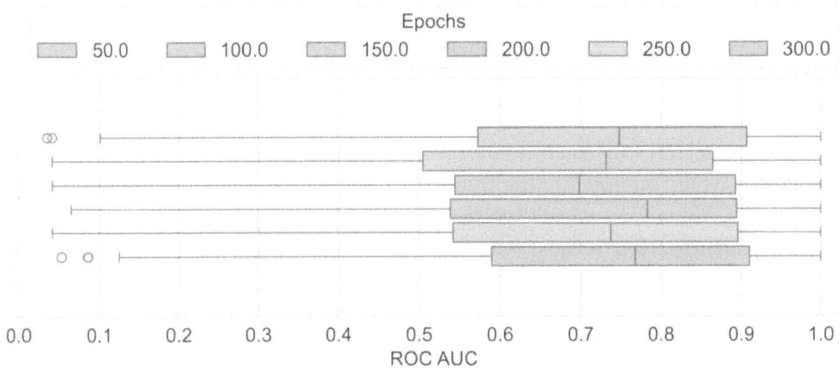

Fig. 2. Model ROC AUC vs Epochs

Figures 2 and 3 shows how ROC AUC and PR AUC respectively are changing when variating epochs parameter, (bandwidth parameter is chosen to be 0.004). Despite values are close to each other, it is clearly seen that 200 epochs provide better scores so we consider this value as standard for that dataset collection.

Another important aspect is model runtime which is controlled mostly by the number of epochs. For 200 epochs, the average runtime is 1.77 ms per data point and it is linearly changing with the number of epochs since it is the most computationally complex stage of the algorithm.

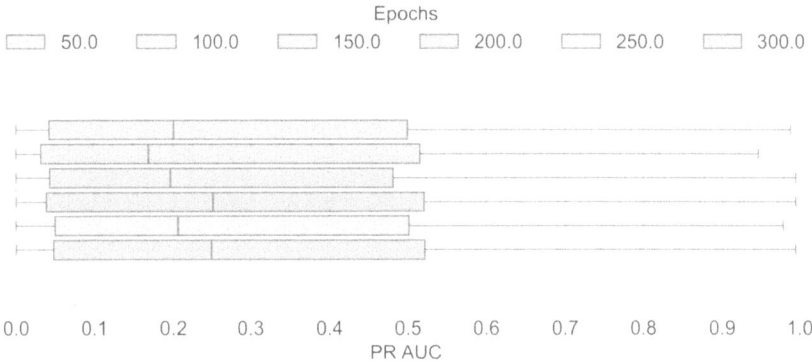

Fig. 3. Model PR AUC vs Epochs

The most important model parameter is bandwidth parameter q. Experiments show that the best value of this parameter in terms of ROC AUC is 0.001, or about the same order of magnitude. If this parameter is increased too much, the model quickly becomes a random guesser. Similarly, too small values decrease efficiency as well. Since the model was tested on time series of the same length from one collection, further experiments are required to identify patterns for proper parameter selection in different cases. Figures 4 and 5 shows how target metrics depends on that bandwidth parameter. Below, unless otherwise noted, the value is selected to be 0.001. It can be also seen that PR AUC is even better with smaller values, but since ROC AUC in that case significantly deteriorates, we do not consider that values.

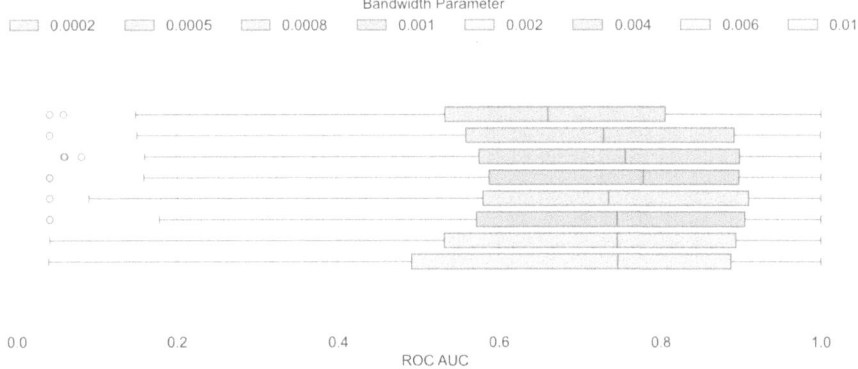

Fig. 4. Model ROC AUC vs Bandwidth Parameter

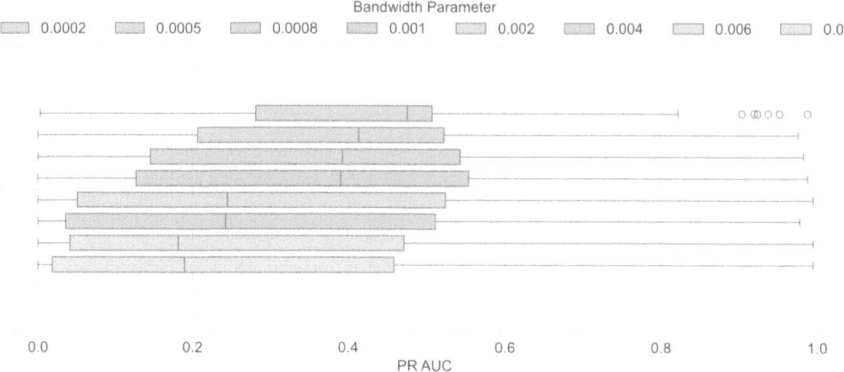

Fig. 5. Model PR AUC vs Bandwidth Parameter

4.2 Comparison with Other Algorithms

The following figures compares our method KDEAE with other 25 unsupervised univariate anomaly detection methods evaluated in [1] on the same data in terms of ROC AUC, PR AUC and runtime.

Figures 6 and 7 demonstrates that KDEAE outperformed 40% of algorithms by ROC AUC and 60% by PR AUC score. These results are promising, and presumably can be improved with further research.

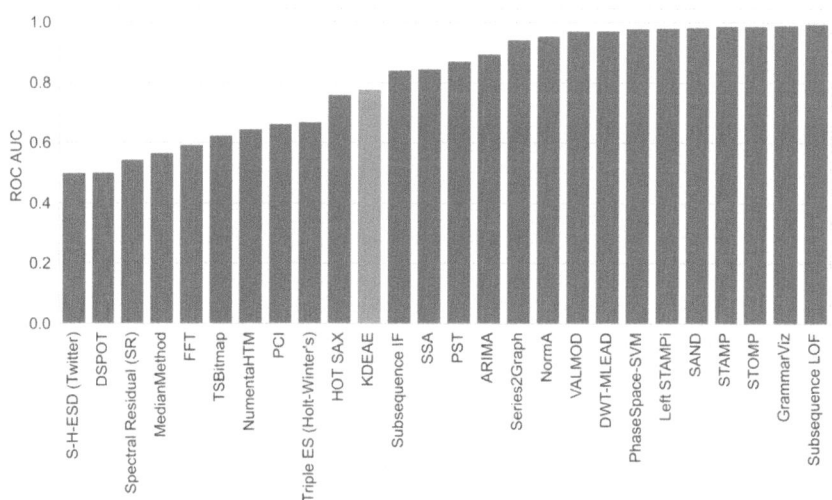

Fig. 6. Median ROC AUC Comparison

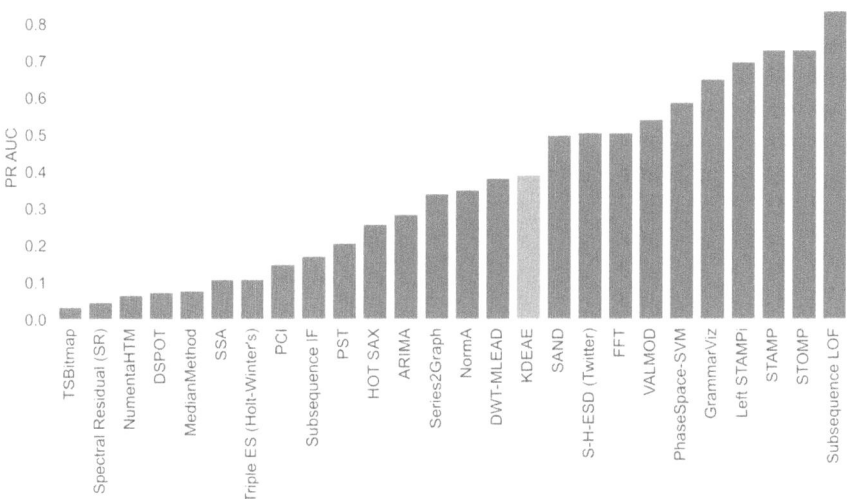

Fig. 7. Median PR AUC Comparison

KDEAE also outperform 60% of algorithms by runtime, which can be seen in Fig. 8. It is also notable that only one algorithm (STOMP) performs better that ours on all three metrics. In most cases, there can be seen a tradeoff runtime-quality.

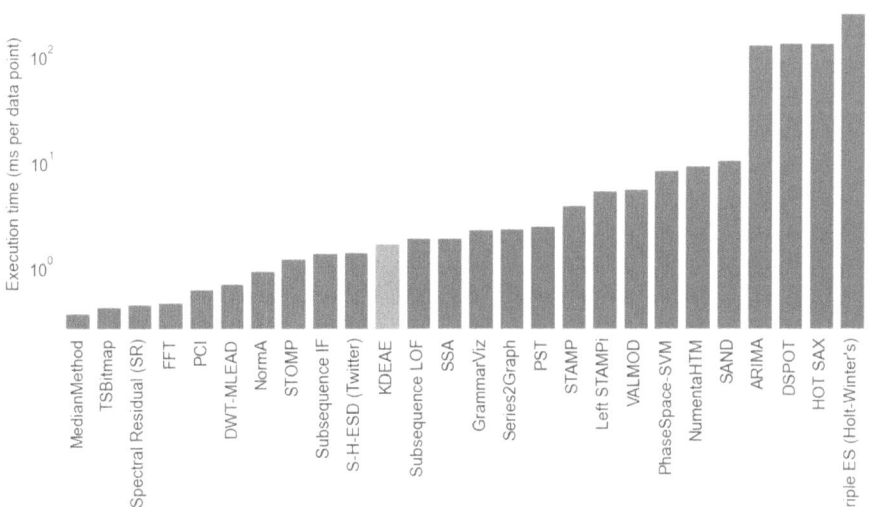

Fig. 8. Runtime Comparison

4.3 Efficiency for Different Types of Anomalies and Base Oscillations

In this section, we evaluate the performance of KDEAE for different types of anomalies and base oscillations, following dataset authors' [6] classification. For base oscillations we use abbreviations: poly – polynomial, rw – random walk, cbf – cylinder-bell-funnel, ecg – electrocardiogram.

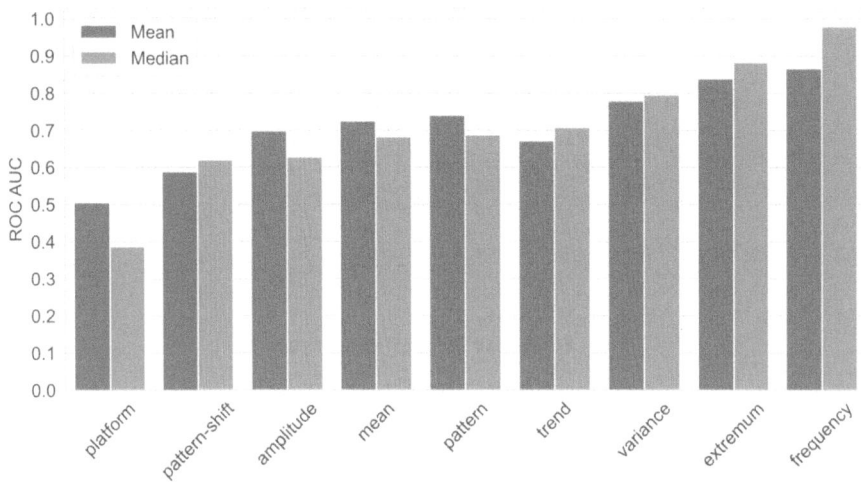

Fig. 9. ROC AUC vs Anomaly Type

Figure 9 shows that KDEAE performs best in terms of ROC AUC for frequency, extremum and variance anomalies. However, it is not suitable for platform anomalies.

Similar pattern can be observed in Fig. 10, but relative to PR AUC. The highest scores are again on frequency anomalies. We see that KDEAE is the least effective to discover trend and platform types.

As for base oscillations, the ROC AUC scores don't vary that much, which can be seen in Fig. 11. Nevertheless, they are generally better for periodic functions. On the other hand, the PR AUC values take a larger range. Figure 12 shows that again the best scores are for periodic series. However, polynomial data have significantly lower metric values in that case.

Overall, experiments demonstrate that KDEAE is suitable to detect anomalies of different types and base oscillations. However, both metrics show low efficiency for platform-type anomalies. It is also notable, that the results are generally better for periodic time series, which is a property of many such algorithms.

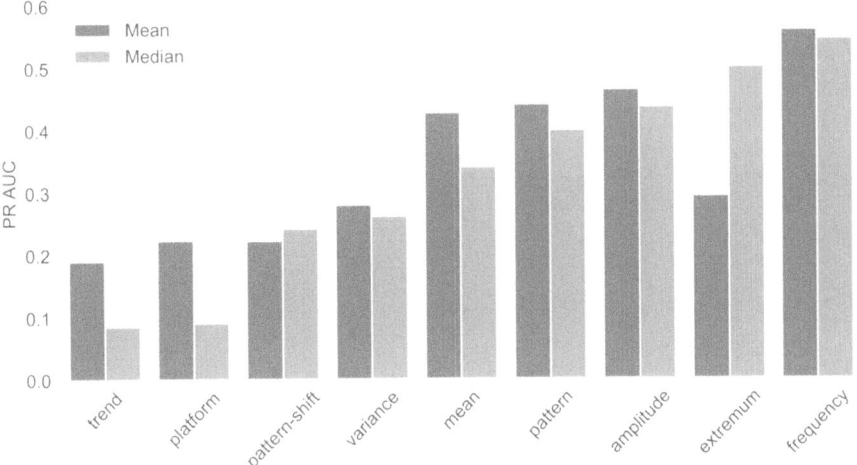

Fig. 10. PR AUC vs Anomaly Type

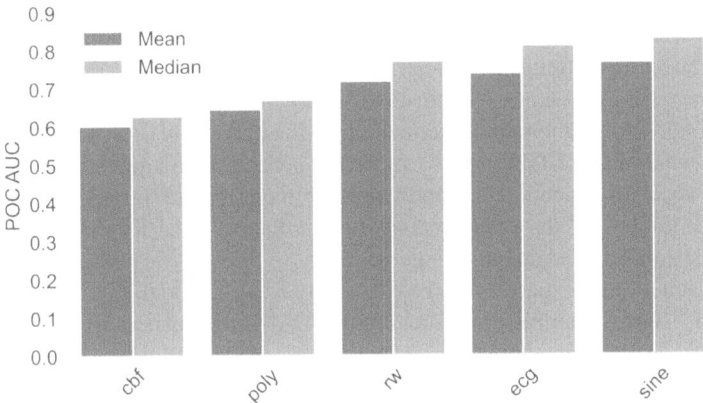

Fig. 11. ROC AUC vs Base Oscillation

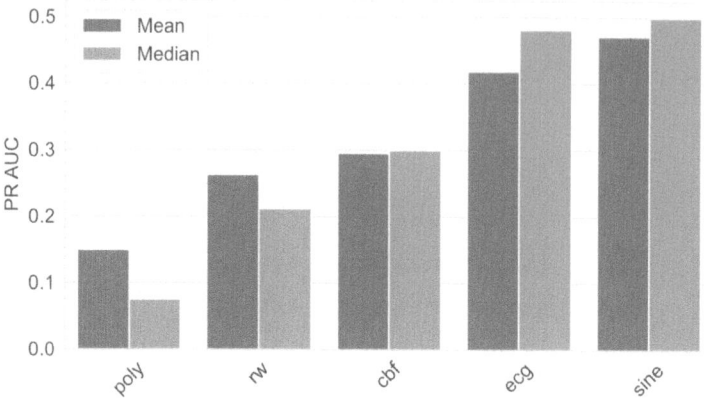

Fig. 12. PR AUC vs Base Oscillation

5   Examples of Model Performance

This section provides examples of anomaly detection using KDEAE. Since time series are too large to display in their entirety, a small section of time series containing anomaly is shown. The anomaly threshold is determined using a specific quantile of the obtained estimates. In general, the larger the threshold quantile is, the better the method performs. Thus, at q = 0.99, true anomalies obtained the highest anomaly scores. As the quantile decreases, the number of false positives increases. The specific quantile used for each plot is shown in its legend. The bandwidth parameter was adjusted to improve the performance. Since the algorithm treats the input data as fixed windows, small shifts between true and detected anomalies are possible.

As was stated before, performance is generally better for periodic time series.

Figure 13 shows example of outstanding KDEAE performance for ECG-type time series with frequency anomaly.

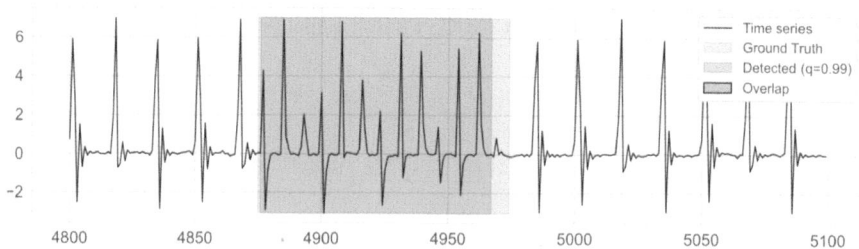

Fig. 13. Sample frequency anomaly detection for ECG type signal

Example of detection pattern anomaly for sine-based time series is depicted in Fig. 14. For that sample true anomaly also obtained the highest anomaly score.

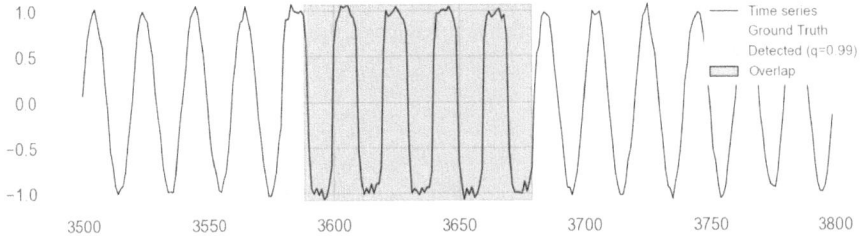

Fig. 14. Sample pattern anomaly detection for sine type signal

For non-periodic series, anomalies can also be discovered, but often with lower thresholds resulting in false positives. For example, Fig. 15 shows example how KDEAE discover anomaly in cbf-based time series.

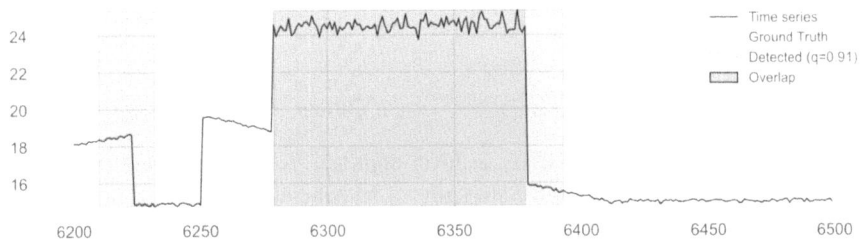

Fig. 15. Sample anomaly detection for cbf-based time series

Figure 16 shows an example of anomaly detection for random-walk-based time series. With high threshold, anomaly was detected only partially.

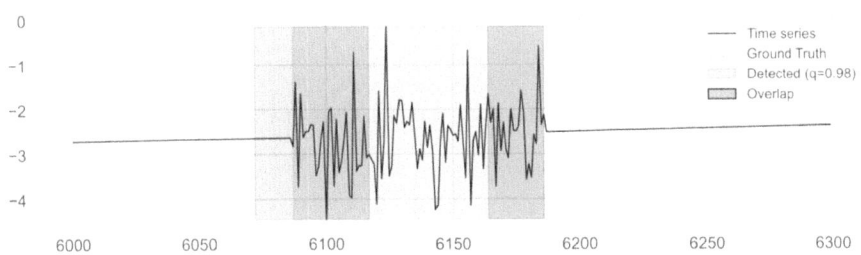

Fig. 16. Sample anomaly detection for random-walk-based time series

The weakness of the algorithm is the detection of platform type anomalies. Since windows related to a platform are very similar to each other, they get similar encodings and hence a higher density estimated by KDE. In this case, the basic assumption of low anomaly density does not work. Anomalies of this type can only be detected if there is a stronger pattern in the time series, such as periodicity or stationarity. Otherwise, their detection is unlikely. An example of this behavior of the algorithm is shown in Fig. 17.

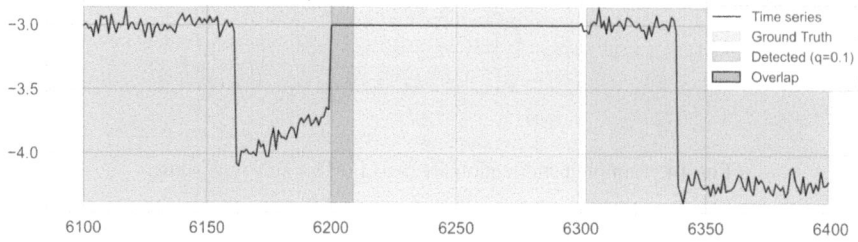

Fig. 17. Sample of platform-type anomaly detection

Overall, KDEAE can be used to discover various anomalies in both periodic and non-periodic time series. The disadvantage of the algorithm is the difficulty in detecting platform-type anomalies.

6 Conclusion

In this paper, we presented KDEAE, a novel approach for unsupervised time series anomaly detection that combines the strengths of autoencoders and kernel density estimation. The methods segments time series into non-overlapping subsequences, utilizing sliding window approach. These parts are then encoded by convolutional autoencoder. Anomaly scores are constructed based on the density of the encoded representations.

We evaluated our method on GutenTAG [6] dataset collection and compared in with 25 algorithms from the same category [1]. The results show that KDEAE is outperforming 40% of them by ROC AUC score, 60% by PR AUC score, and 60% by runtime. The results of the study demonstrate that combining AE and KDE is a promising approach for time series anomaly detection. The directions for further research could be optimizing the process of choosing parameters for the improvement of performance and extending the method to multivariate time series.

Acknowledgement. Supported by Saint Petersburg State University, project ID: 95438429.

References

1. Schmidl, S., Wenig, P., Papenbrock, T.: Anomaly detection in time series: a comprehensive evaluation. PVLDB **15**(9), 1779–1797 (2022). https://doi.org/10.14778/3538598.3538602
2. Belay, M.A., Blakseth, S.S., Rasheed, A., Salvo Rossi, P.: Unsupervised anomaly detection for IoT-based multivariate time series: existing solutions, performance analysis and future directions. Sensors **23**(5), 2844 (2023). https://doi.org/10.3390/s23052844
3. Wang, F., Jiang, Y., Zhang, R., Wei, A., Xie, J., Pang, X.: A survey of deep anomaly detection in multivariate time series: taxonomy, applications, and directions. Sensors **25**(1), 190 (2025). https://doi.org/10.3390/s25010190

4. Choi, K., Yi, J., Park, C., Yoon, S.: Deep learning for anomaly detection in time-series data: review, analysis, and guidelines. IEEE Access **9**, 120043–120065 (2021). https://doi.org/10.1109/ACCESS.2021.3107975

5. Bouman, R., Heskes, T.: Autoencoders for Anomaly Detection are Unreliable. arXiv preprint arXiv: 2501.13864 (2025)

6. Wenig, P., Schmidl, S., Papenbrock, T.: TimeEval: a benchmarking toolkit for time series anomaly detection algorithms. PVLDB **15**(12), 3678–3681 (2022). https://doi.org/10.14778/3554821.3554873

7. Project repository. https://github.com/UnicornTowa/KDEAE. Accessed 28 Mar 2025

8. Hsieh., R.-J., Chou, J., Ho, C.-H.: Unsupervised online anomaly detection on multivariate sensing time series data for smart manufacturing. In: 2019 IEEE 12th Conference on Service-Oriented Computing and Applications (SOCA), pp. 90–97. IEEE, Kaohsiung (2019). https://doi.org/10.1109/SOCA.2019.00021

9. Park, D., Hoshi, Y., Kemp, C.C.: A multimodal anomaly detector for robot-assisted feeding using an LSTM-based variational autoencoder. IEEE Robot. Automation Lett. **3**(3), 1544–1551 (2018). https://doi.org/10.1109/LRA.2018.2801475

10. Cao, V.L., Nicolau, M., McDermott, J.: A hybrid autoencoder and density estimation model for anomaly detection. In: Handl, J., Hart, E., Lewis, P., López-Ibáñez, M., Ochoa, G., Paechter, B. (eds.) Parallel Problem Solving from Nature – PPSN XIV. PPSN 2016. Lecture Notes in Computer Science(), vol. 9921. Springer, Cham (2016). https://doi.org/10.1007/978-3-319-45823-6_67

11. Frehner, R., Wu, K., Sim, A., Kim, J., Stockinger, K.: Detecting anomalies in time series using kernel density approaches. IEEE Access **12**, 33420–33439 (2024). https://doi.org/10.1109/ACCESS.2024.3371891

12. Yeh, C.-C.M. et al.: Matrix profile I: all pairs similarity joins for time series: a unifying view that includes motifs, discords and shapelets. In: 2016 IEEE 16th International Conference on Data Mining (ICDM), Barcelona, Spain, pp. 1317–1322 (2016). https://doi.org/10.1109/ICDM.2016.0179

13. Boniol, P., Paparrizos, J., Palpanas T., Franklin, M.J.: SAND: streaming subsequence anomaly detection. Proc. VLDB Endow. **14**(10), 1717–1729 (2021). https://doi.org/10.14778/3467861.3467863

14. Hyndman, R.J., Athanasopoulos, G.: Forecasting: Principles and Practice, (2nd edn.) OTexts (2018)

15. Boniol, P., Palpanas, T.: Series2Graph: graph-based subsequence anomaly detection for time series. Proc. VLDB Endow. **13**(12), 1821–1834 (2020). https://doi.org/10.14778/3407790.3407792

16. Thill, M., Konen, W., Bäck, T.: Time series anomaly detection with discrete wavelet transforms and maximum likelihood estimation. In: Proceedings of the International Conference on Time Series (ITISE) (2019)

Automated Classification and Segmentation of Brain Tumors on MRI Images Using Superpixel-Based Machine Learning

Nadezhda Shchegoleva[1]([✉]) [ID], Nadezhda Pronina[1] [ID], Nataliya Zalutskaya[2] [ID], and Jasur Kiyamov[3] [ID]

[1] Saint Petersburg State University, St.Petersburg, Russia
n.shchegoleva@spbu.ru, st105895@student.spbu.ru
[2] Federal State Budgetary Institution «Bekhterev National Medical Research Psychiatry and Neurology Center», Ministry of Health of the Russian Federation, St. Petersburg, Russia
[3] Samarkand Branch of Tashkent University of Information Technologies, Tashkent, Uzbekistan
z.kiyamov@spbu.ru

Abstract. Brain tumor detection remains one of the most pressing challenges in medical image analysis due to the complexity and variability of tumor structures. This study presents an automated approach for analyzing magnetic resonance imaging (MRI) scans, aimed at identifying pathological cases and localizing abnormal regions. A hybrid classification model based on support vector machines and k-nearest neighbors is used to distinguish between normal and pathological images. For segmentation, a superpixel-based method is applied to highlight tumor areas. The system combines traditional image preprocessing with statistical and textural feature extraction to enhance diagnostic accuracy. Experimental results confirm the effectiveness of the proposed two-stage pipeline in supporting early diagnosis and reducing the cognitive workload of clinicians.

Keywords: brain tumor · MRI · hybrid classifier

1 Introduction

Brain tumors represent one of the most complex and dangerous pathologies of the central nervous system. According to the World Health Organization (WHO), 20 million new cancer cases were registered worldwide in 2022, with 9.7 million cancer-related deaths. Brain tumors remain among the most challenging forms of cancer, requiring early diagnosis and treatment (WHO).

According to recent statistical data published on the "Main Oncological Portal of Russia" [8], the share of malignant brain tumors in the structure of oncological diseases among the male population in 2023 was approximately 1.4%, and 1.2% among women. Although these figures are lower compared to other cancer localizations (such as prostate cancer in men or breast cancer in women), the dynamics from 2013 to 2023 indicate an increase in the incidence of central nervous system (CNS) tumors. In particular, the

O. Gervasi et al. (Eds.): ICCSA 2025 Workshops, LNCS 15894, pp. 264–281, 2026.
https://doi.org/10.1007/978-3-031-97648-3_18

estimated average annual growth rate for this group of diseases reaches approximately 0.9–1%.

Despite advances in modern medicine, the diagnosis of brain tumors remains a challenging task. Magnetic resonance imaging (MRI) is the gold standard for brain imaging, but interpreting the results requires highly qualified specialists and significant time investment. Furthermore, human factors, physician fatigue, and image quality can negatively affect diagnostic accuracy.

In this context, the development of automated methods for analyzing medical images, utilizing machine learning and computer vision technologies, becomes especially relevant. These algorithms make it possible to identify pathological changes at early stages, minimize the influence of subjective factors, and increase the speed and accuracy of diagnosis.

Analyzing brain tumor structures is a complex task, as not all formations have clear boundaries and distinct visual features. In such cases, traditional diagnostic methods may not be sufficiently accurate, which increases the importance of algorithms that analyze the textural and morphological features of images.

2   Overview

2.1   Research Objectives

Main Objective. The primary goal of this study is to develop an automated system that, in the first stage, determines the presence or absence of pathological changes in the brain, and in the second stage, if such changes are detected, identifies their localization. This two-stage approach to MRI result processing helps optimize the required computational resources and, in some cases, simplifies the interpretation of the results.

The research tasks aimed at achieving this goal can be formulated as follows:

1. Data Preparation. Collection and analysis of an MRI image dataset in compliance with licensing requirements. Preliminary image preprocessing: noise removal, contrast and brightness adjustment, histogram equalization.
2. Classification. Analysis of existing machine learning methods and identification of their advantages and disadvantages for solving the tumor detection task (binary classification: "normal" or "pathology"). Comparison of various algorithms and evaluation of result quality using accuracy, recall, and F1-score metrics.
3. Segmentation of Detected Pathologies. Analysis of existing segmentation algorithms and evaluation of their suitability for detecting pathologies (thresholding methods, superpixels). Generation of masks for pathological areas and assessment of segmentation quality using appropriate metrics.
4. Comparative Analysis and Evaluation of Results. Comparison of results based on selected metrics and search for the optimal combination of "classifier → segmentation method".

2.2   Literature Review

The automation of detection and segmentation of low-grade gliomas in brain MRI scans remains one of the most in-demand tasks in the field of medical imaging. Various approaches to solving this problem are reflected in scientific studies, where each group of authors proposes their own set of algorithms and methods, tailored to different aspects of image processing, computational capabilities, and the specific characteristics of medical data.

One of the earliest fundamental approaches to image segmentation is the work by Felzenszwalb and Huttenlocher [4], in which the authors described a graph-based model that allows for clustering pixels based on proximity measures and controlling the "breaks" within potential segments. The proposed method is characterized by relatively high processing speed and flexible tuning of the scale parameter, which determines the level of detail in the final segmentation. In the context of brain MRI analysis, this algorithm can be applied for preliminary separation of homogeneous regions; however, its effectiveness highly depends on proper hyperparameter selection and preliminary image preprocessing.

The work of Kalavathi [7] is devoted to studying a multi-threshold modification of the Otsu algorithm. The application of this method demonstrated that using multiple thresholds allows for more accurate differentiation of various brain tissues—white matter, gray matter, and cerebrospinal fluid. However, when it comes to heterogeneous tumor regions with low contrast, this approach may lead to inaccurate results, and additional procedures (such as clustering or machine learning) are required to improve accuracy.

At the classification stage—i.e., determining the presence of pathological tissue—hybrid algorithms often prove to be effective solutions. For example, Machhale et al. [5] showed that a combination of support vector machines (SVM) and k-nearest neighbors (KNN) outperforms each of these techniques individually when detecting tumors in MRI scans. The SVM-KNN hybrid takes into account both the global feature structure and their local neighborhood, which is especially important when analyzing highly variable medical data.

At the same time, the emergence of large open image datasets and the increase in computational power have driven the development of neural network-based methods. Menze and colleagues [6] created the benchmark BRATS, a reference dataset for evaluating brain tumor segmentation algorithms across multiple MRI modalities (T1, T1c, T2, FLAIR). This study demonstrated the advantages of deep convolutional neural networks (CNNs), especially when sufficient data and diverse contrast types are available. The authors thoroughly examine the Dice Similarity Coefficient and Intersection over Union (IoU) metrics [6], as well as challenges encountered when processing images of varying quality and resolution.

An important aspect of modern oncological diagnostics is radiogenomics—a field focused on correlating radiological and genetic characteristics of tumors. Buda, Saha, and Mazurowski [3] showed that certain shape parameters derived from deep image analysis models correlate with molecular subtypes of low-grade gliomas. A similar conclusion was reached in the work by Pedano et al. [2], where data from The Cancer Genome Atlas (TCGA) were analyzed alongside MRI results. Both studies confirm that accurate segmentation and detailed extraction of features describing the shape of a tumor can provide additional insights into the tumor's nature, which in turn can influence prognosis and treatment planning.

Thus, the analysis indicates that successful neoplasm diagnosis requires three key components: a reliable classification system (such as SVM-KNN or Random Forest), an accurate segmentation method tailored to data quality (e.g., Felzenszwalb's algorithm, SLIC, or U-Net), and the integration of imaging features with genetic information to enhance the understanding of tumor characteristics and improve treatment strategies.

2.3 Overview of Classification Approaches

The task of classification in the context of medical image analysis typically involves making a binary decision: "tumor present" or "no tumor." The accuracy of this step largely determines the effectiveness of subsequent processing stages, as it allows either the immediate exclusion of healthy cases or the forwarding of images with signs of pathology for more detailed processing (segmentation). Several main groups of methods are commonly used for classification in medical applications:

Traditional Methods.

Support Vector Machine (SVM). SVMs perform well with high-dimensional data and can construct both linear and non-linear decision boundaries by using appropriate kernels (e.g., RBF, polynomial). The method focuses on examples located near the decision boundary, enabling it to build robust models even with a limited amount of data, especially when classes are well-separated. However, the effectiveness of SVM greatly depends on proper hyperparameter tuning.

k-Nearest Neighbors (KNN). KNN assigns a data point to the class most common among its k nearest neighbors in the feature space. The method is simple to understand and implement but may become relatively slow with large datasets. Additionally, KNN is sensitive to feature scaling and the choice of distance metric.

Ensemble Methods (Random Forest, Gradient Boosting).

Ensemble algorithms build multiple decision trees, each trained on a random subset of the data. In the case of Random Forest, the final result is determined by the majority vote of all trees, which reduces overfitting and increases robustness to noise. A major advantage of this approach is its high interpretability, particularly when analyzing feature importance.

Hybrid Approaches.

SVM-KNN. Hybrid methods combine the strengths of multiple algorithms—for example, SVM and KNN. The data is first separated using the support vector machine, and then information about the nearest neighbors (KNN) is used to refine the boundaries between classes or to handle ambiguous cases near the decision margin. According to several experiments (e.g., Machhale et al. [5]), this approach often yields higher accuracy and F1-scores than using either SVM or KNN alone.

Modern Neural Networks.

In recent years, convolutional neural networks (CNNs) have gained popularity due to their ability to automatically extract the most relevant features, minimizing the need for expert-driven feature selection. Convolutional layers are capable of capturing spatial relationships between pixels in brain images, which is particularly important in the medical domain. However, training neural networks requires large volumes of labeled data and significant computational resources.

Thus, the choice of classification method depends on data volume, processing speed requirements, and computational resources. Traditional methods offer predictability and transparency, while hybrid and neural network approaches can achieve higher accuracy if properly tuned and supported by sufficient training data.

2.4   Overview of Segmentation Approaches

Once the presence of a tumor has been established, the next step is to determine its exact location and size—that is, segmentation and delineation of the pathological region. The complexity of this task lies in the heterogeneity of MRI scans, varying tissue contrast, and possible noise, artifacts, and variations in brain characteristics across different patients. Below are the main groups of segmentation algorithms commonly used in medical image analysis.

Thresholding Methods.

Otsu's Algorithm (and its modifications). A classic thresholding segmentation technique where the optimal threshold is selected to maximize inter-class variance between pixel intensities. Multi-threshold extensions (e.g., Kalavathi, 2013 [7]) allow for the differentiation of multiple tissue types (e.g., white matter, gray matter, cerebrospinal fluid). However, in the presence of tumors whose contrast may overlap with that of normal tissues, thresholding methods often produce results that require refinement.

Clustering- and Superpixel-Based Methods.

SLIC (Simple Linear Iterative Clustering). SLIC divides the image into compact super-pixels—small regions grouping adjacent pixels with similar visual characteristics, such as color or brightness. Superpixels significantly reduce the dimensionality of the task: instead of pixel-level analysis, groups of similar pixels are considered. In medical applications, this approach simplifies classification by aggregating homogeneous regions. However, the final result is highly dependent on proper parameter selection (e.g., the number of superpixels, compactness factor).

Felzenszwalb's Method. A graph-based segmentation algorithm where pixels are treated as vertices connected by similarity-based edges (brightness, color, spatial coordinates). Vertices are merged into clusters if the gap between them exceeds a threshold. The method offers high computational efficiency ($O(n \log n)$) [4] and can detect heterogeneous regions, but its performance is sensitive to the scale parameter and input image characteristics.

Neural Network-Based Algorithms.

U-Net and FCN. Segmentation architectures based on convolutional neural networks are widely used in medical applications (e.g., Menze et al., 2015 [6]). Neural networks can automatically detect complex patterns but require large amounts of labeled data and significant computational resources. With sufficient training data, they often achieve the highest scores on metrics such as Dice and IoU.

In practice, the choice of segmentation approach is usually determined by data quality (e.g., presence of contrast or noise), research goals (e.g., preliminary segmentation vs. precise boundary extraction), and available computational resources. Classical and graph-based methods are often sufficient for cases with clear contrast and limited data, while neural networks offer superior accuracy when large, well-annotated datasets are available.

3   Description of Methods

This chapter is dedicated to a detailed examination of the methods for automatic analysis of brain MRI images, as well as the justification for parameter choices at each processing stage. The system developed in this study is based on a two-stage scheme: classification (determining the presence of a tumor) and segmentation (precise delineation of the pathological region) [5, 7].

The implemented system follows these data processing stages:

Preprocessing (noise removal, gamma correction, morphological operations).

Feature extraction and classification (detection of the presence of a tumor).

Segmentation (refining the tumor boundaries if the classifier result is positive).

Postprocessing of the final mask (morphological operations, noise removal).

3.1   Image Preprocessing

Noise Removal and Gamma Correction. The system receives MRI images in.tif format, which may potentially contain a high level of noise [1]. To improve image quality, the following algorithms are most commonly used:

Median filter (with a 3×3 or 5×5 window), which replaces the value of each pixel with the median of its surrounding neighborhood:

$$I^I(x, y) = \text{median } \{I(i, j)|(i, j)\epsilon N(x, y)\} \tag{1}$$

where $N(x,y)$ is the neighborhood window around the pixel (x,y), and III is the original image. This approach reduces salt-and-pepper noise without significantly blurring the edges [5].

Gamma correction.

$$I^I(x, y) = I(x, y)^\gamma \tag{2}$$

where γ is a parameter that determines the degree of brightness enhancement. In this study, γ values in the range of 0.5–2.0 were used to adjust low-contrast regions of the image. Lower values ($\gamma < 1$\gamma < 1$\gamma < 1$) increase the contrast in darker areas of the image, which facilitates tumor detection against the background of healthy tissue [7].

Morphological Operations and Artifact Removal.   After gamma correction, morphological operations such as erosion and dilation are typically applied to remove small noise artifacts or, conversely, to fill in small gaps within the tumor volume. Specifically, the opening and closing methods from the scikit-image library were used. The first is defined as erosion followed by dilation, and the second as dilation followed by erosion [9]. Erosion and dilation are defined by a kernel (structuring element B) and can be described by the following formulas [10]:

Erosion:

$$(A \ominus B) = \{z \,|B_z \subseteq A\} \tag{3}$$

Dilation:

$$(A \oplus B) = \{Z | B_{-z} \cap A \neq \varnothing\} \tag{4}$$

Here, A is a set (a binary mask), and B_z is a shifted copy of the structuring element.

3.2 Feature Extraction and Classification

Feature Vector Construction. To solve the classification task, it is necessary to extract the most informative features from the images. The main groups of features used in this work are listed below:

1. Statistical characteristics [6]:

The most basic and widely used measure is the **mean**, defined by the formula:

$$mean = \frac{1}{N} \sum_{i=1}^{N} x_i \tag{5}$$

This parameter reflects the average brightness level in the analyzed region. However, it can be sensitive to outliers (very bright or very dark pixels).

Variance characterizes the spread of values around the mean:

$$variance = \sigma^2 = \frac{1}{N} \sum_{i=1}^{N} (x_i - mean)^2 \tag{6}$$

This parameter indicates how much the pixel intensity values deviate from the mean.

Standard Deviation (STD) is the square root of the variance:

$$std = \sigma = \sqrt{variance} \tag{7}$$

Higher values of variance and standard deviation indicate that the brightness levels in the analyzed image region are more heterogeneous (variable).

Median

$$median = \begin{cases} x_{\left(\frac{N+1}{2}\right)}, & \text{if N odd} \\ \frac{x_{\left(\frac{N}{2}\right)} + x_{\left(\frac{N}{2}+1\right)}}{2}, & \text{if N even} \end{cases} \tag{8}$$

where x_k is the k-th element in the sorted set $\{x_1, x_2, ..., x_N\}$. The median represents the central value that divides the sample into two equal parts. It is less sensitive to outliers compared to the mean.

Entropy is estimated based on the image intensity histogram. Let the histogram be divided into M intervals (bins), and p_k be the probability that a pixel falls into the k-th bin (the sum of all p_k is 1). Then entropy is defined as:

$$entropy = -\sum_{i=1}^{M} p_k \log_2 p_k \tag{9}$$

Entropy measures the level of "uncertainty." A high value indicates that the region contains a wide range of intensity values (i.e., it has a complex structure).

Skewness. This measures the asymmetry of the distribution relative to the mean (left-skewed or right-skewed). A common formula (without bias correction) is:

$$\text{skewness} = \frac{\frac{1}{N} \sum_{i=1}^{N} (x_i - \text{mean})^3}{\left(\frac{1}{N} \sum_{i=1}^{N} (x_i - \text{mean})^2\right)^{\frac{3}{2}}} \tag{10}$$

If skewness > 0, the distribution has a longer tail on the right, indicating a tendency toward brighter pixels. If skewness < 0, the tail is shifted to the left.

Kurtosis evaluates how "heavy" the tails of the distribution are compared to a normal (Gaussian) distribution. There are several formulas; the most common one (Pearson's definition) gives a value of 0 for a normal distribution.

$$\text{kurtosis} = \frac{\frac{1}{N} \sum_{i=1}^{N} (x_i - \text{mean})^4}{\left(\frac{1}{N} \sum_{i=1}^{N} (x_i - \text{mean})^2\right)^2} - 3 \tag{11}$$

2. Textural features – Haralick features based on the gray-level co-occurrence Matrix (GLCM) [4]. For example:

$$C = \sum_{i=1}^{L-1} \sum_{j=1}^{L-1} (i - j)^2 p(i, j) \tag{12}$$

where $p(i, j)$ is the probability of the co-occurrence of intensity values i and j, and L is the number of gray levels. Other features such as Energy, Homogeneity, Correlation, etc., are computed in a similar way.

All these features are combined into a feature vector x, which is then normalized, for example, using the StandardScaler method:

$$x_{scaled} = \frac{x - \mu_x}{\sigma_x} \tag{13}$$

where σ_x and μ_x are the mean and standard deviation of the feature x across the training dataset.

3. LBP features (Local Binary Patterns) is another widely used method for texture description, computed at the neighborhood level for each pixel [7]. Let P be the number of sampling points around the center, and R the radius of the circle. Then for each pixel at coordinates (x_c, y_c). Determine the intensity of the central point:

$$I_c = I(x_c, y_c) \tag{14}$$

Select P neighboring points I_p, $p \in \{0, ..., P - 1\}$, lying within the radius R. Compare each neighboring intensity I_p with the central intensity I_c:

$$s(I_p - I_c) = \begin{cases} 1, & \text{if } I_p \geq I_c \\ 0, & \text{else} \end{cases} \tag{15}$$

Form a binary number where each bit corresponds to the result of the comparison $s(I_p - I_c)$ for the corresponding neighboring pixel:

$$LBP_{P,R}(x_c, y_c) = \sum_{p=0}^{P-1} s(I_p - I_c)2^p \tag{16}$$

The resulting code (usually $P = 8$ or $P = 16$) is interpreted as the index of a bin in a histogram. Thus, for the entire ROI (Region of Interest) or image, an LBP histogram is constructed, which describes local texture patterns (such as edges, corners, spots). Since the comparison is done bitwise, the method is less sensitive to global changes in lighting or contrast.

Textural features allow for a deeper analysis of the internal structure of the tumor and surrounding tissues, in addition to statistical characteristics (mean, std, etc.). GLCM/Haralick metrics analyze the co-occurrence of intensity values in the pixel neighborhood, making it possible to detect texture changes. LBP reflects micro-local changes in brightness, while Gabor filters are aimed at detecting structural features (lines, contours) in specific orientations. All of these methods together form a sufficient set of features that serves as a basis for more accurate and reliable decisions in brain tumor classification and segmentation tasks [4, 7].

3.3   Classification Algorithms

Support Vector Machine (**SVM**) is one of the classic and reliable machine learning algorithms, well-proven in medical applications [5]. The core idea is to find a hyperplane that best separates objects of one class from those of another, taking into account the margin. The margin is defined as the distance from the separating hyperplane to the closest objects from both classes (support vectors); maximizing this distance improves the model's generalization ability and robustness to noise.

The mathematical formulation in the linear case is:

$$\min \frac{1}{2}||w||^2 \text{ subject to } y_i(w^T x_i + b) \geq 1, i = 1, ..., N. \tag{17}$$

where $x_i \in R^d$ is the feature vector of the i-th object, $y_i \epsilon \{-1; +1\}$ is the class label (typically 0/1 in medicine, though it can be reformatted to $-1/+1$), and w and b define the position of the separating hyperplane in the feature space. During training, values of w and b are selected such that the margin between classes on the training data is maximized.

In the nonlinear case, kernel functions are introduced. The most commonly used is the RBF kernel:

$$K(x_i, y_j) = \exp(-\gamma||x_i - y_j||^2) \tag{18}$$

which allows the construction of complex decision boundaries between classes. Key hyperparameters of SVM include:

C (regularization): controls the balance between maximizing the margin and minimizing classification errors; γ (for the RBF kernel): defines the "influence radius" of individual training samples.

k-Nearest Neighbors (**KNN**) is an algorithm that classifies a new object based on the majority class among its k nearest neighbors in feature space [5, see Sect. 2.3]:

$$\hat{y} = \text{majority}\{y_{(1)}, y_{(2)}, ..., y_{(k)}\} \tag{19}$$

where $y_{(j)}$ is the class of the j-th nearest neighbor. The main parameter is the number of neighbors k. If k is too small, the algorithm may overfit; if too large, it loses local sensitivity.

Random Forest is an ensemble of decision trees [6]. Each tree is trained on a random subset of samples and features, and the final class label is determined by majority voting:

$$\hat{y} = \text{majority}\{\hat{y}_1, ..., \hat{y}_T\} \tag{20}$$

where T is the number of trees in the forest. Key parameters include: n_estimators – number of trees; max_depth – maximum allowed depth of a tree; max_features – number of features to consider at each split. This algorithm is resistant to overfitting and often demonstrates high accuracy when hyperparameters are properly tuned.

3.4 Segmentation Methods

The **SLIC** (Simple Linear Iterative Clustering) algorithm partitions an image into N superpixels, taking into account not only similarity in brightness l, but also spatial coordinates (x, y). Each cluster is represented by a center $c_k = (l_k, x_k, y_k)$. During the iterative process, cluster centers are updated to minimize the combined distance:

$$D(c_k, p) = \sqrt{\left(\frac{l_k - l_p}{\lambda_l}\right)^2 + \left(\frac{x_k - x_p}{\lambda_s}\right)^2 + \left(\frac{y_k - y_p}{\lambda_s}\right)^2} \tag{21}$$

where λ_l is the intensity (brightness) distance, λ_s is the spatial distance [4]. In medical applications, SLIC is often used to reduce analysis to regional (superpixel-based) rather than pixel-level processing.

To evaluate the quality of segmentation, Dice and Intersection over Union (IoU) metrics are used [6].

$$DSC(A, B) = \frac{2|A \cap B|}{|A| + |B|} \tag{22}$$

$$IoU(A, B) = \frac{|A \cap B|}{|A \cup B|} \tag{23}$$

where A is the ground truth tumor mask, and B is the predicted region by the algorithm [2, 3]. Values above 0.8–0.9 are generally considered to indicate good segmentation performance.

3.5 Parameter Selection and Tuning

Classification. Optimal hyperparameters (e.g., number of trees for Random Forest, values of γ and C for SVM, number of neighbors k for KNN, etc.) were selected using 5-fold cross-validation and grid search [5, 7]. The metrics Accuracy, Precision, and Recall were computed as follows:

$$\text{Accuracy} = \frac{TP + TN}{TP + TN + FP + FN} \quad (24)$$

$$\text{Precision} = \frac{TP}{TP + FP} \quad (25)$$

$$\text{Reccal} = \frac{TP}{TP + FN} \quad (26)$$

where TP (True Positives) is the number of tumor-containing images correctly classified as "pathology"; TN, FP, and FN denote the number of true negatives, false positives, and false negatives, respectively.

For SLIC, the number of superpixels (n_segments) ranged from 100 to 300, and the compactness parameter from 5 to 30. After generating the binary tumor mask, hole filling (binary_fill_holes) and removal of small connected components (smaller than 50–100 pixels) were applied. Final parameters were selected experimentally on a training subset, and results were evaluated using the Dice coefficient and Intersection over Union (IoU) metrics [2, 6].

3.6 Most Promising Solution

Novelty of the Proposed Approach. The proposed method implements a two-stage pipeline that combines a hybrid SVM-KNN classifier with superpixel-based segmentation (SLIC) to optimize brain tumor detection on MRI scans. Unlike traditional single-step approaches [5, 6], our system first filters healthy cases, reducing computational load, and applies segmentation only to suspected pathological images. By integrating classical statistical (mean, variance, entropy) and textural (Haralick, LBP) features [4, 6] extracted from superpixels, the system enhances robustness and interpretability compared to deep learning models that require large labeled datasets [6]. This approach provides a balance between efficiency and diagnostic accuracy, making it particularly suitable for clinical settings with limited data.

Original Dataset. In this study, the "LGG MRI Segmentation" dataset published on the Kaggle platform by Mateusz Buda [1] was used. The dataset is distributed under the CC BY-NC-SA 4.0 license and contains brain MRI scans for 110 patients from the TCGA-LGG collection stored in The Cancer Imaging Archive (TCIA). The original tomographic data were obtained as part of The Cancer Genome Atlas (TCGA) project and are accompanied by corresponding genetic and clinical information [2]. A full description of the dataset and related studies is available in the author's publications [3]. The Kaggle version of "LGG MRI Segmentation" includes manually labeled masks of pathological areas. To comply with licensing and TCGA requirements, it is recommended to cite the TCGA-LGG collection [2] when referencing this dataset and to follow the citation guidelines outlined on the TCGA Research Network website. An example of an original MRI scan in.tif format is shown in Fig. 1 (e.g., TCGA_CS_5393_19990606_8).

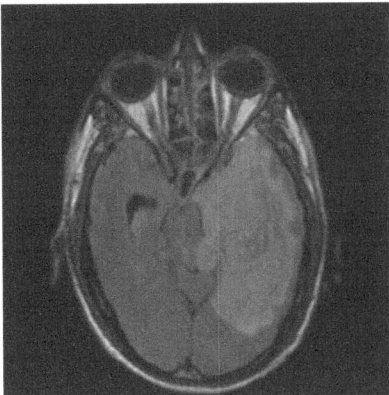

Fig. 1. MRI-scan

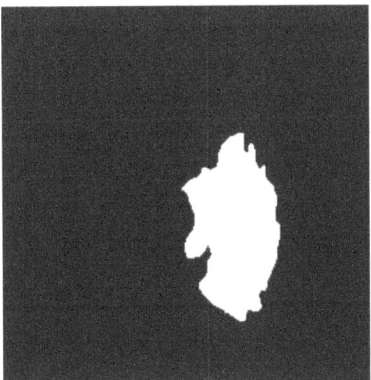

Fig. 2. Corresponding tumor annotation mask of the MRI scan

The corresponding manually created tumor annotation mask is shown in Fig. 2 (Example: TCGA_CS_5393_19990606_8_mask).

The analysis of processing methods and the characteristics of experimental data obtained during this study led to the implementation of the two-stage scheme "classi-fication → segmentation" as the optimal approach. The study employed both classical algorithms (Random Forest) and a hybrid model (SVM-KNN). According to the exper-imental results, the hybrid method demonstrated high accuracy with a limited amount of data, taking into account both the global structure of the feature space (via SVM) and local characteristics (via KNN). At this stage, the SLIC (Simple Linear Iterative Clustering) algorithm was applied, allowing the original image to be reduced to a set of superpixels.

3.7 Results Analysis

Baseline Comparison. To evaluate the effectiveness of the proposed system, simple baseline methods were tested on the same dataset. The visual results reveal key limitations of the Otsu thresholding approach. In the first example (Fig. 3), the algorithm falsely detects large anatomical regions as tumor tissue, despite the absence of any pathology, resulting in a false positive. In the second case (Fig. 4), although a tumor is clearly visible and correctly annotated in the ground truth, Otsu fails to segment it and instead highlights peripheral skull structures—a typical false negative. These outcomes illustrate that global thresholding techniques are insufficiently reliable for medical image segmentation, particularly in cases with low contrast or complex morphology, reinforcing the need for more robust and context-aware hybrid methods.

Example 1: TCGA_HT_A61A_20000127_19.tif

Original_image   True_mask   Otsu

Fig. 3. Example of misclassification by Otsu: the true mask is empty, but the thresholding method incorrectly detects large anatomical regions as tumor.

Example 2: TCGA_DU_6401_19831001_26.tif

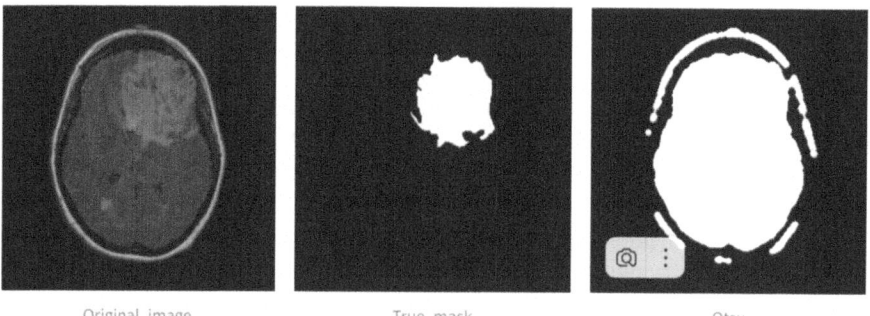

Original_image   True_mask   Otsu

Fig. 4. False negative by Otsu: the method misses the tumor and segments only peripheral structures.

Segmentation Results and Analysis. Experiments have shown that the two-stage data processing procedure "classification → segmentation" offers the following advantages:

reduced segmentation time for images that do not contain tumors, due to early filtering of standard (healthy) cases.

Based on extracted statistical (Mean, Std, Entropy, Skewness, etc.) and textural (Haralick, LBP) features, several machine learning methods were trained, including SVM, KNN, Random Forest, and a hybrid SVM-KNN model.

According to the experimental results, the hybrid SVM-KNN model demonstrated high accuracy and balanced predictions, even in the presence of class imbalance in the dataset. The final confusion matrix and classification metrics are shown in Table 1 and Table 2, respectively.

Table 1. Confusion matrix for SVM-KNN.

	Predicted 0	Predicted 1
True 0	511	0
True 1	1	274

Table 2. SVM-KNN classification metrics.

	0	1
Precision	0.998	1
Recall	1	0.996
F1-score	0.999	0.998
Support	511	275

Overall Accuracy: 0.999.
Macro-averaged: Precision $= 0.999$, Recall $= 0.998$, F1-score $= 0.999$.

The model's high sensitivity to pathological cases (Recall $= 0.996$) indicates that virtually no tumors were missed—only one out of 275 cases was misclassified. At the same time, specificity on healthy images remained perfect: all 511 class 0 examples were correctly classified, meaning no false positives were detected. This behavior is particularly important in the context of medical diagnostics, where the cost of error is extremely high. The results demonstrate that the classifier can be effectively used as a primary filter: healthy images are excluded without requiring further segmentation, while suspicious cases proceed to the next processing stage, optimizing computational resource usage.

As part of the comparative analysis, the Random Forest model was also tested and showed perfect performance on the test set. The algorithm correctly classified all examples, with zero errors in both healthy and pathological cases. The final confusion matrix and classification metrics are shown in Table 3 and Table 4.

The perfect match between predictions and ground truth confirms that the Random Forest model performed excellently on this binary classification task. Its high robustness

Table 3. Confusion matrix for Random Fores

	Predicted 0	Predicted 1
True 0	511	0
True 1	0	275

Table 4. Random Forest classification metrics.

	0	1
Precision	1	1
Recall	1	1
F1-score	1	1
Support	511	275

Overall Accuracy: 1.000
Balanced Accuracy: 1.000
ROC-AUC: 1.000
Class-averaged: Precision = 1.000, Recall = 1.000, F1-score = 1.000

to noise, interpretability, and ability to evaluate feature importance make it an attractive choice—especially on clean, balanced datasets.

However, it should be noted that such ideal results may be due to the quality and structure of the dataset. In real-world scenarios, where data is more diverse and may contain artifacts or borderline cases, model performance may vary. Nonetheless, the obtained results highlight the strong potential of Random Forest as a classifier for medical imaging tasks, particularly during the initial screening and diagnostic stages.

In the segmentation phase, the Random Forest classifier was combined with the SLIC algorithm, and experiments were conducted to evaluate segmentation performance with varying numbers of clusters (2, 3, and 4), while the number of segments was fixed at 380, and compactness at 14.

The segmentation results demonstrated the following performance metrics:

2. Clusters: dice Coefficient (mean): 0.0374; IoU (mean): 0.0198 (Fig. 5, Fig. 6, Fig. 7)

3. Clusters: dice Coefficient (mean): 0.0182; IoU (mean): 0.0099 (Fig. 8)

4. Clusters: dice Coefficient (mean): 0.0125; IoU (mean): 0.0069 (Fig. 9)

These relatively low segmentation metrics indicate that, while the Random Forest classifier perfectly identifies the presence or absence of tumors at the classification stage, the current approach to segmentation using the SLIC algorithm needs further improvement. However, the current segmentation approach consistently includes significant background areas along with the targeted tumor regions. Specifically, the segmentation method does not adequately differentiate between relevant brain structures and irrelevant background or skull areas.

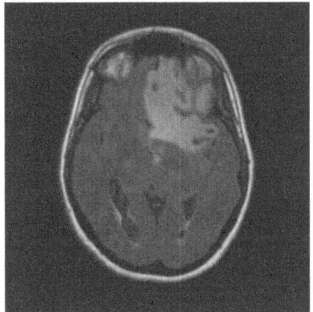

Fig. 5. MRI-scan

Fig. 6. Results using 2 clasters

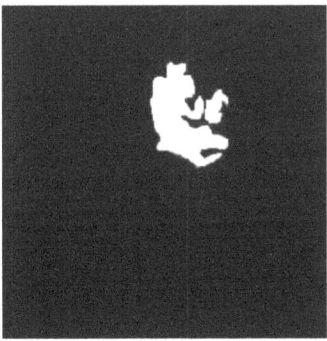

Fig. 7. Corresponding tumor annotation mask of the MRI scan

Fig. 8. Results using 3 clasters

Fig. 9. Results using 4 clasters

4   Conclusions

The developed automated system significantly accelerates the analysis of medical images, helping doctors promptly detect pathological changes in brain MRI scans. At this stage of research, the system already successfully identifies neoplasms, substantially easing the doctor's workload and enabling faster examination of a greater number of patients. In the future, we plan to improve the algorithm by excluding cranial bones from the analysis process. While the current superpixel-based segmentation demonstrates promising results, further research involving clinical validation and evaluation on larger, more diverse datasets is necessary to fully establish the robustness and diagnostic reliability of this approach.

However, regardless of automation level, the final diagnosis must always be made by a medical professional—relying not only on the results of automatic MRI analysis, but also on the original scans and additional tests such as blood work, EEG, the Wechsler test, and others.

Thus, the proposed approach is already enhancing the efficiency of medical diagnostics today, enabling the timely detection of tumors and the initiation of necessary treatment.

References

1. Buda, M.: LGG MRI Segmentation (Brain MRI Segmentation). Kaggle, License: CC BY-NC-SA 4.0 (2019). https://www.kaggle.com/datasets/mateuszbuda/lgg-mri-segmentation/data. Access 28 Mar 2025
2. Pedano, N., Flanders, A.E., Scarpace, L., Mikkelsen, T., Eschbacher, J., Hermes, B., et al.: The Cancer Genome Atlas Low Grade Glioma Collection (TCGA-LGG) (Version 3). Cancer Imaging Archive (2016). https://doi.org/10.7937/K9/TCIA.2016.L4LTD3TK
3. Buda, M., Saha, A., Mazurowski, M.A.: Association of genomic subtypes of lower-grade gliomas with shape features automatically extracted by a deep learning algorithm. Comput. Biol. Med. (2019)
4. Felzenszwalb, P.F., Huttenlocher, D.P.: Efficient graph-based image segmentation. Int. J. Comput. Vision **59**(2), 167–181 (2004)
5. Machhale, K., Nandpuru, H.B., Kapur, V., Kosta, L.: MRI brain cancer classification using hybrid classifier (SVM-KNN). In: 2015 International Conference on Industrial Instrumentation and Control (ICIC), pp. 60–65. IEEE, Pune, India (2015). https://doi.org/10.1109/IIC.2015.7150592
6. Menze, B.H., Jakab, A., Bauer, S., et al.: The multimodal brain tumor image segmentation benchmark (BRATS). IEEE Trans. Med. Imaging **34**(10), 1993–2024 (2015)
7. Kalavathi, P.: Brain tissue segmentation in MR brain images using multiple Otsu's thresholding technique. In: 2013 8th International Conference on Computer Science & Education (ICCSE), pp. 639–642. IEEE (2013)
8. Glavny Onkologichesky Portal Rossii (Main Oncological Portal of Russia): Official Statistics on Malignant Neoplasms Incidence in 2023. https://glavonco.ru/cancer_register/. Accessed 13 Feb 2025
9. Scikit-image Documentation: Morphological Filtering (2025). https://scikit-image.org/docs/stable/auto_examples/applications/plot_morphology.html. Accessed 25 Mar 2025
10. Gonzales, R.C., Woods, R.E.: Digital Image Processing, 4th edn., pp. 638–648. Publisher, Location (2018)

Neural Ordinary Differential Equations with TM-Solver to Predict Time Series Data

Anna Golovkina$^{(\boxtimes)}$ and Anna Vashukova

Saint Petersburg State University, Saint Petersburg, Russia
a.golovkina@spbu.ru

Abstract. The paper aims to analyze the performance of Neural ODE model based solutions for time-series prediction. The original paper from 2018 gave the opportunity for continuous-time modeling of long-time processes. Since then, lots of different modifications were proposed, like ODE-RNN and p-node ODE-RNN, augmented neural ODE, Hamiltonian Neural Networks, Neural Controlled differential equations, etc. All these modifications try to modify the form of ODE lying behind the NN layers. However, the performance of these approaches is still strongly influenced by the choice of numerical solvers, with conventional methods often compromising computational efficiency, stability, or precision. This paper introduces the Taylor Mapping (TM) solver, a numerical integrator that leverages polynomial approximations of the ODE general solution for Neural ODEs. The TM-solver adaptively truncates higher-order terms to balance accuracy and computational cost. What is more, the TM-solver explicitly constructs interpretable maps to reveal local dynamics and can be integrated with automatic differentiation frameworks for efficient training. Evaluations show that the TM-solver improves Neural ODEs by increasing prediction accuracy for synthetic data and real-world datasets.

Keywords: TM-solver · Neural ODE · time-series prediction

1 Introduction

Time-series modeling and prediction, a critical task in domains such as finance, engineering, or energy forecasting, requires models that are capable of capturing complex time dynamics despite possible irregularities in data sampling and scale of temporal resolution. Conventional methods, including autoregressive models and recurrent neural architectures, often impose rigid discrete-time structures, limiting their adaptability to irregularly sampled sequences or continuous latent processes. Neural ordinary differential equations (Neural ODEs) [6] have emerged as a transformative framework for modeling temporal evolution via continuous-time dynamics governed by differential equations. By parameterizing the derivative of hidden states via a neural network, neural ODEs inherently adapt to

The authors acknowledge Saint Petersburg State University for a research project 121061000159-6.

variable time intervals, learn smooth trajectories, and reduce architectural complexity compared to their discrete-layer counterparts.

One of the key parameters strongly influencing the performance of Neural ODEs is the choice of numerical solver that approximates the integration of the learned differential equations [19–22]. Although conventional solvers such as explicit Runge-Kutta or adaptive step size methods (e.g., Dopri5) are widely adopted [3], their computational cost, stability, and precision trade-offs pose challenges for gradient-based training and long-horizon forecasting. This work introduces the Taylor Mapping (TM) solver, a numerical integrator that combines a polynomial representation of the solution derived from Taylor series expansions [11]. Unlike generic methods for an ODE solution, the TM-solver explicitly constructs a local polynomial approximation of the ODE solution by a straightforward procedure at each step. This approach enables precise, high-order approximations of the state trajectory while keeping analytical tractability, a critical feature for efficient gradient propagation in neural ODE training.

The TM-solver offers numerous advantages for modeling time-series data. The polynomial representation facilitates the adaptive truncation of higher-order terms, striking a balance between accuracy and computational efficiency [10]. Second, the explicit computation of Taylor map coefficients (compare to the learned coefficients in traditional solver's approximation formulas) provides information on the local dynamics of the system, improving the interpretability of the learned ODE. Third, compatibility of the method with automatic differentiation frameworks (e.g., PyTorch, TensorFlow) ensures seamless integration with neural network training pipelines [16]. Thus, when combined with Neural ODEs, the TM-solver is well suited for time series applications requiring high precision and smoothness, such as forecasting chaotic systems or interpolating irregularly sampled data (e.g., from sensors).

The polynomial-based methodology of the TM-solver improves interpretability and conforms to the requirements of contemporary scientific computer infrastructure. The solver is optimized for deployment in distributed systems, including extensive climate simulations and real-time sensor networks, due to its provision of closed-form solutions and effective parallelization. This research further investigates its application to real-time vibration sensor data forecasting.

This work explores the synergy between Neural ODEs and the TM-solver, focusing on its capacity to (1) improve prediction accuracy by leveraging high-order Taylor terms for fine-grained trajectory approximation, (2) reduce sensitivity to solver hyperparameters through adaptive polynomial truncation, and (3) enable scalable training via gradient-compatible Taylor coefficient computation. By unifying the continuous-time modeling flexibility of neural ODEs with the analytical rigor of Taylor-based solvers, this framework aims to advance methods in time-series prediction, offering a mathematically grounded and computationally feasible tool for real-world applications. Subsequent sections evaluate the performance of the TM solver against the other Neural ODE modifications.

The rest of the paper is organized as follows: we summarize the related work in Sect. 2. Section 3 presents the description of the combined model. Section 4 introduces the details of the experiment and the experimental results; Sect. 5 explains the conclusions and future work.

2 Related Work

2.1 Neural ODE

Basic Concept. Neural Ordinary Differential Equations (NODEs) are a novel type of model that can be thought of as endless residual blocks connecting the model's input and output [6]. NODEs are an appropriate tool for learning complicated systems over extended periods of time due to their property of continuous infinite depth [20]. In recent years, the NODE has been widely researched in theory and methods to improve its efficiency and robustness. It has been shown to be effective in a variety of applications, including image recognition, point cloud learning, and time series prediction [13].

NODE concept presents deep learning as dynamic systems governed by differential equations so that the hidden state evolves via an ODE that is parameterized by a neural network:

$$\frac{d\mathbf{X}(t)}{dt} = f(\mathbf{X}(t), t, \theta), \tag{1}$$
$$\mathbf{X}(0) = (t_0),$$

where the function f models the dynamics with the initial condition $f(0)$, parameter θ is utilized to optimally approximate f in the ODE model.

Thus, we can compute the terminal value $\mathbf{X}(T)$ of the process started from t_0 $(T > t_0)$ by integrating ODEs:

$$\mathbf{X}(T) = \mathbf{X}(t_0) + \int_{t_0}^{T} f(\mathbf{X}(t), \theta) dt. \tag{2}$$

To test and train the model, a loss function can be defined as the distance between the prediction and training set

$$\mathcal{L}(\mathbf{X}(T), \mathcal{Y}_{\text{train}}) = d(\mathbf{X}(T), \mathcal{Y}_{\text{train}}),$$

where $d(\cdot, \cdot)$ is a metric function for distance such as $d(x, \mathcal{Y}) = \inf_{y \in \mathcal{Y}} ||x - y||^2$. The adjoint approach [21] allows for parameter θ updates by gradient descent, which can be described as the following dynamical system:

$$\frac{d\mathcal{L}(\mathbf{X}(T))}{d\theta} = \int_{t_0}^{T} \psi(t) \frac{\partial f(\mathbf{X}(t), \theta)}{\partial \theta} dt, \tag{3}$$

where $\psi(t) = \frac{\partial \mathcal{L}}{\partial \mathbf{X}}$ is the adjoint state that satisfies the adjoint equation:

$$\frac{d\psi(t)}{dt} = -\psi(t) \frac{\partial f(\mathbf{X}(t), \theta)}{\partial \mathbf{X}}, \tag{4}$$
$$\psi(T) = \frac{\partial \mathcal{L}}{\partial \mathbf{X}}(T).$$

To sum up the points above, NODEs solve (2) to obtain the predicted value in forward inference while solving Eqs. (3) and (4) in backward training utilizing black-box ODE solvers [3,14] to update the weights.

Nevertheless, when addressing extensive machine learning models or learning long-term dependencies in intricate dynamic systems [9,17], NODEs necessitate a substantial quantity of function evaluations during both inference (1) and training (4) to attain a minimal error tolerance of ODEs, thereby impacting the computational efficiency and efficacy of ODE-based models. To alleviate the diminished efficiency caused by elevated function evaluations, dimension-lifting techniques can be incorporated with NODEs to augment the representational capability of such models [7,9]. Also, some authors propose incorporating physical laws or acceleration techniques inspired by physics [5,12]. Let us describe some of the proposed modifications in more detail below.

P-Node Neural ODE and RNN. This method combines two models, vanilla Neural ODE and RNN, giving the possibility to flexibly combine advantages of continuous and discrete models [18]. The hidden state is defined either by Eq. (1) in the case of Neural ODE or by

$$\mathbf{X_t} = \sigma(W_X \mathbf{X}_{t-1} + W_\mathcal{Y} \mathcal{Y}_t + b),$$

in the case of RNN. Here $\mathcal{Y}_t$ is the input data, W_X and $W_\mathcal{Y}$ are the weight matrices, b a bias term, σ is an activation function.

The choice between these two models is done according to the probability: RNN is chosen with probability $1 - p$, while Neural ODE – with p.

It is theoretically proven that when $p(t) = 1/t$ (here t denotes training time), the model's hidden state may be considered as a random process with all of its properties. This probability selection is further justified by the fact that the neural ODE model trains faster than the RNN during the first epochs. Furthermore, this switching allows for fewer function evaluations, lowering total training time.

Augmented Neural ODE (ANODE). This model augments the input state with extra dimensions to learn richer dynamics [7,9]. For example, a 2-dim input might be expanded to 5-dim before solving the ODE:

$$\frac{d}{dt} \begin{bmatrix} \mathbf{X}(t) \\ \hat{\mathbf{X}}(t) \end{bmatrix} = \begin{bmatrix} f(\mathbf{X}(t), t, \theta) \\ g(\hat{\mathbf{X}}(t), t, \phi) \end{bmatrix},$$

where $\hat{\mathbf{X}}(t)$ is an augmented state. Thus, ANODE addresses original Neural ODEs problems related to complex transformations (e.g., rotations, separations) and input space's topology due to limited state space. This provides a variety of benefits; among those are improved expressivity: thanks to additional dimensions, the system is capable of modeling more complex flows. The second is the absence of over-parameterization: expanding state space helps to avoid increasing network width/depth. Additionally, ANODE outperforms vanilla Neural ODEs on some tasks like image classification that require complex feature transformations.

Hamiltonian Neural Networks (HNN). HNN enforces Hamiltonian mechanics (energy conservation) in the ODE structure by learning dynamics that preserve symplectic structure (e.g., position and momentum) [12]. In Hamiltonian mechanics q and p represent generalized coordinates and momenta, respectively. These variables are used to describe the state of the system and its dynamics:

$$\dot{q}(t) = \frac{\partial H}{\partial p}, \quad \dot{p}(t) = -\frac{\partial H}{\partial q},$$

where $H(q, p, t)$ is the Hamiltonian of the system. The Hamiltonian H is a function that describes the total energy of the system. In HNN, the Hamiltonian is parameterized by a neural network:

$$H(q, p) = \text{NN}(q, p; \theta),$$

where NN is a neural network with parameters θ. This helps to model systems where it is important to preserve the physical laws while training, e.g., the energy conservation law.

Thus, HNN addresses original Neural ODE limitations; for instance, with physical plausibility, original Neural ODEs may violate physical laws. Also, standard models require large datasets to learn dynamics, while HNNs exploit the known physics priors. Thanks to physical constraints, HNN exhibits long-term stability of the predictions. All these facts result in better generalization ability and interpretability.

Neural Controlled Differential Equations (NCDE). NCDE extends Neural ODEs to handle controlled dynamical systems, where the derivative depends on an external control signal (e.g., time-series inputs) [15]. Governed by:

$$\frac{d\mathbf{X}(t)}{dt} = f(\mathbf{X}(t), u(t), t, \theta),$$

where $u(t)$ is an external control signal. This allows modeling systems where the state depends not only on the current state but also on external input data. The control action $u(t)$ can be represented as a function of time or as the output of another neural network.

Thus, compared to vanilla Neural ODE, NCDE provides an explicit mechanism to incorporate external inputs handling also time-varying, discontinuous, or sparse control signals. Thanks to the mentioned points, NCDE captures dependence on the entire history of controls (like RNNs but continuous) and models sequential data with irregular sampling.

2.2 TM-Solver

Consider the autonomous system of ordinary differential equations:

$$\frac{d\mathbf{X}}{dt} = f(\mathbf{X}(t)). \tag{5}$$

Here t is an independent variable (time), $\mathbf{X} \in \mathbb{R}^n$ is a n-dimensional state of the system, and $f : \mathbb{R}^n \to \mathbb{R}^n$ a smooth vector field. A non-autonomous system $\frac{d\mathbf{X}}{dt} = f(\mathbf{X}(t), t)$ can be brought to this form by adding a variable $X_{n+1} = t$ and appending the equation $\frac{d}{dt} t = 1$.

For the fixed time t, $\mathbf{Y}(t)$ can be regarded as a function of its initial value $\mathbf{X}(t_0) = \mathbf{X}_0$:

$$\mathbf{X}(t, \mathbf{X}_0) = \mathcal{M}_F^t(\mathbf{X}_0) = \mathbf{X}_0 + \int_{t_0}^{t} F(\tau, \mathbf{X}(\tau)) d\tau. \tag{6}$$

Mapping $\mathcal{M}_F^t$ defines the system's state propagator from the time moment t_0 to t. In general, we pick a numerical integrator Φ_h that approximates $\mathcal{M}_F^t(\mathbf{X}_0)$ and compose it to produce the numerical solution. The pleiades of traditional solvers are based on dividing the interval $[t_0, t]$ into several steps and numerical computing integrals in (6). For example, the common choice is the Runge-Kutta method [2]:

$$\mathbf{X}(t_{k+1}) = \mathbf{X}(t_k) + h \sum_{i=1}^{I} b_i f(t_k, \mathbf{X}(v_i)), \tag{7}$$

$$v_i = \mathbf{X}(t_k) + h \sum_{j=1}^{I} a_{ij} f(v_j), i = 1..I.$$

Here h is a discrete step and coefficients a_{ij} and b_i with $i, j = 1..I$ fully describe particular method. For instance, the simplest procedure is the explicit Euler method, where a single step takes the following form:

$$\mathbf{X}(t_{k+1}) = \mathbf{X}(t_k) + h F(t_k, \mathbf{X}(t_k)). \tag{8}$$

The formula (7)–(8) shows that the state vector values at the previous time step are typically not multiplicatively separable in the nonlinear function f. This indicates that numerical computation should be repeated for each new initial condition when solving a forward problem for (5).

TM-solver aims to build an expression of the flow (similar idea to [4]) $\mathcal{M}_F^t(\mathbf{X}_0)$ in the polynomial form

$$\mathbf{X}(t) = \sum_{i=1}^{m} R^{1i}(t, t_0) \mathbf{X}_0^{[i]}, \tag{9}$$

where $\mathbf{X}^{[k]}$ is k-th Kronecker power of the vector $\mathbf{X}$ (means $\mathbf{X} \otimes \mathbf{X}^{[k-1]}$ after removing duplicate terms). The advantage of representation (9) is that it is linear with respect to the matrices $R^{1i}(t, t_0)$.

The procedure to construct unknown $R^{1i}(t, t_0)$, $i = \overline{1..m}$ matrices based on the system (5) is described in detail in [10].

Using such a method for ODE solution in NODE can bring several potential advantages:

- (Closed-Form Efficiency) Polynomial solutions provide exact or approximate closed-form expressions, eliminating iterative numerical integration. This reduces computational costs during inference; additionally, evaluation of polynomials is typically faster than solving an ODE step-by-step.
- (Simpler Gradient Computation) Gradients might be calculated simply using symbolic differentiation of a polynomial, eliminating the requirement for adjoint sensitivity approaches. This prevents memory-intensive backpropagation using solver stages.
- (Interpretability) In contrast to black-box numerical solvers, polynomial solutions are explicit and provide insights into learnt dynamics.
- (Stability) Polynomial approximations can help to avoid the stability concerns that come with iterative approaches, particularly for stiff systems.

3   Model

Despite the mentioned advantages of TM-solver, when it is applied to Neural ODE there could be some potential problems [8]. For instance, most ODEs do not admit exact polynomial solutions; also, Neural ODEs learn arbitrary dynamics via flexible neural networks. If we force the network to produce ODEs solvable by polynomials, it would severely limit expressivity, undermining their universal approximation capability. At the same time, higher accuracy might require high-degree polynomials, thus introducing computational complexity and numerical instability. Furthermore, fixed polynomial forms lack the adaptive step-sizing required to handle irregular or stiff dynamics, which is a strength of conventional solvers such as dopri5.

Thus, inspired by the p-Node Neural ODE + RNN, the following hybrid architecture can be proposed:

1. Hybrid solver system:
   - *TM-solver*: constructs solution in the form (9) according to the deterministic procedure for the given ODE;
   - *Dopri*: a traditional adaptive ODE solver (e.g., dopri5) for regions where polynomial approximations fail;
   - *Gating Network*: a classifier based on MLP that decides which solver to use for a given input/time window.
2. Neural ODE core: the main network that defines dynamics (1).

The training procedure includes the following steps aside from those provided by the original model for each input/time window $[t_i, t_{i+1}]$:

- Extract dynamics features $\varphi_i = $ feature_extractor$(f_\theta, \mathcal{Y}_i, t_i)$
- Compute gating probability $p_i = $ gating_network(φ_i)
- **if** $p_i > \tau$ (threshold): use TM-solver to predict $\mathcal{Y}_{i+1}$
- **else**: use Dopri to compute $\mathcal{Y}_{i+1}$.

4   Results

The mentioned models in the first section were compared to the proposed TM-solver-based NODE in this paper for two testing scenarios: univariate and multivariate time-series prediction.

4.1   Univariate Time-Series Prediction

We consider two datasets in the univariate time-series scenario: synthetic data defined with a simple formula:

$$\sin(t) + 0.1 \cdot Random(t),$$

and the time-series data of weather conditions in Delhi [1]. For testing, we chose humidity index only.

Table 1 presents the results of experiments on synthetic data and real data (humidity in Delhi) [1]. For each method, the training time and the value of the loss function (MSE) at the test set are indicated.

Table 1. Result of experiments with univariate time series prediction

Method	Synthetical data		Real data	
	train time (s)	MSE	train time (s)	MSE
Neural ODE	12.21	0.0127	31.05	0.0157
P-Node + RNN	10.27	0.0142	30.01	0.0126
Augmented ODE	9.58	0.0123	40.18	0.0089
HNN	7.05	0.0135	33.97	0.0104
NCDE	11.94	0.0193	41.88	0.0150
TM-solver-NODE	10.21	0.0134	35.03	0.0122

Figures 1–2 illustrate the best of the analyzed models (ANODE) with respect to the MSE metric.

 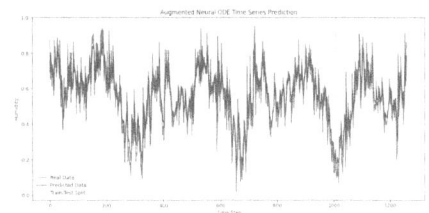

Fig. 1. ANODE for synthetic data.   **Fig. 2.** ANODE for humidity data.

4.2   Multivariate Time-Series Prediction

As for an example of multivariate time-series data, we considered the real dataset collected at the vibration testbed at SPbSU. The dataset consists of acceleration of vibrations measured within three perpendicular directions (X, Y, Z) for 4 points of interest. Figure 3 illustrates the phase portrait of the vibration for the first point.

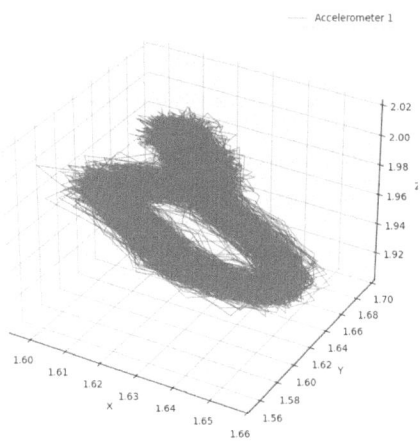

Fig. 3. Vibration phase portrait for the first point of measurements.

Table 2 aggregates the computational results for the different models being investigated in the current research. The best results, both with respect to the training time and MSE Hamiltonian neural network demonstrates. Figure 4 shows the prediction for the vibration signal with HNN model.

Table 2. Result of experiments with multivariate time series prediction

Method	train time (s)	MSE
Neural ODE	31.61	0.0159
P-Node + RNN	55.17	0.0124
Augmented ODE	90.71	0.0123
HNN	2.77	0.0095
NCDE	32.84	0.0247
TM-solver-NODE	11.04	0.0112

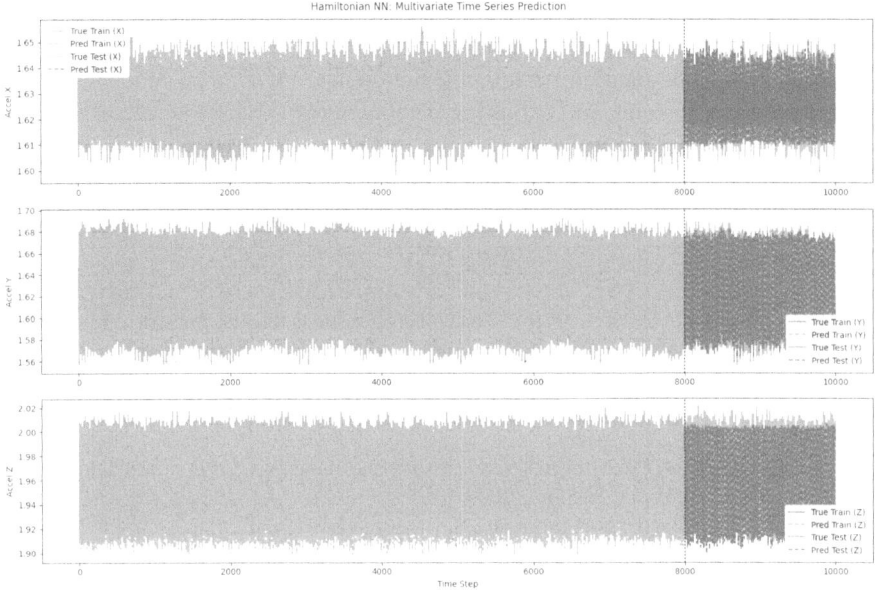

Fig. 4. HNN for the vibration acceleration signal.

5   Conclusion

In this study, we examined how well neural ODE-based models performed in time series forecasting, focusing on how the Taylor Mapping (TM) solver enhanced numerical integration. We considered many versions, such as Neural ODE, P-Node + RNN, Augmented Neural ODE (ANODE), Hamiltonian Neural Networks (HNN), Neural Controlled Differential Equations (NCDE), and the proposed TM-solver-NODE, using both synthetic and real univariate and multivariate datasets. Thanks to the enlarged state space, ANODE achieved the greatest prediction accuracy. Nevertheless, TM-solver-NODE showed competitive performance with clear benefits: its adaptable truncation balanced accuracy and computational cost, its polynomial-based solver structure allowed for interpretable local dynamics, and its smooth integration with automatic differentiating frameworks allowed for effective training.

The proposed strategy to unify the advantages of both approaches is a hybrid design that uses a gate network to dynamically select between a TM solver and conventional solvers (Dopri). The analytical rigor of the TM solver makes it a useful tool for the cases when interpretability and stability are required, including modeling stiff systems or irregularly sampled data, even if HNN and P-Node+RNN are better in terms of training efficiency. Future research might introduce an adaptive truncation criterion to higher-order approximations in TM solver method. Due to the combination of computationally efficient and interpretable solutions joint with the flexibility of continuous modeling, the proposed approach demonstrates an interesting potential of hybrid numerical approaches to develop neural ODEs.

Future directions include optimizing the Neural ODE type models for distributed memory systems and exploring its synergy with GPU-accelerated automatic differentiation frameworks, further bridging the gap between machine learning and scientific computing.

References

1. Delhi Weather Data. https://www.kaggle.com/datasets/mahirkukreja/delhi-weather-data
2. Solving Ordinary Differential Equations I, Springer Series in Computational Mathematics, vol. 8. Springer Berlin Heidelberg, Berlin, Heidelberg (1993). https://doi.org/10.1007/978-3-540-78862-1
3. Atkinson, K., Han, W., Stewart, D.E.: Numerical Solution of Ordinary Differential Equations. John Wiley & Sons (2009)
4. Biloš, M., Sommer, J., Rangapuram, S.S., Januschowski, T., Günnemann, S.: Neural Flows: Efficient Alternative to Neural ODEs (2021). https://doi.org/10.48550/arXiv.2110.13040, http://arxiv.org/abs/2110.13040, arXiv:2110.13040 [cs]
5. Botev, A., Jaegle, A., Wirnsberger, P., Hennes, D., Higgins, I.: Which priors matter? Benchmarking models for learning latent dynamics (2021). https://doi.org/10.48550/arXiv.2111.05458, http://arxiv.org/abs/2111.05458, arXiv:2111.05458 [stat]
6. Chen, R.T.Q., Rubanova, Y., Bettencourt, J., Duvenaud, D.: Neural Ordinary Differential Equations (2019). https://doi.org/10.48550/arXiv.1806.07366, http://arxiv.org/abs/1806.07366, arXiv:1806.07366 [cs]
7. Dupont, E., Doucet, A., Teh, Y.W.: Augmented Neural ODEs. In: Advances in Neural Information Processing Systems. vol. 32. Curran Associates, Inc. (2019)
8. Fronk, C., Petzold, L.: Interpretable polynomial neural ordinary differential equations. Chaos **33**(4) (2023). https://doi.org/10.1063/5.0130803, https://www.ncbi.nlm.nih.gov/pmc/articles/PMC10076068/
9. Gholami, A., Keutzer, K., Biros, G.: ANODE: Unconditionally Accurate Memory-Efficient Gradients for Neural ODEs (2019). https://doi.org/10.48550/arXiv.1902.10298, http://arxiv.org/abs/1902.10298, arXiv:1902.10298 [cs]
10. Golovkina, A., Kozynchenko, V.: Neural network representation for ordinary differential equations. In: Artificial Intelligence in Models, Methods and Applications, Studies in Systems, Decision and Control, vol. 457. Springer International Publishing (2022)
11. Golovkina, A., Kozynchenko, V., Kulabukhova, N.: Reconstruction and identification of dynamical systems based on Taylor maps. In: Gervasi, O., et al. (eds.) Computational Science and Its Applications – ICCSA 2021, vol. 12956, pp. 360–369. Springer International Publishing, Cham (2021).https://doi.org/10.1007/978-3-030-87010-2_26, https://link.springer.com/10.1007/978-3-030-87010-2_26, series Title: Lecture Notes in Computer Science
12. Greydanus, S., Dzamba, M., Yosinski, J.: Hamiltonian Neural Networks (2019). https://doi.org/10.48550/arXiv.1906.01563, arXiv:1906.01563 [cs]
13. Huang, Z., Sun, Y., Wang, W.: Learning Continuous System Dynamics from Irregularly-Sampled Partial Observations (2020). https://doi.org/10.48550/arXiv.2011.03880

14. Kidger, P.: On Neural Differential Equations (2022). https://doi.org/10.48550/arXiv.2202.02435, http://arxiv.org/abs/2202.02435

15. Kidger, P., Morrill, J., Foster, J., Lyons, T.: Neural Controlled Differential Equations for Irregular Time Series (2020). https://doi.org/10.48550/arXiv.2005.08926, http://arxiv.org/abs/2005.08926, arXiv:2005.08926 [cs]

16. Klimenko, I., Golovkina, A., Ruzhnikov, V.: Polynomial neural layers for numerical modeling of dynamical processes. In: Gervasi, O., Murgante, B., Rocha, A.M.A.C., Garau, C., Scorza, F., Karaca, Y., Torre, C.M. (eds.) Computational Science and Its Applications – ICCSA 2023 Workshops, vol. 14109, pp. 261–273. Springer Nature Switzerland, Cham (2023https://doi.org/10.1007/978-3-031-37120-2_17, https://link.springer.com/10.1007/978-3-031-37120-2_17, series Title: Lecture Notes in Computer Science

17. Lechner, M., Hasani, R.: Learning Long-Term Dependencies in Irregularly-Sampled Time Series (2020). https://doi.org/10.48550/arXiv.2006.04418, http://arxiv.org/abs/2006.04418, arXiv:2006.04418 [cs]

18. Margasov, A.: Neural ordinary differential equations and their probabilistic extension. In: Proceedings of the Komi Science Centre of the Ural Division of the Russian Academy of Sciences, vol. 6, pp. 14–19 (2021). https://doi.org/10.19110/1994-5655-2021-6-14-19, https://www.elibrary.ru/item.asp?id=47501514

19. Pal, A., Ma, Y., Shah, V., Rackauckas, C.: Opening the Blackbox: Accelerating Neural Differential Equations by Regularizing Internal Solver Heuristics (2022). https://doi.org/10.48550/arXiv.2105.03918, http://arxiv.org/abs/2105.03918, arXiv:2105.03918 [cs]

20. Poli, M., Massaroli, S., Yamashita, A., Asama, H., Park, J.: Hypersolvers: Toward Fast Continuous-Depth Models (2020). https://doi.org/10.48550/arXiv.2007.09601, http://arxiv.org/abs/2007.09601

21. Pontryagin, L.: Mathematical Theory of Optimal Processes. Routledge, 1 edn. (2018). https://doi.org/10.1201/9780203749319, https://www.taylorfrancis.com/books/9780203749319

22. Zhu, A., Jin, P., Zhu, B., Tang, Y.: On Numerical Integration in Neural Ordinary Differential Equations (2022). https://doi.org/10.48550/arXiv.2206.07335, http://arxiv.org/abs/2206.07335, arXiv:2206.07335 [cs]

Optimization of Fresco Assembly
for Accuracy

Nadezhda Shchegoleva[1]($\boxtimes$)(ID), Maria Gladkaya[1](ID), and Gennady Dik[2](ID)

[1] St. Petersburg University, St. Petersburg, Russia
n.shchegoleva@spbu.ru, st102678@student.spbu.ru
[2] St. Petersburg LLC "System Technologies", St. Petersburg, Russia
g.dick@systechnologies.ru

Abstract. This study introduces a novel approach to the puzzle assembly problem, leveraging textural features and geometric constraints. The texture in regions extending beyond the boundaries of puzzle pieces is estimated using inpainting and texture synthesis techniques. Feature descriptors are extracted from both the original and the synthesized images. An affinity metric is defined to quantify the correspondence between puzzle pieces, and the assembly process is formulated as an optimization problem aimed at maximizing the overall affinity score. To accelerate the alignment procedure, an image registration technique based on the Fast Fourier Transform (FFT) is employed. Experiments were conducted using different image features to study the impact of their use on assembly quality. Experimental results are presented on real and artificial data sets.

Keywords: Archeological reconstruction · Puzzle solving · Partial matching

1 Introduction

In the modern world, more and more importance is attached to the preservation of cultural heritage. Archaeological artifacts are unique materials that can tell us about the culture and lifestyle of our ancestors. Their study allows us to understand the features of the technologies used, crafts, religious beliefs and the daily life of people who lived before us.

A significant part of archaeological artifacts comes to the disposal of researchers in a damaged state, which is due to erosion processes, mechanical defects, loss of individual fragments and other destructive factors. The process of reconstruction of such objects is a complex scientific and technical task that requires the development of effective algorithms for automated restoration. The development and improvement of such methods is an urgent problem of great importance for the preservation of the cultural heritage of mankind.

It is worth noting that restoring broken artifacts manually is usually a very time-consuming task that requires a lot of time. The use of algorithms that can automatically "assemble" pieces of artifacts together can significantly speed up research and allow archaeologists to focus on other more important aspects.

O. Gervasi et al. (Eds.): ICCSA 2025 Workshops, LNCS 15894, pp. 294–308, 2026.
https://doi.org/10.1007/978-3-031-97648-3_20

One of the key problems in the reconstruction of frescoes is the destruction of the edges of the fragments due to erosion and mechanical damage, which leads to their unevenness and deformation. As a result, critical data for the task of reconstruction can be lost under the influence of time, natural factors or acts of vandalism that cause irreparable damage to the historical and cultural heritage.

As noted earlier, the destroyed frescoes are characterized not only by the geometric parameters of the fragments, but also by visual characteristics such as texture, color, continuity and shape of lines. In this regard, the development of effective reconstruction algorithms requires an integrated approach that takes into account not only geometric correspondences and coincidences of images in different fragments, but also their spatial location relative to each other.

All of the above makes the task of developing algorithms that restore archaeological artifacts from several fragments extremely relevant and important for modern society.

2   Algorithms for Automatic Reconstruction of Images from Their Fragments

Over the past few years, a large number of different algorithms have been proposed that use textural and geometric features to automatically reconstruct images from their fragments.

The simplest case of reconstruction of images divided into uniform square fragments is considered by authors in the work [3]. The authors proposed a system capable of simultaneous reconstruction of several objects whose fragments are chaotically mixed.

The absence of some fragments is also not a critical factor for the algorithm, since the proposed method is based on identifying and sequentially combining the most compatible pairs of fragments. In the course of the algorithm, new elements are iteratively attached to the formed pairs based on an assessment of the degree of their compliance. This evaluation takes into account changes in pixel brightness along the boundary of the tiles being joined, as well as derivative information along the adjacent tiles boundaries. The developed algorithm demonstrated a high accuracy of recovery, reaching 95.3%.

Authors of article [8] considered a solution to a problem where the fragments are connected in the form of a "brick wall", which is essentially a set of rectangular parts that can have different sizes and can be placed next to each other with an arbitrary displacement. In their work, they showed that the solution can be reduced to finding the correct displacement between two adjacent parts. The method is based on the use of a number of metrics to assess the difference and compatibility of correlations between all sides of the fragments. The difference score is calculated based on the L_2 norm and color channels of the images. The compatibility score is a key metric when deciding whether to attach a pair of fragments. The compatibility score is calculated by estimating the difference between the ith fragment and the jth fragment and estimating the difference between the ith fragment and the kth fragment, where i is the number of the fragment for which the best match is calculated, j is the number of the fragment that is considered at the current iteration of the algorithm, and k is the number of the fragment with which the ith fragment had the best correlation in previous iterations. The accuracy of the algorithm was 99.8%.

In 2019, group of researchers [5] proposed a method for reconstructing objects consisting of rectangular fragments of arbitrary sizes, provided that the orientation of all parts is known, but their position remains uncertain. To solve this problem, an algorithm was developed based on the comparison of the angles of fragments using the MatchLift framework. MatchLift provides a convex optimization method for finding cyclically consistent matches from a set of noisy inputs. The accuracy of the algorithm was 87%. The system developed in 2021 [4] solves the problem where the fragments are convex polygons obtained by the intersection of an arbitrary number of lines. The solution is a greedy algorithm, simple but reliable. The algorithm starts the search with a randomly selected edge of the fragment and looks for a match with the edge of some other free fragment based on the Euclidean transformation of this fragment. The accuracy of the algorithm is 100%, but the computational complexity is $O(M^4)$, where M is the number of fragments.

In their 2018 study [6], research group proposed an algorithm for solving a problem in which fragments have erased boundaries and do not have a specific shape, and the range of permissible transformations between parts is continuous, that is, the number of ways to place fragments relative to each other is infinite. The algorithm proposed by the authors involves restoring the image at the edges of the fragments and arranging the fragments relative to each other in such a way so that the extrapolated slice edges intersect, but the original slice regions do not. The best placement is found through an iterative process. The area around one fragment that defines the set of possible placements for the second fragment is determined by the Minkovsky sum. Textural, statistical, and the length of the joined sides are used to assess the similarity between the tiles. The accuracy of the algorithm is 100% if the number of fragments $M < 10$, for $M \in [11; 20]$—92.6%, for $M \in [21; 30]$—98.5%.

In 2016, two authors [7] published a paper in which the problem of searching for neighboring fragments is solved using a genetic algorithm. They proposed their own algorithm that creates sets of combined fragments (partial reconstruction pool). The pool of partial reconstructions grows as a result of recombination and selection over generations. Which is resistant to noise and emissions, and a new genetic algorithm selection procedure has been proposed that balances fitness and diversity in the population.

A group of researchers proposed to solve the problem of assembling fragments of Turanian wall paintings on the basis of calculating the normals of 2D scans [9]. To determine the most likely connection of fragments into a single painting, the points of the surface obtained by transforming the fragments into a single surface are used. The same thickness.

The above list of studies allows us to conclude that depending on the features of the fragments (identical square, arbitrary fragments in the shape of a polygon, the presence of damage at the edges of the fragments), as well as on the presence or absence of information about the orientation of the fragments, researchers use different approaches to solve this problem.

The most promising methods use algorithms based on heuristic approaches (greedy algorithms, minimal spanning tree), optimization methods (MatchLift, convex optimization), probabilistic models (genetic algorithms), and machine learning methods. Many modern works demonstrate high accuracy when assembling images from fragments, but the complexity of the algorithms can vary significantly. Algorithms that allow processing fragments that have a shape that is closest to real fragments of archaeological artifacts are usually based on the use of geometric characteristics.

It is worth noting that the neglect of some authors to use the color and texture of neighboring fragments is an ineffective tactic, since graphic information contains many features that can be useful in solving the reconstruction of archaeological artifacts. The graphic information contained in the images of fragments is very diverse and can include many features and components, and depending on the field of study, the informative value of certain features varies. In archaeology, the most informative features of images include the direction of marble veins, the pattern of carving on the surface, painting on the external and internal surface of the object, recesses and horizontal circles formed as a result of smoothing clay with fingers when rotating the pot on the wheel during the manufacturing process.

In archaeology, erosion and damage from impacts lead to the disappearance or destruction of fragments, changes in their boundaries. This makes it necessary to use all available information (including image features) to solve the problem of reconstructing frescoes, since geometric approaches based on the exact coincidence of the edges of fragments are not applicable for assembly if the boundaries of the fragments have not been preserved for a number of reasons.

3 Methods Used for Reassembly of Broken Frescoes

This section describes the methods used to restore broken frescoes. The recovery process consists of three main parts:

- extrapolation of graphic information from the edges of the fragments to the area around the fragment; The main task of this part of the software package is to predict graphic information on the erased edges of fragments. The implementation of this part is represented as an algorithm that determines the color value of pixels in an area outside the boundaries of the tiles with a confidence measure.
- finding a measure of affinity to determine the compatibility of fragments; The characteristics obtained from the predicted texture outside the fragment correlate with the graphical characteristics of the original region of possible neighboring fragments. To effectively compare the textures of fragments, a similarity measure has been introduced, which uses edge continuity, texture

patterns, and color similarity, and the task of assembling is set as its optimization.
- fragment placement using Fast Fourier Transform.

The proposed approach to automated mural restoration is based on a fast and reliable method that finds the best fragment placement that maximizes the overlap and continuity of the fragment textures while respecting geometric constraints (the original areas of the fragments cannot overlap).

After preprocessing the data, the first step is to predict the pixel values in the band around the fragment boundary; This step applies to all fragments separately. The prediction algorithm automatically fills in the extrapolation area using the information from the central part of the fragment. The basic idea behind extrapolating the image/texture of the original region of the fragment outward is that the correlation between the characteristics of the extrapolated region and its true adjacent region is significantly higher than between alternative pairs of fragments.

In extrapolation, the confidence of the extrapolated region is entered as a parameter. This parameter reflects the confidence level for each predicted pixel and is used by subsequent processes. The validity depends on the texture structure, such as edge continuity, texture roughness, and distance to the original fragment boundary.

The feature values are then calculated, both in the original fragment and in the extrapolated region. The proposed approach does not limit the number of features and does not limit the type of features of the image that can be used in the restoration of a fresco. Any textural feature that is thought to improve the success of an assembly can be incorporated into the process. The combination of feature values and image confidence is used to create a measure of the similarity of the corresponding fragments.

Finding the best placement of fragments during assembly is done using the Fast Fourier Transform. Initially, each fragment has a random position in space. FFT is used to iteratively find the fragment placements relative to each other that maximize the correlation between the fragments. To improve the assembly, the algorithm must be able to determine whether a particular arrangement of parts improves the assembly or not; This is done through a common measure of affinity, defined as the sum of the similarity measures of all points in space. During the assembly process, the similarity measure is optimized. In this way, the best placement of the fragments is found.

3.1 Extrapolation of Graphic Information of Fragments

The first step in the assembly process is to extrapolate each fragment to the area around its boundary by predicting graphical information [2]. Image extrapolation refers to the process of filling the area around a fragment in the form of a strip n pixels wide. The task is to fill the strip with a texture sample from the original region of the slice.

3.2 Cost Function to Determine Build Quality

When comparing or calculating the similarity of possible two adjacent fragments, a pixel-by-pixel comparison does not make sense. Therefore, a measure to determine the quality of the side is proposed, described below. Let us call it the function of cost F_{cost}. [1]

The total cost is the sum of similarity conditions and geometric constraints for all points on a predefined board or space. The only parameter of this indicator, which reflects the quality of the assembly of the parts based on textural features and geometric shape, is the transformation of T_i parts.

The F_{cost} value becomes negative if there is a good match between the images in the tiles. The correspondence between the parts increases, while the cost function is optimized.

3.3 Correlation and Fragment Placement with Fast Fourier Transform

The problem of assembling a broken fresco can be formulated as the optimization of the above cost function, the optimization task requires too much computational cost. Note that minimizing the distance function, D, is equivalent to maximizing the correlation between the fragments. [1]

Thus, the algorithm for assembling frescoes looks like this:

Algorithm 1. Fresco Assembly Algorithm

1: Extrapolate all fragments.
2: Restore the images in the extrapolated regions.
3: Place all fragments on a sufficiently large board B.
4: **while** the puzzle is not unambiguously assembled **do**
5:    Find the best transformation for a randomly selected fragment t using FFT and move it accordingly.
6: **end while**

The main disadvantage of this algorithm is that there can be multiple solutions to the problem. These multiple decisions depend on the initial placement of the fragments on the (B) and the random selection of the tth fragment. In such situations, a developed measure of similarity is used. For the possible placement specified by the proposed methodology, F_{cost} is calculated. If the algorithm achieves a new solution that has a lower cost than the previous one, then the new solution becomes the best way to place the mural fragments relative to each other. Iterations continue until the last possible placement is the lowest cost.

4 Extract Features from Images

One of the most informative types of data that can be extracted from fragments is graphical and visual data. In this regard, the development of computer systems to simplify the work of archaeologists using methods of extracting textural and structural features from an image and applying these features in algorithms for assembling archaeological artifacts is becoming widespread.

This approach allows you to more fully and accurately present information about the content of the image. Features allow you to highlight the most significant parts of the image to solve the problem of assembling murals, ignoring less important or noisy data. This makes the algorithms more efficient.

4.1 Histogram of Oriented Gradients

Histogram of Oriented Gradients (HOG) is a feature extraction technique widely used in computer vision tasks such as object recognition and human detection. HOG features are extracted from images to represent them as vectors that contain information about gradients and orientations. The calculated HOG features of the two images can be compared using various methods, such as cosine or Euclidean distance.

You can determine whether one image is relative to another based on the maximum correlation or the bias score.

4.2 Local Binary Patterns

Local binary patterns are a descriptor with low computational complexity proposed by T. Oyala in 1996 to extract texture features [11]. Due to its simplicity and resistance to changes in brightness and small image rotations, this method is a common and effective way to solve computer vision problems, in particular, face recognition.

4.3 Halftone Adjacency Matrix

A grayscale contiguity matrix (sometimes Gray Level Co-Occurence Matrix (GLCM) is a matrix that shows the distribution of gray levels between adjacent pixels in an image. GLCM describes the distribution of pairs of pixels based on their brightness or intensity. For each pair of pixel values, the number of times they occur in a particular relative position in the image is calculated.

Such matrices represent the texture properties of an image, but are sensitive to its scaling and rotation. They are not convenient for direct use in image analysis due to their large size; therefore, they are often only used to calculate various metrics for a more compact representation of textures. In this case, 14 characteristics proposed by R. Haralik in 1973 [10] and used for the task of texture classification are extracted for each image.

4.4 Gabor Filter

A Gabor filter is a linear filter used in computer vision and image processing to analyze texture, highlight edges, and detect structural features of an image. It is based on the Gabor function, which is a harmonic wave (sinusoidal function) with a Gaussian shell.

5   Description of Experiments

5.1   Preparation of Input Data

To simulate the separation of frescoes, the algorithm for extrapolating the graphic information of fragments described in 1.1 is implemented in the work. The algorithm is fed an image of the source fragment and a mask that indicates the target area that the algorithm will fill (Fig. 1). An example of the result is shown in Fig. 2.

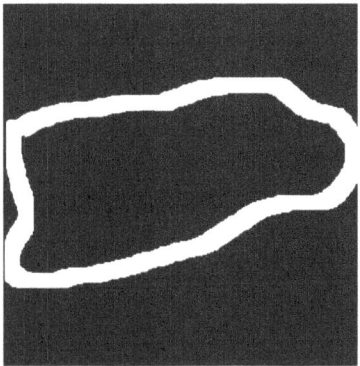

Fig. 1. Image of the source fragment and target area.

Fig. 2. Result of the algorithm for image extrapolation.

In addition, a script has been implemented that automates the division of the fresco into fragments. An image of the fresco and a mask are supplied to the input, which indicates where the cuts will be (Fig. 3). The output is several images - one for each fragment (Fig. 4).

Fig. 3. Image of the original image and the fragment mask.

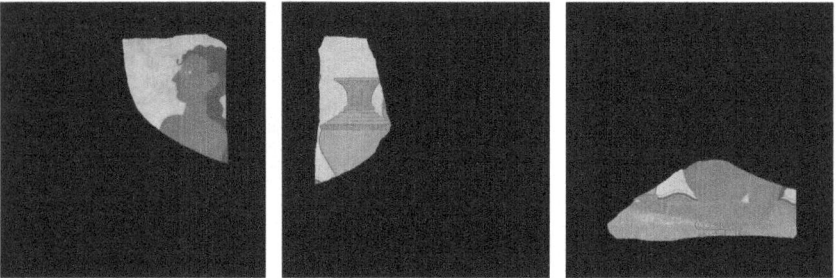

Fig. 4. Results of the algorithm.

5.2   Selection of Image Features

Experiments were carried out on two fragments to determine which features of the images give the highest quality of assembly. The results are presented in Table 1.

The algorithm is based on the textural features of the images, so the following features gave the maximum accuracy during assembly: Local Binary Pattern (LBP), Histogram of Oriented Gradients (HOG), Gabor filter. They were chosen as features of the images that will be used in further experiments.

An example of how the algorithm works with the selected features: the initial placement of fragments is shown in Fig. 5, and the result of the work using HOG, LBP and Gabour filter in the listed order is shown in Fig. 6.

Table 1. Results of the experiment.

Sign	Proposed offset, (x, y)
HOG	(304, 96)
LBP	(300, 100)
Gabour filter	(300, 100)
GLCM	(0, 0)

Fig. 5. Initial arrangement of fragments.

Fig. 6. Results of the algorithm for two fragments using HOG, LBP, Gabour filter, respectively.

5.3   Build Quality Metrics

Texture Affinity Index. The Textural Similarity Index (TSI) is a metric that is used to quantify the degree of similarity between the textures of two images. Unlike traditional metrics such as MSE (root mean square error) or SSIM (structural similarity index), TSI takes into account the textural characteristics of the image, such as gradient histograms or statistical properties of local textures. TSI measures the difference between the textures of two images using texture descriptors such as:

- GLCM (Gray-Level Co-occurrence Matrix)
- LBP (Local Binary Patterns)

These descriptors are described in Chap. 2.
In general, the TSI index can be defined as follows:

$$TSI(I_r, I_t) = 1 - D(T_r, T_t)$$

where:

- I_r—reference image,
- I_t—image under test,
- T_r, T_t—texture image descriptors,
- $D(T_r, T_t)$—function of distance between texture descriptors.

To compute TSI based on GLCM, you can use the cosine distance between feature vectors:

$$D(T_r, T_t) = \frac{\sum_i T_r^i T_t^i}{\sqrt{\sum_i (T_r^i)^2} \sqrt{\sum_i (T_t^i)^2}}$$

The LBP-based method uses the Hellinger distance between the histograms of the reference image and the image under test:

$$D_H(T_r, T_t) = \sqrt{1 - \sum_i \sqrt{T_r^i T_t^i}}$$

Interpretation of the results:
$TSI \approx 1$ means that the textures are almost identical.
$TSI \approx 0$ indicates a complete difference in textures.

Euclidean Matching Accuracy. Euclidean Matching Accuracy (MA) is a metric used to measure the accuracy of predicted coordinates (or points) relative to their true values

For the coordinate prediction problem, the accuracy of the match (MA) is usually defined as the Euclidean mean distance between the predicted and true coordinates.

Interpretation of the results:
$MA \approx 0 \rightarrow$ predicted points perfectly match the reference points (excellent accuracy).
$MA < 1$ pixel $\rightarrow$ a good match.
$MA > 1$ pixel $\rightarrow$ degradation of the prediction quality.
The lower the MA, the higher the accuracy of the prediction.

5.4   Results of Experiments

Let's consider the first experiment. 6 fragments were served at the entrance (Fig. 7).

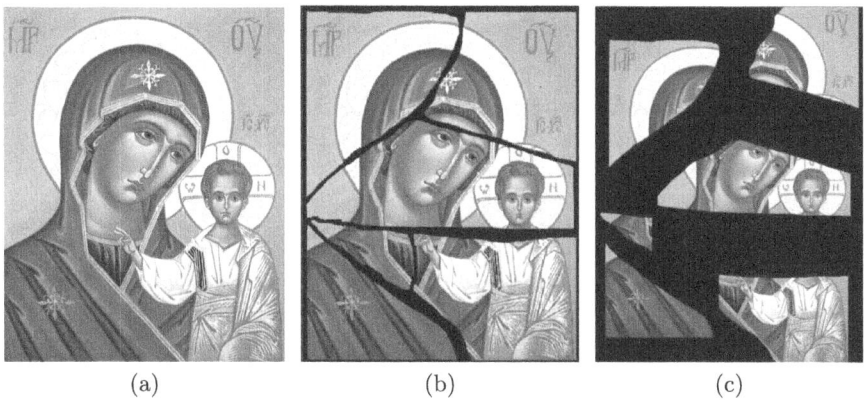

(a)   (b)   (c)

Fig. 7. (a) Original image, (b) Sections imitating fragments of a broken fresco (c) Image prepared for the input of the algorithm.

The result of the program using HOG (a), LBP(b) and Gabour filter(c) in the listed order in Fig. 8.

Fig. 8. The result of the work when using various features.

The effectiveness of the assembly using various features of the image can be evaluated in Table 2:

Table 2. Metrics of the quality of the algorithm

Metrics	HOG	LBP	Gabour filter
Euclidean precision (MA)	0.9px	1.5px	1.2px
TSI Ratio (GLCM)	0.945	0.894	0.928
TSI Ratio (LBP)	0.9762	0.9756	0.9761

At the next stage, an image with a lost fragment was fed to the input of the algorithm (Fig. 9). Such features of the input data are less informative, since graphical information is the most important aspect for the most accurate assembly, which, in turn, complicates the task for the algorithm.

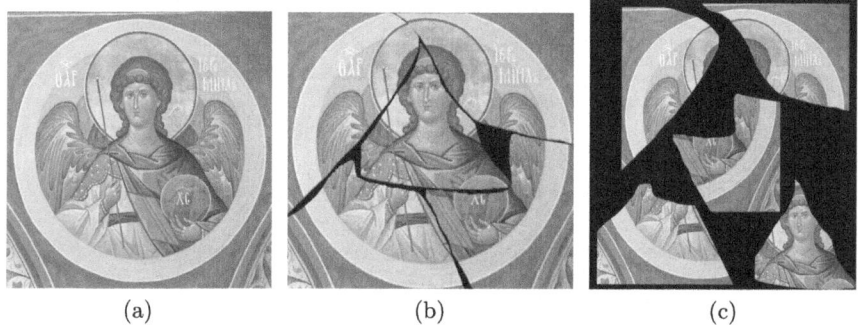

(a)   (b)   (c)

Fig. 9. (a) Original image, (b) Sections imitating fragments of a broken fresco (c) Image prepared for the input of the algorithm.

The result of the program using HOG (a), LBP(b) and Gabour filter(c) in the listed order in Fig. 10.

The effectiveness of the assembly using various features of the image can be evaluated in Table 3:

Table 3. Metrics of the quality of the algorithm

Metrics	HOG	LBP	Gabour filter
Euclidean precision (MA)	1.9px	3.1px	2.7px
TSI Ratio (GLCM)	0.923	0.885	0.91
TSI Ratio (LBP)	0.9786	0.9682	0.9787

Fig. 10. The result of the work when using various features.

6   Conclusion

Summing up the work done, it can be noted that an algorithm has been developed that automatically restores the frescoes. The proposed approach allows you to find the best placement of fragments, which maximizes the coincidence and continuity of the fragment textures while respecting the geometric constraints that consist in ensuring that the fragments do not intersect with each other.

References

1. Ercil, A.: Optimization for automated assembly of puzzles. In: Proceedings of of EUROPT (2008). https://doi.org/10.1007/s11750-010-0156-6
2. Criminisi, A., Perez, P., Toyama, K.: Object removal by exemplar-based inpainting. In: CVPR, pp. 721–728 (2003)
3. Son, K., Moreno, D., Hays, J., Cooper, D.B.: Solving small-piece jigsaw puzzles by growing consensus. In: Proceedings of IEEE Conference on Computer Vision and Pattern Recognition (CVPR) (2016)
4. Kreis, B., Dengler, N., de Heuvel, J., Menon, R., Perur, H., Bennewitz, M.: Compact multi-object placement using adjacency-aware reinforcement learning. In: 2024 IEEE-RAS 23rd International Conference on Humanoid Robots (Humanoids), pp. 698–705 (2024)
5. Wang, T., et al.: Robust and flexible puzzle solving with corner-based cycle consistent correspondences. In: Proceedings of EG UK Computer Graphics and Visual Computing (2019)
6. Derech, N., Tal, A., Shimshoni, I.: Solving archaeological puzzles. Pattern Recogn. **119**, 108065 (2021). https://doi.org/10.1016/j.patcog.2021.108065
7. Sizikova, E., Funkhouser, T.: Wall painting reconstruction using a genetic algorithm. In: Proceedings of EUROGRAPHICS Workshop on Graphics and Cultural Heritage (2016)
8. Gur, S., Ben-Shahar, O.: From square pieces to brick walls: the next challenge in solving jigsaw puzzles. In Proceedings of IEEE International Conference on Computer Vision (ICCV) (2017)
9. Brown, B.J., et al.: A system for high-volume acquisition and matching of fresco fragments: reassembling Theran wall paintings. In: ACM Transactions on Graphics (Proc. SIGGRAPH), vol. 27, no. 3 (2008)

10. Haralick R.M., Shanmugam K., Dinstein I.: Textural features for image classification. In: Proc. IEEE Trans. Syst. Man Cybern. **SMC-3**(6), 610–621 (1973)
11. Ojala, T., Pietikainen, M., Harwood, D.: A comparative study of texture measures with classification based on featured distributions. Pattern Recogn. **26**(1), 51–59 (1996). https://www.sciencedirect.com/science/article/abs/pii/0031320395000674. Accessed 20 May 2022

Intelligent Browser Window System for Visualizing Events Detected from Video in Distributed Fog Computing Environment

Alexey Subbotin[1]([✉]) [iD], Nataly Zhukova[2] [iD], and Elena Stankova[3] [iD]

[1] Saint-Petersburg State Electrotechnical University, Professor Popov Street 5, 197376 St. Petersburg, Russia
alesu1543@gmail.com
[2] St. Petersburg Federal Research Center of the Russian Academy of Sciences, 14Th Line V.O. 39, 199178 St. Petersburg, Russia
[3] St. Petersburg State University, 7-9, Universitetskaya nab., 199034 St. Petersburg, Russia

Abstract. The article discusses a distributed container-based fog computing that powers the window system. Distributed fog computing can significantly increase the speed of window system rendering. The article proposes an intelligent window system for a browser for visualization events detected in a fog computing environment. An overview of visualization tools and settings for video servers is presented. Disadvantages of existing solutions are identified. A new system for visualizing events and editing settings in a browser for a video server in fog is created. The novelty lies in the fact that windows with information in the browser are formed by a neural network based on the user's preferences defined using personal information that is collected with user's consent. The window system in the browser is mobile, high-speed and universal and supports the possibility of configuration. The proposed system was tested in subway subject domain. Its usage made it possible to increase the reaction rate of personnel in the subway by 20.3%. The created window system for the browser can be applied in different areas: airports, shopping centers, hospital buildings, cruise liners and other areas of limited space to improve the consistency of services and the speed of staff interaction.

Keywords: Fog computing · Distributed computing · Window system creation · Event visualization · Intelligent subway video surveillance system · Intelligent assistant · Event and pattern recognition

1 Introduction

Today it is important to create a window system in the browser, as the standard window systems have a long history and are overloaded with a huge number of service functions. Popular window systems are not modern and do not support the intelligent video surveillance system at the core, in particular, event visualization and neural networks. Support for a video server in a fog computing environment should be a priority, in the core of the window system in the browser.

© The Author(s), under exclusive license to Springer Nature Switzerland AG 2026
O. Gervasi et al. (Eds.): ICCSA 2025 Workshops, LNCS 15894, pp. 309–324, 2026.
https://doi.org/10.1007/978-3-031-97648-3_21

1.1   History of Window Systems

The first window system appeared in the Multics-MIT operating system in 1964 for the monitor, before that, in 1955, the GM-NAA operating system was created for the printer for the GE 645 computer in 1955. The window system for the monitor running Multics resembled a space divided into parts from four green windows. There was a primitive status line at the top of the screen. The size of its source code in assembly language is only 120 thousand lines and is available for study (https://www.multicians.org/). The second popular UNIX system appeared in 1970, it is distinguished by minimalism and does not have even a primitive window system in the kernel, but only a command line due to the limitations of PDP-11 and VAX computers. The size of the UNIX kernel is only about 10 thousand lines and is available for study (https://github.com/dspinellis/unix-history-repo). The minimalistic UNIX kernel is the basis for popular operating systems: Linux, BSD, Solaris, QNX, MacOS and Windows, starting with version XP SP3, and version 11 supports the Linux kernel through the WSL command with display of Linux applications on a single Windows desktop. The first version of Linux 0.01 (https://github.com/zavg/linux-0.01) appeared in 1991 based on MINIX (https://www.minix3.org/), each system contains about 10 thousand lines of code, which is comparable to the size of the program code of a small website. The author of the MINIX operating system describes in detail the functions of the kernel and working with memory, that any programmer in the C language can create an operating system in six months (the first version of Linux based on MINIX was created in six months) [1]. The main difficulty in creating an operating system is device support (creating drivers). UNIX utilities for working with memory, directory structure, file system are very simple and can be easily recreated in the C language. The X-Window graphical subsystem is designed in such a way that it can work with drivers and kernel functions of any UNIX-compatible operating system (Linux, BSD, etc.). Like Windows 3.11 and Windows 95, the X.org window system based on the X11 protocol is an application to the UNIX-class operating system, just like Windows 95 and DOS 6.22. The X-Window window system provides only basic functions; to interact with programs, it needs to install a desktop environment (for example, GNOME or KDE based on widgets: GTK + or QT) [6–8].

1.2   Distributed Computing

Fog and distributed computing can significantly increase the speed of an application, in particular, it can increase the speed of information processing (video images, cryptocurrency mining, data processing for intelligent video surveillance systems, etc.). Visualization of events in a window system in a browser can also work faster using distributed computing. Computations can be executed both on containers and on virtual machines. In distributed computing the load is distributed dynamically depending on the load of each container or virtual machine. The manager of such computing is considered to be an orchestrator program. A popular program for distributed computing is Docker (https://www.docker.com/), which is a container manager similar to virtual machines (PC), but it interacts with the operating system environment. It is possible to transfer files and directories, devices and much more from the host system directly at the start of the program. The container can be in the cloud, a local computer or a fog server.

The manager can work only with one type of container. For example, Docker work only with DockerImage and sends containers to DockerHub using the Dockerfile utility. An example of creating a container: "docker container create -a subcontwin".

Many software manufacturers abandon containers in favor of virtual machines due to greater isolation and code security. The speed of a virtual machine is sometimes no different from containers, and sometimes it surpasses when starting a virtual machine from sleep mode, which is not supported by container technologies. A window system in a browser can greatly speed up work using distributed computing technologies due to working on a series of virtual machines managed by an orchestrator. Popular virtual machines are VirtualBox (https://www.virtualbox.org/), VMware (https://www.vmware.com/) and Parallels Desktop (https://www.parallels.com/), which can run under popular operating systems: MacOS Sequoia, Windows 11, Linux Debian 12.

1.3 Modern Browser Interfaces

The majority of existing window systems are programs loaded from the command line or they are automatically loaded on top of the operating system. However, starting with Windows 98, Microsoft developers made deep integration of Explorer with Windows and Explorer became a windowing system [9]. After loading drivers and checking devices, Internet starts Explorer 5 (or MSIE 6.0), which opens a site with a window system. Up to the latest version of Windows 11, a developer can install an application that will patch the Windows kernel, which will allow to minimize the desktop to the taskbar, maximize it to a window on a blue background, and maximize it to full screen, like full-screen mode on the Internet Explorer using F11 button. Theoretically, instead of Internet Explorer one can download Mozilla Firefox, Google Chrome or any other browser with a website that simulates a window system. The Explore window system website can be loaded from the local disk "C:\Windows\System32" (the default, set by Microsoft developers Windows) or a webserver, such as "http://localhost/windows". It is not difficult to create a site that imitates the window system in a browser, but according to Bill Gates, full duplication of the Windows window interface is prohibited by Microsoft copyright. There are several window systems in the Internet that work instead of the Explore task, which is a running copy of Internet Explorer with a window system. After the Explore task is destroyed, the desktop and all applications completely disappear from the screen. It is possible to restart a website with the Windows window system (taskbar, shortcuts, etc.) by running the "explorer" command in the command line, after which the zero task Internet will start Explorer with desktop and all applications [10–12].

The window system in the browser does not necessarily have to be created using ready-made libraries: Bootstrap, Vue.js, React, jQuery and many others, which are common for creating interfaces: buttons, fields, forms, windows and other graphic elements. It is possible to create a window system website on the modern Chromium 44.x engine based on JavaScript, which forms a dynamic DOM on HTML5 and CSS3.2 with dynamic loading through the element " < iframe > … < /iframe >", available in new browsers [13–15].

1.4   Video Analytics and Visualization

Hitachi VSP 5500 video servers have pre-installed software from Microsoft: Windows 7 operating system and a program Windows Media Player (WMP) for viewing video files on the server. The video server has the following characteristics: performance of 21 million IOPS (operations per second) and a throughput of 149 GB/s. The video server is very powerful compared to the client computer.

A very popular video server is the Cisco UCS C480 ML M5 Rack Server, which is also used as a server for machine learning and neural networks. The server developers have implemented the Cisco Unified Computing System (UCS) program, which provides virtual environments at the core level of the Intel Xeon Scalable processor with 28 cores and a motherboard for two such processors. The UCS version server supports up to eight NVIDIA SXM2 V100 32G video cards, which can be combined via NVLink. The C480 series server supports up to 7.5 TB of DDR4 2933 MHz RAM and 24 DIMM slots for shared memory. The Cisco ML M5 modification server supports PCI Express (PCIe) 3.0 slots with 10 Gigabit Ethernet LAN-On-Motherboard (LOM) ports and expansion slots for connecting external devices: video cameras, sensors, etc. intelligent video surveillance system devices. The Cisco server has pre-installed programs for combining computing, virtualization, and statistics (UCS Manager, SingleConnect technology, Integrated Management Controller). The Management Software Development Kits (SDKs) and DevOps software package contains examples for working with neural networks and machine learning. The Cisco server comes with detailed documentation (https://developer.cisco.com/).

Another popular video server HPE DL384 Gen12 (https://hpe-servers.ru/) has a NVIDIA GH200 NVL2 Grace Hopper 144GB HBM3e video card, 960GB LPDDR5X RAM with a capacity of up to 1.2 TB and a throughput of up to 5 TB/s. The server is optimized for machine learning (ML), the creation of language models with intensive use of RAM, requiring a large amount of memory. The HPE server is optimized for building very detailed models and forecasting using ML. It has pre-installed Retrieval Augmented Generation (RAG) programs to improve performance. GPU management on the HPE ProLiant Compute DL384 Gen12 occurs through the HPE ProLiaProLiant Compute DL384 program and the HPE iLO profile. The HPE ProLiant server has expansion ports (EDSFF Gen5 x4 NVME, USB 3.1, iLO Service, Serial, VGA, OCP 3.0) for connecting various devices. The NVIDIA GH200 Grace Hopper graphics chip is also a central processor with artificial intelligence (AI) functions with NVIDIA OVX certification.

Existing systems have a number of limitations that appear when they are used for visualization of events that are the low speed of the application, lack of mobility, configurability and lack of universality (work only under Windows 7). The problem is proposed to be solved by creating an intelligent window system in the browser for visualization of events and video server settings in a fog computing environment.

2   Window Systems Overview

A popular program for viewing events from a video server is Milestone XProtect, which is a suite of video analytics programs. For example, the Smart Client 7.0 program provides a list of objects and assigned video cameras, each video camera can be opened in a conditional workspace divided into four parts. Perhaps this limitation was created by the developers, since high-resolution 4k video with more than four streams at the same time will greatly slow down the client computer. Video recording and saving of individual frames are available. The alarm manager is opened by password, it is possible to create an HTML site with button navigation and a link map based on data from Smart Client. Milestone program Federated Architecture can work with not one, but several video servers at once. XProtect Enterprise version is capable of recognizing audio events. XProtect Express version works with PTZ surveillance cameras. XProtect Go version can save frames in JPEG/PNG format. All versions of XProtect allow to create a map and HTML site with video fragments in the designer mode. Each video camera has three indicators: event, movement and work. It allows configure the quality of the transmitted video MPEG (I-frame) H.264 and JPEG with a frame rate per second (from 0.2 to 20). A detailed guide is available on the website (https://www.milestone-spb.ru/). Currently, the system is used in the State Unitary Enterprise "Petersburg Subway" (https://metro. spb.ru/) [17, 18].

There are a number of other popular programs for viewing events and configuring a video server. An example of such a system is Xeoma (https://felenasoft.com/), which does not require installation and works under all popular operating systems: iOS and Android, Mac OS X, Linux ARM and Windows. The Xeoma program recognizes images well: faces, emotions, license plates and can work in a hospital ward, recreates 3D-objects and allows to draw maps for video surveillance points. The Xeoma window system is very primitive and resembles Windows. NT, and the blue-green pop-up settings windows have no inner edges. The windows have only one icon for closing. The confirmation buttons are darkened with white text and rounded edges.

Another program Zoneminder (https://zoneminder.com/) can work from any browser and there is a compilation for Linux with open-source code with the ability to study and edit the code for the tasks of any company. Zoneminder can detect movement in video and provides sensitivity settings, sends messages to a smartphone and/or email. The system is oriented for home use, can recognize images. The window system resembles GNOME or KDE in style, depending on which version of Ubuntu it is installed. Pop-up windows resemble tables with editable fields and blue inscriptions. Settings are allowed in the same window with the video image. Work is possible through Mozilla Firefox.

iSpy program (https://www.ispyconnect.com/) works only on Android, iOS and Windows. iSpy can recognize barcodes, license plates and overlay text on a video stream. The program has an open-source code, and it can connect an unlimited number of video cameras and video files. There is support for motion sensors, support for network broadcasting on YouTube and support of notifications. The window system resembles Windows 7, and the main menu of the application resembles Windows XP and older versions of Windows. There are large buttons in the menu. The screen is divided into blue sectors with settings. Pop-up windows and viewing video cameras with settings are made in the standard Windows 7 style.

Sighthound Video program (https://www.sighthound.com/) works under all operating systems except Linux. It is possible to work only with one video source. Sighthound Video has motion sensors and distinguishes a person from an animal. The Sighthound video surveillance system is aimed for country houses and can be integrated into the smart home. The system works well with IP video cameras. The appearance of the windows is designed in the standard Macintosh style Sequoia 15.2, on the left side there is an area with certain fragments, and indicators are located above the video viewing, which occupies the main part of the screen. There is a chronometer under the video.

Another program AtHome Video Streamer (https://www.ichano.com/) can work with all popular operating systems. It works well with cloud services and can save video fragments on a schedule. AtHome can work with different types of devices: SmartTV, USB, IP, iOS, which is an undeniable advantage over other programs. The window system is very bright yellow, red with rounded buttons of the same color. At the top and left there is a light red menu with large gray buttons and bookmarks from video cameras (four per tab). At the bottom of the four videos there is a choice of viewing angles (three in total). The entire program window can only be minimized to the taskbar and closed, but it is not possible to open it on full screen.

EyeLine Program Video Surveillance (https://www.nchsoftware.com/) has the advantage of supporting more than 100 channels from different devices at the same time. The EyeLine program can send video to FTP and send SMS, has an archive manager and can send messages by e-mail. The window system has a Windows XP SP1 style with a large red "Stop" button on the video. On the left side of the video there is a directory with a mini view of five video cameras. At the top of the video is a menu for adding video cameras, settings and searching for saved fragments. There is a main menu of the application in the style of old versions of Windows (98/ME).

Netcam Studio program (https://www.netcamstudio.com/) can send notifications and can work with two video cameras. Netcam supports watermarks and consists of two components: the server part and the client part for Android, iOS and Windows 10. The program can work with analog video and combine recording with IP video cameras. There is support for audio signals and sound processing by neural networks. The window system is vaguely reminiscent of Windows NT with a design in gray tones. The menu at the top is made in the form of buttons with pictures and bookmarks (which are named as objects: home, work, office, workshop, warehouse, etc.). Each tab contains video cameras with a preview. At the bottom of the video there is statistical information. At the top of the window, it is possible to select the date and time of viewing, as well as update and preview the picture. At the top, there is also a menu for adding video cameras to tabs and searching in the library of the program that contains objects that should be identified. The settings can be defined on a separate tab. There is detailed information on the objects on each video camera. Pop-up windows are made in gray and instead of buttons there is a check mark and a cross to confirm or cancel. It is possible to configure the parameters of each video camera in the pop-up windows (manufacturer, model, resolution, IP-address, HTTP-port, login/password) and check the connection. The mobile application has two large buttons for recording and turning on the sound, and two switches for detecting motion and audio events. The main program for the PC has an event log. It is possible to work from a browser, but authorization is required (https://localhost:8100). There are indicators of server and client load, number of connections and amount of free space on the video server HDD. There is automatic synchronization with the cloud, remote control, connection indicator (at the bottom of the main window).

The considered systems have different capabilities. XProtect provides basic features in the Go version, but the features become much more with the acquisition of advanced versions of XProtect. XProtect is slow and requires installation, while Xeoma works without installation and runs very fast on weak computers. Without the program, they only work under Windows, but Zoneminder can also work under Linux. iSpy can work with mobile devices. Sighthound Video runs on Linux and Mac OS. At Home Video Streamer can work with devices. EyeLine runs on older versions of Windows. Netcam Studio works through a browser.

Comparison of the features of the considered systems is presented in Table 1. The systems are compared using the following parameters: p1 – operation of the system without installation; p2 – work on Linux; p3 – work with mobile devices; p4 – work on macOS; p5 – work with smart home devices; p6 – work with older versions of Windows; p7 – work in the browser; p8 – high speed of visualization; p9 – mobility; p10 – configurability; p11 – universality.

Table 1. Comparison of the considered features and limitations of the considered systems.

Name of the system	p1	p2	p3	p4	p5	p6	p7	p8	p9	p10	p11
XProtect	−	+	−	+	−	−	+	−	−	+	−
Xeoma	+	+	−	+	−	−	−	−	−	−	+
Zoneminder	−	+	−	−	−	−	−	−	−	+	+
iSpy	−	+	+	+	−	−	−	+	+	+	+
Sighthound Video	−	+	−	+	−	−	−	+	−	+	+
AtHome Video Streamer	−	−	−	−	+	−	−	+	+	+	−
EyeLine Video Surveillance	−	−	−	−	−	+	−	+	−	+	−
Netcam Studio	−	+	+	−	−	−	+	+	+	+	+

According to the results of analyzes of existing systems (Xprotect, Xeoma, Zoneminder, iSpy, Sighthound Video, AtHome Video Streamer, EyeLine Video Surveillance, Netcam Studio) there is no system that meets all the parameters.

3   Problem Definition

Reasons why window systems are created in the browser to visualize events and video server settings:

1) Faster loading and operation of a windowed web site on slow and technological computers (embedded systems) where the standard Explore task from Microsoft works slow.
2) Support for drivers of complex technological devices and monitors.
3) Custom applications based on widgets, function graphs, complex tables, tooltips, running lines and mini applications [3, 4, 16].

The user's preferences are taken from the activity of his profile. It is possible to use the user's interests by IP address (open HTML pages, like Google ads) and other service information to train the neural network [19–22]. The option to use personal information is commonly proposed when installing the program (in the license agreement). The received contextual information can be used to create windows of the intelligent video surveillance system.

The browser's window system should be characterized by high speed of work, mobility, configurability and universality. It should be possible to open the window system on the KENSHI H10 LTE 4 GB RAM tablet with a resolution of 1280x800 (and a 10.1" diagonal) under Android 13.x, and on the MacBook Air M1 8 GB RAM with the macOS Sequoia 15.2 operating system in the Safari 18.2 browser, and on the VivoBook Asus R522M 4 GB RAM under Windows 11. The window system must work equally well as a primary task and a secondary task, like a webpage in a browser. The application must issue events and allow make settings on the video server under all modern operating systems and devices with a wide display [23–25]. It must be configurable depending on the user's preferences.

It is impossible to use the standard UNIX or Linux environment, because the computers have hardware adaptations for macOS and the standard UNIX and Linux kernels do not support Apple chips (M1, M2, M3, M4). Apple chips have non-standard processor registers, a different LLVM linker (https://llvm.org/), which can only work with Apple hardware. In addition, UNIX and Linux are overloaded with redundant functions that are not needed for a specific task (for example, for event visualization). By excluding additional functions, it is possible to increase the speed of the application (window system). In addition, the window system in the browser is well portable to other operating systems: QNX 6 Neutrino and QNX Software Development Platform 8.0 (https://blackberry.qnx.com/en), Debian Linux 12.10 (https://www.debian.org/), Open Solaris 11.4 SRU72 (https://www.oracle.com/solaris/solaris11/) and other less popular systems.

The results of the analysis of analogs showed that they lack mobility, speed, versatility and configurability. This can be achieved only if the window system is used instead of the standard Explore task. It will allow to ensures high speed and also mobility and versatility since the browser can be used on all devices and operating systems. All three criteria directly affect the speed of personnel interaction when solving applied tasks.

4   Solution Method

The authors of the article propose creating a website that imitates a window system. The website contains a status bar, a drop-down menu, and a window factory created in the Windows XP SP 3 style with the ability to move a window when hovering over the title (function «Drage-and-Drop»). The window contains icons for closing (cross) and centering or positioning the window in the center of the screen vertically and horizontally (circle). Windows are configured depending on the user's preferences. The user receives information that is a priority for him/her (an object entered the door; a dog ran along the playground). Binary incompatibility (Fig. 1) can be solved by creating a window system in the browser. First, the kernel functions are loaded, then the drivers, the graphical environment functions, and then not the application is launched, but the browser, which connects instead of the application to the video server in the fog and visualizes the events and settings in the window system.

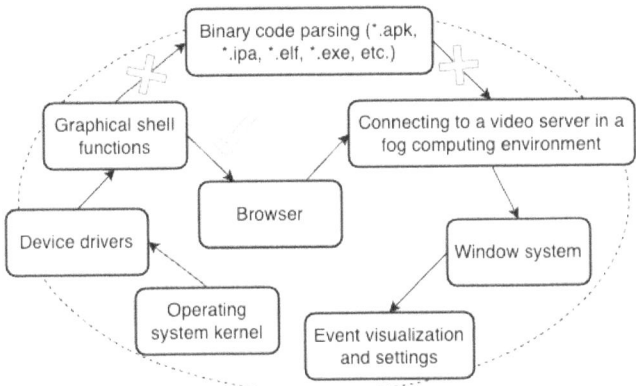

Fig. 1. Solution to the indicated problems in the browser.

Icons (Fig. 2) are located along the edges of the window title. The title and icons change color when hovered over, and when dragging the window, they change transparency to accurately determine the location on the screen. It is enough to use JS for development v.1.5 without «Node.js» on the client side with the formation of a tree structure DOM (Document Object Model) from basic elements in HTML/CSS. Dynamic queries to the database «MariaDB-v.10.4.28» are created through «iFrame», without AJAX technology and basic jQuery technology, because of which the website works much faster. The script «win.js» is built in such a way that the number of child windows is not limited. New windows are created at the «factory» in the file «index.html», where each DIV with the class «WinSettingsSpace» is a new window, regardless of whether it is written in the file «index.html» or created using JS-v.1.71 from the file «win.js». The CSS-v.2.0 properties of the DOM object are the same in both the "*.html" file and the "*.css" file and have event handling from the method of any object of the hierarchical structure. An example of an event handler when pressing the mouse button: «addEventListener ('click', function () {CreateWindow (3, 'Event statistics');});». JS technology is very easy to learn and is considered to have the next level in complexity after HTML/XML and HTML-tag properties with CSS styles.

Processing of dynamic requests (working with DBMS, uploading and processing files on the video server in fog) is done through the PHP language, since it is very fast in execution and easy to understand, with good and reliable documentation (https://www. php.net/docs.php). In the child frame of the "iFrame" type, the "dync.php" page opens, which is a PHP script with parameters. A typical example of such a script (Fig. 3) receives an array of data from one table "subEvents", but at the beginning creates a connection through the PDO object with parameters for connecting to the database "$pdoSet", switches to the "WinSubs" database. In case of an error in the "try… Catch" block, it issues an error message and terminates the work through the "die ();" method. Next, there is code for forming a query to the "subEvents" table. The final two-dimensional

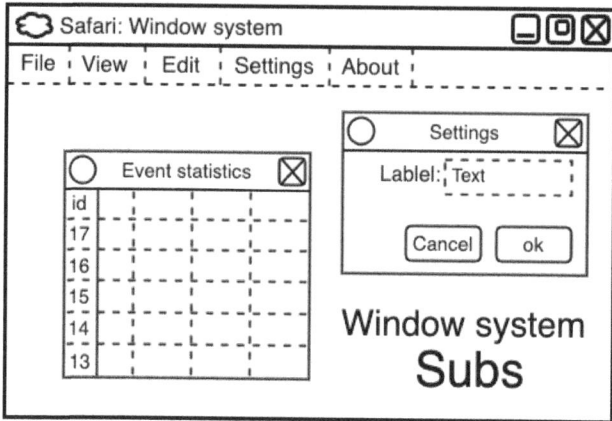

Fig. 2. A prototype of a developed window system named WinSubs-v.4.98a.

array "$resultMF[][]" of rows and columns contains only numeric indices, thanks to the "PDO::FETCH_NUM" modifier. Then the DOCTYPE header is formed in HTML5 format, after opening and closing the PHP code (" < ?php ... ? > "). Next, the table is formed in a loop iterating over a two-dimensional array. The table has an "id" tag with the value "iTableGet" and the content is passed from the child frame to the main page "index.html", where the first frame in the DOM document was assigned to the "iframe" variable via the global object "document" of the method "getElementsByTag-Name ('iframe')[0]" and was called via the modifier "iframe.src = './dync.php?event';". Instead of PHP, one can use another programming language, for example, SubScript [2].

5   Case Study

The authors of the study developed a website that runs entirely on JavaScript 1.7, implementing a window system in the browser. In the center (Fig. 4) of the website there are two windows. The window at the top shows the version of the website, and the second window at the bottom of the screen visualizes events. At the top of the screen there is a status bar, reminiscent of macOS or the main menu of the application (a form element in the Windows application designer). In the upper left corner additional information about the detected event is shown in a small sub-window. Sub-windows are created according to the factory principle, very quickly, almost instantly. Visualization of events is based on using fog distributed computing and containers or virtual machines. In this example, the Parallels Desktop for Mac 20.0.0 (https://www.parallels.com/products/desktop/) virtual machine type based on Qt Creator version 6.0.2 (https://www.qt.io/product/develo pment-tools) was used.

An important element of the proposed solution is the possibility to take into account the user's preferences, which are configured in additional windows that can be opened through the main menu of the application in the browser. It allows to set the color, size, position of windows and much more using a neural network or all these settings can be changed manually using buttons, checkboxes, drop-down lists, etc.

```php
<?php
if (isset($_GET['event']))
        try {
                $pdoSet = new PDO('mysql:dbname=test;host=localhost','root','');
                $pdoSet ->query('SET NAMES utf8;USE WinSubs;');
        } catch (PDOException $e) {
                print "Error!:".$e->getMessage ()."< br />";
                die();
        }
        $sql = "SELECT * FROM subEvents WHERE id>=498 ORDER BY id DESC";
        $stmt =$pdoSet ->query($sql);
        $resultMF = $stmt -> fetchAll (PDO::FETCH_NUM);
        if (Count($resultMF) == 0) {
                ?>
        <!DOCTYPE html><html><head></head><body>
<div id=' iTableGet '>none</div></body></html>
        <?php
        } else {
                $sHTML = '<table>';
                for ($i = 0; $i < Count($resultMF); ++$i) {
                        $sHTML.='<tr>';
                        for ($iCol = 0; $iCol < Count($resultMF [$i]);  ++$iCol)
                                $sHTML.= '<td>'.$resultMF [$i][$iCol].'</td>';
                        $sHTML.='</tr>';
                }
                $sHTML.='</table>';
                GetHTML($sHTML, 'good');
        }
}
?>
```

Fig. 3. PHP code for dynamic loading of information (downloading one table from the DBMS and transferring it to the main frame).

The developed window system was tested in the St. Petersburg Subway (https://metro.spb.ru/). The neural network for detecting events that occur in the subway, such as broken escalator steps, was trained using dataset of 34812 images and a control dataset of 873 images. The dataset contains the images of the following classes: broken steps, fire, flooding, etc. The architecture of the neural network based on NumPy 2.2.0 (https://numpy.org/) with 14 layers: subsampling, max-pooling, and convolution was used.

The features of the NumPy algorithm are: homogeneity of the data array elements, multidimensionality of NumPy arrays with an unlimited number of changes, fixed array dimension after its creation, efficiency in terms of simultaneous operations on the data array, a wide choice of convenient methods for working with array data. NumPy tools work very quickly and have a higher data processing speed in «C/C ++» than in Python. There are no problems with training using the NumPy algorithm in the process of machine

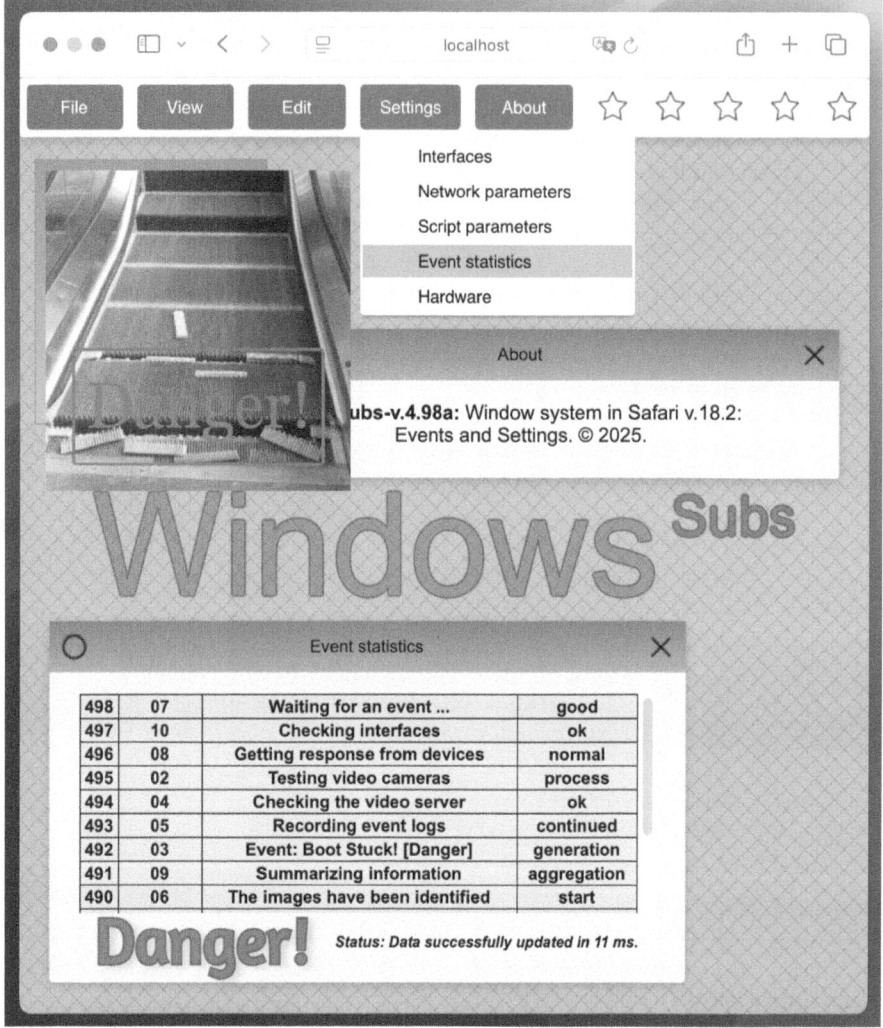

Fig. 4. Windowing system in Safari v.18.2 browser for settings and visualization of events.

learning, since NumPy is implemented very well. A dataset with images that were used to train the model can serve as a visual graphical material. To examine the images carefully, just download the project, run the application build and the datasets will be loaded into the project on NumPy 2.2 in the directory with the source codes. The following image processing libraries were used in the process of using the NumPy 2.2.0 script: Scikit-image 0.25.2 (https://scikit-image.org/), OpenCV 4.11.0 (https://opencv.org/), Mahotas 1.4.16 (https://mahotas.readthedocs.io/).

The neural network model was trained to identify patterns during 12 h on NVIDIA GeForce RTX 4090 (https://www.nvidia.com/en-eu/geforce/graphics-cards/40-series/rtx-4090/). WinSubs window system classified correctly more than 92% of images and showed high efficiency which was estimated based on 5 parameters (p1-p5) shown in Table 2: p1 – fire service; p2 – ambulance (urgent service); p3 – water supply and sanitation; p4 – subway police; p5 – train repair and track workers. The overall increase in the speed of reaction on detected events has increased by 20.3%.

Table 2. Comparison of window systems by response time of various services (p1-p5) in the subway upon occurrence of an event (in sec.).

Window system	p1	p2	p3	p4	p5	More than WinSubs (%)
Explore	137	251	893	192	1739	30.3
XProtect[a]	132	241	857	189	1548	**20.3**
Xeoma	148	259	942	193	1687	30.9
Zoneminder	151	273	1019	214	1819	41
iSpy	147	256	938	185	1635	28.2
Sighthound Video	161	284	982	201	1719	35.7
AtHome Video Streamer	157	278	1124	224	1842	47
EyeLine Video Surveillance	159	287	1207	231	1947	55.4
Netcam Studio	143	251	904	192	1629	26.5
WinSubs	116	219	691	147	1293	0

a) The default system in the subway (now).

The bar chart created based on the experimental data visually illustrates (Fig. 5) how faster WinSubs is (%) compared to other visualization and event monitoring systems. The slowest compared to WinSubs was EyeLine Video Surveillance (55.4%), and the real competition is XProtect (20.3%). Netcam Studio and iSpy programs are at approximately the same level (26–29%). Xeoma and Explore programs are also at approximately the same level (30–31%). After the EyeLine Video Surveillance program (55.4%), the second place for the slowest operation is taken by AtHome Video Streamer (47%), perhaps due to the adaptation of the program for home use.

To reproduce the experiment, it is necessary to install the WinSubs-v.4.98a window system (https://github.com/alex1543/wincat) instead of the desktop (disable the Explore Windows x64 desktop via the "Regedit.exe" utility in the directory "C:\Windows\System32", delete the startup parameter for the Explore task). Collect statistics on one object, where there are more than 159 Axis video cameras P13, P33 and P1365MKII (https://www.axis.com/). Technical specifications of the computer for collecting statistics: ASUS VivoBook R522M with 4 GB RAM, 128 GB ROM under Windows 11.

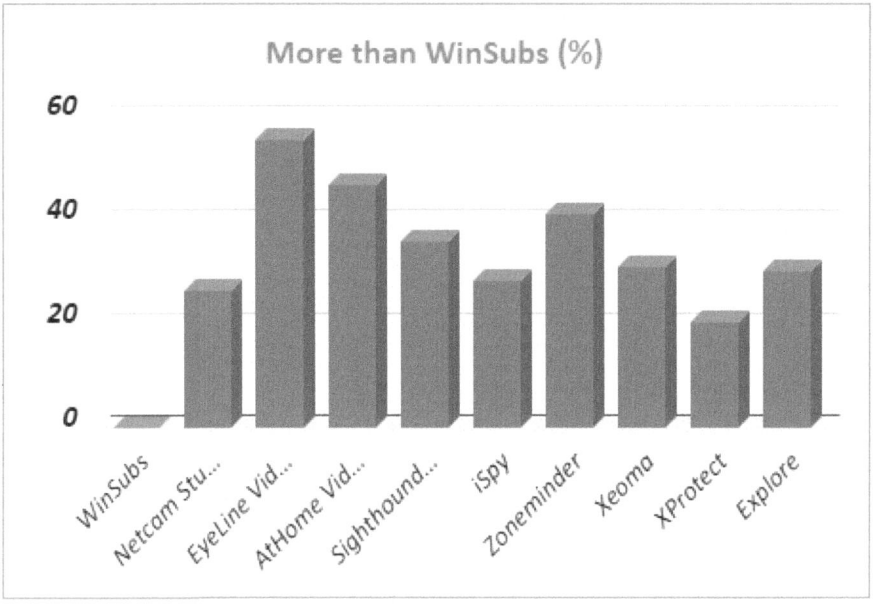

Fig. 5. Visual representation of how much faster WinSubs is (%) than others.

6   Conclusion

The authors of the article consider the creation of a window system in a browser instead of the standard Windows desktop. The key advantage of the proposed system is the high speed of window system rendering. Another distinctive feature of the new WinSubs window system is the versatility, since it can work on all devices and operating systems. In addition, the system is mobile and easily portable, so it can be launched by a video surveillance operator on a tablet. The program is easily configured.

Event visualization based on distributed fog computing has made it possible to significantly increase the speed of the window system in the browser and improve the performance of services.

The usage of the developed system in subway showed an increase in the efficiency (speed of performance) of personnel by 20.3%.

The scientific component of the study is in the method for solving a wide range of problems where it is necessary to determine events in systems with limited resources or non-standard hardware.

Load testing of the system was performed on a control dataset for two weeks with 47 Axis P3384-V IP-cameras (https://www.axis.com/) with positive results and the system did not show any operational failures.

In future it is planned to use a neural network with controlled elements (RNN-CE network), which will allow consider an extended list of parameters such as color, location on the screen, window size, frame event (a person entered the door) and many other for adaptive dynamic configuration of the window system according to the user's preferences. The choice fell on this neural network, since it supports additional training in dynamics and the neural network algorithm works well in recognizing images in motion [5]. Such neural network will be deployed on the video server in the next version of the program.

The proposed approach can be applied not only in the subway, but also in other areas of limited space: a cruise liner, a submarine, a school, a kindergarten, a shopping center, a wholesale warehouse, where it is necessary to conduct investigations and monitoring.

Acknowledgments. This work was supported by the state budget, project No. FFZF-2025–0019.

References

1. Tanenbaum, Andrew S., Woodhull, A.S.: Operating Systems: Design and Implementation. ISBN 9780131429383, January 2006
2. Subbotin, A., Delhibabu, R., Zhukova, N.: A script language creation for event visualization and data storage in an intelligent video surveillance system. Adv. Artif. Intell. Mach. Learn. **4**(4), 3161–3172 (2024)
3. Osipov, V., Zhukova, N., Subbotin, A., et al.: Intelligent escalator passenger safety management. Sci. Rep. **12**, 5506 (2022). https://doi.org/10.1038/s41598-022-09498-x
4. Tianxing, M., Vodyaho, A., Zhukova, N., Subbotin, A., et al.: Urban intelligent assistant on the example of the escalator passenger safety management at the subway stations. Sci. Rep. **13**, 15914 (2023). https://doi.org/10.1038/s41598-023-42535-x
5. Osipov, V., Nikiforov, V.: Recurrent neural networks with controlled elements in restoring frame flows. Inf. Control Syst., 10–17 (2019). https://doi.org/10.31799/1684-8853-2019-5-10-17
6. Yokoyama, N., Tanaka, K.: Container auto-scaling system using sliding-window regression with fuzzy entropy. J. Inf. Process. **32**, 916–928 (2024). https://doi.org/10.2197/ipsjjip.32.916
7. Liu, Y., Yanjun, F.: Design of the nonlinear system predictor driven by the bayesian-gaussian neural network of sliding window data. Comput. Inf. Sci. **2**, 26 (2024). https://doi.org/10.5539/cis.v2n2p26
8. Liang, Z.: Anti-pollution intelligent window control system based on air detection. J. Phys. Conf. Ser. **2810**, 012004 (2024). https://doi.org/10.1088/1742-6596/2810/1/012004
9. Ko, W., Burgess, I., Chung, S., Macnaughton, P., Um, C.Y.: Assessing the impact of glazing and window shade systems on view clarity. Sci. Rep. 14 (2024). https://doi.org/10.1038/s41598-024-69026-x
10. Sisi, C.: Empirical study on functional defects in multi-window Android systems. Appl. Comput. Eng. **73**, 288–294 (2024). https://doi.org/10.54254/2755-2721/73/20240413
11. Koay, H.-H., Thien, G., Wen Cheun, B., Hamed, A., Ruthramurthy, B., Ng, Z., Chan, K.: An IoT-enabled monitoring and control system for electrochromic smart windows. Discover Internet Things 4 (2024). https://doi.org/10.1007/s43926-024-00086-1
12. Deng, L., Shi, Z., Wang, Y., Yu, X., Guan, Y., Xu, Z.: Hybrid window decoding for joint source channel anytime coding system. Entropy **26**, 940 (2024). https://doi.org/10.3390/e26110940
13. Wang, F.-C., Huang, H.-T.: Extended-window algorithms for model prediction applied to hybrid power systems. Technologies. **12**, 6 (2024). https://doi.org/10.3390/technologies12010006
14. Febriyanti, R., Ranti, B., Shihab, M., Wicaksana, I., Mekkawati, H., Salbari, F., Diarto, N.: Transformation of business licensing through a single submission system on public service efficiency: a case study of the Indonesia National Single Window Agency (LNSW). Indonesian J. Comput. Sci. 13 (2024). https://doi.org/10.33022/ijcs.v13i5.4411

15. Wang, A.: Engineering design and implementation of AI-driven single window systems for international trade. J. AI-Driven Trade Facilitation Eng. Single Window Syst. **1**, 21–34 (2024). https://doi.org/10.6914/sw.010102

16. Gunasegran, S., et al.: IoT-based smart window and temperature control system for optimized thermal comfort. 020018 (2024). https://doi.org/10.1063/5.0230083

17. Subbotin, A., Zhukova, N., Gudilov, M.: Problems of building digital twins of escalators at subway stations based on machine learning. In: Arai, K. (eds.) Intelligent Computing. SAI 2024. Lecture Notes in Networks and Systems, vol. 1018. Springer, Cham (2024). https://doi.org/10.1007/978-3-031-62269-4_13

18. Zhang, W., et al.: Design and development of a new biped robotic system for exoskeleton-structure window cleaning. IEEE Trans. Automation Sci. Eng. PP, 1–12 (2024). https://doi.org/10.1109/TASE.2024.3390030

19. Liu, L., Li, F., Liu, W., Xia, H.: Sliding window iterative identification for nonlinear closed-loop systems based on the maximum likelihood principle. Int. J. Robust Nonlinear Control **35** (2024). https://doi.org/10.1002/rnc.7705

20. Zhou, Q.: Frequency-domain characterization of finite sample linear systems with uniform window inputs. Signals. **6**. 1 (2025). https://doi.org/10.3390/signals6010001

21. Pietzsch, A., Woerd, J., Andrae, M., Gebbeken, N.: Analysis of the load-bearing behavior of catcher-cable systems for hazard prevention for windows under blast loads (2024)

22. Xiao, H., Peng, H., Zhao, Y., Hou, L.: Magnetic field energy harvesting and power management with transfer window modulation. IEEE Trans. Power Electron. PP, 1–13. https://doi.org/10.1109/TPEL.2025.3528110

23. Tung, T.-J., Al-Hussein, M., Martinez, P.: Vision-based guiding system for autonomous robotic corner cleaning of window frames. Buildings **13**, 2990 (2023). https://doi.org/10.3390/buildings13122990

24. Zhao, F., et al.: Continuous solar energy conversion windows integrating zinc anode-based electrochromic device and IoT system. Adv. Mater. **36**, e2405035 (2024). https://doi.org/10.1002/adma.202405035

25. Gao, L., Zong, R.: Design of intelligent window automatic monitoring system based on microcontroller control. J. Electron. Res. Appl. **8**. 34–40 (2024). https://doi.org/10.26689/jera.v8i4.7922

MLE-RBA: A Machine Learning-Empowered Risk-Based Authentication Algorithm

Iurii Matiushin$^{(\boxtimes)}$ ⓘ and Vladimir Korkhov ⓘ

St Petersburg State University, St Petersburg 199034, Russia
{y.matyushin,v.korkhov}@spbu.ru

Abstract. Risk-Based Authentication (RBA) is a dynamic authentication app-roach that assesses login attempts based on contextual risk factors. Traditional RBA implementations, such as Freeman et al.'s Naïve Bayes method, provide adaptive security but have limitations in precision and adaptability. In this study, we propose an enhanced RBA method leveraging machine learning to improve risk assessment accuracy.

We design and implement MLE-RBA, an ML-empowered RBA system using a LightGBM classifier trained on a user login dataset, incorporating feature engineering, anomaly detection, and data balancing techniques. Our approach is eval-uated against Freeman's method and the SIMPLE heuristic, with performance measured in terms of Equal Error Rate (EER) and other key metrics. Experimen-tal results show that our ML-based approach achieves a lower EER, demonstrating improved authentication accuracy while maintaining usability.

Despite its effectiveness, we emphasize that RBA, even when enhanced with ML, should not replace primary authentication mechanisms but rather serve as a supplementary layer to improve security. Our findings contribute to the ongoing development of adaptive authentication strategies, highlighting ML's potential in optimizing RBA systems.

Keywords: Risk-Based Authentication · Machine Learning · Cybersecurity

1 Introduction

1.1 The Need for Risk-Based Authentication

As cyber threats continue to evolve, traditional password-based authentication meth-ods have become increasingly inadequate. Simple password authentication is vulner-able to attacks such as credential stuffing, phishing, and brute force attacks, lead-ing to widespread security breaches. Two-factor authentication (2FA) and multi-factor authentication (MFA) offer additional security layers, yet they introduce usability chal-lenges, often frustrating users with frequent secondary verifications. To balance security and usability, modern authentication systems must adopt adaptive and context-aware mechanisms [1].

One of these approaches is known as **risk-based authentication**, or **RBA**. The essence of this approach is calculating a risk score associated with a particular login

O. Gervasi et al. (Eds.): ICCSA 2025 Workshops, LNCS 15894, pp. 325–339, 2026.
https://doi.org/10.1007/978-3-031-97648-3_22

attempt, based on such factors as the connecting device's geographic location, the device's OS and browser version, IP address, and others.

Based on the risk score calculated by the RBA mechanism, the security system can make a decision on how to proceed: if the perceived risk is low enough, the user can be allowed to connect without requiring any additional steps, but if the risk score exceeds a certain threshold – either static or dynamic – additional verification steps are required, such as one-time passwords, biometric authentication, or other approaches.

This means that RBA possesses the following advantages:

- **Increased usability:** since RBA works in the background from the user's perspective, and only triggers additional security steps when necessary, legitimate users can continue their work uninterrupted in the majority of cases.
- **Learning potential:** based on past sessions, an RBA system can create a more and more comprehensive user profile, becoming better at predicting whether the user is legitimate or not over time.
- **Integration potential:** RBA can – and, indeed, should – be combined with other existing authentication approaches, making the system more secure while not unnecessarily compromising usability [2].

1.2   Historical Background for RBA

The RBA concept was introduced in order to mitigate the issues associated with widely used authentication mechanisms, such as passwords, which often do not offer a high enough degree of security, and 2FA/MFA, which often requires the users to take additional steps in order to access a system, decreasing usability.

In particular, Freeman et al. conducted one of the fundamental studies in the field in 2016, using a Naïve Bayes classifier in order to detect account hijacking [3]. Their approach, based on behaviour patterns associated with a given user, is described in further detail in Part 3 of this work.

Freeman's work was followed by subsequent research by Wiefling, Dürmuth, and Lo Iacono. In particular, by analysing real-world authentication system, they came to the conclusion that several popular online services, such as Google, Facebook, LinkedIn, and GOG.com are using RBA in one form of another, despite frequently obscuring the details of their approach to user authentication [4].

Further studies by the same researchers analysed RBA's benefits and shortcomings in deployed systems; in particular, it was revealed that RBA is often perceived by users to be more user-friendly while maintaining a high level of protection [5,6]. This makes RBA particularly appealing for the situations where balancing security and user experience is crucial, such as large-scale web applications.

1.3   The Potential for Machine Learning in RBA

Early implementations of risk-based authentication (RBA), such as Freeman et al.'s algorithm, primarily relied on rule-based heuristics and traditional statistical models. However, the ongoing development of machine learning (ML) offers significant potential to increase the effectiveness of RBA systems. In particular, ML algorithms can analyse large volumes of authentication data and uncover complex behavioural patterns that earlier methods might find harder to capture. By training on historical login data, ML-based RBA systems can improve over time in several ways, such as dynamically adjusting risk thresholds and re-evaluating the importance of a given risk score factor.

Furthermore, recent advancements such as federated learning have enabled privacy-preserving applications of ML in the context of user authentication, which means that RBA algorithms can utilize user data to improve their accuracy without compromising sensitive user data [7].

Collectively, these developments suggest that ML-driven RBA has the potential to offer several important advantages, such as improved security, usability, and privacy.

1.4 Our Contribution

In this work, we design, implement, and test a machine learning-empowered risk-based authentication method, as well as comparing it to certain existing approaches. More specifically, we:

- Develop an ML-empowered RBA model (MLE-RBA), incorporating advanced feature selection and classification techniques in order to calculate risk scores and determine if a particular user is legitimate or not.
- Evaluate our method using a real-world authentication dataset.
- Benchmark our approach against Freeman's Naïve Bayes-based method, as implemented by the Data & Application Security (DAS) Group [8], and a SIMPLE heuristic-based RBA method, as described by Wiefling, Dürmuth, and Lo Iacono in their 2021 study [5].

The results of our comparative analysis demonstrate that ML-empowered RBA has advantages over other approaches when it comes to accuracy, availability, and adaptability. The findings offer valuable insights into the practical integration of machine learning within risk-based user authentication systems, laying a foundation for future research in this area.

1.5 Article Structure

The article is organized as follows.

In Part 1, we introduce the concept of risk-based authentication and discuss the need for RBA and the potential for using ML in such authentication algorithms, as well as our contribution.

In Part 2, we conduct a literature review on the topic of risk-based user authentication.

In Part 3, we propose and describe MLE-RBA, a machine learning-empowered risk-based authentication algorithm.

In Part 4, we conduct comparative analysis, which includes modifying Freeman's algorithm and implementing a SIMPLE risk-based algorithm for comparison purposes.

In Part 5, we conclude our work, discuss our findings, offer considerations for using ML-empowered RBA as a part of a user authentication system, and list future research directions.

2   Related Work

This section provides a brief review of the current RBA-related research.

"Who Are You? A Statistical Approach to Measuring User Authenticity" (2016) by Freeman et al. is one of the foundational studies in the field of risk-based authentication. It introduces a probabilistic, Bayesian approach to authentication, developing a statistical framework to detect account hijacking and non-legitimate login attempts based on previous user behaviour. The framework is then tested on a sample of real-life login data from LinkedIn as well as simulated attacks, and a systematic study of possible attackers is also provided [3].

Several more recent studies explored RBA and Freeman's algorithm further, focusing on such topics as real-life usage, user perception, and usability of such an approach.

In particular, Wiefling et al. conducted a study on RBA algorithms used in eight popular online services (**"Is this really you? An empirical study on risk-based authentication applied in the wild"**, 2019). In order to achieve that, they have developed an automated browser testing framework capable of simulating human-like user behaviour within each service. They found that an IP address is a particularly relevant piece of information in the risk-based authentication context and discovered three distinct RBA models (single-feature, multi-feature, and VIP). Their work has also led to discovery and fixing of a vulnerability within Facebook's authentication protocol [4].

In **"What's in score for website users: A data-driven long-term study on risk-based authentication characteristics"** (2021), Wiefling et al. provide further analysis of an RBA system's practical deployment. The results of this study demonstrate that RBA should be tailored to each service, and even small configuration adjustments can greatly impact security and usability. They also identify a new, previously unused RBA feature, as well as factors that could potentially affect RBA performance [5].

"F-RBA: A Federated Learning-based Framework for Risk-based Authentication" (2024) by Fereidouni et al. integrates RBA with another emerging technology in the field of ML, particularly, federated learning. The study introduces a distributed architecture that provides local risk assessment on user devices instead of centralizing this functionality. The authors also provide empirical evaluation of their proposed approach using a real-world multi-user dataset [7].

"RLAuth: A Risk-Based Authentication System Using Reinforcement Learning" (2023) by C. Picard and S. Pierre provides an example of using binary anomaly detection in a risk-based authentication system. The authors propose a system consisting of an anomaly detector, a risk engine, and an authentication manager, and conducted empirical testing to prove its effectiveness. It should be noted that this study focuses specifically on mobile application security [9].

The study **"Evaluation of Real-World Risk-Based Authentication at Online Services Revisited: Complexity Wins"** by Jan-Phillip Makowski, Daniela Pöhn (2023) re-evaluates the RBA systems of major online services such as Google, Amazon, and Facebook. The authors' research partly verifies the earlier findings of Wiefling et al. They note that the risk-based authentication systems employed by certain popular services, Amazon in particular, seem insufficiently strong, failing to provide alternative ways to safely verify a user's identity and seemingly not reacting to several suspicious user behaviour patterns [10].

Overall, the evolution of RBA reflects a concerted effort to develop authentication systems that are both secure and user-friendly. By using contextual information and adaptive mechanisms, RBA offers a promising alternative to traditional authentication methods, providing high level of security while not compromising usability.

3 The Proposed ML-Based Algorithm

We propose **MLE-RBA (Machine Learning–Empowered Risk-Based Authentication)**, a novel risk-based algorithm inspired by Freeman's work but leveraging the capabilities of machine learning in order to provide more accurate user identity verification based on contextual factors and behavioural data.

MLE-RBA is designed to dynamically assess the risk of authentication attempts by combining classical risk-based heuristics with modern machine learning techniques. The algorithm leverages both anomaly detection and supervised classification to estimate a numerical risk score for each login attempt, which is then used to determine whether additional verification is warranted.

In this work, the algorithm is implemented using a multi-stage pipeline that includes target encoding, class imbalance handling, anomaly detection, and classifier calibration.

3.1 The Rationale for Our Algorithm

As stated above, our algorithm was originally inspired by Freeman's Naïve Bayes-based method.

The method estimates the risk of a login attempt based on statistical rarity. It assigns a risk score to login attempts based on how unusual certain attributes (e.g., IP address, User-Agent, ASN) are compared to past logins from the same user and the global distribution of all users. The risk score is then compared to a predefined threshold. If the risk score is below the threshold, the login succeeds; if it is above the threshold, additional authentication (e.g., MFA) is required. The underlying principle is to flag anomalous activities while minimizing friction for regular users.

While effective, this approach has limitations:

1. **Feature weighting is fixed:** each feature contributes equally or is manually weighted, regardless of actual importance.
2. **Static thresholds:** the risk threshold is predefined and does not adapt to different attack patterns or user behaviours.
3. **Lack of advanced behavioural analysis:** the model does not fully utilize time-based or frequency-based behavioural features.

Our algorithm enhances Freeman's approach while preserving its core idea:

1. **Machine learning-based feature weighting:** instead of manually assigning feature importance, we train a model to learn the impact of each feature on login success. This ensures that important features (such as IP changes) influence the risk score more than less relevant ones.

2. **Adaptive threshold selection:** instead of using a fixed threshold, we dynamically adjust it based on Precision-Recall curves, minimizing both false positives and false negatives.
3. **Enhanced feature engineering:** we introduce behavioural metrics like time since last login, improving risk assessment.

The source code is available at our GitHub repository [11].

The following sections explain the algorithm's work in more detail.

3.2 MLE-RBA Algorithm Pipeline

Feature Engineering and Data Preprocessing

Initially, the input dataset (e.g., collected login records) is pre-processed to handle missing values and standardize feature formats. Categorical features such as "country", "region", "city", "ASN", "user agent string", "browser name and version", "OS name and version", and "device type" are first imputed for missing values and then encoded using a target encoding method with smoothing. A time-based feature, "time_since_last_login," is derived by calculating the time difference between successive login attempts for each user.

Handling Class Imbalance

Authentication datasets typically suffer from class imbalance, with genuine logins vastly outnumbering attack attempts. To address this, the algorithm employs SMOTETomek – a hybrid resampling method that both oversamples the minority class and cleans the majority class by removing ambiguous samples [12, 13]. This balancing step is applied exclusively on the training data to avoid data leakage.

Anomaly Detection

To capture irregularities in user behaviour, the MLE-RBA algorithm incorporates two complementary anomaly detection methods:

- **Local Outlier Factor (LOF):** configured with a tuned number of neighbours and a specified contamination rate, LOF identifies local deviations in the data using a cosine similarity metric.
- **Isolation Forest:** this global anomaly detector isolates observations by recursively partitioning the data.

Both methods are trained on the balanced, encoded training data. Their output scores are normalized and then combined with equal weighting to produce an aggregate anomaly score, which is appended as an additional feature to the original feature matrix. This hybrid approach enhances the algorithm's sensitivity to both local and global anomalies.

Classifier Training and Calibration

The final feature matrix, which includes both the encoded features and the combined anomaly score, is used to train a LightGBM classifier. The classifier is configured with optimized hyperparameters, including an increased maximum depth (to capture more complex interactions), regularization terms, and class weights that favour the minority (attack) class.

LightGBM was chosen because of its efficiency and scalability when handling large datasets, which are important advantages in a real-world authentication scenario. It also offers excellent speed and accuracy, as well as superior performance over such classifiers as Random Forest and traditional gradient boosting methods, especially when working with large amounts of data and high-dimensional feature spaces.

Due to the imbalanced nature of the problem, the classifier's raw output probabilities are further calibrated using sigmoid calibration (via CalibratedClassifierCV) to ensure that the risk scores are well-calibrated and reflect true likelihoods.

Threshold Selection and Evaluation Metrics

To translate continuous risk scores into a binary decision (e.g., whether to trigger additional authentication), a decision threshold must be determined.

The algorithm computes the Receiver Operating Characteristic (ROC) curve, from which it calculates both the False Acceptance Rate (FAR) and False Rejection Rate (FRR). The optimal threshold is selected discretely by identifying the threshold at which the absolute difference between FAR and FRR is minimized. This threshold is then used to classify login attempts.

Evaluation metrics such as the Area Under the ROC Curve (AUC-ROC), confusion matrix, classification report, and Equal Error Rate (EER) are computed to assess the model's performance.

3.3 Visual Representation

Visual representation of the MLE-RBA algorithm is shown in Fig. 1.

Fig. 1. ML-empowered RBA algorithm pipeline.

4 Algorithm Testing and Evaluation

4.1 Dataset

In order to train and test our algorithm, as well as to perform comparative testing, we use the login data set for risk-based authentication provided by the Data & Application Security Group (DAS) [14]. The dataset is available at the DAS Group's GitHub page [15].

The authors describe the dataset as follows: "Synthesized login feature data of >33 M login attempts and >3.3 M users on a large-scale online service in Norway. Original data collected between February 2020 and February 2021."

Each record in the dataset represents a single login attempt and includes a variety of features such as:

- **User identifiers and timestamps:** a unique user ID and the corresponding login timestamp allow for the reconstruction of user-specific login histories and the analysis of temporal patterns.
- **Network information:** attributes like the IP address, Autonomous System Number (ASN), and geographical indicators (country, region, and city) provide context regarding the network origin of the login attempt.
- **Device and client data:** the dataset captures details from the user agent, including the browser name and version, operating system name and version, and the device type. These features are critical for establishing a behavioural profile for each user.
- **Authentication outcome:** it includes a binary label indicating whether the login was successful.

4.2 Freeman's Algorithm

The first algorithm we compare MLE-RBA to is Freeman's RBA algorithm.

For comparative testing purposes, we used the implementation of Freeman's algorithm by Data & Application Security Group, which is freely accessible on GitHub [8].

To provide a comprehensive evaluation and direct comparison with our approach, we enhanced the above implementation with additional evaluation code. Specifically, after obtaining risk scores for each login attempt, our evaluation module computes the AUC-ROC score using standard libraries and visualizes the ROC curve. The confusion matrix is generated to provide an error breakdown, and a custom function calculates the EER by finding the intersection point of the false acceptance and false rejection rates.

Our variation of the DAS Group's implementation can be found in our GitHub repository [11].

4.3 SIMPLE Algorithm

We also implement another risk-based algorithm as a benchmark – a simple feature-based model, described by Wiefling et al. as follows [5]:

"The simple model (SIMPLE) extends the single-feature model used in the open source single sign-on solution OpenAM [31] and is assumed to be used at GOG.com [46]. It also partly reflects models given in literature [42,24,16]. We based our implementation on OpenAM, since it is freely available and probably widely used. The SIMPLE algorithm checks a number of features for an exact match in the user's login history. The risk score is the number of inspected features with at least one match in the login history divided by the total number of considered features. Thus, the risk score granularity increases with the number of observed features."

Our implementation uses the same dataset as for Freeman's algorithm and our MLE-RBA approach. The data is indexed by login timestamps and is grouped by user to ensure that the authentication history for each individual is processed in chronological order. The algorithm focuses on a fixed set of features:

For each user, the algorithm maintains a history of observed values for these features. When processing each login attempt, the algorithm compares the current feature values with those previously recorded. The risk score is determined by the ratio of familiar values (the ones already seen in a given user's login history) to the total number of features.

To facilitate a robust comparison with other RBA methods, we enhanced our implementation of SIMPLE by integrating evaluation metrics, including the AUC-ROC score, confusion matrix, and Equal Error Rate (EER). This evaluation framework provides a comprehensive view of the algorithm's performance, allowing us to contrast its behaviour with both Freeman's probabilistic method and our ML-empowered RBA approach.

Our implementation of the SIMPLE algorithm is also accessible at our GitHub repository [11].

4.4 Evaluation Metrics

We use several different metrics in order to evaluate the authentication algorithms' accuracy.

- **AUC-ROC score** shows how well a model can produce relative scores to discriminate between positive and negative results – in our case, between legitimate and fraudulent authentication attempts – across all classification thresholds.
- **Confusion matrix** demonstrates the number of true positives (legitimate login attempts flagged as such), false positives (attacks successfully passing as legitimate login attempts), true negatives (accurately detected attack attempts), and false negatives (legitimate login attempts flagged as attacks).
- **EER (equal error rate)** shows the point at which the false acceptance rate (FAR) and false rejection rate (FRR) are equal – in our case, we can change FAR and FRR values by adjusting the risk score threshold.

Overall, these metrics offer complementary perspectives: AUC-ROC for overall discrimination performance, the confusion matrix for detailed error analysis, and EER for understanding the balance between security and user experience.

4.5   Evaluation Results

In this section, we demonstrate the results of the comparative analysis via two types of graphs.

FAR, FRR, and EER graph for the SIMPLE algorithm can be seen in Fig. 2.

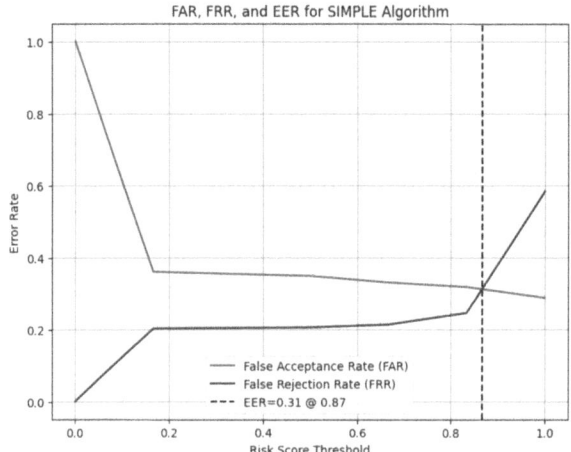

Fig. 2. FAR, FRR, and EER graph for the SIMPLE algorithm.

Confusion matrix for the SIMPLE algorithm can be seen in Fig. 3.

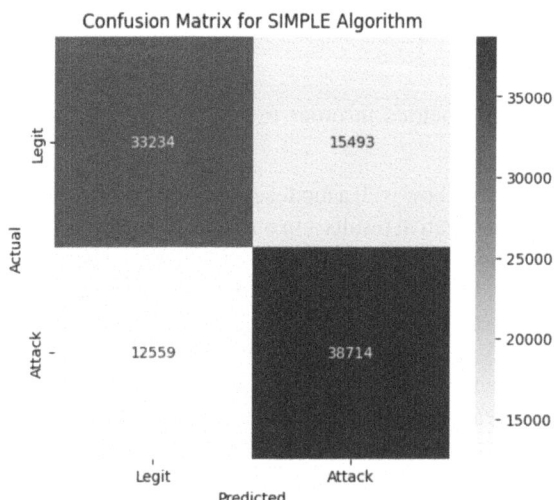

Fig. 3. Confusion matrix for the SIMPLE algorithm.

FAR, FRR, and EER graph for Freeman's algorithm can be seen in Fig. 4.

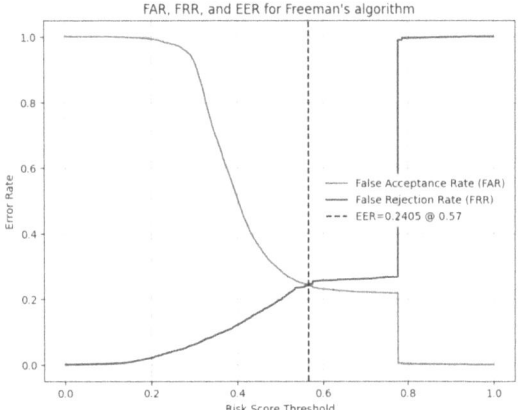

Fig. 4. FAR, FRR, and EER graph for Freeman's algorithm.

Confusion matrix for Freeman's algorithm can be seen in Fig. 5.

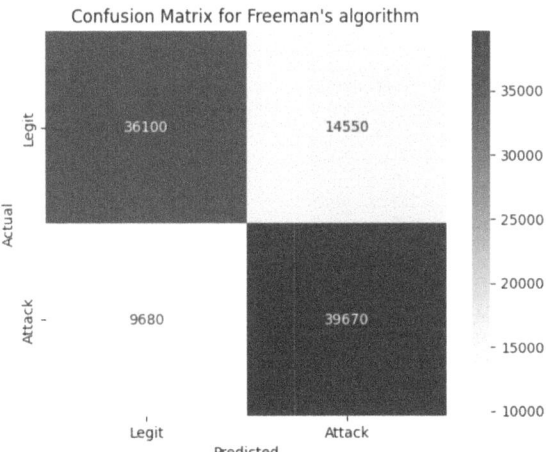

Fig. 5. Confusion matrix for Freeman's algorithm.

FAR, FRR, and EER graph for the MLE-RBA algorithm can be seen in Fig. 6.

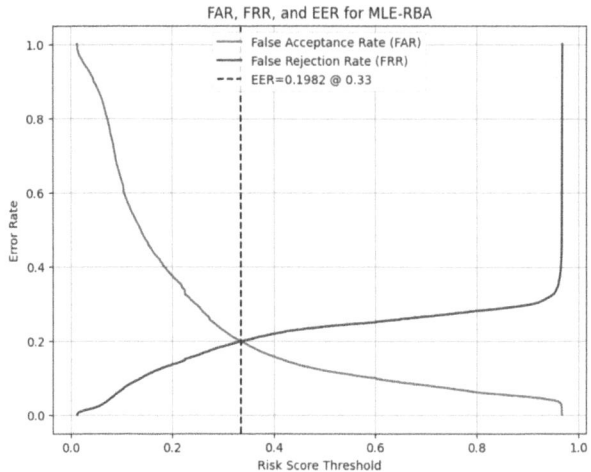

Fig. 6. FAR, FRR, and EER graph for MLE-RBA.

Confusion matrix for the MLE-RBA algorithm can be seen in Fig. 7.

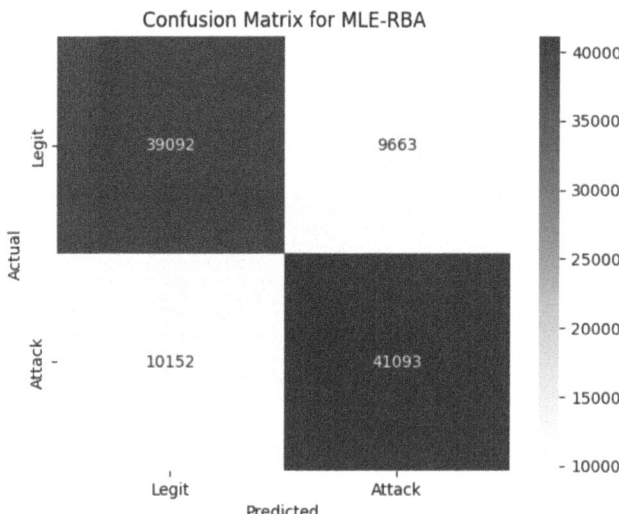

Fig. 7. Confusion matrix for MLE-RBA.

4.6 Results Summary

A summary of evaluation metrics for SIMPLE, Freeman's, and MLE-RBA algorithms is presented in Table 1.

Table 1. Evaluation metrics summary.

Metric	SIMPLE	Freeman	MLE-RBA
EER	0.3100	0.2405	0.1982
AUC-ROC	0.6862	0.7600	0.8721

5 Conclusions and Future Work

5.1 Results Discussion

Our experimental evaluation indicates that the MLE-RBA approach demonstrates improved performance compared to both Freeman's algorithm and the SIMPLE heuristic. The metrics show that MLE-RBA achieves a better balance between false acceptances and false rejections, and it has a higher ability to distinguish between legitimate and fraudulent login attempts.

In practical terms, these improvements suggest that the ML-based model is more effective at adapting to dynamic behavioural patterns, which is crucial for maintaining security without compromising usability. The enhanced discrimination performance implies that the system can more reliably detect anomalous behaviour, which reduces the risk of unauthorized access while minimizing unnecessary authentication challenges.

5.2 Considerations for the Algorithm's Usage

However, it should be noted that the MLE-RBA algorithm, even while outperforming other RBA approaches, still shows a relatively high EER, especially compared to the more classical authentication methods.

This shows that RBA should not be relied upon as the sole way to confirm a user's identity; instead, it should be implemented as a part of a hybrid authentication system incorporating multiple authentication factors. As discussed at the beginning of the article, if the RBA method outputs a risk score exceeding the chosen threshold, approaches such as OTP (one-time passwords) can be used to make the final decision on whether to allow continued access to the system or deny it.

Moreover, MLE-RBA can coexist with a wide range of commonly used authentication methods, from classic password protection to biometrics. It can be used as one of the levels of a multi-factor authentication (MFA) system triggering additional defence layers if the risk threshold is reached, or as a part of a hybrid method calculating login risk scores based on a variety of factors – for instance, by combining it with a keystroke or mouse movement recognition algorithm.

That said, an important point of consideration is ensuring that MLE-RBA integrates smoothly with other systems to avoid conflicts, such as triggering redundant MFA requests or producing conflicting risk evaluation outputs. For example, if MLE-RBA flags a login as high-risk, but biometric or password-based systems do not, this could lead to inconsistent results.

By carefully calibrating risk thresholds and establishing clear protocols for prioritizing or reconciling conflicting assessments, MLE-RBA can ensure a coherent, unified decision-making process and enhance security without sacrificing usability and overburdening the user with unnecessary checks.

5.3 Future Work Directions

As shown above, MLE-RBA shows promise, providing better results in terms of accuracy compared to other approaches, but there is still room for further improvement.

We plan to continue improving our approach by conducting experiments with a wide variety of ML models and classifiers, such as ensemble methods, deep learning architectures, hybrid models combining several algorithms, etc. The end goal is to determine the optimal combination of steps to accurately calculate login risk scores, separating the attackers from the legitimate users.

In addition, it should be noted that we are currently working with a single, albeit extensive and high-quality dataset. Should we gain access to a wider range of user login data, we also plan to incorporate it into our work, making sure the system we are developing can be effectively implemented in a variety of real-world scenarios.

One possible direction of further improvement is the interpretability of MLE-RBA's decisions. Machine learning models can often appear as "black box" systems, which can make it hard for human users to understand how exactly the authentication system decides whether a given login attempt is "risky" or not. A way of addressing this is to integrate explainable AI (XAI) techniques, such as SHAP (SHapley Additive Explanations) and LIME (Local Interpretable Model-agnostic Explanations), which provide clearer insights into the model's decision-making process [16]. This will make it easier for administrators to identify why MLE-RBA flags certain login attempts as risky and adjust the model as necessary – for instance, if a legitimate user is wrongly identified as a possible threat.

Another promising direction is the integration of the ML-RBA system into a continuous authentication framework. By incorporating a CA method like dynamic keystroke recognition, which demonstrates superior accuracy relative to other similar methods [17], the system could continuously validate user identity rather than relying solely on point-of-entry checks. This hybrid approach has the potential to significantly enhance both security and usability by providing ongoing assurance of user authenticity while remaining relatively unobtrusive to the end user.

Acknowledgement. Supported by Saint Petersburg State University, project ID: 95438429.

References

1. Rashidi, B., Garg, V.: Open sesame: lessons in password-based user authentication. Cyber Secur. A Peer-Reviewed J. **4**(4), 317–329 (2021)
2. Security vs. usability: Pros and cons of risk-based authentication. https://www.infosecin stitute.com/resources/management-compliance-auditing/security-vs-usability-pros-cons-of-risk-based-authentication. Accessed 01 Mar 2025

3. Freeman, D., et al.: Who are you? a statistical approach to measuring user authenticity. NDSS, vol. 16 (2016)
4. Wiefling, S., Iacono, L.L., Dürmuth, M.: "Is this really you? An empirical study on risk-based authentication applied in the wild. In: ICT Systems Security and Privacy Protection: 34th IFIP TC 11 International Conference, SEC 2019, Lisbon, Portugal, June 25–27, 2019, Proceedings 34. Springer (2019)
5. Wiefling, S., Dürmuth, M., Iacono, L.L.: What's in score for website users: a data-driven long-term study on risk-based authentication characteristics. In: Financial Cryptography and Data Security: 25th International Conference, FC 2021, Virtual Event, March 1–5, 2021, Revised Selected Papers, Part II 25. Springer, Heidelberg (2021)
6. Wiefling, S., Dürmuth, M., Iacono, L.L.: "More than just good passwords? a study on usability and security perceptions of risk-based authentication. In: Proceedings of the 36th Annual Computer Security Applications Conference (2020)
7. Fereidouni, H., et al.: F-RBA: A Federated Learning-based Framework for Risk-based Authentication. arXiv preprint arXiv:2412.12324 (2024)
8. rba-algorithm. https://github.com/das-group/rba-algorithm. Accessed 20 Mar 2025
9. Picard, C., Pierre, S.: RLAuth: A risk-based authentication system using reinforcement learning. IEEE Access 11, 61129–61143 (2023)
10. Makowski, J.-P., Pöhn, D.: Evaluation of real-world risk-based authentication at online services revisited: complexity wins. In: Proceedings of the 18th International Conference on Availability, Reliability and Security (2023)
11. MLE-RBA. https://github.com/YuriyM-SPB/MLE-RBA. Accessed 23 Mar 2025
12. Chawla, N.V., et al.: SMOTE: synthetic minority over-sampling technique. J. Artif. Intell. Res. 16, 321–357 (2002)
13. SMOTETomek. https://imbalanced-learn.org/stable/references/generated/imblearn.combine. SMOTETomek.html. Accessed 23 Mar 2025
14. Wiefling, S., et al.: Pump up password security! Evaluating and enhancing risk-based authentication on a real-world large-scale online service. ACM Trans. Privacy Secur. 26(1), 1–36 (2022)
15. rba-dataset. https://github.com/das-group/rba-dataset. Accessed 21 Mar 2025
16. Angelov, P.P., et al.: Explainable artificial intelligence: an analytical review. Wiley Interdisciplinary Reviews: Data Mining and Knowledge Discovery 11(5), e1424 (2021)
17. Matiushin, I., Korkhov, V.: Continuous authentication methods for zero-trust cybersecurity architecture. In: International Conference on Computational Science and Its Applications. Springer, Cham (2023)

Investigating Alzheimer's Disease Using a Sequential Analytical Pipeline for High-Dimensional, Low-Sample Biomedical Data

Nadezhda Shchegoleva[1]($\boxtimes$) (ID), Petr Tonka[1] (ID), and Natalia Zalutskaya[2] (ID)

[1] Saint Petersburg State University, St. Petersburg, Russia
n.shchegoleva@spbu.ru, st102620@student.spbu.ru
[2] Federal State Budgetary Institution «Bekhterev National Medical Research Psychiatry and Neurology Center», Saint-Petersburg, Russia

Abstract. Dementia, particularly Alzheimer's disease, is a growing global medical and economic problem exacerbated by increasing life expectancy and aging population. This study demonstrates the critical need for efficient data processing methods in biomedical research, focusing on scenarios where the number of observations is smaller than the dimensionality of the data. Based on a dataset of patients with various neurodegenerative diseases including Alzheimer's disease, this paper describes a comprehensive data processing pipeline including dimensionality reduction and clustering. The methodology is based on the combined use of principal component analysis (PCA) and uniform manifold approximation and projection (UMAP) for dimensionality reduction, followed by clustering with optimized parameters. The study demonstrates how these methods can mitigate problems such as data sparsity and the curse of dimensionality, providing a pipeline to gain insights into potential biomarkers for early diagnosis of neurodegenerative diseases. Although this study does not directly interpret clustering results, it lays the groundwork for experts in the field to explore new hypotheses and improve diagnostic tools.

Keywords: Alzheimer's disease · dimensionality reduction · clustering · PCA · UMAP · HDBSCAN

1 Introduction

Dementia, particularly Alzheimer's disease (AD), is a critical global health issue, rapidly increasing in prevalence due to rising life expectancy and aging of the population [1, 2]. It represents a significant medical and economic burden worldwide [3, 4], posing substantial challenges to healthcare systems. While the scale of the problem is substantial, with millions affected globally and projections indicating continued growth [2], the urgent need for effective diagnosis and treatment methods is widely acknowledged.

Current diagnostic approaches involve various biomarkers such as cerebrospinal fluid (CSF) analysis of amyloid beta (Aβ), total tau (t-tau), and phosphorylated tau

O. Gervasi et al. (Eds.): ICCSA 2025 Workshops, LNCS 15894, pp. 340–355, 2026.
https://doi.org/10.1007/978-3-031-97648-3_23

(p-tau) accumulation, and positron emission tomography (PET) scans (amyloid PET and tau PET) [5]. However, these methods often have drawbacks, including high cost, complexity, and invasiveness [5–8]. In this regard, alternative diagnostic methods are being developed, for example, the development of biomarkers based on the patients' blood analysis, mainly also relying on the analysis of Aβ and tau pathologies, looks quite promising [5–9]. However, the amyloid cascade theory itself, built around the toxic action of amyloid-β, is still a subject of controversy and debate, so there remains a need to search for and investigate other factors of disease onset in parallel with the amyloid hypothesis [5].

Despite growing interest and advances in diagnostic strategies, research into Alzheimer's disease continues to face considerable methodological difficulties, particularly in relation to data acquisition and analysis. Biomedical studies in this domain typically generate large volumes of complex and heterogeneous data derived from a variety of sources, including clinical records, patient histories, neuropsychological testing, and instrumental methods such as electroencephalography (EEG) and magnetic resonance imaging (MRI). These multimodal data sources differ significantly in structure and often contain missing values, which adds layers of complexity to data integration and analysis workflows [14].

Moreover, the high dimensionality of such data – especially in the case of neuroimaging, where thousands of features can be extracted from a single scan – presents further analytical challenges [15]. These are compounded by the limited number of observations that are characteristic of clinical research, resulting in scenarios where the number of variables dramatically exceeds the number of observations. Such conditions hinder the applicability of conventional statistical and machine learning methods, necessitating the development and implementation of specialized approaches for robust and interpretable data analysis [10–12].

This paper proposes a methodological approach specifically tailored to analyze this type of complex medical data characterized by limited dataset size and high dimensionality. Based on a dataset of patients with various neurodegenerative diseases, including AD, our study details a comprehensive data processing pipeline. This pipeline includes preprocessing, a two-stage dimensionality reduction using Principal Component Analysis (PCA) and Uniform Manifold Approximation and Projection (UMAP), and subsequent clustering with optimized parameters. This methodology is designed to effectively manage the curse of dimensionality while preserving meaningful underlying structures in the data. A main outcome of this study is to lay the technical foundation for a diagnostician's workplace by building the basis of a decision support system, enabling domain experts to explore new hypotheses about potential disease biomarkers for early diagnosis of neurodegenerative diseases.

2   Methods

2.1   Data Description

The dataset used in this study was obtained from the St. Petersburg Bekhterev Psychoneurological Research Institute. This institution-specific dataset contains detailed clinical information on patients diagnosed with various neuropsychiatric disorders. While the original dataset is not publicly available due to the inclusion of non-anonymized patient information, the analysis for this study was performed on data accessed and processed within a secure, distributed private cloud environment designed for handling sensitive health data, including anonymized forms of the data. The dataset comprises demographic and background data (such as gender, age, education level, and work history), medical histories (anamneses), results from patient assessments, instrumental diagnostic findings, and clinical diagnoses provided by expert practitioners. The dataset encompasses six diagnostic categories: dementia, vascular dementia, depression, Alzheimer's disease, Parkinson's disease, and a control group.

The available assessments include laboratory blood tests, experimental psychological evaluations, neuropsychological testing, as well as neuroimaging data from MRI and EEG studies. Notably, MRI results were processed using voxel-based morphometry [13] and formatted into structured tabular data, consistent with the rest of the dataset. The dataset includes a total of 254 patients. The distribution of patients across diagnostic categories is presented in Table 1.

Next, the stages of processing and analyzing the dataset under consideration will be described. The complete process cycle is illustrated in Fig. 1.

Table 1. The distribution of patients by diagnoses

Clinical Diagnosis	No. of Observations
Alzheimer's disease	60
Vascular Dementia	58
Control Group	54
Depression	45
Dementia	36
Parkinson's disease	1

2.2 Data Preparation

Considering all available patient information, the sample contains 714 features—almost three times the number of records. For analysis, we focused on EEG and MRI data. The EEG results are divided into two parts: the first includes averaged electrode values, relative indices, and measurement correlations, while the second provides aggregated values per electrode. Initially, the subsample was split into three independent datasets: MRI (MRI), general EEG (EEG), and aggregated EEG (EEG_sumup).

Data quality checks were performed on each subsample. No partial missing values were detected. Incomplete rows (reflecting unperformed procedures) were discarded. The data were also examined for duplicate rows and negative values, with none identified.

Following data cleaning, two additional subsets were created by merging the original three: a mixed EEG subset (EEG + EEG_sumup) and a combined EEG and MRI subset

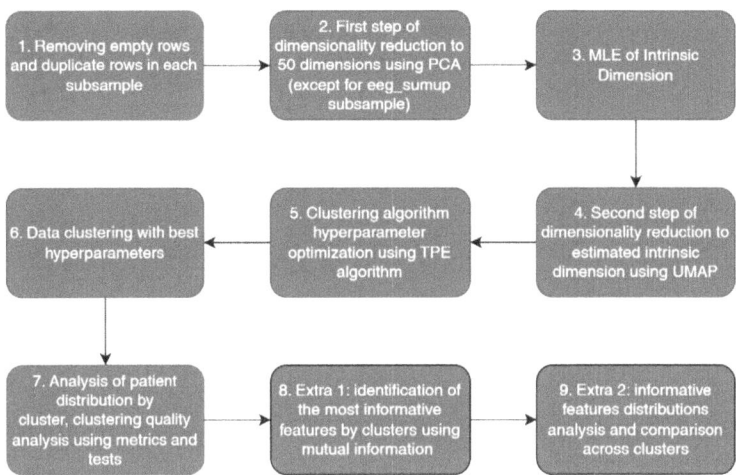

Fig. 1. Data preparation and analysis steps

(EEG + EEG_sumup + MRI). Only patients present in both source subsamples were retained (inner join). Table 2 summarizes the sizes of all five resulting subsamples.

Table 2. Final subsample sizes

Subsample Name	No. of Samples	No. of Features
MRI	117	315
EEG	176	192
EEG_sumup	177	15
EEG + EEG_sumup	172	207
EEG + EEG_sumup + MRI	94	522

Table 3. Distribution of patients by cluster using HDBSCAN

Cluster Label	No. of cases	No. of Clinician Diagnoses in clusters	Clinician Diagnoses Across Clusters (%)	Clinician Diagnoses Within Clusters (%)
−1	31	6/6/6/7/6/0	14/17.1/23.1/19.4/17.1/0.0	19.4/19.4/19.4/22.6/19.4/0.0
0	73	15/13/13/18/13/1	34.9/37.1/50.0/50.0/37.1/100.0	20.5/17.8/17.8/24.7/17.8/1.4
1	4	1/1/0/1/1/0	2.3/2.9/0.0/2.8/2.9/0.0	25.0/25.0/0.0/25.0/25.0/0.0
2	25	8/2/3/5/7/0	18.6/5.7/11.5/13.9/20.0/0.0	32.0/8.0/12.0/20.0/28.0/0.0
3	7	3/2/0/1/1/0	7/5.7/0.0/2.8/2.9/0.0	42.9/28.6/0.0/14.3/14.3/0.0
4	9	3/3/2/0/1/0	7/8.6/7.7/0.0/2.9/0.0	33.3/33.4/22.2/0.0/11.1/0.0
5	27	7/8/2/4/6/0	16.3/22.9/7.7/11.1/17.1/0.0	25.9/29.6/7.4/14.8/22.2/0.0

Table 4. Distribution of patients by cluster using Agglomerative Clustering

Cluster Label	No. of cases	No. of Clinician Diagnoses in clusters	Clinician Diagnoses Across Clusters (%)	Clinician Diagnoses Within Clusters (%)
0	91	25/19/8/18/21/0	58.1/54.3/30.8/50.0/60.0/0.0	27.5/20.9/8.9/19.8/23.1/0.0
1	85	18/16/18/18/14/1	41.9/45.7/69.2/50.0/40.0/100.0	21.2/18.8/21.2/21.2/16.5/1.2

Table 5. Percentage labeled, metrics and cluster stability scores (EEG)

Algorithm	Labeled (%)	DBCV	Silhouette	ARI	AMI
HDBSCAN	82.39	0.47	0.32	0.56	0.68
Agglomerative	100.00	0.21	0.45	0.71	0.68
Spectral	100.00	0.17	0.40	0.74	0.79

2.3 Dimensionality Reduction with PCA

After the first step - selection of three separate subsamples and cleaning them from irrelevant strings - each of them was further subjected to the same processing and analysis steps, except for the EEG_sumup subsample, to which the second step was not applied due to its small dimensionality. The second step of data processing is primary dimensionality reduction using principal component analysis (PCA) with preliminary data normalization. Data normalization ensures that all features contribute equally, which is critical for distance-based methods. PCA is used to reduce the dimensionality of the original data to a set of principal components that preserve the underlying variance. This reduces the impact of the curse of dimensionality in the data. In addition, PCA combats noise and redundancy in the data, and forms a space of uncorrelated features [16]. This step subsequently not only speeds up the algorithms used in the subsequent steps, but also helps to stabilize their results. In this step, the number of principal components to be selected was set to a fixed value of 50 components for both subsamples. In the case of EEG, this number of principal components preserved 97% of the variance in the data, while for MRI - 90% of the variance.

2.4 Calculation of Internal Dimensionality of Data

To objectively determine the optimal number of dimensions for a low-dimensional representation that preserves the essential structure of the original space, we computed the intrinsic dimensionality of subsamples using the MLE estimator (Maximum Likelihood Estimator of Intrinsic Dimension) [17].

It is believed that in most cases any methods applied in very high dimensions work only because the data are not really truly high dimensional, but rather they are embedded in a high dimensional space, but can be effectively generalized to a space of much lower dimensionality. Evaluating the intrinsic dimensionality reveals the minimum number of dimensions sufficient to describe the underlying structure of the data [16, 17]. This approach helps to select the number of components that simultaneously minimizes noise and redundancy, providing a more accurate representation of the real relationships between objects. This, in turn, improves subsequent analysis, for example, in clustering or building predictive models.

The choice of this estimator is justified by its simplicity and sufficiency within the framework of this work. It should be noted that the main problem of the estimator is the underestimation of the real dimensionality of the data when this dimensionality is actually large. However, as the experimental results showed, the estimated intrinsic dimensionality for each of the subsamples did not exceed 10, which is relatively small, especially when compared to the original dimensionality of the data.

Another problem can be the bias of the estimator results from the real internal dimensionality in case of calculating too large number of nearest neighbors for each of the points. This number is regulated by two hyperparameters – $k1$ and $k2$ – that set a range of values for the number of nearest neighbors computed during the algorithm. This problem is partially solved by simply averaging the estimators over a range of values $k = k1 \ldots k2$. The problem is also mitigated by choosing optimal values of $k1$ and 2, which can be chosen empirically based on the sample size and scale of values obtained by the estimator over an arbitrary range of values k.

2.5   Dimensionality Reduction with UMAP

After applying PCA and estimating the intrinsic dimensionality of the data, the use of UMAP [18] follows to further reduce the dimensionality. UMAP is often used in biomedical research and has proven itself in biomedical research as a versatile tool for creating low-dimensional representations [19–22], also due to the fact that it is nonparametric and, as a consequence, it does not require a large amount of data for its application.

By minimizing the noise and the number of irrelevant features using PCA, UMAP can model the internal structure of the data more effectively. By further reducing the dimensionality after applying PCA (50 features) and after applying UMAP equal to the value of internal dimensionality obtained in the previous step, algorithm better preserves the local and global relationships of the original data in the lower dimensionality space, which makes the subsequent data analysis results more reliable.

UMAP, as a nonlinear dimensionality reduction method, has a number of strengths. Unlike linear methods such as PCA, LDA (Linear Discriminant Analysis) or FA (Factor Analysis), it is able to account for complex, nonlinear relationships between objects, which is particularly relevant for biomedical data where the true structure may be hidden as a low-dimensional manifold. The nonlinearity of UMAP allows the local topology of the original space to be preserved, ensuring accurate recovery of local relationships between objects. This is critical for subsequent analysis, as it is in such a compact and informative representation that biologically relevant groups are easier to identify.

Within the scope of this work, the parameter for the number of nearest neighbors of the algorithm was chosen to be relatively large (30 neighbors) to avoid too much emphasis on local structures. The minimum distance between points in the low-dimensional space was chosen to be 0 in order to increase the density of clusters.

2.6 Clustering Algorithms

Given that the goal of the analysis, as stated above, is to generate new hypotheses about biomarkers of Alzheimer's disease, this analysis process is organized, relying as much as possible on the data themselves, rather than on human partitioning, to use clustering seems a logical choice. Clustering was chosen as the primary analysis tool for the reason that clustering, as a method of learning without a teacher, does not require proper data partitioning and is capable of searching the data for structure on its own. However, the automatic partitioning of the data does not mean that there is no need of validation of the results obtained by a specialist. On the contrary, the presence of clinical diagnoses and comparison of clustering results with the available partitioning can also be valuable information, especially if the obtained clusters overlap with the opinion of doctors. However, the absence of such overlaps can also be informative, but in such a case a more thorough analysis of the obtained clusters is needed to validate the value of the obtained partitions in the data.

Three clustering algorithms considered in this work are: HDBSCAN [23, 24], agglomerative clustering and spectral clustering [25]. The choice of these three methods is justified by the balance between the complementary principles underlying each algorithm, providing a more complete view of different aspects of the internal structure of the data. HDBSCAN and agglomerative clustering, among others, are able to determine the number of clusters in the data. Moreover, the use of multiple algorithms provides additional information about the stability of the clusters in the case where there are strong overlaps between the clustering results of the algorithms, i.e., stable partitions are formed. At the same time, a larger number of methods generates more hypotheses and adds reliability to the process of data analysis, since we do not have to rely on the correct operation of a single algorithm.

2.7 Hyperparameter Optimization

To evaluate the result of clustering, a more objective way than simply checking whether clusters correspond to clinical diagnoses is to select metrics that would reflect the quality of clustering and could be used to evaluate the results of the algorithms used. These same metrics could then be used to optimize the hyperparameters of the models fit by the algorithms. Two metrics were chosen as part of this work, DBCV [26] and Silhouette Score [27]. These metrics are the minimum set needed to get an overview of the internal structure of the data and to evaluate the clustering algorithms under consideration. DBCV considers both density and structural features of clusters, assuming their arbitrary shape (e.g., non-convex), and is also able to deal with noise points, which is important for HDBSCAN. Silhouette Score in turn assumes convex compact clusters. Using the two metrics together gives a general idea of the convexity/non-convexity of the clusters and the consistency of the algorithms' assumptions about the structure of the data. Both metrics, moreover, have the same range of values $[-1, 1]$ and in both cases higher values of the metric mean better clustering.

Based on these metrics, we can optimize the hyperparameters of each clustering method by maximizing each of the metrics. The Tree-Structured Parzen Estimator (TPE) method [28] is well suited for this purpose. TPE is a versatile and widely used hyperparameter optimization method that outperforms simpler Random Search and Grid Search due to the probabilistic model of the target function after each iteration [29, 30]. TPE iteratively models the probability distribution of the best performing hyperparameters based on previous trials. It identifies priority regions of the hyperparameter space that are more likely to yield good (in terms of the metrics being optimized) clusters, which significantly reduces the number of evaluations required for convergence to optimal configurations. In convergence, the results of TPE are better than those of Random Search and Grid Search.

Thus, the use of TPE within the study allowed us to select the optimal set of hyperparameters for each clustering model, maximizing the values of the selected metrics. At the same time, the target function was further modified to impose constraints on the resulting clustering models during optimization. First, separately for HDBSCAN, a constraint on the fraction of noise points was imposed - no more than 35%. Second, for all algorithms, a test for statistical significance of the resulting clustering was added ($p < 0.005$).

For the spectral and agglomerative clustering methods, a label reassignment test was conducted using Silhouette Score as the clustering quality metric. Here, the null hypothesis $H0$ states that there is no internal clustering structure, and any observed score of the metric is not different from the scores obtained by randomly reassigning the labels of the clusters (while preserving the noise assignments). By repeatedly reassigning labels and re-calculating the metric, a null distribution is formed. The P-value is determined by the fraction of permutation estimates that are the same or higher, than the observed estimate. A significant result supports the alternative hypothesis that the clustering structure is non-random and statistically significant.

For HDBSCAN, a data-level statistical significance test was used with DBCV as a validation metric. The null hypothesis $H0$ states that the clustering structure revealed by HDBSCAN is no better than the structure derived from the uniformly distributed data. In other words, the observed clusters are neither denser nor more separable than the clusters found in the random data. To test this assertion, null data sets were generated from a uniform sample within the observed data boundaries, and each was clustered using HDBSCAN to calculate the corresponding DBCV value. A right-sided test of the observed DBCV value from the original clustering was then performed using the generated empirical distribution. A low p-value would indicate that the observed clustering pattern was statistically significant, thereby rejecting H0 in favor of the alternative hypothesis that the observed clustering quality exceeds what would be expected by chance.

It is worth noting that the optimization was performed using both metrics simultaneously, in other words, the optimization was multi-objective. Since in such a case there can be many optimal combinations of hyperparameters, each set of which corresponds to one of the compromise solutions (Pareto front), for simplicity in such a case two sets of hyperparameters were selected, each of which would achieve the maximum value of one of the metrics. At the same time, the value of the second metric was not taken into account in this approach.

2.8   Clustering and Testing the Stability of Clusters

Determining the optimal parameters that maximize the selected metrics allows us to perform clustering using the methods described above more efficiently. But before giving an example of clustering algorithms' performance after all the preparatory works, it is also worth describing the last step of validation of clustering results, applied to the results of the model with the best hyperparameters. The last test is the validation of clusters for stability.

The clustering robustness test evaluates the robustness and reproducibility of the clustering solution by generating bootstrap samples. For each of several bootstrap iterations, a random subsample of data is clustered using the same algorithm, and the cluster labels are aggregated for each data point present in that iteration. Each pair of clustered subsamples is then compared using Adjusted Rand Index (ARI) and Adjusted Mutual Information (AMI) [31, 32].

ARI and AMI are widely used normalized metrics for comparing clustering results that are invariant to label permutation. Both metrics range from 0 (no agreement) to 1 (complete agreement) and make allowance for randomness, which is very important when assessing stability. High ARI or AMI values indicate that cluster distributions are replicated across subsamples, indicating that the underlying cluster structure is reliable. Stability is important for research because it is evidence that the clusters found are not artifacts of random sampling or parameter selection, but reflect stable patterns in the data.

3   Example of Analysis

Let us consider the clustering results and some summary tables describing the distribution of patients within clusters based on clinical diagnoses. We will not consider all the experiments, since describing the results of each of them would be too cumbersome. We will give two examples. The first is on a subsample of EEG, and the second is with a subsample of EEG + EEG_sumup + MRI.

3.1   Example 1. Clustering of a Subsample of EEG

PCA is used to first reduce the sample dimensionality to 50 principal components, preserving in this case 97% of the variance in the data. Next, the MLE-estimator is used to calculate the internal dimensionality, which determines that it is equal to 6. The hyperparameters of the clustering models are then optimized and the clustering with the best set of hyperparameters is applied on the data. The clustering is done in 6-dimensional space. After that, to get a visual representation of the result, two graphs of 3D projection of the data are plotted with point markup according to the clustering results. The projection in both cases is generated using UMAP. The first plot shows the mapping of the six-dimensional space into a three-dimensional space, i.e. UMAP, when building the low-level vector representation (embedding), optimizes the already optimized data structure obtained after the first application of UMAP. This sequential mapping of the data may lead to some artifacts in the 3D case, but better demonstrates the structure of the space in which the clustering was performed. The second graph will be a direct mapping of the 50-dimensional space obtained immediately after the application of PCA into the three-dimensional space, labeling the points with the same cluster labels. This graph aims more at showing the clustering results in a space closer to the initial data structure. Considering that PCA was used to remove noise in the data and remove low-information features while preserving most of the variance, displaying this particular representation of the data seems logical. In addition to the visual representation, cluster stability analysis (which was not performed during the optimization phase) is performed, key metrics are calculated, and two summary tables containing the distribution of patients into clusters based on clinical diagnoses are displayed. The first table shows the proportion of patients of each diagnosis in each individual cluster, while the second table shows the distribution of patients of each diagnosis across clusters. An example visualization of the clustering of the selected subsample, as well as the metrics and (merged) supporting tables, are presented in Figs. 2–3 and Tables 3, 4 and 5. The order of diagnoses in the column of patient distribution across clusters is the same for all of the following tables: Alzheimer's disease, dementia, depression, vascular dementia, control group and Parkinson's disease, if presented.

In addition to the clustering visualization and summary table, the most informative features for each cluster were identified, and the distributions of data values for the features within each individual cluster were visualized to see how the values of the features forming differ from cluster to cluster. To assess the importance of the traits for each cluster, Mutual Information (MI) was calculated between each feature and the binary indicator of membership in each individual cluster. Mutual Information is well suited for this task, as it captures both linear and non-linear dependencies without assuming any particular distribution of the data [33]. To account for the differences in uncertainty inherent in clusters, MI estimates were normalized by the entropy of the cluster's binary label. This normalization brings MI to a range [0, 1], which facilitates interpretation by showing the fraction of the maximum possible information contained in each feature [34]. A graph with the most informative features, defined in the above-described way, for each cluster for the two algorithms is shown in Fig. 4.

3.2 Example 2. Clustering of Intersection of All Results

Lastly, we examine the results of analyzing the subsample with the smallest number of patients and the largest initial feature space. To avoid cluttering of graphs and tables, let us consider only the most visually interesting clustering and distribution of patients into clusters, as well as the obtained metrics for all three algorithms. We will omit the list of the most informative features of each cluster and compare it with clustering of other algorithms.

The visualization shows the clustering results using the spectral clustering algorithm. As can be seen in Fig. 5, the algorithm was able to identify three clusters in the data. And on the left plot of the Fig. 5 it is noticeable that each of the clusters is mostly located in one of the corners of the figure formed by all points. The zero cluster, judging by the same visualization, is better separated from the other two clusters. If we look on the right plot of the same Figure, we can conclude that all clusters are convex or almost convex. With the exception of cluster 1, which is slightly bulging toward cluster zero, no

3D with UMAP hdbscan   3D with UMAP (direct projection) hdbscan

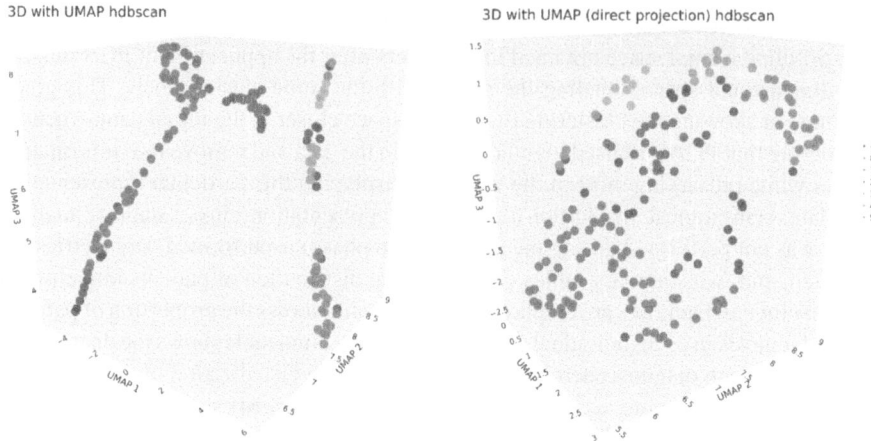

Fig. 2. Visualization of clustering results using HDBSCAN

3D with UMAP agglomerative   3D with UMAP (direct projection) agglomerative

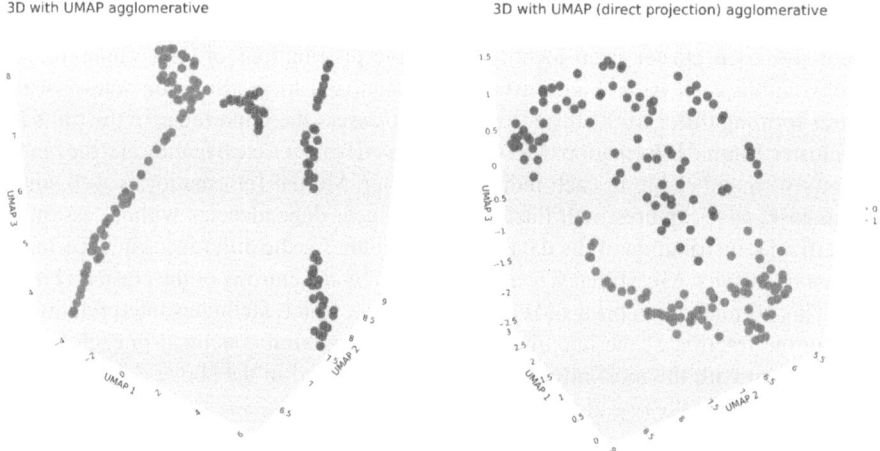

Fig. 3. Visualization of clustering results using Agglomerative Clustering

other "intersections" are visually apparent. The assumption that the clusters are convex is confirmed by the relatively high value of the Silhouette Score metric. It is noteworthy that in the resulting clustering we managed to identify a cluster that included 60% of patients with clinical diagnosis of Alzheimer's disease. The sizes of the clusters were almost identical (Figs. 6, 7 and Tables 6, 7).

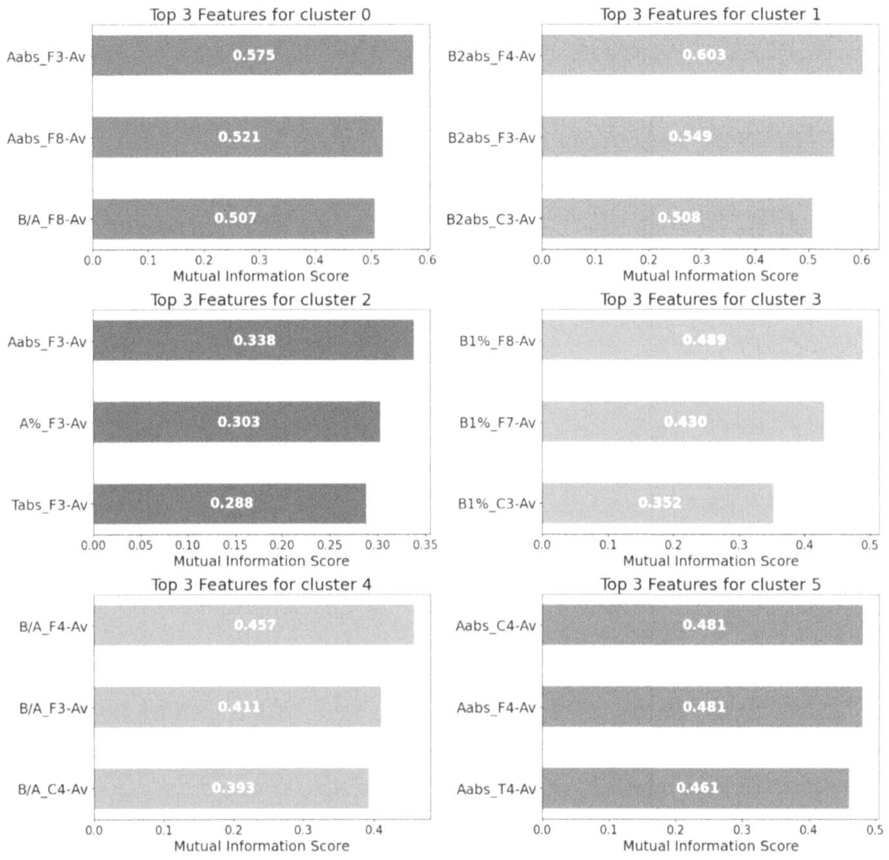

Top 3 Features for cluster 0

Aabs_F3-Av 0.575
Aabs_F8-Av 0.521
B/A_F8-Av 0.507

0.0   0.1   0.2   0.3   0.4   0.5   0.6
Mutual Information Score

Top 3 Features for cluster 1

B2abs_F4-Av 0.603
B2abs_F3-Av 0.549
B2abs_C3-Av 0.508

0.0   0.1   0.2   0.3   0.4   0.5   0.6
Mutual Information Score

Top 3 Features for cluster 2

Aabs_F3-Av 0.338
A%_F3-Av 0.303
Tabs_F3-Av 0.288

0.00   0.05   0.10   0.15   0.20   0.25   0.30   0.35
Mutual Information Score

Top 3 Features for cluster 3

B1%_F8-Av 0.489
B1%_F7-Av 0.430
B1%_C3-Av 0.352

0.0   0.1   0.2   0.3   0.4   0.5
Mutual Information Score

Top 3 Features for cluster 4

B/A_F4-Av 0.457
B/A_F3-Av 0.411
B/A_C4-Av 0.393

0.0   0.1   0.2   0.3   0.4
Mutual Information Score

Top 3 Features for cluster 5

Aabs_C4-Av 0.481
Aabs_F4-Av 0.481
Aabs_T4-Av 0.461

0.0   0.1   0.2   0.3   0.4   0.5
Mutual Information Score

Fig. 4. Most informative features of HDBSCAN clusters

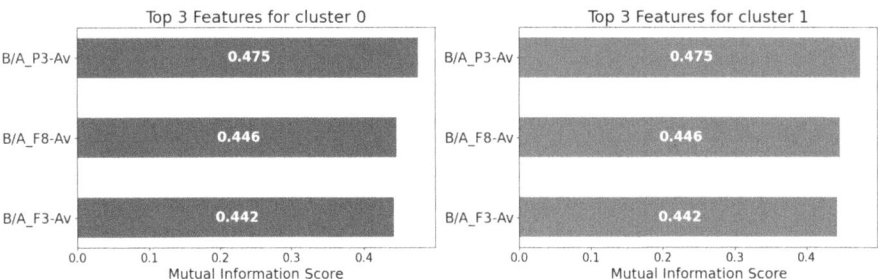

Top 3 Features for cluster 0

B/A_P3-Av 0.475
B/A_F8-Av 0.446
B/A_F3-Av 0.442

0.0   0.1   0.2   0.3   0.4
Mutual Information Score

Top 3 Features for cluster 1

B/A_P3-Av 0.475
B/A_F8-Av 0.446
B/A_F3-Av 0.442

0.0   0.1   0.2   0.3   0.4
Mutual Information Score

Fig. 5. Most informative features of agglomerative clustering clusters

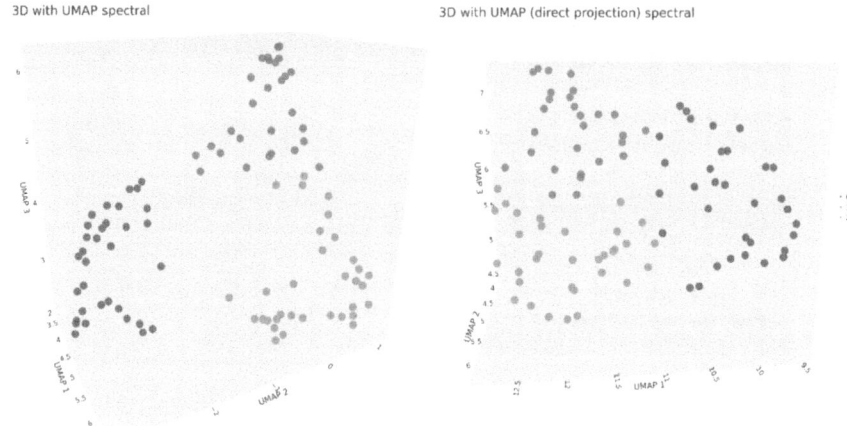

Fig. 6. Visualization of clustering results using Spectral Clustering

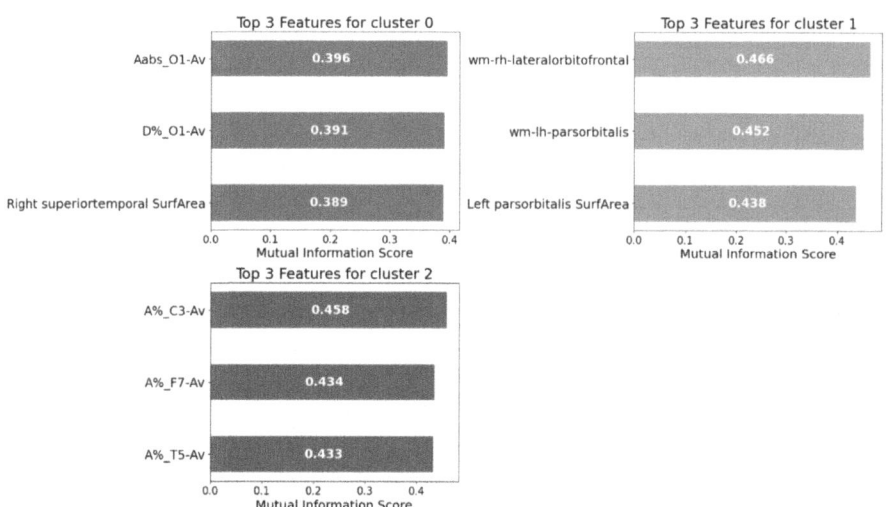

Fig. 7. Most informative features of spectral clustering clusters

Table 6. Distribution of patients by cluster using Spectral Clustering

Cluster Label	No. of cases	No. of Clinician Diagnoses in clusters	Clinician Diagnoses Across Clusters (%)	Clinician Diagnoses Within Clusters (%)
0	33	15/3/6/5/4	60.0/33.3/28.6/29.4/18.2	45.5/9.1/18.2/15.2/12.1
1	28	4/3/7/6/8	16.0/33.3/33.3/35.3/36.4	14.3/10.7/25.0/21.4/28.6
2	33	6/3/8/6/10	24.0/33.3/38.1/35.3/45.5	18.2/9.1/24.2/18.2/30.3

Table 7. Percentage labeled, metrics and cluster stability scores (EEG + EEG_sumup + MRI)

Algorithm	Labeled (%)	DBCV	Silhouette	ARI	AMI
HDBSCAN	70.21	0.25	0.25	0.66	0.72
Agglomerative	100.00	0.22	0.34	0.51	0.51
Spectral	100.00	-0.06	0.40	0.85	0.85

4   Conclusion

Analyzing medical data, especially in the context of neurodegenerative diseases such as Alzheimer's disease, is challenging with limited sample size and high dimensionality. This paper discusses a methodological approach to tackle this problem, focusing on data preprocessing, dimensionality reduction and clustering techniques. The clustering results, although not interpreted in terms of subject matter in this study, highlight the potential for generating new hypotheses about disease biomarkers. By using PCA and UMAP for dimensionality reduction and optimizing the clustering algorithms, the proposed approach effectively handles data sparsity while preserving meaningful structures in the data. These methods have the potential to identify novel biomarkers for the diagnosis of Alzheimer's disease without resorting to invasive procedures. Continued research on larger, more diverse datasets and additional biomarkers will be critical to improve these methods and make them effective clinical tools for early detection and prevention of severe Alzheimer's disease.

It is important to acknowledge, however, that the proposed methodology is not intended as a universal solution. The findings are based on a single, institution-specific dataset. As a result, direct generalization to other datasets – even within the same domain – should be approached with caution. Nevertheless, the broader concept of structured, sequential data processing, with an emphasis on intermediate validation and data-driven decision-making, offers a flexible framework. With appropriate adaptation, this approach may be applicable to similar medical research efforts and even extend to other domains where complex, high-dimensional datasets are encountered.

References

1. Li, X., Feng, X., Sun, X., Hou, N., Han, F., Liu, Y.: Global, regional, and national burden of Alzheimer's disease and other dementias, 1990–2019. Front. Aging Neurosci. **14**, 937486 (2022)
2. GBD 2019 Dementia Forecasting Collaborators: Estimation of the global prevalence of dementia in 2019 and forecasted prevalence in 2050: an analysis for the Global Burden of Disease Study 2019. Lancet Public Health **7**, e105–e125 (2022)
3. Alzheimer's disease facts and figures: Alzheimers Dement. **20**(5), 3708–3821 (2024)
4. Alzheimer's Disease International: World Alzheimer's Report 2015: The Global Impact of Dementia. Alzheimer's Disease International (2015), https://www.alzint.org/resource/world-alzheimer-report-2015/, last accessed 2025/03/16
5. Hardy-Sosa, A., León-Arcia, K., Llibre-Guerra, J.J., et al.: Diagnostic accuracy of blood-based biomarker panels: a systematic review. Front. Aging Neurosci. **14**, 683689 (2022)

6. Brand, A.L., Lawler, P.E., Bollinger, J.G., et al.: The performance of plasma amyloid beta measurements in identifying amyloid plaques in Alzheimer's disease: a literature review. Alz Res Therapy **14**, 195 (2022)

7. Barthélemy, N.R., Salvadó, G., Schindler, S.E., et al.: Highly accurate blood test for Alzheimer's disease is similar or superior to clinical cerebrospinal fluid tests. Nat. Med. **30**, 1085–1095 (2024)

8. Park, S.A., Jang, Y.J., Kim, M.K., et al.: Promising blood biomarkers for clinical use in Alzheimer's disease: a focused update. J. Clin. Neurol. **18**(4), 401–409 (2022)

9. Krix, S., Wilczynski, E., Falgàs, N., et al.: Towards early diagnosis of Alzheimer's disease: advances in immune-related blood biomarkers and computational approaches. Front. Immunol. **15**, 1343900 (2024)

10. Hastie, T., Tibshirani, R., Friedman, J.: The Elements of Statistical Learning: Data Mining, Inference, and Prediction, 2nd edn. Springer, New York (2009)

11. van der Ploeg, T., Austin, P.C., Steyerberg, E.W.: Modern modelling techniques are data hungry: a simulation study for predicting dichotomous endpoints. BMC Med. Res. Methodol. **14**, 137 (2014)

12. Silvey, S., Liu, J.: Sample size requirements for popular classification algorithms in tabular clinical data: an empirical study. J. Med. Internet Res. **26** (2024)

13. Andreev, E., Ananieva, N., Zalutskaya, N., Beltceva, I.A., Neznanov, N.: Use of the voxel-based morphometry method in the diagnosis of dementia of the Alzheimer type. V.M. BEKHTEREV REVIEW OF PSYCHIATRY AND MEDICAL PSYCHOLOGY (4), 66–72 (2017)

14. Lemoine, B., Rayburn, S., Benton, R.: Data fusion and feature selection for Alzheimer's diagnosis. In: Overgaard, N.C., Smedegaard, A.Ø., Rendsvig, R.K. (eds.) Medical Information Extraction and Mining, LNCS, vol. 6232, pp. 320–327. Springer, Heidelberg (2010)

15. Korkhov, V., et al.: Data storage, processing and analysis system to support brain research. In: Gervasi, O., et al. (eds.) Computational Science and Its Applications – ICCSA 2018, LNCS, vol 1 10943, pp. 78–90. Springer, Cham (2018)

16. Ros, F., Riad, R.: Feature and Dimensionality Reduction for Clustering with Deep Learning, 1st edn. Springer, Cham (2024)

17. Levina, E., Bickel, P.J.: Maximum Likelihood estimation of intrinsic dimension. In: Proceedings of the 18th International Conference on Neural Information Processing Systems, pp. 777–784. MIT Press, Cambridge (2004)

18. McInnes, L., Healy, J., Melville, J.: UMAP: uniform manifold approximation and projection for dimension reduction. arXiv:1802.03426 (2018)

19. Chari, T., Pachter, L.: The Specious Art of Single-Cell Genomics. bioRxiv (2022)

20. Castellano-Escuder, P., Zachman, D.K., Han, K., Hirschey, M.D.: Interpretable multi-omics integration with UMAP embeddings and density-based clustering. bioRxiv (2024)

21. Busch, E.L., et al.: Multi-view manifold learning of human brain state trajectories. bioRxiv (2022)

22. Diaz-Papkovich, A., Anderson-Trocmé, L., Gravel, S.: A review of UMAP in population genetics. J. Hum. Genet. **66**, 85–91 (2021)

23. Campello, R.J.G.B., Moulavi, D., Sander, J.: Density-based clustering based on hierarchical density estimates. In: Pei, J., Tseng, V.S., Cao, L., Motoda, H., Xu, G. (eds) Advances in Knowledge Discovery and Data Mining. PAKDD 2013. LNCS, vol. 7819. Springer, Heidelberg (2013)

24. McInnes, L., Healy, J.: Accelerated Hierarchical Density Clustering. arXiv:1705.07321 (2017)

25. Wierzchoń, S., Kłopotek, M.: Modern Algorithms of Cluster Analysis, 1st edn. Springer, Cham (2018)

26. Moulavi, D., Jaskowiak, P.A., Campello, R.J.G.B., Zimek, A., Sander, J.: Density-based clustering validation. In: Proceedings of the 2014 SIAM International Conference on Data Mining (SDM), pp. 839–847. SIAM, Philadelphia (2014)

27. Rousseeuw, P.J.: Silhouettes: a graphical aid to the interpretation and validation of cluster analysis. J. Comput. Appl. Math. **20**(1), 53–65 (1987)

28. Bergstra, J., Bardenet, R., Kégl, B., Bengio, Y.: Algorithms for hyper-parameter optimization. In: Shawe-Taylor, J., Zemel, R.S., Bartlett, P.L., Pereira, F., Weinberger, K.Q. (eds.) Advances in Neural Information Processing Systems 24, pp. 2546–2554. Curran Associates Inc, Red Hook (2011)

29. Watanabe, S.: Tree-Structured Parzen Estimator: Understanding Its Algorithm Components and Their Roles for Better Empirical Performance. arXiv:2304.11127 (2023)

30. Turner, R., et al.: Bayesian Optimization is Superior to Random Search for Machine Learning Hyperparameter Tuning: Analysis of the Black-Box Optimization Challenge 2020. arXiv: 2104.10201 (2021)

31. Romano, S., Vinh, N.X., Bailey, J., Verspoor, K.: Adjusting for Chance Clustering Comparison Measures. arXiv:1512.01286 (2015)

32. Vinh, N.X., Epps, J., Bailey, J.: Information theoretic measures for clusterings comparison: variants, properties, normalization and correction for chance. J. Mach. Learn. Res. **11**, 2837–2854 (2010)

33. La, V., Lee, S., Park, Y.T., d'Auriol, B.: A novel feature selection method based on normalized mutual information. Appl. Intell. **37**(2), 219–237 (2012)

34. Nagel, D., Diez, G., Stock, G.: Accurate estimation of the normalized mutual information of multidimensional data. J. Chem. Phys. **161**(5), 054107 (2024)

Sustainable evolution of long-Distance frEight and paSsenger Transport (SOLIDEST 2025)

Mode Choice at National Level: Revealed and Stated Preference Survey for High-Speed Rail Realization

Francesco Russo⬤ and Marialuisa Moschella⁽⊠⁾ ⬤

DIIES, Università Mediterranea of Reggio Calabria, 89100 Reggio Calabria, Italy
marialuisa.moschella@unirc.it

Abstract. The high-speed rail (HSR) system is becoming increasingly important, on a world scale, for national travel. Some 130.000 km of lines are built in operation or under planning/construction. In the realization of new lines or in the improvement of existing ones to bring them up to a high-speed level it is increasingly important to study the passenger demand and therefore the distribution between the available modes. It is therefore necessary to provide accurate surveys that allow for immediately usable statistics or develop appropriate behavioral models.

Attention is therefore given to the way in which the structure of the survey to be carried out, which must contain both the acquisition of information of type Revealed Preference and of type Stated.

The result obtained is a first structure which has been subjected to a prototype sample. The survey has been tested in South of Italy, where is proposed the realisation of a HSR line.

Based on the results obtained with the prototype, the different sections are updated, in particular those relating to SP information for planned lines.

The interpretation of the result is particularly important because the structure established allows an ex-ante analysis of the questions to be asked by the respondents in relation to the specifications of the induced demand of the various levels to be obtained, and which are not available in literature because of their complexity.

The result is interesting for analysts, for planners and researchers because it defines a structure that can be used or appropriately modified in relation to the study to be carried out in a reality where HSR has to be built or where an upgrade of the conventional line to HSR is planned.

Keywords: mode choice · High Speed Rail (HSR) · Revealed Preference (RP) · Stated Preference (SP) · Survey · Demand analysis

1 Introduction

The environmental, social and economic benefits of high-speed rail (HSR) infrastructure are driving the opening of new lines around the world. In line with Agenda 2030 goals, HSR contributes to promote the energy efficiency and to afford the sustainability challenges by reducing environmental impact in terms of CO2 emissions [1, 2]. In addition

© The Author(s), under exclusive license to Springer Nature Switzerland AG 2026
O. Gervasi et al. (Eds.): ICCSA 2025 Workshops, LNCS 15894, pp. 359–374, 2026.
https://doi.org/10.1007/978-3-031-97648-3_24

to its environmental benefits, HSR transport plays a strategic role for the economic and social development, contributing to Gross Domestic Product (GDP) growth and economic competitiveness, and promoting social inclusion. For instance, HSR service is known to facilitate the access to job opportunities and essential services and to improve the connection between the most underdeveloped areas with the main centers [3–11].

The 9th Report on Economic, Social and Territorial Cohesion of the European Commission highlights how the improvement of transport networks is crucial for reducing territorial disparities within the European Union. In regions such as Southern Italy, Greece, Spain and Eastern Europe, per capita GDP is currently less than 75% of the EU average, and the lack of infrastructure is one of the main barriers to economic growth [12]. HSR has been recognized as one of the most important infrastructure solutions for reducing territorial inequalities, taking its place in the European TEN-T (Trans-European Transport Network) regulations [13, 14] that aim to distribute transport infrastructure across Europe through the planning of strategic corridors and priority projects. The significant reduction in travel times has led many states around the world to invest in HSR networks with the prospect of extending the current 59.000 km of lines with an additional 70.000 km [15]. However, the implementation of an HSR network brings up issues of social equity, as increased accessibility does not always mean a reduction in territorial inequalities.

Several studies analyzed the effects of HSR on social inclusion, highlighting the link between accessibility and distribution of economic benefits [16]. Accessibility is a key variable in the interaction between land use and transport and is defined as the ease with which people or goods can reach certain destinations [17]. While greater accessibility facilitates the connection between territories and increases economic growth, the experience of countries such as China and Spain has demonstrated that the implementation of HSR lines can also increase economic disparities between urban and rural areas [18–21]. Indeed, in cities directly served by HSR there is an increase in economic competitiveness, while areas excluded from HSR face demographic and social decline. In some contexts, HSR has accentuated the gap between the main urban centers and the peripheral ones worsening economic inequality [16].

This aspect emerges clearly in the Italian context where the economic gap between North and South is accentuated by differences in access to transport infrastructure [14, 22]. The presence of an under-dimensioned transport network in Southern Italy is one of the main constraints for the growth of these areas, limiting economic opportunities and attractiveness for investments and productive activities. The planning and implementation of an HSR network in the Southern Italy represents a strategic priority, as it allows the integration of these regions into national and international economic flows [4].

For the new infrastructure to generate the expected benefits, it is essential to conduct a transport demand analysis to predict its impact on mobility. Analyzing travel demand means estimating three components (Fig. 1) [23]:

- Diverted demand, which estimates the shift of users from other modes of transport or services to HSR. It is influenced by endogenous factors such as fares, frequency of service and, above all, travel time, which is the major factor in competitiveness between modes. As it involves a change in modal or service choice for existing users, mode-service models are used to estimate diverted demand using data collected on Revealed Preferences (current situation) and Stated Preferences (assumed future situation);

- Induced demand, which estimates the increase in travel frequency on a given origin–destination pair or the change of final destination by the same users who travelled before the introduction of the high-speed service. It is closely linked to the improvement of spatial accessibility, made possible by an improvement in service levels such as increased speed, which results in a significant reduction in travel time. It leads to a net increase in mobility that may include additional travel for personal and professional reasons, which is why the induced demand is estimated with trip frequency and destination models based on stated user behaviour data with respect to a scenario not yet realised (SP);

- Economy growth demand, which estimates the new trips generated by the economic growth of the territory due to the introduction of the high-speed service. It is related to the interactions between transport and economic development and is not directly related to the improvement of transport services, but to the economic and social impacts generated over time by the presence of HSR. For this reason, it emerges in the long term as a result of structural changes in the territory and is estimated with Spatial Economic Transport Interaction (SETI) models.

In particular, induced demand represents an aspect which is still poorly investigated in the scientific literature but of crucial importance for assessing the medium- to long-term effects of HSR on passenger mobility [24].

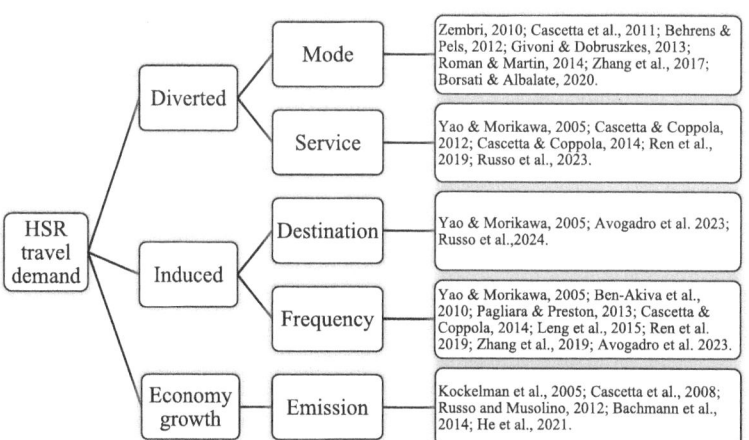

Fig. 1. HSR travel demand component.

Another key element in the study of demand concerns the evolution of HSR services. Four operational models exist according to [45] (Fig. 2), the 'exclusive exploitation' model where HSR and conventional trains have a separate infrastructure, the 'mixed high-speed' model where HSR trains run on dedicated sections and conventional lines, the 'mixed conventional' model where conventional trains run on dedicated sections and high-speed lines, the 'fully mixed conventional' model where HSR and conventional trains run on both dedicated and non-dedicated sections.

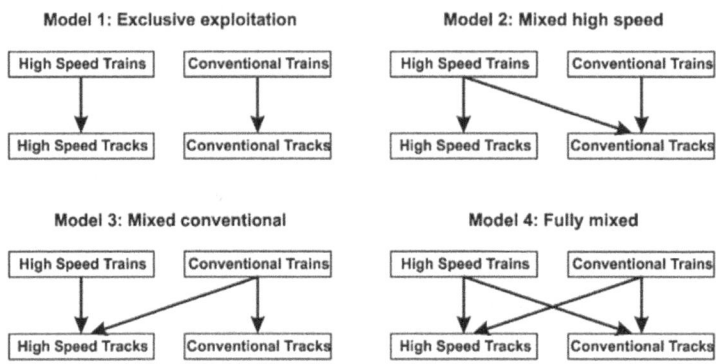

Fig. 2. HSR operational models [45].

Currently, many HSR networks operate in a mixed context, with high-speed trains running on both dedicated lines and conventional infrastructure (Model 2). The introduction of a new specially built HSR line, which is designed for speeds equal or higher than 250 km/h according to the EU 2016/797 European Directive [46], may change the demand structure by increasing the attractiveness of the service. The realization of the line leads to a decisive evolution of services from Model 2 to Model 1. This transition involves a drastic reduction in time distances for the same spatial distances. Furthermore, HSR becomes competitive with air transport up to distances of around 1000 km [28].

The methodological approach used to estimate transport demand involves collecting information on the travel behavior of users before the new infrastructure is built and on the behavior they would adopt after the infrastructure is built. To apply the methodology, the class of Revealed Preference (RP) surveys, which are useful for analyzing actual user behavior in the current transport system, are combined with Stated Preference (SP) surveys, which explore user choices in hypothetical but also realistic scenarios.

The objective of this paper is to provide a methodological structure for the realization of questionnaires on Revealed and Stated Preferences in order to collect the necessary data for applying both descriptive and behavioral Transport System Models (TSMs) [47, 48]. TSMs need general formulations [47, 48] and specific advancement for supply [49–51] and demand [24, 36, 52–54]. Hence, current and future travel demand can be estimated with particular reference to the diverted and induced demand components that emerge in the short and medium term respectively after the implementation of HSR lines.

This work is addressed to transport analysts and planners, as it provides the tools to carry out a survey that can be reproduced in any socio-economic context, and is structured as follows: Sect. 2 presents the description of the methodology for the design of a mixed RP/SP survey; Sect. 3 describes the experimental survey conducted in Southern Italy; Sect. 4 summarizes the objectives and results of the research.

2   Methodology for Survey Design

2.1   Travel Demand Models Considered in the Study

The methodology for analysing travel demand is based on the survey structures available in the literature and on various attributes considered important from a social, economic and modal point of view which are reported or not in the literature. Current and future demand can be estimated by applying models belonging to the class of TSMs, which also include models used to study supply and the interaction between supply and demand [47, 48]. The mathematical models in the literature belong to two categories that differ according to the approach used to forecast demand. Models based on statistical-descriptive approaches to analyze the relationships between socio-economic attributes and transport demand give an aggregate estimate of travel demand, useful for large-scale analyses. Whilst, models based on a probabilistic-behavioral approach to simulate user choices follow the discrete choice theory, generating a disaggregated demand estimate, which makes them suitable for the study of competition between different transport modes or services. Random utility models (RUM), fuzzy utility models (FUM) and quantum utility models (QUM) belong to this category [55–65]. The study presented in this paper takes place within the context of the MOST - spoke 4 project, which focuses on both demand [24, 36, 53, 54, 66, 67] and supply [7, 50, 52, 68–75] analysis of HSR services.

Data required for calibration of demand models are obtained from information on actual user choices in the current transport context and their decisions in hypothetical scenarios involving the introduction of new infrastructures. This information is gathered by conducting combined RP/SP surveys of representative samples of users of the transport system.

2.2   Revealed Preferences (RP) and Stated Preferences (SP) Survey

The RP and SP questionnaires must contain specific questions for investigating user behavior in relation to different alternative choices presented in different contexts. In RP questionnaires, respondents are asked to answer specific questions about their real journeys, such as origin and destination of the trip, the schedule, the mode of transport and the followed path. These data allow the calibration of demand models representative of actual user behavior (Table 1). On the other hand, SP questionnaires present to the respondents hypothetical scenarios with different variables, such as cost, travel time or frequency of a service. Such data allow to estimate how users will react to changes in the transport system, analyzing the impact of alternatives not yet available (Table 2). Moreover, SP surveys allow to investigate different components of induced demand, as well as the most common and widespread components of diverted demand.

Both types of surveys have advantages and disadvantages. RP provides fairly accurate information reflecting reality. However, they present a critical issue concerning the time and cost of conduction. With regards to SP surveys, a significant advantage is the possibility of collecting more information with the same cost and time, as each respondent is generally presented with several choice scenarios. However, these surveys are limited by the reliability of the answers, which may be influenced by the discrepancy between the hypothesized scenarios and the actual behavior of users in the future.

Table 1. Classification of information to be included in the RP questionnaire.

Data	Question	Purpose
Socio-economic	- Gender and age	Sample segmentation by demographic categories
	- Residence	Analyzing the relationship between travel choices and residence location
	- Education level	Assessing the influence of income on travel choices
	- Employment	Analyzing the relationship between travel choices and job profile
	- Economic indicators (n. of household members cars owned…)	Sample segmentation by expenditure potential categories
Travel habits	- Origin–Destination pair	Identify the different origins and destinations of travel to define flows
	- Trip purpose	Identify the main purposes of travel on the O-D pair
	- Frequency of travel	Quantifying existing demand
Current transport choices	- Transport mode	Identify the current modal split
	- Travel period	Analyzing the relationship between the transport choice and the period in which the travel occurs
	- Cost of travel	Assessing the economic and time impact on travel behavior
	- Factors influencing choice of transport mode (level of service, cost refund…)	Identify critical variables in the choice of transport

2.3 Modification of Attributes

As mentioned above, the scenarios presented in the SP questionnaire are characterized by different attribute values. Since each scenario represents a combination of relevant attributes, it is necessary to identify in advance the most significant attributes, the levels associated with each attribute, and whether the choice involves different transport modes (between modes) or different configurations of the same mode (within modes) [76–80]. The total number of possible combinations of attributes and levels can be extremely large. This number (N) can be determined through the Complete Factorial Plan (CFP)

Table 2. Classification of information to be included in the SP questionnaire

Data	Question	Purpose
Socio-economic	(Same questions as RP questionnaire)	Coherence between the two datasets for comparison
Hypothetical transport choice scenarios	- Availability of a new transport mode or service	Identifying the future modal split and estimating diverted demand
	- Different time travel and fares scenarios in comparison with current alternatives	Measuring the impact of main variables on future demand
Future behavior	- Increase in travel frequency	Estimating induced demand
	- Variations in overall journey length	Assessing the effect on travel choices
	- Willingness to change the travel purpose, residence, job location	Measuring the impact of changes in life opportunities (e.g. work)

which combines the number of attributes (n_i) and the number of levels of each attribute (m_i).

$$N = \prod_{i=1}^{k} m_i^{n_i} \tag{1}$$

The number of scenarios, i.e. the combination of attributes of interest, increases with increasing number of attributes and levels. In case of a large number of scenarios, factorialisation (Factorialisation Fractal Plan, FFP) and subdivision of the scenarios into several groups can be applied. Factorialisation eliminates some scenarios while maintaining the orthogonality of attributes variations between scenarios. The orthogonality represent the independence among the variations of attributes in different scenarios, which is an essential condition for isolating and correctly estimating the effect of each attribute on the choice [77]. Block splitting allows all scenarios to be split into groups, so that each individual respondent can answer a different set of questions with a limited number of scenarios submitted [48].

3   Experimental Survey

Following the above discussion, this chapter presents the survey designed to analyze user choice behavior in relation to real and hypothetical travel options after the introduction of an HSR line along the Reggio Calabria-Salerno route in Southern Italy. To achieve this aim, the questionnaire is designed by integrating RP and SP approaches. This dual perspective makes it possible to analyze current travel preferences and predict potential behavioral changes after the introduction of HSR.

In Italy, the HSR railway system includes 921 km of operational lines, with an additional 327 km under construction [14, 15]. For the connection between Southern

Italy and Rome, the available transport modes include car, bus, plane, conventional train and a hybrid service combining high-speed trains on dedicated lines from Salerno to Rome and traditional lines from Reggio Calabria to Salerno [11, 49–51].

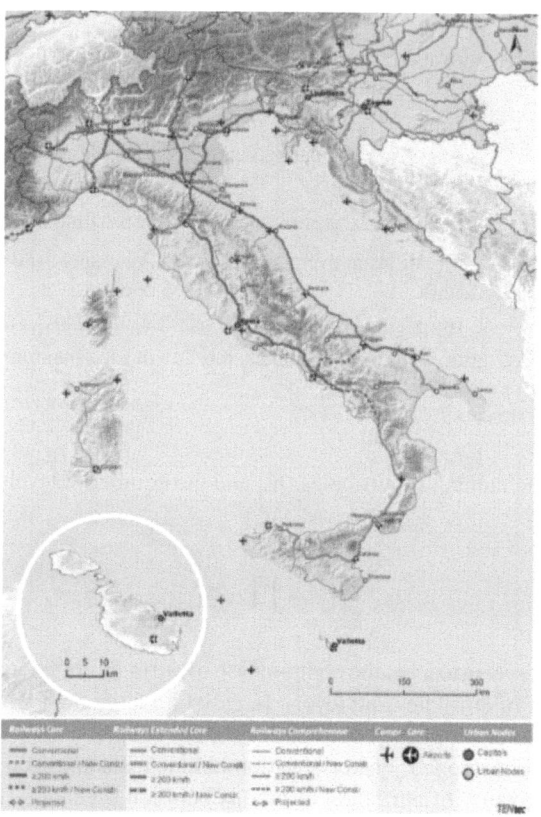

Fig. 3. Core, Extended Core and Comprehensive Networks: Rail Passengers, airports [14].

Figure 3 illustrates the current status of the high-speed railway network in Southern Italy. The segment already completed from Rome to Battipaglia is shown in purple, while the one currently under construction, from Battipaglia to Praia, is shown in dashed purple. Finally, the segment analysed in this study, which extends from Praia to Reggio Calabria, is shown in green.

This survey focuses on the hypothesis of a railway infrastructure for HSR trains directly connecting Reggio Calabria to Salerno, creating a continuous service.

The questionnaire is divided into four main sections, each designed to collect specific information (Fig. 4).

The first part has two sections constructed following the RP methodology. The first section collects the socio-economic profile of the user through questions investigating variables such as gender, age, education level, employment status, residence and domicile, family composition and number of cars owned. The second section aims to gather

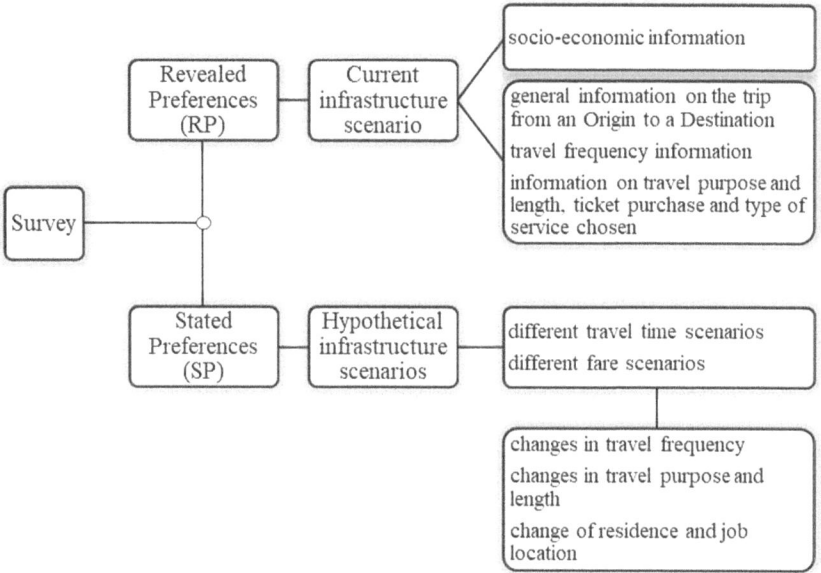

Fig. 4. Framework of the RP/SP survey.

information on the context in which the interview is conducted, including information on the place and date of the interview and the mode of transport being used. This section includes detailed questions about the current journey referring to travel purpose, travel frequency and length of stay at the destination. Both the two sections provide the basis for the analysis of current user behavior.

The second part of the survey is represented by the SP questionnaires. The Origin–Destination (O-D) pairs considered in the survey include connections between Rome and several cities in Southern Italy. The city of Rome (capital of Italy), represents the origin or destination of the trips. This part can be divided into two sections: the first one aims to estimate diverted demand and the second one the induced demand.

In order to estimate the diverted demand, two HSR train travel time scenarios with several fare scenarios are associated with each of the analyzed O-D pairs. The choice of the two travel times was determined on the basis of the meta-analysis of [28], which shows a direct correlation between travel time and preference for a specific transport mode. In addition, to investigate the market share of HSR, among the five alternatives available to connect the cities of southern Italy and Rome, a 10% and 20% increase in fares compared to current averages for air, conventional train and high-speed train modes is proposed to the interviewed users.

To realize the CFP explained in the previous chapter and compose the scenarios to be presented in the first part of the SP section, the fare attribute and three levels are chosen (current average fare, 10% and 20% increase). The FFP is applied to reduce the number of scenarios to be submitted to each respondent by eliminating the first-order interactions followed by the block splitting method. The final number of scenarios presented for each

O-D pair is thirty, subdivided into six groups, each comprising five fare scenarios that can be submitted to the individual user.

The second section of the SP questionnaire is dedicated to the estimation of induced demand and includes a series of questions to investigate the increase in frequency of trips for the same segment travelled in the RP part, the change in travel purpose and/or in length of stay at the destination, also possible new job and residence opportunities. Table 3 shows the results of the modal split of a pilot sample of users in the current situation for only one of the analyzed O-D pairs. These results derived from the data collected through the RP questionnaire (Table 1) with the aim of assessing the understanding of the questions and making some preliminary evaluations for testing the effectiveness of the methodology.

Table 3. Modal choice in current situation (RP)

Modal choice					
Socio-economic classification		Conventional train	Mixed HSR train	Air	Car
Gender	Male	22%	38%	24%	16%
	Female	18%	41%	18%	23%
Age	18–25	42%	28%	8%	22%
	26–45	-	60%	40%	-
	Over45	-	46%	35%	19%
Level of education	Graduate	38%	32%	8%	22%
	Master's degree	3%	46%	37%	14%
Employment status	Bachelor student	37%	32%	12%	19%
	Master's student				
	Ph.D student				
	Professor/Researcher	-	48%	36%	16%
	Employee				
Total		21%	39%	22%	18%

This prototypical survey has been useful for the construction of a survey including a larger and more significant number of participants interviewed at railway stations and airports in the selected cities to ensure adequate coverage of the target population. The interviewers follow a standardized protocol to ensure uniformity in data collection and consistency of responses. The questionnaires are divided according to the time scenarios presented in the SP sections and are only submitted to users travelling between the O-D pairs selected for the study. The data collected through the RP/SP survey are essential for the construction and calibration of descriptive and behavioral models, useful for estimating current and future demand for HSR services.

4 Conclusions

This study describes a methodology for building a survey to investigate the change in travel demand following the introduction of an HSR line in a territory. In order to study user behavior in the presence of modal alternatives not yet available, the survey collects RP information, relating to actual user behavior, and SP information, relating to scenarios not yet realized.

In particular, the survey investigates the impact on travel demand after the realization of a continuous HSR line between Reggio Calabria and Roma, which is currently served by a mixed system: HSR train with dedicated line from Salerno to Rome; HSR train with conventional line from Reggio Calabria to Salerno. The questionnaire is divided into two parts: the first one collects socio-economic information and details on the current journey (RP), the second one investigates preferences with respect to hypothetical future scenarios (SP). The purpose of the RP part is to study the actual behavior of users and to understand the factors influencing their transport choices in order to estimate the current travel demand. Whilst, the SP part aims to study user behavior in a future scenario in order to estimate diverted demand (shift from other modes or services to HSR) and induced demand (increase in travel frequency on the same O-D pair investigated in the RP). Two travel times are presented to the users of each selected O-D pair for the analysis of induced demand. For both of the travel times, thirty fare scenarios are generated, divided into six groups, obtained by increasing the value of the fares by 10% and 20% compared to current averages. Questions are asked to detect changes in travel frequency, travel length, travel purpose and job or residential opportunities.

Data collected can be used to develop aggregated and disaggregated forecast models belonging to the category of TSMs. These models are necessary to estimate future demand concerning HSR services, with particular regard to the induced demand component representing the net increase in travel on O-D fixed pairs, which is still poorly investigated in the existing literature.

Three types of future developments can be identified from the work performed. The first type concerns the implementation of the survey structure with a high sample size, verifying the goodness of the results already obtained. The second type concerns the possibility of calibrating diverted and induced models with different attribute structures. Finally, the third typology deals with the advancement of knowledge in the transition from full interview structures to reduced structures while maintaining orthogonality.

The methodology adopted makes it possible to analyze both the actual and the stated future behavior of users, to assess the impact of new infrastructures and to provide tools to support planning and decision-making in the transport sector. Thus, the integrated RP/SP approach allows a solid estimation of induced and diverted demand, which is crucial for the ex-ante evaluation of the effects of the realization of an HSR line in underdeveloped areas, such as Southern Italy.

Acknowledgements. This study was carried out within the MOST – Sustainable Mobility National Research

Center and received funding from the European Union Next-Generation EU (PIANO NAZIONALE DI RIPRESA E RESILIENZA (PNRR) – MISSIONE 4 COMPONENTE 2, INVESTIMENTO 1.4 – D.D. 1033 17/06/2022, CN00000023).

This manuscript reflects only the authors' views and opinions, neither the European Union nor the European Commission can be considered responsible for them.

References

s1.European Commission: Sustainable and Smart Mobility Strategy – putting European transport on track for the future, https://transport.ec.europa.eu/document/download/be22d311-4a07-4c29-8b72-d6d255846069_en?filename=2021-mobility-strategy-and-action-plan.pdf. (2021).

European Environment Agency: National emissions reported to the UNFCCC and to the EU Greenhouse Gas Monitoring Mechanism, April 2024, https://sdi.eea.europa.eu/catalogue/srv/api/records/6331f651-8863-4656-a911-669f2a332a1e?language=all. (2024). https://doi.org/10.2909/6331F651-8863-4656-A911-669F2A332A1E.

Santilli, G.: Italia divisa in due dalla Tav: Pil a +7% nelle città collegate, https://www.ilsole24ore.com/art/italia-divisa-due-tav-pil-7percento-citta-collegate-ACCZKIFB. (2020).

Russo, F.: Which high-speed rail? larg approach between plan and design. Future Transportation. 1, 202–226 (2021). https://doi.org/10.3390/futuretransp1020013

Raicu, S., Costescu, D., Popa, M., Dragu, V.: Dynamic Intercorrelations between transport/traffic infrastructures and territorial systems: from economic growth to sustainable development. Sustainability. 13, 11951 (2021). https://doi.org/10.3390/su132111951

He, S., Mei, L., Wang, L.: The dynamic influence of high-speed rail on the spatial structure of economic networks and the underlying mechanisms in northeastern china. IJGI. 10, 776 (2021). https://doi.org/10.3390/ijgi10110776

Praticò, F.G., Fedele, R.: Economic sustainability of high-speed and high-capacity railways. Sustainability. 15, 725 (2022). https://doi.org/10.3390/su15010725

Ji, C., Yao, Y., Duan, J., Li, W.: Sustainable mechanism of the entrusted transportation management mode on high-speed rail and the impact of covid-19: a case study of the beijing-shanghai high-speed rail. Sustainability. 14, 1171 (2022). https://doi.org/10.3390/su14031171

Li, D., Jiang, R., Lu, Z., Sun, S., Wang, L.: Does the construction of high-speed rail change the development of regional finance? Sustainability. 15, 10641 (2023). https://doi.org/10.3390/su151310641

Prakongwittaya, S., Liangrokapart, J.: Integrating LARG measures to improve supply chain transparency performance. Asia Pacific Manage. Rev. 30, 100324 (2025). https://doi.org/10.1016/j.apmrv.2024.09.002

Surmařová, S., Neumannová, M., Pařil, V., Vrána, M., Chmelík, J.: Do I really like to shift to rail? Influence of rail modernisation on passenger preferences. Res. Transport. Business Manage. 59, 101284 (2025). https://doi.org/10.1016/j.rtbm.2024.101284

European Commission: 9th Report on Economic, Social and Territorial Cohesion. (2024).

European Union: Regulation (EU) No 1315/2013 of the European Parliament and of the Council. (2013).

European Union: Regulation (EU) 2024/1679 of the European Parliament and of the Council. (2024).

UIC: High-Speed Rail Atlas 4 Edition. International Union of Railways (UIC) - Paris 2023 (2023).

Cascetta, E., Cartenì, A., Henke, I., Pagliara, F.: Economic growth, transport accessibility and regional equity impacts of high-speed railways in Italy: ten years ex post evaluation and future perspectives. Transport. Res. Part A: Policy Pract. 139, 412–428 (2020). https://doi.org/10.1016/j.tra.2020.07.008

Russo, F., Musolino, G.: A unifying modelling framework to simulate the Spatial Economic Transport Interaction process at urban and national scales. J. Transp. Geography. 24, 189–197 (2012). https://doi.org/10.1016/j.jtrangeo.2012.02.003

Monzón, A., Ortega, E., López, E.: Efficiency and spatial equity impacts of high-speed rail extensions in urban areas. Cities **30**, 18–30 (2013). https://doi.org/10.1016/j.cities.2011.11.002

Pagliara, F., Biggiero, L., Patrone, A., Peruggini, F.: An analysis of spatial equity concerning investments in high-speed rail systems: the case study of Italy. Transport Problems. 11, 55–68 (2016). https://doi.org/10.20858/tp.2016.11.3.6.

Biggiero, L., Pagliara, F., Patrone, A., Peruggini, F.: Spatial equity and high-speed rail systems. Int. J. TDI. **1**, 194–202 (2017). https://doi.org/10.2495/TDI-V1-N2-194-202

Yu, W., Yao, Y.: The Route of Development in intra-regional Income Equality via High-Speed Rail: Evidence from China. Agricultural&Applied Economics Association, Annual Meeting. Atlanta, GA, July, 21–23 (2019).

European Commission: 2019 European Semester: Country Reports and Communication - Italy. (2019).

Ben-Akiva, M., Cascetta, E., Coppola, P., Papola, P., Velardi, V.: High speed rail demand forecasting in a competitive market: the Italian case study. Presented at the (2010).

Russo, F., Moschella, M., Musolino, G.: Railway demand evaluation: HSR induced component. In: Gervasi, O., Murgante, B., Garau, C., Taniar, D., C. Rocha, A.M.A., and Faginas Lago, M.N. (eds.) Computational Science and Its Applications – ICCSA 2024 Workshops, pp. 173–187. Springer Nature Switzerland, Cham (2024). https://doi.org/10.1007/978-3-031-65318-6_12.

Zembri, P.: New objectives of the French high-speed rail system within the framework of a highly centralized network: a substitute for the domestic air transport market? Presented at the Collection of open conferences in research transport (2010) (2010).

Cascetta, E., Papola, A., Pagliara, F., Marzano, V.: Analysis of mobility impacts of the high speed Rome-Naples rail link using withinday dynamic mode service choice models. J. Transp. Geogr. **19**, 635–643 (2011). https://doi.org/10.1016/j.jtrangeo.2010.07.001

Behrens, C., Pels, E.: Intermodal competition in the London-Paris passenger market: High-Speed Rail and air transport. J. Urban Econom. **71**, 278–288 (2012). https://doi.org/10.1016/j.jue.2011.12.005

Givoni, M., Dobruszkes, F.: A review of ex-post evidence for mode substitution and induced demand following the introduction of high-speed rail. Transp. Rev. **33**, 720–742 (2013). https://doi.org/10.1080/01441647.2013.853707

Román, C., Martín, J.C.: Integration of HSR and air transport: understanding passengers' preferences. Transport. Res. Part E: Logist. Transport. Rev. **71**, 129–141 (2014). https://doi.org/10.1016/j.tre.2014.09.001

Zhang, Q., Yang, H., Wang, Q.: Impact of high-speed rail on China's Big Three airlines. Transport. Res. Part A: Policy Pract. **98**, 77–85 (2017). https://doi.org/10.1016/j.tra.2017.02.005

Borsati, M., Albalate, D.: On the modal shift from motorway to high-speed rail: evidence from Italy. Transport. Res. Part A: Policy Pract. **137**, 145–164 (2020). https://doi.org/10.1016/j.tra.2020.04.006

Yao, E., Morikawa, T.: A study of on integrated intercity travel demand model. Transport. Res. Part A: Policy Pract. **39**, 367–381 (2005). https://doi.org/10.1016/j.tra.2004.12.003

Cascetta, E., Coppola, P.: An elastic demand schedule-based multimodal assignment model for the simulation of high speed rail (HSR) systems. EURO J. Transport. Logist. **1**, 3–27 (2012). https://doi.org/10.1007/s13676-012-0002-0

Cascetta, E., Coppola, P.: Competition on fast track: an analysis of the first competitive market for HSR services. Proc. - Social Behav. Sci.. **111**, 176–185 (2014). https://doi.org/10.1016/j.sbspro.2014.01.050

Ren, X.,et al.: Impact of high-speed rail on intercity travel behavior change: The evidence from the Chengdu-Chongqing Passenger Dedicated Line. JTLU. 12, (2019). https://doi.org/10.5198/jtlu.2019.1302.

Russo, F., Sgro, D., Musolino, G.: Sustainable development of railway corridors: methods and models for High Speed Rail (HSR) demand analysis. In: Gervasi, O., Murgante, B., Rocha, A.M.A.C., Garau, C., Scorza, F., Karaca, Y., and Torre, C.M. (eds.) Computational Science and Its Applications – ICCSA 2023 Workshops. pp. 527–538. Springer Nature Switzerland, Cham (2023). https://doi.org/10.1007/978-3-031-37123-3_36.

Avogadro, N., Pels, E., Redondi, R.: Policy impacts on the propensity to travel by HSR in the Amsterdam – London market. Socio-Econom. Plann. Sci. **87**, 101585 (2023). https://doi.org/10.1016/j.seps.2023.101585

Pagliara, F., Preston, J.: An induced demand model for high speed 1 in UK. JTTs. **03**, 44–51 (2013). https://doi.org/10.4236/jtts.2013.31005

Cascetta, E., Coppola, P.: High Speed Rail (HSR) induced demand models. Proc. - Social Behav. Sci. **111**, 147–156 (2014). https://doi.org/10.1016/j.sbspro.2014.01.047

Leng, N., Nie, L., Guo, G., Wu, X.: Passenger flow forecasting for Chinese high speed rail network. In: Proceedings of the 2015 International Conference on Mechatronics, Electronic, Industrial and Control Engineering. Atlantis Press, Shenyang, China (2015). https://doi.org/10.2991/meic-15.2015.153.

Zhang, A., Wan, Y., Yang, H.: Impacts of high-speed rail on airlines, airports and regional economies: a survey of recent research. Transp. Policy **81**, A1–A19 (2019). https://doi.org/10.1016/j.tranpol.2019.06.010

Kockelman, K.M., Jin, L., Zhao, Y., Ruíz-Juri, N.: Tracking land use, transport, and industrial production using random-utility-based multiregional input–output models: applications for Texas trade. J. Transp. Geography. **13**, 275–286 (2005). https://doi.org/10.1016/j.jtrangeo.2004.04.009

Cascetta, E., Marzano, V., Papola, A.: Multi-regional input-output models for freight demand simulation at a national level. In: Ben-Akiva, M., Meersman, H., and Van De Voorde, E. (eds.) Recent Developments in Transport Modelling, pp. 93–116. Emerald Group Publishing Limited (2008). https://doi.org/10.1108/9781786359537-006.

Bachmann, C., Kennedy, C., Roorda, M.J.: Applications of random-utility-based multi-region input-output models of transport and the spatial economy. Transp. Rev. **34**, 418–440 (2014). https://doi.org/10.1080/01441647.2014.907369

Campos, J., De Rus, G.: Some stylized facts about high-speed rail: a review of HSR experiences around the world. Transp. Policy **16**, 19–28 (2009). https://doi.org/10.1016/j.tranpol.2009.02.008

European Parliament: DIRECTIVE (EU) 2016/797 OF THE EUROPEAN PARLIAMENT AND OF THE COUNCIL of 11 May 2016 on the interoperability of the rail system within the European Union, https://eur-lex.europa.eu/legal-content/EN/TXT/?uri=CELEX:32016L0797. (2016).

Ortúzar, J.D.D., Willumsen, L.G.: Modelling Transport. Wiley (2011). https://doi.org/10.1002/9781119993308

Cascetta, E.: Transportation systems engineering: theory and methods. Springer Science & Business Media (2013).

Tesoriere, G., Russo, A., De Cet, G., Vianello, C., Campisi, T.: The centrality of Italian airports before and after the COVID-19 period: what happened? European Transport/Trasporti Europei, pp. 1–16 (2023). https://doi.org/10.48295/ET.2023.93.2.

Rindone, C., Russo, A.: A network analysis for HSR services in the south of Italy. In: Gervasi, O., Murgante, B., Garau, C., Taniar, D., C. Rocha, A.M.A., and Faginas Lago, M.N. (eds.) Computational Science and Its Applications – ICCSA 2024 Workshops. pp. 217–232. Springer Nature Switzerland, Cham (2024). https://doi.org/10.1007/978-3-031-65318-6_15.

Campisi, T., Russo, A., Trwdy, E., Zanne, M., Tesoriere, G.: Some considerations on the analysis of port centrality in the Adriatic basin for tourist transport purposes. Transport. Res. Proc. **83**, 125–132 (2025). https://doi.org/10.1016/j.trpro.2025.02.018

Di Gangi, M., Russo, F.: Potentiality of rail networks: Integrated services on conventional and high-speed lines. Presented at the COMPRAIL 2022 , Valencia, Spain November 30 (2022). https://doi.org/10.2495/CR220091.

Russo, F., Sgro, D., Musolino, G.: Dynamic structure of fares for high speed rail services. In: Gervasi, O., Murgante, B., Garau, C., Taniar, D., C. Rocha, A.M.A., and Faginas Lago, M.N. (eds.) Computational Science and Its Applications – ICCSA 2024 Workshops, pp. 188–201. Springer Nature Switzerland, Cham (2024). https://doi.org/10.1007/978-3-031-65318-6_13.

Moschella, M.: Domanda passeggeri High Speed Rail (HSR) in aree in ritardo di sviluppo: analisi sperimentale per la relazione Roma-Reggio Calabria. Presented at the Approfondimenti sulla mobilità terrestre , Roma (2025).

McFadden, D.: The measurement of urban travel demand. J. Public Econom. **3**, 303–328 (1974). https://doi.org/10.1016/0047-2727(74)90003-6

Ben-Akiva, M.E., Lerman, S.R.: Discrete choice analysis: theory and application to travel demand. MIT Press, Cambridge, Mass (1985)

Anderson, S.P., De Palma, A., Thisse, J.-F.: Discrete choice theory of product differentiation. The MIT Press (1992). https://doi.org/10.7551/mitpress/2450.001.0001

Tversky, A., Shafir, E.: The disjunction effect in choice under uncertainty. Psychol. Sci. **3**, 305–309 (1992)

Russo, F.: Fuzzy theory in transportation field: fuzzy sets for simulating path choice behaviour. 279–283 (1997).

McFadden, D.: Disaggregate Behavioral Travel Demand's RUM Side - A 30-Year Retrospective. (2001).

Train, K.E.: Discrete choice methods with simulation. Cambridge University Press, Cambridge (2009)

Quattrone, A., Vitetta, A.: Random and fuzzy utility models for road route choice. Transport. Res. Part E: Logist. Transport. Rev. **47**, 1126–1139 (2011). https://doi.org/10.1016/j.tre.2011.04.007

Busemeyer, J.R., Bruza, P.D.: Quantum models of cognition and decision. Cambridge Univ. Press (2012). https://doi.org/10.1017/CBO9780511997716

Vitetta, A.: A quantum utility model for route choice in transport systems. Travel Behav. Society. **3**, 29–37 (2016). https://doi.org/10.1016/j.tbs.2015.07.003

Ben-Akiva, M., McFadden, D., Train, K.: Foundations of stated preference elicitation: consumer behavior and choice-based conjoint analysis. FNT in Econom. **10**, 1–144 (2019). https://doi.org/10.1561/0800000036

Pellicanò, D.S., Trecozzi, M.R.: Methodologies for sustainable development of TEN-T/RFC corridors and core ports: public incentives for industrial activities location in port related areas. In: Gervasi, O., Murgante, B., Rocha, A.M.A.C., Garau, C., Scorza, F., Karaca, Y., and Torre, C.M. (eds.) Computational Science and Its Applications – ICCSA 2023 Workshops, pp. 635–646. Springer Nature Switzerland, Cham (2023). https://doi.org/10.1007/978-3-031-37123-3_44.

Panuccio, P.: State of the art of sustainable development of railway nodes: the High Speed Rail stations in Italy. (submitted to) International Conference on Computational Science and Its Applications-ICCSA 2024. (2024).

Musolino, G., Cartisano, A., Fortugno, G.: Methodologies for Sustainable Development of TEN-T/RFC Corridors and Core Ports: Estimation of Time-Series Economic Impact. In: Gervasi, O., Murgante, B., Rocha, A.M.A.C., Garau, C., Scorza, F., Karaca, Y., and Torre, C.M. (eds.) Computational Science and Its Applications – ICCSA 2023 Workshops, pp. 551–562. Springer Nature Switzerland, Cham (2023). https://doi.org/10.1007/978-3-031-37123-3_38.

Russo, F., Chilà, G., Zito, C.: Methodologies for Sustainable Development of TEN-T/RFC Corridors and Core Ports: Settlement Capacity of Industrial Firms in Port Related Areas. In: Gervasi, O., Murgante, B., Rocha, A.M.A.C., Garau, C., Scorza, F., Karaca, Y., and Torre, C.M. (eds.)

Computational Science and Its Applications – ICCSA 2023 Workshops, pp. 539–550. Springer Nature Switzerland, Cham (2023). https://doi.org/10.1007/978-3-031-37123-3_37.

Russo, F., Pellicanò, D.S.: Methodologies for sustainable development of TEN-T/RFC corridors and core ports: The role of governance in the export time optimization. In: Gervasi, O., Murgante, B., Rocha, A.M.A.C., Garau, C., Scorza, F., Karaca, Y., and Torre, C.M. (eds.) Computational Science and Its Applications – ICCSA 2023 Workshops, pp. 622–634. Springer Nature Switzerland, Cham (2023). https://doi.org/10.1007/978-3-031-37123-3_43.

Russo, F., Musolino, G.: Methodologies for sustainable development of TEN-T/RFC corridors and core ports: economic impacts generated in port-related areas. In: Gervasi, O., Murgante, B., Rocha, A.M.A.C., Garau, C., Scorza, F., Karaca, Y., and Torre, C.M. (eds.) Computational Science and Its Applications – ICCSA 2023 Workshops, pp. 515–526. Springer Nature Switzerland, Cham (2023). https://doi.org/10.1007/978-3-031-37123-3_35.

Rindone, C., Panuccio, P., Sgro, D.: Methodologies for sustainable development of TEN-T/RFC corridors and core ports: workers mobility between urban and port-related areas. In: Gervasi, O., Murgante, B., Rocha, A.M.A.C., Garau, C., Scorza, F., Karaca, Y., and Torre, C.M. (eds.) Computational Science and Its Applications – ICCSA 2023 Workshops, pp. 608–621. Springer Nature Switzerland, Cham (2023). https://doi.org/10.1007/978-3-031-37123-3_42.

Di Gangi, M., Russo, F.: Design of hybrid rail services on conventional and high-speed lines. IJTDI. 7, 113–121 (2023). https://doi.org/10.18280/ijtdi.070206.

Giunta, M.: Trends and challenges in railway sustainability: the state of the art regarding measures, strategies, and assessment tools. Sustainability. **15**, 16632 (2023). https://doi.org/10.3390/su152416632

Giunta, M., Leonardi, G.: Framework for life cycle railway sustainability assessment: a methodological approach based on advanced methods and tools. In: Gervasi, O., Murgante, B., Garau, C., Taniar, D., C. Rocha, A.M.A., and Faginas Lago, M.N. (eds.) Computational Science and Its Applications – ICCSA 2024 Workshops. pp. 233–244. Springer Nature Switzerland, Cham (2024). https://doi.org/10.1007/978-3-031-65318-6_16.

Cascetta, E., Nuzzolo, A., Biggiero, L., Russo, F.: A system of a within-day dynamic demand and assignment models for scheduled inter-city services. In: Presented at the Seminar D&E on Transportation Planning Methods at the 24th PTRC Summer Annual Meeting , England. University of Sussex. (1996).

Biggiero, L., Russo, F.: Il progetto di una indagine combinata rp-sp per la calibrazione congiunta di modelli di domanda intercity passeggeri e merci. In: IL TRASPORTO PUBBLICO NEI SISTEMI URBANI E METROPOLITANI. F. Angeli, Milano (1997).

Biggiero, L., Pagliara, F.: Calibrating residential location choice model: SP and RP data. VI (2000) 16, 5–9 (2000).

Deflorio, F., Dalla Chiara, B., Gonzalez Feliu, J.: Autostrada ferroviaria e trasporto stradale lungo la direttrice del Frejus: analisi di scenari mediante un modello di rete. (2005).

Dalla Chiara, B., Deflorio, F.P., Spione, D.: The rolling road between the Italian and French Alps: modeling the modal split. Transport. Res. Part E: Logist. Transport. Rev. **44**, 1162–1174 (2008). https://doi.org/10.1016/j.tre.2007.10.001

Inter-urban Transit Connections: A Network Analysis in an Italian Region

Antonio Russo[1] (ID), Giovanni Tesoriere[1] (ID), Corrado Rindone[2] (ID),
and Tiziana Campisi[1(✉)] (ID)

[1] Department of Engineering and Architecture, University of Enna Kore, 94100 Enna, Italy
{antonio.russo,tiziana.campisi}@unikore.it
[2] DIIES, Università Mediterranea di Reggio Calabria, 89100 Reggio Calabria, Italy

Abstract. Connectivity between urban centers is a key element for the development of territories. Public transport by road and rail are the two modes of transport most affected by extra-urban connections by land on a regional scale. To analyze these connections, it is interesting to refer to the methods offered by Network Analysis (NA).

In this paper, we want to study the centrality characteristics of interurban transport networks - both bus and train - on a regional scale, taking as a reference the direct connections between cities. This allows us to identify gaps and define hierarchies of network nodes, starting from the movement possibilities present in a node compared to the others.

NA is the methodology used; it allows to obtain synthetic centrality indicators in a network. In this article, two of the main indicators of NA (i.e., Degree Centrality, Strength Centrality) are applied to a test case of regional extension. Methodology used involves evaluation of Degree Centrality in a time-constrained network. Two different networks are considered and compared: the railway and the extra-urban bus transport network. The methodology considered allows to evaluate the centrality of the urban nodes considered with respect to each of the two networks; in this way, it is possible to compare the centrality values on the two networks between them. The case study highlighted is the Sicilian region, in Southern Italy. The analysis involves the study of centrality of the region's main cities. The results highlight asymmetrical differences between the different territories considered and large margins for improvement of the network. Furthermore, among the conclusions, it is interesting to recall the distortions present between the two modes of transport studied.

Keywords: Sustainable mobility · Network Analysis · Extra-urban transportation · Centrality · Accessibility

1 Introduction

The development of an efficient transport system that allows for faster connections and brings territories closer together is an objective consistent with the SDGs of Agenda 2030. In the European Union, connectivity plays a central role. The TEN-T network,

O. Gervasi et al. (Eds.): ICCSA 2025 Workshops, LNCS 15894, pp. 375–390, 2026.
https://doi.org/10.1007/978-3-031-97648-3_25

within its Comprehensive network, aims to make even the most peripheral territories of the Union connected to the network, through the development of key infrastructures [1, 2]. Accessibility to the transport system, and connectivity within it, are central elements in the sustainable development of Agenda 2030. Several objectives are directly linked to the transport system [3]. It is particularly useful to recall three of them. SDG 13 *"Take urgent action to combat climate change and its impacts"* focuses on decarbonisation; with regard to land transport, a modal shift from rubber to rail is essential, in a logic of reducing CO_2 emissions [4]. In light of SDG 9 *"Build resilient infrastructure, promote sustainable industrialization and foster innovation"* it is clear how sustainable infrastructure is at the heart of the Sustainability Agenda: interventions on railways (construction of new lines, electrification of pre-existing lines) fall within this scope. Finally, SDG 11 *"Make cities inclusive, safe, resilient and sustainable"* concerns the transport system, especially in light of Target 11.2 *"By 2030, provide access to safe, affordable, accessible and sustainable transport systems for all, improving road safety, notably by expanding public transport, with special attention to the needs of those in vulnerable situations, women, children, persons with disabilities and older persons"*, for the implications of the modal shift from road to rail on road safety and the quality of transport on an urban and extra-urban scale [4].

In this context, the study of the transport infrastructural and services subsystems of the most peripheral and less developed areas of the EU is particularly useful. This paper investigates the centrality of a public transport system on a regional scale, by referring to the EU classification Nomenclature of Territorial Units for Statistics (NUTS), and in particular the NUTS-2 class [5]. In this specific case, the region investigated is Sicily, one of the poorest regions in Italy and in the entire EU [6].

It is of fundamental importance, on a regional scale, to define the aggregate characteristics of the networks for extra-urban transport, considering the environmental needs of a modal shift towards more sustainable modes of transport. Sicily is characterized by an extension of 25,832.4 km^2 [7], the absence of inland waterways and a more concentrated population in coastal areas. For this case study the comparison between transit by road and transit by rail is essential to understand how much the latter can be "dominant" compared to the former and how much, instead, development opportunities are still necessary.

Recent scientific literature proposes a set of methodologies for analysing transport supply systems.

Transport supply models commonly known in literature are part of the broader Transportation System Models (TSM) field of study. They give several methods to analyze and measure structure of existing transportation supply network, allowing ex-ante evaluations of project configurations [8]. Classical TSM methods are used to study problems related to railway transport [9–11]. However, these methodologies often lack the capabilities to produce complete and aggregate indicators of supply structure. Methods from Network Analysis (NA) and classical graph theory may offer synthetic indicators to describe supply network's structure, giving details about operations on transportation network [12, 13].

Through the tools provided by network analysis, the study intends to evaluate two supply subsystems: the railway services subsystem and the extra-urban public transport services subsystem by road, considering the provincial capitals of the studied region as a reference.

The study is primarily oriented towards planners, managers of infrastructure companies and public administrators, due to the implications offered by the synthetic nature of the indicators proposed for the analysis of complex networks.

The work is structured as follows. Section 2 recalls the main literature references of the considered field. Section 3 describes the methodological tools of network analysis adopted. Section 4 describes the case study and presents the results obtained. Finally, Sect. 5 discusses the results, and the main conclusions.

2 Background

The analysis of the centrality of a network focuses on the classification of the analysed network nodes according to synthetic and analytical criteria. NA allows the importance of a node within a network to be defined [14]. NA can be used in those contexts in which a system can be represented as a network of point elements and their relationships. The applications in the literature are diverse: geopolitical studies, economic [15, 16], and social network analysis [17, 18].

In the transport sector, it has found wide application in public transport [19, 20] as well as in maritime and air transport [21, 22].

In this sense, transport networks are analysed through the representation of relationships between nodes and the estimation of centrality.

In transport networks, centrality measures are useful to obtain synthetic information on the topology and organisations of the network, with reference to both infrastructure and services. NA indicators determine the level of importance of transport nodes, their centrality in the network and the characteristics of their interactions. These elements are useful for identifying any criticalities in existing networks and then designing interventions to overcome them.

Various applications are present in the railway case and have been applied to networks in Asian [23–25] and European countries [26]. The proposed analyses have made it possible to analyse large-scale railway networks and to assess their connectivity and centrality characteristics.

In the study under examination, a central element is the study of the relationships between cities and the possibilities of movement that the supply system offers to users. In this sense, the research is directed towards the study of service networks and not towards the network of infrastructures.

In the following, for the treatment of network analysis in the railway sector, reference is made to the following treatment reported in the literature. Referring to [27], there are two main methods for representing a network of railway relations:

- The first method models the network as a bipartite graph, where nodes are divided into two distinct sets: a set S representing stations and a set T representing train services. A link between a station s ∈ S and a train service t ∈ T exists only if train t stops at station s;
- The second method constructs a graph in which the nodes directly represent the stations of the railway network. Two stations, i and j, belonging to set S, are connected

to each other if there is at least one railway service that stops at both of them. The network obtained in this way is called a *weighted station-station network*. This approach is widely used in railway network modelling, as it offers a more immediate representation of the structure of the connections between the stations.

In the following sections, the second method for representing the railway network will be considered, and the same criterion is adopted for the extra-urban public transport network.

3   Methodology

The main element of the study is the characterization of the centrality of the network nodes. Network analysis allows, as defined in Sect. 2, to quantitatively characterize and classify the nodes of a network. The proposed study for the application of network analysis to the two transport systems is divided into three sequential moments: data acquisition, data preparation, network analysis indicators.

The "data acquisition" is necessary to define the criteria of the study and the acquisition of data useful for the analysis of the transport system considered. In the case in question, two public transport systems are to be studied: the railway service network and the extra-urban road public transport service network. The elements to be defined and the data to be acquired are the following:

- The geographical area of reference (nation, region, city);
- The geographic aggregation needed. Depending on the nature of the study, it may be useful to provide a different degree of aggregation or to analyze the system in a completely disaggregated way;
- Time interval t;
- Public transport operators;
- The timetable of services operating within the reference area in the time period considered;
- The criterion for defining the existence of a relationship between two nodes of the network.

First two points define the nodes of the network. The remaining ones characterize the arcs of the network. Last point is linked to the type of territorial aggregation considered. In this study, all provincial capitals are considered, and the single node is expressed by the generic provincial capital of the study area defined in the first point. There is a relationship with the transport mode m between two provincial capitals i, j if there is, at time t, a direct service managed by the operator k $r_{ij,m,k}(t)$ that links having origin in node i and destination in node j, or a service $r_{ji,m,k}(t)$ having origin in node j an destination in node i. The analyzed services, both railway and road transport, are generally balanced; it is possible to assume that there are as many inbound as outbound services. As a consequence, we will work on undirected graphs.

The "data preparation" defines, for each mode of transport considered, the adjacency matrix $A_{ij,m}(t)$ and their generic element $a_{ij,m}(t)$ defined as:

$$a_{ij,m}(t) = \begin{cases} 1, & \text{if } \exists r_{ij,m,k}(t) V r_{ji,m,k}(t), i \neq j \\ 0, & \textit{otherwise} \end{cases} \tag{1}$$

The relationship analytically represents the transport network of mode m, and the existence of direct services enabled by the available services in the time t. The definition provided for the adjacency matrix allows to evaluate, with the same criterion, both the public transport network on the road and the railway transport network. In this work, the focus is on the possibilities of movement, from city to city, through direct connections. Therefore, between the two structures typically present in the literature of network analysis, L-space and P-space, the latter is used, because of its capability to represent relations between nodes [28, 29]. The definition provided for $a_{ij,m}(t)$ allows to define the graph in P-space from the presence of at least one direct connection. Once the adjacency matrix has been defined, it is then possible to describe the graph $G = (V, E)$, with V set of nodes and E set of edges, that characterizes the network for transport mode m. Let N be the number of nodes in the graph. Considering the direct connections between nodes i and j, it is also possible to define the value of $f_{ij,m}(t)$, frequency of service of mode m, expressed as the sum, extended to all operators k of mode m, of the existing services.

The third step is the application of network analysis indicators. In the study in question, three indicators are proposed: Degree Centrality, Strength Centrality and Constrained Degree Centrality.

The Degree Centrality (DC) is expressed as

$$c_{i,m}(t) = \frac{\sum_j a_{ij,m}(t)}{N - 1} \qquad (2)$$

DC defines the ratio between the sum of the connections of node i with the other nodes of the network compared to the total potential connections (N-1), referred to the mode m. The DC evaluates the degree of connection of each node of the network. A high DC value, close to 1, indicates that the generic node has many connections; a low value indicates that the node has few connections. It is also possible to evaluate the distribution of the degree centrality among the different nodes, evaluating the percentage of nodes that have a certain degree value. The reconstruction of the distribution of the DC allows to obtain overall information on the degree of interconnection of the network.

The limit of Degree Centrality is that it only provides a condition of existence for the connection between two nodes, without defining its entity.

Since it has been specified that the graphs considered for the study are undirected, it is necessary to specify a quantitative measure to define the Strength Centrality that takes into account both the path from i to j and the opposite path. In this work the formulation of Strength Centrality (SC) proposed is

$$s_{i,m}(t) = \sum_j f_{ij,m}(t) + \sum_j f_{ji,m}(t) \qquad (3)$$

SC evaluates the centrality of the generic node i considering the sum of the frequencies entering and exiting node i. SC therefore allows to correct the distortion induced by DC, whereby two nodes could share the value of connections even though they have completely different frequencies by orders of magnitude.

The third proposed indicator, the Constrained Degree Centrality (CDC), allows to provide an aggregate quantitative value on the connections in a specific Δ. Given $\tau_{ij,m}$, the time considered as a reference for the service with mode m to connect nodes i and j, it is possible to define the generic $a_{ij,m}(t)^\Delta$; Its value is 1 if $\tau_{ij,m} < \Delta$, 0 otherwise. In this way, it is possible to define the indicator as:

$$cc_{i,m}(t)^\Delta = \frac{\sum_j a_{ij,m}(t)^\Delta}{N-1} \tag{4}$$

The cc indicator measures the number of direct connections that respects a specific time constraint. The proposed formulation takes up the one expressed in Eq. (2) adapting it to the case of a temporal cutoff Δ.

The paper studies the characteristics of the direct connections between the nodes of the considered network. Therefore, the methodology described is focused on the two indicators that allow to provide synthetic measures of the direct connec-tions of a node on a network represented in P-space. Other indicators commonly used within the NA (Closeness, Betweenness, Eigenvector Centrality) refer to the study of paths that, in a railway network, represent interchanges and transfers, outside the scope of the research.

4 Results

This Section presents the results of the analysis. Section 4.1 describes the case study; Sect. 4.2 presents the obtained results by applying the formulations presented in Sect. 3.

4.1 Case Study

The analysis focuses on the study of extra-urban connections by train and bus between the nine former provincial capitals of the Sicilian Region. Sicily is the fifth Italian region by population, with 4,797,359 inhabitants [30]; with around 40% of its inhabitants at risk of poverty, it is among the poorest regions in Europe [31]. It has a motorway network of approximately 400 km managed by ANAS [32] and approximately 320 km managed by CAS [33] and a railway network of 1,370 km managed by Rete Ferroviaria Italiana (RFI) and 110 km managed by Ferrovia Circumetnea (FCE) [34, 35] (Fig. 1).

The transport operators consulted for the analysis of the problem are reported in Table 1. The other railway company operating in Sicily, FCE, is not present in the study because the line on which it operates does not connect different provincial capitals. The road transport companies considered in the study are all those that have at least one direct connection between two provincial capitals.

The criterion for defining a connection between two capitals, given the two modes of transport considered (train and bus) is the existence of a direct connection between the two corresponding nodes. As a case study, the services present on a generic winter weekday were considered.

Data were provided by the operators reported in Table 1; the timetables used as a reference are freely available on the respective sites. The study considers daily intervals. The services considered are all those with a departure time within the date considered. The choice of the weekday allows to study the case in which there are the greatest number of services.

Only direct services were indicated on all the relations considered.

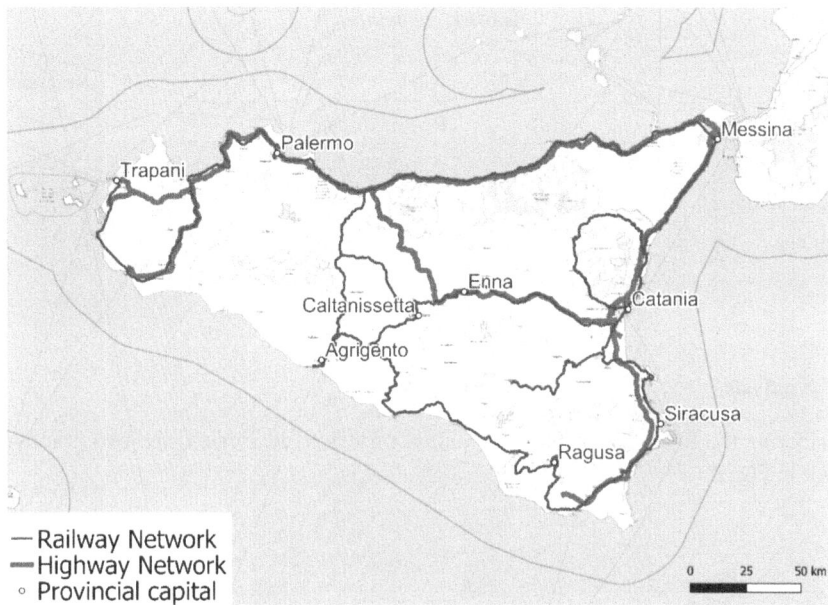

Fig. 1. Railway and Highway Network of Sicily. Source: Openstreetmap; QGIS [36, 37].

As of 2025, there are two lines with suspended circulation (Trapani-Palermo and Gela-Caltagirone) not shown in the image. Furthermore, on the stretch between Catania and Enna, circulation is temporarily suspended due to work on the doubling of the line [36–40].

Due to the temporary interruption on the Palermo-Catania railway line, for the connections from Catania to Enna, Caltanissetta and Palermo, the services that include a replacement bus from the Trenitalia company were considered.

Table 1. Transportation companies considered in the study.

Company	Train/Bus	Area	Reference
AST	Bus	Catania-Siracusa, Siracusa-Ragusa, Palermo-Ragusa	[41]
Astra autolinee	Bus	Caltanissetta-Enna	[42]
Autolinee lumia	Bus	Trapani-Agrigento	[43]
Autoservizi Cuffaro	Bus	Palermo-Agrigento	[44]
Camilleri Argento & Lattuca	Bus	Palermo-Agrigento	[45]
Etna trasporti	Bus	Catania-Ragusa	[46]
Flixbus	Bus	Regional scale	[47]
Interbus	Bus	Siracusa-Enna, Siracusa-Catania	[48]

(*continued*)

Table 1. (*continued*)

Company	Train/Bus	Area	Reference
SAIS	Bus	Regional scale	[49, 50]
SAL Autolinee	Bus	Agrigento-Palermo	[51]
Segesta autolinee	Bus	Palermo-Trapani	[52]
Trenitalia	Train	Regional scale	[53]

4.2 Analysis

Considering the timetable of the companies considered in Table 1, the two graphs are shown in Fig. 2.

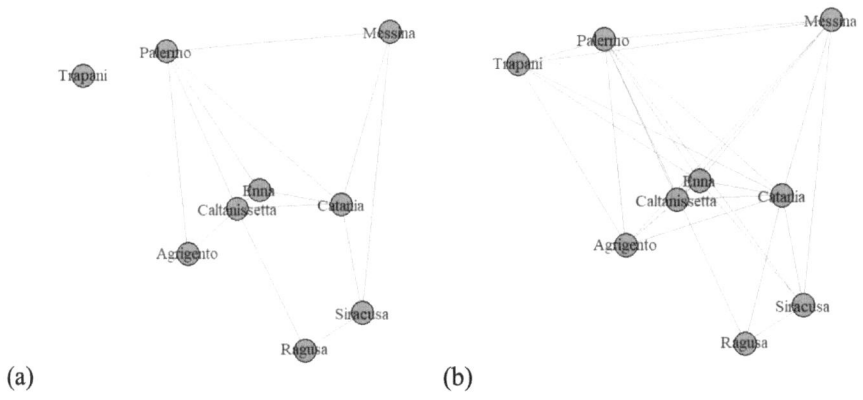

(a)   (b)

Fig. 2. (a) Railway and (b) Bus network.

The Degree Centrality values for the nodes of the two networks under examination are reported in Fig. 3.

Figure 4 defines the statistical distribution of the DC for the two networks.

The representation in Fig. 4 shows the cumulative DC for the two transport modes considered. For the railway network, the cumulative reaches 100% of the nodes at the value of 5 connections. This indicates that all the nodes have 5 connections, or less, out of the 8 total. The cumulative value of the bus network has a less steep trend and reaches 100% of the nodes at the value of $c_i = 8$, indicating that at least one node has all the possible connections. This further confirms that the bus network shows a greater interconnection than the railway network. The maximum value of DC for the train network (5) is reached by three nodes (Palermo, Catania, Caltanissetta), while the

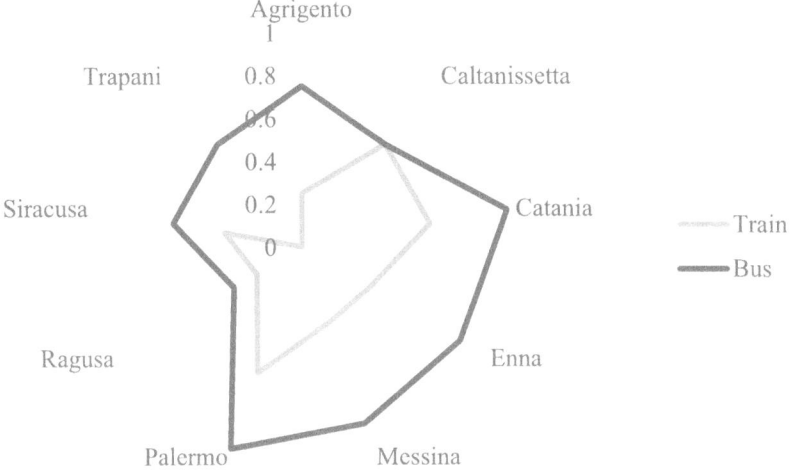

Fig. 3. Rail and bus network node degree centrality (ci)

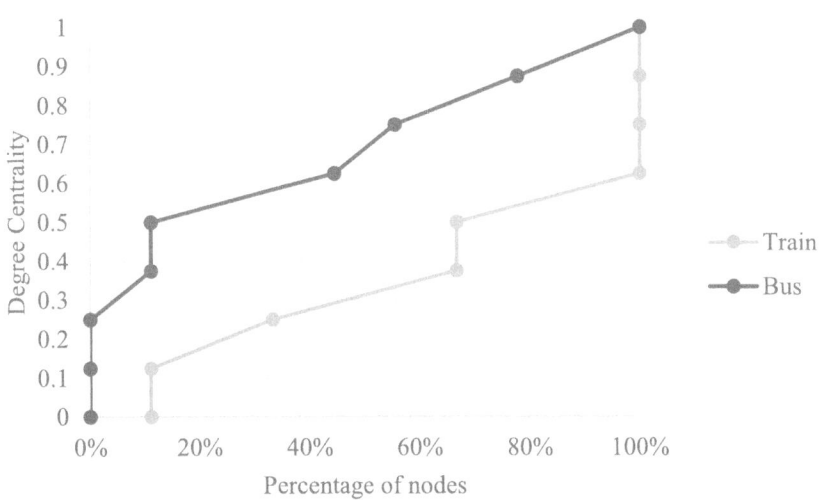

Fig. 4. Railway and Bus network cumulated DC

maximum value of DC for the bus is 8 (the Catania and Palermo nodes are connected with all the other possible nodes), but the value of 7 is reached by Enna and Messina. The result therefore shows a greater interconnection of the bus network.

The result regarding Strength Centrality is reported in Fig. 5.

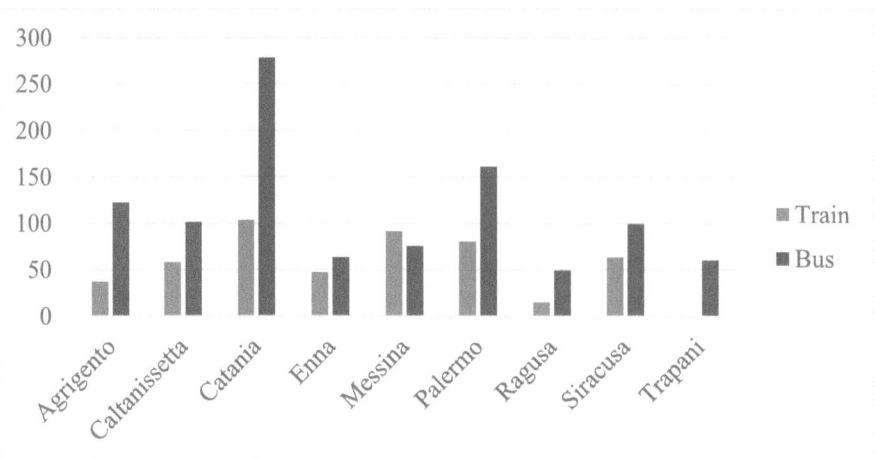

Fig. 5. Strength Centrality

The strength centrality relative to the two networks considered sees a higher value for the bus for all the nodes of the network, except for Messina for which there are more train connections than bus connections. This is mainly because the two most heavily trafficked railway lines converge on Messina; this is due to the particular geographical conformation and demographic distribution of the Messina area, where most of the population lives close to the coast near the railway. We also note the high number of bus connections to and from Catania, also linked to the presence of the airport.

The distributions of the Constrained Degree Centrality for the two modes of transport are reported in Figs. 6 and 7, comparing them with the Degree Centrality of the basic case. The interval considered as a time cutoff is $\Delta = 2$ h. The two-hour time threshold considered is compatible with a return trip during the day, associated with various types of travel reasons (regional commuting, occasional trips). The times taken as reference for each relationship are the minimum times among those declared by the companies.

For both networks and for most nodes, a significant decrease in the number of connections is appreciable. This is due both to the large geographical distances between some capitals, but also, and above all, to the travel times that can be greatly improved, especially in the case of rail. It is in this sense that the intervention on the doubling of the PA-CT railway line should be considered favorably, which should bring the travel time of the Catania-Palermo connection to 1 h 45 min, making it possible to connect Catania with Palermo, Caltanissetta and Enna in less than 2 h by rail. Similarly, the reopening of the Palermo-Trapani line should allow for a rapid connection between the two capitals. Currently, Trapani is not connected by rail to other regional capitals.

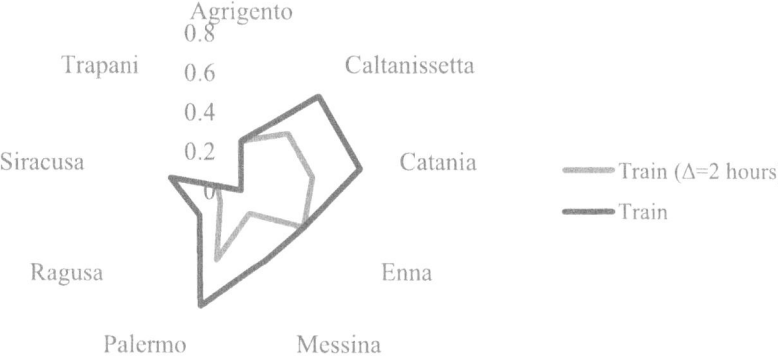

Fig. 6. Degree centrality vs. Constrained Degree Centrality ($\Delta = 2$ h, m $=$ train)

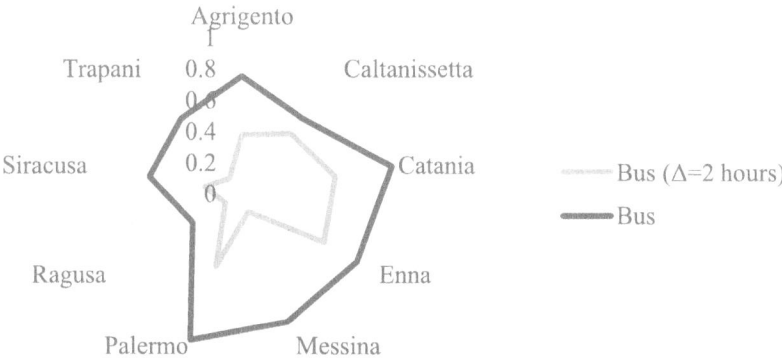

Fig. 7. Degree centrality vs. Constrained Degree Centrality ($\Delta = 2$ h, m $=$ bus)

5 Discussion and Conclusion

In the evaluation process of transport systems, there are several elements that must be taken into consideration. The most connected nodes of the network, with the highest centrality values, are those linked to the three metropolitan cities (Palermo, Messina, Catania), where the largest quantities of residents are also recorded. An overall poorly interconnected network emerges; the exceptions are two central nodes (Catania and Palermo) which, due to the greater population and the presence of key infrastructures, such as airports, are connected to all the other nodes of the network.

The value of Strength Centrality for the bus mode is higher for all the cities considered, with the exception of Messina, which is located at the convergence of two lines (the eastern Tyrrhenian and the Ionian) that have better infrastructural characteristics; the geography of the province of Messina, moreover, has determined the presence of the largest share of the population close to the railway.

The Constrained Degree Centrality for the 2-h case highlights a worsening of the connection conditions between cities, especially in the railway case, where a significant general worsening of the values can be observed for all connections, even though the geographical distances are often not excessive. In the case of the railway, this is mainly linked to the low travel speeds along the lines. Agrigento, Ragusa and Trapani are the cities with the lowest centrality values in the constrained case. This is due to the fact that, in addition to being the most geographically peripheral, they are linked to specific infrastructural interventions (such as the aforementioned intervention on the Palermo-Trapani railway line) that affect the number of connections and the speed of services.

The other ley element is the dominance of the bus network over the railway network. Travel between Sicilian cities, using public transport, mainly takes place via bus. This is due to the conformation of the territory, the distribution of the population and the presence of infrastructure. In Sicily there are numerous disused railway lines, mainly in the western and south-eastern parts of the island; conversely, the motorway system is expanding: among the planned interventions are the Catania-Ragusa and the completion of the Siracusa-Gela, which would complete the connections in the eastern part of the island. In this sense, the railway interventions already mentioned are recalled, including the doubling of the Palermo-Catania line, which would bring the travel time to approximately 1 h and 45 min. The structural limits remain: some railway lines seem to be more affected by flows; in particular the lines that converge on the city of Messina, thanks to the presence of the Strait and the connections with the peninsula; others, however, seem to mainly serve local or provincial mobility.

The policy implications of the contribution can be summarized. The study shows how, for both systems (bus and train) the typical basin structure of the Sicilian Region is confirmed; the region is typically divided into two macro-areas, a western one centered on Palermo and an eastern one centered on Catania. The two-basin structure of the Region struggles to find overall integration precisely because of the high internal travel times. In this regard, the role of the speeding up of the Palermo-Catania railway line is evident. The role, in the railway sector, of the city of Messina is also evident, being the only one of the nine nodes of the network to have a greater number of train connections than bus connections. The role of Messina must be further paid attention to precisely because of its geographical position as a pivot of the Sicilian Region in the case of a speeding up of the crossing of the Strait of Messina; as emerged from the contribution, the railway lines that converge on Messina are already the busiest. Finally, it is evident that the bus covers the majority of the connections in the smaller capitals, often, as in the case of Trapani, being the only possible alternative to reach other cities. In this regard, the main interest of regional and local authorities must be to strengthen the service in these areas, in order to guarantee, even where there is no railway line, stable connections.

In light of the objectives of Agenda 2030, the modernization of railway infrastructures and the attempt to shift the modal shift towards rail, compared to the bus, are certainly in line with Goals 9 and 13. The predominant role of the bus in the infrastructure network remains to be defined.

The work has provided generalized indicators for railway and bus networks at regional level. In the highlighted case study, a region of just under 5 million inhabitants was considered, with 9 cities considered. The indicators provided allow for the synthesis of numerous information relating to the networks and travel times. The characteristics of the work carried out are of particular interest to public transport operators and for regional scale territorial and transport planners who, thanks to synthetic indicators, can define lines of intervention. The work represents a first step in an evaluation at regional scale in which the main indicators have been proposed. The research can be expanded with other aggregations, more specific to individual countries or public transport stations/stops. Further development regard demand analyses for supporting planning and programming of a new transport system configurations.

Acknowledgments. This study was carried out within the MOST – Sustainable Mobility National Re-search Center and received funding from the European Union Next-GenerationEU (PIANO NAZIONALE DI RIPRESA E RESILIENZA (PNRR) – MISSIONE 4 COMPONENTE 2, INVESTIMENTO 1.4 – D.D. 1033 17/06/2022, CN00000023). This manuscript reflects only the authors' views and opinions, neither the European Union nor the European Commission can be considered responsible for them. We authorise the MUR to reproduce and distribute reprints for Governmental purposes, notwithstanding any copyright notations thereon. Any opinions, findings, and conclusions, or recommendations expressed in this material are those of the authors and do not necessarily reflect the views of the MUR.

Credit Author Statement. This paper is the result of the joint work of the authors. In particular, the "Abstract" were jointly written by the authors. AR and CR wrote "Background".AR and TC wrote "Methodology". AR and CR wrote "Results" and related subparagraphs. AR, CR and TC wrote "Discussion and Conclusion".

Disclosure of Interests. N.t.d.

References

1. Regulation (EU) No 1316/2013 of the European Parliament and of the Council of 11: Establishing the Connecting Europe Facility, amending Regulation (EU) No 913/2010 and repealing Regulations (EC) No 680/2007 and (EC) No 67/2010. Off. J. L 348, 129–171 (2013) Author, F.: Article title. Journal 2(5), 99–110 (2016)

2. Regulation (EU) No1315, 2013 of the European Parliament and of the Council of 11,: On Union guidelines for the development of the trans-European transport network and repealing Decision No 661/2010/EU. Off. J. L 348, 1 (2013) Author, F.: Article title. Journal 2(5), 99–110 (2016)

3. United Nations: The sustainable development goals. United Nations Publications (2017). https://unstats.un.org/sdgs/files/report/2017/thesustainabledevelopmentgoalsreport2017.pdf

4. Van Essen, H., et al.: Handbook on the External Costs of Transport, Version 2019 , no. 18.4 K83. 131 (2019)

5. European Parliament: Common classification of territorial units for statistics (NUTS) (2024). https://www.europarl.europa.eu/factsheets/en/sheet/99/nomenclatura-comune-delle-unita-territoriali-statistiche-nuts-

6. Eurostat: Living conditions in Europe - income distribution and income inequality (2025). https://ec.europa.eu/eurostat/statistics-explained/index.php?title=Living_condit ions_in_Europe_-_income_distribution_and_income_inequality#Key_findings

7. ISTAT: Superfici delle unità amministrative (2011). https://www.istat.it/comunicato-stampa/la-superficie-dei-comuni-delle-province-e-delle-regioni-italiane-dati-al-9-ottobre-2011/

8. Cascetta, E.: Transportation Systems Engineering: Theory and Methods, vol. 49. Springer Science & Business Media (2013)

9. Russo, F., Sgro, D., Musolino, G.: Sustainable development of railway corridors: methods and models for high speed rail (HSR) demand analysis. In: Gervasi, O., et al. Computational Science and Its Applications – ICCSA 2023 Workshops. ICCSA 2023. Lecture Notes in Computer Science, vol. 14110. Springer, Cham (2023)

10. Russo, F., Moschella, M., Musolino, G.: Railway demand evaluation: HSR induced component. In: Gervasi, O., Murgante, B., Garau, C., Taniar, D., C. Rocha, A.M.A., Faginas Lago, M.N. (eds.) Computational Science and Its Applications – ICCSA 2024 Workshops. ICCSA 2024. Lecture Notes in Computer Science, vol. 14822. Springer, Cham (2024). https://doi.org/10.1007/978-3-031-65318-6_12

11. Russo, F., Sgro, D., Musolino, G.: Dynamic structure of fares for high speed rail services. In: Gervasi, O., Murgante, B., Garau, C., Taniar, D., C. Rocha, A.M.A., Faginas Lago, M.N. (eds.) Computational Science and Its Applications – ICCSA 2024 Workshops. ICCSA 2024. Lecture Notes in Computer Science, vol. 14822. Springer, Cham (2024). https://doi.org/10.1007/978-3-031-65318-6_13

12. Bamakan, S.M.H., Nurgaliev, I., Qu, Q.: Opinion leader detection: a methodological review. Expert Syst. Appl. **115**, 200–222 (2019)

13. Freeman, L.C.: Centrality in social networks conceptual clarification. Social Networks **1**(3), 215–239 (1978)

14. Rodrigues, F.A.: Network centrality: an introduction. A Mathematical Modeling Approach from Nonlinear Dynamics to Complex Systems, pp. 177–196 (2019)

15. Iapadre, P.L., Tajoli, L.: Emerging countries and trade regionalization. A network analysis. J. Policy Model. **36**, S89–S110 (2014). https://doi.org/10.1016/j.jpolmod.2013.10.010

16. De Benedictis, L., Tajoli, L.: The world trade network. World Econ. **34**, 1417–1454 (2011). https://doi.org/10.1111/j.1467-9701.2011.01360.x

17. Tabassum, S., Pereira, F.S.F., Fernandes, S., Gama, J.: Social network analysis:a overview. WIREs Data Min. Knowl. **8**, e1256 (2018). https://doi.org/10.1002/widm.1256

18. Borgatti, S.P., Mehra, A., Brass, D.J., Labianca, G.: Network analysis in the social sciences. Science **323**, 892–895 (2009). https://doi.org/10.1126/science.1165821

19. Haznagy, A., Fi, I., London, A., Nemeth, T.: Complex network analysis of public transportation networks: a comprehensive study. In: 2015 International Conference on Models and Technologies for Intelligent Transportation Systems (MT-ITS), pp. 371–378. IEEE, Budapest, Hungary (2015). https://doi.org/10.1109/MTITS.2015.7223282

20. VonFerber, C., Holovatch, T., Holovatch, Y., Palchykov, V.: Public transport networks: empirical analysis and modeling. Eur. Phys. J. B. **68**, 261–275 (2009). https://doi.org/10.1140/epjb/e2009-00090-x
21. Campisi, T., Russo, A., Tesoriere, G., Bouhouras, E., & Basbas, S.: The evolution of Italy-Greece passenger maritime transport: a multi-level study to estimate the factors influencing the demand and supply of passenger ferry transport. Transactions on Maritime Science, **13**(2). (2024)
22. Tesoriere, G., Russo, A., De Cet, G., Vianello, C., Campisi, T.: The centrality of Italian airports before and after the COVID-19 period: what happened? European Transport/Trasporti Europei **93**, 1–16 (2023)
23. Ghosh, S., et al.: Statistical analysis of the Indian railway network: a complex network approach. Acta Phys. Pol. B Proc. Suppl. **4**(2), 123–138 (2011)
24. Mohmand, Y.T., Wang, A.: Complex network analysis of Pakistan railways. Discret. Dyn. Nat. Soc. **2014**, 1–5 (2014). https://doi.org/10.1155/2014/126261
25. Wang, W., et al.: Analysis of the Chinese railway system as a complex network. Chaos Solitons Fractals **130**, 109408 (2020). https://doi.org/10.1016/j.chaos.2019.109408
26. Rindone, C., Russo, A.: A network analysis for HSR services in the south of Italy. In: International Conference on Computational Science and Its Applications, pp. 217–232. Cham: Springer Nature Switzerland (2024)
27. Sen, P., Dasgupta, S., Chatterjee, A., Sreeram, P.A., Mukherjee, G., Manna, S.S. :Small-world properties of the Indian railway network. Phys. Rev. E **67**, 036106 (2003). https://doi.org/10.1103/PhysRevE.67.036106
28. Zhang, Y., Zhang, Q., Qiao, J.: Analysis of Guangzhou metro network based on L-space and P-space using complex network. In: 2014 22nd International Conference on Geoinformatics, pp. 1–6. IEEE (2014)
29. Cai, W., Liang, F., Wan, Y., Zhong, H., Gu, Y.: An innovative approach for constructing a shipping index based on dynamic weighted complex networks. Physica A **578**, 126101 (2021). https://doi.org/10.1016/j.physa.2021.126101
30. ISTAT: Popolazione residente al 1° Gennaio 2024. http://dati.istat.it/
31. Eurostat, (2025). Living conditions in Europe - income distribution and income inequality (2024). https://ec.europa.eu/eurostat/statistics-explained/index.php?title=Living_conditions_in_Europe_-_income_distribution_and_income_inequality#Key_findings. Accessed 31 Jan 2025. Author, F.: Article title. Journal **2**(5), 99–110 (2016)
32. ANAS: Itinerari siciliani (2024). https://www.stradeanas.it/it/le-strade/la-rete-anas/i-grandi-itinerari-anas/itinerari-siciliani
33. Autostrade Siciliane (2025). https://www.autostradesiciliane.it/
34. Rete Ferroviaria Italiana, Sicilia (2025). https://www.rfi.it/it/rete/la-rete-oggi/La_rete_oggi_regione_per_regione/sicilia.html
35. Ferrovia Circumetnea: La missione (2025). https://www.circumetnea.it/la-missione/
36. OpenStreetMap: About OpenStreetMap (2025). https://wiki.openstreetmap.org/wiki/About_OpenStreetMap
37. QGIS.org: QGIS Geographic Information System. Open Source Geospatial Foundation Project (2025). http://qgis.org
38. Ferrovie dello Stato Italiane, Ripristino della linea Palermo-Trapani via Milo (2025). https://www.fsitaliane.it/content/fsitaliane/it/opere-strategiche/linea--palermo---trapani-via-milo.html
39. Ferrovia dello Stato Italiane, Caltagirone-Gela ripristino e ammodernamento (2025). https://www.fsitaliane.it/content/fsitaliane/it/opere-strategiche/caltagirone-gela.htmlAuthor, F.: Article title. Journal 2(5), 99–110 (2016)

40. Ferrovie dello Stato Italiane, RFI - Sicilia: lavori sulla linea Catania-Palermo (2025). https://www.rfi.it/it/news-e-media/comunicati-stampa-e-news/2023/3/6/rfi---sicilia--lavori-sulla-linea-catania-palermo.htmlAuthor, F.: Article title. Journal 2(5), 99–110 (2016)
41. Azienda Siciliana Trasporti (2025). http://www.aziendasicilianatrasporti.it/
42. Astra Autolinee (2025). https://www.astraautolinee.com/
43. Autolinee Salvatore Lumia (2025). https://autolineelumia.com/
44. Autoservizi Cuffaro (2025). https://www.cuffaro.info/
45. Camilleri Argento & Lattuca (2025). https://www.camilleriargentoelattuca.it/
46. Etna trasporti (2025). https://www.etnatrasporti.it/
47. Flixbus (2025). https://www.flixbus.it/
48. Interbus (2025). https://www.interbus.it/
49. SAIS trasporti (2025). https://www.saistrasporti.it/
50. SAIS Autolinee (2025). https://www.saisautolinee.it/
51. Società Autolinee Licata SRL (2025). https://www.autolineesal.it/
52. Segesta Autolinee (2025). https://www.segesta.it/
53. Trenitalia (2025). https://www.trenitalia.com/it.html

Circular Economy in Rail Track: Estimating the Environental Burdens of the Use of Recycled Material and EoL Processing Through Life Cycle Assessment

Marinella Giunta(✉), Patrizia Frontera, and Mohammed Er Rouisse

University Mediterranea of Reggio Calabria, Reggio Calabria, Italy
{marinella.giunta,patrizia.frontera}@unirc.it

Abstract. The paper focuses on the application of the principles of the circular economy (CE) to the rail track systems by considering two main aspects: the use of recycled materials for the construction and maintenance and the environmental items associated with the End-of-Life (EoL). CE is an alternative approach to the linear model, promoting reduced raw material consumption and encouraging waste reuse through recycling or the development of new products. However, the waste materials require some pre-treatments before their use for which it is necessary to estimate the environmental consequences to properly estimate the benefits of the application. On the other hand, the EoL of the tracks requires careful considerations on the destination of the decommissioned components. This is an aspect often not fully considered in previous studies. This research focuses on the application of the Life Cycle Assessment (LCA) methodology to the two critical phases of the rail track life cycle: material production and EoL. In the stage of material production, the study looks at a comparison of sourcing and processing of the recycled material into the track construction. For EoL phase, the environmental implication brought by reusing/recycling materials from old tracks versus land filling or incineration have been considered. The results show that, in construction, material recycling and re-use can significantly reduce the environmental burdens related to natural resource depletion, human health and ecosystem protection. The findings are strongly dependent on the quality and efficiency of the recycling processes and on the logistical challenges of reprocessing materials.

Keywords: Railways · Sustainability · LCA · Circular Economy · Recycled Materials

1 Introduction

Climate change requires an extensive application of the circular economy (CE) principles in the railway sector [1]. The conscious use of resources, the reduction of waste and the promotion of sustainable construction and maintenance practices can significantly lower emissions and energy consumption and contribute to a more environmental-friendly rail transportation network for future generations.

O. Gervasi et al. (Eds.): ICCSA 2025 Workshops, LNCS 15894, pp. 391–406, 2026.
https://doi.org/10.1007/978-3-031-97648-3_26

In the European Union, the annual waste generated by construction and demolition (CDW) amounts to around 180 million tons, which equals more than 480 kg per person per year. Of this, approximately 75% is still landfilled. While Denmark, the Netherlands, and Belgium recycle about 80% of CDW, Italy, Spain, Portugal, and Greece recycle significantly less by comparison. [2, 3]. The great importance that material recycling has acquired nowadays, has prompted researchers to work on increasing and improving the recycling potential. In the railway sector, some studies have investigated the possibility of replacing natural aggregates (i.e., for ballast or sub ballast) with recycled ones, comparing their properties and assessing their impact on the final product [4–6]. Maintaining the track geometry produces ballast waste, which is important to reuse as much as possible. This can be done by sieving, cleaning and inserting back into new or renewed tracks the ballast particles with appropriate size (i.e. 30–63 mm). Usually, an average of 70% of removed ballast is suitable for reuse.

In recent years, interesting initiatives have been developed in response to the increasing demand for new construction and network renewal programs on the one hand, and the reduction in the use of virgin materials on the other. These factors have highlighted the need to explore methods for sourcing ballast from alternative materials such as steel slag [7, 8], tire-derived aggregate [9], crumb rubber, as well as innovative solutions to increase the service life of ballast layer including stabilization with bitumen [10], use of polyurethane, cement, and geopolymer [11, 12].

In particular, steel slag when used as railway ballast or blended with traditional crushed stone, provides a layer with excellent mechanical properties and lower permanent deformation under train loads. The slag is delivered as "waste" by the steel production cycle and is subjected to a specific recovery treatment in an authorized plant, from which are produced secondary raw materials (MPS) in different grain sizes, including ballast for railway use. Italy is the second-largest steel producer in Europe, with a 16% share of the entire EU production. In 2024, Italian steel mills produced 20 million tons of steel, generating about 2.6 million tons of black slag or steel slag—roughly 13% of the total production by weight. If this quantity were used to create the ballast layer at a rate of 50% of its total volume, it could support the construction of approximately 900 km of single track. This length could double if the proportion of black slag used were reduced to 25%.

The main steel mills in Italy are concentrated in the Northen Region, with a significant plant in Puglia, South Italy. Smaller plants are spread across the country. This uneven distribution raises concerns about the impact of transporting black slag for recycling in the railway industry, especially considering the distance from steel production hubs to construction sites.

Another important and vulnerable component of the track is the sleeper, which is responsible for load bearing and load distribution. Various materials are used for sleepers, including timber, concrete, and steel. Currently, prestressed concrete sleepers have become one of the most common types of railway sleepers installed worldwide owing to their increased lifespan and strong structural performance. However, due to the larger quantities of CO_2 released in their manufacture, researchers are exploring alternative materials such as recycled plastics, recycled rubber, fiber-reinforced foamed urethane (FFU), epoxy polymer resin [13, 14]. The outcomes of the studies carried out demonstrate that the use of recycled plastic and reinforced material can reduce overall environmental impacts of the sleepers in terms of carbon emissions and resource use.

Another area of improvement is related to the use of recycled aggregates for concrete sleeper manufacturing [15, 16]; this practice, while limited by the percentage of use of recycled material [17], exhibits high environmental performances.

All studies emphasized the importance of assessing environmental impacts across railway components to identify the most sustainable options and consider the entire life-cycle of the infrastructure. Several studies have been conducted to assess the environmental effect of the railway industry. They exhibit significant variety in methodological approaches, analytic periods, railway types, software, and datasets employed [18–21]. Few studies consider different rail track substructure solutions, and the environmental impacts associated with the design, construction, maintenance, and dismantlement of the track. Pons [22] examines and compares the potential environmental implications associated with the life cycle of three distinct track systems: ballasted track, cast-in sleeper track system, and embedded track system, revealing that ballasted tracks cause the lowest environmental impact for service lives of up to 75 years. Conversely, the embedded track beds generate the most significant environmental impacts, irrespective of their operational lifespan. The primary contributor to the impacts is steel manufacturing. The life-cycle energy consumption and global warming potential associated with ballasted and generic concrete track beds, including cast-in sleeper and embedded track systems were evaluated by [23] indicating that concrete slab track beds do not correlate with increased life-cycle energy consumption or global warming potential when compared to ballast track beds. The utilization of materials with elevated embodied energy in concrete systems is counterbalanced by their anticipated extended lifespan. Significant discrepancies exist between the lowest and highest embodied energy values provided for materials, such as aggregate, which undermines the conclusiveness of any comparisons.

This research focuses on two key track components, ballast and sleepers, and aims to assess the environmental impact associated with two specific life cycle phases: production and EoL. The appraisal was conducted by applying the Life Cycle Assessment methodology in accordance with [24]. The analysis of the production and EoL stages of these two components is crucial due to the growing demand for the expansion of railway transport, whether through the construction of new lines or the upgrading of existing ones. Additionally, these two components require frequent maintenance and replacement activities throughout the operational life of the railway track. This study introduces two main innovations with respect to the existing literature on railway infrastructure and life cycle assessment (LCA). First, it explicitly considers the upstream processes associated with the use of recycled materials, including the environmental impacts of collection, treatment, and preparation steps required prior to their integration into new production cycles, stages that are often neglected or only partially addressed in previous studies. Second, it provides a detailed examination of the EoL phase, hypothesizing scenarios in which both ballast and sleepers undergo recovery processes that enable their re-entry into the construction cycle as secondary raw materials. To identify sustainable pathways, the environmental impacts of using virgin materials were compared with those of using recycled materials, with particular emphasis on the pre-processing stages required for the latter. This comprehensive approach allows for a more accurate and holistic assessment of the environmental trade-offs associated with material choices, thereby addressing critical gaps in traditional LCA studies that frequently overlook both upstream burdens and realistic circularity scenarios at end-of-life.

2 Life Cycle Assessment of Rail Track Components: Ballast and Sleepers

2.1 Description of Objectives, Product System, Boundaries and Functional Unit

Ballasted track (Fig. 1) is a layered structure composed mainly of rails and sleepers, which are supported by a crushed stone bed called ballast. This, in turn, rests on an underlying layer, called sub ballast, usually made of bituminous mixture that acts as a transition between the ballast and the underlying subgrade.

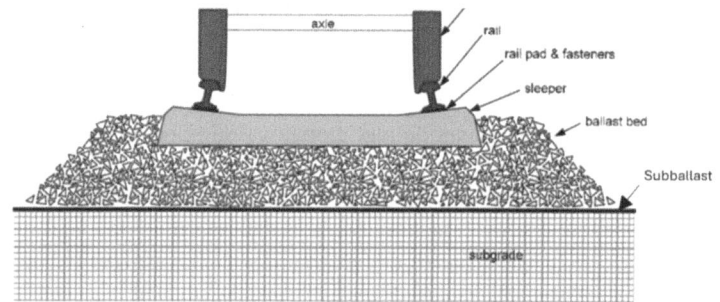

Fig. 1. Ballasted Track System

The purpose of this study is to compare the life cycle emissions of sleepers and ballast made from alternative recycled materials appropriately pre-treated with those of traditional components made from virgin materials. Attention is given to the environmental impacts arising from the pre-treatment processes necessary to make recycled materials suitable for use. This aspect is often underestimated or entirely overlooked in previous studies. By explicitly addressing it, the present approach seeks to evaluate whether the adoption of such alternative products is both environmentally justified and operationally feasible.

To achieve these goals, the specific objectives of this study are:

a. To conduct a life cycle assessment (LCA) on the emissions of sleepers and ballast made with virgin materials (base scenario) compared to those produced with recycled material.

b. To compare the results and determine whether the alternative ballast and sleepers are more environmentally friendly than the base scenario.

By adopting this approach, it is therefore possible to verify whether the application of the principles of CE in the railway sector allows for the reduction of global emissions from the system. The critical phases on which we will focus the most are the production phase of the elements and their end of life.

Two essential elements to define before proceeding with the system analysis are: the system boundaries and the functional unit (FU).

FU is a quantitative description of the service performance (the needs fulfilled) of the investigated product system(s). In the railway sector, FU is usually the length of the track expressed in kilometers (it is necessary to specify whether the track is single or double) [24, 25]. In this study the FU considered is 1 km of single-track line. The time boundaries in which the analysis is carried out correspond to a 30-year time frame.

The different life cycle system boundary models implemented are:

- *Cradle to gate,* this is a life cycle assessment that only considers the resource extraction phase up to the construction site.
- *End-of-life,* this is an assessment from dismantling to grave, where the EoL disposal phase coincides with a recycling process that makes the materials or components reusable for another product, thus allowing for the "closing of the loop".

2.2 Inventory

The inventory is a crucial phase of the LCA that refers to a quantitative analysis aimed at evaluating the resource use, energy consumption, and environmental emissions associated with a product, process, or activity throughout its entire life cycle. Data used are referred to a case study.

Ballast

In the subsequent analyses, three scenarios have been considered:

- Base Scenario B0: 100% virgin aggregate.
- Scenario B1: 50% virgin aggregate + 50% recycled aggregate.
- Scenario B2: 50% virgin aggregate + 25% recycled aggregate + 25% steel slag.

The data for the materials and energy used in the construction of the ballast layer in the different scenarios are shown in Table 1.

Table 1. Quantities and distances for ballast layer

Input	B0		B1		B2	
	t/FU	km	t/FU	km	t/FU	km
Virgin	13167	45	6583,5	45	6583,5	45
Recycled	-	-	6583,5	30	3291,8	30
Steel slag	-	-		-	3291,8	50
Energy Required for Primary Production (MJ)	5.18E + 04		3.28E + 04		3.50E + 04	

Embodied primary energy, expressed in MJ, includes all energy, direct and indirect, used to transform or transport raw materials into products, including inherent energy contained in raw or feedstock materials that are also used as common energy sources. The database used for the estimate is Ecoinvent v3.10.

It was assumed that the distance between the quarry, where the virgin material is extracted, and the installation site is 45 km, and transport takes place via EURO5 trucks. Recycled material was analyzed by accounting for the fuel required for machinery to screen and wash particles from the EoL of the traditional ballast (70% of which is recoverable), while assuming a total transport distance of 30 km from the EoL ballast processing facility to the construction site. Transportation is modelled with reference to EURO5 lorries. So, the designing was based on an analysis of the energy required for processing the stone component that is removed from the life cycle, whether it be the ballast or the sleepers.

Steel slag was modelled with respect to the input flow referred to as "blast furnace slang," which encompasses the deposition of material (landfill of residuals from steel manufacturing). The modelling incorporates the fuel required for the machines to screen and clean the material, as well as the overall distance of 50 km from the slag treatment facility to the disposal location. Transport is modelled using a EURO5 vehicle, and the treatment system consumes 2000 kWh.

The modelling of the EoL of the ballast (Table 2) takes into consideration the following aspects:

i. Transport of the recovered ballast to the treatment site, via EURO 5 lorry for 40% of the distance and by train for the remaining 60%.
ii. Power supply for the machines necessary for the treatment of the ballast.

The equipment considered are:

- HOBCS (High Output Ballast Cleaner System) to sift the particles. The particular model used is RM-900-RT, with a flow rate of 900 m^3/h and power of 1500 kW.
- Ballast Washer for washing. The model adopted is the CLSB-24, with a flow rate of 125 m^3/h and power of 44 kW.

The distance from the processing site to the construction site is assumed to be equal to 100 km. The ballast recovered is 70% of the total dismantled.

All the scenarios have the same EoL.

Table 2. Quantities for ballast EoL

Input		All Scenarios
Transport (km)	lorry	40
	rail	60
Recovery (kW)	HOBCS	1500
	BW	44

Sleepers

Concerning the sleeper production, in Italy, sleepers are categorized according to a fundamental list established by RFI (Italian Railway Network), with RFI 260 being one of the types examined. The primary components of a sleeper cement (Portland, type 1), water, virgin aggregates, additives (this contribution includes various types of additives included in the basic bill of materials formulated by RFI, as ethylene vinyl acetate, carboxylates), and steel. The model incorporates transport from the production site to the construction site via EURO5 lorry over a distance of 20 km. This scenario is called Base Scenario S0.

The modified sleepers (Scenario S1) were constructed using recycled materials (from the EoL of the ballast or of the sleepers themselves), instead of virgin aggregates.

The data for the materials and energy used for construction of the sleepers are shown in Table 3.

Table 3. Quantities and distances for sleepers

Input	S0	S1
	t/FU	t/FU
Virgin aggregate	500	-
Recycled aggregate	-	500
Water	36,2	36,2
Cement	100	100
Steel	18,8	18,8
Additives	15	15
Transport (km)	20	20
Energy Required for Primary Production (MJ)	2,49E + 05	1,51E + 05

The EoL modeling (Table 4) of the sleepers takes into account two aspects:

i. Transport to the treatment site, with 40% of the distance covered by EURO 5 lorry and 60% by train.
ii. Power supply of the machine needed to treat the sleepers.

For the final treatment of the sleepers the use of M100 machine is considered [26]. This machine has a processing capacity of 400 sleepers/h and requires a power of 500 kW. The recycling of concrete railway sleepers is facilitated by the caterpillar conveyor belt. The machine gradually feeds the sleepers into the crusher, which crushes them into very small pieces in a short amount of time. These pieces are then separated by a system of conveyor belts. The long iron is expelled from the front end of the machine. On the left side of the machine, the fine-grained aggregate material is separated from the short iron (plates) and is possibly moistened through nozzles to prevent the formation of dust.

These recycled aggregates can have a second life, not only in the railway industry but also in other construction sectors, thereby reducing emissions associated with processing raw materials that would otherwise be used.

The distance from the sleeper treatment site to the construction site is assumed to be equal to 100 km.

Both base and modified sleepers have the same EoL.

Table 4. Quantities for sleepers EoL

Input		S0, S1
Transport (km)	lorry	40
	rail	60
Recovery (kW)	M-100	500

2.3 Life Cycle Impact Assessment and Interpretation

The impact assessment method used is the ReCiPe 2016 Endpoint (H) used within open-source software OpenLCA 10.2. The adoption of an endpoint methodology over a midpoint methodology provides a more comprehensive understanding of the overall effects on the environment. Endpoint assessments allow for the evaluation of environmental impacts in terms of their ultimate consequences on human health, ecosystem quality, and resource depletion, which can be more meaningful for stakeholders and decision-makers. Unit of measure for human health is DALYs (disability adjusted life years), that represents the years that are lost or that a person is disabled due to a disease or accident. The unit for ecosystem quality is the local species loss integrated over time (species year). The unit for resource scarcity is the USD 2013 (US dollars, base year 2013), which represents the extra costs involved for future mineral and fossil resource extraction [27]. By focusing on these broader outcomes, the authors aimed to illustrate the significance of their findings in a way that transcends specific environmental metrics.

Ballast

Figure 2 illustrates the environmental impact in the area of protection of natural resources, human health and ecosystem of ballast production and transport across the different scenarios.

Concerning ballast production, for all Scenarios, the more consistent environmental impacts are ascribed at the area of protection of naturals resources. It suggests that the extraction of raw materials significantly affects natural landscapes and environmental raw systems. Additionally, high energy consumption during production, often sourced from non-renewable resources, further depletes natural resources and emphasizes the impact in the area of the natural resources.

The impact on the category of natural resources is significantly influenced by the choice between using virgin (B0) or recycled materials (B1, B2) in ballast production.

Production   **Transport**

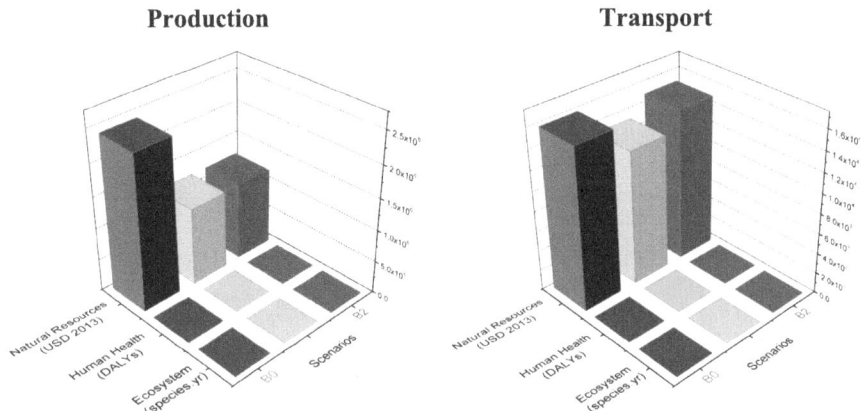

Fig. 2. Environmental impact for alternative types of ballast in production and transport phases

Utilizing virgin materials typically entails higher environmental costs due to the extraction processes, which can lead to habitat destruction and resource depletion. In contrast, incorporating recycled materials can mitigate these impacts by reducing the demand for new resources and minimizing waste.

In the transport phase of ballast, a similar pattern emerges regarding environmental impacts. Just as with the production phase, the choice of materials can significantly influence the area of protection of natural resources. Transporting virgin materials typically entails higher energy consumption and associated emissions, which contribute to the depletion of natural resources and overall ecological impact. On the other hand, using recycled materials can lead to reduced transportation distances and lower energy requirements, thereby minimizing emissions and resource use. This shift underscores the importance of sustainability not only in material selection but also in logistical considerations.

The comparison between the production and transport phases (Fig. 3) regarding the areas of protection for human health reveals that the contributions from both phases are comparable. Each phase plays a significant role in influencing environmental impacts, and their effects on human health and transportation safety are similarly significant.

In scenarios (B1, B2) where recycled materials are used, the transport phase tends to have a more significant impact on environmental outcomes.

Since the production phase in scenarios B1 and B2 presents lower contributions due to the lower exploitation and demand for raw materials which reduces natural resources, necessarily, from a percentage and not an absolute point of view, transport, compared to total emissions, will present a more significant impact in the alternative scenarios.

In the assessment of impacts of the EoL of ballast for all areas of protection valued, the transport process exhibits greater value ($95 \pm 5\%$) with respect recovery ballast process due to a range of factors associated with logistics and the processes involved in both activities.

One of the primary reasons is that transportation emissions, which largely stem from fuel consumption, generate significant greenhouse gas emissions and air pollutants. The

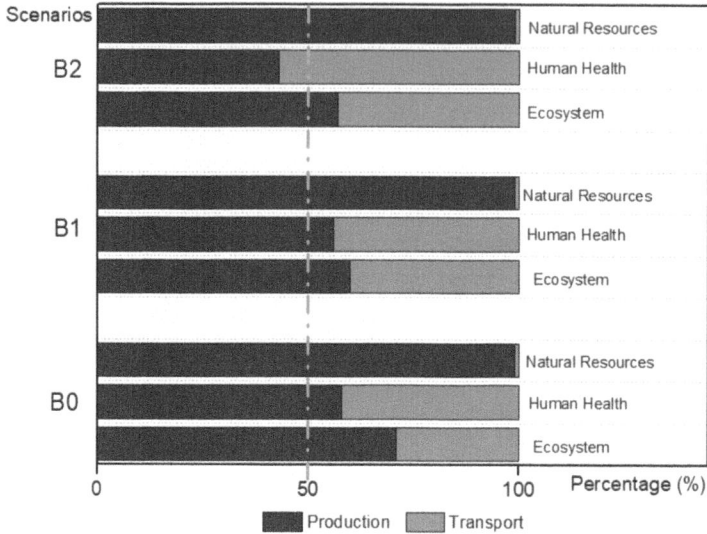

Fig. 3. Comparison of percentage emissions for different types of ballast in production and transport phases

impact of these emissions increases sharply with the distance traveled, meaning that transporting heavy materials like ballast over long distances can lead to a substantial cumulative environmental impact.

In contrast, the recovery of ballast, which typically involves processes such as cleaning, sorting, and reusing of existing materials, is generally less energy intensive. This means that the associated emissions from recovery processes are usually lower than those from transportation.

Recovery minimizes the need for the extraction and processing of new materials, making it a more sustainable option for managing ballast waste.

At the end of their useful life, recovered materials can often be repurposed or recycled, further mitigating environmental impacts by extending the lifespan of existing resources.

Moreover, transportation can also contribute to infrastructure impacts, such as road wear and maintenance, increased traffic congestion, and potential disruption to local habitats and ecosystems.

The logistical requirements for moving heavy materials not only involve high fuel consumption but also can lead to additional environmental consequences related to land use and habitat degradation.

These logistical challenges translate into higher operational costs and broader environmental impacts, compounding the overall impacts associated with transport.

Sleepers

Figure 4 illustrates the environmental impact of production and transport of sleepers in the area of protection of natural resources, human health, and ecosystem, across the scenario that considers the use of virgin materials (S0) and its with recycled aggregates (S1).

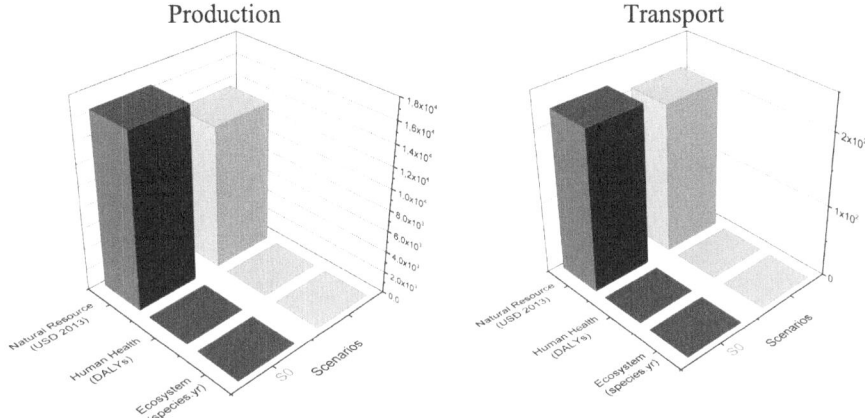

Fig. 4. Environmental impact for two types of sleepers in production and transport phases

In the production and transport of sleepers, the higher impacts related to natural resources compared to human health and ecosystem factors can be attributed to several key reasons. The extraction and processing of raw materials often lead to significant resource depletion which directly affects the environment. Moreover, while human health and ecosystem impacts are important, they may be less immediately apparent in the context of production and transport compared to the visible effects on natural resources. The comparison between the production and transport for all areas of protection and in all scenarios reveals that the production phase of sleepers exerts an impact of over $98 \pm 2\%$ compared to transportation, which highlights the critical role that materials play in this context. This significant influence is primarily due to the resource-intensive processes involved in manufacturing sleepers, where materials such as cement, steel, and various additives require substantial energy and raw materials. The extraction, processing, and transformation of these materials not only generate considerable greenhouse gas emissions but also lead to environmental degradation.

In contrast, transportation, while important, generally has a lower impact in comparison because it constitutes a smaller fraction of the overall life cycle emissions associated with the production of sleepers.

The demand for resources in the production, like concrete, steel and all materials included, create different pressures on the areas of the protection (see Fig. 5).

Considering the natural resources in both scenarios, the significant contribution of additives, specifically polyurethane, ethylene vinyl acetate, and polycarboxylate, reflects the resource-intensive processes involved in their production. Polyurethane, commonly used for its durability and flexibility, is derived from petroleum-based resources, which inherently require extensive fossil fuel extraction and processing.

Similarly, ethylene vinyl acetate (EVA) is produced through the polymerization of ethylene, a byproduct of crude oil refining. The production of EVA necessitates significant energy input, further straining natural resources and contributing to environmental impacts related to fossil fuel extraction. The high demand for energy and raw materials

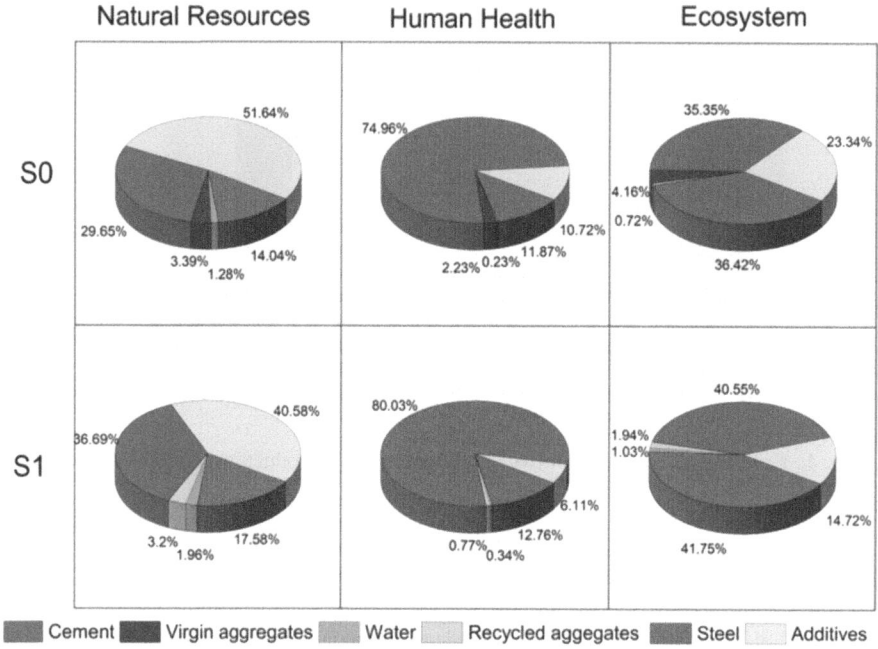

Fig. 5. Analysis of material contributions for two types of sleepers

during the manufacturing process of these plastics can lead to increased greenhouse gas emissions, which exacerbate climate change.

Polycarboxylate, often used as a superplasticizer in concrete and other construction materials, also has a considerable environmental footprint. Its production involves chemical processes that may involve additional energy-intensive steps and the use of non-renewable resources, contributing further to the overall impact on natural resources.

For the area of protection of Human Health, the major contributor is steel.

The steel industry significantly impacts human health due to several interrelated factors. Firstly, the production process generates various pollutants, including particulate matter and nitrogen oxides, which can adversely affect respiratory health for those living near steel plants. Additionally, the release of toxic substances, such as heavy metals, can contaminate surrounding environments and water supplies, exposing local communities to health risks. The resource-intensive nature of steel production often relies on unsustainable energy sources, contributing to pollution and climate change, which further threaten public health. Moreover, workers in the steel industry face direct occupational hazards, including exposure to harmful chemicals and physically demanding conditions. Together, these elements highlight the multifaceted ways in which steel production impacts human health.

In the ecosystem category, cement, additives, and steel contribute similarly to environmental impacts due to their resource-intensive production processes and the associated ecological consequences. Cement production is notorious for its high carbon dioxide emissions and significant energy consumption, leading to habitat loss and degradation of natural environments. Similarly, the manufacturing of additives, such as polyurethane and ethylene vinyl acetate, often entails chemical processes that can lead to pollution and disruption of local ecosystems.

Steel production also shares these challenges, involving resource extraction that can cause habitat destruction, and emissions that contribute to air and water pollution. The entire supply chain for these materials—including extraction, processing, and transportation—exerts cumulative pressure on ecosystems, contributing to biodiversity loss and ecosystem imbalance.

Moreover, all three materials can have lasting effects on soil and water quality, impacting the flora and fauna that depend on these resources.

The environmental assessment of the end-of-life management of sleepers reveals a significant challenge, with transport accounting for $88 \pm 5\%$ of the total impact across all areas of protection, including natural resources, human health, and ecosystems. This overwhelming contribution from transport underscores the substantial emissions and resource consumption associated with moving heavy materials. Such a high percentage indicates that logistics play a crucial role in the overall environmental impacts of sleepers.

The remaining $12 \pm 5\%$ attributable to recovery and recycling processes highlights that, while these efforts are valuable, they currently account for only a small fraction of the total impact. This suggests there is considerable room for improvement in enhancing recovery practices and increasing the efficiency of recycling processes.

3 Discussion and Conclusion

This life cycle assessment (LCA) provides a comprehensive evaluation of the environmental impacts associated with the production and end-of-life management of railway ballast and sleepers. The analysis reveals a complex interplay of factors influencing various impact categories, highlighting the need for a holistic approach to sustainable railway infrastructure development.

The study demonstrates that material selection significantly affects the overall environmental performance. While utilizing recycled materials offers considerable advantages in reducing the depletion of virgin resources, it also introduces trade-offs, primarily impacting other environmental aspects. This underscores the importance of carefully considering the full environmental profile of both virgin and recycled materials and optimizing their processing to minimize negative consequences. Simply substituting one material for another without a thorough assessment of the entire life cycle can lead to unintended shifts in environmental burdens.

Transportation emerges as a critical factor impacting the overall environmental footprint, consistently ranking as a major contributor across all life cycle stages for both ballast and sleepers. This emphasizes the need for optimizing logistics, exploring alternative transportation modes, and potentially redesigning supply chains to minimize transportation distances and emissions. The substantial influence of transport highlights the interconnectedness of environmental impacts and the importance of considering the broader context beyond material choices alone.

The analysis also reveals that the manufacturing processes themselves, particularly for key components like cement and steel in sleeper production, contribute significantly to various environmental impacts. This indicates the potential for further improvements through technological advancements and the adoption of more environmentally friendly production methods. Investing in research and development to reduce the environmental impacts of manufacturing processes is crucial for advancing sustainable railway practices.

Finally, end-of-life management significantly impacts on the overall environmental performance. A comprehensive strategy for managing the end-of-life phases of both ballast and sleepers is essential for minimizing environmental burdens. This requires not only efficient recycling and disposal methods but also innovative solutions to minimize transportation needs during this phase. The integration of end-of-life considerations into the design and production phases is vital for achieving truly sustainable railway infrastructure.

The limitations of this work are primarily related to the use of a case study, with parameters specific to that context; nonetheless, the results remain valid as they offer meaningful insights and highlight key trends that are broadly applicable to similar scenarios.

In conclusion, achieving truly sustainable railway infrastructure requires a holistic approach that integrates material selection, manufacturing processes, transportation optimization, and efficient end-of-life management strategies. The findings of this LCA highlight the complex trade-offs involved and the need for continuous innovation and improvement across all stages of the life cycle to minimize environmental impacts and build a more sustainable future for the railway industry. Furthermore, there is an interesting outlook for the transition to a more circular economy in the rail track systems, basically due to the recycling of materials instead of landfilling, as it will decrease the general environmental impact while pursuing sustainability within the railway infrastructure industry.

Acknowledgments. This study was carried out within the MOST – Sustainable Mobility National Research Center and received funding from the European Union Next-Generation EU (PIANO NAZIONALE DI RIPRESA E RESILIENZA (PNRR) – MISSIONE 4 COMPONENTE 2, INVESTIMENTO 1.4 – D.D. 1033 17/06/2022, CN00000023). This manuscript reflects only the authors' views and opinions, neither the European Union nor the European Commission can be considered responsible for them.

Disclosure of Interests. The authors have no competing interests to declare that are relevant to the content of this article.

References

1. International Union of Railway. UIC SUSTAINABILITY Circular Practices in the Railway and Ways Forward REUSE Project Final Report 2021. Available online: https://uic.org/IMG/pdf/reuse_project_final_report.pdf (Accessed 31 Oct. 2023)
2. Damgaard, A., et al.: Background data collection and life cycle assessment for construction and demolition (CDW) waste management (2022) https://doi.org/10.2760/772724

3. Caro, D., et al.: Environmental and socio-economic effects of building construction and demolition waste recycling in the European Union. Sci. Total Environ. 168295 (2024). https://doi.org/10.1016/j.scitotenv.2023.168295

4. Bressi, S., Santos, J., Giunta, M., Pistonesi, L., Lo Presti, D.: A comparative life cycle assessment of asphalt mixtures for railway sub-ballast containing alternative materials. Resour. Conserv. Recycl. **137**, 76–88 (2018)

5. Guo, Y., Xie, J., Fan, Z., Markine, V., Connolly, D.P., Jing, G.: Railway ballast material selection and evaluation: a review. Constr. Build. Mater. **344**, 128218 (2022)

6. Allacker, K., Mathieux, F., Pennington, D., Pant, R.: The search for an appropriate end-of-life formula for the purpose of the European Commission Environmental Footprint initiative. Int. J. Life Cycle Assess. **22**(9), 14411458 (2017). https://doi.org/10.1007/s11367-016-1244-0

7. Jing, G., Wang, J., Wang, H., Siahkouhi, M.: Numerical investigation of the behavior of stone ballast mixed by steel slag in ballasted railway track. Constr. Build. Mater. **262**, 120015 (2020)

8. Esmaeili, M., Askari, A.: Laboratory investigation of the cyclic behavior of rock ballast mixed with slag ballast for use in railway tracks. Constr. Build. Mater. **365**, 130136 (2023)

9. Fathali, M., Chalabii, J., Astaraki, F., Esmaeili, M.: A new degradation model for life cycle assessment of railway ballast materials. Constr. Build. Mater. **270**, 121437 (2021)

10. D'Angelo, G., Bressi, S., Giunta, M., Presti, D., Thom, N.: Novel performance-based technique for predicting maintenance strategy of bitumen stabilised ballast. Constr. Build. Mater. **161**, 1–8 (2018)

11. Jing, G., Qie, L., Markine, V.L., Jia, W.: Polyurethane reinforced ballasted track: review, innovation and challenge. Constr. Build. Mater. **208**, 734–774 (2019)

12. Sweta, K., Hussaini, S.K.K.: Effect of geogrid on deformation response and resilient modulus of railroad ballast under cyclic loading. Constr. Build. Mater. **264**, 120690 (2020)

13. Dolci, G., Rigamonti, L., Grosso, M.: Potential for improving the environmental performance of railway sleepers with an outer shell made of recycled materials. Transp. Res. Interdiscip. Perspect. **6**, 100160 (2020)

14. Thompson, S., King, C., Rodwell, J., Rayburg, S., Neave, M.: Life cycle cost and assessment of alternative railway sleeper materials. Sustainability **14**, 8814 (2022)

15. Gonzalez-Corominas, A., Etxeberria, M., Fernandez, I. Structural behaviour of prestressed concrete sleepers produced with high performance recycled aggregate concrete. Mater. Struct. **50** (1) (2017)

16. Imtiaz, L., et al.: Life cycle impact assessment of recycled aggregate concrete, geopolymer concrete, and recycled aggregate-based geopolymer concrete. Sustainability **13**, 13515 (2021). https://doi.org/10.3390/su132413515

17. Ministero delle infrastrutture e dei trasporti. Norme tecniche per le costruzioni. (2018)

18. Chang, B., Kendall, A.: Life cycle greenhouse gas assessment of infrastructure construction for california's high-speed rail system. Transp. Res. Part D Transp. Environ. **16**, 429–434 (2011)

19. International Union of Railway. Carbon Footprint of Railway Infrastructure Comparing Existing Methodologies on Typical Corridors Recommendations for Harmonized Approach; International Union of Railway: Paris, France (2016)

20. Olugbenga, O., Kalyviotis, N., Saxe, S.: Embodied emissions in rail infrastructure: a critical literature review. Environ. Res. Lett. **14**, 123002 (2019)

21. Giunta, M., Bressi, S., Losa, M.: Sustainability in Railway Construction: LCA-LCC Based Assessment of Alternative Solutions for Track-Bed. In: Proceedings of the 2020 Joint Rail Conference JRC2020, St. Louis, MO, USA, 20–22 April (2020)

22. Pons, J.J., Villalba Sanchis, I., Insa Franco, R., Yepes, V.: Life cycle assessment of a railway tracks substructures: comparison of ballast and ballastless rail tracks. Environ. Impact Assess. Rev. **85**, 106444 (2020)

23. Kiani, M., Parry, T., Ceney, H.: Environmental life-cycle assessment of railway track beds. Eng. Sustain. **161**, 135–142 (2008)
24. ISO14040; Environmental Management—Life-Cycle Assessment—Principles and Framework. International Organization for Standardization: Geneva, Switzerland (2006)
25. Giunta, M., Leonardi, M.: Framework for life cycle railway sustainability assessment: a methodological approach based on advanced methods and tools. In: Gervasi, O., Murgante, B., Garau, C., Taniar, D., C. Rocha, A.M.A., Faginas Lago, M.N. (eds) Computational Science and Its Applications – ICCSA 2024 Workshops. ICCSA 2024. Lecture Notes in Computer Science, vol 14822. Springer, Cham. https://doi.org/10.1007/978-3-031-65318-6_16
26. DeconX official website, "M100 Riciclaggio di traverse ferroviarie" (2025)
27. Huijbregts, M.A.J., et al.: ReCiPe 2016 A harmonized life cycle impact assessment method at midpoint and endpoint level. Int. J. Life Cycle Assess **22**:138–147 (2017)

Comprehensive Railway Track Monitoring Using Unmanned Aerial Systems (UASs) and Building Information Modeling (BIM)

Marinella Giunta$^{(\boxtimes)}$ ⓘ, Vincenzo Barrile ⓘ, Giovanni Leonardi ⓘ, and Emanuela Genovese ⓘ

University Mediterranea of Reggio Calabria, 89124 Reggio Calabria, Italy
{marinella.giunta,vincenzo.barrile,giovanni.leonardi,
emanuela.genovese}@unirc.it

Abstract. The increasing adoption of UAV-based inspections in railway infrastructures stems from the demand for more efficient, cost-effective, and safer alternatives to conventional track monitoring practices, which typically rely on manual inspections or dedicated rail vehicles. UAVs offer the possibility to capture high-resolution images and detailed data from multiple perspectives, which can then be analyzed using cutting-edge computer software. In this way, a comprehensive assessment of various track components, such as rails, sleepers, fastening systems, and ballast, can be done. Additionally, combining drones with technologies like Building Information Modeling (BIM) allows for the development of precise digital representations of railway infrastructure. This research reports the results of the monitoring of the state of the track based on the images captured by a drone equipped with a video camera and the point cloud created by means of appropriate advanced software that uses photogrammetric techniques to transform a series of images into 3D spatial data. Advantages and limitations of UAVs for monitoring railway track conditions are highlighted as well as the optimization needed for reaching the precision suitable for the assessments. Results demonstrated the appropriateness of using the drone for monitoring and assessing track conditions, in terms of geometric and structural integrity, as well as maintenance requirements.

Keywords: Rail track · Preventive maintenance · Monitoring · Imaging · UAS

1 Introduction

Railways are an integral part of both passenger transport and freight logistics, becoming more and more crucial for the effective and sustainable movement of people and goods over short, medium and long distances. With the growth of traffic, axle load and speed in the railway network, the preservation of the infrastructure in terms of safety, integrity and overall functionality is an undiscussed priority [1, 2].

This requires diligent maintenance activities of the railway tracks, which are exposed to a lot of wear and tear in use, adequately supported by monitoring of their conditions [3]. Railway operators face several challenges in monitoring. Conventional track monitoring

© The Author(s), under exclusive license to Springer Nature Switzerland AG 2026
O. Gervasi et al. (Eds.): ICCSA 2025 Workshops, LNCS 15894, pp. 407–419, 2026.
https://doi.org/10.1007/978-3-031-97648-3_27

practices, which typically rely on manual inspections or dedicated rail vehicles, have supported the railway industry for many years. However, due to the increased need for maintenance and optimization of resources and time the demand for more efficient, cost-effective, and safer alternatives has become increasingly pressing [4, 5].

The adoption of new technologies such as unmanned aerial vehicles (UAVs) and image elaboration is changing the way track monitoring is performed [6]. The UAVs application in track monitoring demonstrated that the advantages of their use include reduced time for inspection, reduced risk for operators, large areas covered quickly, a wide dataset acquired, reliability and simplicity, and digital reconstruction of assets.

UAVs can be used to inspect railroad components such as bridges [7, 8], tunnels [9], vegetation [10], and track conditions [11–14].

As regards the defect of rail superstructure, the horizontal, vertical or composite track irregularities can greatly affect the safety and the comfort of passengers.

Ravitharan [12] proposed a novel approach for monitoring various aspects of track geometry by means UAVs, with a particular focus on rail vertical alignment, twist, curvature, and running surface issues, including discrete defects and rail corrugation.

Qui [13] developed a UAV-LiDAR-based platform capable of performing track geometry measurements. It demonstrated high accuracy in gauge measurement, although its performance in curvature and profile measurement was less effective.

Wu [14] explored the use of UAVs for track gauge measurement. They generate a point cloud of the railway scene and apply a hybrid segmentation algorithm combining augmented region-growing and improved alpha-shape techniques to extract rails from chaotic data. Rails features are compared with a pre-built rail BIM model. The validation of the proposed method demonstrated its superiority in safety, efficiency, speed, and accuracy.

The high-resolution images and detailed data from multiple perspectives, captured by drones, can be analyzed using cutting-edge computer software. In this way, a comprehensive assessment of various track components, such as rails, sleepers, fastening systems, and ballast, can be done. Additionally, combining drones with technologies like Building Information Modeling (BIM) allows for the development of precise digital representations of railway infrastructure [15, 16].

This paper proposes in Sect. 2 a methodology for monitoring track conditions using images captured by a drone equipped with a camera, which are then used to reconstruct a digital representation of the track within a BIM environment. The methodology is applied to a case study referring to a 1 km-long railway line section, flown over with the drone. Using advanced software utilizing photogrammetric techniques, the series of images captured with the drone was transformed into 3D spatial data, as reported in Sect. 3. Section 4 discusses the results of the application and highlights both the advantages and limitations of using UAVs for monitoring railway track conditions, as well as the optimization needed to achieve the precision required for accurate assessments.

2 Methodology for Monitoring Railway Track Conditions

This research focuses mainly on the potential of using drones to monitor a railway infrastructure by emphasizing the pros and cons of this technology in accurately identifying damages, subsidence or other deterioration conditions affecting the railway section.

The methodology proposed for this purpose and applied to 1-km of existing track railway section is divided into three phases: the *data collection*, involving the planning and execution of the drone survey, the *data elaboration*, were the acquired imaged are processed by means of advanced software, and the *results evaluation*, in which in which the rail track is modeled to enable geometric and structural assessments.

Figure 1 reports the flowchart of the proposed methodology described in more detail below.

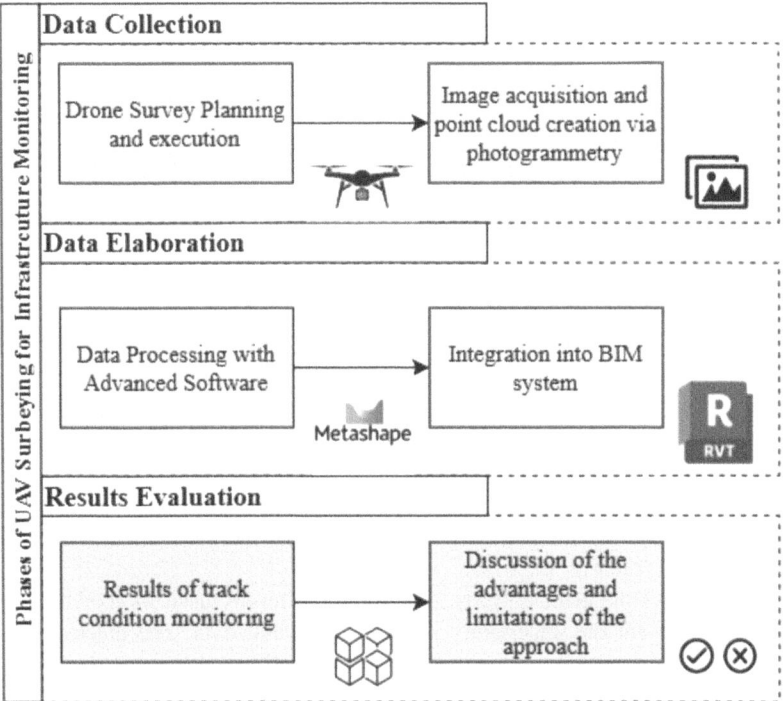

Fig. 1. Flowchart of the proposed methodology for monitoring of the state of the track based on the images captured by drone.

The first phase involved the data acquisition necessary for the analysis to be carried out in the following phases. For the case study under investigation, the survey was conducted using a DJI Mavic 3 Enterprise drone, equipped with a high-resolution quadrangular CMOS 4/3 camera, offering 20 effective megapixels, a field of view (FOV) of 84°, and an aperture of f/2.8 to f/11. This family of drones is well-known for its agility, relatively low cost, and high-precision results thanks for its specific configuration.

The acquisition of the drone's images was carried out based on a detailed flight plan, properly designed and optimized for this specific case study to ensure a level of detail and precision required for the planned experimentation.

To this end, the Pix4D application was used, which allowed setting flight parameters including flight altitude, Ground Sampling Distance (GSD), number of captured frames, longitudinal and transverse overlap, as well as path and speed that the drone must follow and maintain during automated flight. This phase is crucial for obtaining a high-quality and correctly georeferenced 3D model.

In this specific case, an inspection and a planimetric framing of the area were carried out, to then establish the flight parameters. The drone flew at an altitude of 69.5 m along a grid path, the GSD was set to 1.82 cm/pixel. A total of 177 nadir images were captured with an overlap of 80% in both directions (see Table 1). Additionally, a separate flight was conducted without programming to take oblique images to better capture the characteristics of the railway.

Table 1. Parameters of flight.

Parameters	Value
Height of flight	70 m
Speed of flight	12 km/h
Covered Area	0.103 km^2
GSD	1.82 cm/pixel
Front overlap	80%
Side overlap	80%
Number of Nadir images	177

The acquired images have a resolution of 4864 x 3648 (camera model). The calculated error in the camera positioning resulted in average errors of $X = 5.45$ mm, $Y = 3.38$ mm, and $Z = 6.32$ mm (see Fig. 2).

Figure 2 shows the error ellipses, a concept commonly used in geodesy and cartography to represent the uncertainty zone of geospatial data. The black dots in the figure indicate the position measurement, while the ellipse represents the probability distribution, highlighting the area where the true position is likely located.

In this case, the ellipse represents the uncertainty in georeferencing of the images. The shape of the ellipse provides information in the X and Y directions, while the color indicates the error in the Z axis. From this, we can estimate an overall mean uncertainty in the georeferencing of the images of approximately 9.00 mm.

Once the data collection phase was completed, images were processed in the Agisoft Metashape environment, which employs Structure from Motion algorithms for the photogrammetric process and the subsequent creation of 3D models. During this second phase, the images were imported into the Agisoft Metashape and aligned. The alignment of the images is the process in which characteristic points are identified and paired in order to create the sparse point cloud.

This process permits the matching of images with a pairwise comparison. For the image alignment, the generic preselection and reference preselection options were used, which rely on selecting the camera positions at the time of image capture. In this case, the images that were closest to each other and had the highest probability of sharing more characteristic points were selected. Having geotagged images available, the source of the

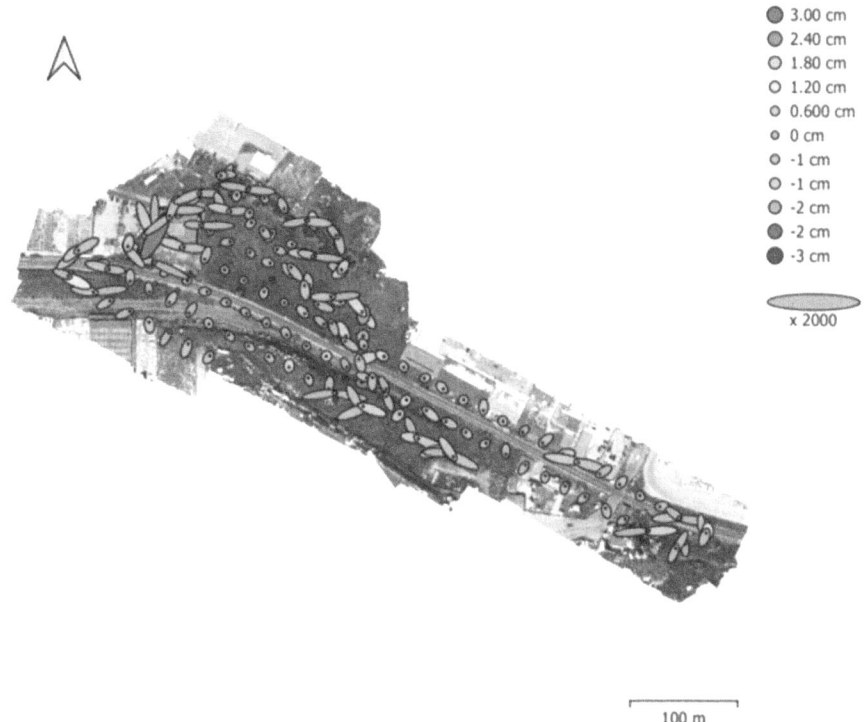

● 3.00 cm
● 2.40 cm
○ 1.80 cm
○ 1.20 cm
○ 0.600 cm
○ 0 cm
○ -1 cm
○ -1 cm
○ -2 cm
● -2 cm
● -3 cm

x 2000

100 m

Fig. 2. Average camera position error.

images was used to calculate the position of the cameras. The end was to give the software the possibility to optimize its process without losing a large amount of information. In fact, the generic preselection reduces the processing and image alignment time. The reference preselection is equally important, as it ensured that images without stable common points were discarded. For the image alignment, high accuracy was chosen, ensuring that the initial resolution of the images was maintained.

After generating the sparse point cloud, scaling and orienting it, according to the aforementioned details, and correcting any distortions, the dense cloud was generated. The dense point cloud provided a high density of information on the ground and on the above elements, which are the focus of the three-dimensional reconstruction. To achieve this, the "high-quality" option was used for generating the point cloud, which affects the resolution of the images considered when identifying points that will become part of the dense cloud (see Fig. 3).

In a Structure from Motion process, the support points (Ground Control Points) alone are not sufficient to determine the accuracy of the point cloud and the subsequent three-dimensional model. In fact, in addition to the support points used to optimize the point cloud and therefore to deform, scale, move, and orient it, it was necessary to have additional points, called check points, measured using GNSS instruments. The check points enable to perform a statistical analysis on the deviations to determine the average error. The average error was calculated by analyzing the root mean square deviations

Fig. 3. Dense Point Cloud generated in Agisoft Metashape environment.

between the X, Y, Z coordinates assigned by the software to the points of the generated sparse cloud and the corresponding coordinates of the check points. The resulting average error across the three coordinates was approximately 2 cm.

The proposed method also includes a series of intermediate steps between the various main phases, which are essential for obtaining the desired results.

The first phase, as previously mentioned, involves programming the flight plan.

In this case, the plan was optimized to ensure the best possible performance in terms of both processing efficiency and the quality and accuracy of the resulting point cloud. During the planned flight, the drone captured a series of frames, which were stored on an external SD card for later transferred to a PC dedicated to processing. In addition to the acquired images, 20 points were surveyed using GNSS equipment, of which 5 served as check points to verify the accuracy of the generated point cloud. Once the process of optimizing the cameras, aligning and importing the GCPs into the sparse cloud for orientation, movement and scaling of the sparse cloud had started, the accuracy of the cloud was assessed using check points.

At the end of these steps, the mesh and texture were generated, moving from a discontinuous point-based visualization to a continuous surface representation. The points of the dense cloud became the vertices of the triangles of a network that constitute the surface inheriting the color information associated with those vertices. Using the same dense point cloud obtained from the photogrammetric processing and the resulting 3D model, the Building Information Model (BIM) of the railway track was then created.

As is known, BIM is a methodology widely used today used in the construction sector for the design and construction of buildings. It allows for the integration of dimensions, materials, and other important technical specifications in the modeling phase. The process to create the BIM model can take place either directly from the point cloud or from the 3D model, producing a real three-dimensional BIM model.

In order to use the model within the software, it was first necessary to export the model in a format compatible with BIM software, i.e., .obj or. fbx, using Autodesk Recap software. This software permits the management, decimation, and merging of clouds not only derived from photogrammetric processes but also from terrestrial laser scanners acquisitions (see Fig. 4).

Fig. 4. Dense Point Cloud from Autodesk Recap environment.

Subsequently, Autodesk Revit software was used for the BIM modeling phase, starting from the generated 3D model and enriching it with specific details such as materials, accurate geometries of the elements, and some structural details. The various components of the railway section were modeled, starting from the terrain, through the "topographic solid" function. For the other components, custom families representing the components of the railway section were defined. In particular, the generated 3D model served as a reference to precisely place BIM objects corresponding to railway components, such as sleepers, tracks, ballast layer, and other features. To this end, the concrete sleepers were inserted, along with the precise geometry and type of attachment, once the steel rails were modeled. The ballast, which plays a crucial role in ensuring the durability and stability of the track, was added at the base of the railway layout. This modeling process enables the identification and assessment of potential defects in the analyzed section of the railway.

It should be noted that manual surveys for infrastructure monitoring require experienced and qualified personnel on site, equipped with total stations and differential GPS to perform precision measurements. These surveys are time-consuming, often requiring several days or even weeks, also due to the interference with rail traffic, as train circulation must be interrupted or slowed down on the day of the survey. Moreover, the data collected refer only to the specific survey and provide solely 2D documentation, which is subject to interpretation errors.

Unlike these methods, the proposed method allows for rapid and automated surveys, reducing the time and costs while covering larger areas in less time. Apart from specific authorizations, altitude limits, and obstacle control in the surveyed area, this type of survey does not interfere with railway operations in any way, making it possible to perform frequent updates and generate a 3D and BIM model that supports structural simulations, analyses, and advanced redevelopment planning. The main drawback lies in the need for advanced skills in Geomatics, particularly in topographic surveys and 3D modeling, as well as cross-disciplinary expertise for evaluating the necessary interventions.

3 Results of Track Condition Monitoring

3.1 3D Modeling

The results of the 3D modeling process, as extensively detailed in Sect. 2, carried out in the Agisoft Metashape environment, are shown in Fig. 5.

Fig. 5. 3D model textured generated in Agisoft Matashape environment.

The process was initiated on a workstation equipped with an Intel Core i7, 32 GB of RAM, and 1 TB of storage, featuring an integrated Intel graphics card. It took approximately 45 min to generate the dense point cloud. The processing time was correlated to the high number of points to be processed (116,712,923 points) and to the parameters set for generating the dense cloud and producing the 3D model. The careful selection of these parameters at this stage was crucial in drastically reducing the computational time.

From the 3D model produced, it was possible to conduct a detailed analysis of the geometry of the railway track, in order to verify compliance with regulations and identify any anomalies in portions of the track that could compromise its safety.

In particular, the 3D model enabled the evaluation of wear and tear on the rails and the state of the concrete sleepers, facilitating informed decisions on the maintenance of the railway section.

From the results obtained, it was possible to precisely measure the standard gauge, which for the entire section taken into consideration is equal to 1435 ± 2 mm, without detecting significant irregular variations (Fig. 6).

Cross-sections were also generated to verify the overhang of the outer rail in the curves; in this case, the railway section did not show significant differences in height between the rails.

Regarding the ballast, it was possible to detect some areas contaminated by vegetation, which could compromise its stability.

The analysis of the slope along the entire section, derived from the generation of the DSM (Digital Surface Model), was equally important, as it enables the visualization of the height fluctuations and slope changes along the stretch. The slope was calculated using a DSM created within Agisoft Metashape, which provides elevation data for the area under examination, including the heights of buildings, vegetation, and any objects

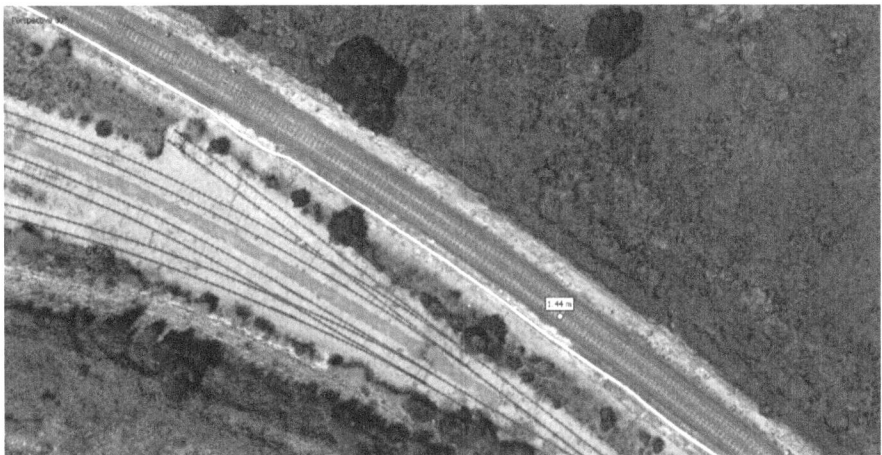

Fig. 6. Detail of the railway track and measurement of the distance between tracks.

above ground level. The software includes a workflow that allows the creation of the DSM starting from the dense cloud. Once the reference system (CRS: WGS84 UTM 33N) and the resolution of the DSM were defined, the DSM creation process was started. The slope analysis was then performed in the QGIS environment. The slopes were found to be within acceptable limits for the flat section, maintaining a gradient of 10‰.

Thanks to the analysis of the three-dimensional model, it was therefore possible to study the actual state of the area being analyzed, obtaining detailed geometry and a realistic texture of the infrastructure useful for topographic analysis of the railway section. In particular, the morphology of the route, the curvatures, the slopes, as well as the longitudinal and transversal profiles, were analyzed for altimetric and planimetric insights. Furthermore, automatic extraction methods of geometric features from the 3D model and automatic segmentation methodologies, based on the use of neural networks, useful for selecting various portions of the infrastructure, are being tested. The use of convolutional neural networks on point clouds, which classify directly without the need for meshing, allows for the automatic classification of rails, sleepers, and ballast. In this case, it would be necessary to optimize the parameters of networks such as PointNet and RandLA-Net to improve the accuracy of segmentation of high-resolution point clouds.

This type of inspection provides valuable insights for planning targeted maintenance activities, enabling more efficient scheduling and contributing to a reduction in both time and operational costs.

3.2 BIM Modeling

BIM is a relevant tool for the management and maintenance of the railway section by enabling the representation of the railway components through parametric elements containing detailed technical information on materials and dimensions, ensuring the possibility of carrying out simulations and planning interventions (Fig. 7).

The 3D model of the section represented in Fig. 7 has a Level Of Detail (LOD) of 300, which guarantees that the objects of the model can be accurately positioned within the

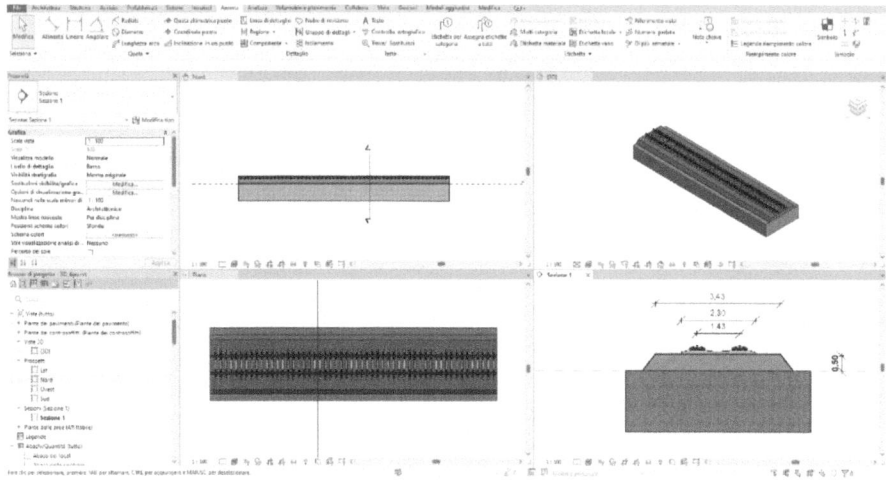

Fig. 7. Autodesk Revit: BIM of the railway track.

project and faithfully reproduce the dimensions, shape, position, and orientation of the represented object. As for the parameters evaluated, these refer to the distance between the rails, the thickness of the ballast, and the slope. There are specific tools within the Agisoft Metashape software that allow the accurate measurement of distances within the 3D model (always considering the average error of the restitution of 2 cm).

BIM modeling, based on the actual state of the railway section, provides important information for intelligent maintenance of the infrastructure, guaranteeing the possibility to simulate the work schedule through the analysis of construction times, the integration of economic data for cost control, and resource management.

In this specific case, the creation of the BIM model starting from the survey carried out with the drone permitted the recreation of the plano-altimetric feature of the railway section and provided useful information for future interventions. For example, the railway line under investigation is not yet electrified, and it could be subject to modernization and electrification interventions, using BIM to simulate the ideal positioning of poles and power cables.

Furthermore, BIM enables the management of information related to environmental sustainability and energy efficiency, supporting the selection of appropriate materials for designing and implementing low environmental impact interventions. Thanks to these capabilities, BIM allows for the management of the entire infrastructure lifecycle, including the monitoring and tracking of the wear condition of each component within the railway section.

4 Conclusions and Future Work

This research focused on the use of drones for constructing 3D and BIM models of a railway section, achieving a high level of precision and detail that enabled significant geometric analyses and demonstrated the potential of these technologies for detecting deterioration and subsidence within the infrastructure.

The advantages of drone-based surveys are well known they allow for the continuous generation of up-to-date 3D models of railway infrastructure, offering detailed, real-time information and enabling the identification of damage and deformations with centimeter-level accuracy. On the other hand, it should be noted that railway areas, especially in Italy, are not always accessible without the necessary permits and certifications, in addition to the specific license required for the drone operator. Additionally, drone surveys are influenced by weather conditions and limited flight autonomy, which tend to decrease in certain areas and conditions. Moreover, drones may not always be able to capture images from all the necessary angles for an accurate reconstruction, making precise and strategic flight planning essential.

The integration of BIM in railway projects offers significant advantages in all phases of the infrastructure's life cycle: in the design phase, BIM enhances the overall quality of the designed infrastructure, improving its performance in terms of safety, security, and resource management; in the construction phase, BIM is useful for optimizing the work scheduling, resource management, time, and costs; and during the operation phase, BIM improves maintenance processes and facilitates the integration of modifications throughout the infrastructure's lifespan.

Therefore, while the 3D model allows for accurate monitoring of the infrastructure's status, the BIM model enables advanced management throughout all phases of design and maintenance. Integrating the BIM design model with the monitoring model permits the identification of potential issues that may arise over time in the railway section, providing valuable insights for planning and optimizing maintenance interventions.

The strength of the proposed methodology lies mainly in the possibility of using rapid procedures and measures for monitoring the railway section. The practical limitations of the entire proposed process lie in the size of the images to be processed and, consequently, in the size of the point cloud at the base of both the 3D model and the creation of the BIM model. A further limitation consists of the need to process the images on a computer that can guarantee the best performance in terms of advanced graphics, in order not to have excessively high processing times. Furthermore, the process requires specific skills in the use of topographical instruments, photogrammetric processing software, and BIM. Regarding the costs of the proposed solution, it is necessary to take into account the initial costs related to the purchase of the equipment and the proprietary software used. The purchase of the drone requires insurance, while the GNSS equipment involves an additional cost for the subscription to the positioning satellites. Regarding the software, the licenses may vary. The cost of such equipment is, however, justified, considering that the monitoring of an entire railway section with traditional methods can end up having the same cost, but with the need for longer times to carry out the survey activities. Finally, the drone operator must acquire the necessary license to operate.

The proposed methodology also provides benefits to several stakeholders. For project managers and construction companies, the combined use of drones and BIM facilitates data collection and monitoring operations, significantly reducing the need for specialized labor. For engineers, this methodology ensures precision and accuracy, allowing for reliable and accurate measurements that are not subject to interpretation errors, also thanks to the possibility of using tools such as drones, equipped with very high-resolution cameras, which allow for more detailed and precise spatial data with minimal average error. This methodology improves collaboration between designers, as the level of detail achieved allows for realistic and geolocalized representations of infrastructures and for a greater understanding of the interventions to be carried out.

Future work could involve the integration of additional geomatics and artificial intelligence techniques to improve advanced analyses on railway infrastructures. Drones equipped with multispectral sensors could be used to identify variations in humidity and ballast grain size, while georadar could be used as a tool to identify any subsidence areas in the section. Furthermore, artificial intelligence techniques could help in the automatic segmentation and classification processes of portions of the point cloud for subsequent BIM modeling. Future analyses could also focus on applying post-processing techniques to convolutional neural networks to further refine the results achieved by global segmentation, by applying morphological filtering algorithms.

Acknowledgments. This study was carried out within the MOST – Sustainable Mobility National Research Center and received funding from the European Union Next-Generation EU (PIANO NAZIONALE DI RIPRESA E RESILIENZA (PNRR) – MISSIONE 4 COMPONENTE 2, INVESTIMENTO 1.4 – D.D. 1033 17/06/2022, CN00000023). This manuscript reflects only the authors' views and opinions, neither the European Union nor the European Commission can be considered responsible for them.

Disclosure of Interests. The authors have no competing interests to declare that are relevant to the content of this article.

References

1. European Commission. Seventh monitoring report on the development of the rail market under Article 15(4) of Directive 2012/34/EU of the European Parliament and of the Council (2021)
2. Giunta, M.: Trends and challenges in railway sustainability: the state of the art regarding measures, strategies, and assessment tools. Sustainability **15**, 16632 (2023)
3. Sedghi, M., Kauppila, O., Bergquista, B., Vanhataloa, E., Kulahcia, M.: A taxonomy of railway track maintenance planning and scheduling: a review and research trends. Reliab. Eng. Syst. Saf. **215**, 107827 (2021)
4. Aela, P., Cai, J., Jing, G., Hung-Lin Chi, H.-L.: Vision-based monitoring of railway superstructure: a review. Constr. Build. Mater. **442**, 137385 (2024)
5. Guerrieri, M., Parla, G., Celauro, C.: Digital image analysis technique for measuring railway track defects and ballast gradation. Measurement **113**, 137–147 (2018)
6. Barrile, V., Fotia, A., Leonardi, G., Pucinotti, R.: Geomatics and soft computing techniques for infrastructural monitoring. Sustainability **12**(4), 1606 (2020)
7. Bolourian, N., Hammad, A.: LiDAR-equipped UAV path planning considering potential locations of defects for bridge inspection. Autom. Constr. **117**, 103250 (2020). https://doi.org/10.1016/j.autcon.2020.103250
8. Cabral, R., et al.: Railway bridge geometry assessment supported by cutting-edge reality capture technologies and 3D as-designed models. Infrastructures **8**(7), 114 (2023)
9. Zhang, R., Hao, G., Zhang, K., Li, Z.: Unmanned aerial vehicle navigation in underground structure inspection: A review. Geol. J. **58** (6) (2023) 2454–2472. ISSN: 0072–1050. https://doi.org/10.1002/gj.4763

10. Rahman, M.A., Mammeri, A.: Vegetation detection in UAV imagery for railway Monitoring, In: Proceedings of the 7th International Conference on Vehicle Technology and Intelligent Transport Systems - VEHITS, pp. 457–464 (2021) ISSN: 978–989–758–513–5. https://doi.org/10.5220/0010439904570464

11. Sherrock, E., Neubecker, K.: Unmanned aircraft system applications in international railroads, in, United States. Federal Railroad Administration. Technical Report DOT/FRA/ORD-18/04 (2018)

12. Ravitharan, R., Chevin, J., Chung, H., C. Vong, Zhang, D.: The Implementation of Unmanned Autonomous Systems for Railway Inspection. In: Proceedings of the International Heavy Haul Association (IHHA), 10–14 June 2019, Narvik, Norway

13. Qiu, L.: Development of UAV-based rail track geometry irregularity monitoring and measuring platform empowered by artificial intelligence, UNLV Theses (2022). https://doi.org/10.34917/31813346 from

14. Wu, J., Limei Peng, L., Sheng, W., Changxin Wang, C., Sun, J.: Track gauge measurement based on model matching using UAV image. Autom. Constr. **155**, 105070 (2023)

15. Sahebdivani, S., Arefi, H., Maboudi, M.: Rail track detection and projection-based 3D modeling from UAV point cloud. Sensors **20**, 5220 (2020)

16. Barrile, V., Genovese, E., Favasuli, F.: Development and application of an integrated BIM-GIS system for the energy management of buildings. WSEAS Trans. Power Syst **18**, 232–240 (2023)

Estimating the Run Choice Behavior in High Speed Rail (HSR) Mode-Service: A Revealed Preference Survey

Giuseppe Musolino🆔 and Domenico Sgro$^{(\boxtimes)}$🆔

DIIES, Università Mediterranea of Reggio Calabria, 89100 Reggio Calabria, Italy
domenico.sgro@unirc.it

Abstract. High Speed Rail (HSR) passenger services cause competition with other rail services, and other modes of transport. The paper presents the structure of a Reveled Preference (RP) survey which has been submitted to travelers in an Italian HSR context. The objective of the survey is to analyze the travelers' choice behavior, among the services, the runs and the ticket levels. Hence, the survey investigates the main behavioral variables of HSR travelers to be adopted for the calibration of discrete choice models in the dimension of run and ticket. The RP survey is organized in several sections to collect different types of data: data about the chosen run (day of travel, number of the run, departure and arrival time); socio-economic data about the traveler and his/her family; data about the purpose and frequency of the trip; data about the chosen ticket. This work is aimed at supporting transport planners and decision-makers in the evaluation of future investment in HSR lines and services, and to analyze the travelers' behavior, by means of methodological and modelling tools to assess the potential HSR travel demand.

Keywords: High Speed Rail (HSR) · demand analysis · run choice behavior · survey · Revealed Preference (RP)

1 Introduction

The extension of High Speed Rail (HSR) lines around the world considerably increased in the last decades. Currently, on the one hand the HSR lines result to be more than 120,000 km. On the other hand, the number of passengers which have been travelled with the HSR services achieved 778,9 billion of passenger-kilometres in year 2021. The main country which contributes to this result is China with 606,4 billion of passenger-kilometres [1].

The design of an HSR line and the organization of the services is dependent of several factors [2–5]. The effects of HSR on passenger mobility have been investigated by means of the travel demand models, which may be segmented into three components [6–8]: diverted, induced and economic-growth. In the context of diverted demand, the fare structures of HSR services play a key role in either intra-modal and inter-modal levels of competition for the intercity passenger mobility. The demand models are part

© The Author(s), under exclusive license to Springer Nature Switzerland AG 2026
O. Gervasi et al. (Eds.): ICCSA 2025 Workshops, LNCS 15894, pp. 420–433, 2026.
https://doi.org/10.1007/978-3-031-97648-3_28

of the Transport System Models (TSMs) [9–11], which simulate a transport system where transport supply and travel demand interact and generate the flows and the performances of the transport system.

In the context of intercity trips and intra-modal competition of HSR, the run choice models estimate the travelers' choices among the available runs, where the relevant attributes generally belong to the class of level of service, for instance the fares, the components of trip time (e.g. departure/arrival times), the company.

The data necessary for the choice models' calibration are traditionally obtained by means of surveys [11, 15]. The surveys may be classified according to different criteria, based on: (a) the level of aggregation of the observed variables: aggregated or disaggregated; the nature of choice: Revealed Preference (RP) or Stated Preference (SP).

The paper presents the structure of a RP survey, which has been submitted to users travelling along the Rome-Milan relationship (Italy) during April 2025, in order to observe the choice behaviour of travelers.

According to the above considerations, the structure of the paper is the following. Section 2 concerns the theoretical background of the run choice models. Section 3 describes the existing classes of survey for collecting data concerning passenger mobility. Section 4 specifies the structure of the questionnaire submitted to the travelers in the experimental context. The last section contains some final remarks.

This work is aimed at supporting transport planners and decision-makers in the evaluation of future investment in HSR lines and services, by means of methodological and modelling tools to assess the potential HSR travel demand and possible future investments in HSR infrastructure and services.

2   Run Choice Model

In the behalf of the TSM framework [9–11], the travel demand models estimate the users' behavior in relation to (congested) costs on the transport network.

Travel demand models may be differently classified in literature. There are two main approaches: aggregate models, where variables are related to group of users (e.g., average origin-destination demand flow of passengers in a reference time period); and disaggregated models, where variables are related to the behavior of single user in terms of different choice dimensions (e.g., making the trip, destination, mode-service, departure time, path, or run).

Aggregated travel demand models may be segmented into three categories. Statistical-descriptive estimate the demand flow among relationships by means of attributes of the socio-economic and level-of-service class. Time series use historical data to estimate demand flows with fixed characteristics (e.g. origin-destination). Partial-share simulate the user choice through a procedure of partial sequential choices, or steps; the more current example regards the multi-stage models, including trip generation, trip distribution, time choice (arrival/departure), service choice, path/run choice.

Disaggregated travel demand models are generally based on discrete choice theory, which have been specified with different formalization of discrete alternatives and related perceived utility, in term of random utility [12], fuzzy utility [13], and quantum utility [14] approaches. From a general point of view, random utility models vary in relation to the perceived utility function, that may be specified according to different functional correlations among, for instance, the levels of choice (hierarchical or factorial), different hypotheses on the formation of choice set of alternatives, and lastly different hypotheses about the distribution of random residuals.

Travel demand models in the context of High Speed Rail (HSR) mode-services may be classified into three main components [6, 8 (and references included)]. The diverted demand is the number of passengers attracted to HSR from other transport modes and/or other rail services. The induced demand is the number of passengers travelling with HSR due to changes in trip frequency and destination. The economy-based demand is the number of passengers travelling with HSR due to the changing structure of the economy, which in its turns generates new trips. The three components are generally estimated before the opening of a HSR line with ex-ante modelling approaches, or after the opening of a HSR line by means of before-after approaches.

According to the above classification, there are several papers in literature which specify, calibrate and validate discrete choice models regarding the three modelling components. The diverted demand is the most investigated among the three components of the demand, whereas the induced component is studied in few papers for the complexity to be identified. Therefore, there is a lack in the literature about the economy-based component, which requires the development of Spatial Economy Transport Interction (SETI) models [16] to be estimated.

As far as concern the diverted demand, several choice dimensions are investigated by plenty of papers, such as the mode, service, company, and run. A set of papers which deal with this topic are reported here. Yao and Morikawa (2005) [17] analyze the intercity travel demand by means of a specification of a multi-level discrete choice model on the dimensions of mode/service/run. The considered modal alternatives are bus, car, airplane. The model uses data provided by RP and SP surveys and aggregate data and has been tested in a Japanese case study. Cascetta et al. (2011) [18] analyse the impacts of the HSR services along the Italian relationship Rome-Naples. The paper concerns the diverted demand analysis towards HSR services from other transport modes and other rail services (e.g., Intercity services). It has been specified a discrete choice model on the dimensions of mode-service-company-run for different trip purposes, such as "home-based trips" and "non-home-based trips". The data has been provided by a RP survey submitted to users travelling by car and with conventional and HSR services. Cascetta and Coppola (2012) [19] work on the national transport competition in the case of a new HSR operator entering. It has been specified and calibrated a discrete choice model, hence a multi-level nested logit model, on the dimensions of mode-service-run for different travel purposes (e.g., business). The data was provided by traffic counts and RP/SP surveys submitted to users between the years 2009 and 2011. Roman and Martin (2014) [20] deal with the simulation of passenger choices between two modes of transport alternatives, hence HSR and air services. In order to achieve the objective, two models have been specified and calibrated, thus the multinomial logit and the mixed logit. Cross elasticity is specified, however not calculated.

The discrete choice models commonly used for the estimation of the users' choices in the path dimension are based upon the specification of Mansky (1977) [12]. In the context of run choice, the probability that a user i chooses a run r, $p^i(r)$, is calculated as the product of two components:

- probability that a user i chooses the set of alternative runs, I_v: $p^i(I_v)$;
- probability that a user i chooses the run r, given the set of alternative runs, I_v: $p^i(r|I_v)$;

where:

r is the perceived run ($r \in I_r$);

$Z = \{1, 2, ..., r, ...\}$ is the set containing a finite number of runs (elementary alternatives);

$G = \{I_1, I_2, , I_v, ...\}$ is the set containing all the sets of runs.

The probability of choosing a run r, considering the two components of probabilities, may be calculated as (Mansky 1977) [12]:

$$p^i(r) = \sum_{I_v \in G} p^i(r) \cdot p^i(r|I_v) \tag{1}$$

Transport users might perceive the sets of runs r, $I_v \in G$, with different probabilities $p^i(I_v)$. It is reasonable that users perceive a limited number of sets $S \subseteq G$. This implies that the probability is $p^i(I_v) > 0$ for the perceived sets $I_v \in S \subseteq G$ and the probability is $p^i(I_v) = 0$ for the non-perceived sets $I_v \notin S$.

In the extreme case where one set, $I_v^* \in G$, is perceived, the probability $p(I_v)$ in Eq. (1) is calculated as:

$$p^i(I_v) = p^i(I_v^*) = \begin{cases} 1 & \text{if } I_v \in G \\ 0 & \text{if } I_v \neq I_v^* \text{ and } I_v^* \in G \end{cases} \tag{2}$$

According to Eqs. (2), (1) is specified as follows:

$$p^i(r) = p^i(r|I_v^*) \tag{3}$$

It is possible to estimate the quantity $p^i(I_v^*) \in [0, 1]$ with choice set perception models, which allow to construct the perceived choice sets (formation level), thus to estimate the quantity $p(I_r)$ associated to each perceived choice set by the user (extraction level) ([21] and references included).

The probability $p^i(r)$ may be specified by means of several categories of discrete choice models existing in literature: random utility models, fuzzy utility models, or quantum utility models. (see Vitetta, 2025 [22] for a comparison among the different categories).

The discrete choice models that rely upon random utility theory [11, 23, 24], are based on the assumptions that a user i chooses the run r, among the set $I_v \in G$, which maximize the associated perceived utility, $U^i(r)$.

Considering that the utility, $U^i(r)$, is a random variable, it is not possible to establish with absolute certainty which run will be chosen by the user i. However, it is possible to specify the probability, $p^i(r|I_v)$ that the run $r \in I_v$ chosen by user i is greater than the perceived utility associated to the other run r', $U^i(r')'$, with r, r' $\in I_v$:

$$p^i(r|I_v) = \text{Prob} (U^i(r|I_v) > U^i(r'|I_v)) \ \forall \ r' \neq r, r \in I_v \tag{4}$$

3   Survey Methods

The census knowledge of trips of each user with her/his own characteristics require so high costs that they are not sustainable by analysts and transport modelers. Therefore, travel demand is estimated by means of surveys on a sample of users.

The methods for surveying passenger (and freight) mobility may be classified in two main categories: disaggregate and aggregate (Fig. 1). The setting of the survey concerns the definition of the location of the detectors and the sampling of the elements to be monitored. The monitoring activities are generally executed by means of ICT tools in the case of aggregate surveys, whereas they are generally executed with the support of interviews to travelers in the case of disaggregate ones. The aim of the disaggregate surveys is the acquisition of data about the trip behavior of individual users; while the aggregate surveys consist in the acquisition of traffic flow data on specific links/nodes, or paths, of the transport network. In both the categories of surveys the attributes estimated rely to socioeconomic characteristics of users, land use, characteristics of users' trips and behavior, and level-of-service of transportation network (e.g. travel costs).

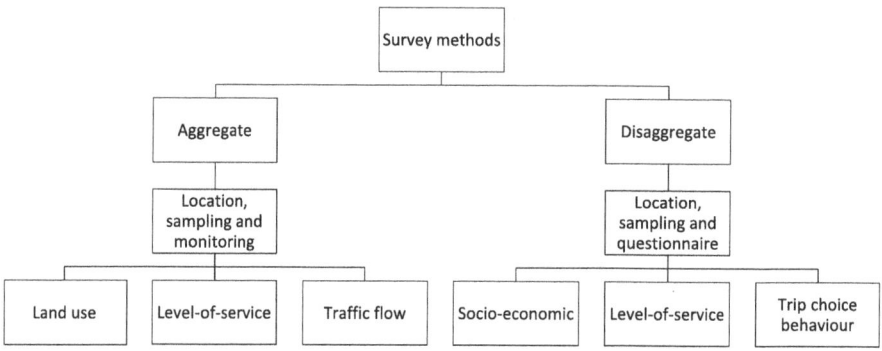

Fig. 1. Classification of survey methods

3.1   Aggregate Survey

The aim of the aggregate surveys is to obtain data about mobility of people inside a given study area.

Location and Sampling. The setting activities concern the correct identification of the elements (links/nodes or paths) of the network to be monitored and their number, in order to obtain a sample of elements which is representative of the whole network (universe). The above element is particularly important in the case of origin-destination matrix updating from traffic counts.

Monitoring. The monitoring consists in the counting and classification of users travelling on the elements of the transport network. These operations are generally executed by means of different Information and Communication Technology (ICT) tools.

A review of monitoring methods of vehicular traffic flow, where vehicles may be private (e.g. cars) or collective (e.g. buses), is reported in the Guide Lines authored by the Italian Ministry of Transport and Infrastructures [25].

Mobility of people (and goods) is generally monitored on two elements of the network: link/node sections and (multi-modal) paths.

The monitoring of on link/node sections may be executed with manual or automatic techniques. The manual techniques consist in travellers/vehicles counting and classification by human operators, that are employed in case of surveys of short time (e.g. hours, days) and on few links/nodes. The automatic techniques are supported by ICT tools and are employed in case of long time extension surveys (e.g. weeks, months) and several links/nodes. Examples of sections in case of transit systems are the entrance/exit of railway stations/bus terminals/airports, the get on/get off to/from the trains or buses.

The monitoring on (multi-modal) paths is today mainly based on data collected from smartphones, smartcards, Points-Of-Interest (POIs) and GPS that trace the travellers along their trip; for example, from the origin to the destination of the trip [26].

Smartphones are potentially capable to provide a great amount of data about travellers' trips for long periods at relative low costs. Nevertheless, the distribution and the shape of phone cells limit their quality. Smartphone data needs to be adequately elaborated and structured to obtain space-time trajectories of travellers.

Smartcards are generally used for Automated Fare Collection (AFC) in public transport systems. They provide space–time based trip data referred to the place where the transactions are executed. They generally record only travellers' boarding and are suitable for the estimation and/or updating of origin-destination matrices of passenger flows.

POIs data may be used to combine data about the locations where systematic trips from home to work originate and have their destination (e.g. provided from smartphones), with data about the locations where not-systematic trips originate/have their destination, such as leisure activities, shopping.

GPS are generally used from insurance companies to monitor private cars, commercial and bus fleets. The challenge of GPS data concerns the association of the discrete row data about vehicle time-space position with the link of the road network (e.g. mapmatching) especially in urban area.

The above ICT tools allow to obtain a great amount of data (big-data) that need to be adequately elaborated and structured before it can be used as input for travel demand models.

The data may be classified into two main groups: land use and level-of-service data (attributes) and flows data of users (and/or vehicles).

Land Use. The land use data concern census data about the population and economic activities inside the study area. The data about the population includes, for instance, the number of residents, employees, students. The data about the economic activities may include the number of workplaces in different economic sectors, the number of shops in urban areas, and schools. The census data are collected during periodic surveys (e.g. every 5 years) form national statistic institutes (e.g. Istituto Nazionale di Statistica-ISTAT in Italy) due to their high costs.

Level-of-Service. The level-of-service data concerns the performance of the transport network. The most common attribute belonging to this class is the travel time. The link travel time may be referred to a road section or to a section of transit line between two stops, while the node travel time is the time necessary for crossing a road intersection or a transit terminal. The path travel time may be the time, let's say, from the origin of the trip to the destination of the trip and it presents several components associated with the phases of the trip (e.g. access, waiting time at the bus stop/station, on-board, egress). There are other level-of service attributes, such as the average speed on the link and nodes of the transport network, in the case of trips with private modes (e.g., car); the frequency of the transit lines, in the case of trips with transit modes (e.g. bus or train).

Flow Data. The flow data are generally related to a sample of links/nodes or paths of the transport network. The flows on links/nodes sections are obtained as the ratio between the observed people that cross the section and the reference time period (e.g. hour, day) and they do not contain any information about the origin/destination of the trip. The flows on the (multi-modal) paths contain several information about the origin/destination of the trip; the portions of the path undertaken with each mode, such as (e.g. car, train, ...), if the path is multimodal.

3.2 Disaggregate Survey

The aim of disaggregate surveys is to obtain data about the choice behavior of each individual traveler, which belongs to a sample in a specific study area.

The setting of the survey concerns the definition of the location of interviewers and the sampling of the travelers.

Location. The location of interviewers may be different: at the origin or the destination of the trip, at home, at workplace, by phone and along the trip and performed by operators in different ways: for instance, at a railway stations, airports, bus terminals, on-board of transport vehicles. The location influences the questionnaire design, in terms of specific questions to be submitted to the travelers. An example is in the medium-long haul services. In the case of railway, different configurations of the question are necessary according to the questionnaire is submitted on-board or at the railway terminal, as some information (e.g. run, departure and arrival time, ...) are implicitly known by the operator when she/he is on-board.

Sampling. It is necessary to define the sampling unit, the procedure for the extraction of the sample and the size of the sample. The individual traveler is generally considered as the sampling unit, but in some cases the family may be also considered. The literature proposes several methods for the extraction of the sample, for instance the simple random sampling, the stratified random sampling, the cluster sampling. The relevance of the latter element is given by the necessity, for instance, to include inside the sample travelers belonging to different socio-economic classes, or to different geographic areas, in order to capture the choice behavior of travelers that may be conditioned by different values of attributes. This consideration is held in the choice of the fare, where two main class of users' behavior may be defined. The time-based user, that chooses the run/flight on the basis of the desired departure/arrival time and the day of trip, regardless to the fare;

and the price-based user, which chooses the run/flight with the lowest fare available, independently of the departure/arrival time or the day of trip (see, among the others [27]). As an example, the students that travel for leisure purposes behave as a price-based users; whereas autonomous workers that travel for business purposes behave as a time-based users.

In addition, the days of observation (or surveying) result to be dependent to the sampling method, to the variable to be estimated and to the statistical significance expected.

Questionnaire. The design of the questionnaire consists, mainly, in the formulation of the questions in order to collect data related to the socio-economic characteristics of the respondents and their trip choices. Two classes of preferences may be asked to the respondents:

- the preferences about the trip they have already undertaken given the current real conditions of the transport system; in this case we talk about a Revealed Preference (RP) approach;
- the preferences about the trip they could undertake given one, or more scenarios, where the conditions of the transport system are realistic but not real; in this case it is intended a Stated Preference (SP) approach.

The Revealed Preference (RP) survey refers to the investigation of the user choice behavior in a real context; while the Stated Preference (SP) survey refers to the investigation of users' choice behavior stated by the user in a hypothetical scenario proposed in the scenario. It is possible to submit one of the latter two (RP/SP) surveys to the user, otherwise there is the possibility to design a questionnaire with a combination of RP and SP questionnaires.

The data obtained from the disaggregate surveys may be classified into: socio-economic data and data about the choice behavior of each individual travelers.

Socio-economic Attributes. The socio-economic attributes of the respondents may concern the gender, the age, the level of education, the working condition, the residence and domicile, the number of family components.

Level-of-Service Attributes. The attributes are generally related to costs (e.g., monetary cost, travel time, …) and attributes concerning service satisfaction. Among these attributes, the fares play a key role in the users' choices. In the literature, the structure of fares are classified into two main approaches, such as static and dynamic. The static approach results to be used mainly for local public transport, whereas the dynamic approach means that the fares are characterized by variations over time, depending on several factors, in particular between the day of travel and the day of ticket purchasing (day of the week).

Trip Choice Behavior. The dimensions of choices of the users are various, thus from the choice to make a trip to the choice of the destination, the choice of the departure time, the choice of the transport mode and the service, and to the choice of the path or the run. Moreover, another dimension of choice results to be the ticket choice, especially in the public transport sector.

4 Survey Design: Italian Case Study

A survey based on the RP approach has been planned to obtain data about the trip choices of users in the dimension of the run and fare. A questionnaire has been submitted to users travelling along the relationship Rome-Milan (Italy) with HSR mode-services.

4.1 Experimental Test Site

The HSR line between Rome and Milan (Italy) was selected as it is the main Italian relationship in terms of volume of passengers and of services. The relationship includes besides the alternative of air services; however, this work does not investigate the mode choice level.

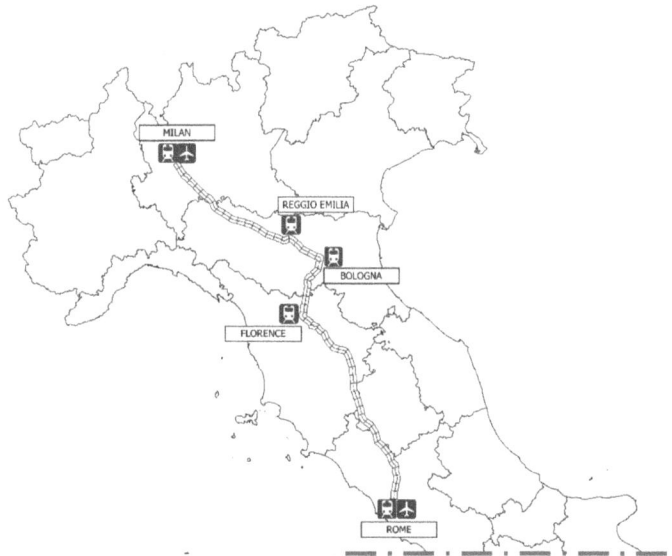

Fig. 2. Rome-Milan relationship (Italy)

The HSR line between Rome and Milan has been operating since 2009. Therefore, it began to generate intra-modal and inter-model competition, causing the diversion of travel demand from air and conventional rail services. Moreover, new travel demand was induced as a result of several factors, such as the increased level of service offered by HSR (e.g. reduction of on-board travel time).

The observation of available traffic before-after the HSR opening [28] shows that the passenger flows in the year 2008 were about 2,4 millions/year by the air mode and 1,0 millions/year by conventional rail mode. The passenger flows in the year 2018 were 1,2 millions/year by air mode and 3,6 millions/year by HSR mode-service.

Two HSR companies operate along this relationship. Trenitalia supplies HSR services and also conventional and local rail services; while Italo Nuovo Trasporto Viaggiatori (Italo NTV) supplies only HSR services. The two companies compete each other at service and run choice levels, hence they both compete at mode choice level with some airline companies.

The frequency of HSR services is about, respectively, 45 runs/day (per direction) for the Trenitalia company, and 32 runs/day for the NTV company, during the year 2024. The scheduled runs are characterized by several elements such as the typology of service, for instance the shuttle runs (with at least one stop), the in-vehicle travel time, and the organization of the fares offered to the travelers. Each HSR company supplies services with higher performances, for instance in terms of minimum number of intermediate stops, in the peak-hours of the day (e.g., 06:00–09:00 am on the working days).

Concerning the fare choice level, both companies operating in Italy organizes and propose the ticket fares into two main categories, which are business and economy, each declined in one or more classes. In particular, Trenitalia company offers a wider set of fares than Italo NTV, thus characterized by numerous combination of services, however both companies offer flexible tickets (e.g., possibility to change day/hour of travel, possibility of refund, …), defined as Classes (e.g., "Super Economy" for Trenitalia and "Low Cost" for Italo NTV) and accommodation offered (e.g., wider seat, faster wi-fi connection, welcome service,..), defined as Quality of service (e.g., "Standard" for Trenitalia and "Smart" for Italo NTV). Each fare is the result of the combination of the latter two elements (class and quality of service), as well as the possibility of adding further services (e.g., seat selection, partial or total refund in case of trip cancellation,…). Consequently, there are lots of variables composing the fare, called dimensions, that determine a multi-dimension structure of the fares [29].

4.2 Questionnaire Design

The questionnaire is organized into 5 sections, described in the following (Fig. 2).

- Section 0 is dedicated to the operator who must fill the fields with specific information related to the location of the interview and about the chosen service;
- Section 1 is composed of 9 questions of a socio-economic nature concerning gender, age, level of education and working status, residence and domicile, number of household members and children under 18 years old, number of cars in the family;
- Section 2 concerns information about the trip from Milan to Rome and from Rome to Milan. It consists of four questions: the purpose of the trip, the purpose for staying in the area of origin of the trip, the frequency with which the same trip takes place and the period of staying in the area of origin/destination of the trip.
- Section 3 regards questions about the company chosen for the trip by the user. It is composed by fifteen questions, questions 1 and 2 concern the choice between the two Italian HSR transport companies and the purpose, while the subsequent questions concern the satisfaction of the chosen service.
- Section 4a and 4b concern the choice of the route and fare for Trenitalia and Italo NTV, respectively. Questions concern the reason for choosing the run, the desired departure time from the origin and desired arrival at the destination, the type of ticket and the services chosen. In addition, the price of the ticket, how many days before departure, as well as on which platform it was purchased (Fig. 3).

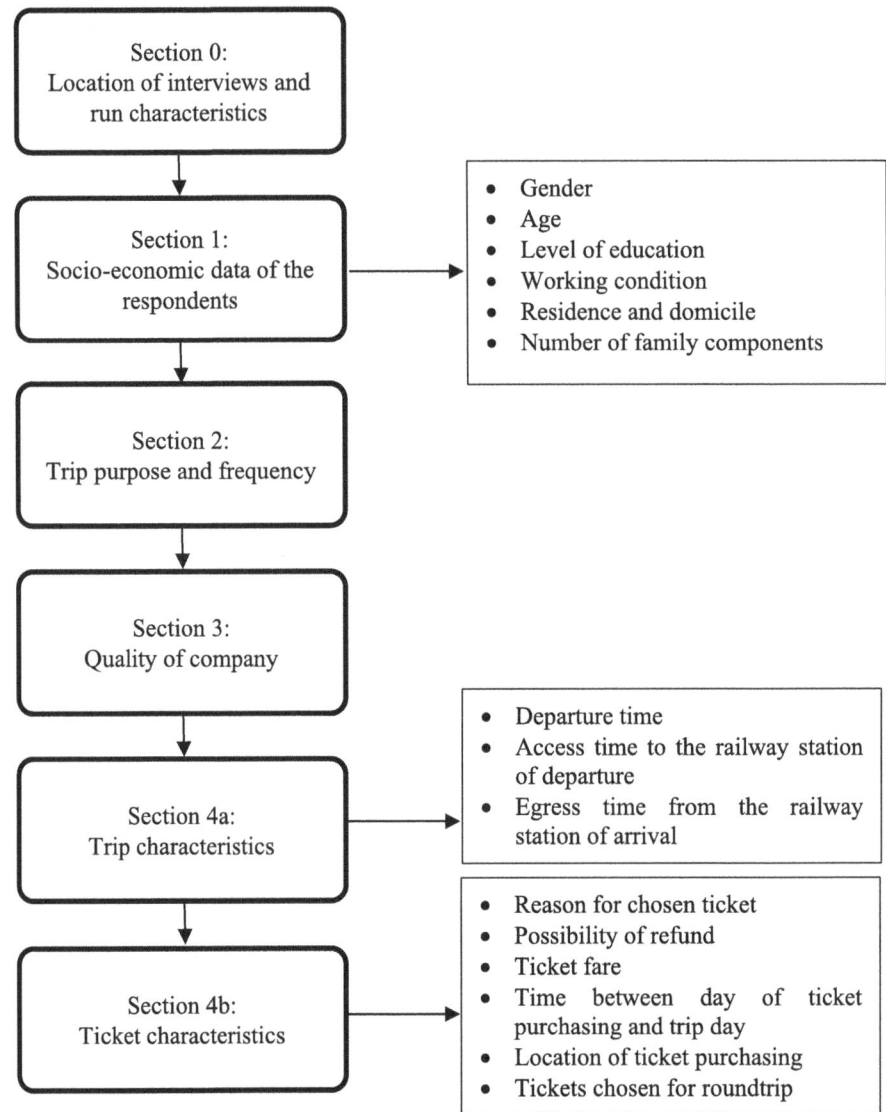

Fig. 3. Sections of the questionnaire organization

The survey has been carried out by submitting questionnaires to users in both directions of the relationship: Rome-Milan and Milan-Rome. Moreover, the sample has been designed in order to interview: at least 40% of workers, at least 40% of males and females, and at least about 40% of people travelling for business purpose. The composition of the sample is useful to better analyze the choices of several types of users. In addition, the questionnaires were submitted during different days of week, to capture the behavior of the users among the working days, weekend days and holydays.

Furthermore, the schedule of the services has been considered among the days of the week, hence the survey has been distributed not among all the scheduled runs, however, between the runs considered as a reference in the time slots of the day (e.g., the runs with at least one intermediate stop).

The submission of the questionnaire was performed onboard; hence the users has been interviewed during the trip. Therefore, a few information results ot be fixed: e.g., number of the run (e.g., also departure time to the railway stations), company, the number of the carriages.

5   Conclusions

The paper presents a RP survey aimed to build a dataset of users' trip behaviour for the specification and calibration of run choice models. The survey aims to investigate the users' choice behavior in an intercity context in which HSR services operate and different companies compete each other. The designed survey was submitted to users which travel among the main Italian route, thus the Rome-Milan relationship, in terms of service and flows, in terms of representativity of the sample.

The obtained data could reveal important information about the behavior of different typology of users in the dimension choice of run and fare that travels with HSR mode-service along this important Italian relationship.

Future research directions of the presented work concerns the use of available data for the specification, calibration and validation of discrete choice models in the dimensions of run choice and fare.

Acknowledgements. This study was carried out within the MOST – Sustainable Mobility National Research Center (CUP C33C22000240001) and received funding from the European Union Next-Generation EU (PIANO NAZIONALE DI RIPRESA E RESILIENZA (PNRR) – MISSIONE 4 COMPONENTE 2, INVESTIMENTO 1.4 – D.D. 1033 17/06/2022, CN00000023). This manuscript reflects only the authors' views and opinions, neither the European Union nor the European Commission can be considered responsible for them.

References

1. High Speed Lines In The World (Summary), Updated 1st October 2023. https://uic.org/pas senger/highspeed/article/high-speed-data-and-atlas. Accessed 26 Feb 2025
2. Russo, F.: Which high-speed rail? LARG approach between plan and design. Future Transport. **1**(2), 202–226 (2021). https://doi.org/10.3390/futuretransp1020013
3. Massimo di Gangi, Francesco Russo. Potentiality of rail networks: integrated services on conventional and high-speed lines. WIT Trans. Built Environ. **213**, 101–112 (2022). https://doi.org/10.2495/CR220091
4. Massimo di Gangi, Francesco Russo, Design of hybrid rail services on conventional and high-speed lines. Int. J. Transp. Develop. Integrat. https://www.iieta.org/journals/ijtdi/paper/https://doi.org/10.18280/ijtdi.070206
5. Corrado Rindone, Antonio Russo. A network analysis for High Speed Rail services in the South of Italy. In: Conference proceedings of the international Conference on Computational Science and ITS Applications ICCSA 2024 July 1–4, 2024, HANOI, Vietnam. https://link.springer.com/chapter/https://doi.org/10.1007/978-3-031-65318-6_15

6. Ben-Akiva, M., Cascetta, E., Coppola, P., Papola, A., Velardi, V.: High Speed Rail demand forecasting in a competitive market: the Italian case study. In: Proceedings of the World Conference of Transportation Research (WCTR). Lisbon, Portugal (2010)

7. Cascetta, E., Coppola, P.: High speed rail (HSR) induced demand models. Procedia-Soc. Behav. Sci. **111**, 147–156 (2014)

8. Russo, F., Sgro, D., Musolino, G.: Sustainable development of railway corridors: methods and models for High Speed Rail (HSR) demand analysis. In: Gervasi, O., et al. (eds.) Computational Science and Its Applications – ICCSA 2023 Workshops. ICCSA 2023. LNCS, vol. 14110. Springer, Cham (2023). https://doi.org/10.1007/978-3-031-37123-3_36

9. Ben-Akiva, M., Bergman, M.J., Daly, A.J., Ramaswamy, R.: Modelling interurban route choice behaviour. In: Proceedings of the 9th International Symposium on Transportation and Traffic Theory, pp. 299–330. VNU Science Press (1984)

10. Ortúzar, J.D.D., Willumsen, L.G.: Modelling transport, 3rd edn. John Wiley, Chichester, NY, USA (2001)

11. Cascetta, E.: Transportation systems analysis: models and applications. Springer (2009)

12. Manski, C.F.: The structure of random utility models. Theor. Decis. **8**, 229–254 (1977)

13. Quattrone, A.; Vitetta, A. Random and Fuzzy Utility Models for Road Route Choice. Transp. Res. Part E Logist. Transp. Rev. 2011, 47, 1126–1139

14. Vitetta, A.: Quantum utility model for route choice in transport systems. Travel Behav. Soc. **3**, 29–37 (2016)

15. Russo, F., Moschella, M., Musolino, G.: Railway demand evaluation: HSR induced component. In: Gervasi, O., Murgante, B., Garau, C., Taniar, D.C., Rocha, A.M.A., Faginas Lago, M.N. (eds.) Computational Science and Its Applications – ICCSA 2024 Workshops. ICCSA 2024. LNCS, vol. 14822. Springer, Cham (2024). https://doi.org/10.1007/978-3-031-65318-6_12

16. Russo, F., Musolino, G.: A unifying modelling framework to simulate the spatial economic transport interaction process at urban and national scales. J. Transp. Geogr. **24**, 9–22 (2012). https://doi.org/10.1016/j.jtrangeo.2012.02.003

17. Yao, E., Morikawa, T.: A study of an integrated intercity travel demand model. Transp. Res. Part A **39**, 367–381 (2005)

18. Cascetta, E., Papola, A., Pagliara, F., Marzano, V.: Analysis of mobility impacts of the high-speed Rome-Naples rail link using within-day dynamic mode service choice models. J. Transp. Geogr. **19**(3), 423–432 (2011). https://doi.org/10.1016/j.jtrangeo.2010.07.001

19. Cascetta, E., Coppola, P.: An elastic demand schedule-based multimodal assignment model for the simulation of high-speed rai(HSR) systems. Assoc. Euro. Oper. Res. Soc. **2012**(1), 3–27 (2012)

20. Román, C., Martín, J.C.: Integration of HSR and air transport: Understanding passengers' preferences. J. Transp. Geogr. **41**, 77–85 (2014). https://doi.org/10.1016/j.jtrangeo.2014.01.001

21. Cascetta, E., Russo, F., Viola, F.A., Vitetta, A.: A model of route perception in urban road networks. Transport. Res. Part B: Methodol. **36**(7), 577–592 (2002)

22. Vitetta, A.: Path choice in transport systems: comparing random, quantum, and fuzzy utility models in a small network. Front. Future Transp. **6**, 1544947 (2025). https://doi.org/10.3389/ffutr.2025.1544947

23. Ben-Akiva, M., Lerman, S.R.: Discrete choice analysis: theory and application to travel demand. MIT Press, Cambridge, MA (1985)

24. McFadden, D.: The measurement of urban travel demand. J. Public Econ. **3**(4), 303–328 (1974). https://doi.org/10.1016/0047-2727(74)90001-7

25. Italian Government. Ministry of Transport and Infrastructures: Sistemi di monitoraggio deltraffico linee guida per la progettazione (2000)

26. Croce, A.I., Musolino, G., Rindone, C., Vitetta, A.: Estimation of travel demand models with limited information: floating car data for parameters' Calibration. Sustainability **13**(16), 8838 (2021). https://doi.org/10.3390/su13168838

27. Xiao, Y.-B., Chen, J., Liu, X.-L.: Joint dynamic pricing for two parallel flights based on passenger choice behavior. Xitong Gongcheng Lilun yu Shijian/Syst. Eng. Theory Pract. **28**(1), 46–55 (2008)

28. Ferrovie dello Stato Italiane. Nota stampa, Fs Italiane: Dieci anni di alta velocità, cambiato il paese e la vita delle persone. FS-Italiane (2019). https://www.fsitaliane.it/content/dam/fsi taliane/Documents/fsnews/comunicati-stam-pa/2019/dicembre/2019_12_05_NS_2_FS_Ita liane_10_anni_AV_cambiato_Paese_e_vita_persone.pdf. Accessed 2 Feb 2024

29. Russo, F., Sgro, D., Musolino, G.: dynamic structure of fares for high speed rail services. In: Gervasi, O., Murgante, B., Garau, C., Taniar, D., C. Rocha, A.M.A., Faginas Lago, M.N. (eds.) Computational Science and Its Applications – ICCSA 2024 Workshops. ICCSA 2024. LNCS, vol. 14822. Springer, Cham (2024). https://doi.org/10.1007/978-3-031-65318-6_13

High Speed Rail Stations in Territorial Areas: Sustainable Development and Quality of New Landscape

Paola Panuccio^(✉)

Università Mediterranea di Reggio Calabria, 89100 Reggio Calabria, Italy
paola.panuccio@gmail.com

Abstract. The High-Speed Rail (HSR) is the new mode of transport and is an opportunity for the sustainable development of the territory it crosses. HSR is an indispensable link to increase social and economic development and an opportunity to environmental sustainability. Transport net reshape the landscape and defines new distributions of functional areas on the territory. The HSR Stations (ST) are the fundamental nodes of connection with the territorial system.

This document analyses existing HSR ST with the aim of outlining the uniform characteristics and the specific characteristics found. This working method allows to define, a basic criterion to be applied in the planning process for new potential HSR ST. It is considered that the synthesis of uniform characteristics and specific characteristics can be useful, validated and replicable reference for potential new HSR ST that the planning process will locate. The main elements characterizing the reference criterion for the choice of a potential high-speed station were applied to the case study of Gioia Tauro. The planning process can use these categories to decide on the location of potential HSR ST. The integrated smart process allows to plan the transformations caused by the new infrastructure node. The planning process leads towards sustainable development of the territory and the composition of new quality landscapes. The paper understands the importance of HSR and proposes some useful references to the smart process for sustainable development of the territory and new quality landscapes by means of new stations. As a result of HSR, the territory becomes sustainable and smart.

Keywords: Hight Speed Rail Stations · sustainable development · new smart landscape · planning process

1 Introduction

High Speed Rail (HSR) is the most innovative national passenger transport system built in the last 30 years. Significant economic investment has been made in the infrastructure system. Around 60,000 kms (km) have been built all over the world: 20,000 km are under construction and 40,000 km, are in the planning phase. Italy has several line planned [1]. The financial programme, National Recovery and Resilience Plan (PNRR) aimed at Next Generation, allows to implement the planning of the HSR [2].

© The Author(s), under exclusive license to Springer Nature Switzerland AG 2026
O. Gervasi et al. (Eds.): ICCSA 2025 Workshops, LNCS 15894, pp. 434–451, 2026.
https://doi.org/10.1007/978-3-031-97648-3_29

One of the objectives of the 2001 National General Transport Plan (GTP) and the 2007 Guidelines for the Mobility Plan [3, 4] was to develop the HSR towards the regions of southern Italy (up to Calabria and Sicily). In fact, it was believed that extending the high-speed system to national territory could promote opportunities for economic and social development, and reduce the gap between the regions of northern Italy and the south, economically very different realities. HSR is a significant factor to the development of territories [5]. HSR is an indispensable mode of connection, for innovation and sustainable development of the national territory and local systems [6]. Transport networks increase connections, stimulate economic growth, assign new functions, redesign a new productive geography with a sustainable environmental development [7]. The location of HSR Stations (ST) is relevant for the integral sustainable development of the territory. The ST is the infrastructural node with which new development opportunities for the surrounding area are triggered. The choice of HSR ST location has a major impact on the added value that infrastructure can bring, and on the quality of the new landscape; it will make a difference for the host territory [8]. In summary, it can be said that the success or failure of HSR investments depends on city-region-nation integration and station - urban area connections [9, 10]. In order to ensure continuity between the HSR ST, the territory and society, it is essential to establish intermodal links, assign integrated functions and provide new territorial services [11]. Transport infrastructures are crucial systems to transform territories in smart direction according to smartness parameters of Commission Smart Cities and Communities [12] and pursue sustainable development, as outlined in the 2030 Agenda for Sustainable Development Goals [13, 14]. If we cross the smartness factors and the goals declined in the 2030 Agenda, with the effects induced on the territory by the construction of HSR, we have a full validation of the positive impact that HSR has to achieve innovation and sustainability. It has been observed that the construction of a high-speed rail allows for direct pursuit of certain objectives, such as: *7: affordable and clean energy; 8: decent work and economic growth; 9: Industry, innovation and infrastructure; 10: reduced inequalities; 13: climate action* [15]. Furthermore, if the HSR is implemented in coherence with the indications of the European cohesion policy, promoting the need to improve territorial accessibility of all regions by supporting the development of the Trans-European Network (TEN-T) [16] sustainable development will be the qualifying condition of HSR. The implementation of HSR causes such extensive developments that it affects the integral sustainable transformation of the territory. All 17 goals are involved, although with different levels of influence. Public decision-makers working on the potential 60,000 km, divided between those to be planned and those to be designed, can find useful proposals in the typological categories discussed in this paper [17].

This work identifies two main types of high-speed stations (Fig. 1). The first type of station constitutes the typology of the Territorial HSR ST; it is the station realized in the territory with two main motivations: may be near to other major transportation infrastructure; it may be a transit node for a neighbouring large city or for nearby medium-sized cities. The realization of a new architectural design has a significant effect to transforming the original territory. The urban planning, together with national policy choices, decide on a new site outside the city centre to build a new transport node. In this case the node is completely dedicated to HSR and the new design has significant consequences on the territorial gravitation system [18, 19].

The second type of station is the Urban HSR ST. The historic stations, located in urban centers, are adapted with adding of new tracks dedicated to high speed. The new high-speed tracks are placed parallel to the traditional, dedicating an adjacent area, or they are built below the existing station. The type of Urban HSR ST does not change the surrounding territory because it fits into an existing node. The interference on the territory remains unaltered: the same infrastructure is used, same services, only the new mode of transport is inserted. The existing node is overloaded with new performance and therefore has the potential to become a node of development.

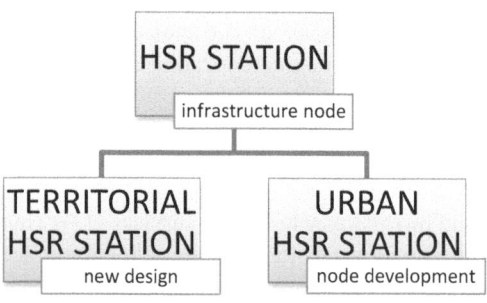

Fig. 1. Two types of HSR ST

The choice of location for the new territorial HSR ST, together with a good project, are decisive to transform the 'nothing' territorial, in smart and sustainable area. However, if the ST is designed without using a smart planning process and without an accurate evaluation, it will be itself the 'nothing' becoming what in literature is called a 'cathedral in the desert'. If the project does not make use of a planning process, instead of triggering opportunities for sustainable development, smart progress and valorization of the territory, it determines degeneration, decay, land consumption, urban sprawl [20]. Urban planning choices must be integrated with transport infrastructure choices, in comprehensive and integrated plan, for determining: benefits innovative; transformation of cities into smart cities [12]; new quality landscapes [21]; sustainable development of territories [17]. In Italy, important planning is underway to provide the country with a development of the HSR network. In this work, based on the observations and analyses of Italian ST, it is proposed a summary list of factors that define an identification protocol for two types of HSR ST. The uniform characters, or factors of similarity, are been differentiated from the specific characters, or exclusive factors; the differences distinguish the typology of the Territorial HSR ST. Some stations located in urban centres, have been adapted to allow the transit of trains. The most important are: Milano Centrale, Roma Termini, Firenze Santa Maria Novella, Bologna Centrale, Torino Porta Susa, Napoli Centrale. In the paper, this type is indicated by the name of Urban HSR ST. Instead, two new stations, Mediopadana-Reggio Emilia e Napoli-Afragola, have been designed ex novo and are totally dedicated to HSR. In the paper, this type is indicated with the name of Territorial HSR ST [8, 22]. The structure of the paper is as follows. Section 2 illustrates methods to planning process for High-Speed Rail Stations. The section consistis of: 2.1 Planning process; 2.2 Organization of territorial systems; 2.3 Organized systems for sustainable territory development; 2.4 The HSR nodes; 2.5 Uniform characters of the Territorial HSR ST; 2.6 Specific characters of the Territorial HSR ST. Section 3 illustrates the Planning process: results for HSR ST and case study. It indicates the factors of sustainable development that the HSR ST can trigger on the territory and the quality of life generated by the new proposed landscapes. The section consists of: 3.1 Planning process: to identify place new HSR ST; 3.2 The case study of Gioia Tauro: organized territorial systems; 3.3 The case study of Gioia Tauro: organized system for sustainable territory development; 3.4 Characteristics: attractiveness and lacks for the future Territorial HSR ST; 3.5. Uniform characters of the HSR ST; 3.6 Specific characters of the HSR ST. Lastly, Sect. 4 shortly draws some conclusions.

2   Methods to Planning Process for High-Speed Rail Station

2.1   The Planning Process in the Territorial System

The planning process considers the territory as a whole: a set of interconnected systems. The planning process structure knowledge to articulate the complex system, in problems and solutions (problem solving), making choices and taking choices, according to the basic principle of strategic planning [23–25]. Furthermore, the smart planning process, following the EU's current Smart City guidelines [12] and sustainable development [13, 14, 16] evaluate systems, crossing smartness characteristics and the Sustainable Development Goals (SDGs), with the resources that characterize the systems. Then assign significant dimensions by value, number, role, function [20, 26]. Following the evaluation of resources, the plan defines strategic objectives and indicates priority project choices. The planning process and its phases are [27]:

- Process of knowledge: Organisational structuring by systems; functional interpretation for the organisation of territory into systems. Resource identification phase; interpretation of significant identities.
- Process of evaluation: Qualification phase of characterizing resources. They are the structuring factors of the planning process.
- Process of signification: Assignment to resources of the typological dimension; it is to determine which resources qualify the landscape. The resources assign signification to the systems, by value and criticality defining the degree of relevance.
- Process decision-making of the vision and consequent strategic quality objectives: Smart design scenarios (balance, coherence, identity). Selection of priorities for the transformation of territories in sustainable, based on the indication of smart characteristics and 2030 goals. Design of new quality smart landscapes.
- Process deliberative: legitimacy of decisions with the approval of the plan; shared policies participatory consensus.

2.2   Organization of Territorial Systems

The territory is a wole of systems connected to each other by infrastructures concerning functions and services. The systems are constituted of elements linked together in different ways to achieve a community objective. The elements, interconnected with each other, adopt a functional behavior to the point of assuming the role of resource and constituting significant entities [28].

The behaviour of the elements is mainly determined by the synapses which are activated with connections and affinity. These interconnections, activated to establish functions and actions, allows the system to be thought of as an organization. The system, although it is formed of several elements, reacts and evolves as a whole, organized with coherent rules, both in terms of characteristics and functions to satisfy [29]. The organized system, composed of internally associated resources for homogeneous functions, is important for that specific territory. It makes the difference between a normal territory and a sustainable territorial heritage [30, 31].

The sustainability of the territory is determined by the internal balance of the system and the stable external connections between the different systems [32]. If the resource does not prevail over the others, but collaborates in an organized and implementative way, the system is in balance and expresses a high value, as well as being immediately recognizable and significant for the territory [33]. For example, an infrastructure node represents a recognizable system. The elements of the system have functionally homogeneous characteristics and contribute to the function to which they are called. The system is therefore organised; the internal balance between resources produces value and reveals to the outside, a new scenario for sustainable development.

Resources are of different types, from natural (exceptional value) to antropic (ordinary value); in both cases are of significant interest because they characterize the territory, assign typical places and constitute the mainstay on which establish the planning process [34]. The size of resources within the system (by role, number and importance) characterizes the system and assigns the name. Each specific territory is made up of several systems. The systems differ in terms of the size of their resources. Resources do not necessarily have to be equal; they are aggregated by function and objective and in this regard, can be described by homogeneous characters.

The components of the set, although different from each other, appear to be uniform regarding the functions they execute. This whole becomes a system, because the interacting elements give rise to a precise function. This function define the system and assigns an identifying name; for example: transport system. The resources are the elements that characterize that territory, which constitute the invariants; the framework for planning decisions. They range from excellence, easily recognizable by high value (e.g.: the nature park is composed of well-defined environmental resources) to common resources, which are essential to daily life; (e.g.: the transport infrastructure system or service infrastructure system or the infrastructure nodes system).

2.3 Organized Systems for Sustainable Territory Development

Resources characterise the identities of territories and assign qualities. The variety of systems expresses the level of the offering. The territory expresses value when there are many organized systems. Systems are organized when they are in balance both internally, between associated resources for coherent functions, and externally between systems. For example, the systems that make up the territory may be of the following types:

landscaped; cultural-historical; archeological; anthropic; transport; service infrastructures; touristic; manufacturing etc. If these systems are integrated with each other, they will produce incremental offerings that increase the quality of a sustainable territory. Normally, behind the integration between systems, there is an effective smart planning process, which plans the sustainable development of the territory [20, 27, 33].

The more each system works in equilibrium, because the resources are coherent compared to the functions to be fulfilled, the greater will be the propositive effects to have sustainable territories and new quality landscapes. When the territory is represented by a few organized systems, it is the task of the planning process to push for the use of the prevailing system (more organized), drawing up new connections in order to make the territory become increasingly functional. The plan uses the prevalent system to achieve progressively, on the basis of the priorities decided, the maximum level of development. The territory in this way increases sustainability and quality. Starting from the few systems in equilibrium, the plan decides the vision to be achieved over time, assigning the list of priorities to be implemented with precise projects. The realization of the projects will produce new quality landscapes to generate, incrementally, by aggregate multiplication, balanced systems, interacting, sufficient to repair the initial degradation of the imbalance. The more systems are organized and connected, the better the quality of life for people living in the territories. Interconnected systems determine the integral development, the connection between opportunities, sustainable development and the transformation of the territory into smart [35].

The study of the transport system is divided into three basic components: demand; supply; demand-supply interaction. The study of demand allows us to know the users who use or will use the reference infrastructure in the scenarios of possible development [6, 36, 37]. The study of the supply allows to know the role that the individual infrastructure assumes or will assume in different scenarios of development, and in the context of the overall multimodal system of transport infrastructures [5, 38]. The supply-demand interaction allows to analyse what is or will be the level of use of the individual infrastructure and then to assess the value of the relative investment in relation to the different objectives that the planning process poses [36, 39]. The network analysis system theory allows to study the centrality of stations in the overall system. It proposes indicators to recall the main quantities relating to connectivity. A basic indicator is:

$$c_i(t) = \frac{\sum_i a_{ij}(t)}{N - 1}$$

on which given a station node i, we intend to define the number of stations, whose generic is j, with which it is connected. This measure is defined starting from Total Degree Centrality. Additional indicators talk about the centrality of the node. For example, a node is more central depending on the total number of services connecting it to other nodes in the network [40–42].

This premise is of conceptual interest to underline the decisive role that the network of transport infrastructures has for each territory and how important what is happening in Italy in recent years. The planning process integrated into the transport plan is key to sustainable development, innovation, economic growth, new quality landscapes [43].

2.4   The HSR Nodes

Rail system is an indispensable condition for the economic, social and environmental development of the territories. The quality of life in cities has always been linked to transport infrastructure and urban planning. The planning process connects the two disciplines and plan sustainable and smart development scenarios [44].

High speed is an important opportunity for the development of territories, both for the new transport supply and for the socio-economic growth of cities. The design of HSR ST is the further input that has a major impact on spatial dynamics. The station draws a new landscape and the territory takes on a new significance, both for the architectural sign and for the functions. The determining factors for successful choice of station place are: to be a node of responsive and flexible networks; to be an intermodal interchange node; have the ability to trigger new functions; offer a range of services and activities in surrounding (obviously interconnected) urban systems. Another important factor is the centrality formulated by the basic indicator referred before which reinforce the 'three competing theories' influencing social development processes [45].

The station becomes a hub of interest, especially for regional and national companies. It is a multi-scale dimension, convergence of multiple factors [46].

In many cases, the station assumes the additional role of location for new urban and territorial functions. The station spaces if they offer new services, could be used by daily users, but could also be used by citizens of neighbouring places. Station area is experienced by travelers, who use similar services and functions as those offered by the city. This new concept of station, urban function, supports the concept that the station, must be designed with function of 'node and place' [47, 48].

From the current analysis of the projects carried out in Italy it is considered interesting to build a reference paradigm to relate to new design approaches. The comparison between the main characteristics of uniformity makes it possible to distinguish two types of stations and synthesizes the basic affinities, which are to be referred to. The reference paradigm is based on case studies already carried out, tested and evaluated.

In Italy, new HSR ST are distinguished, usually on a territorial scale, from existing stations adapted to the transit of HSR. The two HSR ST Mediopadana-Reggio Emilia and Napoli-Afragola are newly built and constitute important infrastructural and architectural nodes. These ST have been located in extra-urban territory; in the remainder of the paper we will indicate them as Territorial HSR ST. Other ST, have been adapted to the needs of HSR. The new high-speed tracks have been positioned or in line with conventional tracks, by dedicating a contiguous area, the main examples are the stations of Milano Centrale and Roma Termini, or, they are in the axis below the pre-existing station. This is the case of Bologna Centrale where a passing railway dedicated exclusively to high speed was built, and Torino Porta Susa, although in this case the passing is not exclusive. These ST are located in the urban centre, potential focal points of urban regeneration; in the paper we will indicate it with the name of Urban HSR ST. In order to catalogue and define the uniform characters and specific characters, which represent the type of Territorial HSR ST, the cases of territorial stations, realized in Italy, were analyzed. The two HSR ST (Napoli-Afragola and Mediopadana-Reggio Emilia) are exemplary constructions, designed by international architects, they are the sign of a further historical moment that the country is going through. The HSR ST is an opportunity to combine new quality smart landscapes, with functional and technological innovation and regeneration projects.

The comparison between the Mediopadana ST and the Napoli-Afragola ST allows to analyze some prevalent characters and differentiate them between uniform (confirmed in both stations and therefore replicable) and specific (found in one of the two ST; therefore, characteristic and exclusive for that given territorial context).

The Fig. 2) represents the two types of characters that describe Territorial HSR ST. Uniform characters are the same in the different analyzed contexts and therefore replicable in new future stations. Specific characters are exclusive of one context analysed.

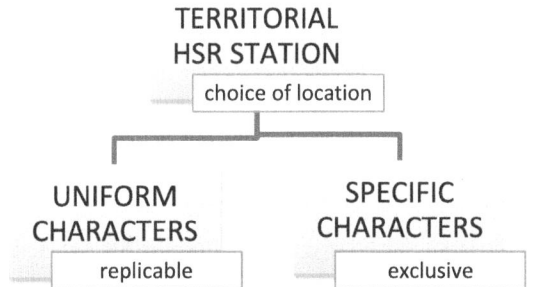

Fig. 2. Two types of characters of Territorial HSR ST in Italy

2.5   Uniform Characters of the Territorial HSR ST

In the following, a whole of uniform characters is proposed. They were deduced by the analysis of the two existing Territorial HSR ST in Italy: the Mediopadana-Reggio Emilia station located in Northern Italy [49, 50] and the Napoli-Afragola station located in southern Italy [51]. The uniform characteristics found in both stations, therefore confirmed and reproposed for the types of territorial HSR ST of future design are below. They constitute a first set of quantitative type characters, which can be developed and deepened with further work.

- International project signed by archistar. The stations are newly built. They are located outside the city centre and have been built on large area available. The Mediopadana Reggio Emilia station was designed by Calatrava and opened in 2013. The total planned cost was about 79 million euros, allocated by the Italian Railways and Emilia-Romagna Region. The Napoli-Afragola station was designed by Zaha Hadid and opened in 2017. The total planned cost has been of approximately 60 million euro, allocated by the Italian Railways. This descriptive synthesis allows to catalogue two constructions structurally and architecturally different, in the same category. Both are impressive signs on the territory, of architecture. The newly designed station is a relevant form of architecture; a new signification that transforms and determines a new landscape. In this case, the parameters are descriptive and the indicators qualitative.

- Railway service area. The railway service area for the transit of the HSR line is newly built. The station Mediopadana occupies an area of about 28.000 m^2; it has 4 tracks, the total length is about 500 m [52]. Napoli-Afragola station occupies an area of about 30,000 m^2; it has 4 tracks, the total length is about 400 m [53].
- Surface of parking areas. The ST have allocated large areas for parking, differentiating their uses between passengers, reserved areas and public transport.
- Surface of commercial areas. The infrastructure node is also diversifying from conventional ST for the new functions it performs. These station assign new signification; they aim to transform the station into an attractive pole, a new site, a new quality smart landscape. The Territorial HSR ST provide new urban functions, complete or replace those present in the surrounding urbanized territory.
- Availability of areas without urban constraints. The station can expand its margin over time, increasing offers and services, because there is a free area available to the boundary. The project has provided for the possibility of successive expansions in contiguous areas.
- Population density in adjacent areas. The surrounding areas have many urban centres. The ray of distance from the node is variable, the density is high.

2.6 Specific Characters of the Territorial HSR ST

From stations analysis, it was found that the Territorial HSR ST Mediopadana, has triggered more opportunities for sustainable development in the surrounding area, compared to the Territorial HSR ST Afragola. The elements of attractiveness and success, while specific and unique to the station analyzed, indicate some assumptions to consider in the choice of location and design of potential new stations [54, 55]. The specific characteristics, indicators of value, quality and development, can be proposed in a new future station, after evaluation.

The specific characters that may be initially proposed are:

- Intermodal node. The station is a node of an organized network linking different parts of the territory, connecting functional infrastructures, offering alternative mode and triggering conditions for development. The node plays its special role because it is interconnected to infrastructure network that distributes services and creates connections. The number and type of connected systems are significant to the role of the node; such as: taxis, private cars, car rental, car sharing; buses and how many lines; metro lines; conventional rail lines.
- Network linking urban areas. The territory near the node is surrounded by urban areas. Reach the localities by public transport, allows the development of smart mobility as well as social and economic sustainability. Service and transport infrastructures are the most important asset for the smart development of the territory. They promote profit in the socio-economic system.
- Connection of territorial supplied. The territory rich in organized systems, if they are connected to each other, implement the offers of services and economic development. If the systems are integrated with each other, they will produce incremental supply. The various places linked together, promote the development of systems and trigger the positive process of demand - supply - convenient allocation for integrated development. The type of systems are indicative for the role of the node; such as: Special

Economic Zone (SEZ), industrial zone; commercial area; areas for services destined by the urban plan; sports centers; etc.

• Areas constrained by the urban plan. It is necessary to specify that the constraint provided by the urban plan, can be a limit for the potential infrastructural node. The constraint obliges to respect the assigned urban destinations and allows to build in compliance with the parameters, and with the modalities, decided by the plan. Therefore, it may happen that around the node the plan has provided for the construction of volumetries not congruent with the future development of the transport node; or that has decided on urban constraints for the station itself, limiting the expansion of volumes and areas. On the other hand, if there is a vision open to the dynamics of socio-economic development of the territory, smart process planning assumes the specific character for the success of the area. For example, in the case of the Mediopadana Station, the plan has allocated some areas to urban regeneration, providing opportunities for territory qualification, new advantageous impulse and smart integration.

3 Planning Process: Results for HSR ST and Case Study

3.1 The Planning Process to Identify Place New HSR ST

The construction of a new HSR ST, if planned, promote socio-economic development but above all ensures the sustainable development of the territory [56]. The project establish new conditions that will impact on existing landscape. How can the Territorial HSR ST be integrated into the existing landscape, with the least possible impact and mitigate overlaps with quality alternative scenarios? To mitigate the impact of the new construction, it is necessary that this trigger benefits. The quality balance must be positive, compared to factors that promote sustainable development (DSG goals) to mitigate the negative effects of land use and degradation. The new infrastructure node mitigates negative impacts, if it offers a new wide range of services and functions; high-quality multifunctional equipment; new benefits for integrated territory development; architectural project, new aesthetic symbol of design, respect the pre-existing landscape. The new station becomes the new system characterizing for that territory; visible expression of a new landscape of quality. The new landscape is of quality when it transforms negative impacts into new forms of proactive landscape. By the term proactive landscape, it is intended to indicate that within the 'beautiful architectural project' are active new functions and supply of services, important elements to trigger sustainable development and smart innovation of the territory. The analysis of the social benefits costs, integrated with the evaluation of the new functions, supply and advantages, confirms the value that the new work imparts on the territory. These elements are guarantee of integral quality and therefore of a new smart quality landscape.

In this regard, it is interesting to recall what Latouche said in 2005 that defined development as the realization of the desires and aspirations of all, outside any historical, economic, social and cultural context [57]. Sustainability is researched by applying models and is certified with the results of evaluation techniques. Sustainability is likely, if the landscape designed by urbanism, produces quality. Planning and assure integral quality through planning is a complex operation; in fact, the quantitative indicator must be integrated with the qualitative indicator. The quantitative evaluation is complemented by the qualitative evaluation; if the systems do not meet the full quality, they cannot be sustainable [58]. Urban planning to design sustainable cities must adopt new criteria. Urban destinations become functional urban areas to the 2030 goals. The integrated urban plan, after identifying and evaluating the resources existing on the territory, must plan smart way. The urban choices include new strategies that will transform the territory, in sustainable [35]. The project actions, coordinated by smart integrated planning, regenerate the comprehensive territory and qualify new smart landscapes.

3.2 The Case Study of Gioia Tauro: Organized Territorial Systems

Gioia Tauro is an urban centre which due to the construction of the port, has expanded increasingly occupying land, originally agricultural. The current population is 19.240 and the workers involved with port activities are about 1400 employees.The port was built in 1970 but commercial operations began in 1995. First Italian port for freight traffic, eighth in Europe, extends over an area of 620 hectares; from 2018 is part of the Special Economic Zone (SEZ) [59, 60]. The territory presents itself with two strong scenarios: on the one hand the port, an imposing infrastructural node for the intercontinental routes of the ships that load and unload goods; on the other hand the urban system. Urban areas have occupied the territory and provoked the urban sprawl phenomenon, causing decay [61]. The lack of process planning has led to excessive land use, causing disorder and degradation. The territory is not organized in systems; it appears to lack connections, services and infrastructure; lack of integration and balance between systems. The port is closed in its own border, it is a gigantic infrastructure without a territory that supports it. The infrastructure and the territory do not communicate; organized systems are not present. The state reveals two separate systems that would need to integrate and collaborate for sustainable development and new quality landscapes.

It is a special case in which the planning process could transform the state of places into smart territory: integrated system between port, urbanized areas and environment [62, 63]. The scenario has great similarities with that determined by the Territorial HSR ST Afragola, also closed in its project, with no connection to the local system.

3.3 The Case Study of Gioia Tauro: Organized Systems for Sustainable Territory Development

The territory of the Gioia Tauro plain is characterized by resources of various type, working in disaggregated way. This means that it is difficult to recognise organised systems and that existing activities are disconnected from each other. These conditions indicate the lack of a urban planning. The territory has grown over time without respecting urban standards and without a vision; without process planning. For this reason the undetermined prevails, the unfinished; the territory remains there as a container, it is not proposed as a heritage. Resources are presented as individual elements, not working together in organized systems. They have their own endogenous value, but do not produce sustainable development; do not collaborate in aggregating actions, do not perform organized functions; the territory is not organized in system of systems. For example, the port system is a closed system in its function, it is not integrated with other of the territory in which it is inserted. Urban areas survive, adapting; they do not react to the opportunities of so presence. In the preceding chapter we underlined the concept that if the territory is not represented by organized systems the degradation overcome.

The method indicated by the planning process, makes the prevailing system the opportunity for development; the focal point on which to set up the planning choices. The plan uses the prevalent system (more organized and balanced) to decide vision and objectives, to assigne project priorities, to achieve with consecutive steps, the maximum level of development. The territory, starting from lighthouse system, will be able to design a new landscape of quality and trigger actions for sustainable development. The choices of the planning process determine the integral development, the integration of infrastructures, the connection between the offers, the sustainable valorization and the transformation of the territory into smart. The plan devises regeneration projects to convert urbanized areas, and equipe the territory for new sustainable offerings, with new development factors and new forms for quality landscape.

3.4 Characteristics: Attractiveness and Lacks for the Future Territorial HSR ST

The study area is characterized by some singularities that constitute the history of the place. They can inspire the name of the future station:

- Station 'Metaurus': to evoke the historic greek town of Gioia Tauro, already mentioned in the III century B.C. and then, in 130 B.C., for the Via Popilia.
- Station 'Medma': the historical archaeological heritage suggests this name. Medma was an ancient Greek city of the V–IV sec a.C. with a population of about 4000 inhabitants, located near the existing city of Rosarno.
- Station 'Eranova': to remember the preexisting town demolished to realize the mega infrastructure of the port of Gioia Tauro.
- 'Station – Porto': this name would give meaning to the need to integrate two important nodes such as the port, already of international level, and the HSR station.

In the following will be named the New Station which integrates two special functions becoming unique great opportunity. Great potential for sustainable territory development, for a huge change in the local, regional and national system. The territory has elements of attractiveness and lacks. The characteristic territorial systems are the intercontinental port; vast urban areas; exceptional environmental systems; resources with potential attractiveness. At present, the territorial system appears to be disaggregated, irregular, fragmented in functions with lack of transport and service infrastructures, of network connections. The citizen does not experience the advantages of the port; does not use public transport; resources are scattered randomly, they do not constitute common heritage. The process planning proposes scenarios of smart innovation, sustainable development, urban regeneration to design new quality landscape. In this paper the New HSR ST is proposed, composed from the infrastructural node of the port, already at international level, and the HSR station infrastructure node, future access core. The new Territorial HSR ST becomes an opportunity for system integration and open borders. The current boundary of the port system, will be integrated with the resources spread over the territory, through a new development project operated by smart process planning. A

New Station architectural sign of value, which integrates two special functions becoming unique great opportunity. High potential for sustainable territory development, for a huge change in the local, regional and national system.

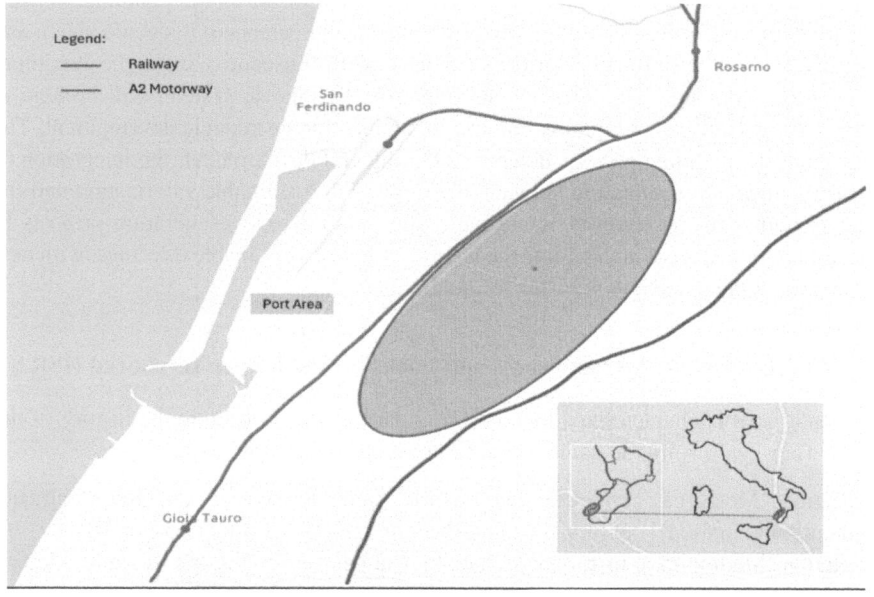

Fig. 3. The study area

The Fig. 3) illustrates the study area with the future area for New HSR ST.

The proposal solves the high-speed node in Calabria, a crucial interchange to connect the South of Italy to Europe. The Calabria Region includes environmental resources at the moment lacking infrastructure network, not connected, difficult to access. It can be cited the exceptional resources of the: Archaeological Park Locri Epizefiri, National archaeological museum of Reggio Calabria and Locri, Aspromonte National Park, Serre Natural Park, Passo della Limina, Special Protection Zone of the Costa Viola, Monte Poro, promontory of Sant'Elia.

3.5   Uniform Characters of the HSR Station

The case study is therefore a special case in which the construction of a new territorial HSR ST can be conceived. Design of a single integrated station, to be done ex novo using the success categories described in Sect. 2. The design of a New HSR ST considers the uniform characteristics, tested and catalogued as a result of the comparison between the analysed HSR ST.

The uniform characteristics identified and replicable for the New HSR ST are:

- International project signed by archistar. The relevant architectural design of a new form to identify a new quality landscape. Creative commitment for a form of aesthetic quality and at the same time, a functional node: Relevant transport infrastructure and location of services and new offers such as in Reggio Calabria: project of the Sea Museum designed by Zaha Hadid; National Museum of Magna Grecia designed by Piacentini; Casa del Fascio of the Razionalist Architecture. Other then the liberty and neoclassical architectures built after 1908 earthquake.

- Railway service area. The railway with 4 tracks HSR about 400 m long. It has the average standards found in the works carried out and tested on the national territory.
- Surface of parking areas. Extensive parking areas should be designed. The development of the area will also depend on the ease of use of the node.
- Surface of commercial areas. The station is a new site: new urban functions turn it into an attractive node, a new smart economy system.
- Availability of areas without urban constraints. It is necessary to have available free areas for future expansions. The vision is structured on a project that is implemented by step and priority. Land use potential is a positive element for development
- Population density in adjacent areas. The catchment area is extensive and is estimated to be around 0.4 million inhabitants. The area is populated; over time the area has been occupied by agglomerations without urban planning, sparsed as a 'leopard spot' without following a regular plan.

3.6 Specific Characters of the HSR ST

The design of a New HSR ST takes into account the specific characteristics already experienced by the comparison between the analysed HSR ST. The specific characteristic proposed for the future HSR station in the territory of Gioia Tauro plains are:

- Intermodal node. The area is served by linear and punctual transport infrastructures. Linear infrastructures comprehend TEN-T railway (Tyrrhenian line) belonging to Scandinavian-Mediterranean core network corridor and motorway roads (A2 Salerno -Reggio Calabria) [43]. The station becomes the important connecting point to link the transport of the Tyrrhenian area with those of the Ionic area; for the airport nodes of Reggio Calabria and Vibo Valentia; in addition to the many possible connections with the territorial system of the Piana of Gioia Tauro with about 165,000 inhabitant.
- Network linking urban areas. The station becomes intermodal interchange hub, for the new infrastructural network of the local system.
- Connection of territorial offers. The station, reference for the integrated network of territorial systems, such as environmental, landscape, historical, cultural and anthropic resources. Opportunity for new infrastructure endowment; new condition for the use of territorial services and landscape resources. The presence of the SEZ is highlighted as an additional element of attention.
- Areas constrained by the urban plan. The process smart planning proposes the node station for regeneration opportunities, qualification of the territorial system, new smart offers.

4 Conclusions

The work develops the analyses proposed in preceding works, on the two existing HSR ST in Italy (Mediopadana-Reggio Emilia and Napoli-Afragola) and on the territorial system of the port of Gioia Tauro, to define uniform and specific characters that can be employed in planning for potential territorial HSR ST.

From the interpretation of the analyses of existing HSR ST in Italy, it was possible to develop a reference paradigm for new design approaches. The choice of place to a new station is crucial to think of new opportunities for sustainable development and new quality smart landscapes. An important factor reference for the choice is the centrality model defined by basic indicator.

Comparison of the uniform and specific characteristics of existing stations provides reference categories for the success of new plans. An elements list is a useful reference for planners; the smart planning process cannot ignore the characteristics designated for the choice of the location of the new node and to include elements of positive attractiveness. The formulation of a reference paradigm for new quality smart landscapes is based on reality, on cases tested in the territory, evaluated and monitored to update and validate the effects on the surrounding territory.

The characters uniform, precisely because they synthesize quantitative data, are replicable for the realization of future Territorial HSR ST. These indications are useful to planners and decisions makers who can cite a working method for the choice of place. The quantitative characteristics and inter modal systems constitute a first step which can be developed and deepened with further work.

Acknowledgements. "This study was carried out within the MOST – Sustainable Mobility National Research Center and received funding from the European Union Next-Generation EU (Piano Nazionale Di Ripresa e Resilienza (PNRR) – Missione 4 Componente 2, Investimento 1.4 – D.D. 1033 17/06/2022, CN00000023). This manuscript reflects only the authors' views and opinions, neither the European Union nor the European Commission can be considered responsible for them."

References

1. UIC 2023. High-speed around the world. International Union of Railways, Paris (2023)
2. CPI 2021. Council presidency of Italy. Piano Nazionale di Ripresa e Resilienza (2021). https://www.governo.it/sites/governo.it/files/PNRR_0.pdf
3. GURI Gazzetta Ufficiale della Repubblica Italiana. Decreto del Presidente della Repubblica 14 marzo 2001. Nuovo piano generale dei trasporti e della logistica. (GU Serie Generale n.163 del 16-07-2001-Suppl. Straordinario) (2001). https://www.gazzettaufficiale.it/eli/id/2001/07/16/001A6017/sg
4. MIT Ministero Infrastrutture e Trasporti. Piano Generale della Mobilità, Linee Guida. Nota Introduttiva Roma (2007)
5. Russo, F.: Which high-speed rail? LARG approach between plan and design. Future Transp. **2021**(1), 202–226 (2021). https://doi.org/10.3390/futuretransp1020013
6. Russo, F., Sgro, D., Musolino, G.: sustainable development of railway corridors: methods and models for High-Speed Rail (HSR) demand analysis. Internaz. Conference on Computational Science and Its Applications, pp. 527–538, Springer (2023)
7. Di Gangi, M., Russo, F.: Design of hybrid rail services on conventional and high-speed lines. Int. J. Transp. Develop. Integrat. (2023)
8. Panuccio, P.: State of the art of sustainable development of railway nodes: the High-Speed Rail (HSR). In Gervasi, O., Murgante, B., Garau, C., Taniar, D., Rocha, A.M., Faginas Lago, N. (eds.) ICCSA 2024. Springer Nature Switzerland (2024). https://hdl.handle.net/20.500.12318/152086

9. Givoni, M., Banister, D.: Moving towards low carbon mobility elgaronline, Social and Political Science, p. 304 (2013)

10. Hall, P.: Magic carpets and seamless webs: opportunities and constraints for high-speed trains in Europe. Built Environ. **35**, 59–69 (2009)

11. Russo, F., Musolino, G.: Methodologies for sustainable development of TEN-T/RFC corridors and core ports: economic impacts generated in port-related areas. In: International Conference on Computational Science and Its Applications, pp. 515–526 (2023)

12. European Commission 2012. Communication from the Commission Smart Cities and Communities. European Innovation Partnership. https://digital-strategy.ec.europa.eu/en/library/smart-cities-and-communities-european-innovation-partnership-communication-commission-c2012-4701. Accessed 27 Feb 2025

13. UN. United Nations. Transforming our world: the 2030 agenda for sustainable development (2015)

14. UN. United Nations. global indicator framework for the sustainable development goals and targets of the 2030 agenda for sustainable development (2018)

15. Rindone, C., Russo, A.: A network analysis for HSR services in the south of Italy. In: Gervasi, O., Murgante, B., Garau, C., Taniar, D., C. Rocha, A.M.A., Faginas Lago, M.N. (eds.) Computational Science and Its Applications – ICCSA 2024 Workshops. ICCSA 2024. LNCS, vol. 14822. Springer, Cham (2023). https://doi.org/10.1007/978-3-031-65318-6_15

16. EU. European Commission, Cohesion in Europe towards 2050: 8th Cohesion Report (2022). https://ec.europa.eu/regional_policy/information-sources/cohesion-report_en

17. Sustainable Development Goals 2030. https://sustainabledevelopment.un.org. Accessed 27 Feb 2025

18. Hull, A.: Policy integration: what will it take to achieve more sustainable transport solutions in cities? Transp. Policy **15**(2), 94–103 (2008). https://doi.org/10.1016/j.tranpol.2007.10.004

19. Wang, X., Liu, J., Zhang, W.: How does the spatial structure of high-speed rail station areas evolve? a case study of zhengzhou east railway station, China. Appl. Sci. **11**(23), 11132 (2021). https://doi.org/10.3390/app112311132

20. Panuccio, P.: Smart planning: from city to territorial system. MDPI Sustain. **11**(24), 7184 (2019). https://doi.org/10.3390/su11247184

21. EU Guidelines for the implementation on the European Landscape Convention (2008). http://www.coe.int/t/dg4/cultureheritage/heritage/Landscape (2008)

22. Panuccio, P.: Framework for sustainable development of High-Speed Railway passengers' stations in Italy. In: EMCEI 6Th Euro-Mediterranean Conference for Environmental integration 2024. Springer (2024)

23. Faludi, A.: A decision-centred view of environmental planning. Pergamon Press, Oxford (1987)

24. Friedmann, J.: Pianificazione e dominio pubblico. Dalla conoscenza all'azione. Edizioni Dedalo, Bari, IT (1993)

25. Friedmann, J.: Planning theory revisited. Eur. Plan. Stud. **6**(3), 245–253 (1998). https://doi.org/10.1080/09654319808720459

26. Giffinger, R., Fertner, C., Kramar, H., Meijers, E., Pichler-Milanović, N.: Smart cities Ranking of European medium-sized cities. Centre of Regional Science, Vienna University Technology (2007). http://www.smart-cities.eu/download/smart_cities_final_report.pdf

27. Albanese G.: Il territorio dell'urbanistica. Gangemi Editore, Roma (1999)

28. Kuhn, D.: A developmental model of critical thinking. Educational Researcher, vol. 28, pp. 16–25 (1999)

29. Bocchi, G., Ceruti, M.: (a cura di) La sfida della complessità, Feltrinelli, MI, IT (1985)

30. Fu, Y., Zhang, X.: Trajectory of urban sustainability concepts: A 35-year bibliometric analysis. Cities **60**(A), pp. 113–123 (2017)

31. Alferj, P., Pilati, A.: Conoscenza e complessità. Edizioni Theoria, Roma, IT (1990)
32. European Commission 2023. Sustainable Urban Development. Cities forum https://ec.eur opa.eu/regional_policy/policy/themes/urban-development_en
33. Panuccio, P.: Urbanistica e Paesaggio. Gangemi Editore, Roma, Italia (2007)
34. Haarstad, H.: Constructing the sustainable city: examining the role of sustainability in the 'smart city' discourse. J. Environ. Policy Plan. **19**(4), 423–437 (2017)
35. Bisello, A., Vettorato, D., Laconte, P., Costa, S.: Smart and sustainable planning for cities and Regions. SSPCR Springer, Bolzano, IT (2017). https://doi.org/10.1007/978-3-319-75774-2
36. Cascetta, E.: Transportation systems analysis, models and applications. Springer (2009)
37. Russo, F., Moschella, M., Musolino, G.: Railway demand evaluation: HSR induced component. In: International Conference on Computational Science and Its Applications, pp. 173–187. Springer (2024). https://doi.org/10.1007/978-3-031-65318-6_12
38. Di Gangi, M., Russo, F.: Potentiality of rail networks: Integrated services on conventional and high-speed lines. WIT Trans. Built Environ. **213**, 101–112 (2022)
39. Russo, F., Sgro, D., Musolino, G: Dynamic structure of fares for High-Speed Rail services. In: Gervasi, O., Murgante, B., Garau, C., Taniar, D., C. Rocha, A.M.A., Faginas Lago, M.N. (eds.) Computational Science and Its Applications – ICCSA 2024 Workshops. ICCSA 2024. LNCS, vol. 14822. Springer, Cham (2024). 10.1007/978-3-031-65318-6_13https://doi.org/ 10.1007/978-3-031-65318-6_13
40. Rindone, C., Russo, A.: A network analysis for HSR services in the south of Italy. In: Gervasi, M., Garau, T., Roca, F.L. (eds.) International Conference on Computational Science, pp. 217–232, vol. I 14822. ICCSA 2024. LNCS. Springer (2024). https://doi.org/10.1007/978-3-031-65318-6_15
41. Tesoriere, G., Russo, A., De Cet, G., Vianello, C., Campisi, T.: The centrality of Italian airports before and after the COVID-19 period what happened. Eur. Transp./Trasp. Eur. **93**, 1–16 (2023)
42. Campisi, T., Russo, A., Trwdy, E., Zanne, M., Tesoriere, G.: Some considerations on the analysis of port centrality in the Adriatic basin for tourist transport purposes, Transport. Res. Procedia **83**. 125–132, ISSN 2352-1465 (2025). https://doi.org/10.1016/j.trpro.2025.02.018
43. Russo, F., Rindone, C., Panuccio, P.: Structural factors for a third-generation port: between hinterland regeneration and smart town in Gioia Tauro. Urban Maritime Transport **XXVII**, 204, 43, ISSN 1743–3509 (2021)
44. Russo, F., Rindone, C., Panuccio, P.: European plans for the smart city: from theories and rules to logistics test case. Eur. Plan. Stud. **24**(9), 1709–1726 (2016)
45. Freeman, L.C.: Centrality in social networks conceptual clarification. Elsevier Sequoia Lausanne, pp. 215–239 (1978/79). https://www.semanticscholar.org/paper/Centrality-in-social-networks-conceptual-Freeman/5d61ef638fd684facc1e68e654053e9bc065b36f
46. Dragan, W.: Development of the urban space surrounding selected railway stations in Poland. Environ. Socio-Econ. Stud. **5**(4), 57–65 (2017)
47. Bertolini L., Pasquier F.: Des gares en transformation. Nœuds de réseaux et lieux dans la ville. Les annales de la recherche urbaine **71**(1), 86–89 (1996)
48. Bertolini, L., Spit, T.: Cities on Rails: The Redevelopment of Railway Stations and their Surroundings Routledge (1998) https://doi.org/10.4324/9780203980439
49. Stazione AV Mediopadana Reggio Emilia. https://www.fsitaliane.it/content/fsitaliane/it/inn ovazione/tecnologie-per-i-trasporti/le-principali-stazioni-av/reggio-emilia-av-mediopdana. html
50. Casabella870 n. 831/2 2017: "Reggio Emilia: un paesaggio ridisegnato. Grandi opere sotto tutela" Alberto Ferlenga
51. Domus Stazione Napoli Afragola (2017). https://www.domusweb.it/it/architettura/2017/06/ 12/stazione_napoli_afragola.html

52. http://structuralweb.it/cms/it300-inaugurata-la-stazione-av-mediopadana-.asp
53. https://www.mit.gov.it/connettere-litalia/nuova-stazione-av-napoli-afragola
54. Lee, K.: The conceptualization of country attractiveness: a review of research. Int. Rev. Adm. Sci. **82**(4), 807–826 (2016)
55. Garmendia, M., Ribalaygua, C., Ureña, J.M.: High speed rail: implication for cities. Cities (2012). https://doi.org/10.1016/j.cities.2012.06.005[GoogleScholar][CrossRef]
56. Lu, H., Jong, M.D., Heuvelhof, E.F.: Explaining the variety in smart eco city development in China – what policy network theory can teach us about overcoming barriers in implementation? J. Clean. Product. **196**, 135e149 (2018)
57. Latouche, S.: Come sopravvivere allo sviluppo: dalla decolonizzazione dell'immaginario economico alla costruzione di una società alternativa, Bollati Boringhieri, IT (2005)
58. Pallante, M.: La decrescita felice: la qualità della vita non dipende dal Pil, Ed. per la decrescita felice (2009)
59. Russo, F., Panuccio, P., Rindone, C.: External interactions for a third-generation port: from urban sustainable planning to research developments. WIT Int. J. Transp. Dev. Integr. **6**(3), 253–270 (2022). https://doi.org/10.2495/EI-V6-N3-253-270
60. Musolino, D.A., Panuccio, P.: Special economic zones planning for sustainable ports: the test case of territorial attractiveness and urban planning in calabria region. In: Gervasi, O., Murgante, B., Misra, S., Rocha, A.M.A.C., Garau, C. (eds.) Computational Science and Its Applications. LNCS, vol. 13381, pp.7284, ISBN 978-3-031-10547-0 (2022). https://doi.org/10.1007/978-3-031-10548-7_6.
61. EEA, Urban sprawl in Europe – The ignored challenge. EEA Report No.10/2006, European Environment Agency, Copenhagen (2006)
62. Karvonen, A., Cugurullo, F., Caprotti, F.: Inside smart cities. Place, politics and urban innovation. Routledge Taylor Francis (2018)
63. Mitchell, W.J.: Smart cities: Vision Available online (2013). http://www.smartcities.media.mit.edu/frameset.html

Author Index

A

Aleksandrov, Aleksandr   205
Amodio, Antonio Minervino   18
Arzha, Anton   249

B

Balena, Pasquale   49
Barrile, Vincenzo   407
Biscione, Marilisa   3, 30, 172
Blečić, Ivan   159
Bogdanov, Alexander   205, 231
Bonazza, Alessandra   18
Borri, Dino   49
Bruno, Maria Francesca   110

C

Campisi, Tiziana   375
Cantatore, Elena   61
Clavé, Salvador Anton   159

D

Danese, Maria   3, 30, 172
De Fino, Mariella   61
Di Ruocco, Irina   125
Dik, Aleksandr   205
Dik, Gennady   205, 294

F

Fatiguso, Fabio   61
Filitti, Domenico   172
Florio, Valentina   30
Fratino, Umberto   49, 110
Frontera, Patrizia   391

G

Gallo, Andrea   142
Gavrilov, Nikita   219
Genovese, Emanuela   407
Giunta, Marinella   391, 407
Gizzi, Fabrizio Terenzio   18

G

Gladkaya, Maria   294
Golovkina, Anna   282

H

Ha, Muon   191

I

Iacobellis, Vito   49, 110
Ibatullin, Evgeniy   231

K

Khvatov, Valery   231
Kiyamov, Jasur   205, 264
Korkhov, Vladimir   219, 249, 325
Kusumegi, Toko   79

L

Lasorella, Margherita   61
Leonardi, Giovanni   407

M

Mascitelli, Alessandra   97
Masini, Nicola   172
Matiushin, Iurii   325
Mazzarino, Marco   125
Molfetta, Matteo Gianluca   110
Moschella, Marialuisa   359
Musolino, Giuseppe   420

N

Nguyen, Xuan-Hien   191

O

Osaragi, Toshihiro   79

P

Panuccio, Paola   434
Pen, Evgenii   219
Pisano, Federica   142
Pronina, Nadezhda   264

O. Gervasi et al. (Eds.): ICCSA 2025 Workshops, LNCS 15894, pp. 453–454, 2026.
https://doi.org/10.1007/978-3-031-97648-3

R
Rindone, Corrado   375
Rouisse, Mohammed Er   391
Russo, Antonio   375
Russo, Francesco   359

S
Saliu, Maria Carla   159
Santoro, Stefania   49, 110
Sardella, Alessandro   18
Savkov, Egor   205
Scaramuzzo, Giovanni   172
Sgro, Domenico   420
Shchegolev, Aleksandr   205
Shchegoleva, Nadezhda   231, 264, 294, 340
Shichkina, Yulia   191
Sonnessa, Alberico   97

Stankova, Elena   309
Subbotin, Alexey   309

T
Tarantino, Eufemia   97
Tesoriere, Giovanni   375
Tokarev, Alexey   219
Tonka, Petr   340
Totaro, Vincenzo   49, 110

V
Vashukova, Anna   282
Villani, Fausto   172

Z
Zalutskaya, Natalia   340
Zalutskaya, Nataliya   264
Zhukova, Nataly   309

The manufacturer's authorised representative in the EU is Springer
Nature Customer Service Centre GmbH, Europaplatz 3, 69115 Heidelberg,
Germany. If you have any concerns regarding our products, please
contact ProductSafety@springernature.com

Printed and bound by CPI Group (UK) Ltd, Croydon, CR0 4YY

01/05/2026

02101080-0005